CELEBRITY DEATH CERTIFICATES

CELEBRITY DEATH CERTIFICATES

by M. F. Steen

McFarland & Company, Inc., Publishers
Jefferson, North Carolina, and London

To the people who are always in my corner:
Bill, Marge, Mim, Judi, Lee and Marian.

To the late Arthur N. Chambers, my first employer, mentor and friend. His love for funeral service and his dedication to the families he was privileged to serve was contagious. He graciously taught me the basics which have held me in good stead throughout my career. He answered a million questions and always seemed ready for more.

To Elliott Mintz and the late Willis G. "Bud" Noakes for reminding me of the importance of perseverance: This book is proof of that concept.

ACKNOWLEDGMENTS

Few projects like this are a one person accomplishment. I would like to acknowledge the work and encouragement of the following: Judi Adams, Lee Adams, Ryan Barron, Warren Beath, Gail Blamires, Margaret Blamires, Matthew Blamire-Romleski, Samuel Combs, Kathy Conner, the late Clyde Curtis, Debby Durham, Darlene Edgington, the late Harry Essex, Jenny Flores, John Gerchas, Steve Goldstein, Christopher Jacobson, Bernard Johnson, Sid Keating, Vern Knuckles, Jonathan Lackey, Jim Lemmon, David Lotz, Anne Mamalyga, Karen McHale, Scott Michales, R. Bart Mruz, Frank Romleski, Phyllis Romleski, Bill Schneid, the late David Schneid, the late Florence Schneid, Millie Skinner, Jim Stepkowski, Kathy Stepkowski, Jim Tipton, Marge Van Meter.

ISBN 0-7864-1641-6 (softcover : 50# alkaline paper) ♾

Library of Congress cataloguing data are available

British Library cataloguing data are available

Manufactured in the United States of America

McFarland & Company, Inc., Publishers
Box 611, Jefferson, North Carolina 28640
www.mcfarlandpub.com

Table of Contents

Preface

A death certificate is an intriguing document. On one page, a person's life is encapsulated. It's all there! Where the person was born and to what parents; amount of education and length of career; place of residence; whether the person was married at the time of death and to whom; what caused the death; and finally, what happened to the "remains."

A death certificate is a state-originated document. The information required on the certificate may vary from year to year and state to state.

Each state looks at a death certificate in a different way. California thinks of them as public documents, available to anyone. Other states, such as Texas and New York, do not consider them public documents. In those states, death certificates are officially available only to family members and others showing a direct need for a copy. Satisfying idle curiosity is not considered a need.

This book contains 170 death certificates of Hollywood's famous and infamous. You will find examples from the Silent Era; some from Hollywood's Golden Era; some recent and others who made their fame on the small screen. To include everyone that a reader might care about would, of course, have been an impossible task.

Many famous people whose certificates I would have liked to include died in New York. The restrictions mentioned above prevented their inclusion.

The certificates are presented in alphabetical order by familiar name. Otherwise, people like Gale Gordon (whose certificate lists his name as Charles J. Aldrich, Jr.) and Audrey Meadows (Audrey Cotter Six) would be hard to find.

It was difficult to decide what certificates to include. I sent my list of death certificates to family members and friends and asked them to list the ones they would be interested in. Whenever several friends suggested the same people, I knew those certificates especially needed to be included. I took their suggestions and added some of my favorite peoples' certificates.

Collecting death certificates is surely an unusual hobby. If you are interested in starting a collection, you do not need to limit it to motion picture people. Sports stars, authors, or presidents of the United States are just a few other possibilities.

I started my collection in July of 1991. I had seen a similar book to this one. It was smaller, but with a wider range of people. It contained motion picture celebrities, captains of industry and U.S. presidents.

I began my collection by ordering the death certificates of my 10 favorite celebrities. Marilyn Monroe was one of the first. I had worked at Pierce Brothers Westwood Memorial Park for 11 years. I had dealt with her fans on a daily basis. I knew how important she was to them. Many of them were not even born when she died, so clearly her legacy continues.

Death certificates are available from the county health department in the county where the death occurred. The fees usually range from $5.00 to $15.00, but they change from time to time, so it is necessary to check before ordering. Many states offer applications for death certificates online.

State health departments are another place to order death certificates but, in most instances, getting them from the state takes a lot longer than ordering them from the county health department.

The county or state often will not search for a certificate if the information provided is incorrect or incomplete. This can provoke guessing games, particularly where women are concerned. Was the certificate filed under a birth name, professional name, or married name? Sometimes several attempts are necessary to get it right.

If you order certificates from the same place over a period of time, you may develop a relationship with the person filling your order. This can be quite beneficial if a problem or question should arise.

Following the 182 pages of actual death certificates is a section containing biographical notes about each of the deceased, providing information essential to understanding the certificates.

THE DEATH CERTIFICATES

CERTIFICATION OF VITAL RECORD

COUNTY OF LOS ANGELES • REGISTRAR-RECORDER/COUNTY CLERK

CERTIFICATE OF DEATH 0190-018789

STATE OF CALIFORNIA—DEPARTMENT OF PUBLIC HEALTH

DECEDENT PERSONAL DATA	1a. Name of deceased—first name: WILLIAM	1b. Middle name: ALEXANDER	1c. Last name: ABBOTT
	2a. Date of death: April 24, 1974	2b. Hour: 5:30 A.M.	
	3. Sex: Male	4. Color or race: Caucasian	5. Birthplace: New Jersey
	6. Date of birth: October 2, 1898	7. Age: 75 years	
	8. Name and birthplace of father: Harry Abbott, Unknown	9. Maiden name and birthplace of mother: Rae Fisher, Unknown	
	10. Citizen of what country: U. S. A.	11. Social security number: 092-09-9869 A	12. Married, never married, widowed, divorced: Married
	13. Name of surviving spouse: Jennie Mae Pratt		
	14. Last occupation: Performer	15. Number of years in this occupation: 45	16. Name of last employing company or firm: Universal Studios
	17. Kind of industry or business: Motion Picture		
PLACE OF DEATH	18a. Place of death—name of hospital or other in-patient facility: -	18b. Street address: 19853 Redwing Street	18c. Inside city corporate limits: Yes
	18d. City or town: Woodland Hills	18e. County: Los Angeles	18f. Length of stay in county of death: 34 years; 18g. Length of stay in California: 34 years
USUAL RESIDENCE	19a. Usual residence: 19853 Redwing Street	19b. Inside city corporate limits: Yes	20. Name and mailing address of informant: Mrs. Jennie M. Abbott, Same
	19c. City or town: Woodland Hills	19d. County: Los Angeles	19e. State: California
PHYSICIAN'S OR CORONER'S CERTIFICATION	21b. Physician: From 5/6/69 to 4/24/74; last saw the deceased alive 4/18/74	21c. Physician or coroner—signature: Harry L. Carnow, MD	21d. Date signed: 4/24/74
	21e. Address: 5312 Comercio Lane, Woodland Hills, Calif.	21f. Physician's California license number: A-18843	
FUNERAL DIRECTOR AND LOCAL REGISTRAR	22a. Specify burial, entombment or cremation: Cremation	22b. Date: 4/29/74	23. Name of cemetery or crematory: Grandview Memorial Park
	24. Embalmer—signature: [signature], License number 4937	25. Name of funeral director: J. T. OSWALD MORTUARY, Re	26. If not certified by coroner, was this death reported to coroner: No
	27. Local registrar—signature: [signature]	28. Date accepted for registration by local registrar: APR 24 1974	
CAUSE OF DEATH	29. Part I. Death was caused by: Immediate cause (A) Respiratory failure		5 min
	Due to, or as a consequence of (B) Acute CVA		2 hrs
	Due to, or as a consequence of (C) Cerebral metastases		6 mos.
	30. Part II. Other significant conditions	31. Was operation or biopsy performed: no	32a. Autopsy: No
INJURY INFORMATION	33. Specify accident, suicide or homicide	34. Place of injury	35. Injury at work
	36a. Date of injury	36b. Hour	
	37a. Place of injury	37b. Distance from place of injury to usual residence	38. / 39. Laboratory tests
	40. Describe how injury occurred		
STATE REGISTRAR	A. B. C. D. E. F.		

*Dr. Statesz: Primary site Prostate, mrc

This is to certify that this document is a true copy of the official record filed with the Registrar-Recorder/County Clerk.

Beatriz Valdez
BEATRIZ VALDEZ
Registrar-Recorder/County Clerk

AUG 25 1995
19-398415

This copy not valid unless prepared on engraved border displaying the Seal and Signature of the Registrar-Recorder/County Clerk.

ANY ALTERATION OR ERASURE VOIDS THIS CERTIFICATE

CERTIFICATION OF VITAL RECORD

COUNTY OF LOS ANGELES • REGISTRAR-RECORDER/COUNTY CLERK

FILED MAR 15 1968 RAY E LEE COUNTY RECORDER

CERTIFICATE OF DEATH 7097-000081

STATE FILE NUMBER — STATE OF CALIFORNIA—DEPARTMENT OF PUBLIC HEALTH — LOCAL REGISTRATION DISTRICT AND CERTIFICATE NUMBER

DECEDENT PERSONAL DATA 5

- 1A. NAME OF DECEASED—FIRST NAME: Nick
- 1B. MIDDLE NAME:
- 1C. LAST NAME: Adams
- 2A. DATE OF DEATH—MONTH, DAY, YEAR: 2-7-68
- 2B. HOUR: 8:00 P.M.
- 3. SEX: male
- 4. COLOR OR RACE: Cauc.
- 5. BIRTHPLACE (STATE OR FOREIGN COUNTRY): Pa.
- 6. DATE OF BIRTH: 7-10-1931
- 7. AGE (LAST BIRTHDAY): 36 YEARS
- 8. NAME AND BIRTHPLACE OF FATHER: Peter Adamshock-Pa.
- 9. MAIDEN NAME AND BIRTHPLACE OF MOTHER: Catherine Kutz-Pa.
- 10. CITIZEN OF WHAT COUNTRY: U.S.A.
- 11. SOCIAL SECURITY NUMBER: 157-20-8333
- 12. MARRIED, NEVER MARRIED, WIDOWED, DIVORCED (SPECIFY): married
- 13. NAME OF SURVIVING SPOUSE (IF WIFE, ENTER MAIDEN NAME): Carol L. Nugent
- 14. LAST OCCUPATION: Actor
- 15. NUMBER OF YEARS IN THIS OCCUPATION: 14
- 16. NAME OF LAST EMPLOYING COMPANY OR FIRM (IF SELF-EMPLOYED, SO STATE): Free lance
- 17. KIND OF INDUSTRY OR BUSINESS: Motion Pictures and T.V.

PLACE OF DEATH

- 18A. PLACE OF DEATH—NAME OF HOSPITAL OR OTHER IN-PATIENT FACILITY:
- 18B. STREET ADDRESS—(STREET AND NUMBER, OR LOCATION): 2126 El Robles Lane
- 18C. INSIDE CITY CORPORATE LIMITS (SPECIFY YES OR NO): Yes
- 18D. CITY OR TOWN: Los Angeles
- 18E. COUNTY: Los Angeles
- 18F. LENGTH OF STAY IN COUNTY OF DEATH: 21 YEARS
- 18G. LENGTH OF STAY IN CALIFORNIA: 21 YEARS

USUAL RESIDENCE (IF DEATH OCCURRED IN INSTITUTION, ENTER RESIDENCE BEFORE ADMISSION)

- 19A. USUAL RESIDENCE—STREET ADDRESS (STREET AND NUMBER OR LOCATION): 2126 El Robles Lane
- 19B. INSIDE CITY CORPORATE LIMITS (SPECIFY YES OR NO): Yes
- 19C. CITY OR TOWN: Los Angeles
- 19D. COUNTY: Los Angeles
- 19E. STATE: Calif.
- 20. NAME AND MAILING ADDRESS OF INFORMANT: Carol L. Adams, 9240 Robin Dr., Los Angeles, California

PHYSICIAN'S OR CORONER'S CERTIFICATION

- 21A. CORONER: I HEREBY CERTIFY THAT DEATH OCCURRED AT THE HOUR, DATE AND PLACE STATED ABOVE FROM THE CAUSES STATED BELOW AND THAT I HAVE HELD AN INVESTIGATION: Investigation (INVESTIGATION OR INQUEST)
- 21B. PHYSICIAN: I HEREBY CERTIFY THAT DEATH OCCURRED AT THE HOUR, DATE, AND PLACE STATED ABOVE, FROM THE CAUSES STATED BELOW AND THAT I ATTENDED THE DECEASED FROM / TO / AND LAST SAW THE DECEASED ALIVE
- 21C. PHYSICIAN OR CORONER SIGNATURE: Thomas T. Noguchi, M.D. Coroner — Wallace Graham MD Deputy
- 21D. DATE SIGNED: 3-4-68
- 21E. ADDRESS: Hall of Justice, Los Angeles
- 21F. PHYSICIAN'S CALIFORNIA LICENSE NUMBER: G-9196

FUNERAL DIRECTOR AND LOCAL REGISTRAR

- 22A. SPECIFY BURIAL, ENTOMBMENT OR CREMATION: burial
- 22B. DATE: Shipped 2-10-68
- 23. NAME OF CEMETERY OR CREMATORY: St. Cyrill and Methodius Cem., Berwick, Pa.
- 24. EMBALMER—SIGNATURE (IF BODY EMBALMED) LICENSE NUMBER: 4109
- 25. NAME OF FUNERAL DIRECTOR (OR PERSON ACTING AS SUCH): Pierce Brothers, Beverly Hills
- 26. IF NOT CERTIFIED BY CORONER, WAS THIS DEATH REPORTED TO CORONER? (SPECIFY YES OR NO):
- 27. LOCAL REGISTRAR SIGNATURE: [signature] MD
- 28. DATE ACCEPTED FOR REGISTRATION BY LOCAL REGISTRAR: MAR 6 1968 — 2-9-68

MEDICAL AND HEALTH DATA — CAUSE OF DEATH 5

29. PART I. DEATH WAS CAUSED BY: ENTER ONLY ONE CAUSE PER LINE FOR A, B, AND C

- IMMEDIATE CAUSE (A): PARALDEHYDE AND PROMAZINE INTOXICATION
- CONDITIONS, IF ANY, WHICH GAVE RISE TO THE IMMEDIATE CAUSE (A), STATING THE UNDERLYING CAUSE LAST. DUE TO, OR AS A CONSEQUENCE OF (B):
- DUE TO, OR AS A CONSEQUENCE OF (C):

APPROXIMATE INTERVAL BETWEEN ONSET AND DEATH

- 30. PART II. OTHER SIGNIFICANT CONDITIONS—CONTRIBUTING TO DEATH BUT NOT RELATED TO THE IMMEDIATE CAUSE GIVEN IN PART I(A):
- 31. WAS OPERATION OR BIOPSY PERFORMED FOR ANY CONDITION IN ITEMS 29 OR 30? (SPECIFY TYPE OF OPERATION AND/OR BIOPSY): No
- 32A. AUTOPSY (SPECIFY YES OR NO): Yes
- 32B. IF YES, WERE FINDINGS CONSIDERED IN DETERMINING CAUSE OF DEATH? (SPECIFY YES OR NO): Yes

INJURY INFORMATION

- 33. SPECIFY ACCIDENT, SUICIDE OR HOMICIDE: Accident; Suicide; Undetermined
- 34. PLACE OF INJURY (SPECIFY HOME, FARM, FACTORY, STREET, OFFICE BUILDING, ETC.): Home
- 35. INJURY AT WORK (SPECIFY YES OR NO): No
- 36A. DATE OF INJURY—MONTH, DAY, YEAR: Prior to 2-7-68
- 36B. HOUR: Prior to 8:00 P.M.
- 37A. PLACE OF INJURY (STREET AND NUMBER OR LOCATION AND CITY OR TOWN): 2126 El Robles, Los Angeles (W.L.A.)
- 37B. DISTANCE FROM PLACE OF INJURY TO USUAL RESIDENCE, ITEM 19: 0 MILES
- 38. WERE LABORATORY TESTS DONE FOR DRUGS OR TOXIC CHEMICALS (SPECIFY YES OR NO): Yes
- 39. WERE LABORATORY TESTS DONE FOR ALCOHOL? (SPECIFY YES OR NO): Yes
- 40. DESCRIBE HOW INJURY OCCURRED (ENTER SEQUENCE OF EVENTS WHICH RESULTED IN INJURY. NATURE OF INJURY SHOULD BE ENTERED IN ITEM 29): AS ABOVE

STATE REGISTRAR

A.	B.	C.	D.	E.	F.
					2611

REV. 1-1-68 FORM VS-11

This is to certify that this document is a true copy of the official record filed with the Registrar-Recorder/County Clerk.

[signature]
CHARLES WEISSBURD
Registrar-Recorder/County Clerk

FEB 03 1992

19-307549

This copy not valid unless prepared on engraved border displaying the Seal and Signature of the Registrar-Recorder/County Clerk.

American Bank Note Company

ANY ALTERATION OR ERASURE VOIDS THIS CERTIFICATE

CERTIFICATION OF VITAL RECORD

COUNTY OF LOS ANGELES • REGISTRAR-RECORDER/COUNTY CLERK

STATE FILE NUMBER

CERTIFICATE OF DEATH

STATE OF CALIFORNIA—DEPARTMENT OF PUBLIC HEALTH

LOCAL REGISTRATION DISTRICT AND CERTIFICATE NUMBER 7053 17247

DECEDENT PERSONAL DATA

1a. NAME OF DECEASED—FIRST NAME: GRACE
1b. MIDDLE NAME: ALLEN
1c. LAST NAME: BURNS
2a. DATE OF DEATH—MONTH, DAY, YEAR: August 27, 1964
2b. HOUR: 11:55 P.M.
3. SEX: Female
4. COLOR OR RACE: Caucasian
5. BIRTHPLACE (STATE OR FOREIGN COUNTRY): California
6. DATE OF BIRTH: July 26, 1902
7. AGE (LAST BIRTHDAY): 62 YEARS
8. NAME AND BIRTHPLACE OF FATHER: George Allen - California
9. MAIDEN NAME AND BIRTHPLACE OF MOTHER: Margaret Darragh - Unknown
10. CITIZEN OF WHAT COUNTRY: U.S.A.
11. SOCIAL SECURITY NUMBER: 568-03-7360
12. LAST OCCUPATION: Actress
13. NUMBER OF YEARS IN THIS OCCUPATION: 40
14. NAME OF LAST EMPLOYING COMPANY OR FIRM: McCadden Productions
15. KIND OF INDUSTRY OR BUSINESS: Television Films
16. IF DECEASED WAS EVER IN U.S. ARMED FORCES, GIVE WAR OR DATES OF SERVICE: None
17. SPECIFY MARRIED, NEVER MARRIED, WIDOWED, DIVORCED: Married
18a. NAME OF PRESENT SPOUSE: George N. Burns
18b. PRESENT OR LAST OCCUPATION OF SPOUSE: Actor

PLACE OF DEATH

19a. PLACE OF DEATH—NAME OF HOSPITAL: Cedars Of Lebanon Hospital
19b. STREET ADDRESS: 4833 Fountain Avenue — INSIDE CITY CORPORATE LIMITS [X]
19c. CITY OR TOWN: Los Angeles
19d. COUNTY: Los Angeles
19e. LENGTH OF STAY IN COUNTY OF DEATH: 30 YEARS
19f. LENGTH OF STAY IN CALIFORNIA: 30 YEARS

LAST USUAL RESIDENCE (WHERE DID DECEASED LIVE—. IN INSTITUTION ENTER RESIDENCE BEFORE ADMISSION)

20a. LAST USUAL RESIDENCE—STREET ADDRESS: 720 N. Maple Drive
20b. IF INSIDE CITY CORPORATE LIMITS: [X] CHECK HERE
20c. CITY OR TOWN: Beverly Hills 12-13
20d. COUNTY: Los Angeles
20e. STATE: California
21a. NAME OF INFORMANT (IF OTHER THAN SPOUSE): William Burns
21b. ADDRESS OF INFORMANT: 364 N. McCadden Place, Los Angeles, California

PHYSICIAN'S OR CORONER'S CERTIFICATION

22a. PHYSICIAN: I HEREBY CERTIFY THAT DEATH OCCURRED AT THE HOUR, DATE AND PLACE STATED ABOVE FROM THE CAUSES STATED BELOW AND THAT I ATTENDED THE DECEASED FROM 5-9-44 TO 8-27-64 AND THAT I LAST SAW THE DECEASED ALIVE ON 8-26-64
22b. CORONER: I HEREBY CERTIFY THAT DEATH OCCURRED AT THE HOUR, DATE AND PLACE STATED ABOVE FROM THE CAUSES STATED BELOW AND THAT I HAVE HELD ON THE REMAINS OF DECEASED AS REQUIRED BY LAW
22c. PHYSICIAN OR CORONER—SIGNATURE: S R Kennamer — DEGREE OR TITLE: MD
22d. ADDRESS: 436 N Roxbury dr.
22e. DATE SIGNED: 8-29-64

FUNERAL DIRECTOR AND LOCAL REGISTRAR

23. SPECIFY BURIAL, ENTOMBMENT OR CREMATION: Entombment
24. DATE: 8-31-64
25. NAME OF CEMETERY OR CREMATORY: Forest Lawn Memorial-Park Mausoleum
26. EMBALMER—SIGNATURE: Marvin C. Frey — LICENSE NUMBER: 4373
27. NAME OF FUNERAL DIRECTOR: FOREST LAWN MEMORIAL-PARK, GLENDALE, CALIFORNIA
28. DATE ACCEPTED FOR REGISTRATION BY LOCAL REGISTRAR: AUG 31 1964
29. LOCAL REGISTRAR—SIGNATURE: K. H. Sutherland M.D.

MEDICAL AND HEALTH DATA

CAUSE OF DEATH

30. CAUSE OF DEATH — ENTER ONLY ONE CAUSE PER LINE FOR (A), (B), AND (C)
PART I. DEATH WAS CAUSED BY: IMMEDIATE CAUSE (A): Acute myocardial infarction — 2 hrs.
CONDITIONS, IF ANY, WHICH GAVE RISE TO THE ABOVE CAUSE (A) STATING THE UNDERLYING CAUSE LAST. DUE TO (B): Arteriosclerotic Heart disease — 5 yrs.
DUE TO (C):
APPROXIMATE INTERVAL BETWEEN ONSET AND DEATH
PART II: OTHER SIGNIFICANT CONDITIONS CONTRIBUTING TO DEATH BUT NOT RELATED TO THE TERMINAL DISEASE CONDITION GIVEN IN PART I (A)

OPERATION AND AUTOPSY

31. OPERATION—CHECK ONE: [X] NO OPERATION PERFORMED
32. DATE OF OPERATION
33. AUTOPSY—CHECK ONE: [X] NO AUTOPSY PERFORMED

INJURY INFORMATION

34a. SPECIFY ACCIDENT, SUICIDE OR HOMICIDE
34b. DESCRIBE HOW INJURY OCCURRED
35a. TIME OF INJURY — HOUR MONTH DAY YEAR M.
35b. INJURY OCCURRED — WHILE AT WORK / NOT WHILE AT WORK
35c. PLACE OF INJURY
35d. CITY, TOWN, OR LOCATION — COUNTY — STATE

Filed OCT 9 1964 RAY E. LEE, COUNTY RECORDER

This is to certify that this document is a true copy of the official record filed with the Registrar-Recorder/County Clerk.

NOV 13 1995

19-065564

This copy not valid unless prepared on engraved border displaying the Seal of the Registrar-Recorder/County Clerk.

ANY ALTERATION OR ERASURE VOIDS THIS CERTIFICATE

CERTIFICATION OF VITAL RECORD

COUNTY OF LOS ANGELES • REGISTRAR-RECORDER/COUNTY CLERK

CERTIFICATE OF DEATH 3911 9046474
STATE OF CALIFORNIA
USE BLACK INK ONLY

STATE FILE NUMBER — LOCAL REGISTRATION DISTRICT AND CERTIFICATE NUMBER

DECEDENT PERSONAL DATA

1A. NAME OF DECEDENT—FIRST (GIVEN): IRWIN
1B. MIDDLE: --
1C. LAST (FAMILY): ALLEN
2A. DATE OF DEATH—MO, DAY, YR: NOVEMBER 2, 1991
2B. HOUR: 0717
3. SEX: MALE
4. RACE: CAUCASIAN
5. HISPANIC—SPECIFY: YES [ ] NO [X]
6. DATE OF BIRTH—MO, DAY, YR: JUNE 12, 1916
7. AGE IN YEARS: 75 (IF UNDER 1 YEAR: MONTHS, DAYS; IF UNDER 24 HOURS: HOURS, MINUTES)
8. STATE OF BIRTH: NY
9. CITIZEN OF WHAT COUNTRY: USA
10A. FULL NAME OF FATHER: JOSEPH ALLEN
10B. STATE OF BIRTH: RUSSIA
11A. FULL MAIDEN NAME OF MOTHER: EVA DAVIS
11B. STATE OF BIRTH: NY
12. MILITARY SERVICE: 19__ TO 19__ [X] NONE
13. SOCIAL SECURITY NO.: 573-20-5978
14. MARITAL STATUS: MARRIED
15. NAME OF SURVIVING SPOUSE (IF WIFE, ENTER MAIDEN NAME): SHEILA MATHEWS
16A. USUAL OCCUPATION: DIRECTOR & PRODUCER
16B. USUAL KIND OF BUSINESS OR INDUSTRY: MOTION PICTURES
16C. USUAL EMPLOYER: WARNER BROTHERS
16D. YEARS IN OCCUPATION: 45
17. EDUCATION—YEARS COMPLETED: 14

USUAL RESIDENCE

18A. RESIDENCE—STREET AND NUMBER OR LOCATION: 21554 PACIFIC COAST HWY
18B. CITY: MALIBU
18C. ZIP CODE: 90265
18D. COUNTY: LOS ANGELES
18E. NUMBER OF YEARS IN THIS COUNTY: 45
18F. STATE OR FOREIGN COUNTRY: CALIFORNIA
20. NAME, RELATIONSHIP, MAILING ADDRESS AND ZIP CODE OF INFORMANT: MRS. SHEILA ALLEN - WIFE, 21554 PACIFIC COAST HWY, MALIBU, CA 90265

PLACE OF DEATH

19A. PLACE OF DEATH: SANTA MONICA HOSPITAL
19B. IF HOSPITAL, SPECIFY ONE: IP, ER/OP, DOA: IP
19C. COUNTY: LOS ANGELES
19D. STREET ADDRESS—STREET AND NUMBER OR LOCATION: 1225 15TH STREET
19E. CITY: SANTA MONICA

CAUSE OF DEATH

21. DEATH WAS CAUSED BY: (ENTER ONLY ONE CAUSE PER LINE FOR A, B, AND C) — TIME INTERVAL BETWEEN ONSET AND DEATH

IMMEDIATE CAUSE (A) CARDIO-PULMONARY ARREST — 5 MINS
DUE TO (B) ACUTE MYOCARDIAL INFARCTION — 10 MINS
DUE TO (C) ATHEROSCLEROTIC HEART DISEASE — 15 YRS

22. WAS DEATH REPORTED TO CORONER? REFERRAL NUMBER: YES [ ] NO [X]
23. WAS BIOPSY PERFORMED? YES [ ] NO [X]
24A. WAS AUTOPSY PERFORMED? YES [ ] NO [X]
24B. WAS IT USED IN DETERMINING CAUSE OF DEATH? YES [ ] NO [ ]
25. OTHER SIGNIFICANT CONDITIONS CONTRIBUTING TO DEATH BUT NOT RELATED TO CAUSE GIVEN IN 21: NONE
26. WAS OPERATION PERFORMED FOR ANY CONDITION IN ITEM 21 OR 25? IF YES, LIST TYPE OF OPERATION AND DATE: CORONARY ARTERY BYPASS GRAFT SURGERY, 1988

PHYSICIAN'S CERTIFICATION

I CERTIFY THAT TO THE BEST OF MY KNOWLEDGE DEATH OCCURRED AT THE HOUR, DATE AND PLACE STATED FROM THE CAUSES STATED.
27A. DECEDENT ATTENDED SINCE (MONTH, DAY, YEAR): AUG. 1, 1978 — DECEDENT LAST SEEN ALIVE (MONTH, DAY, YEAR): OCT. 28, 1991
27B. SIGNATURE AND DEGREE OR TITLE OF CERTIFIER: Jay J. Jordan, MD
27C. CERTIFIER'S LICENSE NUMBER: A025646
27D. DATE SIGNED: 11-4-1991
27E. TYPE ATTENDING PHYSICIAN'S NAME AND ADDRESS: JAY L. JORDAN, M.D., 8631 WEST 3RD STREET, SUITE 445E, LOS ANGELES, CA 90048

CORONER'S USE ONLY

I CERTIFY THAT IN MY OPINION DEATH OCCURRED AT THE HOUR, DATE AND PLACE STATED FROM THE CAUSES STATED.
28A. SIGNATURE AND TITLE OF CORONER OR DEPUTY CORONER
28B. DATE SIGNED
29. MANNER OF DEATH—specify one: natural, accident, suicide, homicide, pending investigation or could not be determined
30A. PLACE OF INJURY
30B. INJURY AT WORK: YES [ ] NO [ ]
30C. DATE OF INJURY—MONTH, DAY, YEAR
31. HOUR
32. LOCATION (STREET AND NUMBER OR LOCATION AND CITY)
33. DESCRIBE HOW INJURY OCCURRED (EVENTS WHICH RESULTED IN INJURY)

FUNERAL DIRECTOR AND LOCAL REGISTRAR

34A. DISPOSITION(S): ENTOMBMENT
34B. PLACE OF FINAL DISPOSITION—NAME AND ADDRESS: MOUNT SINAI MEMORIAL-PARK, 5950 FOREST LAWN DRIVE, LOS ANGELES, CA
34C. DATE MO, DAY, YEAR: NOV. 6, 1991
35A. SIGNATURE OF EMBALMER: Richard D. Wasserman
35B. LICENSE NUMBER: 6563
36A. NAME OF FUNERAL DIRECTOR (OR PERSON ACTING AS SUCH): MOUNT SINAI MORTUARY
36B. LICENSE NO.: FD-1010
37. SIGNATURE OF LOCAL REGISTRAR: Robert C. Bate Jr
38. REGISTRATION DATE: NOV 06 1991

STATE REGISTRAR: A. B. C. D. E. F. CENSUS TRACT

VS-11 (REV. 3-91) — MAKE NO ERASURES, WHITEOUTS, OR OTHER ALTERATIONS

This is to certify that this document is a true copy of the official record filed with the Registrar-Recorder/County Clerk.

CHARLES WEISSBURD
Registrar-Recorder/County Clerk

JAN 22 1992
19-298625

This copy not valid unless prepared on engraved border displaying the Seal and Signature of the Registrar-Recorder/County Clerk.

American Bank Note Company

ANY ALTERATION OR ERASURE VOIDS THIS CERTIFICATE

CERTIFICATION OF VITAL RECORD

SANTA BARBARA COUNTY

SANTA BARBARA, CALIFORNIA

CERTIFICATE OF DEATH

STATE OF CALIFORNIA
USE BLACK INK ONLY

3-92-42-000001

STATE FILE NUMBER — LOCAL REGISTRATION DISTRICT AND CERTIFICATE NUMBER

DECEDENT PERSONAL DATA

1A. NAME OF DECEDENT—FIRST (GIVEN): FRANCES
1B. MIDDLE: MARGARET
1C. LAST (FAMILY): ANDERSON
2A. DATE OF DEATH—MO, DAY, YR: JANUARY 3, 1992
2B. HOUR: 0330
3. SEX: F
4. RACE: WHITE
5. HISPANIC—SPECIFY: ☐ YES ☒ NO
6. DATE OF BIRTH—MO, DAY, YR: FEBRUARY 10, 1897
7. AGE IN YEARS: 94
IF UNDER 1 YEAR: MONTHS / DAYS; IF UNDER 24 HOURS: HOURS / MINUTES
8. STATE OF BIRTH: AUSTRAL
9. CITIZEN OF WHAT COUNTRY: AUSTRALIA
10A. FULL NAME OF FATHER: JAMES ANDERSON ANDERSON
10B. STATE OF BIRTH: SCOTLAND
11A. FULL MAIDEN NAME OF MOTHER: JESSE MARGARET SALTMARSH
11B. STATE OF BIRTH: AUSTRALIA
12. MILITARY SERVICE?: 19__ TO 19__ ☒ NONE
13. SOCIAL SECURITY NO.: 555-09-3841
14. MARITAL STATUS: DIVORCED
15. NAME OF SURVIVING SPOUSE (IF WIFE, ENTER MAIDEN NAME): ---
16A. USUAL OCCUPATION: ACTRESS
16B. USUAL KIND OF BUSINESS OR INDUSTRY: THEATRE
16C. USUAL EMPLOYER: SELF
16D. YEARS IN OCCUPATION: 70
17. EDUCATION—YEARS COMPLETED: 9

USUAL RESIDENCE

18A. RESIDENCE—STREET AND NUMBER OR LOCATION: 808 SAN YSIDRO LANE
18B. CITY: SANTA BARBARA
18C. ZIP CODE: 93108
18D. COUNTY: SANTA BARBARA
18E. NUMBER OF YEARS IN THIS COUNTY: 40
18F. STATE OR FOREIGN COUNTRY: CALIFORNIA
20. NAME, RELATIONSHIP, MAILING ADDRESS AND ZIP CODE OF INFORMANT: JENIFER BROWN - NIECE, P.O. BOX 8, MIDLAND SCHOOL, LOS OLIVOS, CA 93441

PLACE OF DEATH

19A. PLACE OF DEATH: RESIDENCE
19B. IF HOSPITAL, SPECIFY ONE: IP, ER/OP, DOA: ---
19C. COUNTY: SANTA BARBARA
19D. STREET ADDRESS—STREET AND NUMBER OR LOCATION: 808 SAN YSIDRO LANE
19E. CITY: SANTA BARBARA

CAUSE OF DEATH

21. DEATH WAS CAUSED BY: (ENTER ONLY ONE CAUSE PER LINE FOR A, B, AND C)
IMMEDIATE CAUSE (A) RESPIRATORY FAILURE — TIME INTERVAL BETWEEN ONSET AND DEATH: MIN.
DUE TO (B) BRAIN TUMOR - PRIMARY — 4 MO.
DUE TO (C)
22. WAS DEATH REPORTED TO CORONER? ☒ YES — REFERRAL NUMBER: CNR-92-008 ☐ NO
23. WAS BIOPSY PERFORMED? ☐ YES ☒ NO
24A. WAS AUTOPSY PERFORMED? ☐ YES ☒ NO
24B. WAS IT USED IN DETERMINING CAUSE OF DEATH? ☐ YES ☒ NO
25. OTHER SIGNIFICANT CONDITIONS CONTRIBUTING TO DEATH BUT NOT RELATED TO CAUSE GIVEN IN 21: NONE
26. WAS OPERATION PERFORMED FOR ANY CONDITION IN ITEM 21 OR 25? IF YES, LIST TYPE OF OPERATION AND DATE: NO

PHYSICIAN'S CERTIFICATION

I CERTIFY THAT TO THE BEST OF MY KNOWLEDGE DEATH OCCURRED AT THE HOUR, DATE AND PLACE STATED FROM THE CAUSES STATED.
27A. DECEDENT ATTENDED SINCE MONTH, DAY, YEAR: 8/1991
DECEDENT LAST SEEN ALIVE MONTH, DAY, YEAR: 10/10/1991
27B. SIGNATURE AND DEGREE OR TITLE OF CERTIFIER: [signature]
27C. CERTIFIER'S LICENSE NUMBER: G 57049
27D. DATE SIGNED: 1/3/1992
27E. TYPE ATTENDING PHYSICIAN'S NAME AND ADDRESS: DAVID FRECKER, MD, 2320 BATH STREET, SANTA BARBARA, CA

CORONER'S USE ONLY

I CERTIFY THAT IN MY OPINION DEATH OCCURRED AT THE HOUR, DATE AND PLACE STATED FROM THE CAUSES STATED.
28A. SIGNATURE AND TITLE OF CORONER OR DEPUTY CORONER
28B. DATE SIGNED
29. MANNER OF DEATH—specify one: natural, accident, suicide, homicide, pending investigation or could not be determined
30A. PLACE OF INJURY
30B. INJURY AT WORK ☐ YES ☐ NO
30C. DATE OF INJURY MONTH, DAY, YEAR
31. HOUR
32. LOCATION (STREET AND NUMBER OR LOCATION AND CITY)
33. DESCRIBE HOW INJURY OCCURRED (EVENTS WHICH RESULTED IN INJURY)

FUNERAL DIRECTOR AND LOCAL REGISTRAR

34A. DISPOSITION(S): CR-RES
34B. PLACE OF FINAL DISPOSITION—NAME AND ADDRESS: 808 SAN YSIDRO LANE, SANTA BARBARA, CA
34C. DATE MO, DAY, YEAR: 1/7/1992
35A. SIGNATURE OF EMBALMER: NOT EMBALMED
35B. LICENSE NUMBER: ---
36A. NAME OF FUNERAL DIRECTOR (OR PERSON ACTING AS SUCH): WELCH-RYCE-HAIDER FUNERAL CHAPELS
36B. LICENSE NO.: 303
37. SIGNATURE OF LOCAL REGISTRAR: Sarah L. Miller (K)
38. REGISTRATION DATE: JAN 0 6 1992

STATE REGISTRAR

A. B. C. D. E. F. CENSUS TRACT

MAKE NO ERASURES, WHITEOUTS, OR OTHER ALTERATIONS

S214703

CERTIFIED COPY OF VITAL RECORDS

STATE OF CALIFORNIA
COUNTY OF SANTA BARBARA } SS

DATE ISSUED JUN 0 5 1998

This is a true and exact reproduction of the document officially registered and placed on file in the office of the SANTA BARBARA COUNTY CLERK-RECORDER.

[signature]
KENNETH A. PETTIT
COUNTY CLERK-RECORDER
SANTA BARBARA, CALIFORNIA

This copy not valid unless prepared on engraved border displaying seal and signature of County Clerk-Recorder.

MIDWEST BANK NOTE COMPANY

ANY ALTERATION OR ERASURE VOIDS THIS CERTIFICATE

CERTIFICATION OF VITAL RECORD

COUNTY OF LOS ANGELES • REGISTRAR-RECORDER/COUNTY CLERK

CERTIFICATE OF DEATH 39019050699
STATE OF CALIFORNIA
USE BLACK INK ONLY

DECEDENT PERSONAL DATA

- 1A. Name of Decedent—First (Given): EVE
- 1B. Middle: ARDEN
- 1C. Last (Family): WEST
- 2A. Date of Death—Mo, Day, Yr: NOVEMBER 12, 1990
- 2B. Hour: 0218
- 3. Sex: FEMALE
- 4. Race: CAUCASIAN
- 5. Hispanic—Specify: Yes ☐ No XX
- 6. Date of Birth—Mo, Day, Yr: APRIL 30, 1908
- 7. Age in Years: 82
- 8. State of Birth: CA
- 9. Citizen of What Country: USA
- 10A. Full Name of Father: CHARLES QUEDENS
- 10B. State of Birth: UNKNOWN
- 11A. Full Maiden Name of Mother: LUCILLE UNKNOWN
- 11B. State of Birth: CALIFORNIA
- 12. Military Service?: 19__ to 19__ ☒ None
- 13. Social Security No.: 568-03-2856
- 14. Marital Status: WIDOWED
- 15. Name of Surviving Spouse (If wife, enter maiden name): ----
- 16A. Usual Occupation: ACTRESS
- 16B. Usual Kind of Business or Industry: ENTERTAINMENT
- 16C. Usual Employer: SELF
- 16D. Years in Occupation: 52
- 17. Education—Years Completed: 12

USUAL RESIDENCE

- 18A. Residence—Street and Number or Location: 9066 ST. IVES DRIVE
- 18B. City: LOS ANGELES
- 18C. Zip Code: 90069
- 18D. County: LOS ANGELES
- 18E. Number of Years in This County: 52
- 18F. State or Foreign Country: CALIFORNIA
- 20. Name, Relationship, Mailing Address and Zip Code of Informant: DOUGLAS WEST (SON) 6451 GREENBUSH AVENUE VAN NUYS, CA 91401

PLACE OF DEATH

- 19A. Place of Death: RESIDENCE
- 19B. If Hospital, Specify One: IP, ER/OP, DOA: --
- 19C. County: LOS ANGELES
- 19D. Street Address—Street and Number or Location: 9066 ST. IVES DR.
- 19E. City: LOS ANGELES

CAUSE OF DEATH

- 21. Death was caused by: (Enter only one cause per line for A, B, and C)
  - Immediate Cause (A): Cardiac Arrest — Time interval between onset and death: Ten minutes
  - Due to (B): Arteriosclerotic Heart Disease — 20 years
  - Due to (C):
- 22. Was Death Reported to Coroner? Yes ☐ No ☒ Referral Number:
- 23. Was Biopsy Performed? Yes ☐ No ☒
- 24A. Was Autopsy Performed? Yes ☐ No ☒
- 24B. Was It Used in Determining Cause of Death? Yes ☐ No ☒
- 25. Other Significant Conditions Contributing to Death But Not Related to Cause Given in 21: none
- 26. Was Operation Performed for Any Condition in Item 21 or 23? If yes, list type of operation and date: no

PHYSICIAN'S CERTIFICATION

- I certify that to the best of my knowledge death occurred at the hour, date and place stated from the causes stated.
- 27A. Decedent Attended Since Month, Day, Year: 2/24/1965 — Decedent Last Seen Alive Month, Day, Year: 11/11/90
- 27B. Signature and Degree or Title of Certifier: [signature], MD
- 27C. Certifier's License Number: G6692
- 27D. Date Signed: 11/14/90
- 27E. Type Attending Physician's Name and Address: ELSIE A. GIORGI, MD 153 LASKY DRIVE, BEVERLY HILLS, CA 90210

CORONER'S USE ONLY

- I certify that in my opinion death occurred at the hour, date and place stated from the causes stated.
- 28A. Signature and Title of Coroner or Deputy Coroner:
- 28B. Date Signed:
- 29. Manner of Death—Specify one: natural, accident, suicide, homicide, pending investigation or could not be determined
- 30A. Place of Injury
- 30B. Injury at Work: Yes ☐ No ☐
- 30C. Date of Injury Month, Day, Year
- 31. Hour
- 32. Location (Street and Number or Location and City)
- 33. Describe How Injury Occurred (Events Which Resulted in Injury)

FUNERAL DIRECTOR AND LOCAL REGISTRAR

- 34A. Disposition(s): CR/BU
- 34B. Place of Final Disposition—Name and Address: WESTWOOD MEMORIAL PARK 1218 GLENDON AVE. LOS ANGELES, CA
- 34C. Date Mo, Day, Year: NOV.15.1990
- 35A. Signature of Embalmer: NOT EMBALMED
- 35B. License Number: NONE
- 36A. Name of Funeral Director (or Person Acting as Such): PIERCE BROS. WESTWOOD VILLAGE
- 36B. License No.: F-951
- 37. Signature of Local Registrar: [signature] R.R.
- 38. Registration Date: NOV 14 1990

10 STATE REGISTRAR: A. B. C. D. E. F. CENSUS TRACT

VS-11 (REV. 1-90) 7140 MAKE NO ERASURES, WHITEOUTS, OR OTHER ALTERATIONS 07-9-1-7005

This is to certify that this document is a true copy of the official record filed with the Registrar-Recorder/County Clerk.

[signature]
CHARLES WEISSBURD
Registrar-Recorder/County Clerk

FEB 03 1992
19-309695

This copy not valid unless prepared on engraved border displaying the Seal and Signature of the Registrar-Recorder/County Clerk.

THE GREAT SEAL OF THE STATE OF CALIFORNIA

REGISTRAR-RECORDER/COUNTY CLERK COUNTY OF LOS ANGELES CALIFORNIA

American Bank Note Company

ANY ALTERATION OR ERASURE VOIDS THIS CERTIFICATE

CERTIFICATE OF DEATH
STATE OF CALIFORNIA

STATE FILE NUMBER

38637 014355
LOCAL REGISTRATION DISTRICT AND CERTIFICATE NUMBER

DECEDENT PERSONAL DATA

1A. NAME OF DECEDENT—FIRST: Desiderio
1B. MIDDLE: Alberto
1C. LAST: Arnaz III
2A. DATE OF DEATH (MONTH, DAY, YEAR): December 2, 1986
2B. HOUR: 0005
3. SEX: Male
4. RACE/ETHNICITY: White
5. SPANISH/HISPANIC: NO ☐ Hispanic
6. DATE OF BIRTH: March 2, 1917
7. AGE: 69 YEARS
IF UNDER 1 YEAR: MONTHS / DAYS
IF UNDER 24 HOURS: HOURS / MINUTES
8. BIRTHPLACE OF DECEDENT (STATE OR FOREIGN COUNTRY): Cuba
9. NAME AND BIRTHPLACE OF FATHER: Desiderio Arnaz II, Cuba
10. BIRTH NAME AND BIRTHPLACE OF MOTHER: Doloras Deacha, Cuba
11A. CITIZEN OF WHAT COUNTRY: USA
11B. IF DECEASED WAS EVER IN MILITARY GIVE DATES OF SERVICE: 19 NA TO 19 NA
12. SOCIAL SECURITY NUMBER: 564-26-7086
13. MARITAL STATUS: Widowed
14. NAME OF SURVIVING SPOUSE (IF WIFE, ENTER BIRTH NAME): -
1508
15. PRIMARY OCCUPATION: Actor/Producer
16. NUMBER OF YEARS THIS OCCUPATION: 50
17. EMPLOYER (IF SELF-EMPLOYED, SO STATE): Self Employed
18. KIND OF INDUSTRY OR BUSINESS: Entertainment

USUAL RESIDENCE

19A. USUAL RESIDENCE—STREET ADDRESS (STREET AND NUMBER OR LOCATION): 1920 Ocean Front
19B.
19C. CITY OR TOWN: Del Mar
19D. COUNTY: San Diego
19E. STATE: CA
20. NAME AND ADDRESS OF INFORMANT—RELATIONSHIP: Lucie Arnaz Luckinbill, Daughter, 271 Central Park West, New York, New York 10024

PLACE OF DEATH

21A. PLACE OF DEATH: Residence
21B. COUNTY: San Diego
21C. STREET ADDRESS (STREET AND NUMBER OR LOCATION): 1920 Ocean Front
21D. CITY OR TOWN: Del Mar

CAUSE OF DEATH

1629 / 629

22. DEATH WAS CAUSED BY: (ENTER ONLY ONE CAUSE PER LINE FOR A, B, AND C)
IMMEDIATE CAUSE (A) Lung Cancer — 9 mons
CONDITIONS, IF ANY, WHICH GAVE RISE TO THE IMMEDIATE CAUSE, STATING THE UNDERLYING CAUSE LAST.
DUE TO, OR AS A CONSEQUENCE OF (B) None
DUE TO, OR AS A CONSEQUENCE OF (C) none
APPROXIMATE INTERVAL BETWEEN ONSET AND DEATH
24. WAS DEATH REPORTED TO CORONER? no
25. WAS BIOPSY PERFORMED? Yes
26. WAS AUTOPSY PERFORMED? no
23. OTHER SIGNIFICANT CONDITIONS—CONTRIBUTING TO DEATH BUT NOT RELATED TO CAUSE GIVEN IN 22A: None
27. WAS OPERATION PERFORMED FOR ANY CONDITION IN ITEMS 22 OR 23? TYPE OF OPERATION / DATE: Bronchoscopy/Thiracebtesas 10/86

PHYSICIAN'S CERTIFICATION

28A. I CERTIFY THAT DEATH OCCURRED AT THE HOUR, DATE AND PLACE STATED FROM THE CAUSES STATED.
I ATTENDED DECEDENT SINCE (ENTER MO. DA. YR.): 3/4/86
I LAST SAW DECEDENT ALIVE (ENTER MO. DA. YR.): 12/1/86
28B. PHYSICIAN—SIGNATURE AND DEGREE OR TITLE: [signature]
28C. DATE SIGNED: 12/2/86
28D. PHYSICIAN'S LICENSE NUMBER: G003113
28E. TYPE PHYSICIAN'S NAME AND ADDRESS: CHARLES G. CAMPBELL, M.D.. 9834 Genesee Ave., La Jolla

INJURY INFORMATION — CORONER'S USE ONLY

29. SPECIFY ACCIDENT, SUICIDE, ETC.
30. PLACE OF INJURY
31. INJURY AT WORK
32A. DATE OF INJURY—MONTH, DAY, YEAR
32B. HOUR
33. LOCATION (STREET AND NUMBER OR LOCATION AND CITY OR TOWN)
34. DESCRIBE HOW INJURY OCCURRED (EVENTS WHICH RESULTED IN INJURY)
35A. I CERTIFY THAT DEATH OCCURRED AT THE HOUR, DATE AND PLACE STATED FROM THE CAUSES STATED. AS REQUIRED BY LAW I HAVE HELD AN (INQUEST-INVESTIGATION)
35B. CORONER—SIGNATURE AND DEGREE OR TITLE
35C. DATE SIGNED

36. DISPOSITION: Cremation
37. DATE—MONTH, DAY, YEAR: 12-2-86
38. NAME AND ADDRESS OF CEMETERY OR CREMATORY: Cypress View Crematory 3953 Imperial Ave. San Diego, CA
39. EMBALMER'S LICENSE NUMBER AND SIGNATURE: Not Embalmed
40A. NAME OF FUNERAL DIRECTOR (OR PERSON ACTING AS SUCH): Encinitas Mortuary
40B. LICENSE NO.: 857
41. LOCAL REGISTRAR—SIGNATURE: [signature], M.D.
42. DATE ACCEPTED BY LOCAL REGISTRAR: DEC 02 1986

STATE REGISTRAR: A. B. C. D. E. F.

VS-11 (1-85)

This is a true certified copy of the record if it bears the seal, imprinted in purple ink, of the Recorder. JUL 12 1995

[signature]

Recorder/County Clerk
San Diego County, California

CERTIFICATION OF VITAL RECORD

COUNTY OF LOS ANGELES • REGISTRAR-RECORDER/COUNTY CLERK

CERTIFICATE OF DEATH
STATE OF CALIFORNIA

STATE FILE NUMBER

387 028156
LOCAL REGISTRATION DISTRICT AND CERTIFICATE NUMBER

DECEDENT PERSONAL DATA

1A. NAME OF DECEDENT—FIRST: FRED
1B. MIDDLE:
1C. LAST: ASTAIRE
2A. DATE OF DEATH (MONTH, DAY, YEAR): June 22, 1987
2B. HOUR: 0425
3. SEX: Male
4. RACE/ETHNICITY: White
5. SPANISH/HISPANIC: NO
6. DATE OF BIRTH: May 10, 1899
7. AGE: 88 YEARS
IF UNDER 1 YEAR: MONTHS / DAYS
IF UNDER 24 HOURS: HOURS / MINUTES
8. BIRTHPLACE OF DECEDENT (STATE OR FOREIGN COUNTRY): Nebraska
9. NAME AND BIRTHPLACE OF FATHER: Fred Austerlitz-Austria
10. BIRTH NAME AND BIRTHPLACE OF MOTHER: Anne Geilus-Nebraska
11A. CITIZEN OF WHAT COUNTRY: U.S.A.
11B. IF DECEASED WAS EVER IN MILITARY GIVE DATES OF SERVICE: 19 n/a TO 19 n/a
12. SOCIAL SECURITY NUMBER: 568-05-4206
13. MARITAL STATUS: Married
14. NAME OF SURVIVING SPOUSE (IF WIFE, ENTER BIRTH NAME): Robyn Smith
15. PRIMARY OCCUPATION: Entertainer
16. NUMBER OF YEARS THIS OCCUPATION: Adult Life
17. EMPLOYER (IF SELF-EMPLOYED, SO STATE): Various Studios
18. KIND OF INDUSTRY OR BUSINESS: Entertainment

USUAL RESIDENCE

19A. USUAL RESIDENCE—STREET ADDRESS (STREET AND NUMBER OR LOCATION): 1155 San Ysidro Drive
19B.
19C. CITY OR TOWN: Beverly Hills
19D. COUNTY: Los Angeles
19E. STATE: California
20. NAME AND ADDRESS OF INFORMANT—RELATIONSHIP: Robyn Smith Astaire-Wife, 1155 San Ysidro Drive, Beverly Hills, California 90210

PLACE OF DEATH

21A. PLACE OF DEATH: Century City Hospital
21B. COUNTY: Los Angeles
21C. STREET ADDRESS (STREET AND NUMBER OR LOCATION): 2070 Century Park East
21D. CITY OR TOWN: Los Angeles

CAUSE OF DEATH

22. DEATH WAS CAUSED BY: (ENTER ONLY ONE CAUSE PER LINE FOR A, B, AND C)
IMMEDIATE CAUSE (A) Pneumonia — APPROXIMATE INTERVAL BETWEEN ONSET AND DEATH: 10 days
CONDITIONS, IF ANY, WHICH GAVE RISE TO THE IMMEDIATE CAUSE, STATING THE UNDERLYING CAUSE LAST.
DUE TO, OR AS A CONSEQUENCE OF (B)
DUE TO, OR AS A CONSEQUENCE OF (C)
24. WAS DEATH REPORTED TO CORONER? NO
25. WAS BIOPSY PERFORMED? No
26. WAS AUTOPSY PERFORMED? No
23. OTHER SIGNIFICANT CONDITIONS—CONTRIBUTING TO DEATH BUT NOT RELATED TO CAUSE GIVEN IN 22A: NO
27. WAS OPERATION PERFORMED FOR ANY CONDITION IN ITEMS 22 OR 23? TYPE OF OPERATION: NO — DATE

PHYSICIAN'S CERTIFICATION

28A. I CERTIFY THAT DEATH OCCURRED AT THE HOUR, DATE AND PLACE STATED FROM THE CAUSES STATED.
I ATTENDED DECEDENT SINCE (ENTER MO, DA, YR): 5-2-87
I LAST SAW DECEDENT ALIVE (ENTER MO, DA, YR): 6/21/87
28B. PHYSICIAN—SIGNATURE AND DEGREE OR TITLE: Neal R. Cutler MD
28C. DATE SIGNED: 6-23-87
28D. PHYSICIAN'S LICENSE NUMBER: G-032762
28E. TYPE PHYSICIAN'S NAME AND ADDRESS: Neal R. Cutler, 8500 Wilshire Blvd., Beverly Hills, Ca.

INJURY INFORMATION / CORONER'S USE ONLY

29. SPECIFY ACCIDENT, SUICIDE, ETC.
30. PLACE OF INJURY
31. INJURY AT WORK
32A. DATE OF INJURY—MONTH, DAY, YEAR
32B. HOUR
33. LOCATION (STREET AND NUMBER OR LOCATION AND CITY OR TOWN)
34. DESCRIBE HOW INJURY OCCURRED (EVENTS WHICH RESULTED IN INJURY)
35A. I CERTIFY THAT DEATH OCCURRED AT THE HOUR, DATE AND PLACE STATED FROM THE CAUSES STATED. AS REQUIRED BY LAW I HAVE HELD AN (INQUEST-INVESTIGATION)
35B. CORONER—SIGNATURE AND DEGREE OR TITLE
35C. DATE SIGNED

36. DISPOSITION: Burial
37. DATE—MONTH, DAY, YEAR: June 24, 1987
38. NAME AND ADDRESS OF CEMETERY OR CREMATORY: Oakwood Memorial Park, Chatsworth, Calif.
39. EMBALMER'S LICENSE NUMBER AND SIGNATURE: #6292 Milton L. Johnson
40A. NAME OF FUNERAL DIRECTOR (OR PERSON ACTING AS SUCH): Pierce Brothers Westwood Village
40B. LICENSE NO.: F-951
41. LOCAL REGISTRAR—SIGNATURE: Robert S. Black
42. DATE ACCEPTED BY LOCAL REGISTRAR: JUN 23 1987

STATE REGISTRAR: A. B. C. D. E. F.

VS-11 (1-85)

This is to certify that this document is a true copy of the official record filed with the Registrar-Recorder/County Clerk.

Charles Weissburd
CHARLES WEISSBURD
Registrar-Recorder/County Clerk

FEB 03 1992
19-309727

This copy not valid unless prepared on engraved border displaying the Seal and Signature of the Registrar-Recorder/County Clerk.

American Bank Note Company

ANY ALTERATION OR ERASURE VOIDS THIS CERTIFICATE

CERTIFICATION OF VITAL RECORD

COUNTY OF LOS ANGELES • REGISTRAR-RECORDER/COUNTY CLERK

CERTIFICATE OF DEATH 38719042272
STATE OF CALIFORNIA

STATE FILE NUMBER — LOCAL REGISTRATION DISTRICT AND CERTIFICATE NUMBER

DECEDENT PERSONAL DATA

1A. NAME OF DECEDENT—FIRST: MARY | 1B. MIDDLE: | 1C. LAST: ASTOR | 2A. DATE OF DEATH (MONTH, DAY, YEAR): September 25, 1987 | 2B. HOUR: 0130

3. SEX: female | 4. RACE/ETHNICITY: white | 5. SPANISH/HISPANIC: NO | 6. DATE OF BIRTH: May 3, 1906 | 7. AGE: 81 YEARS

8. BIRTHPLACE OF DECEDENT (STATE OR FOREIGN COUNTRY): Illinois | 9. NAME AND BIRTHPLACE OF FATHER: Otto Langhanke - Germany | 10. BIRTH NAME AND BIRTHPLACE OF MOTHER: Unknown Unknown - Portugal

11A. CITIZEN OF WHAT COUNTRY: USA | 11B. IF DECEASED WAS EVER IN MILITARY GIVE DATES OF SERVICE: 19 X X TO 19 X X | 12. SOCIAL SECURITY NUMBER: 562-18-9904 | 13. MARITAL STATUS: Divorced | 14. NAME OF SURVIVING SPOUSE: None

15. PRIMARY OCCUPATION: Actress | 16. NUMBER OF YEARS THIS OCCUPATION: 40 Years | 17. EMPLOYER: Various studios | 18. KIND OF INDUSTRY OR BUSINESS: Motion Picture Industry

USUAL RESIDENCE

19A. USUAL RESIDENCE—STREET ADDRESS: 23388 Mulholland Drive | 19B. | 19C. CITY OR TOWN: Woodland Hills

19D. COUNTY: Los Angeles | 19E. STATE: California | 20. NAME AND ADDRESS OF INFORMANT—RELATIONSHIP: Anthony Del Campo - Son, 10413 Egret Avenue, Fountain Valley, CA 92708

PLACE OF DEATH

21A. PLACE OF DEATH: Motion Picture/TV Hospital | 21B. COUNTY: Los Angeles

21C. STREET ADDRESS: 23388 Mulholland Drive | 21D. CITY OR TOWN: Woodland Hills

CAUSE OF DEATH

22. DEATH WAS CAUSED BY: (ENTER ONLY ONE CAUSE PER LINE FOR A, B, AND C)

IMMEDIATE CAUSE (A) Respiratory Failure — APPROXIMATE INTERVAL BETWEEN ONSET AND DEATH: 2 days

DUE TO, OR AS A CONSEQUENCE OF (B) Pulmonary Emphysema — 5 years

DUE TO, OR AS A CONSEQUENCE OF (C)

CONDITIONS, IF ANY, WHICH GAVE RISE TO THE IMMEDIATE CAUSE, STATING THE UNDERLYING CAUSE LAST.

24. WAS DEATH REPORTED TO CORONER? NO | 25. WAS BIOPSY PERFORMED? NO | 26. WAS AUTOPSY PERFORMED? NO

23. OTHER SIGNIFICANT CONDITIONS—CONTRIBUTING TO DEATH BUT NOT RELATED TO CAUSE GIVEN IN 22A: Arteriosclerotic Heart Disease | 27. WAS OPERATION PERFORMED FOR ANY CONDITION IN ITEMS 22 OR 23? NO

PHYSICIAN'S CERTIFICATION

28A. I CERTIFY THAT DEATH OCCURRED AT THE HOUR, DATE AND PLACE STATED FROM THE CAUSES STATED. ATTENDED DECEDENT SINCE: 11/30/81 | LAST SAW DECEDENT ALIVE: 09/25/87 | 28B. PHYSICIAN—SIGNATURE: Otto H. Lange | 28C. DATE SIGNED: 09/25/87 | 28D. PHYSICIAN'S LICENSE NUMBER: A-09619

28E. TYPE PHYSICIAN'S NAME AND ADDRESS: Otto H. Lange, M.D., 23388 Mulholland Drive, Woodland Hills, CA 91364

INJURY INFORMATION

29. SPECIFY ACCIDENT, SUICIDE, ETC. | 30. PLACE OF INJURY | 31. INJURY AT WORK | 32A. DATE OF INJURY—MONTH, DAY, YEAR | 32B. HOUR

33. LOCATION | 34. DESCRIBE HOW INJURY OCCURRED

CORONER'S USE ONLY

35A. I CERTIFY THAT DEATH OCCURRED AT THE HOUR, DATE AND PLACE STATED FROM THE CAUSES STATED, AS REQUIRED BY LAW I HAVE HELD AN (INQUEST-INVESTIGATION) | 35B. CORONER—SIGNATURE AND DEGREE OR TITLE | 35C. DATE SIGNED

36. DISPOSITION: Burial | 37. DATE: Sept. 28, 1987 | 38. NAME AND ADDRESS OF CEMETERY OR CREMATORY: Holy Cross Cemetery, 5835 W. Slauson Ave., Los Angeles, CA | 39. EMBALMER'S LICENSE NUMBER AND SIGNATURE: 4350 James E. Austin

40A. NAME OF FUNERAL DIRECTOR: Pierce Brothers' Cunningham & O'Connor Hollywood Mortuary | 40B. LICENSE NO.: F - 168 | 41. LOCAL REGISTRAR: Robert R. Mate | 42. DATE ACCEPTED BY LOCAL REGISTRAR: SEP 28 1987

STATE REGISTRAR A. B. C. D. E. F.

VS-11 (1-86)

This is to certify that this document is a true copy of the official record filed with the Registrar-Recorder/County Clerk.

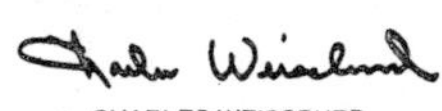

CHARLES WEISSBURD
Registrar-Recorder/County Clerk

FEB 05 1992
19-312847

This copy not valid unless prepared on engraved border displaying the Seal and Signature of the Registrar-Recorder/County Clerk.

ANY ALTERATION OR ERASURE VOIDS THIS CERTIFICATE

CERTIFICATION OF VITAL RECORD

COUNTY OF LOS ANGELES • REGISTRAR-RECORDER/COUNTY CLERK

CERTIFICATE OF DEATH
STATE OF CALIFORNIA
USE BLACK INK ONLY

STATE FILE NUMBER — 39119049875 — LOCAL REGISTRATION DISTRICT AND CERTIFICATE NUMBER

DECEDENT PERSONAL DATA

1A. NAME OF DECEDENT—FIRST (GIVEN): Eleanor
1B. MIDDLE: --
1C. LAST (FAMILY): Audley
2A. DATE OF DEATH—MO, DAY, YR: November 25, 1991
2B. HOUR: 0949
3. SEX: F
4. RACE: CAUCASIAN
5. HISPANIC—SPECIFY: [ ] YES [X] NO
6. DATE OF BIRTH—MO, DAY, YR: NOVEMBER 19, 1905
7. AGE IN YEARS: 86
8. STATE OF BIRTH: UNK
9. CITIZEN OF WHAT COUNTRY: USA
10A. FULL NAME OF FATHER: WILLIAM ZELLMAN
10B. STATE OF BIRTH: UNK
11A. FULL MAIDEN NAME OF MOTHER: RUTH SIMMONS.
11B. STATE OF BIRTH: NY
12. MILITARY SERVICE? 19__ TO 19__ [X] NONE
13. SOCIAL SECURITY NO.: 114-07-6014
14. MARITAL STATUS: NEVER MARRIED
15. NAME OF SURVIVING SPOUSE (IF WIFE, ENTER MAIDEN NAME): NONE
16A. USUAL OCCUPATION: ACTRESS
16B. USUAL KIND OF BUSINESS OR INDUSTRY: FILM & T.V.
16C. USUAL EMPLOYER: DISNEY STUDIOS
16D. YEARS IN OCCUPATION: 50
17. EDUCATION—YEARS COMPLETED: 12

USUAL RESIDENCE

18A. RESIDENCE—STREET AND NUMBER OR LOCATION: 10749 ACAMA STREET
18B. CITY: NO. HOLLYWOOD
18C. ZIP CODE: 91602
18D. COUNTY: LOS ANGELES
18E. NUMBER OF YEARS IN THIS COUNTY: 40
18F. STATE OR FOREIGN COUNTRY: CALIFORNIA
20. NAME, RELATIONSHIP, MAILING ADDRESS AND ZIP CODE OF INFORMANT: PETER ENTIN-NEPHEW, 505 WEST END AVENUE #4A, NEW YORK, NY 10024

PLACE OF DEATH

19A. PLACE OF DEATH: Residence
19B. IF HOSPITAL, SPECIFY ONE: IP, ER/OP, DOA: --
19C. COUNTY: Los Angeles
19D. STREET ADDRESS—STREET AND NUMBER OR LOCATION: 10749 ACAMA STREET
19E. CITY: NO. HOLLYWOOD

CAUSE OF DEATH

21. DEATH WAS CAUSED BY: (ENTER ONLY ONE CAUSE PER LINE FOR A, B, AND C)

		Time interval between onset and death
IMMEDIATE CAUSE (A)	ACUTE CARDIORESPIRATORY ARREST	MINS
DUE TO (B)	ACUTE MYOCARDIAL INFARCTION	HRS
DUE TO (C)	CHRONIC HYPERTENSIVE HEART DISEASE	YRS

22. WAS DEATH REPORTED TO CORONER? [X] YES — REFERRAL NUMBER 91-55240 [ ] NO
23. WAS BIOPSY PERFORMED? [ ] YES [X] NO
24A. WAS AUTOPSY PERFORMED? [ ] YES [X] NO
24B. WAS IT USED IN DETERMINING CAUSE OF DEATH? [ ] YES [X] NO
25. OTHER SIGNIFICANT CONDITIONS CONTRIBUTING TO DEATH BUT NOT RELATED TO CAUSE GIVEN IN 21: COPD, ARTERIOSCLEROSIS
26. WAS OPERATION PERFORMED FOR ANY CONDITION IN ITEM 21 OR 25? IF YES, LIST TYPE OF OPERATION AND DATE: NO

PHYSICIAN'S CERTIFICATION

I CERTIFY THAT TO THE BEST OF MY KNOWLEDGE DEATH OCCURRED AT THE HOUR, DATE AND PLACE STATED FROM THE CAUSES STATED.
27A. DECEDENT ATTENDED SINCE MONTH, DAY, YEAR: 3/6/73 — DECEDENT LAST SEEN ALIVE MONTH, DAY, YEAR: 10/22/91
27B. SIGNATURE AND TITLE OF CERTIFIER: [signature]
27C. CERTIFIER'S LICENSE NUMBER: A 28224
27D. DATE SIGNED: 11/26/91
27E. TYPE ATTENDING PHYSICIAN'S NAME AND ADDRESS: SANDER W. ZUCKERMAN, M.D. 4314 WEST VICTORY BLVD. BURBANK, CA 91505

CORONER'S USE ONLY

I CERTIFY THAT IN MY OPINION DEATH OCCURRED AT THE HOUR, DATE AND PLACE STATED FROM THE CAUSES STATED.
28A. SIGNATURE AND TITLE OF CORONER OR DEPUTY CORONER
28B. DATE SIGNED
29. MANNER OF DEATH—specify one: natural, accident, suicide, homicide, pending investigation or could not be determined
30A. PLACE OF INJURY
30B. INJURY AT WORK [ ] YES [ ] NO
30C. DATE OF INJURY MONTH, DAY, YEAR
31. HOUR
32. LOCATION (STREET AND NUMBER OR LOCATION AND CITY)
33. DESCRIBE HOW INJURY OCCURRED (EVENTS WHICH RESULTED IN INJURY)

FUNERAL DIRECTOR AND LOCAL REGISTRAR

34A. DISPOSITION(S): BURIAL
34B. PLACE OF FINAL DISPOSITION—NAME AND ADDRESS: MOUNT SINAI MEMORIAL PARK, 5950 FOREST LAWN DR. L.A., CA 90068
34C. DATE MO, DAY, YEAR: NOV 27, 1991
35A. SIGNATURE OF EMBALMER: NOT EMBALMED
35B. LICENSE NUMBER: - -
36A. NAME OF FUNERAL DIRECTOR (OR PERSON ACTING AS SUCH): MOUNT SINAI MORTUARY
36B. LICENSE NO.: FD-1010
37. SIGNATURE OF LOCAL REGISTRAR: [signature]
38. REGISTRATION DATE: NOV 27 1991

STATE REGISTRAR: A. B. C. D. E. F. CENSUS TRACT

VS-11 (REV. 3-91) 410 — MAKE NO ERASURES, WHITEOUTS, OR OTHER ALTERATIONS — 01-9-1-7005

This is to certify that this document is a true copy of the official record filed with the Registrar-Recorder/County Clerk.

MAR 12 1996
19-217437

CONNY B. McCORMACK
Registrar-Recorder/County Clerk

This copy not valid unless prepared on engraved border displaying the Seal and Signature of the Registrar-Recorder/County Clerk.

ANY ALTERATION OR ERASURE VOIDS THIS CERTIFICATE

STATE OF CALIFORNIA
CERTIFICATION OF VITAL RECORD

COUNTY OF LOS ANGELES
DEPARTMENT OF HEALTH SERVICES

CERTIFICATE OF DEATH
STATE OF CALIFORNIA
USE BLACK INK ONLY/NO ERASURES, WHITEOUTS OR ALTERATIONS
VS-11 (REV. 7/97)

STATE FILE NUMBER — LOCAL REGISTRATION NUMBER

DECEDENT PERSONAL DATA

1. NAME OF DECEDENT—FIRST (GIVEN)	2. MIDDLE	3. LAST (FAMILY)
ORVON	GENE	AUTRY

4. DATE OF BIRTH MM/DD/CCYY	5. AGE YRS.	IF UNDER 1 YEAR (MONTHS, DAYS)	IF UNDER 24 HOURS (HOURS, MINUTES)	6. SEX	7. DATE OF DEATH MM/DD/CCYY	8. HOUR
09/29/1907	91			M	10/02/1998	0724

9. STATE OF BIRTH	10. SOCIAL SECURITY NO.	11. MILITARY SERVICE	12. MARITAL STATUS	13. EDUCATION—YEARS COMPLETED
TX	565-16-0614	[X] YES [ ] NO [ ] UNK	MARRIED	12

14. RACE	15. HISPANIC—SPECIFY	16. USUAL EMPLOYER
WHITE	[ ] YES [X] NO	SELF EMPLOYED

17. OCCUPATION	18. KIND OF BUSINESS	19. YEARS IN OCCUPATION
CHAIRMAN OF THE BOARD	ENTERTAINMENT	60

USUAL RESIDENCE

20. RESIDENCE—(STREET AND NUMBER OR LOCATION): 3171 BROOKDALE ROAD

21. CITY	22. COUNTY	23. ZIP CODE	24. YRS IN COUNTY	25. STATE OR FOREIGN COUNTRY
STUDIO CITY	LOS ANGELES	91604	64	CALIFORNIA

INFORMANT

26. NAME, RELATIONSHIP	27. MAILING ADDRESS (STREET AND NUMBER OR RURAL ROUTE NUMBER, CITY OR TOWN, STATE, ZIP)
JACQUELINE AUTRY-WIFE	3171 BROOKDALE ROAD, STUDIO CITY, CA, 91604

SPOUSE AND PARENT INFORMATION

28. NAME OF SURVIVING SPOUSE—FIRST	29. MIDDLE	30. LAST (MAIDEN NAME)	
JACQUELINE	EVELYN	ELLAM	
31. NAME OF FATHER—FIRST	32. MIDDLE	33. LAST	34. BIRTH STATE
DELBERT	-	AUTRY	TX
35. NAME OF MOTHER—FIRST	36. MIDDLE	37. LAST (MAIDEN)	38. BIRTH STATE
NORA	-	OZMENT	TX

DISPOSITION(S)

39. DATE MM/DD/CCYY	40. PLACE OF FINAL DISPOSITION
10/02/1998	FOREST LAWN MEMORIAL PARK, LOS ANGELES, CA, 90068

FUNERAL DIRECTOR AND LOCAL REGISTRAR

41. TYPE OF DISPOSITION(S)	42. SIGNATURE OF EMBALMER		43. LICENSE NO.
BURIAL	Damon De La Cruz		8310
44. NAME OF FUNERAL DIRECTOR	45. LICENSE NO.	46. SIGNATURE OF LOCAL REGISTRAR	47. DATE MM/DD/CCYY
FOREST LAWN HOLLYWOOD HILLS	F-904	[signature]	10/02/1998

PLACE OF DEATH

101. PLACE OF DEATH	102. IF HOSPITAL, SPECIFY ONE	103. FACILITY OTHER THAN HOSPITAL	104. COUNTY
RESIDENCE	[ ] IP [ ] ER/OP [ ] DOA	[ ] CONV. HOSP. [ ] RES. CARE [ ] OTHER	LOS ANGELES

105. STREET ADDRESS—(STREET AND NUMBER OR LOCATION)	106. CITY
3171 BROOKDALE ROAD	STUDIO CITY

CAUSE OF DEATH

107. DEATH WAS CAUSED BY: (ENTER ONLY ONE CAUSE PER LINE FOR A, B, C, AND D)

	Cause	TIME INTERVAL BETWEEN ONSET AND DEATH
IMMEDIATE CAUSE (A)	CARDIOPULMONARY ARREST	MINS
DUE TO (B)	RESPIRATORY FAILURE	HOURS
DUE TO (C)	LYMPHOMA	YEARS
DUE TO (D)		

108. DEATH REPORTED TO CORONER: [ ] YES [X] NO — REFERRAL NUMBER
109. BIOPSY PERFORMED: [X] YES [ ] NO
110. AUTOPSY PERFORMED: [ ] YES [X] NO
111. USED IN DETERMINING CAUSE: [ ] YES [X] NO

112. OTHER SIGNIFICANT CONDITIONS CONTRIBUTING TO DEATH BUT NOT RELATED TO CAUSE GIVEN IN 107: ASCVD

113. WAS OPERATION PERFORMED FOR ANY CONDITION IN ITEM 107 OR 112? IF YES, LIST TYPE OF OPERATION AND DATE.
PACEMAKER --/--/1986, BIOPSY 07/--/1996

PHYSICIAN'S CERTIFICATION

114. I CERTIFY THAT TO THE BEST OF MY KNOWLEDGE DEATH OCCURRED AT THE HOUR, DATE AND PLACE STATED FROM THE CAUSES STATED.

DECEDENT ATTENDED SINCE MM/DD/CCYY	DECEDENT LAST SEEN ALIVE MM/DD/CCYY	115. SIGNATURE AND TITLE OF CERTIFIER	116. LICENSE NO.	117. DATE MM/DD/CCYY
09/01/1996	09/27/1998	S Drell MD	G035439	10/02/1998

118. TYPE ATTENDING PHYSICIAN'S NAME, MAILING ADDRESS, ZIP: STEVEN A DRELL MD., 13320 RIVERSIDE DR, SHERMAN OAKS, CA, 91423

CORONER'S USE ONLY

I CERTIFY THAT IN MY OPINION DEATH OCCURRED AT THE HOUR, DATE AND PLACE STATED FROM THE CAUSES STATED.

119. MANNER OF DEATH: [ ] NATURAL [ ] SUICIDE [ ] HOMICIDE [ ] ACCIDENT [ ] PENDING INVESTIGATION [ ] COULD NOT BE DETERMINED

120. INJURY AT WORK: [ ] YES [ ] NO | 121. INJURY DATE MM/DD/CCYY | 122. HOUR | 123. PLACE OF INJURY

124. DESCRIBE HOW INJURY OCCURRED (EVENTS WHICH RESULTED IN INJURY)

125. LOCATION (STREET AND NUMBER OR LOCATION AND CITY, ZIP)

126. SIGNATURE OF CORONER OR DEPUTY CORONER | 127. DATE MM/DD/CCYY | 128. TYPED NAME, TITLE OF CORONER OR DEPUTY CORONER

STATE REGISTRAR

A | B | C | D | E | F | G | H | FAX AUTH. # | CENSUS TRACT

090181040

This is a true certified copy of the record filed in the County of Los Angeles Department of Health Services if it bears the Registrar's signature in purple ink.

DATE ISSUED OCT 16 1998

Director of Health Service and Registrar

This copy not valid unless prepared on engraved border displaying seal and signature of Registrar.

DE LA RUE

ANY ALTERATION OR ERASURE VOIDS THIS CERTIFICATE

CERTIFICATION OF VITAL RECORD

COUNTY OF LOS ANGELES • REGISTRAR-RECORDER/COUNTY CLERK

CERTIFICATE OF DEATH
STATE OF CALIFORNIA

STATE FILE NUMBER

LOCAL REGISTRATION DISTRICT AND CERTIFICATE NUMBER: 3861 [illegible]

DECEDENT PERSONAL DATA

1A. NAME OF DECEDENT—FIRST: HERMIONE
1B. MIDDLE: NMN.
1C. LAST: BADDELEY
2A. DATE OF DEATH (MONTH, DAY, YEAR): August 19, 1986
2B. HOUR: 1602
3. SEX: Female
4. RACE/ETHNICITY: White
5. SPANISH/HISPANIC: NO
6. DATE OF BIRTH: November 13, 1908
7. AGE: 77 YEARS
IF UNDER 1 YEAR: MONTHS / DAYS
IF UNDER 24 HOURS: HOURS / MINUTES
8. BIRTHPLACE OF DECEDENT (STATE OR FOREIGN COUNTRY): England
9. NAME AND BIRTHPLACE OF FATHER: Wm. H. Clinton-Baddeley-England
10. BIRTH NAME AND BIRTHPLACE OF MOTHER: Louise Bourdin-France
11A. CITIZEN OF WHAT COUNTRY: England
11B. IF DECEASED WAS EVER IN MILITARY GIVE DATES OF SERVICE: 19 NA TO 19 NA
12. SOCIAL SECURITY NUMBER: 095 - 34 - 5888
13. MARITAL STATUS: Divorced
14. NAME OF SURVIVING SPOUSE (IF WIFE, ENTER BIRTH NAME): None
15. PRIMARY OCCUPATION: Actress
16. NUMBER OF YEARS THIS OCCUPATION: 60 Yrs.
17. EMPLOYER (IF SELF-EMPLOYED, SO STATE): Self - Employed
18. KIND OF INDUSTRY OR BUSINESS: Entertainment

USUAL RESIDENCE

19A. USUAL RESIDENCE—STREET ADDRESS (STREET AND NUMBER OR LOCATION): 2686 Carmar Drive
19B.
19C. CITY OR TOWN: Los Angeles
19D. COUNTY: Los Angeles
19E. STATE: CA
20. NAME AND ADDRESS OF INFORMANT—RELATIONSHIP: Mr. David Tennant - Son, The Old Vickerage, Hempnall, Norwich, England Nr. 152AD

PLACE OF DEATH

21A. PLACE OF DEATH: Cedars-Siani Medical Center
21B. COUNTY: Los Angeles
21C. STREET ADDRESS (STREET AND NUMBER OR LOCATION): 8700 Beverly Blvd.
21D. CITY OR TOWN: Los Angeles

CAUSE OF DEATH

22. DEATH WAS CAUSED BY: (ENTER ONLY ONE CAUSE PER LINE FOR A, B, AND C)

	Cause	Approximate interval between onset and death
IMMEDIATE CAUSE (A)	CARDIO-RESPIRATORY ARREST	SUDDEN
CONDITIONS, IF ANY, WHICH GAVE RISE TO THE IMMEDIATE CAUSE, STATING THE UNDERLYING CAUSE LAST. DUE TO, OR AS A CONSEQUENCE OF (B)	CORTICAL NECROSIS	21 DAYS
DUE TO, OR AS A CONSEQUENCE OF (C)	CEREBRAL ARTERIAL OCCLUSION	25 DAYS

24. WAS DEATH REPORTED TO CORONER? NO
25. WAS BIOPSY PERFORMED? YES
26. WAS AUTOPSY PERFORMED? NO
23. OTHER SIGNIFICANT CONDITIONS—CONTRIBUTING TO DEATH BUT NOT RELATED TO CAUSE GIVEN IN 22A: DIABETES MELLITUS; ATRIAL FIBRILLATION; POORLY DIFFERENTIATED LYMPHOMA
27. WAS OPERATION PERFORMED FOR ANY CONDITION IN ITEMS 22 OR 23? TYPE OF OPERATION: YES, LYMPH NODE EXCISION; DATE: 2-2-1981

PHYSICIAN'S CERTIFICATION

28A. I CERTIFY THAT DEATH OCCURRED AT THE HOUR, DATE AND PLACE STATED FROM THE CAUSES STATED.
I ATTENDED DECEDENT SINCE (ENTER MO. DA. YR.): 2-2-1965
I LAST SAW DECEDENT ALIVE (ENTER MO. DA. YR.): 8-19-1986
28B. PHYSICIAN—SIGNATURE AND DEGREE OR TITLE: [signature]
28C. DATE SIGNED: 8-22-1986
28D. PHYSICIAN'S LICENSE NUMBER: A15079
28E. TYPE PHYSICIAN'S NAME AND ADDRESS: GERALD W. LABRINER, M.D., 8920 WILSHIRE BLVD., BEVERLY HILLS, CA

INJURY INFORMATION

29. SPECIFY ACCIDENT, SUICIDE, ETC.
30. PLACE OF INJURY
31. INJURY AT WORK
32A. DATE OF INJURY—MONTH, DAY, YEAR
32B. HOUR
33. LOCATION (STREET AND NUMBER OR LOCATION AND CITY OR TOWN)
34. DESCRIBE HOW INJURY OCCURRED (EVENTS WHICH RESULTED IN INJURY)

CORONER'S USE ONLY

35A. I CERTIFY THAT DEATH OCCURRED AT THE HOUR, DATE AND PLACE STATED FROM THE CAUSES STATED. AS REQUIRED BY LAW I HAVE HELD AN (INQUEST-INVESTIGATION)
35B. CORONER—SIGNATURE AND DEGREE OR TITLE
35C. DATE SIGNED

36. DISPOSITION: Burial
37. DATE—MONTH, DAY, YEAR: August 30, 1986
38. NAME AND ADDRESS OF CEMETERY OR CREMATORY: Amesbury Church Yard, Amesbury, England
39. EMBALMER'S LICENSE NUMBER AND SIGNATURE: 6662 [signature]
40A. NAME OF FUNERAL DIRECTOR (OR PERSON ACTING AS SUCH): AKES FAMILY FUNERAL HOME
40B. LICENSE NO.: F1276
41. LOCAL REGISTRAR—SIGNATURE: [signature]
42. DATE ACCEPTED BY LOCAL REGISTRAR: AUG 25 1986

STATE REGISTRAR: A. B. C. D. E. F.

VS-11 (1-85) 4349 — 9-1-0555

This is to certify that this document is a true copy of the official record filed with the Registrar-Recorder/County Clerk.

[signature] Beatriz Valdez
BEATRIZ VALDEZ
Registrar-Recorder/County Clerk

AUG 10 1995
19-389408

This copy not valid unless prepared on engraved border displaying the Seal and Signature of the Registrar-Recorder/County Clerk.

American Bank Note Company

ANY ALTERATION OR ERASURE VOIDS THIS CERTIFICATE

STATE OF CALIFORNIA

CERTIFICATION OF VITAL RECORD

COUNTY OF LOS ANGELES • REGISTRAR-RECORDER/COUNTY CLERK

CERTIFICATE OF DEATH 3 200119027857

STATE OF CALIFORNIA

USE BLACK INK ONLY/NO ERASURES, WHITEOUTS OR ALTERATIONS

STATE FILE NUMBER — LOCAL REGISTRATION NUMBER

Decedent Personal Data	1. Name of decedent—First (Given)	Bonny
	2. Middle	Lee
	3. Last (Family)	Bakley
	4. Date of birth MM/DD/CCYY	06/07/1956
	5. Age yrs.	44
	6. Sex	F
	7. Date of death MM/DD/CCYY	05/04/2001
	8. Hour	2215
	9. State of birth	N.J.
	10. Social security no.	193-48-3503
	11. Military service	X No
	12. Marital status	Married
	13. Education—years completed	12
	14. Race	Caucasian
	15. Hispanic	X No
	16. Usual employer	Self Employed
	17. Occupation	Mail Order
	18. Kind of business	Mail
	19. Years in occupation	29
Usual Residence	20. Residence—street and number or location	11604 Dillings St.
	21. City	Studio City
	22. County	Los Angeles
	23. Zip code	91604
	24. Yrs in county	Unknown
	25. State or foreign country	California
Informant	26. Name, relationship	Margerry Lisa Bakley Sister
	27. Mailing address	51 Berry st.#6 Dover, New Jersey 07801
Spouse and Parent Information	28. Name of surviving spouse—First	Robert
	29. Middle	-
	30. Last (maiden name)	Blake
	31. Name of father—First	Edward
	32. Middle	John
	33. Last	Bakley
	34. Birth state	N.J.
	35. Name of mother—First	Marjorie
	36. Middle	Lois
	37. Last (maiden)	Unknown
	38. Birth state	N.J.
Disposition(s)	39. Date MM/DD/CCYY	05/23/2001
	40. Place of final disposition	Forest Lawn Hollywood Hills Cemetery 6300 Forest Lawn Dr.Los Angeles,Ca.
Funeral Director and Local Registrar	41. Type of disposition(s)	Burial
	42. Signature of embalmer	[signature]
	43. License no.	5799
	44. Name of funeral director	Armstrong Family Malloy-Mitten
	45. License no.	Fd-380
	46. Signature of local registrar	[signature]
	47. Date MM/DD/CCYY	05/22/2001
Place of Death	101. Place of death	ST. JOSEPH'S MEDICAL CENTER
	102. If hospital, specify one	X ER/OP
	104. County	LOS ANGELES
	105. Street address	501 SOUTH BUENA VISTA
	106. City	BURBANK
Cause of Death	107. Death was caused by: Immediate cause (A)	DEFERRED
	Due to (B)	
	Due to (C)	
	Due to (D)	
	108. Death reported to coroner	X Yes; Referral number 2001-03348
	109. Biopsy performed	
	110. Autopsy performed	X Yes
	111. Used in determining cause	
	112. Other significant conditions contributing to death but not related to cause given in 107	
	113. Was operation performed for any condition in item 107 or 112? If yes, list type of operation and date	
Physician's Certification	114.–118.	
Coroner's Use Only	119. Manner of death	X Pending investigation
	120.–125.	
	126. Signature of coroner or deputy coroner	[signature] Regina Augustine
	127. Date MM/DD/CCYY	05/16/2001
	128. Typed name, title of coroner or deputy coroner	REGINA AUGUSTINE DEPUTY CORONER
State Registrar	A B C D E F G H / Fax Auth. # / Census Tract	

1 of 2

This is to certify that this document is a true copy of the official record filed with the Registrar-Recorder/County Clerk.

[signature]

CONNY B. McCORMACK
Registrar-Recorder/County Clerk

This copy not valid unless prepared on engraved border displaying the Seal and Signature of the Registrar-Recorder/County Clerk.

APR 17 2002
19-195918

THE GREAT SEAL OF THE STATE OF CALIFORNIA EUREKA

MIDWEST BANK NOTE COMPANY

ANY ALTERATION OR ERASURE VOIDS THIS CERTIFICATE

STATE OF CALIFORNIA

CERTIFICATION OF VITAL RECORD

COUNTY OF LOS ANGELES • REGISTRAR-RECORDER/COUNTY CLERK

AMENDMENT OF MEDICAL AND HEALTH DATA—DEATH 02-000699

3 052001 137607 — STATE FILE NUMBER

USE BLACK INK ONLY—NO ERASURES, WHITEOUT, OR ALTERATIONS

3200119027857 — LOCAL REGISTRATION DISTRICT AND CERTIFICATE NUMBER

STATE/LOCAL REGISTRAR USE ONLY: 1 | 2 | 3

TYPE OR PRINT IN BLACK INK ONLY

PART I — INFORMATION TO LOCATE RECORD

1. NAME—FIRST (GIVEN)	2. MIDDLE	3. LAST (FAMILY)	4. SEX
BONNY	LEE	BAKLEY	F
5. DATE OF EVENT—MM/DD/CCYY	6. CITY OF OCCURENCE	7. COUNTY OF OCCURRENCE	
05/04/2001	Burbank	Los Angeles	

PART II — INFORMATION AS IT APPEARS ON RECORD

107. DEATH WAS CAUSED BY (ENTER ONLY ONE CAUSE PER LINE FOR A, B, C, AND D)

IMMEDIATE CAUSE (A) DEFERRED

(B) 2 OF 2

(C)

DUE TO (D)

TIME INTERVAL BETWEEN ONSET AND DEATH:

108. DEATH REPORTED TO CORONER [X] YES [ ] NO — REFERRAL NUMBER 2001-03348

109. BIOPSY PERFORMED [ ] YES [ ] NO

110. AUTOPSY PERFORMED [X] YES [ ] NO

111. USED IN DETERMINING CAUSE [ ] YES [ ] NO

112. OTHER SIGNIFICANT CONDITIONS CONTRIBUTING TO DEATH BUT NOT RELATED TO CAUSE GIVEN IN 107

113. WAS OPERATION PERFORMED FOR ANY CONDITION IN ITEM 107 or 112? IF YES, LIST TYPE OF OPERATION AND DATE.

119. MANNER OF DEATH [ ] NATURAL [ ] SUICIDE [ ] HOMICIDE [ ] ACCIDENT [X] PENDING INVESTIGATION [ ] COULD NOT BE DETERMINED

120. INJURY AT WORK [ ] YES [ ] NO | 121. INJURY DATE—MM/DD/CCYY | 122. HOUR | 123. PLACE OF INJURY

124. DESCRIBE HOW INJURY OCCURED (EVENTS WHICH RESULTED IN INJURY)

125. LOCATION (STREET AND NUMBER OR LOCATION AND CITY AND ZIP CODE)

PART III — INFORMATION AS IT SHOULD APPEAR

107. DEATH WAS CAUSED BY (ENTER ONLY ONE CAUSE PER LINE FOR A, B, C, AND D)

IMMEDIATE CAUSE (A) MULTIPLE GUNSHOT WOUNDS — TIME INTERVAL BETWEEN ONSET AND DEATH: Unk

(B)

(C)

DUE TO (D)

108. DEATH REPORTED TO CORONER [X] YES [ ] NO — REFERRAL NUMBER 2001-03348

109. BIOPSY PERFORMED [ ] YES [X] NO

110. AUTOPSY PERFORMED [X] YES [ ] NO

111. USED IN DETERMINING CAUSE [X] YES [ ] NO

112. OTHER SIGNIFICANT CONDITIONS CONTRIBUTING TO DEATH BUT NOT RELATED TO CAUSE GIVEN IN 107

None

113. WAS OPERATION PERFORMED FOR ANY CONDITION IN ITEM 107 or 112? IF YES, LIST TYPE OF OPERATION AND DATE.

No

119. MANNER OF DEATH [ ] NATURAL [ ] SUICIDE [X] HOMICIDE [ ] ACCIDENT [ ] PENDING INVESTIGATION [ ] COULD NOT BE DETERMINED

120. INJURY AT WORK [ ] YES [X] NO | 121. INJURY DATE—MM/DD/CCYY 05/04/2001 | 122. HOUR 2140 | 123. PLACE OF INJURY Street

124. DESCRIBE HOW INJURY OCCURRED (EVENTS WHICH RESULTED IN INJURY)

Shot By Assailant (s)

125. LOCATION (STREET AND NUMBER OR LOCATION AND CITY AND ZIP CODE)

4346 N. Kraft Street Los Angeles, CA 90001

DECLARATION OF CERTIFYING PHYSICIAN OR CORONER

I HEREBY DECLARE UNDER PENALTY OF PERJURY THAT THE ABOVE INFORMATION IS TRUE AND CORRECT TO THE BEST OF MY KNOWLEDGE.

8. SIGNATURE OF CERTIFYING PHYSICIAN OR CORONER	9. DATE SIGNED—MM/DD/CCYY	10. TYPED OR PRINTED NAME AND DEGREE/TITLE OF CERTIFIER	
Jeffrey P. Gutstadt MD	01/29/2002	JEFFREY P. GUTSTADT, M.D. DME	
11. ADDRESS—STREET AND NUMBER	12. CITY	13. STATE	14. ZIP CODE
1104 North Mission Road	Los Angeles	Ca	90033

STATE/LOCAL REGISTRAR USE ONLY: 15. OFFICE OF THE STATE REGISTRAR OF VITAL STATISTICS | 16. DATE ACCEPTED FOR REGISTRATION—MM/DD/CCYY 02/08/2002

STATE OF CALIFORNIA, DEPARTMENT OF HEALTH SERVICES, OFFICE OF STATE REGISTRAR

This is to certify that this document is a true copy of the official record filed with the Registrar-Recorder/County Clerk.

Conny B. McCormack

CONNY B. McCORMACK
Registrar-Recorder/County Clerk

This copy not valid unless prepared on engraved border displaying the Seal and Signature of the Registrar-Recorder/County Clerk.

APR 17 2002
19-195917

MIDWEST BANK NOTE COMPANY

ANY ALTERATION OR ERASURE VOIDS THIS CERTIFICATE

CERTIFICATION OF VITAL RECORD

COUNTY OF LOS ANGELES • REGISTRAR-RECORDER/COUNTY CLERK

CERTIFICATE OF DEATH
STATE OF CALIFORNIA
USE BLACK INK ONLY

STATE FILE NUMBER

LOCAL REGISTRATION DISTRICT AND CERTIFICATE NUMBER: 38919017430

DECEDENT PERSONAL DATA

1A. NAME OF DECEDENT—FIRST (GIVEN): Lucille
1B. MIDDLE: Ball
1C. LAST (FAMILY): Morton
2A. DATE OF DEATH—MONTH, DAY, YEAR: April 26, 1989
2B. HOUR: 0547
3. SEX: F
4. RACE: White
5. SPANISH/HISPANIC: ☐ YES ___ SPECIFY ☒ NO
6. DATE OF BIRTH—MONTH, DAY, YEAR: August 6, 1911
7. AGE IN YEARS: 77
IF UNDER 1 YEAR: MONTHS / DAYS
IF UNDER 24 HOURS: HOURS / MINUTES
8. STATE OF BIRTH: NY
9. CITIZEN OF WHAT COUNTRY: U.S.A.
10A. FULL NAME OF FATHER: Henry Ball
10B. STATE OF BIRTH: NY
11A. FULL MAIDEN NAME OF MOTHER: Desiree Hunt
11B. STATE OF BIRTH: NY
12. MILITARY SERVICE? 19 ___ TO 19 ___ ☒ NONE
13. SOCIAL SECURITY NUMBER: 568-05-1624
14. MARITAL STATUS: Married
15. NAME OF SURVIVING SPOUSE (IF WIFE, ENTER MAIDEN NAME): Gary Morton
16A. USUAL OCCUPATION: Actress
16B. USUAL KIND OF BUSINESS OR INDUSTRY: T.V. Actress
16C. USUAL EMPLOYER: self-employed
16D. YEARS IN USUAL OCCUPATION: 50
17. NUMBER OF HIGHEST GRADE COMPLETED (1–12 OR COLLEGE 13–17+): 12

USUAL RESIDENCE

18A. RESIDENCE—STREET AND NUMBER OR LOCATION: 1000 No. Roxbury
18B. CITY: Beverly Hills
18C. ZIP CODE: 90210
18D. COUNTY: Los Angeles
18E. NUMBER OF YEARS IN THIS COUNTY: 56
18F. STATE OR FOREIGN COUNTRY: California
20. NAME, RELATIONSHIP, MAILING ADDRESS AND ZIP CODE OF INFORMANT: Mr. Gary Morton, Husband, 1000 No. Roxbury, Beverly Hills, California 90210

PLACE OF DEATH

19A. PLACE OF DEATH: Cedars-Sinai Medical Center
19B. IF HOSPITAL, SPECIFY ONE: IP, ER/OP, DOA: IP
19C. COUNTY: Los Angeles
19D. STREET ADDRESS—STREET AND NUMBER OR LOCATION: 8700 Beverly Blvd.
19E. CITY: Los Angeles

CAUSE OF DEATH

21. DEATH WAS CAUSED BY: (ENTER ONLY ONE CAUSE PER LINE FOR A, B, AND C)—TYPE OR PRINT

	Cause	Time interval between onset and death
IMMEDIATE CAUSE (A)	Acute Rupture of the Abdominal Aorta	1½ hr
DUE TO (B)	Acute Aortic Dissection	8 days
DUE TO (C)	Cystic Medial Necrosis of Aorta	8 ds

22. WAS DEATH REPORTED TO CORONER? ☐ YES ___ REFERRAL NUMBER ☒ NO
23. WAS BIOPSY PERFORMED? ☒ YES ☐ NO
24A. WAS AUTOPSY PERFORMED? ☐ YES ☒ NO
24B. IF YES, WAS IT USED IN DETERMINING CAUSE OF DEATH? ☐ YES ☐ NO
25. OTHER SIGNIFICANT CONDITIONS CONTRIBUTING TO DEATH BUT NOT RELATED TO CAUSE GIVEN IN 21: Hypertension
26. WAS OPERATION PERFORMED FOR ANY CONDITION IN ITEM 21 OR 25? MONTH, DAY, YEAR: April 18, 1989 TYPE: Replacement of Aortic Valve & Ascending Aorta

PHYSICIAN'S CERTIFICATION

I CERTIFY THAT DEATH OCCURRED AT THE HOUR, DATE AND PLACE STATED FROM THE CAUSES STATED.
27A. DECEDENT ATTENDED SINCE MONTH, DAY, YEAR: Apr. 1 15, 1989
DECEDENT LAST SEEN ALIVE MONTH, DAY, YEAR: April 26, 1989
27B. SIGNATURE AND DEGREE OR TITLE OF PHYSICIAN: [signature]
27C. PHYSICIAN'S LICENSE NUMBER: G-35162
27D. DATE SIGNED: Apr 1 26, 1989
27E. TYPE ATTENDING PHYSICIAN'S NAME AND ADDRESS: Robert M. Kass, M.D. 8700 Beverly Blvd. Room 6215, Los Angeles, CA 90048

CORONER'S USE ONLY

I CERTIFY THAT DEATH OCCURRED AT THE HOUR, DATE AND PLACE STATED FROM THE CAUSES STATED.
28A. SIGNATURE OF CORONER OR DEPUTY CORONER
28B. DATE SIGNED
29. MANNER OF DEATH—specify one: natural, accident, suicide, homicide, pending investigation or could not be determined
30A. PLACE OF INJURY
30B. INJURY AT WORK ☐ Yes ☐ No
30C. DATE OF INJURY MONTH, DAY, YEAR
31. HOUR
32. LOCATION (STREET AND NUMBER OR LOCATION AND CITY)
33. DESCRIBE HOW INJURY OCCURRED (EVENTS WHICH RESULTED IN INJURY)

FUNERAL DIRECTOR AND LOCAL REGISTRAR

34A. DISPOSITION: Cremation/BU
34B. PLACE OF FINAL DISPOSITION: Forest Lawn 6300 Forest Lawn Dr., L.A., CA
34C. DATE OF DISPOSITION MONTH, DAY, YEAR: 4/28/89
35A. SIGNATURE OF EMBALMER: No Embalming
35B. LICENSE NUMBER: —
36A. NAME OF FUNERAL DIRECTOR (OR PERSON ACTING AS SUCH): Forest Lawn - Glendale
36B. LICENSE NO.: 656
37. SIGNATURE OF LOCAL REGISTRAR: [signature]
38. REGISTRATION DATE: APR 27 1989

STATE REGISTRAR

A. B. C. D. E. F. CENSUS TRACT

VS-11 (REV. 1-89) 4410 MAKE NO ERASURES, WHITEOUTS, OR OTHER ALTERATIONS

This is to certify that this document is a true copy of the official record filed with the Registrar-Recorder/County Clerk.

AUG 0 8 1991

[signature]
CHARLES WEISSBURD
Registrar-Recorder/County Clerk

19-139053

This copy not valid unless prepared on engraved border displaying the Seal and Signature of the Registrar-Recorder/County Clerk.

American Bank Note Company

ANY ALTERATION OR ERASURE VOIDS THIS CERTIFICATE

STATE OF CALIFORNIA

CERTIFICATION OF VITAL RECORD

COUNTY OF LOS ANGELES • REGISTRAR-RECORDER/COUNTY CLERK

FILED JUL 17 1959 RAY E. LEE COUNTY RECORDER

STATE FILE NUMBER

CERTIFICATE OF DEATH

STATE OF CALIFORNIA—DEPARTMENT OF PUBLIC HEALTH

LOCAL REGISTRATION DISTRICT AND CERTIFICATE NUMBER 7013 10168

DECEDENT PERSONAL DATA

1A. NAME OF DECEASED—FIRST NAME: ETHEL
1B. MIDDLE NAME: BARRYMORE
1C. LAST NAME: COLT
2A. DATE OF DEATH—MONTH, DAY, YEAR: JUNE 18, 1959
2B. HOUR: 9:00 A.M.
3. SEX: Female
4. COLOR OR RACE: White
5. BIRTHPLACE (STATE OR FOREIGN COUNTRY): Pennsylvania
6. DATE OF BIRTH: Aug. 15, 1879
7. AGE (LAST BIRTHDAY): 79 YEARS — IF UNDER 1 YEAR: MONTHS, DAYS — IF UNDER 24 HOURS: HOURS, MINUTES
8. NAME AND BIRTHPLACE OF FATHER: Maunze Barrymore, India
9. MAIDEN NAME AND BIRTHPLACE OF MOTHER: Georgia Drew, Penna.
10. CITIZEN OF WHAT COUNTRY: USA
11. SOCIAL SECURITY NUMBER: 130-12-6033
12. LAST OCCUPATION: Actress
13. NUMBER OF YEARS IN THIS OCCUPATION: 64
14. NAME OF LAST EMPLOYING COMPANY OR FIRM: National Broadcasting Co.
15. KIND OF INDUSTRY OR BUSINESS: Radio Broadcasting & Television
16. IF DECEASED WAS EVER IN U.S. ARMED FORCES GIVE WAR OR DATES OF SERVICE: None
17. SPECIFY MARRIED, NEVER MARRIED, WIDOWED, DIVORCED: Widowed
18A. NAME OF PRESENT SPOUSE
18B. PRESENT OR LAST OCCUPATION OF SPOUSE

PLACE OF DEATH

19A. PLACE OF DEATH—NAME OF HOSPITAL: (None)
19B. STREET ADDRESS—(GIVE STREET OR RURAL ADDRESS OR LOCATION. DO NOT USE P.O. BOX NUMBERS): 135½ So. Linden Drive — [X] INSIDE CITY CORPORATE LIMITS [ ] OUTSIDE CITY CORPORATE LIMITS
19C. CITY OR TOWN: Beverly Hills 1-12-13
19D. COUNTY: Los Angeles
19E. LENGTH OF STAY IN COUNTY OF DEATH: 12 YEARS
19F. LENGTH OF STAY IN CALIFORNIA: 12 YEARS

LAST USUAL RESIDENCE (WHERE DID DECEASED LIVE—IF IN INSTITUTION ENTER RESIDENCE BEFORE ADMISSION)

20A. LAST USUAL RESIDENCE—STREET ADDRESS: 135½ So. Linden Dr.
20B. IF INSIDE CITY CORPORATE LIMITS CHECK HERE [X] — IF OUTSIDE CITY CORPORATE LIMITS CHECK ONE: [ ] ON A FARM [ ] NOT ON A FARM
20C. CITY OR TOWN: Beverly Hills 12-13
20D. COUNTY: Los Angeles
20E. STATE: Calif.
21A. NAME OF INFORMANT (IF OTHER THAN SPOUSE): Sam Colt
21B. ADDRESS OF INFORMANT (IF DIFFERENT FROM LAST USUAL RESIDENCE OF DECEDENT)

PHYSICIAN'S OR CORONER'S CERTIFICATION

22A. PHYSICIAN: I HEREBY CERTIFY THAT DEATH OCCURRED AT THE HOUR, DATE AND PLACE STATED ABOVE FROM THE CAUSES STATED BELOW AND THAT I ATTENDED THE DECEASED FROM May 55 TO 18 June 59 AND THAT I LAST SAW THE DECEASED ALIVE ON 18 June 59
22B. CORONER: I HEREBY CERTIFY THAT DEATH OCCURRED AT THE HOUR, DATE AND PLACE STATED ABOVE FROM THE CAUSES STATED BELOW AND THAT I HAVE HELD AN INVESTIGATION, AUTOPSY, INQUEST ON THE REMAINS OF DECEASED AS REQUIRED BY LAW
22C. PHYSICIAN OR CORONER—SIGNATURE: H. Clay Barton M.D. — DEGREE OR TITLE
22D. ADDRESS: 5505 Ocean Front Walk
22E. DATE SIGNED: 19 June 59

FUNERAL DIRECTOR AND LOCAL REGISTRAR

23. SPECIFY BURIAL, ENTOMBMENT OR CREMATION: Entombment
24. DATE: 6/22/59
25. NAME OF CEMETERY OR CREMATORY: Calvary Mausaleum, L.A.
26. EMBALMER—SIGNATURE (IF BODY EMBALMED): Robert [illegible] — LICENSE NUMBER 3272
27. NAME OF FUNERAL DIRECTOR (OR PERSON ACTING AS SUCH): CALLANAN MORTUARY
28. DATE ACCEPTED FOR REGISTRATION BY LOCAL REGISTRAR: JUN 22 1959
29. LOCAL REGISTRAR—SIGNATURE: Roy O. Gilbert [illegible] Tsuyuko Miyagi

MEDICAL AND HEALTH DATA

CAUSE OF DEATH

30. CAUSE OF DEATH — ENTER ONLY ONE CAUSE PER LINE FOR (A), (B), AND (C)

		APPROXIMATE INTERVAL BETWEEN ONSET AND DEATH
PART I. DEATH WAS CAUSED BY: IMMEDIATE CAUSE (A)	Pulmonary infarction	1 hour
CONDITIONS, IF ANY, WHICH GAVE RISE TO THE ABOVE CAUSE (A), STATING THE UNDERLYING CAUSE LAST — DUE TO (B)	Arteriosclerotic heart disease	20 yrs
DUE TO (C)	Generalized arteriosclerosis	25 yrs

PART II. OTHER SIGNIFICANT CONDITIONS CONTRIBUTING TO DEATH BUT NOT RELATED TO THE TERMINAL DISEASE CONDITION GIVEN IN PART I (A)

CC 6-30-59

OPERATION AND AUTOPSY

31. OPERATION—CHECK ONE: [✓] OPERATION PERFORMED [ ] OPERATION PERFORMED—FINDINGS USED IN DETERMINING ABOVE STATED CAUSES OF DEATH [ ] OPERATION PERFORMED—FINDINGS NOT USED IN DETERMINING ABOVE STATED CAUSES OF DEATH
32. DATE OF OPERATION
33. AUTOPSY—CHECK ONE: [✓] AUTOPSY PERFORMED [ ] AUTOPSY PERFORMED—GROSS FINDINGS USED IN DETERMINING ABOVE STATED CAUSES OF DEATH [ ] AUTOPSY PERFORMED—GROSS FINDINGS NOT USED IN DETERMINING ABOVE STATED CAUSES OF DEATH

INJURY INFORMATION

34A. SPECIFY ACCIDENT, SUICIDE OR HOMICIDE
34B. DESCRIBE HOW INJURY OCCURRED
35A. TIME OF INJURY: HOUR, MONTH, DAY, YEAR
35B. INJURY OCCURRED: [ ] WHILE AT WORK [ ] NOT WHILE AT WORK
35C. PLACE OF INJURY (E.G., IN OR ABOUT HOME, FARM, FACTORY, STREET, OFFICE BUILDING)
35D. CITY, TOWN, OR LOCATION — COUNTY — STATE

This is to certify that this document is a true copy of the official record filed with the Registrar-Recorder/County Clerk.

Conny B. McCormack

CONNY B. McCORMACK
Registrar-Recorder/County Clerk

SEP 30 2002
19-539653

This copy not valid unless prepared on engraved border displaying the Seal and Signature of the Registrar-Recorder/County Clerk.

MIDWEST BANK NOTE COMPANY

ANY ALTERATION OR ERASURE VOIDS THIS CERTIFICATE

CERTIFICATION OF VITAL RECORD

COUNTY OF LOS ANGELES • REGISTRAR-RECORDER/COUNTY CLERK

DISTRICT NO. 1901 REGISTRAR'S NO. 7883

1. FULL NAME JOHN BARRYMORE

2. PLACE OF DEATH: (A) COUNTY LOS ANGELES
(B) CITY OR TOWN LOS ANGELES
IF OUTSIDE CITY OR TOWN LIMITS, WRITE RURAL
(C) NAME OF HOSPITAL OR INSTITUTION HOLLYWOOD HOSPITAL
IF NOT IN HOSPITAL OR INSTITUTION, GIVE STREET NUMBER OR LOCATION
(D) LENGTH OF STAY: (SPECIFY WHETHER YEARS, MONTHS OR DAYS)
IN HOSPITAL OR INSTITUTION 11 DAYS
IN THIS COMMUNITY 20 YRS. IN CALIFORNIA 20 YRS.
(E) IF FOREIGN BORN, HOW LONG IN THE U. S. A.? YEARS

3. USUAL RESIDENCE OF DECEASED:
(A) STATE CALIFORNIA
(B) COUNTY LOS ANGELES
(C) CITY OR TOWN LOS ANGELES
IF OUTSIDE CITY OR TOWN LIMITS, WRITE RURAL
(D) STREET NO. 6 TOWER GROVE DRIVE

20. DATE OF DEATH: MONTH MAY DAY 29
YEAR 1942 HOUR 10 MINUTE 30 P.M.

3. (E) IF VETERAN, NAME OF WAR NONE
3. (F) SOCIAL SECURITY NO. 569-18-9124
4. SEX MALE
5. COLOR OR RACE CAUC.
6. (A) SINGLE, MARRIED, WIDOWED OR DIVORCED DIVORCED
6. (B) NAME OF HUSBAND OR WIFE ELAINE BARRYMORE
6. (C) AGE OF HUSBAND OR WIFE IF ALIVE UNK. YEARS

21. MEDICAL CERTIFICATE
I HEREBY CERTIFY, THAT I ATTENDED THE DECEASED FROM Oct-1-1940 TO May-29-42, THAT I LAST SAW HIM ALIVE ON May 29 1942 AND THAT DEATH OCCURRED ON THE DATE AND HOUR STATED ABOVE.

22. CORONER'S CERTIFICATE
I HEREBY CERTIFY, THAT I HELD AN AUTOPSY, INQUEST OR INVESTIGATION ON THE REMAINS OF THE DECEASED AND FIND FROM SUCH ACTION THAT DECEASED CAME TO H DEATH ON THE DATE AND HOUR STATED ABOVE.

7. BIRTHDATE OF DECEASED FEB. 15 1882 (MONTH DAY YEAR)
8. AGE 60 YRS. 3 MOS. 14 DAYS IF LESS THAN ONE DAY OLD HRS. MIN.
9. BIRTHPLACE PHILADELPHIA, PENN.
10. USUAL OCCUPATION ACTOR
11. INDUSTRY OR BUSINESS STAGE, SCREEN & RADIO
FATHER 12. NAME MAURICE BARRYMORE
13. BIRTHPLACE UNKNOWN, INDIA
MOTHER 14. MAIDEN NAME GEORGIA DREW
15. BIRTHPLACE PHILADELPHIA, PENN.
16. (A) INFORMANT MR. LIONEL BARRYMORE
(B) ADDRESS 11050 INDEPENDENCE AVE. CHATSWORTH, CALIF.

	DURATION
IMMEDIATE CAUSE OF DEATH Myocarditis (acute)	48 hrs.
DUE TO Chronic nephritis	yrs.
DUE TO Cirrhosis of liver	yrs.
OTHER CONDITIONS [illegible] Heart (INCLUDE PREGNANCY WITHIN THREE MONTHS OF DEATH)	yrs.

MAJOR FINDINGS: OF OPERATIONS 0 DATE OF OPERATION 0
OF AUTOPSY none

PHYSICIAN UNDERLINE THE CAUSE TO WHICH DEATH SHOULD BE CHARGED STATISTICALLY.

17. (A) ENTOMBMENT (BURIAL, CREMATION OR REMOVAL) (B) DATE 6.2.1942
(C) PLACE CALVARY MAUS.
18. (A) EMBALMER'S SIGNATURE Elmer Gault LICENSE NO. 1472
(B) FUNERAL DIRECTOR PIERCE BROS.
ADDRESS 720 W. WASHINGTON BLVD.
BY C. H. Hess

23. IF DEATH WAS DUE TO EXTERNAL CAUSES, FILL IN THE FOLLOWING:
(A) ACCIDENT, SUICIDE, OR HOMICIDE? 0 (B) DATE OF INJURY 0
(C) WHERE DID INJURY OCCUR? 0 CITY OR TOWN COUNTY STATE
(D) DID INJURY OCCUR IN OR ABOUT HOME, ON FARM, IN INDUSTRIAL PLACE, OR IN PUBLIC PLACE? — WHILE AT WORK? — SPECIFY TYPE OF PLACE
(E) MEANS OF INJURY —

19. (A) JUN 1 1942 DATE FILED (B) George M. Uhl M.D. REGISTRAR'S REGISTRAR

24. CORONER'S OR PHYSICIAN'S SIGNATURE (SPECIFY WHICH) Hugo M. Kersten MD
ADDRESS 956 S. Norton DATE 6/1/42

STATE OF CALIFORNIA DEPARTMENT OF PUBLIC HEALTH CERTIFICATE OF DEATH U. S. DEPT. OF COMMERCE

This is to certify that this document is a true copy of the official record filed with the Registrar-Recorder/County Clerk.

Beatriz Valdez
BEATRIZ VALDEZ
Registrar-Recorder/County Clerk

AUG 25 1995
19-398640

This copy not valid unless prepared on engraved border displaying the Seal and Signature of the Registrar-Recorder/County Clerk.

American Bank Note Company ANY ALTERATION OR ERASURE VOIDS THIS CERTIFICATE

CERTIFICATION OF VITAL RECORD

COUNTY OF LOS ANGELES • REGISTRAR-RECORDER/COUNTY CLERK

STATE FILE NO.

CERTIFICATE OF DEATH

STATE OF CALIFORNIA—DEPARTMENT OF PUBLIC HEALTH

REGISTRATION DISTRICT NO. 1901 REGISTRAR'S NUMBER 19425

DECEDENT PERSONAL DATA (TYPE OR PRINT NAME)

1a. NAME OF DECEASED—FIRST NAME: Lionel
1b. MIDDLE NAME:
1c. LAST NAME: Barrymore
2a. DATE OF DEATH—MONTH, DAY, YEAR: November 15, 1954
2b. HOUR: 7:15P.M.
3. SEX: Male
4. COLOR OR RACE: Cauc
5. SPECIFY MARRIED, NEVER MARRIED, WIDOWED, DIVORCED: Widowed
6. DATE OF BIRTH: April 28, 1878
7. AGE (LAST BIRTHDAY): 76 YEARS — IF UNDER 1 YEAR: MONTHS, DAYS — IF UNDER 24 HOURS: HOURS, MINUTES
8a. USUAL OCCUPATION (GIVE KIND OF WORK DONE DURING MOST OF WORKING LIFE, EVEN IF RETIRED): Actor
8b. KIND OF BUSINESS OR INDUSTRY: Stage &Screen Radio
9. BIRTHPLACE (STATE OR FOREIGN COUNTRY): Philadelphia Pennsylvania
10. CITIZEN OF WHAT COUNTRY: U.S.A.
11. NAME AND BIRTHPLACE OF FATHER: Maurice Barrymore-India
12. MAIDEN NAME AND BIRTHPLACE OF MOTHER: Georgie Drew - Unk
13. NAME OF PRESENT SPOUSE (IF MARRIED):
14. WAS DECEASED EVER IN U. S. ARMED FORCES? SPECIFY YES, NO, UNKNOWN: No — IF YES, GIVE WAR OR DATES OF SERVICE:
15. SOCIAL SECURITY NUMBER: 569-18-9721
16. INFORMANT: Miss Florence Wheeler

PLACE OF DEATH

17a. COUNTY: Los Angeles
17b. CITY OR TOWN: Los Angeles (Van Nuys) — ☐ OUTSIDE CORPORATE LIMITS ☒ INSIDE CORPORATE LIMITS
17c. LENGTH OF STAY IN THIS CITY OR TOWN: 30 Years
17d. FULL NAME OF HOSPITAL OR INSTITUTION: Valley Hospital
17e. ADDRESS (IF NOT IN HOSPITAL OR INSTITUTION, GIVE STREET OR RURAL ADDRESS OR LOCATION. DO NOT USE P. O. BOX NUMBERS): 14500 Valley Circle

LAST USUAL RESIDENCE (WHERE DECEASED LIVED. IF INSTITUTION, RESIDENCE BEFORE ADMISSION)

18a. STATE: Calif
18b. COUNTY: Los Angeles
18c. CITY OR TOWN: Los Angeles (Chatsworth) — ☐ OUTSIDE CORPORATE LIMITS ☒ INSIDE CORPORATE LIMITS
18d. STREET OR RURAL ADDRESS (DO NOT USE P. O. BOX NUMBERS): 11050 Independence Ave.

PHYSICIAN'S OR CORONER'S CERTIFICATION

19a. CORONER: I HEREBY CERTIFY THAT DEATH OCCURRED AT THE HOUR, DATE AND PLACE STATED ABOVE FROM THE CAUSES STATED BELOW AND THAT I HAVE HELD AN ______ (INVESTIGATION, AUTOPSY, INQUEST) ON THE REMAINS OF DECEASED AS REQUIRED BY LAW.
19b. PHYSICIAN: I HEREBY CERTIFY THAT DEATH OCCURRED AT THE HOUR, DATE AND PLACE STATED ABOVE FROM THE CAUSES STATED BELOW AND THAT I ATTENDED THE DECEASED FROM 9-11-54 TO 11-15-54 AND THAT I LAST SAW THE DECEASED ALIVE ON 11-15-54
19c. SIGNATURE / DEGREE OR TITLE: John Paul Ewing, M.D.
19d. ADDRESS: 8366 Reseda Blvd Northridge
19e. DATE SIGNED: 11-15-54

FUNERAL DIRECTOR AND REGISTRAR

20a. SPECIFY BURIAL, CREMATION OR REMOVAL: Burial
20b. DATE: Nov 18, 1954
20c. CEMETERY OR CREMATORY: Calvary Cemetery
21. SIGNATURE OF EMBALMER (IF BODY EMBALMED): John L. Reed — LICENSE NUMBER: 249[illegible]
22. FUNERAL DIRECTOR: Pierce Brothers Valley
23. DATE RECEIVED BY LOCAL REGISTRAR: NOV 17 1954
24. SIGNATURE OF LOCAL REGISTRAR: George M. Uhl, M.D.

MEDICAL AND HEALTH DATA

CAUSE OF DEATH (ENTER ONLY ONE CAUSE PER LINE FOR (A), (B) AND (C).)

THIS DOES NOT MEAN THE MODE OF DYING SUCH AS HEART FAILURE, ASTHENIA, ETC. IT MEANS THE DISEASE, INJURY OR COMPLICATIONS WHICH CAUSED DEATH.

25. DISEASE OR CONDITION DIRECTLY LEADING TO DEATH (A): Myocarditis Chronic 93D — Years
ANTECEDENT CAUSES — MORBID CONDITIONS, IF ANY, GIVING RISE TO THE ABOVE CAUSE (A) STATING THE UNDERLYING CAUSE LAST.
DUE TO (B): Edema Lung, Acute 1.11 B — 20 hrs
DUE TO (C): Nephritis chronic, Parenchymatous — 10 Yrs

APPROXIMATE INTERVAL BETWEEN ONSET AND DEATH

OTHER SIGNIFICANT CONDITIONS

26. CONDITIONS CONTRIBUTING TO THE DEATH BUT NOT RELATED TO THE DISEASE OR CONDITION CAUSING DEATH.

OPERATIONS

27a. DATE OF OPERATION
27b. MAJOR FINDINGS OF OPERATION
28. AUTOPSY ☐ YES ☒ NO

DEATH DUE TO EXTERNAL VIOLENCE

29a. SPECIFY ACCIDENT, SUICIDE OR HOMICIDE
29b. PLACE OF INJURY (E.G., IN OR ABOUT HOME, FARM, FACTORY, STREET, OFFICE BUILDING)
29c. LOCATION — CITY OR TOWN, COUNTY, STATE
29d. TIME OF INJURY — MONTH DAY YEAR HOUR M.
29e. INJURY OCCURRED ☐ WHILE AT WORK ☐ NOT WHILE AT WORK
29f. HOW DID INJURY OCCUR?

REV. 1-1-52. FORM R69-11

This is to certify that this document is a true copy of the official record filed with the Registrar-Recorder/County Clerk.

Beatriz Valdez
BEATRIZ VALDEZ
Registrar-Recorder/County Clerk

AUG 0 4 1994

19-390018

This copy not valid unless prepared on engraved border displaying the Seal and Signature of the Registrar-Recorder/County Clerk.

American Bank Note Company

ANY ALTERATION OR ERASURE VOIDS THIS CERTIFICATE

CERTIFICATION OF VITAL RECORD

COUNTY OF LOS ANGELES • REGISTRAR-RECORDER/COUNTY CLERK

CERTIFICATE OF DEATH
STATE OF CALIFORNIA

0190-012729

STATE FILE NUMBER — LOCAL REGISTRATION DISTRICT AND CERTIFICATE NUMBER

DECEDENT PERSONAL DATA

1A. NAME OF DECEDENT—FIRST: John
1B. MIDDLE: Adam
1C. LAST: Belushi
2A. DATE OF DEATH (MONTH, DAY, YEAR): FOUND MARCH 5, 1982
2B. HOUR: 1245
3. SEX: Male
4. RACE: Cauc.
5. ETHNICITY: not stated
6. DATE OF BIRTH: January 24, 1949
7. AGE: 33 YEARS
8. BIRTHPLACE OF DECEDENT (STATE OR FOREIGN COUNTRY): Illinois
9. NAME AND BIRTHPLACE OF FATHER: Adam Belushi., Albania
10. BIRTH NAME AND BIRTHPLACE OF MOTHER: Agnes Samaras., Ohio
11. CITIZEN OF WHAT COUNTRY: United States
12. SOCIAL SECURITY NUMBER: 327.42.1315
13. MARITAL STATUS: Married
14. NAME OF SURVIVING SPOUSE (IF WIFE, ENTER BIRTH NAME): Judith Jacklin
15. PRIMARY OCCUPATION: Actor
16. NUMBER OF YEARS THIS OCCUPATION: 8
17. EMPLOYER (IF SELF-EMPLOYED, SO STATE): Self
18. KIND OF INDUSTRY OR BUSINESS: Motion Pictures/ T.V.

USUAL RESIDENCE

19A. USUAL RESIDENCE—STREET ADDRESS (STREET AND NUMBER OR LOCATION): South Road
19B.
19C. CITY OR TOWN: Chilmark
19D. COUNTY: Duke
19E. STATE: Massachusetts
20. NAME AND ADDRESS OF INFORMANT—RELATIONSHIP: John Mucci - Friend, 9200 Sunset Blvd. Los Angeles, California

AMENDED 1 OF 2

PLACE OF DEATH

21A. PLACE OF DEATH: HOTEL-BUNGALOW B-#3
21B. COUNTY: LOS ANGELES
21C. STREET ADDRESS (STREET AND NUMBER OR LOCATION): 8221 SUNSET BLVD.
21D. CITY OR TOWN: HOLLYWOOD

CAUSE OF DEATH

22. DEATH WAS CAUSED BY: (ENTER ONLY ONE CAUSE PER LINE FOR A, B, AND C)
IMMEDIATE CAUSE (A) DEFERRED
CONDITIONS, IF ANY, WHICH GAVE RISE TO THE IMMEDIATE CAUSE, STATING THE UNDERLYING CAUSE LAST
DUE TO, OR AS A CONSEQUENCE OF (B)
DUE TO, OR AS A CONSEQUENCE OF (C)
APPROXIMATE INTERVAL BETWEEN ONSET AND DEATH
24. WAS DEATH REPORTED TO CORONER? 82-3036
25. WAS BIOPSY PERFORMED?
26. WAS AUTOPSY PERFORMED? YES
23. OTHER CONDITIONS CONTRIBUTING BUT NOT RELATED TO THE IMMEDIATE CAUSE OF DEATH
27. WAS OPERATION PERFORMED FOR ANY CONDITION IN ITEMS 22 OR 23? TYPE OF OPERATION — DATE

PHYSICIAN'S CERTIFICATION

28A. I CERTIFY THAT DEATH OCCURRED AT THE HOUR, DATE AND PLACE STATED FROM THE CAUSES STATED. I ATTENDED DECEDENT SINCE (ENTER MO, DA, YR.) I LAST SAW DECEDENT ALIVE (ENTER MO, DA, YR.)
28B. PHYSICIAN—SIGNATURE AND DEGREE OR TITLE
28C. DATE SIGNED
28D. PHYSICIAN'S LICENSE NUMBER
28E. TYPE PHYSICIAN'S NAME AND ADDRESS

INJURY INFORMATION

29. SPECIFY ACCIDENT, SUICIDE, ETC.
30. PLACE OF INJURY
31. INJURY AT WORK
32A. DATE OF INJURY—MONTH, DAY, YEAR
32B. HOUR
33. LOCATION (STREET AND NUMBER OR LOCATION AND CITY OR TOWN)
34. DESCRIBE HOW INJURY OCCURRED (EVENTS WHICH RESULTED IN INJURY)

CORONER'S USE ONLY 18

35A. I CERTIFY THAT DEATH OCCURRED AT THE HOUR, DATE AND PLACE STATED FROM THE CAUSES STATED. AS REQUIRED BY LAW I HAVE HELD AN INVESTIGATION
35B. CORONER—SIGNATURE AND DEGREE OR TITLE: THOMAS T. NOGUCHI, M.D. CORONER, LOS ANGELES, CALIF. 90033 — Robert D. Arteaga, DEPUTY
35C. DATE SIGNED: 3-6-82

36. DISPOSITION: Burial
37. DATE—MONTH, DAY, YEAR: Mar. 10, 82
38. NAME AND ADDRESS OF CEMETERY OR CREMATORY: Abel's Hill Cemetery, Chilmark, Mass.
39. EMBALMER'S LICENSE NUMBER AND SIGNATURE: William L. Pierce 5595
40. NAME OF FUNERAL DIRECTOR (OR PERSON ACTING AS SUCH): Westwood Village Mortuary
41. LOCAL REGISTRAR—SIGNATURE: Robert Wolfe
42. DATE ACCEPTED BY LOCAL REGISTRAR: MAR 8 1982

STATE REGISTRAR: A. B. C. D. E. F.

6 VS-11 (10-78)

01-12-4-7007

This is to certify that this document is a true copy of the official record filed with the Registrar-Recorder/County Clerk.

Charles Weissburd
CHARLES WEISSBURD
Registrar-Recorder/County Clerk

FEB 12 1992

19-312714

This copy not valid unless prepared on engraved border displaying the Seal and Signature of the Registrar-Recorder/County Clerk.

American Bank Note Company

ANY ALTERATION OR ERASURE VOIDS THIS CERTIFICATE

CERTIFICATION OF VITAL RECORD

COUNTY OF LOS ANGELES • REGISTRAR-RECORDER/COUNTY CLERK

THIS FORM MUST BE COMPLETED IN BLACK INK
AMENDMENT OF MEDICAL AND HEALTH SECTION DATA-DEATH
(INSTRUCTIONS ON REVERSE)

STATE CERTIFICATE NUMBER 823454

LOCAL REGISTRATION DISTRICT AND CERTIFICATE NUMBER 0190-012129

IDENTIFICATION OF THE RECORD

1a. FIRST NAME: John
1b. MIDDLE NAME: Adam
1c. LAST NAME: Belushi
2. PLACE OF OCCURRENCE—CITY OR COUNTY: Los Angeles
3. DATE OF EVENT: Found March 5, 1982
4. DATE ORIGINAL FILED: March 8, 1982

ORIGINALLY REPORTED INFORMATION

INFORMATION AS REPORTED ON THE ORIGINALLY REGISTERED CERTIFICATE

21. DEATH WAS CAUSED BY: (ENTER ONLY ONE CAUSE PER LINE FOR A, B, AND C)
IMMEDIATE CAUSE (A) Deferred
CONDITIONS, IF ANY, WHICH GAVE RISE TO THE IMMEDIATE CAUSE STATING THE UNDERLYING CAUSE LAST
DUE TO, OR AS A CONSEQUENCE OF (B)
DUE TO, OR AS A CONSEQUENCE OF (C)
2 OF 2
APPROXIMATE INTERVAL BETWEEN ONSET AND DEATH
24. WAS DEATH REPORTED TO CORONER? 82-3036
25. WAS BIOPSY PERFORMED?
26. WAS AUTOPSY PERFORMED? Yes
23. OTHER CONDITIONS CONTRIBUTING BUT NOT RELATED TO THE IMMEDIATE CAUSE OF DEATH
27. WAS OPERATION PERFORMED FOR ANY CONDITION IN ITEMS 21 OR 23? OPERATION DATE
29. SPECIFY ACCIDENT, SUICIDE, ETC.
30. PLACE OF INJURY
31. INJURY AT WORK
32A. DATE OF INJURY—MONTH, DAY, YEAR
32B. HOUR
33. LOCATION (STREET AND NUMBER OR LOCATION AND CITY OR TOWN)
34. DESCRIBE HOW INJURY OCCURRED (EVENTS WHICH RESULTED IN INJURY)

INFORMATION AS IT SHOULD BE STATED ON THE ORIGINALLY REGISTERED CERTIFICATE

INFORMATION AS IT SHOULD BE STATED ON THE ORIGINALLY REGISTERED CERTIFICATE

21. DEATH WAS CAUSED BY: (ENTER ONLY ONE CAUSE PER LINE FOR A, B, AND C)
IMMEDIATE CAUSE (A) ACUTE COCAINE AND HEROIN INTOXICATION
CONDITIONS, IF ANY, WHICH GAVE RISE TO THE IMMEDIATE CAUSE, STATING THE UNDERLYING CAUSE LAST
DUE TO, OR AS A CONSEQUENCE OF (B)
DUE TO, OR AS A CONSEQUENCE OF (C)
APPROXIMATE INTERVAL BETWEEN ONSET AND DEATH
24. WAS DEATH REPORTED TO CORONER? 82-3036
25. WAS BIOPSY PERFORMED? No
26. WAS AUTOPSY PERFORMED? Yes
23. OTHER CONDITIONS CONTRIBUTING BUT NOT RELATED TO THE IMMEDIATE CAUSE OF DEATH
27. WAS OPERATION PERFORMED FOR ANY CONDITION IN ITEMS 21 OR 23? OPERATION DATE No
29. SPECIFY ACCIDENT, SUICIDE, ETC.: Accident
30. PLACE OF INJURY: Hotel - Bungalow
31. INJURY AT WORK: No
32A. DATE OF INJURY—MONTH, DAY, YEAR: 3-5-82
32B. HOUR: Unk.
33. LOCATION (STREET AND NUMBER OR LOCATION AND CITY OR TOWN): 8221 Sunset Blvd - Los Angeles
34. DESCRIBE HOW INJURY OCCURRED (EVENTS WHICH RESULTED IN INJURY): INTRAVENOUS DRUG INJECTION

DECLARATION OF CERTIFYING PHYSICIAN OR CORONER

5. I, THE CERTIFYING PHYSICIAN OR CORONER HAVING PERSONAL KNOWLEDGE OF SUPPLEMENTAL INFORMATION WHICH MODIFIES THE INFORMATION ORIGINALLY REPORTED, DECLARE UNDER PENALTY OF PERJURY THAT THE ABOVE INFORMATION IS TRUE AND CORRECT TO THE BEST OF MY KNOWLEDGE

6a. SIGNATURE OF PHYSICIAN OR CORONER: N. Palmer
6b. DATE SIGNED: 3-12-82
7a. NAME OF PHYSICIAN OR CORONER (PRINT OR TYPE): THOMAS T. NOGUCHI, M.D., CORONER
BY N. Palmer DEPUTY
7b. DEGREE OR TITLE
7c. ADDRESS—STREET, CITY, STATE: 1104 N. MISSION ROAD LOS ANGELES, CALIFORNIA 90033

REGISTRAR'S OFFICE

8a. OFFICE OF STATE OR LOCAL REGISTRAR
8b. DATE ACCEPTED: MAR 19 1982

STATE OF CALIFORNIA, DEPARTMENT OF HEALTH SERVICES, OFFICE OF THE STATE REGISTRAR OF VITAL STATISTICS

FORM VS-24B (REV. 10-79)

This is to certify that this document is a true copy of the official record filed with the Registrar-Recorder/County Clerk.

CHARLES WEISSBURD
Registrar-Recorder/County Clerk

19-312794

This copy not valid unless prepared on engraved border displaying the Seal and Signature of the Registrar-Recorder/County Clerk.

American Bank Note Company

ANY ALTERATION OR ERASURE VOIDS THIS CERTIFICATE

CERTIFICATION OF VITAL RECORD

COUNTY OF LOS ANGELES • REGISTRAR-RECORDER/COUNTY CLERK

CERTIFICATE OF DEATH 0190-058330

STATE OF CALIFORNIA—DEPARTMENT OF HEALTH
OFFICE OF THE STATE REGISTRAR OF VITAL STATISTICS

DECEDENT PERSONAL DATA

- 1a. Name of deceased—first name: Jack Benjamin
- 1c. Last name: Benny, aka Kubelsky
- 2a. Date of death: December 26, 1974
- 2b. Hour: 11:30 P.M.
- 3. Sex: Male
- 4. Color or race: Cauc.
- 5. Birthplace: Illinois
- 6. Date of birth: February 14, 1894
- 7. Age: 80 years
- 8. Name and birthplace of father: Meyer Kubelsky, Russia
- 9. Maiden name and birthplace of mother: Naomi Sachs, Russia
- 10. Citizen of what country: USA
- 11. Social security number: 561-09-5488
- 12. Married, never married, widowed, divorced: Married
- 13. Name of surviving spouse: Mary Marks
- 14. Last occupation: Actor
- 15. Number of years in this occupation: 65
- 16. Name of last employing company or firm: Self Employed
- 17. Kind of industry or business: Entertainment

PLACE OF DEATH

- 18a. Place of death:
- 18b. Street address: 10231 Charing Cross Rd.
- 18c. Inside city corporate limits: yes
- 18d. City or town: Los Angeles
- 18e. County: Los Angeles
- 18f. Length of stay in county of death: 37 years
- 18g. Length of stay in California: 37 years

USUAL RESIDENCE

- 19a. Usual residence: 10231 Charing Cross Rd.
- 19b. Inside city corporate limits: yes
- 19c. City or town: Los Angeles
- 19d. County: Los Angeles
- 19e. State: California
- 20. Name and mailing address of informant: Irving Fein, 9808 Wilshire Blvd., Beverly Hills, California

PHYSICIAN'S OR CORONER'S CERTIFICATION

- 21b. Physician: from 7-1-52 to 12-26-74; last saw 12-26-74
- 21c. Physician or coroner—signature: [signature] MD
- 21d. Date signed: 12-27-74
- 21e. Address: 436 N Roxbury
- 21f. Physician's California license number: G1805

FUNERAL DIRECTOR AND LOCAL REGISTRAR

- 22a. Specify burial, entombment or cremation: Entombment
- 22b. Date: 12/29/74
- 23. Name of cemetery or crematory: Hillside Memorial Park
- 24. Embalmer—signature: David George Rice 5229
- 25. Name of funeral director: Groman Mortuary bb
- 26. If not certified by coroner, was this death reported to coroner: NO
- 27. Local registrar—signature: [signature]
- 28. Date received for registration: DEC 28 1974

MEDICAL AND HEALTH DATA — CAUSE OF DEATH

- 29. Part I. Death was caused by: (A) Immediate cause: Carcinoma of Pancreas — approximate interval between onset and death: 3 mos.
- (B) Due to, or as a consequence of:
- (C) Due to, or as a consequence of:
- 30. Part II. Other significant conditions: Arteriosclerosis, Mellitus, mild
- 31. Was operation or biopsy performed: No
- 32a. Autopsy: No

INJURY INFORMATION

- 33. Specify accident, suicide or homicide:
- 34. Place of injury:
- 35. Injury at work:
- 36a. Date of injury:
- 36b. Hour:
- 37a. Place of injury:
- 40. Describe how injury occurred:

STATE REGISTRAR A. B. C. D. E. F.

This is to certify that this document is a true copy of the official record filed with the Registrar-Recorder/County Clerk.

Beatriz Valdez
BEATRIZ VALDEZ
Registrar-Recorder/County Clerk

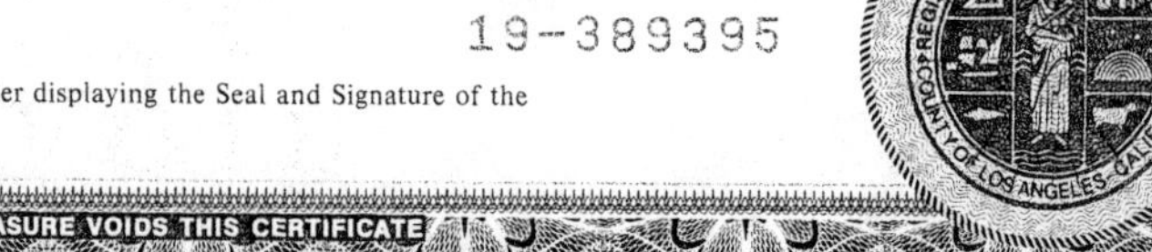

This copy not valid unless prepared on engraved border displaying the Seal and Signature of the Registrar-Recorder/County Clerk.

ANY ALTERATION OR ERASURE VOIDS THIS CERTIFICATE

STATE OF CALIFORNIA

CERTIFICATION OF VITAL RECORD

COUNTY OF LOS ANGELES

DEPARTMENT OF HEALTH SERVICES

CERTIFICATE OF DEATH

STATE OF CALIFORNIA
USE BLACK INK ONLY/NO ERASURES, WHITEOUTS OR ALTERATIONS
VS-11 (REV. 1/00)

STATE FILE NUMBER | LOCAL REGISTRATION NUMBER

DECEDENT PERSONAL DATA

1. NAME OF DECEDENT—FIRST (GIVEN): Milton
2. MIDDLE: -
3. LAST (FAMILY): Berle
4. DATE OF BIRTH MM/DD/CCYY: 07/12/1908
5. AGE YRS.: 93
IF UNDER 1 YEAR: MONTHS | DAYS — IF UNDER 24 HOURS: HOURS | MINUTES
6. SEX: M
7. DATE OF DEATH MM/DD/CCYY: 03/27/2002
8. HOUR: 1430
9. STATE OF BIRTH: NY
10. SOCIAL SECURITY NO.: 568-07-6710
11. MILITARY SERVICE: ☐ YES ☒ NO ☐ UNK
12. MARITAL STATUS: Married
13. EDUCATION—YEARS COMPLETED: 12
14. RACE: White
15. HISPANIC—SPECIFY: ☐ YES ☒ NO
16. USUAL EMPLOYER: Self Employed
17. OCCUPATION: Entertainer
18. KIND OF BUSINESS: Entertainment
19. YEARS IN OCCUPATION: 88

USUAL RESIDENCE

20. RESIDENCE—(STREET AND NUMBER OR LOCATION): 10490 Wilshire Boulevard #1603
21. CITY: Los Angeles
22. COUNTY: Los Angeles
23. ZIP CODE: 90024
24. YRS IN COUNTY: 41
25. STATE OR FOREIGN COUNTRY: California

INFORMANT

26. NAME, RELATIONSHIP: Lorna Berle, Wife
27. MAILING ADDRESS (STREET AND NUMBER OR RURAL ROUTE NUMBER, CITY OR TOWN, STATE, ZIP): 10490 Wilshire Boulevard, #1603, Los Angeles, CA 90024

SPOUSE AND PARENT INFORMATION

28. NAME OF SURVIVING SPOUSE—FIRST: Lorna
29. MIDDLE: -
30. LAST (MAIDEN NAME): Shaw
31. NAME OF FATHER—FIRST: Moses
32. MIDDLE: -
33. LAST: Berlinger
34. BIRTH STATE: New York
35. NAME OF MOTHER—FIRST: Sarah
36. MIDDLE: -
37. LAST (MAIDEN): Glanz
38. BIRTH STATE: New York

DISPOSITION(S)

39. DATE MM/DD/CCYY: 03/29/2002
40. PLACE OF FINAL DISPOSITION: Hillside Memorial Park 6001 Centinela Avenue, Los Angeles, CA 90045

FUNERAL DIRECTOR AND LOCAL REGISTRAR

41. TYPE OF DISPOSITION(S): CR/BU
42. SIGNATURE OF EMBALMER: Not Embalmed
43. LICENSE NO.: -
44. NAME OF FUNERAL DIRECTOR: Hillside Mortuary
45. LICENSE NO.: FD 1358
46. SIGNATURE OF LOCAL REGISTRAR: Fred Leaf
47. DATE MM/DD/CCYY: 03/29/2002

PLACE OF DEATH

101. PLACE OF DEATH: Residence
102. IF HOSPITAL, SPECIFY ONE: ☐ IP ☐ ER/OP ☐ DOA
103. FACILITY OTHER THAN HOSPITAL: ☐ CONV. HOSP. ☐ RES. CARE ☐ OTHER
104. COUNTY: Los Angeles
105. STREET ADDRESS—(STREET AND NUMBER OR LOCATION): 10490 Wilshire Boulevard #1603
106. CITY: Los Angeles

CAUSE OF DEATH

107. DEATH WAS CAUSED BY: (ENTER ONLY ONE CAUSE PER LINE FOR A, B, C, AND D)

	Cause	Time interval between onset and death
IMMEDIATE CAUSE (A)	Cardiopulmonary Arrest	Minutes
DUE TO (B)	Colon Cancer	Months
DUE TO (C)		
DUE TO (D)		

108. DEATH REPORTED TO CORONER: ☐ YES ☒ NO — REFERRAL NUMBER
109. BIOPSY PERFORMED: ☒ YES ☐ NO
110. AUTOPSY PERFORMED: ☐ YES ☒ NO
111. USED IN DETERMINING CAUSE: ☐ YES ☐ NO
112. OTHER SIGNIFICANT CONDITIONS CONTRIBUTING TO DEATH BUT NOT RELATED TO CAUSE GIVEN IN 107: Aortic Stenosis, Cerebrovascular Disease, Sick Sinus Syndrome
113. WAS OPERATION PERFORMED FOR ANY CONDITION IN ITEM 107 OR 112? IF YES, LIST TYPE OF OPERATION AND DATE.: No

PHYSICIAN'S CERTIFICATION

114. I CERTIFY THAT TO THE BEST OF MY KNOWLEDGE DEATH OCCURRED AT THE HOUR, DATE AND PLACE STATED FROM THE CAUSES STATED. DECEDENT ATTENDED SINCE MM/DD/CCYY: 01/01/1992 — DECEDENT LAST SEEN ALIVE MM/DD/CCYY: 03/07/2002
115. SIGNATURE AND TITLE OF CERTIFIER: Alexander Ford
116. LICENSE NO.: G 057387
117. DATE MM/DD/CCYY: 03/28/2002
118. TYPE ATTENDING PHYSICIAN'S NAME, MAILING ADDRESS, ZIP: Alexander Ford, M.D., 1125 South Beverly Dr., Los Angeles, CA 90035

CORONER'S USE ONLY

25

C189

119. I CERTIFY THAT IN MY OPINION DEATH OCCURRED AT THE HOUR, DATE AND PLACE STATED FROM THE CAUSES STATED. MANNER OF DEATH: ☐ NATURAL ☐ SUICIDE ☐ HOMICIDE ☐ ACCIDENT ☐ PENDING INVESTIGATION ☐ COULD NOT BE DETERMINED
120. INJURY AT WORK: ☐ YES ☐ NO
121. INJURY DATE MM/DD/CCYY
122. HOUR
123. PLACE OF INJURY
124. DESCRIBE HOW INJURY OCCURRED (EVENTS WHICH RESULTED IN INJURY)
125. LOCATION (STREET AND NUMBER OR LOCATION AND CITY, ZIP)
126. SIGNATURE OF CORONER OR DEPUTY CORONER
127. DATE MM/DD/CCYY
128. TYPED NAME, TITLE OF CORONER OR DEPUTY CORONER

STATE REGISTRAR: A | B | C | D | E | F | G | H | FAX AUTH. # | CENSUS TRACT

0517338

This is a true certified copy of the record filed in the County of Los Angeles Department of Health Services if it bears the Registrar's signature in purple ink.

DATE ISSUED APR 02 2002

Director of Health Services and Registrar

This copy not valid unless prepared on engraved border displaying seal and signature of Registrar.

THE GREAT SEAL OF THE STATE OF CALIFORNIA — EUREKA

MIDWEST BANK NOTE COMPANY

ANY ALTERATION OR ERASURE VOIDS THIS CERTIFICATE

STATE OF CALIFORNIA
CERTIFICATION OF VITAL RECORD

COUNTY OF LOS ANGELES • REGISTRAR-RECORDER/ COUNTY CLERK

CERTIFICATE OF DEATH
STATE OF CALIFORNIA
USE BLACK INK ONLY

39319049663

STATE FILE NUMBER — LOCAL REGISTRATION DISTRICT AND CERTIFICATE NUMBER

DECEDENT PERSONAL DATA

1A. NAME OF DECEDENT—FIRST (GIVEN): WILFRED
1B. MIDDLE: BAILEY
1C. LAST (FAMILY): BIXBY
2A. DATE OF DEATH—MO. DAY. YR: 11/21/1993
2B. HOUR: 1533
3. SEX: M
4. RACE: CAUCASIAN
5. HISPANIC—SPECIFY: YES [ ] NO [X]
6. DATE OF BIRTH—MO. DAY. YR: 01/22/1934
7. AGE IN YEARS: 59 — IF UNDER 1 YEAR: MONTHS, DAYS — IF UNDER 24 HOURS: HOURS, MINUTES
8. STATE OF BIRTH: CA
9. CITIZEN OF WHAT COUNTRY: USA
10A. FULL NAME OF FATHER: WILFRED BIXBY
10B. STATE OF BIRTH: CA
11A. FULL MAIDEN NAME OF MOTHER: JANE McFARLAND
11B. STATE OF BIRTH: CA
12. MILITARY SERVICE: 19UNK TO 19UNK [ ] NONE
13. SOCIAL SECURITY NO.: UNK
14. MARITAL STATUS: MARRIED
15. NAME OF SURVIVING SPOUSE (IF WIFE, ENTER MAIDEN NAME): JUDITH KAMMAN
16A. USUAL OCCUPATION: ACTOR
16B. USUAL KIND OF BUSINESS OR INDUSTRY: ENTERTAINMENT
16C. USUAL EMPLOYER: WITT-THOMAS-HARRIS
16D. YEARS IN OCCUPATION: 30
17. EDUCATION—YEARS COMPLETED: 16

USUAL RESIDENCE

18A. RESIDENCE—STREET AND NUMBER OR LOCATION: 10100 GALAXY WAY
18B. CITY: CENTURY CITY
18C. ZIP CODE: 90067
18D. COUNTY: LOS ANGELES
18E. NUMBER OF YEARS IN THIS COUNTY: UNK
18F. STATE OR FOREIGN COUNTRY: CALIFORNIA
20. NAME, RELATIONSHIP, MAILING ADDRESS AND ZIP CODE OF INFORMANT: JUDITH KLIBAN BIXBY, WIFE, 10100 GALAXY WAY, LOS ANGELES, CA. 90067

PLACE OF DEATH

19A. PLACE OF DEATH: RESIDENCE
19B. IF HOSPITAL, SPECIFY ONE: IP, ER/OP, DOA: --
19C. COUNTY: LOS ANGELES
19D. STREET ADDRESS—STREET AND NUMBER OR LOCATION: 10100 GALAXY WAY
19E. CITY: CENTURY CITY

CAUSE OF DEATH

21. DEATH WAS CAUSED BY: (ENTER ONLY ONE CAUSE PER LINE FOR A, B, AND C)
IMMEDIATE CAUSE (A) METASTATIC CARCINOMA OF PROSTATE — TIME INTERVAL BETWEEN ONSET AND DEATH: 32 MOS.
DUE TO (B)
DUE TO (C)
22. WAS DEATH REPORTED TO CORONER: REFERRAL NUMBER — YES [ ] NO [X]
23. WAS BIOPSY PERFORMED: YES [X] NO [ ]
24A. WAS AUTOPSY PERFORMED: YES [ ] NO [X]
24B. WAS IT USED IN DETERMINING CAUSE OF DEATH: YES [ ] NO [X]
25. OTHER SIGNIFICANT CONDITIONS CONTRIBUTING TO DEATH BUT NOT RELATED TO CAUSE GIVEN IN 21: NONE
26. WAS OPERATION PERFORMED FOR ANY CONDITION IN ITEM 21 OR 25. IF YES, LIST TYPE OF OPERATION AND DATE: NO

PHYSICIAN'S CERTIFICATION

I CERTIFY THAT TO THE BEST OF MY KNOWLEDGE DEATH OCCURRED AT THE HOUR, DATE AND PLACE STATED FROM THE CAUSES STATED.
27A. DECEDENT ATTENDED SINCE MONTH, DAY, YEAR: 03/08/1991 — DECEDENT LAST SEEN ALIVE MONTH, DAY, YEAR: 11/21/1993
27B. SIGNATURE AND DEGREE OR TITLE OF CERTIFIER: Leon I Bender MD
27C. CERTIFIER'S LICENSE NUMBER: G15668
27D. DATE SIGNED: 11-21-93
27E. TYPE ATTENDING PHYSICIAN'S NAME AND ADDRESS: LEON I. BENDER,MD,8631 W.3RD,LOS ANGELES,CA.

CORONER'S USE ONLY

I CERTIFY THAT IN MY OPINION DEATH OCCURRED AT THE HOUR, DATE AND PLACE STATED FROM THE CAUSES STATED.
28A. SIGNATURE AND TITLE OF CORONER OR DEPUTY CORONER
28B. DATE SIGNED
29. MANNER OF DEATH—specify one: natural, accident, suicide, homicide, pending investigation or could not be determined
30A. PLACE OF INJURY
30B. INJURY AT WORK: YES [ ] NO [ ]
30C. DATE OF INJURY MONTH, DAY, YEAR
31. HOUR
32. LOCATION (STREET AND NUMBER OR LOCATION AND CITY)
33. DESCRIBE HOW INJURY OCCURRED (EVENTS WHICH RESULTED IN INJURY)

FUNERAL DIRECTOR AND LOCAL REGISTRAR

34A. DISPOSITION(S): CR/RES
34B. PLACE OF FINAL DISPOSITION—NAME AND ADDRESS: RES: 10100 GALAXY WAY LOS ANGELES, CA. 90067
34C. DATE MO. DAY. YR.: 11/26/1993
35A. SIGNATURE OF EMBALMER: Kim Evans
35B. LICENSE NO.: 7417
36A. NAME OF FUNERAL DIRECTOR (OR PERSON ACTING AS SUCH): FOREST LAWN HOLLYWOOD HILLS
36B. LICENSE NO.: F 904
37. SIGNATURE OF LOCAL REGISTRAR: Robert C. Hate
38. REGISTRATION DATE: NOV 26 1993

STATE REGISTRAR: A. B. C. D. E. F. CENSUS TRACT

VS-11 (REV. 7-92) MAKE NO ERASURES, WHITEOUTS, OR OTHER ALTERATIONS

This is to certify that this document is a true copy of the official record filed with the Registrar-Recorder/County Clerk.

Conny B. McCormack

CONNY B. McCORMACK
Registrar-Recorder/County Clerk

This copy not valid unless prepared on engraved border displaying the Seal and Signature of the Registrar-Recorder/County Clerk.

NOV 09 1995
19-604809

ANY ALTERATION OR ERASURE VOIDS THIS CERTIFICATE

STATE OF CALIFORNIA
CERTIFICATION OF VITAL RECORD

SACRAMENTO COUNTY
SACRAMENTO, CALIFORNIA

CERTIFICATE OF DEATH 38934 007056
STATE OF CALIFORNIA
USE BLACK INK ONLY

STATE FILE NUMBER — LOCAL REGISTRATION DISTRICT AND CERTIFICATE NUMBER

DECEDENT PERSONAL DATA
1A. NAME OF DECEDENT—FIRST (GIVEN): BEVERLY
1B. MIDDLE: LOUISE
1C. LAST (FAMILY): NEILL
2A. DATE OF DEATH—MONTH, DAY, YEAR: August 16, 1989
2B. HOUR: 1910
3. SEX: Female
4. RACE: White
5. SPANISH/HISPANIC: ☐ YES ☒ NO (SPECIFY)
6. DATE OF BIRTH—MONTH, DAY, YEAR: May 20, 1929
7. AGE IN YEARS: 60 — IF UNDER 1 YEAR: MONTHS - DAYS - — IF UNDER 24 HOURS: HOURS - MINUTES -
8. STATE OF BIRTH: NY
9. CITIZEN OF WHAT COUNTRY: USA
10A. FULL NAME OF FATHER: Jesse C. Neill
10B. STATE OF BIRTH: AL
11A. FULL MAIDEN NAME OF MOTHER: Louise P. unknown
11B. STATE OF BIRTH: AL
12. MILITARY SERVICE: 19__ TO 19__ ☒ NONE
13. SOCIAL SECURITY NUMBER: 573-38-0599
14. MARITAL STATUS: Divorced
15. NAME OF SURVIVING SPOUSE (IF WIFE, ENTER MAIDEN NAME): - - -
16A. USUAL OCCUPATION: Actress
16B. USUAL KIND OF BUSINESS OR INDUSTRY: Television
16C. USUAL EMPLOYER: Screen Actors Guild
16D. YEARS IN USUAL OCCUPATION: 30
17. NUMBER OF HIGHEST GRADE COMPLETED (1–12 OR COLLEGE 13–17+): 12

Amended 1 of 2

USUAL RESIDENCE
18A. RESIDENCE—STREET AND NUMBER OR LOCATION: 11435 Simmerhorn Road
18B. CITY: Galt
18C. ZIP CODE: 95632
18D. COUNTY: Sacramento
18E. NUMBER OF YEARS IN THIS COUNTY: 2
18F. STATE OR FOREIGN COUNTRY: CA
20. NAME, RELATIONSHIP, MAILING ADDRESS AND ZIP CODE OF INFORMANT: Patricia Derby-Power-of-Attorney, 11435 Simmerhorn Road, Galt, CA 95632

PLACE OF DEATH
19A. PLACE OF DEATH: Mercy General
19B. IF HOSPITAL, SPECIFY ONE: IP, ER/OP, DOA: IP
19C. COUNTY: Sacramento
19D. STREET ADDRESS—STREET AND NUMBER OR LOCATION: 4001 J Street
19E. CITY: Sacramento

CAUSE OF DEATH
21. DEATH WAS CAUSED BY: (ENTER ONLY ONE CAUSE PER LINE FOR A, B, AND C) — TIME INTERVAL BETWEEN ONSET AND DEATH
IMMEDIATE CAUSE (A): Cardiopulmonary arrest — 7 min
DUE TO (B): Hepatic failure — 2 wks.
DUE TO (C): CMV Hepatitis — 2 mos.
22. WAS DEATH REPORTED TO CORONER? ☒ YES ☐ NO — REFERRAL NUMBER: 89-2543
23. WAS BIOPSY PERFORMED? ☐ YES ☒ NO
24A. WAS AUTOPSY PERFORMED? ☐ YES ☒ NO
24B. IF YES, WAS IT USED IN DETERMINING THE CAUSE OF DEATH? ☐ YES ☒ NO
25. OTHER SIGNIFICANT CONDITIONS CONTRIBUTING TO DEATH BUT NOT RELATED TO CAUSE GIVEN IN 21: Acquired immunodeficiency syndrome; head & neck cancer
26. WAS OPERATION PERFORMED FOR ANY CONDITION IN ITEM 21 OR 25? MONTH, DAY, YEAR — TYPE: no

PHYSICIAN'S CERTIFICATION
I CERTIFY THAT DEATH OCCURRED AT THE HOUR, DATE AND PLACE STATED FROM THE CAUSES STATED.
27A. DECEDENT ATTENDED SINCE (MONTH, DAY, YEAR): Sept, 88 — DECEDENT LAST SEEN ALIVE (MONTH, DAY, YEAR): 8-16-89
27B. SIGNATURE AND DEGREE OR TITLE OF PHYSICIAN: [signature]
27C. PHYSICIAN'S LICENSE NUMBER: G46283
27D. DATE SIGNED: 8-18-89
27E. TYPE ATTENDING PHYSICIAN'S NAME AND ADDRESS: Lou T. Nishimura, MD, 3160 Folsom Blvd., Sacramento, CA 95816

CORONER'S USE ONLY
I CERTIFY THAT DEATH OCCURRED AT THE HOUR, DATE AND PLACE STATED FROM THE CAUSES STATED.
28A. SIGNATURE OF CORONER OR DEPUTY CORONER
28B. DATE SIGNED
29. MANNER OF DEATH—specify one: natural, accident, suicide, homicide, pending investigation or could not be determined
30A. PLACE OF INJURY
30B. INJURY AT WORK: ☐ YES ☐ NO
30C. DATE OF INJURY—MONTH, DAY, YEAR
31. HOUR
32. LOCATION (STREET AND NUMBER OR LOCATION AND CITY)
33. DESCRIBE HOW INJURY OCCURRED (EVENTS WHICH RESULTED IN INJURY)

FUNERAL DIRECTOR AND LOCAL REGISTRAR
34A. DISPOSITION: Cremation /Res
34B. PLACE OF FINAL DISPOSITION: 11435 Simmerhorn Road, Galt, CA 95632
34C. DATE OF DISPOSITION—MONTH, DAY, YEAR: Aug. 23, 1989
35A. SIGNATURE OF EMBALMER: Not Embalmed
35B. LICENSE NUMBER: - - -
36A. NAME OF FUNERAL DIRECTOR (OR PERSON ACTING AS SUCH): Sacramento Memorial Lawn
36B. LICENSE NO.: F974
37. SIGNATURE OF LOCAL REGISTRAR: Bette G. Hinton, M.D.
38. REGISTRATION DATE: AUG 22 1989

STATE REGISTRAR: A. B. C. D. E. F. CENSUS TRACT

VS-11 (REV. 1-89) — MAKE NO ERASURES, WHITEOUTS, OR OTHER ALTERATIONS

SEE ATTACHED AMENDMENT

456851

CERTIFIED COPY OF VITAL RECORDS

STATE OF CALIFORNIA
COUNTY OF SACRAMENTO } SS — DATED ISSUED DEC 13 2000

This is a true and exact reproduction of the document officially registered and placed on file in the office of the SACRAMENTO COUNTY CLERK-RECORDER.

Mark Norris
SACRAMENTO COUNTY CLERK-RECORDER

This copy not valid unless prepared on engraved border displaying date, seal and signature of the County Clerk-Recorder.

MIDWEST BANK NOTE COMPANY — ANY ALTERATION OR ERASURE VOIDS THIS CERTIFICATE

CERTIFICATION OF VITAL RECORD

COUNTY OF LOS ANGELES • REGISTRAR-RECORDER/COUNTY CLERK

CERTIFICATE OF DEATH
STATE OF CALIFORNIA

0190-058494

STATE FILE NUMBER — LOCAL REGISTRATION DISTRICT AND CERTIFICATE NUMBER

DECEDENT PERSONAL DATA

1A. NAME OF DECEDENT—FIRST: JOAN
1B. MIDDLE: - - -
1C. LAST: BLONDELL
2A. DATE OF DEATH (MONTH, DAY, YEAR): December 25, 1979
2B. HOUR: 0425
3. SEX: Female
4. RACE: White
5. ETHNICITY: American
6. DATE OF BIRTH: August 30, 1906
7. AGE: 73 YEARS
8. BIRTHPLACE OF DECEDENT (STATE OR FOREIGN COUNTRY): New York
9. NAME AND BIRTHPLACE OF FATHER: Edward Blondell - France
10. BIRTH NAME AND BIRTHPLACE OF MOTHER: Kathryn Cain - New York
11. CITIZEN WHAT COUNTRY: USA
12. SOCIAL SECURITY NUMBER: 573-03-9019
13. MARITAL STATUS: divorced
14. NAME OF SURVIVING SPOUSE (IF WIFE, ENTER BIRTH NAME): - - -
15. PRIMARY OCCUPATION: Actress
16. NUMBER OF YEARS THIS OCCUPATION: 70
17. EMPLOYER (IF SELF-EMPLOYED, SO STATE): Spelling-Goldberg Co.
18. KIND OF INDUSTRY OR BUSINESS: T. V. Productions

USUAL RESIDENCE

19A. USUAL RESIDENCE—STREET ADDRESS (STREET AND NUMBER OR LOCATION): 1221 Ocean Ave.
19C. CITY OR TOWN: Santa Monica
19D. COUNTY: Los Angeles
19E. STATE: Calif.
20. NAME AND ADDRESS OF INFORMANT—RELATIONSHIP: Mr. Norman S. Powell - Son, 4621 Ocean Front Walk, Marina Del Rey, Calif. 90291

PLACE OF DEATH

21A. PLACE OF DEATH: St. John's Hospital
21B. COUNTY: Los Angeles
21C. STREET ADDRESS (STREET AND NUMBER OR LOCATION): 1328 22nd Street
21D. CITY OR TOWN: Santa Monica

CAUSE OF DEATH

22. DEATH WAS CAUSED BY: (ENTER ONLY ONE CAUSE PER LINE FOR A, B, AND C)
IMMEDIATE CAUSE (A) Myeloid Leukemia — APPROXIMATE INTERVAL BETWEEN ONSET AND DEATH: 3½ yrs
CONDITIONS, IF ANY, WHICH GAVE RISE TO THE IMMEDIATE CAUSE, STATING THE UNDERLYING CAUSE LAST — DUE TO, OR AS A CONSEQUENCE OF (B) — DUE TO, OR AS A CONSEQUENCE OF (C)
24. WAS DEATH REPORTED TO CORONER? No
25. WAS BIOPSY PERFORMED? No
26. WAS AUTOPSY PERFORMED? NO
23. OTHER CONDITIONS CONTRIBUTING BUT NOT RELATED TO THE IMMEDIATE CAUSE OF DEATH:
27. WAS OPERATION PERFORMED FOR ANY CONDITION IN ITEMS 22 OR 23? TYPE OF OPERATION: NONE — DATE

PHYSICIAN'S CERTIFICATION

28A. I CERTIFY THAT DEATH OCCURRED AT THE HOUR, DATE AND PLACE STATED FROM THE CAUSES STATED. I ATTENDED DECEDENT SINCE: 4-10-75; I LAST SAW DECEDENT ALIVE: 12-24-79
28B. PHYSICIAN—SIGNATURE AND DEGREE OR TITLE: [signature]
28C. DATE SIGNED: 12-26-79
28D. PHYSICIAN'S LICENSE NUMBER: A-65-525
28E. TYPE PHYSICIAN'S NAME AND ADDRESS: W. L. Marmer, 2021 Santa Monica Blvd. Santa Monica

INJURY INFORMATION — CORONER'S USE ONLY

29. SPECIFY ACCIDENT, SUICIDE, ETC.
30. PLACE OF INJURY
31. INJURY AT WORK
32A. DATE OF INJURY—MONTH, DAY, YEAR
32B. HOUR
33. LOCATION (STREET AND NUMBER OR LOCATION AND CITY OR TOWN)
34. DESCRIBE HOW INJURY OCCURRED (EVENTS WHICH RESULTED IN INJURY)
35A. I CERTIFY THAT DEATH OCCURRED AT THE HOUR, DATE AND PLACE STATED FROM THE CAUSES STATED. AS REQUIRED BY LAW I HAVE HELD AN (INQUEST-INVESTIGATION)
35B. CORONER—SIGNATURE AND DEGREE OR TITLE
35C. DATE SIGNED

36. DISPOSITION: Cremation
37. DATE—MONTH, DAY, YEAR: 12/28/79
38. NAME AND ADDRESS OF CEMETERY OR CREMATORY: FOREST LAWN MEMORIAL PARK, 1712 S. GLENDALE AVE., GLENDALE, CA
39. EMBALMER'S LICENSE NUMBER AND SIGNATURE: Not embalmed
40. NAME OF FUNERAL DIRECTOR (OR PERSON ACTING AS SUCH): FOREST LAWN MEMORIAL PARK, 1712 S. GLENDALE AVE, GLENDALE, CA
41. LOCAL REGISTRAR: [signature]
42. DATE ACCEPTED BY LOCAL REGISTRAR: DEC 27 1979

STATE REGISTRAR A. B. C. D. E. F.

VS-11 (10-78)

01-8-1-0756

This is to certify that this document is a true copy of the official record filed with the Registrar-Recorder/County Clerk.

OCT 1 1996

19-381949

Conny B. McCormack
CONNY B. McCORMACK
Registrar-Recorder/County Clerk

This copy not valid unless prepared on engraved border displaying the Seal and Signature of the Registrar-Recorder/County Clerk.

ANY ALTERATION OR ERASURE VOIDS THIS CERTIFICATE

CERTIFICATION OF VITAL RECORD

COUNTY OF LOS ANGELES • REGISTRAR-RECORDER/COUNTY CLERK

CERTIFICATE OF DEATH 3 7 19002663

STATE OF CALIFORNIA

STATE FILE NUMBER | LOCAL REGISTRATION DISTRICT AND CERTIFICATE NUMBER

DECEDENT PERSONAL DATA

1A. NAME OF DECEDENT—FIRST: RAYMOND | 1B. MIDDLE: WALLACE | 1C. LAST: BOLGER | 2A. DATE OF DEATH (MONTH, DAY, YEAR): January 15, 1987 | 2B. HOUR: 1500

3. SEX: Male | 4. RACE/ETHNICITY: White | 5. SPANISH/HISPANIC: NO ☒ | 6. DATE OF BIRTH: January 10, 1904 | 7. AGE: 83 YEARS | IF UNDER 1 YEAR: MONTHS, DAYS | IF UNDER 24 HOURS: HOURS, MINUTES

8. BIRTHPLACE OF DECEDENT (STATE OR FOREIGN COUNTRY): Massachusetts | 9. NAME AND BIRTHPLACE OF FATHER: James E. Bolger-Massachusetts | 10. BIRTH NAME AND BIRTHPLACE OF MOTHER: Ann Wallace-Massachusetts

11A. CITIZEN OF WHAT COUNTRY: U.S.A. | 11B. IF DECEASED WAS EVER IN MILITARY GIVE DATES OF SERVICE: 19__ TO 19__ | 12. SOCIAL SECURITY NUMBER: 083-05-6270 A | 13. MARITAL STATUS: Married | 14. NAME OF SURVIVING SPOUSE (IF WIFE, ENTER BIRTH NAME): Gwendolyn Rickard

15. PRIMARY OCCUPATION: Actor | 16. NUMBER OF YEARS THIS OCCUPATION: 65 | 17. EMPLOYER (IF SELF-EMPLOYED, SO STATE): Self-employed | 18. KIND OF INDUSTRY OR BUSINESS: Entertainment

USUAL RESIDENCE

19A. USUAL RESIDENCE—STREET ADDRESS (STREET AND NUMBER OR LOCATION): 618 N. Beverly Drive | 19B. | 19C. CITY OR TOWN: Beverly Hills

19D. COUNTY: Los Angeles | 19E. STATE: California | 20. NAME AND ADDRESS OF INFORMANT—RELATIONSHIP: Gwendolyn Bolger-Wife, 618 N. Beverly Drive, Beverly Hills, California 90210

PLACE OF DEATH

21A. PLACE OF DEATH: Nazareth House | 21B. COUNTY: Los Angeles

21C. STREET ADDRESS (STREET AND NUMBER OR LOCATION): 3333 Manning Avenue | 21D. CITY OR TOWN: Los Angeles

CAUSE OF DEATH

22. DEATH WAS CAUSED BY: (ENTER ONLY ONE CAUSE PER LINE FOR A, B, AND C)

IMMEDIATE CAUSE (A): Metastatic Transitional Cell Cancer of Bladder | APPROXIMATE INTERVAL BETWEEN ONSET AND DEATH: 2 years

CONDITIONS, IF ANY, WHICH GAVE RISE TO THE IMMEDIATE CAUSE, STATING THE UNDERLYING CAUSE LAST. DUE TO, OR AS A CONSEQUENCE OF (B) | DUE TO, OR AS A CONSEQUENCE OF (C)

24. WAS DEATH REPORTED TO CORONER? No | 25. WAS BIOPSY PERFORMED? No | 26. WAS AUTOPSY PERFORMED? No

23. OTHER SIGNIFICANT CONDITIONS—CONTRIBUTING TO DEATH BUT NOT RELATED TO CAUSE GIVEN IN 22A: None | 27. WAS OPERATION PERFORMED FOR ANY CONDITION IN ITEMS 22 OR 23? TYPE OF OPERATION: Bladder Surgery | DATE: 11/84

PHYSICIAN'S CERTIFICATION

28A. I CERTIFY THAT DEATH OCCURRED AT THE HOUR, DATE AND PLACE STATED FROM THE CAUSES STATED. ATTENDED DECEDENT SINCE (ENTER MO, DA, YR): 5/18/84 | LAST SAW DECEDENT ALIVE (ENTER MO, DA, YR): 1/14/87 | 28B. PHYSICIAN—SIGNATURE AND DEGREE OR TITLE: [signature] MD | 28C. DATE SIGNED: 1/16/87 | 28D. PHYSICIAN'S LICENSE NUMBER: C24698

28E. TYPE PHYSICIAN'S NAME AND ADDRESS: Richard R. Hawley, 2021 Santa Monica Blvd., Santa Monica, Ca.

INJURY INFORMATION

29. SPECIFY ACCIDENT, SUICIDE, ETC. | 30. PLACE OF INJURY | 31. INJURY AT WORK | 32A. DATE OF INJURY—MONTH, DAY, YEAR | 32B. HOUR

33. LOCATION (STREET AND NUMBER OR LOCATION AND CITY OR TOWN) | 34. DESCRIBE HOW INJURY OCCURRED (EVENTS WHICH RESULTED IN INJURY)

CORONER'S USE ONLY

35A. I CERTIFY THAT DEATH OCCURRED AT THE HOUR, DATE AND PLACE STATED FROM THE CAUSES STATED. AS REQUIRED BY LAW I HAVE HELD AN (INQUEST-INVESTIGATION) | 35B. CORONER—SIGNATURE AND DEGREE OR TITLE | 35C. DATE SIGNED

36. DISPOSITION: Burial | 37. DATE—MONTH, DAY, YEAR: Jan. 20, 1987 | 38. NAME AND ADDRESS OF CEMETERY OR CREMATORY: Holy Cross Cemetery, Culver City, Calif. | 39. EMBALMER'S LICENSE NUMBER AND SIGNATURE: #4350 [signature]

40A. NAME OF FUNERAL DIRECTOR (OR PERSON ACTING AS SUCH): Pierce Brothers Cunningham & O'Connor-Hollywood | 40B. LICENSE NO.: F-168 | 41. LOCAL REGISTRAR: [signature] | 42. DATE ACCEPTED BY LOCAL REGISTRAR: JAN 20 1987

STATE REGISTRAR: A. | B. | C. | D. | E. | F.

VS-11 (1-85)

This is to certify that this document is a true copy of the official record filed with the Registrar-Recorder/County Clerk.

OCT 02 1995

19 033396

This copy not valid unless prepared on engraved border displaying the Seal of the Registrar-Recorder/County Clerk.

THE GREAT SEAL OF THE STATE OF CALIFORNIA

BANKNOTE CORPORATION OF AMERICA

ANY ALTERATION OR ERASURE VOIDS THIS CERTIFICATE

CERTIFICATION OF VITAL RECORD

COUNTY OF LOS ANGELES • REGISTRAR-RECORDER/COUNTY CLERK

Filed NOV 5 1965 / RAY E. LEE, COUNTY RECORDER

CERTIFICATE OF DEATH

STATE OF CALIFORNIA—DEPARTMENT OF PUBLIC HEALTH

STATE FILE NUMBER

LOCAL REGISTRATION DISTRICT AND CERTIFICATE NUMBER 7053 41205

DECEDENT PERSONAL DATA

1A. NAME OF DECEASED—FIRST NAME	CLARA
1B. MIDDLE NAME	BOW
1C. LAST NAME	BELDAM
2A. DATE OF DEATH—MONTH, DAY, YEAR	SEPT. 27, 1965
2B. HOUR	12:06 A.M.
3. SEX	Female
4. COLOR OR RACE	Caucasian
5. BIRTHPLACE (STATE OR FOREIGN COUNTRY)	New York
6. DATE OF BIRTH	July 29, 1907
7. AGE (LAST BIRTHDAY)	58 YEARS
8. NAME AND BIRTHPLACE OF FATHER	Robert Walter Bow-New York
9. MAIDEN NAME AND BIRTHPLACE OF MOTHER	Sarah Frances Gordon-New York
10. CITIZEN OF WHAT COUNTRY	U.S.A.
11. SOCIAL SECURITY NUMBER	None
12. LAST OCCUPATION	Motion Picture Actress
13. NUMBER OF YEARS IN THIS OCCUPATION	14
14. NAME OF LAST EMPLOYING COMPANY OR FIRM	Self-Employed
15. KIND OF INDUSTRY OR BUSINESS	Motion Pictures
16. IF DECEASED WAS EVER IN U.S. ARMED FORCES, GIVE WAR OR DATES OF SERVICE	No
17. SPECIFY MARRIED, NEVER MARRIED, WIDOWED, DIVORCED	Widowed
18A. NAME OF PRESENT SPOUSE	---
18B. PRESENT OR LAST OCCUPATION OF SPOUSE	---

PLACE OF DEATH

19A. PLACE OF DEATH—NAME OF HOSPITAL	None
19B. STREET ADDRESS	12214 Aneta Street (X inside city corporate limits)
19C. CITY OR TOWN	Los Angeles
19D. COUNTY	Los Angeles
19E. LENGTH OF STAY IN COUNTY OF DEATH	26 YEARS
19F. LENGTH OF STAY IN CALIFORNIA	26 YEARS

LAST USUAL RESIDENCE (WHERE DID DECEASED LIVE—IF IN INSTITUTION, ENTER RESIDENCE BEFORE ADMISSION)

20A. LAST USUAL RESIDENCE—STREET ADDRESS	12214 Aneta Street
20B. IF INSIDE CITY CORPORATE LIMITS	X
20C. CITY OR TOWN	Los Angeles
20D. COUNTY	Los Angeles
20E. STATE	California
21A. NAME OF INFORMANT (IF OTHER THAN SPOUSE)	Rex Anthony Bell
21B. ADDRESS OF INFORMANT	1885 Mayberry Drive, Reno, Nevada

PHYSICIAN'S OR CORONER'S CERTIFICATION

22A. PHYSICIAN. I HEREBY CERTIFY THAT DEATH OCCURRED AT THE HOUR, DATE AND PLACE STATED ABOVE FROM THE CAUSES STATED BELOW AND THAT I ATTENDED THE DECEASED FROM ___ AND THAT I LAST SAW THE DECEASED ALIVE ON ___

22B. CORONER. I HEREBY CERTIFY THAT DEATH OCCURRED AT THE HOUR, DATE AND PLACE STATED ABOVE FROM THE CAUSES STATED BELOW AND THAT I HAVE HELD AN autopsy ON THE REMAINS OF DECEASED AS REQUIRED BY LAW

22C. PHYSICIAN OR CORONER — Theodore J. Curphey, M.D., Coroner [signature] — Deputy

22D. ADDRESS — HALL OF JUSTICE, LOS ANGELES

22E. DATE SIGNED — 10-1965

FUNERAL DIRECTOR AND LOCAL REGISTRAR

23. SPECIFY BURIAL, ENTOMBMENT OR CREMATION	Entombment
24. DATE	10-1-65
25. NAME OF CEMETERY OR CREMATORY	Forest Lawn Memorial-Park
26. EMBALMER—SIGNATURE / LICENSE NUMBER	[signature] / 4206
27. NAME OF FUNERAL DIRECTOR	FOREST LAWN MEMORIAL-PARK ASSN. GLENDALE, CALIFORNIA
28. DATE ACCEPTED FOR REGISTRATION BY LOCAL REGISTRAR	OCT 2 1965
29. LOCAL REGISTRAR—SIGNATURE	K.H. Sutherland M.D.

#21445 Clara Bow Beldam W. Arterberry M.D.

MEDICAL AND HEALTH DATA

CAUSE OF DEATH

30. CAUSE OF DEATH — ENTER ONLY ONE CAUSE PER LINE FOR (A), (B) AND (C)

PART I. DEATH WAS CAUSED BY IMMEDIATE CAUSE (A) Coronary thrombosis.

CONDITIONS, IF ANY, WHICH GAVE RISE TO THE ABOVE CAUSE (A) STATING THE UNDERLYING CAUSE LAST. DUE TO (B) Coronary atherosclerosis.

DUE TO (C)

APPROXIMATE INTERVAL BETWEEN ONSET AND DEATH

PART II. OTHER SIGNIFICANT CONDITIONS CONTRIBUTING TO DEATH BUT NOT RELATED TO THE TERMINAL DISEASE CONDITION GIVEN IN PART I (A)

Acute drug intoxication.

OPERATION AND AUTOPSY

31. OPERATION—CHECK ONE: [X] NO OPERATION PERFORMED
32. DATE OF OPERATION
33. AUTOPSY—CHECK ONE: [X] AUTOPSY PERFORMED—GROSS FINDINGS USED IN DETERMINING ABOVE STATED CAUSES OF DEATH

INJURY INFORMATION

34A. SPECIFY ACCIDENT, SUICIDE OR HOMICIDE — PROBABLE NATURAL

34B. DESCRIBE HOW INJURY OCCURRED

35A. TIME OF INJURY — HOUR MONTH DAY YEAR

35B. INJURY OCCURRED — WHILE AT WORK / NOT WHILE AT WORK

35C. PLACE OF INJURY

35D. CITY, TOWN OR LOCATION — COUNTY — STATE

final Oct 19, 1965 os

This is to certify that this document is a true copy of the official record filed with the Registrar-Recorder/County Clerk.

SEP 20 1996

19-376754

[signature]
CONNY B. McCORMACK
Registrar-Recorder/County Clerk

This copy not valid unless prepared on engraved border displaying the Seal and Signature of the Registrar-Recorder/County Clerk.

ANY ALTERATION OR ERASURE VOIDS THIS CERTIFICATE

CERTIFICATION OF VITAL RECORD

COUNTY OF LOS ANGELES • REGISTRAR-RECORDER/COUNTY CLERK

REGISTRATION DISTRICT NO. 1901 REGISTRAR'S NUMBER 9181 **CERTIFICATE OF DEATH** STATE FILE NO.

DECEDENT PERSONAL DATA (TYPE OR PRINT NAME)

1A. NAME OF DECEASED—FIRST NAME: FANNY
1B. MIDDLE NAME:
1C. LAST NAME: BRICE
2A. DATE OF DEATH — MONTH, DAY, YEAR: May 29, 1951
2B. HOUR: 11:15
3. SEX: Female
4. COLOR OR RACE: Cauc.
5. MARRIED, NEVER MARRIED, WIDOWED, DIVORCED: Divorced
6. DATE OF BIRTH: October 29, 1891
7. AGE (LAST BIRTHDAY): 59 YEARS; IF UNDER 1 YEAR: MONTHS, DAYS; IF UNDER 24 HOURS: HOURS, MINUTES
8A. USUAL OCCUPATION (GIVE KIND OF WORK DONE DURING MOST OF WORKING LIFE, EVEN IF RETIRED): Actress
8B. KIND OF BUSINESS OR INDUSTRY: Motion Pictures Radio
9. BIRTHPLACE (STATE OR FOREIGN COUNTRY): New York
10. CITIZEN OF WHAT COUNTRY?: United States of America
11. NAME AND BIRTHPLACE OF FATHER: Charles Borach, France
12. MAIDEN NAME AND BIRTHPLACE OF MOTHER: Rose Stern, Hungary
13. NAME OF SPOUSE (IF MARRIED): William Rose, Divorced
14. WAS DECEASED EVER IN U.S. ARMED FORCES? SPECIFY YES, NO, UNKNOWN: No. IF YES, GIVE WAR OR DATES OF SERVICE: No
15. SOCIAL SECURITY NUMBER: Unknown
16. INFORMANT: Frances Stark

PLACE OF DEATH

17A. PLACE OF DEATH — CITY OR TOWN (IF OUTSIDE CORPORATE LIMITS, WRITE RURAL AND NAME OF NEAREST TOWN): Los Angeles
17B. LENGTH OF STAY (IN THIS PLACE): 13 Years
17C. COUNTY: Los Angeles
17D. FULL NAME AND ADDRESS OF HOSPITAL OR INSTITUTION — (IF NOT IN HOSPITAL OR INSTITUTION, GIVE STREET ADDRESS OR LOCATION): Cedars of Lebanon Hospital 4833 Fountain Street

USUAL RESIDENCE (WHERE DECEASED LIVED) (IF INSTITUTION, RESIDENCE BEFORE ADMISSION)

18A. STREET ADDRESS (IF RURAL, GIVE LOCATION): 312 N. Faring Road
18B. CITY OR TOWN (IF OUTSIDE CORPORATE LIMITS, WRITE RURAL AND NAME OF NEAREST TOWN): Los Angeles 24
18C. COUNTY: Los Angeles
18D. STATE: Calif.

CAUSE OF DEATH (ENTER ONLY ONE CAUSE PER LINE FOR (A), (B) AND (C))

THIS DOES NOT MEAN THE MODE OF DYING SUCH AS HEART FAILURE, ASTHENIA, ETC. IT MEANS THE DISEASE, INJURY OR COMPLICATIONS WHICH CAUSED DEATH.

19-I. DISEASE OR CONDITION DIRECTLY LEADING TO DEATH (A): Cerebral Hemorrhage — 6 days
ANTECEDENT CAUSES — MORBID CONDITIONS, IF ANY, GIVING RISE TO THE ABOVE CAUSE (A) STATING THE UNDERLYING CAUSE LAST. DUE TO (B) DUE TO (C)
APPROXIMATE INTERVAL BETWEEN ONSET AND DEATH
19-II. OTHER SIGNIFICANT CONDITIONS — CONDITIONS CONTRIBUTING TO THE DEATH BUT NOT RELATED TO THE DISEASE OR CONDITION CAUSING DEATH.

OPERATIONS

20A. DATE OF OPERATION
20B. MAJOR FINDINGS OF OPERATION
21. AUTOPSY: [X] YES [ ] NO

DEATH DUE TO EXTERNAL VIOLENCE

22A. ACCIDENT, SUICIDE, HOMICIDE (SPECIFY)
22B. PLACE OF INJURY (E.G., IN OR ABOUT HOME, FARM, FACTORY, STREET, OFFICE BUILDING, ETC.)
22C. LOCATION — CITY OR TOWN, COUNTY, STATE
22D. TIME OF INJURY — MONTH, DAY, YEAR, HOUR M
22E. INJURY OCCURRED — [ ] WHILE AT WORK [ ] NOT WHILE AT WORK
22F. HOW DID INJURY OCCUR?

PHYSICIAN'S OR CORONER'S CERTIFICATION

23A. CORONER'S: I HEREBY CERTIFY THAT I HAVE HELD AN [ ] AUTOPSY, [ ] INQUEST, OR [ ] INVESTIGATION ON THE REMAINS OF THE DECEASED AND FIND THAT THE DECEASED CAME TO DEATH AT THE HOUR AND DATE STATED ABOVE.
23B. PHYSICIAN'S: I HEREBY CERTIFY THAT I ATTENDED THE DECEASED FROM Jan 1947 TO 5/29 1951, THAT I LAST SAW THE DECEASED ALIVE ON 5/29 1951 AND THAT DEATH OCCURRED FROM THE CAUSES AND AT THE HOUR AND DATE STATED ABOVE.
23C. SIGNATURE: Myron Prinzmetal
DEGREE OR TITLE: M.D.
23D. ADDRESS: 300 So. Beverly Drive
23E. DATE SIGNED: 5-29-51

FUNERAL DIRECTOR AND REGISTRAR

24A. [ ] BURIAL [X] CREMATION [ ] REMOVAL
24B. DATE: 5/31/51
24C. CEMETERY OR CREMATORY: Rosedale Crematory
25. SIGNATURE OF EMBALMER: Francis H Palmieri — LICENSE NUMBER 330
26. FUNERAL DIRECTOR: MALINOW & SIMONS, LOS ANGELES
27. DATE RECEIVED BY LOCAL REGISTRAR: MAY 31 1951
28. SIGNATURE OF LOCAL REGISTRAR: [signature]
By [signature]

STATE OF CALIFORNIA — DEPARTMENT OF PUBLIC HEALTH

This is to certify that this document is a true copy of the official record filed with the Registrar-Recorder/County Clerk.

Beatriz Valdez
BEATRIZ VALDEZ
Registrar-Recorder/County Clerk

AUG 8 4 1995

19-390016

This copy not valid unless prepared on engraved border displaying the Seal and Signature of the Registrar-Recorder/County Clerk.

American Bank Note Company

ANY ALTERATION OR ERASURE VOIDS THIS CERTIFICATE

CERTIFICATION OF VITAL RECORD

COUNTY OF LOS ANGELES • REGISTRAR-RECORDER/COUNTY CLERK

39619011679

CERTIFICATE OF DEATH
STATE OF CALIFORNIA
USE BLACK INK ONLY/NO ERASURES, WHITEOUTS OR ALTERATIONS
VS-11 (REV. 7/93)

STATE FILE NUMBER — LOCAL REGISTRATION NUMBER

DECEDENT PERSONAL DATA

1. NAME OF DECEDENT—FIRST (GIVEN): GEORGE
2. MIDDLE: -
3. LAST (FAMILY): BURNS
4. DATE OF BIRTH MM/DD/CCYY: 01/20/1896
5. AGE YRS.: 100
6. SEX: MALE
7. DATE OF DEATH MM/DD/CCYY: 03/09/1996
8. HOUR: 1000
9. STATE OF BIRTH: NY
10. SOCIAL SECURITY NO.: 568-03-7361
11. MILITARY SERVICE: 19__ TO 19__ [ ] NONE
12. MARITAL STATUS: WIDOWED
13. EDUCATION—YEARS COMPLETED: 3
14. RACE: CAUC.
15. HISPANIC: [ ] YES [X] NO
16. USUAL EMPLOYER: SELF EMPLOYED
17. OCCUPATION: ENTERTAINER
18. KIND OF BUSINESS: ENTERTAINMENT
19. YEARS IN OCCUPATION: 95

USUAL RESIDENCE

20. RESIDENCE—STREET AND NUMBER OR LOCATION: 720 N. MAPLE DR.
21. CITY: BEVERLY HILLS
22. COUNTY: LOS ANGELES
23. ZIP CODE: 90210
24. YRS IN COUNTY: 61
25. STATE OR FOREIGN COUNTRY: CALIFORNIA

INFORMANT

26. NAME, RELATIONSHIP: RONALD J. BURNS - SON
27. MAILING ADDRESS: 720 N. MAPLE DR., BEVERLY HILLS,CA. 90210

SPOUSE AND PARENT INFORMATION

28. NAME OF SURVIVING SPOUSE—FIRST: -
29. MIDDLE: -
30. LAST (MAIDEN NAME): -
31. NAME OF FATHER—FIRST: LOUIS
32. MIDDLE: P.
33. LAST: BIRNBAUM
34. BIRTH STATE: AUSTRIA
35. NAME OF MOTHER—FIRST: DORA
36. MIDDLE: -
37. LAST (MAIDEN): BLUTH
38. BIRTH STATE: AUSTRIA

DISPOSITION(S)

39. DATE MM/DD/CCYY: 03/12/1996
40. PLACE OF FINAL DISPOSITION: FOREST LAWN MEM. PARK 1712 S. GLENDALE AVE., GLENDALE,CA. 91205

FUNERAL DIRECTOR AND LOCAL REGISTRAR

41. TYPE OF DISPOSITION(S): BURIAL
42. SIGNATURE OF EMBALMER: NOT EMBALMED
43. LICENSE NO.: -
44. NAME OF FUNERAL DIRECTOR: FOREST LAWN MTY GLENDALE
45. LICENSE NO.: FD 656
46. SIGNATURE OF LOCAL REGISTRAR: [signature]
47. DATE MM/DD/CCYY: 03/12/1996

PLACE OF DEATH

101. PLACE OF DEATH: RESIDENCE
102. IF HOSPITAL, SPECIFY ONE: [ ] IP [ ] ER/OP [ ] DOA
103. FACILITY OTHER THAN HOSPITAL: [ ] CONV. HOSP. [X] RES. [ ] OTHER
104. COUNTY: LOS ANGELES
105. STREET ADDRESS—STREET AND NUMBER OR LOCATION: 720 N. MAPLE DRIVE
106. CITY: BEVERLY HILLS

CAUSE OF DEATH

107. DEATH WAS CAUSED BY: (ENTER ONLY ONE CAUSE PER LINE FOR A, B, C, AND D)

	Cause	Time interval between onset and death
IMMEDIATE CAUSE (A)	CARDIO RESPIRATORY ARREST	30MINS.
DUE TO (B)	CONGESTIVE HEART FAILURE	1YEAR
DUE TO (C)	CORONARY ARTERY DISEASE	20YEARS
DUE TO (D)		

108. DEATH REPORTED TO CORONER: [ ] YES [X] NO — REFERRAL NUMBER
109. BIOPSY PERFORMED: [ ] YES [X] NO
110. AUTOPSY PERFORMED: [ ] YES [X] NO
111. USED IN DETERMINING CAUSE: [ ] YES [ ] NO
112. OTHER SIGNIFICANT CONDITIONS CONTRIBUTING TO DEATH BUT NOT RELATED TO CAUSE GIVEN IN 107: NONE
113. WAS OPERATION PERFORMED FOR ANY CONDITION IN ITEM 107 OR 112? IF YES, LIST TYPE OF OPERATION AND DATE: NO

PHYSICIAN'S CERTIFICATION

114. I CERTIFY THAT TO THE BEST OF MY KNOWLEDGE DEATH OCCURRED AT THE HOUR, DATE AND PLACE STATED FROM THE CAUSES STATED. DECEDENT ATTENDED SINCE MM/DD/CCYY: 07/01/1974 — DECEDENT LAST SEEN ALIVE MM/DD/CCYY: 03/09/1996
115. SIGNATURE AND TITLE OF CERTIFIER: [signature]
116. LICENSE NO.: G20608
117. DATE MM/DD/CCYY: 03/11/1996
118. TYPE ATTENDING PHYSICIAN'S NAME, MAILING ADDRESS, ZIP: GARY SUGARMAN,MD 436 N.ROXBURY DR.BEVERLY HILLS,CA 90210

CORONER'S USE ONLY

I CERTIFY THAT IN MY OPINION DEATH OCCURRED AT THE HOUR, DATE AND PLACE STATED FROM THE CAUSES STATED.

119. MANNER OF DEATH: [ ] NATURAL [ ] SUICIDE [ ] HOMICIDE [ ] ACCIDENT [ ] PENDING INVESTIGATION [ ] COULD NOT BE DETERMINED
120. INJURY AT WORK: [ ] YES [ ] NO
121. INJURY DATE MM/DD/CCYY
122. HOUR
123. PLACE OF INJURY
124. DESCRIBE HOW INJURY OCCURRED (EVENTS WHICH RESULTED IN INJURY)
125. LOCATION (STREET AND NUMBER OR LOCATION AND CITY AND ZIP CODE)
126. SIGNATURE OF CORONER OR DEPUTY CORONER
127. DATE MM/DD/CCYY
128. TYPED NAME, TITLE OF CORONER OR DEPUTY CORONER

STATE REGISTRAR: A B C D E F G H — FAX AUTH. #: 273/24039 — CENSUS TRACT

This is to certify that this document is a true copy of the official record filed with the Registrar-Recorder/County Clerk.

JUL 9 1996

19-318580

[signature]
CONNY B. McCORMACK
Registrar-Recorder/County Clerk

This copy not valid unless prepared on engraved border displaying the Seal and Signature of the Registrar-Recorder/County Clerk.

ANY ALTERATION OR ERASURE VOIDS THIS CERTIFICATE

STATE OF CALIFORNIA
CERTIFICATION OF VITAL RECORD
COUNTY OF LOS ANGELES • REGISTRAR-RECORDER/COUNTY CLERK

DISTRICT NO. 1901 REGISTRAR'S NO. 7081

1. FULL NAME Mae Busch Tate

2. PLACE OF DEATH: (A) COUNTY Los Angeles
(B) CITY OR TOWN Los Angeles
(C) NAME OF HOSPITAL OR INSTITUTION Motion Picture Country Home
(D) LENGTH OF STAY: IN HOSPITAL OR INSTITUTION 7 weeks
IN THIS COMMUNITY 28 yrs IN CALIFORNIA 28 yrs
(E) IF FOREIGN BORN, HOW LONG IN THE U. S. A.? 37 yrs YEARS

3. USUAL RESIDENCE OF DECEASED
(A) STATE California
(B) COUNTY Los Angeles
(C) CITY OR TOWN Los Angeles
(D) STREET NO. 1219 N. Beachwood Dr.

20. DATE OF DEATH: MONTH April DAY 20 YEAR 1946 HOUR 2 MINUTE 20 am

3. (E) IF VETERAN, NAME OF WAR no
3. (F) SOCIAL SECURITY NO. 568-12-1560
4. SEX female
5. COLOR OR RACE cauc
6. (A) SINGLE, MARRIED, WIDOWED OR DIVORCED married
6. (B) NAME OF HUSBAND OR WIFE Thomas Tate
6. (C) AGE OF HUSBAND OR WIFE IF ALIVE 39 YEARS
7. BIRTHDATE OF DECEASED June 19 1901
8. AGE 44 YRS. 10 MOS. 1 DAYS
9. BIRTHPLACE Melbourne Australia
10. USUAL OCCUPATION actress
11. INDUSTRY OR BUSINESS silent motion pictures
FATHER 12. NAME William Busch
13. BIRTHPLACE Melbourne Australia
MOTHER 14. MAIDEN NAME Dora unknown
15. BIRTHPLACE Melbourne Australia
16. (A) INFORMANT Thomas Tate
(B) ADDRESS 1219 N Beachwood Dr.
17. (A) cremation (B) DATE 4 24 46
(C) PLACE Pierce Bros. Crematorium
18. (A) EMBALMER'S SIGNATURE Joseph E. Wiley LICENSE NO. 2561
(B) FUNERAL DIRECTOR Pierce Bros. Hollywood
ADDRESS 5959 Santa Monica Blvd.
BY [signature]
19. (A) APR 23 1946 DATE FILED (B) [signature] M.D. REGISTRAR'S SIGNATURE

21. MEDICAL CERTIFICATE
I HEREBY CERTIFY, THAT I ATTENDED THE DECEASED FROM Jan 2 1946 TO April 20 1946 THAT I LAST SAW HER ALIVE ON April 16 1946 AND THAT DEATH OCCURRED ON THE DATE AND HOUR STATED ABOVE.
IMMEDIATE CAUSE OF DEATH Carcinomatosis — DURATION 3 mos
DUE TO Carcinoma of Rectum — ?
DUE TO
OTHER CONDITIONS (INCLUDE PREGNANCY WITHIN THREE MONTHS OF DEATH)
MAJOR FINDINGS: OF OPERATIONS DATE OF OPERATION
OF AUTOPSY
PHYSICIAN UNDERLINE THE CAUSE TO WHICH DEATH SHOULD BE CHARGED STATISTICALLY

22. CORONER'S CERTIFICATE
I HEREBY CERTIFY, THAT I HELD AN AUTOPSY, INQUEST OR INVESTIGATION ON THE REMAINS OF THE DECEASED AND FIND FROM SUCH ACTION THAT DECEASED CAME TO H DEATH ON THE DATE AND HOUR STATED ABOVE.

23. IF DEATH WAS DUE TO EXTERNAL CAUSES, FILL IN THE FOLLOWING:
(A) ACCIDENT, SUICIDE, OR HOMICIDE? (B) DATE OF INJURY
(C) WHERE DID INJURY OCCUR? CITY OR TOWN COUNTY STATE
(D) DID INJURY OCCUR IN OR ABOUT HOME, ON FARM, IN INDUSTRIAL PLACE, OR IN PUBLIC PLACE? SPECIFY TYPE OF PLACE WHILE AT WORK?
(E) MEANS OF INJURY

24. CORONER'S OR PHYSICIAN'S SIGNATURE (SPECIFY WHICH) Francis E. Browne MD
ADDRESS 9730 Wilshire Beverly DATE 4-22-46

STATE OF CALIFORNIA DEPARTMENT OF PUBLIC HEALTH
CERTIFICATE OF DEATH
U. S. DEPT. OF COMMERCE BUREAU OF THE CENSUS

This is to certify that this document is a true copy of the official record filed with the Registrar-Recorder/County Clerk.

Conny B. McCormack
CONNY B. McCORMACK
Registrar-Recorder/County Clerk

JAN 9 2002
19-007647

This copy not valid unless prepared on engraved border displaying the Seal and Signature of the Registrar-Recorder/County Clerk.

MIDWEST BANK NOTE COMPANY — ANY ALTERATION OR ERASURE VOIDS THIS CERTIFICATE

CERTIFICATION OF VITAL RECORD

COUNTY OF LOS ANGELES • REGISTRAR-RECORDER/COUNTY CLERK

STATE FILE NUMBER

CERTIFICATE OF DEATH

STATE OF CALIFORNIA—DEPARTMENT OF PUBLIC HEALTH

LOCAL REGISTRATION DISTRICT AND CERTIFICATE NUMBER 7097-036479

DECEDENT PERSONAL DATA	1a. NAME OF DECEASED—FIRST NAME	FRANCIS
	1b. MIDDLE NAME	XAVIER
	1c. LAST NAME	BUSHMAN
	2a. DATE OF DEATH—MONTH, DAY, YEAR	8-23-66
	2b. HOUR	10:00 A.M.
	3. SEX	Male
	4. COLOR OR RACE	Caucasian
	5. BIRTHPLACE (STATE OR FOREIGN COUNTRY)	Maryland
	6. DATE OF BIRTH	January 10, 1883
	7. AGE (LAST BIRTHDAY)	83 YEARS
	8. NAME AND BIRTHPLACE OF FATHER	John H. Bushman-Pennsylvania
	9. MAIDEN NAME AND BIRTHPLACE OF MOTHER	Mary Norbeck-Pennsylvania
	10. CITIZEN OF WHAT COUNTRY	U.S.A.
	11. SOCIAL SECURITY NUMBER	571-14-1353
	12. LAST OCCUPATION	Actor
	13. NUMBER OF YEARS IN THIS OCCUPATION	70
	14. NAME OF LAST EMPLOYING COMPANY OR FIRM	Self-employed
	15. KIND OF INDUSTRY OR BUSINESS	Screen, Stage & Radio
	16. IF DECEASED WAS EVER IN U.S. ARMED FORCES, GIVE WAR OR DATES OF SERVICE	None
	17. SPECIFY MARRIED, NEVER MARRIED, WIDOWED, DIVORCED	Married
	18a. NAME OF PRESENT SPOUSE	Iva M. Bushman
	18b. PRESENT OR LAST OCCUPATION OF SPOUSE	Housewife
PLACE OF DEATH	19a. PLACE OF DEATH—NAME OF HOSPITAL	(None)
	19b. STREET ADDRESS	17500 Posetano Road — [X] Inside city corporate limits
	19c. CITY OR TOWN	Pacific Palisades
	19d. COUNTY	Los Angeles
	19e. LENGTH OF STAY IN COUNTY OF DEATH	51 YEARS
	19f. LENGTH OF STAY IN CALIFORNIA	51 YEARS
LAST USUAL RESIDENCE	20a. LAST USUAL RESIDENCE—STREET ADDRESS	17500 Posetano Road
	20b. IF INSIDE CITY CORPORATE LIMITS	[X] CHECK HERE
	20c. CITY OR TOWN	Pacific Palisades 2626
	20d. COUNTY	Los Angeles
	20e. STATE	California
	21a. NAME OF INFORMANT (IF OTHER THAN SPOUSE)	—
	21b. ADDRESS OF INFORMANT	—
PHYSICIAN'S OR CORONER'S CERTIFICATION	22b. CORONER	Autopsy
	22c. PHYSICIAN OR CORONER—SIGNATURE	Theo. J. Curphey, M.D., Chief Medical Examiner-Coroner, By [signature], Deputy
	22d. ADDRESS	Hall of Justice, Los Angeles
	22e. DATE SIGNED	9-4-66
FUNERAL DIRECTOR AND LOCAL REGISTRAR	23. SPECIFY BURIAL, ENTOMBMENT OR CREMATION	Entombment
	24. DATE	8-26-66
	25. NAME OF CEMETERY OR CREMATORY	Forest Lawn Memorial-Park
	26. EMBALMER—SIGNATURE / LICENSE NUMBER	Ralph M. Bailey 3433
	27. NAME OF FUNERAL DIRECTOR	FOREST LAWN MEMORIAL-PARK ASSN. GLENDALE CALIFORNIA
	28. DATE ACCEPTED FOR REGISTRATION BY LOCAL REGISTRAR	SEP 7 1966
	29. LOCAL REGISTRAR—SIGNATURE	[signature] M.D.

CAUSE OF DEATH	30. PART I. DEATH WAS CAUSED BY: IMMEDIATE CAUSE (A)	MASSIVE HEMOPERICARDIUM
	DUE TO (B)	MYOCARDIAL INFARCTION WITH RUPTURE, RECENT.
	DUE TO (C)	CORONARY THROMBOSIS
	PART II: OTHER SIGNIFICANT CONDITIONS CONTRIBUTING TO DEATH BUT NOT RELATED TO THE TERMINAL DISEASE CONDITION GIVEN IN PART I (A)	DIABETES MELLITUS
OPERATION AND AUTOPSY	31. OPERATION	[X] No operation performed
	32. DATE OF OPERATION	
	33. AUTOPSY	[X] Autopsy performed—gross findings used in determining above stated causes of death
INJURY INFORMATION	34a. SPECIFY ACCIDENT, SUICIDE OR HOMICIDE	
	34b. DESCRIBE HOW INJURY OCCURRED	
	35a. TIME OF INJURY	
	35b. INJURY OCCURRED	
	35c. PLACE OF INJURY	
	35d. CITY, TOWN, OR LOCATION	

Margin: Filed SEP 30 1966 RAY E. LEE, COUNTY RECORDER — Francis X. Bushman #66-8596 — J. Nelson M.D. — Final 9-26-66

This is to certify that this document is a true copy of the official record filed with the Registrar-Recorder/County Clerk.

Beatriz Valdez
BEATRIZ VALDEZ
Registrar-Recorder/County Clerk

AUG 16 1995

19-389288

This copy not valid unless prepared on engraved border displaying the Seal and Signature of the Registrar-Recorder/County Clerk.

American Bank Note Company

ANY ALTERATION OR ERASURE VOIDS THIS CERTIFICATE

CERTIFICATION OF VITAL RECORD

COUNTY OF LOS ANGELES • REGISTRAR-RECORDER/COUNTY CLERK

CERTIFICATE OF DEATH 7097-037821

STATE FILE NUMBER — STATE OF CALIFORNIA—DEPARTMENT OF PUBLIC HEALTH — LOCAL REGISTRATION DISTRICT AND CERTIFICATE NUMBER

DECEDENT PERSONAL DATA 9

1a. Name of deceased—first name	Spring
1b. Middle name	Dell
1c. Last name	Byington
2a. Date of death—month, day, year	Sept. 7, 1971
2b. Hour	6:00 P.M
3. Sex	Female
4. Color or race	Cauc.
5. Birthplace (state or foreign country)	Colorado
6. Date of birth	Oct. 17, 1886
7. Age (last birthday)	84 years
8. Name and birthplace of father	Edwin Lee Byington, Canada
9. Maiden name and birthplace of mother	Helene Cleghorn, Canada
10. Citizen of what country	U.S.A.
11. Social Security number	565 14 8522
12. Married, never married, widowed, divorced (specify)	Divorced
13. Name of surviving spouse (if wife enter maiden name)	-----
14. Last occupation	Actress
15. Number of years in this occupation	50
16. Name of last employing company or firm (if self employed so state)	National Broadcasting Co.
17. Kind of industry or business	Television

PLACE OF DEATH

18a. Place of death—name of hospital or other in-patient facility	At Home
18b. Street address—(street and number or location)	2946 N. Beachwood Dr.
18c. Inside city corporate limits (specify yes or no)	Yes
18d. City or town	Hollywood
18e. County	Los Angeles
18f. Length of stay in county of death	35 years
18g. Length of stay in California	35 years

USUAL RESIDENCE (if death occurred in institution enter residence before admission)

19a. Usual residence—street address (street and number or location)	2946 N. Beachwood Dr.
19b. Inside city corporate limits (specify yes or no)	Yes
19c. City or town	Hollywood
19d. County	Los Angeles
19e. State	California
20. Name and mailing address of informant	Self, pre-need

PHYSICIAN'S OR CORONER'S CERTIFICATION

21a. Coroner	
21b. Physician — I hereby certify that death occurred at the hour, date and place stated above from the causes stated below and that I attended the deceased from / to / and last saw her alive on	9/1/70 / 9/7/71 / 9/7/71
21c. Physician or coroner—signature and degree or title	George Nesola MD
21d. Date signed	9/7/71
21e. Address	1157 Wilshire Blvd
21f. Physician's California license number	[illegible]196

FUNERAL DIRECTOR AND LOCAL REGISTRAR

22a. Specify burial, entombment or cremation	Specimen
22b. Date	9/13/71
23. Name of cemetery or crematory	UCI-College of Medicine
24. Embalmer—signature (if body embalmed)	Raymond M. Zeller
License number	4112
25. Name of funeral director (or person acting as such)	UCI-College of Medicine
26. If not certified by coroner was this death reported to coroner? (specify yes or no)	No
27. Local registrar—signature	[signature] MD
28. Date accepted for registration by local registrar	SEP 15 1971

MEDICAL AND HEALTH DATA — CAUSE OF DEATH 9

29. Part I. Death was caused by: (enter only one cause per line for A, B and C)

	Cause	Approximate interval between onset and death
Immediate cause (A)	Adenocarcinoma Rectum	1½ yrs
Due to or as a consequence of (B)	Pelvic Cellulitis	3 mos
Due to or as a consequence of (C)		

30. Part II. Other significant conditions—contributing to death but not related to the immediate cause given in Part I:

31. Was operation or biopsy performed for any condition in items 29 or 30? (specify) Yes – operation

32a. Autopsy (specify yes or no) No

32b. If yes were findings considered in determining cause of death?

INJURY INFORMATION

33. Specify accident, suicide or homicide

34. Place of injury (specify home, farm, factory, street, office building, etc.)

35. Injury at work (specify yes or no)

36a. Date of injury—month, day, year

36b. Hour

37a. Place of injury (street and number or location and city or town)

37b. Distance from place of injury to usual residence (item 19) — miles

38. Were laboratory tests done for drugs or toxic chemicals? (specify yes or no)

39. Were laboratory tests done for alcohol? (specify yes or no)

40. Describe how injury occurred (enter sequence of events which resulted in injury. Nature of injury should be entered in item 29)

STATE REGISTRAR A | B | C | D | E | F 1814

REV. 1-1-69 FORM VS-11

This is to certify that this document is a true copy of the official record filed with the Registrar-Recorder/County Clerk.

THE GREAT SEAL OF THE STATE OF CALIFORNIA — EUREKA

OCT 02 1995

19 034104

This copy not valid unless prepared on engraved border displaying the Seal of the Registrar-Recorder/County Clerk.

ANY ALTERATION OR ERASURE VOIDS THIS CERTIFICATE

CERTIFICATION OF VITAL RECORD

COUNTY OF LOS ANGELES • REGISTRAR-RECORDER/COUNTY CLERK

STATE FILE NUMBER

CERTIFICATE OF DEATH

STATE OF CALIFORNIA—DEPARTMENT OF PUBLIC HEALTH

LOCAL REGISTRATION DISTRICT AND CERTIFICATE NUMBER 7013 20771

DECEDENT PERSONAL DATA

1a. Name of deceased—first name	Eddie
1b. Middle name	
1c. Last name	Cantor
2a. Date of death—month, day, year	October 10, 1964
2b. Hour	7:25P M.
3. Sex	Male
4. Color or race	Cauc.
5. Birthplace (state or foreign country)	New York
6. Date of birth	January 31, 1892
7. Age (last birthday)	72 years
8. Name and birthplace of father	Michael Cantor, Russia
9. Maiden name and birthplace of mother	Maite (Unknown), Russia
10. Citizen of what country	U.S.A.
11. Social security number	568_01_7037
12. Last occupation	Actor
13. Number of years in this occupation	40
14. Name of last employing company or firm	Self Employed
15. Kind of industry or business	Motion Picture, TV & Stage
16. If deceased was ever in U.S. armed forces, give war or dates of service	No
17. Specify married, never married, widowed, divorced	Widowed
18a. Name of present spouse	
18b. Present or last occupation of spouse	

PLACE OF DEATH

19a. Place of death—name of hospital	(not in a hospital)
19b. Street address	9360 Monte Leon Lane [x] inside city corporate limits [ ] outside city corporate limits
19c. City or town	Beverly Hills
19d. County	Los Angeles
19e. Length of stay in county of death	34 years
19f. Length of stay in California	34 years

LAST USUAL RESIDENCE (where did deceased live—if in institution enter residence before admission)

20a. Last usual residence—street address	9360 Monte Leon Lane
20b. If inside city corporate limits	[X] check here [ ] on a farm [ ] not on a farm
20c. City or town	Beverly Hills 1213
20d. County	Los Angeles
20e. State	California
21a. Name of informant (if other than spouse)	Natalie Metzger
21b. Address of informant	1455 S Edris Dr. Los Angeles

PHYSICIAN'S OR CORONER'S CERTIFICATION

22a. Physician: I hereby certify that death occurred at the hour, date and place stated above, from the causes stated below and that I attended the deceased from Nov 12-15[?] to 10-10-64 and that I last saw the deceased alive on 10-10-64

22b. Coroner: I hereby certify that death occurred at the hour, date and place stated above from the causes stated below and that I have held an investigation, autopsy, inquest on the remains of deceased as required by law

22c. Physician or coroner—signature: Herbert Gold[?] — Degree or title: M.D

22d. Address: 436 N. Roxbury Drive, B.H. Beverly Hills

22e. Date signed: 10-11-64

FUNERAL DIRECTOR AND LOCAL REGISTRAR

23. Specify burial, entombment or cremation	Entombment
24. Date	10/12/64
25. Name of cemetery or crematory	Hillside Memorial Park
26. Embalmer—signature (if body embalmed) / License number	Meredith Westwood 4629
27. Name of funeral director (or person acting as such)	Groman Mortuary BF
28. Date accepted for registration by local registrar	OCT 12 1964
29. Local registrar—signature	R. H. Sutherland M.D.

MEDICAL AND HEALTH DATA

CAUSE OF DEATH 10-23-64

30. Cause of death. Enter only one cause per line for (a), (b), and (c)

	Cause	Approximate interval between onset and death
Part I. Death was caused by: Immediate cause (a)	Myocardial Infarction	Minutes
Conditions, if any, which gave rise to the above cause (a) stating the underlying cause last. Due to (b)	Arteriosclerotic Heart Disease	Years
Due to (c)		

Part II: Other significant conditions contributing to death but not related to the terminal disease condition given in Part I (a)

OPERATION AND AUTOPSY

31. Operation—check one: [X] No operation performed [ ] Operation performed—findings used in determining above stated causes of death [ ] Operation performed—findings not used in determining above stated causes of death

32. Date of operation

33. Autopsy—check one: [X] No autopsy performed [ ] Autopsy performed—gross findings used in determining above stated causes of death [ ] Autopsy performed—gross findings not used in determining above stated causes of death

INJURY INFORMATION 6 cc (2)

34a. Specify accident, suicide or homicide

34b. Describe how injury occurred

35a. Time of injury: Hour Month Day Year M.

35b. Injury occurred: [ ] While at work [ ] Not while at work

35c. Place of injury

35d. City, town, or location County State

Filed NOV 12 1964 RAY E. LEE, COUNTY RECORDER

This is to certify that this document is a true copy of the official record filed with the Registrar-Recorder/County Clerk.

Beatriz Valdez
BEATRIZ VALDEZ
Registrar-Recorder/County Clerk

AUG 10 1995

19-389281

This copy not valid unless prepared on engraved border displaying the Seal and Signature of the Registrar-Recorder/County Clerk.

ANY ALTERATION OR ERASURE VOIDS THIS CERTIFICATE

CERTIFICATION OF VITAL RECORD

COUNTY OF LOS ANGELES • REGISTRAR-RECORDER/COUNTY CLERK

CERTIFICATE OF DEATH 0190-044036
STATE OF CALIFORNIA

STATE FILE NUMBER — LOCAL REGISTRATION DISTRICT AND CERTIFICATE NUMBER

DECEDENT PERSONAL DATA

1A. Name of Decedent—First	Truman
1B. Middle	
1C. Last	Capote
2A. Date of Death (Month, Day, Year)	August 25, 1984
2B. Hour	1221
3. Sex	Male
4. Race/Ethnicity	Caucasian
5. Spanish/Hispanic	No
6. Date of Birth	Sept. 30, 1924
7. Age	59 years
8. Birthplace of Decedent (State or Foreign Country)	Louisiana
9. Name and Birthplace of Father	Julian A. Persons - Alabama
10. Birth Name and Birthplace of Mother	Lillie Mae Faulk - Ala.
11. Citizen of What Country	United States
12. Social Security Number	102-20-9733
13. Marital Status	Never Married
14. Name of Surviving Spouse (If wife, enter birth name)	
15. Primary Occupation	Author-Writer
16. Number of Years This Occupation	Adult Life
17. Employer (If self-employed, so state)	Self- Employed
18. Kind of Industry or Business	Literary & Motion Picture

USUAL RESIDENCE

19A. Usual Residence—Street Address (Street and number or location)	870 United Nations Plaza
19B.	
19C. City or Town	New York
19D. County	New York
19E. State	New York
20. Name and Address of Informant—Relationship	Joanne Carson - Friend, 11001 Sunset Blvd., Los Angeles, California

AMENDED 1 OF 2

PLACE OF DEATH

21A. Place of Death	A residence
21B. County	Los Angeles
21C. Street Address (Street and number or location)	11001 Sunset Blvd.
21D. City or Town	Los Angeles

CAUSE OF DEATH

22. Death was caused by: (Enter only one cause per line for A, B, and C) Immediate Cause (A)	DEFERRED
Due to, or as a consequence of (B)	
Due to, or as a consequence of (C)	
Approximate interval between onset and death	
24. Was death reported to coroner?	84-10675
25. Was biopsy performed?	
26. Was autopsy performed?	YES
23. Other significant conditions—contributing to death but not related to cause given in 22A	
27. Was operation performed for any condition in items 22 or 23? Type of operation / Date	

Conditions, if any, which gave rise to the immediate cause, stating the underlying cause last.

PHYSICIAN'S CERTIFICATION

28A. I certify that death occurred at the hour, date and place stated from the causes stated. I attended decedent since (Enter Mo. Da. Yr.) | I last saw decedent alive (Enter Mo. Da. Yr.)
28B. Physician—Signature and degree or title | 28C. Date signed | 28D. Physician's license number
28E. Type physician's name and address

INJURY INFORMATION

29. Specify accident, suicide, etc. | 30. Place of injury | 31. Injury at work | 32A. Date of injury—Month, Day, Year | 32B. Hour
33. Location (Street and number or location and city or town) | 34. Describe how injury occurred (Events which resulted in injury)

CORONER'S USE ONLY

35A. I certify that death occurred at the hour, date and place stated from the causes stated. As required by law I have held an investigation
35B. Coroner—Signature and degree or title: [signature] Deputy Coroner
35C. Date signed: 8-26-84

36. Disposition	Cremation
37. Date—Month, Day, Year	Aug. 28, 1984
38. Name and Address of Cemetery or Crematory	Grandview Crematory, Glendale, Ca
39. Embalmer's License Number and Signature	Not Embalmed
40A. Name of Funeral Director (or person acting as such)	Westwood Village Mortuary
40B. License No.	951
41. Local Registrar—Signature	[signature]
42. Date Accepted by Local Registrar	AUG 28 1984

STATE REGISTRAR A. B. C. D. E. F.

VS-11 (7-83) 571.3 01-19-4-7005 87604-449 8-83 400M DUP OSP

This is to certify that this document is a true copy of the official record filed with the Registrar-Recorder/County Clerk.

OCT 26 1995

19-048127

THE GREAT SEAL OF THE STATE OF CALIFORNIA EUREKA

This copy not valid unless prepared on engraved border displaying the Seal of the Registrar-Recorder/County Clerk.

BANKNOTE CORPORATION OF AMERICA

ANY ALTERATION OR ERASURE VOIDS THIS CERTIFICATE

CERTIFICATION OF VITAL RECORD

COUNTY OF LOS ANGELES • REGISTRAR-RECORDER/COUNTY CLERK

CERTIFICATE OF DEATH

STATE OF CALIFORNIA—DEPARTMENT OF HEALTH
OFFICE OF THE STATE REGISTRAR OF VITAL STATISTICS

STATE FILE NUMBER

0190-052000
LOCAL REGISTRATION DISTRICT AND CERTIFICATE NUMBER

DECEDENT PERSONAL DATA

Field	Entry
1A. NAME OF DECEASED—FIRST NAME	RICHARD
1B. MIDDLE NAME	DUTOIT
1C. LAST NAME	CARLSON
2A. DATE OF DEATH—MONTH, DAY, YEAR	NOVEMBER 25,1977
2B. HOUR	9:45 P.M.
3. SEX	Male
4. COLOR OR RACE	Cauc
5. BIRTHPLACE (STATE OR FOREIGN COUNTRY)	Minn.
6. DATE OF BIRTH	April 29, 1912
7. AGE (LAST BIRTHDAY)	65 YEARS
IF UNDER 1 YEAR	
IF UNDER 24 HOURS	
8. NAME AND BIRTHPLACE OF FATHER	Henry Carlson-Sweden
9. MAIDEN NAME AND BIRTHPLACE OF MOTHER	Mabel DuToit-Minn.
10. CITIZEN OF WHAT COUNTRY	U.S.A.
11. SOCIAL SECURITY NUMBER	092-05-6736
12. MARRIED, NEVER MARRIED, WIDOWED, DIVORCED (SPECIFY)	Married
13. NAME OF SURVIVING SPOUSE (IF WIFE, ENTER MAIDEN NAME)	Mona Mayfield
14. LAST OCCUPATION	Actor
15. NUMBER OF YEARS IN THIS OCCUPATION	35
16. NAME OF LAST EMPLOYING COMPANY OR FIRM (IF SELF EMPLOYED, SO STATE)	Free Lance
17. KIND OF INDUSTRY OR BUSINESS	Motion Pictures

PLACE OF DEATH

Field	Entry
18A. PLACE OF DEATH—NAME OF HOSPITAL OR OTHER IN-PATIENT FACILITY	Encino Hospital
18B. STREET ADDRESS—(STREET AND NUMBER, OR LOCATION)	16237 Ventura Blvd
18C. INSIDE CITY CORPORATE LIMITS (SPECIFY YES OR NO)	
18D. CITY OR TOWN	Encino
18E. COUNTY	Los Angeles
18F. LENGTH OF STAY IN COUNTY OF DEATH	37 YEARS
18G. LENGTH OF STAY IN CALIFORNIA	37 YEARS

USUAL RESIDENCE (IF DEATH OCCURRED IN INSTITUTION, ENTER RESIDENCE BEFORE ADMISSION)

Field	Entry
19A. USUAL RESIDENCE—STREET ADDRESS (STREET AND NUMBER OR LOCATION)	14101 Valley Vista
19B. INSIDE CITY CORPORATE LIMITS (SPECIFY YES OR NO)	
19C. CITY OR TOWN	Sherman Oaks
19D. COUNTY	Los Angeles
19E. STATE	California
20. NAME AND MAILING ADDRESS OF INFORMANT	Christopher H Carlson, 525 Muskingum Pl, Pac. Palisades, Ca

PHYSICIAN'S OR CORONER'S CERTIFICATION

Field	Entry
21A. CORONER: I HEREBY CERTIFY THAT DEATH OCCURRED AT THE HOUR, DATE AND PLACE STATED ABOVE FROM THE CAUSES STATED BELOW AND THAT I HAVE HELD AN INVESTIGATION OR INQUEST ON THE REMAINS OF DECEASED AS REQUIRED BY LAW	
21B. PHYSICIAN: I HEREBY CERTIFY THAT DEATH OCCURRED AT THE HOUR, DATE, AND PLACE STATED ABOVE FROM THE CAUSES STATED BELOW AND THAT I ATTENDED THE DECEASED FROM (ENTER MONTH, DAY, YEAR)	11-15-77
TO (ENTER MONTH, DAY, YEAR)	11-24-77
AND LAST SAW THE DECEASED ALIVE ON (ENTER MONTH, DAY, YEAR)	11-24-77
21C. PHYSICIAN OR CORONER—SIGNATURE AND DEGREE OR TITLE	[illegible] M.D.
21D. DATE SIGNED	11/28/77
21E. ADDRESS	16237 Ventura Bl. Encino
21F. PHYSICIAN'S CALIFORNIA LICENSE NUMBER	G 22362

FUNERAL DIRECTOR AND LOCAL REGISTRAR

Field	Entry
22A. SPECIFY BURIAL, ENTOMBMENT OR CREMATION	Cremation
22B. DATE	11-29-77
23. NAME OF CEMETERY OR CREMATORY	Chapel of the Pines
24. EMBALMER—SIGNATURE (IF BODY EMBALMED) LICENSE NUMBER	Not Embalmed
25. NAME OF FUNERAL DIRECTOR (OR PERSON ACTING AS SUCH)	PIERCE BROS. SANTA MONICA
26. IF NOT CERTIFIED BY CORONER WAS THIS DEATH REPORTED TO CORONER? (SPECIFY YES OR NO)	
27. LOCAL REGISTRAR—SIGNATURE	Morrison E. Chamberlin [illegible]
28. DATE RECEIVED FOR REGISTRATION BY LOCAL REGISTRAR	NOV 29 1977

MEDICAL AND HEALTH DATA

CAUSE OF DEATH

29. PART I. DEATH WAS CAUSED BY: ENTER ONLY ONE CAUSE PER LINE FOR A, B, AND C

	Cause	Approximate interval between onset and death
IMMEDIATE CAUSE (A)	Sub Arachnoid [illegible]	2wks
CONDITIONS, IF ANY, WHICH GAVE RISE TO THE IMMEDIATE CAUSE (A), STATING THE UNDERLYING CAUSE LAST. DUE TO, OR AS A CONSEQUENCE OF (B)		
DUE TO, OR AS A CONSEQUENCE OF (C)		

Field	Entry
30. PART II: OTHER SIGNIFICANT CONDITIONS—CONTRIBUTING TO DEATH BUT NOT RELATED TO THE IMMEDIATE CAUSE GIVEN IN PART I	
31. WAS OPERATION OR BIOPSY PERFORMED FOR ANY CONDITION IN ITEMS 29 OR 30? (SPECIFY TYPE OF OPERATION AND/OR BIOPSY)	NO
32A. AUTOPSY (SPECIFY YES OR NO)	NO
32B. IF YES WERE FINDINGS CONSIDERED IN DETERMINING CAUSE OF DEATH? (SPECIFY YES OR NO)	

INJURY INFORMATION

Field	Entry
33. SPECIFY ACCIDENT, SUICIDE OR HOMICIDE	
34. PLACE OF INJURY (SPECIFY HOME, FARM, FACTORY, STREET, OFFICE BUILDING, ETC.)	
35. INJURY AT WORK (SPECIFY YES OR NO)	
36A. DATE OF INJURY—MONTH, DAY, YEAR	
36B. HOUR	
37A. PLACE OF INJURY (STREET AND NUMBER OR LOCATION AND CITY OR TOWN)	
37B. DISTANCE FROM PLACE OF INJURY TO USUAL RESIDENCE, ITEM 19. MILES	
38. WERE LABORATORY TESTS DONE FOR DRUGS OR TOXIC CHEMICALS (SPECIFY YES OR NO)	
39. WERE LABORATORY TESTS DONE FOR ALCOHOL (SPECIFY YES OR NO)	
40. DESCRIBE HOW INJURY OCCURRED (ENTER SEQUENCE OF EVENTS WHICH RESULTED IN INJURY. NATURE OF INJURY SHOULD BE ENTERED IN ITEM 29)	

70 / Free

STATE REGISTRAR

A.	B.	C.	D.	E.	F.
					01-9-1-0280

VS 11 (8-73)

This is to certify that this document is a true copy of the official record filed with the Registrar-Recorder/County Clerk.

Beatriz Valdez
BEATRIZ VALDEZ
Registrar-Recorder/County Clerk

AUG 10 1995

19-389402

This copy not valid unless prepared on engraved border displaying the Seal and Signature of the Registrar-Recorder/County Clerk.

American Bank Note Company

ANY ALTERATION OR ERASURE VOIDS THIS CERTIFICATE

CERTIFICATION OF VITAL RECORD

COUNTY OF LOS ANGELES • REGISTRAR-RECORDER/COUNTY CLERK

CERTIFICATE OF DEATH

STATE OF CALIFORNIA—DEPARTMENT OF PUBLIC HEALTH

LOCAL REGISTRATION DISTRICT AND CERTIFICATE NUMBER 7053 17639

DECEDENT PERSONAL DATA

1a. NAME OF DECEASED—FIRST NAME: LEO; 1b. MIDDLE NAME: ANTONIO; 1c. LAST NAME: CARRILLO; 2a. DATE OF DEATH: September 10, 1961; 2b. HOUR: 5:55 p.m.

3. SEX: Male; 4. COLOR OR RACE: White; 5. BIRTHPLACE: California; 6. DATE OF BIRTH: August 6, 1881; 7. AGE: 80 YEARS

8. NAME AND BIRTHPLACE OF FATHER: Juan J. Carrillo - California; 9. MAIDEN NAME AND BIRTHPLACE OF MOTHER: Frances Doldon Spain; 10. CITIZEN OF WHAT COUNTRY: U.S.A.; 11. SOCIAL SECURITY NUMBER: 562-12-4981

12. LAST OCCUPATION: Actor; 13. NUMBER OF YEARS IN THIS OCCUPATION: 60; 14. NAME OF LAST EMPLOYING COMPANY OR FIRM; 15. KIND OF INDUSTRY OR BUSINESS: Motion & Television

16. IF DECEASED WAS EVER IN U.S. ARMED FORCES, GIVE WAR OR DATES OF SERVICE: No; 17. SPECIFY MARRIED, NEVER MARRIED, WIDOWED, DIVORCED: Widowed; 18a. NAME OF PRESENT SPOUSE; 18b. PRESENT OR LAST OCCUPATION OF SPOUSE

PLACE OF DEATH

19a. PLACE OF DEATH—NAME OF HOSPITAL: None; 19b. STREET ADDRESS: 639 East Channel Road; 19c. CITY OR TOWN: Los Angeles; 19d. COUNTY: Los Angeles; 19e. LENGTH OF STAY IN COUNTY OF DEATH: 80 YEARS; 19f. LENGTH OF STAY IN CALIFORNIA: 80 YEARS

LAST USUAL RESIDENCE

20a. LAST USUAL RESIDENCE—STREET ADDRESS: 639 East Channel Road; 20b. IF INSIDE CITY CORPORATE LIMITS: X; 20c. CITY OR TOWN: Los Angeles; 20d. COUNTY: Los Angeles; 20e. STATE: California; 21a. NAME OF INFORMANT: Antoinette Carrillo; 21b. ADDRESS OF INFORMANT: 639 E. Channel Rd

PHYSICIAN'S OR CORONER'S CERTIFICATION

22a. PHYSICIAN: I HEREBY CERTIFY THAT DEATH OCCURRED AT THE HOUR, DATE AND PLACE STATED ABOVE FROM THE CAUSES STATED BELOW AND THAT I ATTENDED THE DECEASED FROM 1937 TO 9-10-61 AND THAT I LAST SAW THE DECEASED ALIVE ON 9-10-61

22b. CORONER: I HEREBY CERTIFY THAT DEATH OCCURRED AT THE HOUR, DATE AND PLACE STATED ABOVE FROM THE CAUSES STATED BELOW AND THAT I HAVE HELD AN INVESTIGATION OR AUTOPSY INQUEST ON THE REMAINS OF DECEASED AS REQUIRED BY LAW

22c. PHYSICIAN OR CORONER—SIGNATURE: Adolph Kooley M.D.; 22d. ADDRESS: Santa Monica; 22e. DATE SIGNED: 9-11-61

FUNERAL DIRECTOR AND LOCAL REGISTRAR

23. SPECIFY BURIAL, ENTOMBMENT OR CREMATION: Burial; 24. DATE: September 14-61; 25. NAME OF CEMETERY OR CREMATORY: Woodlawn Cemetery; 26. EMBALMER—SIGNATURE: Robert Mashmeyer; LICENSE NUMBER 1878

27. NAME OF FUNERAL DIRECTOR: BOGGS & MASHMEYER Wilshire Funeral Home; 28. DATE ACCEPTED FOR REGISTRATION BY LOCAL REGISTRAR: SEP 1 2 1961; 29. LOCAL REGISTRAR—SIGNATURE: George M. Uhl, M.D.

MEDICAL AND HEALTH DATA

CAUSE OF DEATH

30. CAUSE OF DEATH. PART I. DEATH WAS CAUSED BY: IMMEDIATE CAUSE (A) Metastatic Carcinoma Recto - Sigmoid - colon - ; APPROXIMATE INTERVAL BETWEEN ONSET AND DEATH: 3 yrs

CONDITIONS, IF ANY, WHICH GAVE RISE TO THE ABOVE CAUSE (A), STATING THE UNDERLYING CAUSE LAST: DUE TO (B); DUE TO (C)

PART II. OTHER SIGNIFICANT CONDITIONS CONTRIBUTING TO DEATH BUT NOT RELATED TO THE TERMINAL DISEASE CONDITION GIVEN IN PART I (A)

OPERATION AND AUTOPSY

31. OPERATION—CHECK ONE: OPERATION PERFORMED—FINDINGS USED IN DETERMINING ABOVE STATED CAUSES OF DEATH: ✓; 32. DATE OF OPERATION: 8-31-59; 33. AUTOPSY—CHECK ONE: NO AUTOPSY PERFORMED: ✓

INJURY INFORMATION

34a. SPECIFY ACCIDENT, SUICIDE OR HOMICIDE; 34b. DESCRIBE HOW INJURY OCCURRED; 35a. TIME OF INJURY: HOUR MONTH DAY YEAR; 35b. INJURY OCCURRED: WHILE AT WORK / NOT WHILE AT WORK; 35c. PLACE OF INJURY; 35d. CITY, TOWN, OR LOCATION; COUNTY; STATE

This is to certify that this document is a true copy of the official record filed with the Registrar-Recorder/County Clerk.

Beatriz Valdez
BEATRIZ VALDEZ
Registrar-Recorder/County Clerk

SEP 0 5 1995
19-000003

This copy not valid unless prepared on engraved border displaying the Seal and Signature of the Registrar-Recorder/County Clerk.

ANY ALTERATION OR ERASURE VOIDS THIS CERTIFICATE

CERTIFICATION OF VITAL RECORD

COUNTY OF LOS ANGELES • REGISTRAR-RECORDER/COUNTY CLERK

CERTIFICATE OF DEATH
STATE OF CALIFORNIA
USE BLACK INK ONLY

STATE FILE NUMBER — LOCAL REGISTRATION DISTRICT AND CERTIFICATE NUMBER: 38919006567

DECEDENT PERSONAL DATA

1A. NAME OF DECEDENT—FIRST (GIVEN): JOHN
1B. MIDDLE: NICHOLAS
1C. LAST (FAMILY): CASSAVETES
2A. DATE OF DEATH—MONTH, DAY, YEAR: FEBRUARY 3, 1989
2B. HOUR: 0950
3. SEX: MALE
4. RACE: CAUC.
5. SPANISH/HISPANIC: ☐ YES SPECIFY ___ X NO
6. DATE OF BIRTH—MONTH, DAY, YEAR: DEC. 9, 1929
7. AGE IN YEARS: 59 — IF UNDER 1 YEAR: MONTHS / DAYS — IF UNDER 24 HOURS: HOURS / MINUTES
8. STATE OF BIRTH: NEW YORK
9. CITIZEN OF WHAT COUNTRY: U.S.A.
10A. FULL NAME OF FATHER: NICHOLAS CASSAVETES
10B. STATE OF BIRTH: GREECE
11A. FULL MAIDEN NAME OF MOTHER: KATHERINE DEMETRE
11B. STATE OF BIRTH: NEW YORK
12. MILITARY SERVICE? 19__ TO 19__ XX NONE
13. SOCIAL SECURITY NUMBER: 131-24-4520
14. MARITAL STATUS: MARRIED
15. NAME OF SURVIVING SPOUSE (IF WIFE, ENTER MAIDEN NAME): GENA ROWLANDS
16A. USUAL OCCUPATION: ACTOR/WRITER/DIRECTOR
16B. USUAL KIND OF BUSINESS OR INDUSTRY: ENTERTAINMENT
16C. USUAL EMPLOYER: SELF
16D. YEARS IN USUAL OCCUPATION: 35
17. NUMBER OF HIGHEST GRADE COMPLETED (1–12 OR COLLEGE 13–17+): 14

USUAL RESIDENCE

18A. RESIDENCE—STREET AND NUMBER OR LOCATION: 8717 WOODROW WILSON DRIVE
1 OF 2
18B. CITY: LOS ANGELES
18C. ZIP CODE: 90046
18D. COUNTY: LOS ANGELES
18E. NUMBER OF YEARS IN THIS COUNTY: 20
18F. STATE OR FOREIGN COUNTRY: CALIFORNIA
20. NAME, RELATIONSHIP, MAILING ADDRESS AND ZIP CODE OF INFORMANT: MRS. GENA CASSAVETES - WIFE, 8717 WOODROW WILSON DRIVE, LOS ANGELES, CALIFORNIA 90046

PLACE OF DEATH

19A. PLACE OF DEATH: CEDARS SINAI MEDICAL CTR.
19B. IF HOSPITAL, SPECIFY ONE: IP, ER/OP, DOA: I.P.
19C. COUNTY: LOS ANGELES
19D. STREET ADDRESS—STREET AND NUMBER OR LOCATION: 8700 BEVERLY BLVD.
19E. CITY: LOS ANGELES
22. WAS DEATH REPORTED TO CORONER? ☐ YES ___ REFERRAL NUMBER X NO

CAUSE OF DEATH

21. DEATH WAS CAUSED BY: (ENTER ONLY ONE CAUSE PER LINE FOR A, B, AND C)—TYPE OR PRINT — TIME INTERVAL BETWEEN ONSET AND DEATH
IMMEDIATE CAUSE (A): Liver failure — Several months
DUE TO (B): cirrhosis of the liver — 5 years
DUE TO (C):
23. WAS BIOPSY PERFORMED? ☐ YES X NO
24A. WAS AUTOPSY PERFORMED? ☐ YES X NO
24B. IF YES, WAS IT USED IN DETERMINING CAUSE OF DEATH? ☐ YES ☐ NO
25. OTHER SIGNIFICANT CONDITIONS CONTRIBUTING TO DEATH BUT NOT RELATED TO CAUSE GIVEN IN 21: NONE
26. WAS OPERATION PERFORMED FOR ANY CONDITION IN ITEM 21 OR 25? MONTH, DAY, YEAR / TYPE: NO

PHYSICIAN'S CERTIFICATION

I CERTIFY THAT DEATH OCCURRED AT THE HOUR, DATE AND PLACE STATED FROM THE CAUSES STATED.
27A. DECEDENT ATTENDED SINCE / DECEDENT LAST SEEN ALIVE — MONTH, DAY, YEAR: 1959 / 2/3/89
27B. SIGNATURE AND DEGREE OR TITLE OF PHYSICIAN: Wilbur S Schwartz MD
27C. PHYSICIAN'S LICENSE NUMBER: G2425
27D. DATE SIGNED: 2/4/89
27E. TYPE ATTENDING PHYSICIAN'S NAME AND ADDRESS: WILBUR S. SCHWARTZ, M.D. 435 NORTH BEDFORD DRIVE BEVERLY HILLS, CALIFORNIA

CORONER'S USE ONLY

I CERTIFY THAT DEATH OCCURRED AT THE HOUR, DATE AND PLACE STATED FROM THE CAUSES STATED.
28A. SIGNATURE OF CORONER OR DEPUTY CORONER
28B. DATE SIGNED
29. MANNER OF DEATH—specify one: natural, accident, suicide, homicide, pending investigation or could not be determined
30A. PLACE OF INJURY
30B. INJURY AT WORK ☐ YES ☐ NO
30C. DATE OF INJURY MONTH, DAY, YEAR
31. HOUR
32. LOCATION (STREET AND NUMBER OR LOCATION AND CITY)
33. DESCRIBE HOW INJURY OCCURRED (EVENTS WHICH RESULTED IN INJURY)

FUNERAL DIRECTOR AND LOCAL REGISTRAR

34A. DISPOSITION: CREMATION
34B. PLACE OF FINAL DISPOSITION: PIERCE BROTHERS WESTWOOD MEMORIAL PARK - LOS ANGELES
34C. DATE OF DISPOSITION MONTH, DAY, YEAR: FEBR. 6, 1989
35A. SIGNATURE OF EMBALMER: NOT EMBALMED
35B. LICENSE NUMBER: -
36A. NAME OF FUNERAL DIRECTOR (OR PERSON ACTING AS SUCH): PIERCE BROS. WESTWOOD VILLAGE
36B. LICENSE NO.: F-951
37. SIGNATURE OF LOCAL REGISTRAR: Robert ... H
38. REGISTRATION DATE: FEB 5 1989

STATE REGISTRAR A. B. C. D. E. F. CENSUS TRACT

VS-11 (REV. 1-89) 5715 MAKE NO ERASURES, WHITEOUTS, OR OTHER ALTERATIONS 0555

This is to certify that this document is a true copy of the official record filed with the Registrar-Recorder/County Clerk.

Beatriz Valdez
BEATRIZ VALDEZ
Registrar-Recorder/County Clerk

AUG 18 1995
19-397062

This copy not valid unless prepared on engraved border displaying the Seal and Signature of the Registrar-Recorder/County Clerk.

THE GREAT SEAL OF THE STATE OF CALIFORNIA — EUREKA

American Bank Note Company

ANY ALTERATION OR ERASURE VOIDS THIS CERTIFICATE

CERTIFICATION OF VITAL RECORD

COUNTY OF LOS ANGELES • REGISTRAR-RECORDER/COUNTY CLERK

CERTIFICATE OF DEATH
STATE OF CALIFORNIA—DEPARTMENT OF HEALTH
OFFICE OF THE STATE REGISTRAR OF VITAL STATISTICS

STATE FILE NUMBER

0190-055251
LOCAL REGISTRATION DISTRICT AND CERTIFICATE NUMBER

DECEDENT PERSONAL DATA

1A. NAME OF DECEASED—FIRST NAME: Jack
1B. MIDDLE NAME: Edward
1C. LAST NAME: Cassidy
2A. DATE OF DEATH—MONTH, DAY, YEAR: December 12, 1976
2B. HOUR: Found 0615 hrs.
3. SEX: Male
4. COLOR OR RACE: Cauc.
5. BIRTHPLACE (STATE OR FOREIGN COUNTRY): New York
6. DATE OF BIRTH: March 5, 1927
7. AGE (LAST BIRTHDAY): 49 YEARS
IF UNDER 1 YEAR: MONTHS / DAYS — IF UNDER 24 HOURS: HOURS / MINUTES
8. NAME AND BIRTHPLACE OF FATHER: William Cassidy - Ireland
9. MAIDEN NAME AND BIRTHPLACE OF MOTHER: Charlotte Kohler - Germany
10. CITIZEN OF WHAT COUNTRY: U.S.A.
11. SOCIAL SECURITY NUMBER: 102-18-3471
12. MARRIED, NEVER MARRIED, WIDOWED, DIVORCED (SPECIFY): Divorced
13. NAME OF SURVIVING SPOUSE (IF WIFE, ENTER MAIDEN NAME): ———
14. LAST OCCUPATION: Actor-Singer
15. NUMBER OF YEARS IN THIS OCCUPATION: 30
16. NAME OF LAST EMPLOYING COMPANY OR FIRM (IF SELF EMPLOYED SO STATE): Self Employed
17. KIND OF INDUSTRY OR BUSINESS: Entertainment

PLACE OF DEATH

18A. PLACE OF DEATH—NAME OF HOSPITAL OR OTHER IN-PATIENT FACILITY:
18B. STREET ADDRESS—(STREET AND NUMBER, OR LOCATION): 1221 North Kings Road
18C. INSIDE CITY CORPORATE LIMITS (SPECIFY YES OR NO): Yes
18D. CITY OR TOWN: Los Angeles
18E. COUNTY: Los Angeles
18F. LENGTH OF STAY IN COUNTY OF DEATH: 17 YEARS
18G. LENGTH OF STAY IN CALIFORNIA: 17 YEARS

USUAL RESIDENCE (IF DEATH OCCURRED IN INSTITUTION, ENTER RESIDENCE BEFORE ADMISSION)

19A. USUAL RESIDENCE—STREET ADDRESS (STREET AND NUMBER OR LOCATION): 1221 North Kings Road
19B. INSIDE CITY CORPORATE LIMITS (SPECIFY YES OR NO): Yes
19C. CITY OR TOWN: Los Angeles
19D. COUNTY: Los Angeles
19E. STATE: California
20. NAME AND MAILING ADDRESS OF INFORMANT: Ronald Karno, 1901 Ave. of the Stars, Los Angeles, Ca. 90067

PHYSICIAN'S OR CORONER'S CERTIFICATION

21A. CORONER: I HEREBY CERTIFY THAT DEATH OCCURRED AT THE HOUR, DATE AND PLACE STATED ABOVE FROM THE CAUSES STATED BELOW AND THAT I HAVE HELD AN Investigation (INVESTIGATION OR INQUEST)
21B. PHYSICIAN: I HEREBY CERTIFY THAT DEATH OCCURRED AT THE HOUR, DATE, AND PLACE STATED ABOVE FROM THE CAUSES STATED BELOW AND THAT I ATTENDED THE DECEASED FROM / TO / AND LAST SAW THE DECEASED ALIVE ON
21C. PHYSICIAN OR CORONER SIGNATURE: Thomas T. Noguchi, M.D., Coroner — [signature] Palmer, Deputy
21D. DATE SIGNED: 12-14-76
21E. ADDRESS: 1104 N. Mission Rd., Los Angeles, Calif. 90033
21F. PHYSICIAN'S CALIFORNIA LICENSE NUMBER:

FUNERAL DIRECTOR AND LOCAL REGISTRAR

22A. SPECIFY BURIAL, ENTOMBMENT OR CREMATION: Cremation
22B. DATE: 12-15-76
23. NAME OF CEMETERY OR CREMATORY: Chapel of the Pines
24. EMBALMER—SIGNATURE (IF BODY EMBALMED) LICENSE NUMBER: Not Embalmed
25. NAME OF FUNERAL DIRECTOR (OR PERSON ACTING AS SUCH): Pierce Bros. Los Angeles
26. IF NOT CERTIFIED BY CORONER WAS THIS DEATH REPORTED TO CORONER? (SPECIFY YES OR NO):
27. LOCAL REGISTRAR—SIGNATURE: [signature]
28. DATE RECEIVED FOR REGISTRATION BY LOCAL REGISTRAR: DEC 14 1976

MEDICAL AND HEALTH DATA — CAUSE OF DEATH

29. PART I. DEATH WAS CAUSED BY: (ENTER ONLY ONE CAUSE PER LINE FOR (A), (B), AND (C))
IMMEDIATE CAUSE (A) EXTENSIVE THERMAL BURNS OF BODY
CONDITIONS, IF ANY, WHICH GAVE RISE TO THE IMMEDIATE CAUSE (A), STATING THE UNDERLYING CAUSE LAST
DUE TO, OR AS A CONSEQUENCE OF (B)
DUE TO, OR AS A CONSEQUENCE OF (C)
APPROXIMATE INTERVAL BETWEEN ONSET AND DEATH
30. PART II: OTHER SIGNIFICANT CONDITIONS—CONTRIBUTING TO DEATH BUT NOT RELATED TO THE IMMEDIATE CAUSE GIVEN IN PART I (A)
31. WAS OPERATION OR BIOPSY PERFORMED FOR ANY CONDITION IN ITEMS 29 OR 30? (SPECIFY OPERATION AND/OR BIOPSY): No
32A. AUTOPSY (SPECIFY YES OR NO): Yes
32B. IF YES WERE FINDINGS CONSIDERED IN DETERMINING CAUSE OF DEATH? (SPECIFY YES OR NO): Yes

INJURY INFORMATION

33. SPECIFY ACCIDENT, SUICIDE OR HOMICIDE: Accident
34. PLACE OF INJURY (SPECIFY HOME, FARM, FACTORY, STREET, OFFICE BUILDING, ETC.): Home
35. INJURY AT WORK (SPECIFY YES OR NO): No
36A. DATE OF INJURY—MONTH, DAY, YEAR: 12-12-76
36B. HOUR: Unk.
37A. PLACE OF INJURY (STREET AND NUMBER OR LOCATION AND CITY OR TOWN): 1221 N. King Road - West Hollywood
37B. DISTANCE FROM PLACE OF INJURY TO RESIDENCE (ITEM 19): 0 MILES
38. WERE LABORATORY TESTS DONE FOR DRUGS OR TOXIC CHEMICALS? (SPECIFY YES OR NO): Yes
39. WERE LABORATORY TESTS DONE FOR ALCOHOL? (SPECIFY YES OR NO): Yes
40. DESCRIBE HOW INJURY OCCURRED (ENTER SEQUENCE OF EVENTS WHICH RESULTED IN INJURY. NATURE OF INJURY SHOULD BE ENTERED IN ITEM 29): As above - Housefire

12

STATE REGISTRAR A. B. C. D. E. F. 01-5-4

VS 11 (9-73)

This is to certify that this document is a true copy of the official record filed with the Registrar-Recorder/County Clerk.

[signature] Beatriz Valdez
BEATRIZ VALDEZ
Registrar-Recorder/County Clerk

AUG 16 1995
19-397053

This copy not valid unless prepared on engraved border displaying the Seal and Signature of the Registrar-Recorder/County Clerk.

ANY ALTERATION OR ERASURE VOIDS THIS CERTIFICATE

CERTIFICATION OF VITAL RECORD

COUNTY OF LOS ANGELES • REGISTRAR-RECORDER/COUNTY CLERK

CERTIFICATE OF DEATH

STATE OF CALIFORNIA—DEPARTMENT OF PUBLIC HEALTH

STATE FILE NUMBER

LOCAL REGISTRATION DISTRICT AND CERTIFICATE NUMBER 7022 10808

DECEDENT PERSONAL DATA

- 1a. Name of Deceased—First Name: Ira aka Jeff
- 1b. Middle Name:
- 1c. Last Name: Grossel Chandler
- 2a. Date of Death: June 17, 1961
- 2b. Hour: 4:35 P. M.
- 3. Sex: Male
- 4. Color or Race: Cauc.
- 5. Birthplace: New York
- 6. Date of Birth: December 15, 1918
- 7. Age (last birthday): 42 Years
- 8. Name and Birthplace of Father: Phillip Grossel-New York
- 9. Maiden Name and Birthplace of Mother: Anna Shapiro-Russia
- 10. Citizen of What Country: U.S.A.
- 11. Social Security Number: 130-10-0476
- 12. Last Occupation: Actor
- 13. Number of Years in This Occupation: 16
- 14. Name of Last Employing Company or Firm: Warner Brothers
- 15. Kind of Industry or Business: Motion Pictures
- 16. If Deceased Was Ever in U.S. Armed Forces, Give War or Dates of Service: World War II
- 17. Specify Married, Never Married, Widowed, Divorced: Divorced
- 18a. Name of Present Spouse:
- 18b. Present or Last Occupation of Spouse:

PLACE OF DEATH

- 19a. Place of Death—Name of Hospital: Culver City Hospital
- 19b. Street Address: 3828 Hughes Avenue (Inside city corporate limits: ☒)
- 19c. City or Town: Culver City
- 19d. County: Los Angeles
- 19e. Length of Stay in County of Death: 17 Years
- 19f. Length of Stay in California: 17 Years

LAST USUAL RESIDENCE

- 20a. Last Usual Residence—Street Address: 1152 San Ysidro Drive
- 20b. If Inside City Corporate Limits: ☒
- 20c. City or Town: Beverly Hills
- 20d. County: Los Angeles
- 20e. State: California
- 21a. Name of Informant: Phillip Grossel
- 21b. Address of Informant: 1427 N. Laurel Ave. Los Angeles

PHYSICIAN'S OR CORONER'S CERTIFICATION

- 22a. Physician: I hereby certify that death occurred at the hour date and place stated above from the causes stated below and that I attended the deceased from 5/1/61 to 6/17/61 and that I last saw the deceased alive on 6/17/61
- 22c. Physician or Coroner—Signature: Robert E. Rakney MD
- 22d. Address: 1015 Gayley Ave Los Angeles
- 22e. Date Signed: 6/18/61

FUNERAL DIRECTOR AND LOCAL REGISTRAR

- 23. Specify Burial, Entombment or Cremation: Entombment
- 24. Date: 6-19-61
- 25. Name of Cemetery or Crematory: Hillside Mausoleum
- 26. Embalmer—Signature: Robert Hengel — License Number 4470
- 27. Name of Funeral Director: Malinow and Silverman
- 28. Date Accepted for Registration by Local Registrar: JUN 19 1961
- 29. Local Registrar—Signature: [signature] Lillian L. McKenzie

CAUSE OF DEATH

30. Part I. Death was caused by:

	Cause	Approximate interval between onset and death
Immediate cause (a)	Shock - peripheral vascular collapse	12 hrs
Due to (b)	Staphylococci septicemia	4 days
Due to (c)	Pneumonitis	4 days

Part II: Other significant conditions contributing to death but not related to the terminal disease condition given in Part I (a): Bone marrow depression

OPERATION AND AUTOPSY

- 31. Operation: ☒ Operation performed—findings used in determining above stated causes of death
- 32. Date of Operation: 6/8/61
- 33. Autopsy: ☒ Autopsy performed—gross findings used in determining above stated causes of death

INJURY INFORMATION

- 34a. Specify Accident, Suicide or Homicide:
- 34b. Describe How Injury Occurred:
- 35a. Time of Injury:
- 35b. Injury Occurred: ☐ While at work ☐ Not while at work
- 35c. Place of Injury:
- 35d. City, Town, or Location:

(Margin annotation: *32: Dr states: For ac. Cholecystitis, 1m 12 cc & 1 cc free for V.A., 6-23-61)

Filed JUL 14 1961 RAY E. LEE, COUNTY RECORDER

This is to certify that this document is a true copy of the official record filed with the Registrar-Recorder/County Clerk.

Beatriz Valdez
BEATRIZ VALDEZ
Registrar-Recorder/County Clerk

AUG 25 1995
19-399112

This copy not valid unless prepared on engraved border displaying the Seal and Signature of the Registrar-Recorder/County Clerk.

ANY ALTERATION OR ERASURE VOIDS THIS CERTIFICATE

CERTIFICATION OF VITAL RECORD

COUNTY OF LOS ANGELES • REGISTRAR-RECORDER/COUNTY CLERK

C-9427

STATE OF CALIFORNIA
DEPARTMENT OF PUBLIC HEALTH
VITAL STATISTICS
STANDARD CERTIFICATE OF DEATH

30-042405

Local Registered No. 9427

1 PLACE OF DEATH. Dist. No. 1901 (To be inserted by Registrar)
County of Los Angeles
City or Town of Los Angeles
or Rural Registration District
(No. St. Vincents Hospital St.; Ward) [If death occurred in a hospital or institution, give its NAME instead of street and number.]

2 FULL NAME Lon F. Chaney

PERSONAL AND STATISTICAL PARTICULARS

3 SEX Male
4 COLOR OR RACE White
5 SINGLE, MARRIED, WIDOWED, OR DIVORCED (Write the word) Married
5a If married, widowed, or divorced HUSBAND of (or) WIFE of Hazel G Chaney
6 DATE OF BIRTH April 1 1883 (Month) (Day) (Year)
7 AGE 47 years 4 months 25 days. If LESS than 1 day, — hrs. or min.
8 OCCUPATION (a) Trade, profession, or particular kind of work (b) General nature of industry, business, or establishment in which employed (or employer) Motion Picture Actor
(c) Name of employer
9 BIRTHPLACE (State or country, city or town) Colorado

PARENTS
10 NAME OF FATHER Frank C. Chaney
11 BIRTHPLACE OF FATHER (city or town) (State or Country) Ohio
12 MAIDEN NAME OF MOTHER Emma Kennedy
13 BIRTHPLACE OF MOTHER (city or town) (State or Country) Colorado

14 LENGTH OF RESIDENCE At Place of Death 18 years months days
(Primary registration district) (If nonresident, give city or town and state)
In California 18 years months days
How long in U.S., if of foreign birth? years months days

15 THE ABOVE IS TRUE TO THE BEST OF MY KNOWLEDGE
(Informant) Hazel G. Chaney
(Address) Beverly Wilshre Hotel
George Parrish Dep. [illegible]

16 Filed AUG 28 1930 [illegible] REGISTRAR
By [illegible] DEPUTY

MEDICAL CERTIFICATE OF DEATH

17 DATE OF DEATH August 26, 1930 (Month) (Day) (Year)

18 I HEREBY CERTIFY, That I attended deceased from April 1925 to Aug 26 1930, that I last saw h[illegible] alive on Aug 26 1930 and that death occurred on the date stated above at 12⁵⁵ a.m.

The CAUSE OF DEATH* was as follows:
Carcinoma of right lower and [illegible] of upper bronchus —
(Duration) years 10 months days
Contributory Pulmonary hemorrhage not T.B.
(Duration) years 4 months days

18a Where was disease contracted ✓
If not at place of death?
Did an operation precede death? no Date of
Was there an autopsy? no
What test confirmed diagnosis? [illegible] and bronchoscopic [illegible]
(Signed) John C. [illegible] M.D.
Aug 26 1930 (Address) 834 Pac. Mut. Bldg.

*State the DISEASE CAUSING DEATH, or, in deaths from VIOLENT CAUSES, state (1) MEANS OF INJURY; and (2) whether (probably) ACCIDENTAL, SUICIDAL, or HOMICIDAL. (See reverse side for additional space.)

19 PLACE OF BURIAL OR REMOVAL Forest Lawn Mausoleum
DATE OF BURIAL Aug 28, 1930
20 UNDERTAKER CUNNINGHAM & O'CONNOR
ADDRESS 2051 SOUTH GRAND AVE
EMBALMER'S LICENSE No. 1968

This is to certify that this document is a true copy of the official record filed with the Registrar-Recorder/County Clerk.

Beatriz Valdez
BEATRIZ VALDEZ
Registrar-Recorder/County Clerk

AUG 04 1995
19-390015

This copy not valid unless prepared on engraved border displaying the Seal and Signature of the Registrar-Recorder/County Clerk.

THE GREAT SEAL OF THE STATE OF CALIFORNIA EUREKA

REGISTRAR-RECORDER/COUNTY CLERK • COUNTY OF LOS ANGELES • CALIFORNIA

American Bank Note Company

ANY ALTERATION OR ERASURE VOIDS THIS CERTIFICATE

CERTIFICATE OF DEATH

STATE OF CALIFORNIA
USE BLACK INK ONLY/NO ERASURES, WHITEOUTS OR ALTERATIONS
VS-11 (REV. 7/93)

STATE FILE NUMBER — LOCAL REGISTRATION NUMBER

DECEDENT PERSONAL DATA

1. NAME OF DECEDENT—FIRST (GIVEN): JOHN
2. MIDDLE: WILLIAM
3. LAST (FAMILY): CONRAD
4. DATE OF BIRTH MM/DD/CCYY: 09/27/1920
5. AGE YRS.: 73
IF UNDER 1 YEAR (MONTHS / DAYS) — IF UNDER 24 HOURS (HOURS / MINUTES)
6. SEX: M
7. DATE OF DEATH MM/DD/CCYY: 02/11/1994
8. HOUR: 1331
9. STATE OF BIRTH: KY
10. SOCIAL SECURITY NO.: 545-28-6151
11. MILITARY SERVICE: 19 42 TO 19 46 ☐ NONE
12. MARITAL STATUS: MARRIED
13. EDUCATION—YEARS COMPLETED: 14
14. RACE: CAUCASIAN
15. HISPANIC—SPECIFY: ☐ YES [X] NO
16. USUAL EMPLOYER: SELF EMPLOYED
17. OCCUPATION: ACTOR
18. KIND OF BUSINESS: ENTERTAINMENT
19. YEARS IN OCCUPATION: 57

USUAL RESIDENCE

20. RESIDENCE—STREET AND NUMBER OR LOCATION: 15250 VENTURA BLVD. #900
21. CITY: SHERMAN OAKS
22. COUNTY: LOS ANGELES
23. ZIP CODE: 91403
24. YRS IN COUNTY: 60
25. STATE OR FOREIGN COUNTRY: CALIFORNIA

INFORMANT

26. NAME, RELATIONSHIP: TIPTON CONRAD, WIFE
27. MAILING ADDRESS (STREET AND NUMBER OR RURAL ROUTE NUMBER, CITY OR TOWN, STATE, ZIP): 15250 VENTURA BLVD. #900, SHERMAN OAKS, CA. 91403

SPOUSE AND PARENT INFORMATION

28. NAME OF SURVIVING SPOUSE—FIRST: LEWIS
29. MIDDLE: TIPTON
30. LAST (MAIDEN NAME): STRINGER
31. NAME OF FATHER—FIRST: WILLIAM
32. MIDDLE: -
33. LAST: CANN
34. BIRTH STATE: AL
35. NAME OF MOTHER—FIRST: IDA
36. MIDDLE: MAE
37. LAST (MAIDEN): UPCHURCH
38. BIRTH STATE: AL

DISPOSITION(S)

39. DATE MM/DD/CCYY: 02/16/1994
40. PLACE OF FINAL DISPOSITION: FOREST LAWN MEMORIAL PARK, LOS ANGELES, CA. 90068

FUNERAL DIRECTOR AND LOCAL REGISTRAR

41. TYPE OF DISPOSITION(S): CREMATION/BURIAL
42. SIGNATURE OF EMBALMER: ▶ Elizabeth Derrick
43. LICENSE NO.: 7435
44. NAME OF FUNERAL DIRECTOR: FOREST LAWN HOLLYWOOD HILLS
45. LICENSE NO.: F 904
46. SIGNATURE OF LOCAL REGISTRAR: ▶ Robert C. [illegible]
47. DATE MM/DD/CCYY: 02/15/1994

PLACE OF DEATH

101. PLACE OF DEATH: MED. CTR. OF N. HOLLYWOOD
102. IF HOSPITAL, SPECIFY ONE: ☐ IP [X] ER/OP ☐ DOA
103. FACILITY OTHER THAN HOSPITAL: ☐ CONV. HOSP. ☐ RES. ☐ OTHER
104. COUNTY: LOS ANGELES
105. STREET ADDRESS—STREET AND NUMBER OR LOCATION: 12629 RIVERSIDE DR.
106. CITY: NORTH HOLLYWOOD

CAUSE OF DEATH

107. DEATH WAS CAUSED BY: (ENTER ONLY ONE CAUSE PER LINE FOR A, B, C, AND D)

		Cause	Time interval between onset and death
IMMEDIATE CAUSE	(A)	CARDIOPULMONARY ARREST	1 MIN
DUE TO	(B)	ARTERIOSCLEROTIC HEART DISEASE	5 YRS
DUE TO	(C)		
DUE TO	(D)		

108. DEATH REPORTED TO CORONER: ☐ YES [X] NO — REFERRAL NUMBER
109. BIOPSY PERFORMED: ☐ YES [X] NO
110. AUTOPSY PERFORMED: ☐ YES [X] NO
111. USED IN DETERMINING CAUSE: ☐ YES ☐ NO
112. OTHER SIGNIFICANT CONDITIONS CONTRIBUTING TO DEATH BUT NOT RELATED TO CAUSE GIVEN IN 107: END STAGE RENAL DISEASE
113. WAS OPERATION PERFORMED FOR ANY CONDITION IN ITEM 107 OR 112? IF YES, LIST TYPE OF OPERATION AND DATE.: PERITONEAL CATHETER RESECTION 03/01/1993

PHYSICIAN'S CERTIFICATION

114. I CERTIFY THAT TO THE BEST OF MY KNOWLEDGE DEATH OCCURRED AT THE HOUR, DATE AND PLACE STATED FROM THE CAUSES STATED.
DECEDENT ATTENDED SINCE MM/DD/CCYY: 02/01/1992 — DECEDENT LAST SEEN ALIVE MM/DD/CCYY: 02/05/1994
115. SIGNATURE AND TITLE OF CERTIFIER: ▶ [signature] MD
116. LICENSE NO.: G033719
117. DATE MM/DD/CCYY: 02/14/1994
118. TYPE ATTENDING PHYSICIAN'S NAME, MAILING ADDRESS + ZIP: ISAAC GORBATY,MD,4835 VAN NUYS BLVD.,SHERMAN OAKS, CA. 91403

CORONER'S USE ONLY

I CERTIFY THAT IN MY OPINION DEATH OCCURRED AT THE HOUR, DATE AND PLACE STATED FROM THE CAUSES STATED.
119. MANNER OF DEATH: ☐ NATURAL ☐ SUICIDE ☐ HOMICIDE ☐ ACCIDENT ☐ PENDING INVESTIGATION ☐ COULD NOT BE DETERMINED
120. INJURY AT WORK: ☐ YES ☐ NO
121. INJURY DATE MM/DD/CCYY
122. HOUR
123. PLACE OF INJURY
124. DESCRIBE HOW INJURY OCCURRED (EVENTS WHICH RESULTED IN INJURY)
125. LOCATION (STREET AND NUMBER OR LOCATION AND CITY AND ZIP CODE)
126. SIGNATURE OF CORONER OR DEPUTY CORONER ▶
127. DATE MM/DD/CCYY
128. TYPED NAME, TITLE OF CORONER OR DEPUTY CORONER

10

STATE REGISTRAR

A	B	C	D	E	F	G	H	FAX AUTH. #	CENSUS TRACT

4110 — 01-7-1-065

CERTIFICATION OF VITAL RECORD

COUNTY OF LOS ANGELES • REGISTRAR-RECORDER/COUNTY CLERK

CERTIFICATE OF DEATH

STATE OF CALIFORNIA—DEPARTMENT OF PUBLIC HEALTH

Local Registration District and Certificate Number: 7053 9361

DECEDENT PERSONAL DATA

1a. Name of Deceased—First Name: Gary
1b. Middle Name:
1c. Last Name: COOPER
2a. Date of Death: May 13, 1961
2b. Hour: 12:27 P.M.
3. Sex: Male
4. Color or Race: White
5. Birthplace: Helena, Montana
6. Date of Birth: May 7, 1901
7. Age: 60 Years
8. Name and Birthplace of Father: Charles H. Cooper, England
9. Maiden Name and Birthplace of Mother: Alice Brazier, England
10. Citizen of What Country: United States
11. Social Security Number: 564 18 4956
12. Last Occupation: Actor
13. Number of Years in This Occupation: 35 Yrs
14. Name of Last Employing Company or Firm: Baroda Productions, Inc.
15. Kind of Industry or Business: Motion Pictures
16. If Deceased Was Ever in U.S. Armed Forces, Give War or Dates of Service: No
17. Specify Married, Never Married, Widowed, Divorced: Married
18a. Name of Present Spouse: Veronica B. Cooper
18b. Present or Last Occupation of Spouse: Housewife

PLACE OF DEATH

19a. Place of Death—Name of Hospital:
19b. Street Address: 200 No. Baroda — [X] Inside City Corporate Limits
19c. City or Town: Los Angeles
19d. County: Los Angeles
19e. Length of Stay in County of Death: 35 Yrs
19f. Length of Stay in California: 35 Yrs

LAST USUAL RESIDENCE

20a. Last Usual Residence—Street Address: 200 No. Baroda
20b. If Inside City Corporate Limits: [X] Check Here
20c. City or Town: Los Angeles 262
20d. County: Los Angeles
20e. State: California
21a. Name of Informant: Mrs. Veronica B. Cooper
21b. Address of Informant: Same

PHYSICIAN'S OR CORONER'S CERTIFICATION

22a. Physician: I hereby certify that death occurred at the hour, date and place stated above from the causes stated below and that I attended the deceased from 12-24-60 to 5/13/61 and that I last saw the deceased alive on 5-13-61
22a. Coroner:
22c. Physician or Coroner—Signature: S R Kennamer M.D.
22d. Address: 436 No. Roxbury Dr., B.H.
22e. Date Signed: 5/15/61

FUNERAL DIRECTOR AND LOCAL REGISTRAR

23. Specify Burial, Entombment, Cremation: Burial
24. Date: 5/16/61
25. Name of Cemetery or Crematory: Holy Cross Cemetery
26. Embalmer—Signature: Charles L. Mercer — License Number 2210
27. Name of Funeral Director: Cunningham & O'Connor, L.A.
28. Date Accepted for Registration by Local Registrar: MAY 15 1961
29. Local Registrar—Signature: George M. Uhl, M.D.

CAUSE OF DEATH

30. Cause of Death — Part I. Death was caused by: Immediate Cause (a): Carcinoma of Colon — Approximate interval between onset and death: 9 mths.
Due to (b):
Due to (c):
Part II. Other significant conditions contributing to death but not related to the terminal disease condition given in Part I (a):

OPERATION AND AUTOPSY

31. Operation—Check One: [X] Operation performed—findings used in determining above stated causes of death
32. Date of Operation: 5/31/60
33. Autopsy—Check One: [X] No autopsy performed

INJURY INFORMATION

34a. Specify Accident, Suicide or Homicide:
34b. Describe How Injury Occurred:
35a. Time of Injury:
35b. Injury Occurred: [ ] While at work [ ] Not while at work
35c. Place of Injury:
35d. City, Town, or Location: County: State:

This is to certify that this document is a true copy of the official record filed with the Registrar-Recorder/County Clerk.

Beatriz Valdez
BEATRIZ VALDEZ
Registrar-Recorder/County Clerk

AUG 04 1995

19-390011

This copy not valid unless prepared on engraved border displaying the Seal and Signature of the Registrar-Recorder/County Clerk.

American Bank Note Company — ANY ALTERATION OR ERASURE VOIDS THIS CERTIFICATE

CERTIFICATION OF VITAL RECORD

COUNTY OF LOS ANGELES • REGISTRAR-RECORDER/COUNTY CLERK

CERTIFICATE OF DEATH

STATE OF CALIFORNIA—DEPARTMENT OF PUBLIC HEALTH

LOCAL REGISTRATION DISTRICT AND CERTIFICATE NUMBER 7053 4694

DECEDENT PERSONAL DATA

1a. Name of deceased—First name: Louis (Lou) 1b. Middle name: Francis 1c. Last name: Cristillo (aka Costello)
2a. Date of death: March 3, 1959 2b. Hour: 3:55P
3. Sex: Male 4. Color or race: cauc 5. Birthplace: New Jersey 6. Date of birth: March 6, 1906 7. Age: 52 years
8. Name and birthplace of father: Sebastian Cristillo-Italy 9. Maiden name and birthplace of mother: Helen Rege-New Jersey 10. Citizen of what country: USA 11. Social security number: 151-07-5152
12. Last occupation: Actor 13. Number of years in this occupation: 35 14. Name of last employing company or firm: DRB Productions Inc. 15. Kind of industry or business: Motion Picture & Stage & Television
16. If deceased was ever in U.S. armed forces: no 17. Specify married, never married, widowed, divorced: Married 18a. Name of present spouse: Anne Cristillo 18b. Present or last occupation of spouse: Housewife

PLACE OF DEATH

19a. Place of death—Name of hospital: Beverly Hills Doctor Hospital 19b. Street address: 10390 Santa Monica Blvd.
19c. City or town: Los Angeles 19d. County: Los Angeles 19e. Length of stay in county of death: 19 years 19f. Length of stay in California: 19 years

LAST USUAL RESIDENCE

20a. Last usual residence—Street address: 4222 Ethel Ave. 20b. If inside city corporate limits: [X]
20c. City or town: Los Angeles (Studio City) 20d. County: Los Angeles 20e. State: California
21a. Name of informant: Anne Cristillo 21b. Address of informant: 4222 Ethel Ave. Studio City

PHYSICIAN'S OR CORONER'S CERTIFICATION

22a. Physician: I hereby certify that death occurred at the hour, date and place stated above from the causes stated below and that I attended the deceased from 2/25/59 to 3/3/59 and that I last saw the deceased alive on 3/3/59
22c. Physician or coroner—Signature: [signature] M.D.
22d. Address: 435 N. Roxbury Dr. Beverly Hills 22e. Date signed: 3/3/59

FUNERAL DIRECTOR AND LOCAL REGISTRAR

23. Specify burial, entombment or cremation: Entombment 24. Date: 3/7/59 25. Name of cemetery or crematory: Calvary Cemetery 26. Embalmer—Signature: [signature] License number: 2508
27. Name of funeral director: Steen's Chapel 28. Date accepted for registration by local registrar: MAR 5 1959 29. Local registrar: [signature]

CAUSE OF DEATH

30. Part I. Death was caused by: Immediate cause (A): Ventricular fibrillation — Approximate interval between onset and death: Final
Due to (B): Hypertension + Rheumatic Heart Disease — 10 yrs
Due to (C): Sub Acute Mesenteric Thrombosis c̄ Ileus and Perforation — 1 wk

OPERATION AND AUTOPSY

31. Operation: [X] No operation performed 33. Autopsy: [X] Gross findings used in determining above stated causes of death

This is to certify that this document is a true copy of the official record filed with the Registrar-Recorder/County Clerk.

OCT 02 1995

19 033995

This copy not valid unless prepared on engraved border displaying the Seal of the Registrar-Recorder/County Clerk.

ANY ALTERATION OR ERASURE VOIDS THIS CERTIFICATE

BOOK 1986 PAGE

CERTIFICATE OF DEATH
STATE OF CALIFORNIA

STATE FILE NUMBER

33 002445
LOCAL REGISTRATION DISTRICT AND CERTIFICATE NUMBER

DECEDENT PERSONAL DATA

1A. NAME OF DECEDENT—FIRST: WILLIAM AKA BRODERICK
1B. MIDDLE: BRODERICK
1C. LAST: CRAWFORD
2A. DATE OF DEATH (MONTH, DAY, YEAR): April 26, 1986
2B. HOUR: 1340 hrs
3. SEX: Male
4. RACE/ETHNICITY: White
5. SPANISH/HISPANIC: NO ☒
6. DATE OF BIRTH: December 9, 1911
7. AGE: 74 YEARS
IF UNDER 1 YEAR: MONTHS / DAYS
IF UNDER 24 HOURS: HOURS / MINUTES
8. BIRTHPLACE OF DECEDENT (STATE OR FOREIGN COUNTRY): Pennsylvania
9. NAME AND BIRTHPLACE OF FATHER: LESTER C. PENDERGAST - NEW YORK
10. BIRTH NAME AND BIRTHPLACE OF MOTHER: HELEN BRODERICK - PA
11A. CITIZEN OF WHAT COUNTRY: U.S.A.
11B. IF DECEASED WAS EVER IN MILITARY GIVE DATES OF SERVICE: 19__ TO 19__
12. SOCIAL SECURITY NUMBER: 565-14-8920
13. MARITAL STATUS: Married
14. NAME OF SURVIVING SPOUSE (IF WIFE, ENTER BIRTH NAME): Mary Alice Moore
15. PRIMARY OCCUPATION: Actor
16. NUMBER OF YEARS THIS OCCUPATION: Adult Life
17. EMPLOYER (IF SELF-EMPLOYED, SO STATE): Screen Actors Guild
18. KIND OF INDUSTRY OR BUSINESS: Entertainment

USUAL RESIDENCE

19A. USUAL RESIDENCE—STREET ADDRESS (STREET AND NUMBER OR LOCATION): 2265 SOUTH BEVERLY GLEN
19B.
19C. CITY OR TOWN: LOS ANGELES
19D. COUNTY: LOS ANGELES
19E. STATE: California
20. NAME AND ADDRESS OF INFORMANT—RELATIONSHIP: Mr. Kelly G. Crawford - Son / CONSERVATOR, 3636 Barham Boulevard, Los Angeles, California 90068

PLACE OF DEATH

21A. PLACE OF DEATH: Eisenhower Medical Center
21B. COUNTY: Riverside
21C. STREET ADDRESS (STREET AND NUMBER OR LOCATION): 39000 Bob Hope Drive
21D. CITY OR TOWN: Palm Desert

CAUSE OF DEATH

22. DEATH WAS CAUSED BY: (ENTER ONLY ONE CAUSE PER LINE FOR A, B, AND C)
IMMEDIATE CAUSE
(A) RESPIRATORY ARREST — APPROXIMATE INTERVAL BETWEEN ONSET AND DEATH: 5 MIN
CONDITIONS, IF ANY, WHICH GAVE RISE TO THE IMMEDIATE CAUSE, STATING THE UNDERLYING CAUSE LAST.
DUE TO, OR AS A CONSEQUENCE OF
(B) PNEUMONIA — 2 WKS
DUE TO, OR AS A CONSEQUENCE OF
(C) -
24. WAS DEATH REPORTED TO CORONER? NO
25. WAS BIOPSY PERFORMED? NO
26. WAS AUTOPSY PERFORMED? NO
23. OTHER SIGNIFICANT CONDITIONS—CONTRIBUTING TO DEATH BUT NOT RELATED TO CAUSE GIVEN IN 22A: MULTIPLE CEREBROVASCULAR ACCIDENTS
27. WAS OPERATION PERFORMED FOR ANY CONDITION IN ITEMS 22 OR 23? TYPE OF OPERATION: NO
DATE

PHYSICIAN'S CERTIFICATION

28A. I CERTIFY THAT DEATH OCCURRED AT THE HOUR, DATE AND PLACE STATED FROM THE CAUSES STATED.
I ATTENDED DECEDENT SINCE (ENTER MO. DA. YR.): 4-7-86
I LAST SAW DECEDENT ALIVE (ENTER MO. DA. YR.): 4-26-86
28B. PHYSICIAN—SIGNATURE AND DEGREE OR TITLE: [signature] MD
28C. DATE SIGNED: 4-27-86
28D. PHYSICIAN'S LICENSE NUMBER: G 29026
28E. TYPE PHYSICIAN'S NAME AND ADDRESS: Robert B. Waterbor 1695 N. Sunrise Wy, Palm Springs, CA

INJURY INFORMATION

29. SPECIFY ACCIDENT, SUICIDE, ETC.
30. PLACE OF INJURY
31. INJURY AT WORK
32A. DATE OF INJURY—MONTH, DAY, YEAR
32B. HOUR
33. LOCATION (STREET AND NUMBER OR LOCATION AND CITY OR TOWN)
34. DESCRIBE HOW INJURY OCCURRED (EVENTS WHICH RESULTED IN INJURY)

CORONER'S USE ONLY

35A. I CERTIFY THAT DEATH OCCURRED AT THE HOUR, DATE AND PLACE STATED FROM THE CAUSES STATED. AS REQUIRED BY LAW I HAVE HELD AN (INQUEST-INVESTIGATION)
35B. CORONER—SIGNATURE AND DEGREE OR TITLE
35C. DATE SIGNED

36. DISPOSITION: BURIAL
37. DATE—MONTH, DAY, YEAR: MAY 6, 1986
38. NAME AND ADDRESS OF CEMETERY OR CREMATORY: GLOVERSVILLE CEMETERY, GLOVERSVILLE. N.Y.
39. EMBALMER'S LICENSE NUMBER AND SIGNATURE: 5377 [signature]
40A. NAME OF FUNERAL DIRECTOR (OR PERSON ACTING AS SUCH): PIERCE BROS.MOELLER MURPHY
40B. LICENSE NO.: F 695
41. LOCAL REGISTRAR—SIGNATURE: [signature]
42. DATE ACCEPTED BY LOCAL REGISTRAR: MAY 01 1986

STATE REGISTRAR: A. B. C. D. E. F.

VS-11 (1-85)

CERTIFICATION OF VITAL RECORD

COUNTY OF LOS ANGELES • REGISTRAR-RECORDER/COUNTY CLERK

Filed DEC 17 1965 RAY E. LEE, COUNTY RECORDER

STATE FILE NUMBER

CERTIFICATE OF DEATH

STATE OF CALIFORNIA—DEPARTMENT OF PUBLIC HEALTH

LOCAL REGISTRATION DISTRICT AND CERTIFICATE NUMBER 7097 46060

1 of 2

DECEDENT PERSONAL DATA

1A. NAME OF DECEASED—FIRST NAME: Dorothy
1B. MIDDLE NAME: Jean
1C. LAST NAME: Dandridge
2A. DATE OF DEATH: Sept. 8, 1965
2B. HOUR: approx. 2:27p M.
3. SEX: Female
4. COLOR OR RACE: Negro
5. BIRTHPLACE: Cleveland, Ohio
6. DATE OF BIRTH: 11/9/22
7. AGE: 42 YEARS
8. NAME AND BIRTHPLACE OF FATHER: Arril Dandridge Ohio
9. MAIDEN NAME AND BIRTHPLACE OF MOTHER: Ruby Jean Butler Miss.
10. CITIZEN OF WHAT COUNTRY: U.S.A.
11. SOCIAL SECURITY NUMBER: Unk.
12. LAST OCCUPATION: Actress- Singer
13. NUMBER OF YEARS IN THIS OCCUPATION: 39
14. NAME OF LAST EMPLOYING COMPANY OR FIRM: Self Employed
15. KIND OF INDUSTRY OR BUSINESS: Show Business
16. IF DECEASED WAS EVER IN U.S. ARMED FORCES, GIVE WAR OR DATES OF SERVICE: None
17. SPECIFY MARRIED, NEVER MARRIED, WIDOWED, DIVORCED: Divorced
18A. NAME OF PRESENT SPOUSE: None
18B. PRESENT OR LAST OCCUPATION OF SPOUSE: None

PLACE OF DEATH

19A. PLACE OF DEATH—NAME OF HOSPITAL:
19B. STREET ADDRESS: 8495 Fountain Ave. Apt. D-2 — [X] OUTSIDE CITY CORPORATE LIMITS
19C. CITY OR TOWN: West Hollywood
19D. COUNTY: Los Angeles
19E. LENGTH OF STAY IN COUNTY OF DEATH: 33 YEARS
19F. LENGTH OF STAY IN CALIFORNIA: 33 YEARS

LAST USUAL RESIDENCE

20A. LAST USUAL RESIDENCE—STREET ADDRESS: 8495 Fountain Avenue
20B. IF INSIDE CITY CORPORATE LIMITS / IF OUTSIDE CITY CORPORATE LIMITS: [X] NOT ON A FARM
20C. CITY OR TOWN: West Hollywood 8797
20D. COUNTY: Los Angeles
20E. STATE: California
21A. NAME OF INFORMANT: Ruby Dandridge
21B. ADDRESS OF INFORMANT: 3737 Homeland Avenue

PHYSICIAN'S OR CORONER'S CERTIFICATION

22A. PHYSICIAN: I HEREBY CERTIFY THAT DEATH OCCURRED AT THE HOUR, DATE AND PLACE STATED ABOVE FROM THE CAUSES STATED BELOW AND THAT I ATTENDED THE DECEASED FROM ___ AND THAT I LAST SAW THE DECEASED ALIVE ON ___
22B. CORONER: I HEREBY CERTIFY THAT DEATH OCCURRED AT THE HOUR, DATE AND PLACE STATED ABOVE FROM THE CAUSES STATED BELOW AND THAT I HAVE HELD AN autopsy ON THE REMAINS OF DECEASED AS REQUIRED BY LAW
22C. PHYSICIAN OR CORONER—SIGNATURE: Theo. J. Curphey, M.D., Chief Medical Examiner-Coroner — Deputy
22D. ADDRESS: Hall of Justice, Los Angeles
22E. DATE SIGNED: 11-19-65

FUNERAL DIRECTOR AND LOCAL REGISTRAR

23. SPECIFY BURIAL, ENTOMBMENT OR CREMATION: Cremation
24. DATE: 9/11/65
25. NAME OF CEMETERY OR CREMATORY: Forest Lawn Crematory
26. EMBALMER—SIGNATURE / LICENSE NUMBER: 3687
27. NAME OF FUNERAL DIRECTOR: Angelus Funeral Home
28. DATE ACCEPTED FOR REGISTRATION BY LOCAL REGISTRAR: NOV 24 1965
29. LOCAL REGISTRAR—SIGNATURE: dep.

20813

Dorothy Dandridge

H. Kade, M.D.

CAUSE OF DEATH

30. CAUSE OF DEATH
PART I. DEATH WAS CAUSED BY: IMMEDIATE CAUSE (A) Acute drug intoxication.
DUE TO (B) Ingestion of Tofranil.
DUE TO (C)
PART II. OTHER SIGNIFICANT CONDITIONS CONTRIBUTING TO DEATH BUT NOT RELATED TO THE TERMINAL DISEASE CONDITION GIVEN IN PART I (A)
APPROXIMATE INTERVAL BETWEEN ONSET AND DEATH

OPERATION AND AUTOPSY

31. OPERATION—CHECK ONE: [X] NO OPERATION PERFORMED
32. DATE OF OPERATION:
33. AUTOPSY—CHECK ONE: [X] AUTOPSY PERFORMED—GROSS FINDINGS USED IN DETERMINING ABOVE STATED CAUSES OF DEATH

INJURY INFORMATION

34A. SPECIFY ACCIDENT, SUICIDE OR HOMICIDE: Accident - Suicide - Undetermined
34B. DESCRIBE HOW INJURY OCCURRED: As Above
35A. TIME OF INJURY: 2:27p M. 9-8-65
35B. INJURY OCCURRED: [X] NOT WHILE AT WORK
35C. PLACE OF INJURY: Home
35D. CITY, TOWN, OR LOCATION / COUNTY / STATE: West Hollywood, L.A., California

Final Nov. 19, 1965

MEDICAL AND HEALTH DATA

This is to certify that this document is a true copy of the official record filed with the Registrar-Recorder/County Clerk.

SEP 09 1996

19-363348

CONNY B. McCORMACK
Registrar-Recorder/County Clerk

This copy not valid unless prepared on engraved border displaying the Seal and Signature of the Registrar-Recorder/County Clerk.

ANY ALTERATION OR ERASURE VOIDS THIS CERTIFICATE

CERTIFICATION OF VITAL RECORD

COUNTY OF LOS ANGELES • REGISTRAR-RECORDER/COUNTY CLERK

66 900

Coroner's Case # 20813

AMENDMENT OF MEDICAL AND HEALTH SECTION DATA

STATE FILE NO. 65-135547 [X] DEATH RECORD [ ] FETAL DEATH RECORD [ ] BIRTH RECORD REGISTRATION DISTRICT NO. 7097 REGISTRAR'S NUMBER 46060

REGISTRANT INFORMATION SEE INSTRUCTIONS ON REVERSE

1A. FIRST NAME	1B. MIDDLE NAME	1C. LAST NAME
Dorothy	Jean	Dandridge

2. PLACE OF OCCURRENCE—CITY OR COUNTY	3. DATE OF EVENT	4. DATE ORIGINAL FILED
Los Angeles	9-8-65	11-24-65

5. NAME OF FATHER	6. MAIDEN NAME OF MOTHER
Arril Dandridge	Ruby Jean Butler

STATEMENT OF AMENDMENTS

7. ITEM NUMBER	8A. INFORMATION EXACTLY AS STATED ON THE ORIGINAL RECORD	8B. INFORMATION AS IT SHOULD BE STATED ON THE ORIGINAL RECORD
34A	Accident-Suicide-Undetermined	34A Probable Accident

DECLARATION OF CERTIFYING PHYSICIAN OR CORONER

9. I, the [ ] certifying physician [X] coroner, having personal knowledge of supplemental information which modifies the information originally furnished, do certify under penalty of perjury that the information listed under 8B is true and correct to the best of my knowledge.

10A. SIGNATURE OF PHYSICIAN OR CORONER	10B. DEGREE OR TITLE	10C. DATE SIGNED
Theo J. Curphey M.D.	Chief Medical Examiner Coroner	June 9, 1966

11A. NAME OF PHYSICIAN OR CORONER (TYPE OR PRINT)	11B. ADDRESS—STREET ADDRESS	11C. CITY AND STATE
Theodore J. Curphey, M.D.	104 Hall of Justice	Los Angeles, Calif. 90012

FOR USE OF STATE REGISTRAR'S OFFICE

12A.		
12B. DATE ACCEPTED	JUN 16 1966	12C. STATE REGISTRAR LESTER BRESLOW, M.D.

STATE OF CALIFORNIA DEPARTMENT OF PUBLIC HEALTH

BUREAU OF VITAL STATISTICS (REV. 8-17-65) FORM VS-24A

D65-135547 6/14 ... WC53

This is to certify that this document is a true copy of the official record filed with the Registrar-Recorder/County Clerk.

CONNY B. McCORMACK
Registrar-Recorder/County Clerk

SEP 09 1998
19-363350

This copy not valid unless prepared on engraved border displaying the Seal and Signature of the Registrar-Recorder/County Clerk.

ANY ALTERATION OR ERASURE VOIDS THIS CERTIFICATE

CERTIFICATION OF VITAL RECORD

COUNTY OF LOS ANGELES • REGISTRAR-RECORDER/COUNTY CLERK

CERTIFICATE OF DEATH
STATE OF CALIFORNIA
USE BLACK INK ONLY

STATE FILE NUMBER

39119037578
LOCAL REGISTRATION DISTRICT AND CERTIFICATE NUMBER

DECEDENT PERSONAL DATA

1A. NAME OF DECEDENT—FIRST (GIVEN): Robert
1B. MIDDLE: --
1C. LAST (FAMILY): Davis
2A. DATE OF DEATH—MO, DAY, YR: September 8, 1991
2B. HOUR: 1645
3. SEX: M
4. RACE: Caucasian
5. HISPANIC—SPECIFY: [ ] YES [X] NO
6. DATE OF BIRTH—MO, DAY, YR: November 6, 1949
7. AGE IN YEARS: 41
IF UNDER 1 YEAR: MONTHS / DAYS
IF UNDER 24 HOURS: HOURS / MINUTES
8. STATE OF BIRTH: FL
9. CITIZEN OF WHAT COUNTRY: USA
10A. FULL NAME OF FATHER: Eugene Davis
10B. STATE OF BIRTH: FL
11A. FULL MAIDEN NAME OF MOTHER: Annie Creel
11B. STATE OF BIRTH: FL
12. MILITARY SERVICE? 19__ TO 19__ [X] NONE
13. SOCIAL SECURITY NO.: 263-86-0332
14. MARITAL STATUS: Married
15. NAME OF SURVIVING SPOUSE (IF WIFE, ENTER MAIDEN NAME): Susan Bluestein
16A. USUAL OCCUPATION: Actor
16B. USUAL KIND OF BUSINESS OR INDUSTRY: Entertainment
16C. USUAL EMPLOYER: Self-Employed
16D. YEARS IN OCCUPATION: 20
17. EDUCATION—YEARS COMPLETED: 14

1 of 3

USUAL RESIDENCE

18A. RESIDENCE—STREET AND NUMBER OR LOCATION: 4259 Rhodes Avenue
18B. CITY: Studio City
18C. ZIP CODE: 91604
18D. COUNTY: Los Angeles
18E. NUMBER OF YEARS IN THIS COUNTY: 14
18F. STATE OR FOREIGN COUNTRY: California
20. NAME, RELATIONSHIP, MAILING ADDRESS AND ZIP CODE OF INFORMANT: Susan Davis - Wife, 4259 Rhodes Avenue, Studio City, California 91604

PLACE OF DEATH

19A. PLACE OF DEATH: Residence
19B. IF HOSPITAL, SPECIFY ONE: IP, ER/OP, DOA: --
19C. COUNTY: Los Angeles
19D. STREET ADDRESS—STREET AND NUMBER OR LOCATION: 4259 Rhodes Avenue
19E. CITY: Studio City

CAUSE OF DEATH

21. DEATH WAS CAUSED BY: (ENTER ONLY ONE CAUSE PER LINE FOR A, B, AND C)

	Cause	Time interval between onset and death
IMMEDIATE CAUSE (A)	Mycobacteria Avium Complex	1 month
DUE TO (B)	Acquired Immunodeficiency Syndrome	2 yrs
DUE TO (C)	Intravenous Drug Abuse By History	Unk.

22. WAS DEATH REPORTED TO CORONER? [X] YES REFERRAL NUMBER 91-8425 [ ] NO
23. WAS BIOPSY PERFORMED? [ ] YES [X] NO
24A. WAS AUTOPSY PERFORMED? [ ] YES [X] NO
24B. WAS IT USED IN DETERMINING CAUSE OF DEATH? [ ] YES [X] NO
25. OTHER SIGNIFICANT CONDITIONS CONTRIBUTING TO DEATH BUT NOT RELATED TO CAUSE GIVEN IN 21: None
26. WAS OPERATION PERFORMED FOR ANY CONDITION IN ITEM 21 OR 25? IF YES, LIST TYPE OF OPERATION AND DATE: No

PHYSICIAN'S CERTIFICATION

I CERTIFY THAT TO THE BEST OF MY KNOWLEDGE DEATH OCCURRED AT THE HOUR, DATE AND PLACE STATED FROM THE CAUSES STATED.
27A. DECEDENT ATTENDED SINCE MONTH, DAY, YEAR / DECEDENT LAST SEEN ALIVE MONTH, DAY, YEAR
27B. SIGNATURE AND DEGREE OR TITLE OF CERTIFIER
27C. CERTIFIER'S LICENSE NUMBER
27D. DATE SIGNED
27E. TYPE ATTENDING PHYSICIAN'S NAME AND ADDRESS

CORONER'S USE ONLY

10

I CERTIFY THAT IN MY OPINION DEATH OCCURRED AT THE HOUR, DATE AND PLACE STATED FROM THE CAUSES STATED.
28A. SIGNATURE AND TITLE OF CORONER OR DEPUTY CORONER: Deputy Coroner Sandra Fitzgerald
28B. DATE SIGNED: 9/13/91
29. MANNER OF DEATH—specify one natural, accident, suicide, homicide, pending investigation or could not be determined: Accident
30A. PLACE OF INJURY: Unknown
30B. INJURY AT WORK: [ ] YES [X] NO
30C. DATE OF INJURY MONTH, DAY, YEAR: Unknown
31. HOUR: Unk.
32. LOCATION (STREET AND NUMBER OR LOCATION AND CITY): Unknown
33. DESCRIBE HOW INJURY OCCURRED (EVENTS WHICH RESULTED IN INJURY): Intravenous Injection

FUNERAL DIRECTOR AND LOCAL REGISTRAR

34A. DISPOSITION(S): CR/BU
34B. PLACE OF FINAL DISPOSITION—NAME AND ADDRESS: FOREST LAWN MEMORIAL PARK, LOS ANGELES, CA 90068
34C. DATE MO, DAY, YEAR: 9-18-1991
35A. SIGNATURE OF EMBALMER: NOT EMBALMED
35B. LICENSE NUMBER: - - -
36A. NAME OF FUNERAL DIRECTOR (OR PERSON ACTING AS SUCH): Forest Lawn Hollywood Hills Mty
36B. LICENSE NO.: F-904
37. SIGNATURE OF LOCAL REGISTRAR: Robert C. [signature]
38. REGISTRATION DATE: SEP 13 1991

STATE REGISTRAR

A. B. C. D. E. F. CENSUS TRACT

VS-11 (REV. 3-91) 8471 MAKE NO ERASURES, WHITEOUTS, OR OTHER ALTERATIONS 7-9-3-2005

This is to certify that this document is a true copy of the official record filed with the Registrar-Recorder/County Clerk.

Beatriz Valdez
BEATRIZ VALDEZ
Registrar-Recorder/County Clerk

This copy not valid unless prepared on engraved border displaying the Seal and Signature of the Registrar-Recorder/County Clerk.

THE GREAT SEAL OF THE STATE OF CALIFORNIA — EUREKA

REGISTRAR-RECORDER/COUNTY CLERK — COUNTY OF LOS ANGELES • CALIFORNIA

ANY ALTERATION OR ERASURE VOIDS THIS CERTIFICATE

CERTIFICATION OF VITAL RECORD

COUNTY OF LOS ANGELES • REGISTRAR-RECORDER/COUNTY CLERK

PHYSICIAN/CORONER'S AMENDMENT FORM

USE BLACK INK ONLY—MAKE NO ERASURES, WHITEOUTS, OR OTHER ALTERATIONS

925007

STATE FILE NUMBER: 91-156900 ☒ DEATH ☐ FETAL DEATH ☐ BIRTH

LOCAL REGISTRATION DISTRICT AND CERTIFICATE NUMBER: 39119037578

INFORMATION AS REPORTED ON ORIGINAL CERTIFICATE

1A. NAME—FIRST (GIVEN)	1B. MIDDLE	1C. LAST (FAMILY)	1D. SEX
ROBERT		DAVIS	M

2. DATE OF EVENT—MONTH, DAY, YEAR	3A. CITY OF OCCURRENCE	3B. COUNTY OF OCCURRENCE
SEPTEMBER 8, 1991	STUDIO CITY	LOS ANGELES

LIST ONE ITEM PER LINE

4. CERTIFICATE ITEM NUMBER	5A. INCORRECT INFORMATION ON ORIGINAL CERTIFICATE	5B. INFORMATION AS IT SHOULD BE STATED
21A	MYOCOBACTERIA AVIUM COMPLEX 1MONTH	ACUTE BARBITURATE INTOXICATION (UNK)
21B	ACQUIRED IMMUNO DEFICIENCY SYNDROME (2 Yrs)	DELETE
21C	INTRAVENOUS DRUG ABUSE BY HISTORY UNK	DELETE
25	NONE	AIDS (I.v. drug abuse)
29	Accident	Suicide

3OF3

DECLARATION OF CERTIFYING PHYSICIAN OR CORONER

6. I, THE CERTIFYING PHYSICIAN OR CORONER HAVING PERSONAL KNOWLEDGE OF SUPPLEMENTAL INFORMATION WHICH MODIFIES THE INFORMATION ORIGINALLY REPORTED, DECLARE UNDER PENALTY OF PERJURY THAT THE ABOVE INFORMATION IS TRUE AND CORRECT TO THE BEST OF MY KNOWLEDGE.

7A. SIGNATURE OF CERTIFYING PHYSICIAN OR CORONER	7B. DATE SIGNED
[signature]	3/4/92

8A. NAME OF CERTIFYING PHYSICIAN OR CORONER (PRINT OR TYPE)	8B. DEGREE OR TITLE
J. LAWRENCE COGAN, M.D.	DME

8C. ADDRESS—STREET AND NUMBER	8D. CITY	8E. STATE
1104 NO. MISSION RD.,	L.A.	CA

STATE/LOCAL REGISTRAR USE ONLY

9. OFFICE OF STATE OR LOCAL REGISTRAR	10. DATE ACCEPTED FOR REGISTRATION
OFFICE OF THE STATE REGISTRAR OF VITAL STATISTICS	APR 06 1992

STATE OF CALIFORNIA, DEPARTMENT OF HEALTH SERVICES, OFFICE OF STATE REGISTRAR

VS 24A (Rev. 1/89)

This is to certify that this document is a true copy of the official record filed with the Registrar-Recorder/County Clerk.

Beatriz Valdez
BEATRIZ VALDEZ
Registrar-Recorder/County Clerk

19-399455

This copy not valid unless prepared on engraved border displaying the Seal and Signature of the Registrar-Recorder/County Clerk.

American Bank Note Company

ANY ALTERATION OR ERASURE VOIDS THIS CERTIFICATE

CERTIFICATION OF VITAL RECORD

COUNTY OF LOS ANGELES • REGISTRAR-RECORDER/COUNTY CLERK

CERTIFICATE OF DEATH
STATE OF CALIFORNIA
USE BLACK INK ONLY

1A. Name of decedent—First (Given)	SAMMY
1B. Middle	--
1C. Last (Family)	Davis, JR.
2A. Date of death—Mo, Day, Yr	May 16, 1990
2B. Hour	0559
3. Sex	MALE
4. Race	BLACK
5. Spanish/Hispanic—Specify	[ ] Yes [X] No
6. Date of birth—Mo, Day, Yr	DECEMBER 8, 1925
7. Age in years	64
8. State of birth	NY
9. Citizen of what country	USA
10A. Full name of father	SAMMY DAVIS
10B. State of birth	NC
11A. Full maiden name of mother	ELVERA SANCHEZ
11B. State of birth	NY
12. Military service?	19 42 to 19 45 [ ] None
13. Social Security No.	362-24-9984
14. Marital status	MARRIED
15. Name of surviving spouse	ALTOVISE GORE
16A. Usual occupation	ENTERTAINER
16B. Usual kind of business or industry	SHOW BUSINESS
16C. Usual employer	SELF EMPLOYED
16D. Years in occupation	60
17. Education—Years completed	NONE
18A. Residence—Street and number or location	1151 SUMMIT DRIVE
18B. City	BEVERLY HILLS
18C. Zip code	90210
18D. County	LOS ANGELES
18E. Number of years in this county	25
18F. State or foreign country	CALIFORNIA
20. Name, relationship, mailing address and zip code of informant	ALTOVISE DAVIS - WIFE, 1151 SUMMIT DRIVE, BEVERLY HILLS, CA. 90210
19A. Place of death	Residence
19B. If hospital, specify one: IP, ER/OP, DOA	- -
19C. County	Los Angeles
19D. Street address	1151 Summit Drive
19E. City	Beverly Hills
22. Was death reported to coroner?	[ ] Yes [X] No

21. Death was caused by		Time interval between onset and death
Immediate cause (A)	Cardio Respiratory Arrest	8 mins
Due to (B)	Gram Negative Pneumonia	4wks
Due to (C)	Laryngeal Carcinoma	8mos

23. Was biopsy performed?	[X] Yes [ ] No
24A. Was autopsy performed?	[ ] Yes [X] No
24B. Was it used in determining cause of death?	[ ] Yes [X] No
25. Other significant conditions contributing to death but not related to cause given in 21	None
26. Was operation performed for any condition in item 21 or 25?	No
27A. Decedent attended since	01/21/90
Decedent last seen alive	05/13/90
27B. Signature and degree or title of physician	[signature] M.D.
27C. Physician's license number	G27436
27D. Date signed	5/16/90
27E. Type attending physician's name and address	Irving Pasalski M.D. 8635 W.Third St.L.A. CA 90048
34A. Disposition(s)	BURIAL
34B. Place of final disposition	FOREST LAWN MEMORIAL PARK 1712 S. GLENDALE AVE., GLENDALE, CA.
34C. Date	5-18-1990
35A. Name of funeral director	FOREST LAWN GLENDALE
35B. License no.	656
35C. License number (embalmer)	7621
37. Signature of local registrar	[signature]
38. Registration date	MAY 17 1990

VS-11 (REV. 3-89) 1619 MAKE NO ERASURES, WHITEOUTS, OR OTHER ALTERATIONS 04-9-1-7505

This is to certify that this document is a true copy of the official record filed with the Registrar-Recorder/County Clerk.

CHARLES WEISSBURD
Registrar-Recorder/County Clerk

JAN 13 1992
19-289046

This copy not valid unless prepared on engraved border displaying the Seal and Signature of the Registrar-Recorder/County Clerk.

ANY ALTERATION OR ERASURE VOIDS THIS CERTIFICATE

CERTIFICATION OF VITAL RECORD

STATE OF CALIFORNIA

DEPARTMENT OF HEALTH SERVICES

STATE FILE No. 55-107590

CERTIFICATE OF DEATH

STATE OF CALIFORNIA—DEPARTMENT OF PUBLIC HEALTH

REGISTRATION DISTRICT No. 4000 REGISTRAR'S NUMBER 441

DECEDENT PERSONAL DATA

1a. NAME OF DECEASED—FIRST NAME: James
1b. MIDDLE NAME: Byron
1c. LAST NAME: Dean
2a. DATE OF DEATH—MONTH, DAY, YEAR: September 30, 1955
2b. HOUR: 5:45P
3. SEX: Male
4. COLOR OR RACE: White
5. MARITAL STATUS: Never Married
6. DATE OF BIRTH: February 8, 1931
7. AGE (LAST BIRTHDAY): 24 YEARS
8a. USUAL OCCUPATION: Actor
8b. KIND OF BUSINESS OR INDUSTRY: Motion Picture
9. BIRTHPLACE: Indiana
10. CITIZEN OF WHAT COUNTRY: United States
11. NAME AND BIRTHPLACE OF FATHER: Winton A. Dean, Indiana
12. MAIDEN NAME AND BIRTHPLACE OF MOTHER: Mildred Wilson, Indiana
13. NAME OF PRESENT SPOUSE:
14. WAS DECEASED EVER IN U.S. ARMED FORCES? No
15. SOCIAL SECURITY NUMBER: 310-28-1959
16. INFORMANT: Winton A. Dean

8164

PLACE OF DEATH

7653

17a. COUNTY: San Luis Obispo
17b. CITY OR TOWN: Cholame
17c. LENGTH OF STAY IN THIS CITY OR TOWN: Transient
17d. FULL NAME OF HOSPITAL OR INSTITUTION:
17e. ADDRESS: One mile east Cholame at highway 466 and 41 junction

LAST USUAL RESIDENCE

18a. STATE: California
18b. COUNTY: Los Angeles
18c. CITY OR TOWN: Sherman Oaks
18d. STREET OR RURAL ADDRESS: 14611 Sutton

PHYSICIAN'S OR CORONER'S CERTIFICATION

19a. CORONER: Investigation
19c. SIGNATURE: Paul E. Merrick, By J. W. Stande, Deputy Coroner
19b. ADDRESS: San Luis Obispo
19c. DATE SIGNED: 10-3-55

FUNERAL DIRECTOR AND REGISTRAR

20a. SPECIFY BURIAL, CREMATION OR REMOVAL: Removal
20b. DATE: 10-3-55
20c. CEMETERY OR CREMATORY: Grant Memorial Park, Marion Indiana
21. SIGNATURE OF EMBALMER: Martin Kuehl
LICENSE NUMBER: 3095
22. FUNERAL DIRECTOR: Kuehl Funeral Home
23. DATE RECEIVED BY LOCAL REGISTRAR: October 5, 1955
24. SIGNATURE OF LOCAL REGISTRAR: H. O. Swartout, M.D.

MEDICAL AND HEALTH DATA

CAUSE OF DEATH

25. DISEASE OR CONDITION DIRECTLY LEADING TO DEATH: (a) Broken neck
ANTECEDENT CAUSES: multiple fractures of upper and lower jaw; multiple fractures of left and right arm; internal injuries

OTHER SIGNIFICANT CONDITIONS: 26.

OPERATIONS: 27a. DATE OF OPERATION; 27b. MAJOR FINDINGS OF OPERATION
28. AUTOPSY: No

DEATH DUE TO EXTERNAL VIOLENCE

29a. SPECIFY ACCIDENT, SUICIDE OR HOMICIDE: Accident
29b. PLACE OF INJURY: Highway
29c. LOCATION: Rural Cholame, San Luis Obispo, California
29d. TIME OF INJURY: 10-3-55 5:45P
29e. INJURY OCCURRED: NOT WHILE AT WORK
29f. HOW DID INJURY OCCUR? 2 car collision

This is to certify that this document is a true copy of the official record filed with the Office of Vital Records and Statistics.

S. Kimberly Belshé, Director and State Registrar of Vital Records and Statistics

by: Michael Davis
MICHAEL DAVIS, CHIEF
OFFICE OF VITAL RECORDS AND STATISTICS

DATE ISSUED SEP 27 1995

113573

This copy not valid unless prepared on engraved border displaying seal and signature of Registrar.

ANY ALTERATION OR ERASURE VOIDS THIS CERTIFICATE

CERTIFICATION OF VITAL RECORD

COUNTY OF LOS ANGELES • REGISTRAR-RECORDER/COUNTY CLERK

7097-021331

CERTIFICATE OF DEATH

STATE FILE NUMBER — STATE OF CALIFORNIA—DEPARTMENT OF PUBLIC HEALTH — LOCAL REGISTRATION DISTRICT AND CERTIFICATE NUMBER

DECEDENT PERSONAL DATA

1a. NAME OF DECEASED—FIRST NAME: Albert | 1b. MIDDLE NAME: | 1c. LAST NAME: Dekker | 2a. DATE OF DEATH—MONTH, DAY, YEAR: MAY 5, 1968 | 2b. HOUR: 1045P.M.

3. SEX: Male | 4. COLOR OR RACE: Cauc. | 5. BIRTHPLACE (STATE OR FOREIGN COUNTRY): New York | 6. DATE OF BIRTH: Dec. 20, 1905 | 7. AGE (LAST BIRTHDAY): 52 YEARS | IF UNDER 1 YEAR: MONTHS, DAYS | IF UNDER 24 HOURS: HOURS, MINUTES

8. NAME AND BIRTHPLACE OF FATHER: Albert Ecke, New York | 9. MAIDEN NAME AND BIRTHPLACE OF MOTHER: Grace Dekker, New York

10. CITIZEN OF WHAT COUNTRY: U.S.A. | 11. SOCIAL SECURITY NUMBER: 112-09-1525 | 12. MARRIED, NEVER MARRIED, WIDOWED, DIVORCED (SPECIFY): Divorced | 13. NAME OF SURVIVING SPOUSE (IF WIFE, ENTER MAIDEN NAME):

14. LAST OCCUPATION: Actor | 15. NUMBER OF YEARS IN THIS OCCUPATION: 39 | 16. NAME OF LAST EMPLOYING COMPANY OR FIRM (IF SELF EMPLOYED, SO STATE): Warner Bros. Studios | 17. KIND OF INDUSTRY OR BUSINESS: Acting

PLACE OF DEATH

18a. PLACE OF DEATH—NAME OF HOSPITAL OR OTHER IN-PATIENT FACILITY: | 18b. STREET ADDRESS—(STREET AND NUMBER, OR LOCATION): 1731 N. Normandie Ave. | 18c. INSIDE CITY CORPORATE LIMITS (SPECIFY YES OR NO): Yes

18d. CITY OR TOWN: Los Angeles | 18e. COUNTY: Los Angeles | 18f. LENGTH OF STAY IN COUNTY OF DEATH: 39 YEARS | 18g. LENGTH OF STAY IN CALIFORNIA: 39 YEARS

USUAL RESIDENCE (IF DEATH OCCURRED IN INSTITUTION, ENTER RESIDENCE BEFORE ADMISSION)

19a. USUAL RESIDENCE—STREET ADDRESS (STREET AND NUMBER OR LOCATION): 1731 N. Normandie Ave. | 19b. INSIDE CITY CORPORATE LIMITS (SPECIFY YES OR NO): Yes | 20. NAME AND MAILING ADDRESS OF INFORMANT: Jan Dekker, 60 Main St., Hastings-on-Hudson, New York

19c. CITY OR TOWN: Los Angeles | 19d. COUNTY: Los Angeles | 19e. STATE: California

PHYSICIAN'S OR CORONER'S CERTIFICATION

21a. CORONER: I HEREBY CERTIFY THAT DEATH OCCURRED AT THE HOUR, DATE AND PLACE STATED ABOVE FROM THE CAUSES STATED BELOW AND THAT I HAVE HELD AN INVESTIGATION OR INQUEST ON THE REMAINS OF DECEASED AS REQUIRED BY LAW: Investigation | 21b. PHYSICIAN: I HEREBY CERTIFY THAT DEATH OCCURRED AT THE HOUR, DATE, AND PLACE STATED ABOVE FROM THE CAUSES STATED BELOW AND THAT I ATTENDED THE DECEASED FROM (ENTER MONTH, DAY, YEAR) TO (ENTER MONTH, DAY, YEAR) AND I LAST SAW THE DECEASED ALIVE ON (ENTER MONTH, DAY, YEAR) | 21c. PHYSICIAN OR CORONER—SIGNATURE AND DEGREE OR TITLE: Thomas T. Noguchi, M.D., Coroner; Albert a Selle Deputy | 21d. DATE SIGNED: 5-22-68

21e. ADDRESS: Hall of Justice, Los Angeles | 21f. PHYSICIAN'S CALIFORNIA LICENSE NUMBER:

FUNERAL DIRECTOR AND LOCAL REGISTRAR

22a. SPECIFY BURIAL, ENTOMBMENT OR CREMATION: Cremation | 22b. DATE: 5-8-68 | 23. NAME OF CEMETERY OR CREMATORY: Odd Fellows Crematory to Garden State Crematory N.J. | 24. EMBALMER—SIGNATURE (IF BODY EMBALMED) LICENSE NUMBER: J. V. Gallagher 4718

25. NAME OF FUNERAL DIRECTOR (OR PERSON ACTING AS SUCH): Edwards Bros. Colonial Mortuary | 26. IF NOT CERTIFIED BY CORONER, WAS THIS DEATH REPORTED TO CORONER? (SPECIFY YES OR NO) | 27. LOCAL REGISTRAR—SIGNATURE: [signature] M.D. | 28. DATE ACCEPTED FOR REGISTRATION BY LOCAL REGISTRAR: MAY 29 1968; 5-8-68

MEDICAL AND HEALTH DATA — CAUSE OF DEATH

29. PART I. DEATH WAS CAUSED BY: ENTER ONLY ONE CAUSE PER LINE FOR (A), (B), AND (C)

IMMEDIATE CAUSE (A): ASPHYXIATION

CONDITIONS, IF ANY, WHICH GAVE RISE TO THE IMMEDIATE CAUSE (A), STATING THE UNDERLYING CAUSE LAST.

DUE TO, OR AS A CONSEQUENCE OF (B): SUFFOCATION AND CONSTRICTION OF NECK BY LIGATURES

DUE TO, OR AS A CONSEQUENCE OF (C):

APPROXIMATE INTERVAL BETWEEN ONSET AND DEATH

30. PART II: OTHER SIGNIFICANT CONDITIONS—CONTRIBUTING TO DEATH BUT NOT RELATED TO THE IMMEDIATE CAUSE GIVEN IN PART I | 31. WAS OPERATION OR BIOPSY PERFORMED FOR ANY CONDITION IN ITEMS 29 OR 30? (SPECIFY TYPE OF OPERATION AND/OR BIOPSY): No | 32a. AUTOPSY (SPECIFY YES OR NO): Yes | 32b. IF YES WERE FINDINGS CONSIDERED IN DETERMINING CAUSE OF DEATH? (SPECIFY YES OR NO): Yes

INJURY INFORMATION

33. SPECIFY ACCIDENT, SUICIDE OR HOMICIDE: Accident | 34. PLACE OF INJURY (SPECIFY HOME, FARM, FACTORY, OFFICE BUILDING, ETC.): HOME | 35. INJURY AT WORK (SPECIFY YES OR NO): NO | 36a. DATE OF INJURY—MONTH, DAY, YEAR: 5-5-68 | 36b. HOUR: 1045P M.

37a. PLACE OF INJURY (STREET AND NUMBER OR LOCATION AND CITY OR TOWN): 1731 N. NORMANDIE, LOS ANGELES | 37b. DISTANCE FROM PLACE OF INJURY TO USUAL RESIDENCE, ITEM 19: 0 MILES | 38. WERE LABORATORY TESTS DONE FOR DRUGS OR TOXIC CHEMICALS? (SPECIFY YES OR NO): Yes | 39. WERE LABORATORY TESTS DONE FOR ALCOHOL? (SPECIFY YES OR NO): Yes

40. DESCRIBE HOW INJURY OCCURRED (ENTER SEQUENCE OF EVENTS WHICH RESULTED IN INJURY. NATURE OF INJURY SHOULD BE ENTERED IN ITEM 29): AS ABOVE

STATE REGISTRAR: A. | B. | C. | D. | E. | F. HCN

REV. 1-1-68 Form VS-11

This is to certify that this document is a true copy of the official record filed with the Registrar-Recorder/County Clerk.

Beatriz Valdez
BEATRIZ VALDEZ
Registrar-Recorder/County Clerk

AUG 18 1995

19-397406

This copy not valid unless prepared on engraved border displaying the Seal and Signature of the Registrar-Recorder/County Clerk.

American Bank Note Company

ANY ALTERATION OR ERASURE VOIDS THIS CERTIFICATE

CERTIFICATION OF VITAL RECORD

COUNTY OF LOS ANGELES • REGISTRAR-RECORDER/COUNTY CLERK

STATE FILE NUMBER

CERTIFICATE OF DEATH

STATE OF CALIFORNIA—DEPARTMENT OF PUBLIC HEALTH

LOCAL REGISTRATION DISTRICT AND CERTIFICATE NUMBER 7053 1299

DECEDENT PERSONAL DATA

1a. NAME OF DECEASED—FIRST NAME: Cecil | 1b. MIDDLE NAME: Blount | 1c. LAST NAME: De Mille | 2a. DATE OF DEATH—MONTH, DAY, YEAR: Jan. 21, 1959 | 2b. HOUR: 5:00 A.M.

3. SEX: Male | 4. COLOR OR RACE: Cauc. | 5. BIRTHPLACE (STATE OR FOREIGN COUNTRY): Massachusetts | 6. DATE OF BIRTH: Aug. 12, 1881 | 7. AGE (LAST BIRTHDAY): 77 YEARS | IF UNDER 1 YEAR | IF UNDER 24 HOURS

8. NAME AND BIRTHPLACE OF FATHER: Henry C. De Mille—No.Carolina | 9. MAIDEN NAME AND BIRTHPLACE OF MOTHER: Beatrice M. Samuel—England | 10. CITIZEN OF WHAT COUNTRY: U.S.A. | 11. SOCIAL SECURITY NUMBER: 560-12-6992

12. LAST OCCUPATION: Director-Producer | 13. NUMBER OF YEARS IN THIS OCCUPATION: 45 | 14. NAME OF LAST EMPLOYING COMPANY OR FIRM (IF SELF-EMPLOYED SO STATE): Paramount Studios | 15. KIND OF INDUSTRY OR BUSINESS: Motion Pictures

16. IF DECEASED WAS EVER IN U.S. ARMED FORCES, GIVE WAR OR DATES OF SERVICE: None | 17. SPECIFY MARRIED, NEVER MARRIED, WIDOWED, DIVORCED: Married | 18a. NAME OF PRESENT SPOUSE: Constance A. De Mille | 18b. PRESENT OR LAST OCCUPATION OF SPOUSE: Housewife

PLACE OF DEATH

19a. PLACE OF DEATH—NAME OF HOSPITAL: — | 19b. STREET ADDRESS—(GIVE STREET OR RURAL ADDRESS OR LOCATION. DO NOT USE P.O. BOX NUMBERS): 2000 De Mille Drive | [X] INSIDE CITY CORPORATE LIMITS | [ ] OUTSIDE CITY CORPORATE LIMITS

19c. CITY OR TOWN: Los Angeles | 19d. COUNTY: Los Angeles | 19e. LENGTH OF STAY IN COUNTY OF DEATH: 40 YEARS | 19f. LENGTH OF STAY IN CALIFORNIA: 40 YEARS

LAST USUAL RESIDENCE (WHERE DID DECEASED LIVE—IF IN INSTITUTION ENTER RESIDENCE BEFORE ADMISSION)

20a. LAST USUAL RESIDENCE—STREET ADDRESS (GIVE STREET OR RURAL ADDRESS OR LOCATION. DO NOT USE P.O. BOX NUMBERS): 2000 De Mille Drive | 20b. IF INSIDE CITY CORPORATE LIMITS CHECK HERE [X] | IF OUTSIDE CITY CORPORATE LIMITS CHECK ONE: [ ] ON A FARM [ ] NOT ON A FARM | 21a. NAME OF INFORMANT (IF OTHER THAN SPOUSE): —

20c. CITY OR TOWN: Los Angeles 0578 | 20d. COUNTY: Los Angeles | 20e. STATE: California | 21b. ADDRESS OF INFORMANT (IF DIFFERENT FROM LAST USUAL RESIDENCE OF DECEDENT): —

PHYSICIAN'S OR CORONER'S CERTIFICATION

22a. PHYSICIAN: I HEREBY CERTIFY THAT DEATH OCCURRED AT THE HOUR, DATE AND PLACE STATED ABOVE FROM THE CAUSES STATED BELOW AND THAT I ATTENDED THE DECEASED FROM 1955 TO 1-21-59 AND THAT I LAST SAW THE DECEASED ALIVE ON 1-21-59 | 22c. PHYSICIAN OR CORONER—SIGNATURE: [signature] M.D. | DEGREE OR TITLE

22a. CORONER: I HEREBY CERTIFY THAT DEATH OCCURRED AT THE HOUR, DATE AND PLACE STATED ABOVE FROM THE CAUSES STATED BELOW AND THAT I HAVE HELD AN ______ INVESTIGATION, AUTOPSY, INQUEST ON THE REMAINS OF DECEASED AS REQUIRED BY LAW. | 22d. ADDRESS: 6317 Wilshire Blvd | 22e. DATE SIGNED: 1-22-1959

FUNERAL DIRECTOR AND LOCAL REGISTRAR

23. SPECIFY BURIAL, ENTOMBMENT OR CREMATION: Entombment | 24. DATE: Jan.23,1959 | 25. NAME OF CEMETERY OR CREMATORY: Hollywood Mausoleum | 26. EMBALMER—SIGNATURE (IF BODY EMBALMED): John Q Lipsey | LICENSE NUMBER: 3843

27. NAME OF FUNERAL DIRECTOR (OR PERSON ACTING AS SUCH): Pierce Brothers Hollywood | 28. DATE ACCEPTED FOR REGISTRATION BY LOCAL REGISTRAR: JAN 22 1959 | 29. LOCAL REGISTRAR—SIGNATURE: George M. Uhl, M.D.

MEDICAL AND HEALTH DATA

CAUSE OF DEATH

30. CAUSE OF DEATH — ENTER ONLY ONE CAUSE PER LINE FOR (A), (B), AND (C)

PART I. DEATH WAS CAUSED BY: IMMEDIATE CAUSE (A): Congestive heart failure — 24 hrs.

CONDITIONS, IF ANY, WHICH GAVE RISE TO THE ABOVE CAUSE (A) STATING THE UNDERLYING CAUSE LAST: DUE TO (B): Coronary thrombosis and myocardial infarction — 6 months

DUE TO (C):

APPROXIMATE INTERVAL BETWEEN ONSET AND DEATH

PART II: OTHER SIGNIFICANT CONDITIONS CONTRIBUTING TO DEATH BUT NOT RELATED TO THE TERMINAL DISEASE CONDITION GIVEN IN PART I (A)

OPERATION AND AUTOPSY

31. OPERATION—CHECK ONE: [X] NO OPERATION PERFORMED [ ] OPERATION PERFORMED—FINDINGS USED IN DETERMINING ABOVE STATED CAUSES OF DEATH [ ] OPERATION PERFORMED—FINDINGS NOT USED IN DETERMINING ABOVE STATED CAUSES OF DEATH | 32. DATE OF OPERATION | 33. AUTOPSY—CHECK ONE: [X] NO AUTOPSY PERFORMED [ ] AUTOPSY PERFORMED—GROSS FINDINGS USED IN DETERMINING ABOVE STATED CAUSES OF DEATH [ ] AUTOPSY PERFORMED—GROSS FINDINGS NOT USED IN DETERMINING ABOVE STATED CAUSES OF DEATH

INJURY INFORMATION

34a. SPECIFY ACCIDENT, SUICIDE OR HOMICIDE | 34b. DESCRIBE HOW INJURY OCCURRED

35a. TIME OF INJURY: HOUR, MONTH, DAY, YEAR, M.

35b. INJURY OCCURRED: [ ] WHILE AT WORK [ ] NOT WHILE AT WORK | 35c. PLACE OF INJURY | 35d. CITY, TOWN, OR LOCATION | COUNTY | STATE

This is to certify that this document is a true copy of the official record filed with the Registrar-Recorder/County Clerk.

Beatriz Valdez
BEATRIZ VALDEZ
Registrar-Recorder/County Clerk

AUG 04 1995

19-390019

This copy not valid unless prepared on engraved border displaying the Seal and Signature of the Registrar-Recorder/County Clerk.

American Bank Note Company

ANY ALTERATION OR ERASURE VOIDS THIS CERTIFICATE

CERTIFICATION OF VITAL RECORD

COUNTY OF MONTEREY

Salinas, California

CERTIFIED COPY OF VITAL RECORDS

CERTIFICATE OF DEATH

STATE OF CALIFORNIA
USE BLACK INK ONLY/NO ERASURES, WHITEOUTS OR ALTERATIONS
VS-11 (REV. 11/96)

STATE FILE NUMBER: 3199727

LOCAL REGISTRATION NUMBER: 001571

DECEDENT PERSONAL DATA

1. NAME OF DECEDENT—FIRST (GIVEN): HENRY
2. MIDDLE: JOHN
3. LAST (FAMILY): DEUTSCHENDORF JR.
4. DATE OF BIRTH MM/DD/CCYY: 12/31/1943
5. AGE YRS.: 53
6. SEX: M
7. DATE OF DEATH MM/DD/CCYY: 10/12/1997
8. HOUR: 1730
9. STATE OF BIRTH: NM
10. SOCIAL SECURITY NO.: 453-70-6010
11. MILITARY SERVICE: [ ] YES [X] NO
12. MARITAL STATUS: Divorced
13. EDUCATION—YEARS COMPLETED: 14
14. RACE: White
15. HISPANIC—SPECIFY: [ ] YES [X] NO
16. USUAL EMPLOYER: Self-employed
17. OCCUPATION: Singer
18. KIND OF BUSINESS: Music industry
19. YEARS IN OCCUPATION: 34

USUAL RESIDENCE

20. RESIDENCE—STREET AND NUMBER OR LOCATION: 0570 Johnson Drive
21. CITY: Aspen
22. COUNTY: Pitkin
23. ZIP CODE: 81611
24. YRS IN COUNTY: 28
25. STATE OR FOREIGN COUNTRY: Colorado

INFORMANT

26. NAME, RELATIONSHIP: Ronald Deutschendorf, brother
27. MAILING ADDRESS: 14422 Corte Lampara San Diego, CA 92129

SPOUSE AND PARENT INFORMATION

28. NAME OF SURVIVING SPOUSE—FIRST: –
29. MIDDLE: –
30. LAST (MAIDEN NAME): –
31. NAME OF FATHER—FIRST: Henry
32. MIDDLE: John
33. LAST: Deutschendorf Sr.
34. BIRTH STATE: OK
35. NAME OF MOTHER—FIRST: Erma
36. MIDDLE: Louise
37. LAST (MAIDEN): Swope
38. BIRTH STATE: OK

DISPOSITION(S)

39. DATE MM/DD/CCYY: 10/15/1997
40. PLACE OF FINAL DISPOSITION: Parker Funeral Home Inc. 10325 Parkglenn Way Parker, CO 80134

FUNERAL DIRECTOR AND LOCAL REGISTRAR

41. TYPE OF DISPOSITION(S): CR/TR
42. SIGNATURE OF EMBALMER: Not embalmed
43. LICENSE NO.: –
44. NAME OF FUNERAL DIRECTOR: Chapel of Seaside, Inc.
45. LICENSE NO.: FD-1363
46. SIGNATURE OF LOCAL REGISTRAR: Robert J Melton MD
47. DATE MM/DD/CCYY: 10/14/1997

PLACE OF DEATH

101. PLACE OF DEATH: pacific ocean
102. IF HOSPITAL, SPECIFY ONE: [ ] IP [ ] ER/OP [ ] DOA
103. FACILITY OTHER THAN HOSPITAL: [ ] CONV HOSP [ ] RES. CARE [ ] OTHER
104. COUNTY: MONTEREY
105. STREET ADDRESS—STREET AND NUMBER OR LOCATION: 150 YARDS OFF SHORE, SOUTH OF LOVERS POINT
106. CITY: PACIFIC GROVE

CAUSE OF DEATH

107. DEATH WAS CAUSED BY: (ENTER ONLY ONE CAUSE PER LINE FOR A, B, C, AND D)

IMMEDIATE CAUSE (A) MULTIPLE BLUNT FORCE TRAUMA — TIME INTERVAL BETWEEN ONSET AND DEATH: SECS.

DUE TO (B)

DUE TO (C)

DUE TO (D)

108. DEATH REPORTED TO CORONER: [X] YES [ ] NO — REFERRAL NUMBER: 97-227
109. BIOPSY PERFORMED: [ ] YES [X] NO
110. AUTOPSY PERFORMED: [X] YES [ ] NO
111. USED IN DETERMINING CAUSE: [X] YES [ ] NO
112. OTHER SIGNIFICANT CONDITIONS CONTRIBUTING TO DEATH BUT NOT RELATED TO CAUSE GIVEN IN 107
113. WAS OPERATION PERFORMED FOR ANY CONDITION IN ITEM 107 OR 112? IF YES, LIST TYPE OF OPERATION AND DATE.

PHYSICIAN'S CERTIFICATION

114. I CERTIFY THAT TO THE BEST OF MY KNOWLEDGE DEATH OCCURRED AT THE HOUR, DATE AND PLACE STATED FROM THE CAUSES STATED. DECEDENT ATTENDED SINCE MM/DD/CCYY — DECEDENT LAST SEEN ALIVE MM/DD/CCYY
115. SIGNATURE AND TITLE OF CERTIFIER
116. LICENSE NO.
117. DATE MM/DD/CCYY
118. TYPE ATTENDING PHYSICIAN'S NAME, MAILING ADDRESS, ZIP

CORONER'S USE ONLY

I CERTIFY THAT IN MY OPINION DEATH OCCURRED AT THE HOUR, DATE AND PLACE STATED FROM THE CAUSES STATED.

119. MANNER OF DEATH: [ ] NATURAL [ ] SUICIDE [ ] HOMICIDE [X] ACCIDENT [ ] PENDING INVESTIGATION [ ] COULD NOT BE DETERMINED
120. INJURY AT WORK: [ ] YES [X] NO
121. INJURY DATE MM/DD/CCYY: 10/12/1997
122. HOUR: 1730
123. PLACE OF INJURY: PACIFIC OCEAN
124. DESCRIBE HOW INJURY OCCURRED (EVENTS WHICH RESULTED IN INJURY): PILOT OF AIRPLANE WHICH CRASHED IN OCEAN.
125. LOCATION (STREET AND NUMBER OR LOCATION AND CITY, ZIP): 150 YARDS OFF SHORE, SOUTH OF LOVERS POINT, PACIFIC GROVE, CA. 93950
126. SIGNATURE OF CORONER OR DEPUTY CORONER: [signature]
127. DATE MM/DD/CCYY: 10/13/1997
128. TYPED NAME, TITLE OF CORONER OR DEPUTY CORONER: ALAN WHEELUS DEPUTY CORONER

STATE REGISTRAR

A B C D E F G H — FAX AUTH. #: 002184 — CENSUS TRACT

MONTEREY CO. DEPT. OF HEALTH
STATE OF CALIFORNIA
COUNTY OF MONTEREY

DATE ISSUED: NOV 03 1997

By: Robert J Melton MD, Local Registrar.

34792

This is a true and exact reproduction of the document officially registered and placed on file in the Office of the Monterey County Vital Records.

This copy is not valid unless prepared on engraved border displaying seal and signature of local Registrar.

MIDWEST BANK NOTE COMPANY

ANY ALTERATION OR ERASURE VOIDS THIS CERTIFICATE

CERTIFICATION OF VITAL RECORD

COUNTY OF LOS ANGELES • REGISTRAR-RECORDER/COUNTY CLERK

CERTIFICATE OF DEATH 7097-055557

STATE OF CALIFORNIA—DEPARTMENT OF PUBLIC HEALTH

DECEDENT PERSONAL DATA	1A Name of deceased—first name: PETER	1B Middle name: ELLSTROM	1C Last name: DEUEL
	2A Date of death: DECEMBER 31, 1971	2B Hour: 0133 Hrs.	
	3 Sex: Male	4 Color or race: Cauc.	5 Birthplace: New York
	6 Date of birth: February 24, 1940	7 Age: 31 years	
	8 Name and birthplace of father: Ellsworth Deuel, New York	9 Maiden name and birthplace of mother: Lillian Ellstrom, Pennsylvania	
	10 Citizen of what country: U.S.A.	11 Social Security number: not available	12 Married, never married, widowed, divorced: never married
	13 Name of surviving spouse: ----		
	14 Last occupation: Actor	15 Number of years in this occupation: 11 yrs.	16 Name of last employing company or firm: Universal Studios
	17 Kind of industry or business: Movie Industry		
PLACE OF DEATH	18A Place of death:	18B Street address: 2552 Glen Green	18C Inside city corporate limits: yes
	18D City or town: (Hollywood) Los Angeles	18E County: Los Angeles	18F Length of stay in county: 8 years; 18G in California: 8 years
USUAL RESIDENCE	19A Usual residence—street address: 2552 Glen Green	19B Inside city corporate limits: yes	20 Name and mailing address of informant: Geoffrey Deuel, 1158 1/2 N. Fuller, Los Angeles, California
	19C City or town: (Hollywood) L.A.	19D County: Los Angeles	19E State: California
PHYSICIAN'S OR CORONER'S CERTIFICATION	21A Coroner: INVESTIGATION	21C Physician or coroner: THOMAS T. NOGUCHI, M.D. CORONER	21D Date signed: 12-31-71
	21E Address: HALL OF JUSTICE, LOS ANGELES		
FUNERAL DIRECTOR AND LOCAL REGISTRAR	22A Burial	22B Date: January 6, 1972	23 Name of cemetery or crematory: Oakwood Cem. Penfield, New York
	25 Name of funeral director: GLASBAND WILLEN MORTUARY	26 Not certified by coroner: YES	28 Accepted for registration: DEC 1971
CAUSE OF DEATH	29 Part I. Death was caused by: Immediate cause (A) DEFERRED		
	31 Was operation or biopsy performed:	32A Autopsy: YES	
INJURY INFORMATION	33–40		
STATE REGISTRAR	F: 1844		

AMENDED OF 2

This is to certify that this document is a true copy of the official record filed with the Registrar-Recorder/County Clerk.

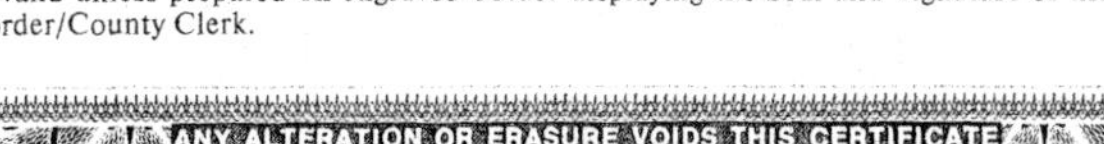

BEATRIZ VALDEZ
Registrar-Recorder/County Clerk

AUG 18 1995

19-397408

This copy not valid unless prepared on engraved border displaying the Seal and Signature of the Registrar-Recorder/County Clerk.

ANY ALTERATION OR ERASURE VOIDS THIS CERTIFICATE

CERTIFICATION OF VITAL RECORD

COUNTY OF LOS ANGELES • REGISTRAR-RECORDER/COUNTY CLERK

72 710

AMENDMENT OF MEDICAL AND HEALTH SECTION DATA—DEATH 7097-055657

(INSTRUCTIONS ON REVERSE)

STATE CERTIFICATE NUMBER — LOCAL REGISTRATION DISTRICT AND CERTIFICATE NUMBER

IDENTIFICATION OF THE RECORD

1A. FIRST NAME	1B. MIDDLE NAME	1C. LAST NAME
PETER	ELLSTROM	DEUEL

2. PLACE OF OCCURRENCE—CITY OR COUNTY	3. DATE OF EVENT	4. DATE ORIGINAL FILED
(HOLLYWOOD) LOS ANGELES	DEC. 31, 1971	12-31-71

2 OF 2

ORIGINALLY REPORTED INFORMATION

INFORMATION AS REPORTED ON THE ORIGINALLY REGISTERED CERTIFICATE

29. PART I. DEATH WAS CAUSED BY: ENTER ONLY ONE CAUSE PER LINE FOR A, B, AND C

IMMEDIATE CAUSE (A) DEFERRED

CONDITIONS, IF ANY, WHICH GAVE RISE TO THE IMMEDIATE CAUSE (A), STATING THE UNDERLYING CAUSE LAST. DUE TO, OR AS A CONSEQUENCE OF (B)

DUE TO, OR AS A CONSEQUENCE OF (C)

APPROXIMATE INTERVAL BETWEEN ONSET AND DEATH

30. PART II: OTHER SIGNIFICANT CONDITIONS—CONTRIBUTING TO DEATH BUT NOT RELATED TO THE IMMEDIATE CAUSE GIVEN IN PART IA | 31. WAS OPERATION OR BIOPSY PERFORMED FOR ANY CONDITION IN ITEMS 29 OR 30? (SPECIFY OPERATION AND/OR BIOPSY) | 32A. AUTOPSY (SPECIFY YES OR NO) YES | 32B. IF YES, WERE FINDINGS CONSIDERED IN DETERMINING CAUSE OF DEATH? (SPECIFY YES OR NO)

33. SPECIFY ACCIDENT, SUICIDE OR HOMICIDE | 34. PLACE OF INJURY (SPECIFY HOME, FARM, FACTORY, FREEWAY, HIGHWAY, STREET, OFFICE BUILDING, ETC.) | 35. INJURY AT WORK (SPECIFY YES OR NO) | 36A. DATE OF INJURY—MONTH, DAY, YEAR | 36B. HOUR M

37A. PLACE OF INJURY (STREET AND NUMBER OR LOCATION AND CITY OR TOWN) | 37B. DISTANCE FROM PLACE OF INJURY TO USUAL RESIDENCE, ITEM 19 MILES | 38. WERE LABORATORY TESTS DONE FOR DRUGS OR TOXIC CHEMICALS? (SPECIFY YES OR NO) | 39. WERE LABORATORY TESTS DONE FOR ALCOHOL? (SPECIFY YES OR NO)

40. DESCRIBE HOW INJURY OCCURRED (ENTER SEQUENCE OF EVENTS WHICH RESULTED IN INJURY. NATURE OF INJURY SHOULD BE ENTERED IN ITEM 29)

INFORMATION AS IT SHOULD BE STATED ON THE ORIGINALLY REGISTERED CERTIFICATE

INFORMATION AS IT SHOULD BE STATED ON THE ORIGINALLY REGISTERED CERTIFICATE

29. PART I. DEATH WAS CAUSED BY: ENTER ONLY ONE CAUSE PER LINE FOR A, B, AND C

IMMEDIATE CAUSE (A) CEREBRAL DESTRUCTION

CONDITIONS, IF ANY, WHICH GAVE RISE TO THE IMMEDIATE CAUSE (A), STATING THE UNDERLYING CAUSE LAST. DUE TO, OR AS A CONSEQUENCE OF (B) GUNSHOT WOUND TO HEAD

DUE TO, OR AS A CONSEQUENCE OF (C)

APPROXIMATE INTERVAL BETWEEN ONSET AND DEATH

30. PART II: OTHER SIGNIFICANT CONDITIONS—CONTRIBUTING TO DEATH BUT NOT RELATED TO THE IMMEDIATE CAUSE GIVEN IN PART IA | 31. WAS OPERATION OR BIOPSY PERFORMED FOR ANY CONDITION IN ITEMS 29 OR 30? (SPECIFY OPERATION AND/OR BIOPSY) NO | 32A. AUTOPSY (SPECIFY YES OR NO) YES | 32B. IF YES, WERE FINDINGS CONSIDERED IN DETERMINING CAUSE OF DEATH? (SPECIFY YES OR NO) YES

33. SPECIFY ACCIDENT, SUICIDE OR HOMICIDE	34. PLACE OF INJURY	35. INJURY AT WORK	36A. DATE OF INJURY—MONTH, DAY, YEAR	36B. HOUR
SUICIDE	HOME	NO	Dec. 31, 1971	0133 M.

37A. PLACE OF INJURY (STREET AND NUMBER OR LOCATION AND CITY OR TOWN)	37B. DISTANCE FROM PLACE OF INJURY TO USUAL RESIDENCE, ITEM 19	38. WERE LABORATORY TESTS DONE FOR DRUGS OR TOXIC CHEMICALS?	39. WERE LABORATORY TESTS DONE FOR ALCOHOL?
2552 Glen Green Ave. Los Angeles	0 MILES	YES	YES

40. DESCRIBE HOW INJURY OCCURRED (ENTER SEQUENCE OF EVENTS WHICH RESULTED IN INJURY. NATURE OF INJURY SHOULD BE ENTERED IN ITEM 29)

AS ABOVE, SELF INFLICTED

DECLARATION OF CERTIFYING PHYSICIAN OR CORONER

5. I, THE CERTIFYING PHYSICIAN OR CORONER HAVING PERSONAL KNOWLEDGE OF SUPPLEMENTAL INFORMATION WHICH MODIFIES THE INFORMATION ORIGINALLY REPORTED, DECLARE UNDER PENALTY OF PERJURY THAT THE ABOVE INFORMATION IS TRUE AND CORRECT TO THE BEST OF MY KNOWLEDGE.

6A. SIGNATURE OF PHYSICIAN OR CORONER: Loverne Butler | 6B. DATE SIGNED: 1-24-72

7A. NAME OF PHYSICIAN OR CORONER (PRINT OR TYPE): THOMAS T. NOGUCHI, M.D., CORONER — Loverne Butler DEPUTY | 7B. DEGREE OR TITLE

7C. ADDRESS—STREET, CITY, STATE: HALL OF JUSTICE LOS ANGELES, CALIFORNIA

REGISTRAR'S OFFICE

8A. OFFICE OF STATE OR LOCAL REGISTRAR: [signature] MD | 8B. DATE ACCEPTED: JAN 26 1972

STATE OF CALIFORNIA, DEPARTMENT OF PUBLIC HEALTH, BUREAU OF VITAL STATISTICS (REV. 1-1-69) FORM VS-24B

This is to certify that this document is a true copy of the official record filed with the Registrar-Recorder/County Clerk.

Beatriz Valdez
BEATRIZ VALDEZ
Registrar-Recorder/County Clerk

AUG 16 1995
19-397409

This copy not valid unless prepared on engraved border displaying the Seal and Signature of the Registrar-Recorder/County Clerk.

American Bank Note Company

ANY ALTERATION OR ERASURE VOIDS THIS CERTIFICATE

CERTIFICATION OF VITAL RECORD

COUNTY OF LOS ANGELES • REGISTRAR-RECORDER/COUNTY CLERK

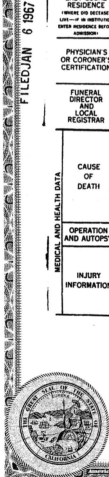

FILED JAN 6 1967 RAY E LEE COUNTY RECORDER

STATE FILE NUMBER

CERTIFICATE OF DEATH

STATE OF CALIFORNIA—DEPARTMENT OF PUBLIC HEALTH

LOCAL REGISTRATION DISTRICT AND CERTIFICATE NUMBER 7097-050719

DECEDENT PERSONAL DATA

1a. NAME OF DECEASED—FIRST NAME: WALTER | 1b. MIDDLE NAME: ELIAS | 1c. LAST NAME: DISNEY | 2a. DATE OF DEATH—MONTH, DAY, YEAR: DECEMBER 15, 1966 | 2b. HOUR: 9:30 A.M.

3. SEX: Male | 4. COLOR OR RACE: Caucasian | 5. BIRTHPLACE (STATE OR FOREIGN COUNTRY): Illinois | 6. DATE OF BIRTH: December 5, 1901 | 7. AGE (LAST BIRTHDAY): 65 YEARS | IF UNDER 1 YEAR | IF UNDER 24 HOURS

8. NAME AND BIRTHPLACE OF FATHER: Elias Disney-Canada | 9. MAIDEN NAME AND BIRTHPLACE OF MOTHER: Flora Call-Canada | 10. CITIZEN OF WHAT COUNTRY: U. S. A. | 11. SOCIAL SECURITY NUMBER: 562-10-0296

12. LAST OCCUPATION: Founder & Creative Head | 13. NUMBER OF YEARS IN THIS OCCUPATION: 30 | 14. NAME OF LAST EMPLOYING COMPANY OR FIRM (IF SELF-EMPLOYED, SO STATE): (Self Employed) Walt Disney Productions | 15. KIND OF INDUSTRY OR BUSINESS: Motion Pictures & Television

16. IF DECEASED WAS EVER IN U.S. ARMED FORCES GIVE WAR OR DATES OF SERVICE: WW I | 17. SPECIFY MARRIED, NEVER MARRIED, WIDOWED, DIVORCED: Married | 18a. NAME OF PRESENT SPOUSE: Lillian Disney | 18b. PRESENT OR LAST OCCUPATION OF SPOUSE: Housewife

PLACE OF DEATH

19a. PLACE OF DEATH—NAME OF HOSPITAL: St. Joseph Hospital | 19b. STREET ADDRESS—(GIVE STREET OR RURAL ADDRESS OR LOCATION. DO NOT USE P.O. BOX NUMBERS): 501 Buena Vista Street | xx INSIDE CITY CORPORATE LIMITS | OUTSIDE CITY CORPORATE LIMITS

19c. CITY OR TOWN: Burbank | 19d. COUNTY: Los Angeles | 19e. LENGTH OF STAY IN COUNTY OF DEATH: 43 YEARS | 19f. LENGTH OF STAY IN CALIFORNIA: 43 YEARS

LAST USUAL RESIDENCE (WHERE DID DECEASED LIVE—IF IN INSTITUTION ENTER RESIDENCE BEFORE ADMISSION)

20a. LAST USUAL RESIDENCE—STREET ADDRESS (GIVE STREET OR RURAL ADDRESS OR LOCATION. DO NOT USE P.O. BOX NUMBERS): 355 Carolwood Drive | 20b. IF INSIDE CITY CORPORATE LIMITS CHECK HERE: XX | IF OUTSIDE CITY CORPORATE LIMITS CHECK ONE: ON A FARM / NOT ON A FARM | 21a. NAME OF INFORMANT (IF OTHER THAN SPOUSE): Mr. Ronald W. Miller

20c. CITY OR TOWN: Los Angeles (Holmby Hills) | 20d. COUNTY: Los Angeles | 20e. STATE: California | 21b. ADDRESS OF INFORMANT (IF DIFFERENT FROM LAST USUAL RESIDENCE): 4750 Louise Avenue Encino, California

PHYSICIAN'S OR CORONER'S CERTIFICATION

22a. PHYSICIAN: I HEREBY CERTIFY THAT DEATH OCCURRED AT THE HOUR DATE AND PLACE STATED ABOVE FROM THE CAUSES STATED BELOW AND THAT I ATTENDED THE DECEASED FROM 11/2/66 TO 12/15/66 AND THAT I LAST SAW THE DECEASED ALIVE ON 12/15/66

22b. CORONER: I HEREBY CERTIFY THAT DEATH OCCURRED AT THE HOUR DATE AND PLACE STATED ABOVE FROM THE CAUSES STATED BELOW AND THAT I HAVE HELD AN INVESTIGATION, AUTOPSY, INQUEST ON THE REMAINS OF DECEASED AS REQUIRED BY LAW

22c. PHYSICIAN OR CORONER—SIGNATURE: [signature] M.D. | 22d. ADDRESS: 111 Congress Street Pasadena, California | 22e. DATE SIGNED: 12/16/66

FUNERAL DIRECTOR AND LOCAL REGISTRAR

23. SPECIFY BURIAL, ENTOMBMENT OR CREMATION: Cremation | 24. DATE: 12-17-66 | 25. NAME OF CEMETERY OR CREMATORY: Forest Lawn Memorial-Park | 26. EMBALMER—SIGNATURE (IF BODY EMBALMED): [signature] | LICENSE NUMBER: 3644

27. NAME OF FUNERAL DIRECTOR (OR PERSON ACTING AS SUCH): Forest Lawn Memorial-Park Association, Glendale | 28. DATE ACCEPTED FOR REGISTRATION BY LOCAL REGISTRAR: DEC 16 1966 | 29. LOCAL REGISTRAR—SIGNATURE: [signature] MD

MEDICAL AND HEALTH DATA

CAUSE OF DEATH

30. CAUSE OF DEATH — ENTER ONLY ONE CAUSE PER LINE FOR (A), (B), AND (C)

PART I DEATH WAS CAUSED BY IMMEDIATE CAUSE (A): Cardiac arrest

CONDITIONS IF ANY WHICH GAVE RISE TO THE ABOVE CAUSE (A) STATING THE UNDERLYING CAUSE LAST — DUE TO (B): Bronchogenic Ca of Lung | 3 mo

DUE TO (C):

APPROXIMATE INTERVAL BETWEEN ONSET AND DEATH

PART II OTHER SIGNIFICANT CONDITIONS CONTRIBUTING TO DEATH BUT NOT RELATED TO THE TERMINAL DISEASE CONDITION GIVEN IN PART I (A)

OPERATION AND AUTOPSY

31. OPERATION—CHECK ONE: NO OPERATION PERFORMED | [X] OPERATION PERFORMED—FINDINGS USED IN DETERMINING ABOVE STATED CAUSES OF DEATH | OPERATION PERFORMED—FINDINGS NOT USED IN DETERMINING ABOVE STATED CAUSES OF DEATH | 32. DATE OF OPERATION: 11/7/66 | 33. AUTOPSY—CHECK ONE: [X] NO AUTOPSY PERFORMED | AUTOPSY PERFORMED—FINDINGS USED IN DETERMINING ABOVE STATED CAUSES OF DEATH | AUTOPSY PERFORMED—FINDINGS NOT USED IN DETERMINING ABOVE STATED CAUSES OF DEATH

INJURY INFORMATION

34a. SPECIFY ACCIDENT, SUICIDE OR HOMICIDE | 34b. DESCRIBE HOW INJURY OCCURRED

35a. TIME OF INJURY: HOUR / MONTH / DAY / YEAR

35b. INJURY OCCURRED: WHILE AT WORK / NOT WHILE AT WORK | 35c. PLACE OF INJURY | 35d. CITY, TOWN, OR LOCATION / COUNTY / STATE

This is to certify that this document is a true copy of the official record filed with the Registrar-Recorder/County Clerk.

Beatriz Valdez

BEATRIZ VALDEZ
Registrar-Recorder/County Clerk

AUG 10 1995

19-389285

This copy not valid unless prepared on engraved border displaying the Seal and Signature of the Registrar-Recorder/County Clerk.

THE GREAT SEAL OF THE STATE OF CALIFORNIA — EUREKA

REGISTRAR-RECORDER/COUNTY CLERK — COUNTY OF LOS ANGELES • CALIFORNIA

American Bank Note Company

ANY ALTERATION OR ERASURE VOIDS THIS CERTIFICATE

CERTIFICATION OF VITAL RECORD

COUNTY OF LOS ANGELES • REGISTRAR-RECORDER/COUNTY CLERK

CERTIFICATE OF DEATH
STATE OF CALIFORNIA

0190-050343
LOCAL REGISTRATION DISTRICT AND CERTIFICATE NUMBER

STATE FILE NUMBER

DECEDENT PERSONAL DATA

1A. NAME OF DECEDENT—FIRST: Dominique | 1B. MIDDLE: Ellen | 1C. LAST: Dunne | 2A. DATE OF DEATH (MONTH, DAY, YEAR): Nov 4 1982 | 2B. HOUR: 1100

3. SEX: female | 4. RACE: cauc | 5. ETHNICITY: not stated | 6. DATE OF BIRTH: Nov 20 1959 | 7. AGE: 22 YEARS

8. BIRTHPLACE OF DECEDENT (STATE OR FOREIGN COUNTRY): California | 9. NAME AND BIRTHPLACE OF FATHER: Dominick Dunne-Conn | 10. BIRTH NAME AND BIRTHPLACE OF MOTHER: Ellen Griffin-Arizona

11. CITIZEN OF WHAT COUNTRY: U.S.A. | 12. SOCIAL SECURITY NUMBER: 545 33 7243 | 13. MARITAL STATUS: never married | 14. NAME OF SURVIVING SPOUSE (IF WIFE, ENTER BIRTH NAME):

15. PRIMARY OCCUPATION: Actress | 16. NUMBER OF YEARS THIS OCCUPATION: 4 | 17. EMPLOYER (IF SELF-EMPLOYED, SO STATE): Freelance | 18. KIND OF INDUSTRY OR BUSINESS: Entertainment

1 OF 2

USUAL RESIDENCE

19A. USUAL RESIDENCE—STREET ADDRESS (STREET AND NUMBER OR LOCATION): 523 N Crescent Drive | 19B. | 19C. CITY OR TOWN: Beverly Hills

19D. COUNTY: Los Angeles | 19E. STATE: Calif | 20. NAME AND ADDRESS OF INFORMANT—RELATIONSHIP: Mrs E. Griffin Dunne (Mother) same address

PLACE OF DEATH

21A. PLACE OF DEATH: Cedar Sinai Hospital | 21B. COUNTY: Los Angeles

21C. STREET ADDRESS (STREET AND NUMBER OR LOCATION): 8700 Beverly Bl. | 21D. CITY OR TOWN: Los Angeles

CAUSE OF DEATH

22. DEATH WAS CAUSED BY: (ENTER ONLY ONE CAUSE PER LINE FOR A, B, AND C)
IMMEDIATE CAUSE (A) ANOXIC ENCEPHALOPTHY
CONDITIONS, IF ANY, WHICH GAVE RISE TO THE IMMEDIATE CAUSE, STATING THE UNDERLYING CAUSE LAST
DUE TO, OR AS A CONSEQUENCE OF (B) STRANGULATION
DUE TO, OR AS A CONSEQUENCE OF (C)
APPROXIMATE INTERVAL BETWEEN ONSET AND DEATH

24. WAS DEATH REPORTED TO CORONER? 82-13890
25. WAS BIOPSY PERFORMED? No
26. WAS AUTOPSY PERFORMED? Yes

23. OTHER CONDITIONS CONTRIBUTING BUT NOT RELATED TO THE IMMEDIATE CAUSE OF DEATH
27. WAS OPERATION PERFORMED FOR ANY CONDITION IN ITEMS 22 OR 23? TYPE OF OPERATION: No | DATE

PHYSICIAN'S CERTIFICATION

28A. I CERTIFY THAT DEATH OCCURRED AT THE HOUR, DATE AND PLACE STATED FROM THE CAUSES STATED. I ATTENDED DECEDENT SINCE (ENTER MO, DA, YR.) I LAST SAW DECEDENT ALIVE (ENTER MO, DA, YR.) | 28B. PHYSICIAN—SIGNATURE AND DEGREE OR TITLE | 28C. DATE SIGNED | 28D. PHYSICIAN'S LICENSE NUMBER
28E. TYPE PHYSICIAN'S NAME AND ADDRESS

INJURY INFORMATION

29. SPECIFY ACCIDENT, SUICIDE, ETC.: Homicide | 30. PLACE OF INJURY: Residence | 31. INJURY AT WORK: No | 32A. DATE OF INJURY—MONTH, DAY, YEAR: 10-30-82 | 32B. HOUR: 2124

33. LOCATION (STREET AND NUMBER OR LOCATION AND CITY OR TOWN): 8723 Rangely , Los Angeles | 34. DESCRIBE HOW INJURY OCCURRED (EVENTS WHICH RESULTED IN INJURY): Assaulted

CORONER'S USE ONLY

35A. I CERTIFY THAT DEATH OCCURRED AT THE HOUR, DATE AND PLACE STATED FROM THE CAUSES STATED. AS REQUIRED BY LAW I HAVE HELD AN XXXXXX INVESTIGATION) 6 | 35B. CORONER—SIGNATURE AND DEGREE OR TITLE: Deputy Coroner | 35C. DATE SIGNED: 11-5-82

36. DISPOSITION: Burial | 37. DATE—MONTH, DAY, YEAR: 11-6-82 | 38. NAME AND ADDRESS OF CEMETERY OR CREMATORY: Westwood Memorial Park Los Angeles Calif not embalmed | 39. EMBALMER'S LICENSE NUMBER AND SIGNATURE

40. NAME OF FUNERAL DIRECTOR (OR PERSON ACTING AS SUCH): Westwood Village Mortuary | 41. LOCAL REGISTRAR—SIGNATURE | 42. DATE ACCEPTED BY LOCAL REGISTRAR: NOV 6 1982

STATE REGISTRAR: A. | B. | C. | D. | E. | F.

VS-11 (10-78)

01-9-4-0555

This is to certify that this document is a true copy of the official record filed with the Registrar-Recorder/County Clerk.

Beatriz Valdez
BEATRIZ VALDEZ
Registrar-Recorder/County Clerk

AUG 15 1995
19-397059

This copy not valid unless prepared on engraved border displaying the Seal and Signature of the Registrar-Recorder/County Clerk.

THE GREAT SEAL OF THE STATE OF CALIFORNIA
EUREKA

American Bank Note Company

ANY ALTERATION OR ERASURE VOIDS THIS CERTIFICATE

CERTIFICATION OF VITAL RECORD

COUNTY OF LOS ANGELES • REGISTRAR-RECORDER/COUNTY CLERK

CERTIFICATE OF DEATH
STATE OF CALIFORNIA

0190-004440

1A. Name of decedent—first: JAMES Aka JIMMY
1B. Middle: FRANCIS
1C. Last: DURANTE DURANTE
2A. Date of death: Jan 29, 1980
2B. Hour: 0427
3. Sex: Male
4. Race: White
5. Ethnicity: American
6. Date of birth: Feb. 10, 1893
7. Age: 86 years
8. Birthplace of decedent: New York
9. Name and birthplace of father: Bartholomew Durante, Italy
10. Birth name and birthplace of mother: Rose Lentino, Italy
11. Citizen of what country: USA
12. Social Security Number: 112-10-9800
13. Marital status: Married
14. Name of surviving spouse: Margaret A. Little
15. Primary occupation: Entertainer
16. Number of years this occupation: 68
17. Employer: Self Employed
18. Kind of industry or business: Stage, Radio, Motion Picture & T.V.
19A. Usual residence—street address: 511 North Beverly Drive
19C. City or town: Beverly Hills
19D. County: Los Angeles
19E. State: California
20. Name and address of informant—relationship: Mrs. Margaret A. Durante, Wife, 511 North Beverly Drive, Beverly Hills, Calif. 90210
21A. Place of death: St John Hospital & Health Center
21B. County: Los Angeles
21C. Street address: 1328 - 22nd Street
21D. City or town: Santa Monica
22. Death was caused by:
(A) Terminal pneumonitis — 21 days
(B) Repeated small cerebral thrombosis since July 1979
(C) Residual of right cerebral thrombosis with left hemiplegia — 7½ yrs
24. Was death reported to coroner? No
25. Was biopsy performed? No
26. Was autopsy performed? No
23. Other conditions contributing but not related to the immediate cause of death: A.S.H.D.w/cardiomegaly; Abdominal aneurysm 4 cm.
27. Was operation performed for any condition in items 22 or 23? No
28A. I certify that death occurred at the hour, date and place stated from the causes stated. Attended decedent since 1-26-73; Last saw decedent alive 1-28-80
28B. Physician—signature and degree or title: John B. McDonald M.D.
28C. Date signed: 1-29-80
28D. Physician's license number: 0A0-7719
28E. Type physician's name and address: JOHN B. MC DONALD, M.D., 133 S. Lasky Drive, Beverly Hills, Calif. 90212
29. Specify accident, suicide, etc.
30. Place of injury
31. Injury at work
32A. Date of injury
32B. Hour
33. Location
34. Describe how injury occurred
35A. I certify that death occurred at the hour, date and place stated from the causes stated. As required by law I have held an (inquest-investigation)
35B. Coroner—signature and degree or title
35C. Date signed
36. Disposition: Burial
37. Date: Feb. 1, 1980
38. Name and address of cemetery or crematory: Holy Cross, 5835 W. Slauson Ave. LA.
39. Embalmer's license number and signature: Francis P. Palmieri 3305
40. Name of funeral director: GODEAU & MARTINONI INC.
41. Local registrar—signature
42. Date accepted by local registrar: JAN 30 1980

State Registrar: A. B. C. D. E. F.

VS-11 (10-78)

01-9-1-0756

This is to certify that this document is a true copy of the official record filed with the Registrar-Recorder/County Clerk.

CONNY B. McCORMACK
Registrar-Recorder/County Clerk

OCT 3 1996
19-386526

This copy not valid unless prepared on engraved border displaying the Seal and Signature of the Registrar-Recorder/County Clerk.

ANY ALTERATION OR ERASURE VOIDS THIS CERTIFICATE

CERTIFICATE OF DEATH

STATE OF CALIFORNIA
USE BLACK INK ONLY/NO ERASURES, WHITEOUTS OR ALTERATIONS
VS-11 (REV. 11/96)

STATE FILE NUMBER | LOCAL REGISTRATION NUMBER

DECEDENT PERSONAL DATA

1. NAME OF DECEDENT—FIRST (GIVEN)	2. MIDDLE	3. LAST (FAMILY)
HARRY	J.	ESSEX

4. DATE OF BIRTH MM/DD/CCYY	5. AGE YRS.	IF UNDER 1 YEAR MONTHS / DAYS	IF UNDER 24 HOURS HOURS / MINUTES	6. SEX	7. DATE OF DEATH MM/DD/CCYY	8. HOUR
11/29/1910	86			M	02/06/1997	1616

9. STATE OF BIRTH	10. SOCIAL SECURITY NO.	11. MILITARY SERVICE	12. MARITAL STATUS	13. EDUCATION—YEARS COMPLETED
NY	559-36-6762	[X] YES [ ] NO	WIDOWED	16

14. RACE	15. HISPANIC—SPECIFY	16. USUAL EMPLOYER
CAUCASIAN	[ ] YES [X] NO	SELF EMPLOYED

17. OCCUPATION	18. KIND OF BUSINESS	19. YEARS IN OCCUPATION
WRITER/DIRECTOR	ENTERTAINMENT	75

USUAL RESIDENCE

20. RESIDENCE—STREET AND NUMBER OR LOCATION: 9303 READCREST DRIVE

21. CITY	22. COUNTY	23. ZIP CODE	24. YRS IN COUNTY	25. STATE OR FOREIGN COUNTRY
BEVERLY HILLS	LOS ANGELES	90210	55	CA

INFORMANT

26. NAME, RELATIONSHIP	27. MAILING ADDRESS (STREET AND NUMBER OR RURAL ROUTE NUMBER, CITY OR TOWN, STATE, ZIP)
DAVID STEPHEN ESSEX - SON	73-373 COUNTRY DR. #2812 PALM DESERT, CA 92260

SPOUSE AND PARENT INFORMATION

28. NAME OF SURVIVING SPOUSE—FIRST	29. MIDDLE	30. LAST (MAIDEN NAME)	
-	-	-	
31. NAME OF FATHER—FIRST	**32. MIDDLE**	**33. LAST**	**34. BIRTH STATE**
WOLFE	-	ESSEX	AUSTRIA
35. NAME OF MOTHER—FIRST	**36. MIDDLE**	**37. LAST (MAIDEN)**	**38. BIRTH STATE**
SARAH	-	BRATTER	AUSTRIA

DISPOSITION(S)

39. DATE MM/DD/CCYY	40. PLACE OF FINAL DISPOSITION
02/11/1997	WESTWOOD MEMORIAL PARK, 1218 GLENDON AVE. LOS ANGELES, CA 90024

FUNERAL DIRECTOR AND LOCAL REGISTRAR

41. TYPE OF DISPOSITION(S)	42. SIGNATURE OF EMBALMER	43. LICENSE NO.
CR/BU	▶ NOT EMBALMED	-

44. NAME OF FUNERAL DIRECTOR	45. LICENSE NO.	46. SIGNATURE OF LOCAL REGISTRAR	47. DATE MM/DD/CCYY
PIERCE BROS. WESTWOOD VILLAGE	F-951	▶ [signature]	02/07/1997

PLACE OF DEATH

101. PLACE OF DEATH	102. IF HOSPITAL, SPECIFY ONE	103. FACILITY OTHER THAN HOSPITAL	104. COUNTY
CEDARS SINAI MEDICAL CTR	[X] IP [ ] ER/OP [ ] DOA	[ ] CONV. HOSP. [ ] RES. CARE [ ] OTHER	LOS ANGELES

105. STREET ADDRESS—STREET AND NUMBER OR LOCATION	106. CITY
8700 BEVERLY BLVD.	LOS ANGELES

CAUSE OF DEATH

107. DEATH WAS CAUSED BY: (ENTER ONLY ONE CAUSE PER LINE FOR A, B, C, AND D)

		TIME INTERVAL BETWEEN ONSET AND DEATH
IMMEDIATE CAUSE (A)	CARDIOPULMONARY ARREST	25 MINS
DUE TO (B)	ARTERIOSCLEROTIC HEART DISEASE	YEARS
DUE TO (C)		
DUE TO (D)		

108. DEATH REPORTED TO CORONER: [ ] YES [X] NO — REFERRAL NUMBER
109. BIOPSY PERFORMED: [ ] YES [X] NO
110. AUTOPSY PERFORMED: [ ] YES [X] NO
111. USED IN DETERMINING CAUSE: [ ] YES [ ] NO

112. OTHER SIGNIFICANT CONDITIONS CONTRIBUTING TO DEATH BUT NOT RELATED TO CAUSE GIVEN IN 107
NONE

113. WAS OPERATION PERFORMED FOR ANY CONDITION IN ITEM 107 OR 112? IF YES, LIST TYPE OF OPERATION AND DATE.
NO

PHYSICIAN'S CERTIFICATION

114. I CERTIFY THAT TO THE BEST OF MY KNOWLEDGE DEATH OCCURRED AT THE HOUR, DATE AND PLACE STATED FROM THE CAUSES STATED.

DECEDENT ATTENDED SINCE MM/DD/CCYY	DECEDENT LAST SEEN ALIVE MM/DD/CCYY	115. SIGNATURE AND TITLE OF CERTIFIER	116. LICENSE NO.	117. DATE MM/DD/CCYY
--/--/1979	02/06/1997	▶ [signature] MD.	G 26101	02/07/1997

118. TYPE ATTENDING PHYSICIAN'S NAME, MAILING ADDRESS, ZIP
DAVID FRISCH, MD 434 S. SAN VICENTE BL. #200, LOS ANGELES, CA

CORONER'S USE ONLY

12

I CERTIFY THAT IN MY OPINION DEATH OCCURRED AT THE HOUR, DATE AND PLACE STATED FROM THE CAUSES STATED.

119. MANNER OF DEATH: [ ] NATURAL [ ] SUICIDE [ ] HOMICIDE [ ] ACCIDENT [ ] PENDING INVESTIGATION [ ] COULD NOT BE DETERMINED

120. INJURY AT WORK	121. INJURY DATE MM/DD/CCYY	122. HOUR	123. PLACE OF INJURY
[ ] YES [ ] NO			

124. DESCRIBE HOW INJURY OCCURRED (EVENTS WHICH RESULTED IN INJURY)

125. LOCATION (STREET AND NUMBER OR LOCATION AND CITY, ZIP)

126. SIGNATURE OF CORONER OR DEPUTY CORONER	127. DATE MM/DD/CCYY	128. TYPED NAME, TITLE OF CORONER OR DEPUTY CORONER
▶		

4140

STATE REGISTRAR

A	B	C	D	E	F	G	H	FAX AUTH. #	CENSUS TRACT

CERTIFICATION OF VITAL RECORD

COUNTY OF LOS ANGELES • REGISTRAR-RECORDER/COUNTY CLERK

12242

STATE OF CALIFORNIA
DEPARTMENT OF PUBLIC HEALTH
VITAL STATISTICS
STANDARD CERTIFICATE OF DEATH

1. PLACE OF DEATH: DIST. NO. 1906
COUNTY OF Los Angeles
LOCAL REGISTERED NO. 682
CITY, OF Santa Monica
STREET AND NO. 705 Ocean Front
IF DEATH OCCURRED IN A HOSPITAL OR INSTITUTION, GIVE ITS NAME INSTEAD OF STREET AND NO.
2. FULL NAME Fairbanks, Douglas Elton, Sr
RESIDENCE: NO. 705 Ocean Front ST. IF NON-RESIDENT, GIVE CITY OR TOWN, AND STATE
USUAL PLACE OF ABODE

3. SEX male
4. COLOR OR RACE cauc
5. SINGLE, MARRIED, WIDOWED OR DIVORCED? (WRITE THE WORD) married
5A. IF MARRIED, WIDOWED OR DIVORCED, NAME OF HUSBAND OR WIFE Sylvia Fairbanks
6. DATE OF BIRTH May 23 1883 (MONTH, DAY, YEAR)
7. AGE 56 YR. 6 MO. 19 DAYS. IF LESS THAN ONE DAY ___ HRS. ___ MIN.
8. TRADE, PROFESSION OR KIND OF WORK DONE AS SPINNER, SAWYER, BOOKKEEPER, ETC. Actor and motion Picture Producer
9. INDUSTRY OR BUSINESS IN WHICH WORK WAS DONE, AS SILKMILL, SAWMILL, BANK, ETC. Motion Pictures
10. DATE DECEASED LAST WORKED AT THIS OCCUPATION (MO. AND YR.) Dec. 1939
11. TOTAL YEARS SPENT IN THIS OCCUPATION 25
12. BIRTHPLACE (CITY OR TOWN) Denver
STATE OR COUNTRY Colorado
FATHER
13. NAME John Fairbanks
14. BIRTHPLACE (CITY OR TOWN) New York
STATE OR COUNTRY New York
MOTHER
15. MAIDEN NAME Ella Adelaide Marsh
16. BIRTHPLACE (CITY OR TOWN) New York
STATE OR COUNTRY New York
17. LENGTH OF RESIDENCE
A. CITY, TOWN OR RURAL DISTRICT OF DEATH 3 YRS. ___ MOS. ___ DAYS
B. IN CALIFORNIA 22 YRS. ___ MOS. ___ DAYS
C. IN U.S., IF OF FOREIGN BIRTH ___ YRS. ___ MOS. ___ DAYS
18. INFORMANT (SIGNATURE) C. E. Erickson
ADDRESS 6924 Oakwood Ave. Los Angeles
19. BURIAL, CREMATION OR REMOVAL? (WRITE THE WORD) burial
PLACE Forest Lawn Cemetery DATE 12/15/39
20. EMBALMER LICENSE NO. 1682
SIGNATURE M Carter Long
FUNERAL DIRECTOR Forest Lawn Memorial-Park Association, Inc.
ADDRESS Glendale, California. Fernand H. Sears
21. FILED 12-14-39 (DATE) J L Pomeroy M D
By Robert H Webster LOCAL REGISTRAR
FILED JAN 12 1940 MAME B. BEATTY, Registrar of Vital Statistics

22. DATE OF DEATH Dec. 12 1939 (MONTH, DAY, YEAR)
23. MEDICAL CERTIFICATE OF DEATH
I HEREBY CERTIFY, THAT I ATTENDED DECEASED FROM 12/10/39 TO 12/12/39;
THAT I LAST SAW H im ALIVE 12/11/39
AND THAT DEATH OCCURRED ON THE ABOVE STATED DATE AT THE HOUR OF 12 45 A. M.
THE PRINCIPAL CAUSE OF DEATH AND RELATED CAUSES OF IMPORTANCE, IN ORDER OF ONSET, WERE AS FOLLOWS: / DATE OF ONSET
Arteriosclerosis 2 yrs.
Coronary Sclerosis 2 yrs
OTHER CONTRIBUTORY CAUSES OF IMPORTANCE:
Coronary occlusion 12/10/39
IF OPERATION, DATE OF none
WAS THERE AN AUTOPSY? No
CONDITION FOR WHICH PERFORMED
NAME LABORATORY TEST CONFIRMING DIAGNOSIS Electrocardiograph
24. CORONER'S CERTIFICATE OF DEATH
I HEREBY CERTIFY, THAT I TOOK CHARGE OF THE REMAINS DESCRIBED ABOVE, HELD AN ___ INQUEST, AUTOPSY OR INQUIRY THEREON, AND FROM SUCH ACTION FIND THAT SAID DECEASED CAME TO H___ DEATH ON THE DATE STATED ABOVE.
25. IF DEATH WAS DUE TO EXTERNAL CAUSES (VIOLENCE) FILL IN THE FOLLOWING:
ACCIDENT, SUICIDE OR HOMICIDE? ___ DATE OF INJURY ___
INJURED AT: CITY OR TOWN OF ___ COUNTY AND STATE OF ___
DID INJURY OCCUR IN HOME, INDUSTRY, OR PUBLIC PLACE? ___
MANNER OF INJURY ___
NATURE OF INJURY ___
26. IF DISEASE/INJURY RELATED TO OCCUPATION, SPECIFY ___
27. SIGNATURE J F Sampson M.D.
PHYSICIAN, AUTOPSY SURGEON
ADDRESS 710 Wilshire Blvd Santa Monica
28. WHEN REQUIRED BY LAW ___ CORONER

This is to certify that this document is a true copy of the official record filed with the Registrar-Recorder/County Clerk.

OCT 1 1996
19-382344

Conny B. McCormack
CONNY B. McCORMACK
Registrar-Recorder/County Clerk

This copy not valid unless prepared on engraved border displaying the Seal and Signature of the Registrar-Recorder/County Clerk.

ANY ALTERATION OR ERASURE VOIDS THIS CERTIFICATE

A

No. 15

DISTRICT NO. 1904 REGISTRAR'S NO. 1384

1. FULL NAME William Claude Fields — Resident

2. PLACE OF DEATH: (A) COUNTY Los Angeles
(B) CITY OR TOWN Pasadena
(IF OUTSIDE CITY OR TOWN LIMITS, WRITE RURAL)
(C) NAME OF HOSPITAL OR INSTITUTION 2900 Blanche Street Las Encinas Sanitarium
(IF NOT IN HOSPITAL OR INSTITUTION, GIVE STREET NUMBER OR LOCATION)
(D) LENGTH OF STAY: (SPECIFY WHETHER YEARS, MONTHS OR DAYS)
IN HOSPITAL OR INSTITUTION 14 months
IN THIS COMMUNITY 14 months IN CALIFORNIA 18 yrs
(E) IF FOREIGN BORN, HOW LONG IN THE U. S. A.? ____ YEARS

3. USUAL RESIDENCE OF DECEASED:
(A) STATE California
(B) COUNTY Los Angeles
(C) CITY OR TOWN Los Angeles
(IF OUTSIDE CITY OR TOWN LIMITS, WRITE RURAL)
(D) STREET NO. 2015 DeMille Drive

20. DATE OF DEATH: MONTH December DAY 25 YEAR 1946 HOUR 12 MINUTE 03 PM

3. (E) IF VETERAN, NAME OF WAR None
3. (F) SOCIAL SECURITY NO. Unknown

4. SEX Male
5. COLOR OR RACE Caucasian
6. (A) SINGLE, MARRIED, WIDOWED OR DIVORCED Married
6. (B) NAME OF HUSBAND OR WIFE Harriet Veronica Fields
6. (C) AGE OF HUSBAND OR WIFE IF ALIVE 66 YEARS

7. BIRTHDATE OF DECEASED January 29 1880 (MONTH, DAY, YEAR)

8. AGE 66 YRS 10 MOS 26 DAYS — IF LESS THAN ONE DAY OLD ____ HRS ____ MIN

9. BIRTHPLACE Philadelphia, Pennsylvania
10. USUAL OCCUPATION Actor
11. INDUSTRY OR BUSINESS Stage and Screen
FATHER 12. NAME James Dukenfield
13. BIRTHPLACE Sheffield, England
MOTHER 14. MAIDEN NAME Kate Felton
15. BIRTHPLACE Philadelphia, Pennsylvania
16. (A) INFORMANT W. Claude Fields, Jr.
(B) ADDRESS 123½ North Cale Drive- Beverly Hills

17. (A) Entombment (BURIAL, CREMATION OR REMOVAL) (B) DATE Jan. 2, 1947
(C) PLACE Forest Lawn Mausoleum
18. (A) EMBALMER'S SIGNATURE Claude Nixon LICENSE NO. 2919
(B) FUNERAL DIRECTOR Forest Lawn Memorial- Park
ADDRESS Association, Inc., Glendale, Calif.
BY H.B. Chenoweth

19. (A) DEC 30 1946 (DATE FILED) (B) CHARLES W. ARTHUR D.M. (REGISTRAR'S SIGNATURE)

21. MEDICAL CERTIFICATE
I HEREBY CERTIFY, THAT I ATTENDED THE DECEASED FROM October 29 1945 TO December 25 1946
THAT I LAST SAW HIM ALIVE ON 25 December 1946 AND THAT DEATH OCCURRED ON THE DATE AND HOUR STATED ABOVE.

22. CORONER'S CERTIFICATE
I HEREBY CERTIFY, THAT I HELD AN AUTOPSY, INQUEST OR INVESTIGATION ON THE REMAINS OF THE DECEASED AND FIND FROM SUCH ACTION THAT DECEASED CAME TO H__ DEATH ON THE DATE AND HOUR STATED ABOVE.

	DURATION
IMMEDIATE CAUSE OF DEATH Cirrhosis of the Liver	5 yrs.
DUE TO	
DUE TO Chronic alcoholism	Unknown
OTHER CONDITIONS (INCLUDE PREGNANCY WITHIN THREE MONTHS OF DEATH)	
MAJOR FINDINGS OF OPERATIONS	DATE OF OPERATION
OF AUTOPSY None	

PHYSICIAN UNDERLINE THE CAUSE TO WHICH DEATH SHOULD BE CHARGED STATISTICALLY

23. IF DEATH WAS DUE TO EXTERNAL CAUSES, FILL IN THE FOLLOWING:
(A) ACCIDENT, SUICIDE, OR HOMICIDE? (B) DATE OF INJURY
(C) WHERE DID INJURY OCCUR? CITY OR TOWN COUNTY STATE
(D) DID INJURY OCCUR IN OR ABOUT HOME, ON FARM, IN INDUSTRIAL PLACE, OR IN PUBLIC PLACE? (SPECIFY TYPE OF PLACE) WHILE AT WORK?
(E) MEANS OF INJURY

24. CORONER'S OR PHYSICIAN'S SIGNATURE Douglas R. Dodge, M.D.
ADDRESS 2900 Blanche Street Pasadena DATE 25 Dec.-46

N. B.—Every item of information should be carefully supplied. AGE should be stated EXACTLY. PHYSICIANS should state CAUSE OF DEATH in plain terms, that it may be properly classified. Exact statement of OCCUPATION is very important.

STATE OF CALIFORNIA DEPARTMENT OF PUBLIC HEALTH — CERTIFICATE OF DEATH — U. S. DEPT. OF COMMERCE BUREAU OF THE CENSUS

CERTIFICATION STATEMENT

This is to certify that the above is a true and correct copy of the DEATH CERTIFICATE of the above named decedent as registered in this office.

Health Officer

Deputy Registrar-Vital Statistics
Pasadena Public Health Department

Furnished for fee of $9.00

Date: 09/22/1995 SEAL OF THE CITY OF PASADENA

CERTIFICATION OF VITAL RECORD

COUNTY OF LOS ANGELES • REGISTRAR-RECORDER/COUNTY CLERK

CERTIFICATE OF DEATH
STATE OF CALIFORNIA

0190-037351

STATE FILE NUMBER — LOCAL REGISTRATION DISTRICT AND CERTIFICATE NUMBER

DECEDENT PERSONAL DATA

1A. NAME OF DECEDENT—FIRST	1B. MIDDLE	1C. LAST	2A. DATE OF DEATH (MONTH, DAY, YEAR)	2B. HOUR
Henry		Fonda	Aug 12 1982	0815

3. SEX	4. RACE	5. ETHNICITY	6. DATE OF BIRTH	7. AGE
male	cauc	not stated	May 16 1905	77 YEARS

8. BIRTHPLACE OF DECEDENT (STATE OR FOREIGN COUNTRY)	9. NAME AND BIRTHPLACE OF FATHER	10. BIRTH NAME AND BIRTHPLACE OF MOTHER
Nebraska	William Brace Fonda- Neb.	Herbertha Jaynes - Wis.

11. CITIZEN OF WHAT COUNTRY	12. SOCIAL SECURITY NUMBER	13. MARITAL STATUS	14. NAME OF SURVIVING SPOUSE (IF WIFE, ENTER BIRTH NAME)
U.S.A.	561-14-7670	married	Shirlee Adams

15. PRIMARY OCCUPATION	16. NUMBER OF YEARS THIS OCCUPATION	17. EMPLOYER (IF SELF-EMPLOYED, SO STATE)	18. KIND OF INDUSTRY OR BUSINESS
Actor	adult life	Self	Entertainment

USUAL RESIDENCE

19A. USUAL RESIDENCE—STREET ADDRESS (STREET AND NUMBER OR LOCATION)	19B.	19C. CITY OR TOWN
10744 Chalon Rd.		Los Angeles

19D. COUNTY	19E. STATE	20. NAME AND ADDRESS OF INFORMANT—RELATIONSHIP
Los Angeles	Calif	Shirlee Fonda (Wife) same address

PLACE OF DEATH

21A. PLACE OF DEATH	21B. COUNTY
Cedars Sinai Hospital	Los Angeles

21C. STREET ADDRESS (STREET AND NUMBER OR LOCATION)	21D. CITY OR TOWN
8700 Beverly Blvd.	Los Angeles

CAUSE OF DEATH

22. DEATH WAS CAUSED BY: (ENTER ONLY ONE CAUSE PER LINE FOR A, B, AND C)

	Cause	Approximate interval between onset and death
IMMEDIATE CAUSE (A)	Cardio-Respiratory Arrest	30 min
DUE TO, OR AS A CONSEQUENCE OF (B)	Chronic Cardiac failure	3 yrs.
DUE TO, OR AS A CONSEQUENCE OF (C)	Restrictive Cardiomyopathy	5 yrs.

CONDITIONS, IF ANY, WHICH GAVE RISE TO THE IMMEDIATE CAUSE, STATING THE UNDERLYING CAUSE LAST.

24. WAS DEATH REPORTED TO CORONER? No
25. WAS BIOPSY PERFORMED? No
26. WAS AUTOPSY PERFORMED? YES

23. OTHER CONDITIONS CONTRIBUTING BUT NOT RELATED TO THE IMMEDIATE CAUSE OF DEATH: Permanent pacemaker, Carcinoma Prostate
27. WAS OPERATION PERFORMED FOR ANY CONDITION IN ITEMS 22 OR 23? TYPE OF OPERATION: Median Sternotomy DATE: May 15, 1981

PHYSICIAN'S CERTIFICATION

28A. I CERTIFY THAT DEATH OCCURRED AT THE HOUR, DATE AND PLACE STATED FROM THE CAUSES STATED.

I ATTENDED DECEDENT SINCE (ENTER MO, DA, YR.)	I LAST SAW DECEDENT ALIVE (ENTER MO, DA, YR.)	28B. PHYSICIAN—SIGNATURE AND DEGREE OR TITLE	28C. DATE SIGNED	28D. PHYSICIAN'S LICENSE NUMBER
July 1974	8-11-82	[signature] MD	8-12-82	G20608

28E. TYPE PHYSICIAN'S NAME AND ADDRESS: Gary Sugarman M.D. 436 N Roxbury Dr Beverly Hills Calif

INJURY INFORMATION

29. SPECIFY ACCIDENT, SUICIDE, ETC. | 30. PLACE OF INJURY | 31. INJURY AT WORK | 32A. DATE OF INJURY—MONTH, DAY, YEAR | 32B. HOUR

33. LOCATION (STREET AND NUMBER OR LOCATION AND CITY OR TOWN) | 34. DESCRIBE HOW INJURY OCCURRED (EVENTS WHICH RESULTED IN INJURY)

CORONER'S USE ONLY

35A. I CERTIFY THAT DEATH OCCURRED AT THE HOUR, DATE AND PLACE STATED FROM THE CAUSES STATED. AS REQUIRED BY LAW I HAVE HELD AN (INQUEST-INVESTIGATION) | 35B. CORONER—SIGNATURE AND DEGREE OR TITLE | 35C. DATE SIGNED

36. DISPOSITION	37. DATE—MONTH, DAY, YEAR	38. NAME AND ADDRESS OF CEMETERY OR CREMATORY	39. EMBALMER'S LICENSE NUMBER AND SIGNATURE
Cremation	8-13-82	Grandview Crematory Glendale Calif	not Embalmed

40. NAME OF FUNERAL DIRECTOR (OR PERSON ACTING AS SUCH)	41. LOCAL REGISTRAR—SIGNATURE	42. DATE ACCEPTED BY LOCAL REGISTRAR
Westwood Village Mortuary	[signature] rb	AUG 13 1982

STATE REGISTRAR: A. | B. | C. | D. | E. | F.

VS-11 (10-70) 4140 — 01-3-2-0555

This is to certify that this document is a true copy of the official record filed with the Registrar-Recorder/County Clerk.

OCT 02 1995

19 033394

This copy not valid unless prepared on engraved border displaying the Seal of the Registrar-Recorder/County Clerk.

THE GREAT SEAL OF THE STATE OF CALIFORNIA — EUREKA

REGISTRAR-RECORDER/COUNTY CLERK — COUNTY OF LOS ANGELES, CALIFORNIA

ANY ALTERATION OR ERASURE VOIDS THIS CERTIFICATE

CERTIFICATION OF VITAL RECORD

COUNTY OF LOS ANGELES • REGISTRAR-RECORDER/COUNTY CLERK

STATE FILE NUMBER

CERTIFICATE OF DEATH

STATE OF CALIFORNIA—DEPARTMENT OF PUBLIC HEALTH

LOCAL REGISTRATION DISTRICT AND CERTIFICATE NUMBER 7097 009739

DECEDENT PERSONAL DATA

1A. NAME OF DECEASED—FIRST NAME: WILLIAM
1B. MIDDLE NAME: CLEMENT
1C. LAST NAME: FRAWLEY
2A. DATE OF DEATH—MONTH, DAY, YEAR: MARCH 3, 1966
2B. HOUR: 5:43 P.M.
3. SEX: Male
4. COLOR OR RACE: Cauc
5. BIRTHPLACE (STATE OR FOREIGN COUNTRY): Iowa
6. DATE OF BIRTH: February 26, 1887
7. AGE (LAST BIRTHDAY): 79 YEARS; IF UNDER 1 YEAR: MONTHS, DAYS; IF UNDER 24 HOURS: HOURS, MINUTES
8. NAME AND BIRTHPLACE OF FATHER: Michael A. Frawley, Conn
9. MAIDEN NAME AND BIRTHPLACE OF MOTHER: Mary E. Brady, Iowa
10. CITIZEN OF WHAT COUNTRY: USA
11. SOCIAL SECURITY NUMBER: 562-05-1177
12. LAST OCCUPATION: Actor
13. NUMBER OF YEARS IN THIS OCCUPATION: 58
14. NAME OF LAST EMPLOYING COMPANY OR FIRM (IF SELF-EMPLOYED, SO STATE): Desi-Lu Studios
15. KIND OF INDUSTRY OR BUSINESS: Motion Picture/TV
16. IF DECEASED WAS EVER IN U.S. ARMED FORCES GIVE WAR OR DATES OF SERVICE: No
17. SPECIFY MARRIED, NEVER MARRIED, WIDOWED, DIVORCED: Divorced
18A. NAME OF PRESENT SPOUSE:
18B. PRESENT OR LAST OCCUPATION OF SPOUSE:

PLACE OF DEATH

19A. PLACE OF DEATH—NAME OF HOSPITAL: DOA @ HOLLYWOOD RECEIVING HOSPITAL
19B. STREET ADDRESS—(GIVE STREET OR RURAL ADDRESS OR LOCATION. DO NOT USE P.O. BOX NUMBERS): 1350 North Wilcox Avenue; INSIDE CITY CORPORATE LIMITS: XX; OUTSIDE CITY CORPORATE LIMITS
19C. CITY OR TOWN: Los Angeles
19D. COUNTY: Los Angeles
19E. LENGTH OF STAY IN COUNTY OF DEATH: 32 YEARS
19F. LENGTH OF STAY IN CALIFORNIA: 32 YEARS

LAST USUAL RESIDENCE (WHERE DID DECEASED LIVE—IF IN INSTITUTION ENTER RESIDENCE BEFORE ADMISSION)

20A. LAST USUAL RESIDENCE—STREET ADDRESS (GIVE STREET OR RURAL ADDRESS OR LOCATION. DO NOT USE P.O. BOX NUMBERS): 450 North Rossmore Avenue
20B. IF INSIDE CITY CORPORATE LIMITS: [X] CHECK HERE; IF OUTSIDE CITY CORPORATE LIMITS CHECK ONE: [ ] ON A FARM [ ] NOT ON A FARM
20C. CITY OR TOWN: Los Angeles 1923
20D. COUNTY: Los Angeles
20E. STATE: California
21A. NAME OF INFORMANT (IF OTHER THAN SPOUSE): Patricia Berry
21B. ADDRESS OF INFORMANT (IF DIFFERENT FROM LAST USUAL RESIDENCE OF DECEDENT): 345 N. Chadbourne, Brentwood

PHYSICIAN'S OR CORONER'S CERTIFICATION

22A. PHYSICIAN: I HEREBY CERTIFY THAT DEATH OCCURRED AT THE HOUR, DATE AND PLACE STATED ABOVE FROM THE CAUSES STATED BELOW AND THAT I ATTENDED THE DECEASED FROM 8/16/58 TO 3/1/66 AND THAT I LAST SAW THE DECEASED ALIVE ON 3/1/66
22B. CORONER: I HEREBY CERTIFY THAT DEATH OCCURRED AT THE HOUR, DATE AND PLACE STATED ABOVE FROM THE CAUSES STATED BELOW AND THAT I HAVE HELD AN ______ (INVESTIGATION, AUTOPSY, INQUEST) ON THE REMAINS OF DECEASED AS REQUIRED BY LAW
22C. PHYSICIAN OR CORONER—SIGNATURE: Wm Weber Smith, M.D. DEGREE OR TITLE
22D. ADDRESS: 133 Lasky Dr, Bev Hills
22E. DATE SIGNED: 3-4-66

FUNERAL DIRECTOR AND LOCAL REGISTRAR

23. SPECIFY BURIAL, ENTOMBMENT OR CREMATION: Burial
24. DATE: 3-8-66
25. NAME OF CEMETERY OR CREMATORY: San Fernando Mission
26. EMBALMER—SIGNATURE (IF BODY EMBALMED): Joseph J. Callanan; LICENSE NUMBER: 2616
27. NAME OF FUNERAL DIRECTOR (OR PERSON ACTING AS SUCH): CALLANAN MORTUARY
28. DATE ACCEPTED FOR REGISTRATION BY LOCAL REGISTRAR: MAR 8 1966
29. LOCAL REGISTRAR—SIGNATURE: Gabriel Bueder M.D.

MEDICAL AND HEALTH DATA

CAUSE OF DEATH

30. CAUSE OF DEATH — ENTER ONLY ONE CAUSE PER LINE FOR (A), (B), AND (C)

PART I. DEATH WAS CAUSED BY: IMMEDIATE CAUSE (A): Myocardial Insufficiency — 5 yr (APPROXIMATE INTERVAL BETWEEN ONSET AND DEATH)

CONDITIONS, IF ANY, WHICH GAVE RISE TO THE ABOVE CAUSE (A) STATING THE UNDERLYING CAUSE LAST: DUE TO (B): Arteriosclerosis, Gen'l

DUE TO (C):

PART II. OTHER SIGNIFICANT CONDITIONS CONTRIBUTING TO DEATH BUT NOT RELATED TO THE TERMINAL DISEASE CONDITION GIVEN IN PART I (A)

OPERATION AND AUTOPSY

31. OPERATION—CHECK ONE: [X] NO OPERATION PERFORMED; [ ] OPERATION PERFORMED—FINDINGS USED IN DETERMINING ABOVE STATED CAUSES OF DEATH; [ ] OPERATION PERFORMED—FINDINGS NOT USED IN DETERMINING ABOVE STATED CAUSES OF DEATH
32. DATE OF OPERATION:
33. AUTOPSY—CHECK ONE: [X] NO AUTOPSY PERFORMED; [ ] AUTOPSY PERFORMED—GROSS FINDINGS USED IN DETERMINING ABOVE STATED CAUSES OF DEATH; [ ] AUTOPSY PERFORMED—GROSS FINDINGS NOT USED IN DETERMINING ABOVE STATED CAUSES OF DEATH

INJURY INFORMATION

34A. SPECIFY ACCIDENT, SUICIDE OR HOMICIDE:
34B. DESCRIBE HOW INJURY OCCURRED
35A. TIME OF INJURY: HOUR M., MONTH, DAY, YEAR
35B. INJURY OCCURRED: [ ] WHILE AT WORK [ ] NOT WHILE AT WORK
35C. PLACE OF INJURY (E.G., IN OR ABOUT HOME, FARM, FACTORY, STREET, OFFICE BUILDING)
35D. CITY, TOWN, OR LOCATION; COUNTY; STATE

Rev. 1-1-58 Form VS-11

This is to certify that this document is a true copy of the official record filed with the Registrar-Recorder/County Clerk.

Beatriz Valdez
BEATRIZ VALDEZ
Registrar-Recorder/County Clerk

AUG 16 1995
19-397407

This copy not valid unless prepared on engraved border displaying the Seal and Signature of the Registrar-Recorder/County Clerk.

American Bank Note Company

ANY ALTERATION OR ERASURE VOIDS THIS CERTIFICATE

CERTIFICATION OF VITAL RECORD

COUNTY OF LOS ANGELES • REGISTRAR-RECORDER/COUNTY CLERK

CERTIFICATE OF DEATH
STATE OF CALIFORNIA—DEPARTMENT OF PUBLIC HEALTH

State File Number: 60-117777
Local Registration District and Certificate Number: 7053 22428

36X

DECEDENT PERSONAL DATA 846 010-3

1a. Name of deceased—first name	Clark
1c. Last name	Gable
2a. Date of death	November 16, 1960
2b. Hour	10:50 P.
3. Sex	Male
4. Color or race	White
5. Birthplace	Ohio
6. Date of birth	February 1, 1901
7. Age	59 years
8. Name and birthplace of father	William H. Gable, Penn.
9. Maiden name and birthplace of mother	Adeline Hershelman, Penn.
10. Citizen of what country	United States
11. Social security number	567 18 9990
12. Last occupation	Actor
13. Number of years in this occupation	30 Yrs
14. Name of last employing company or firm	Self-Employed
15. Kind of industry or business	Motion Pictures
16. If deceased was ever in U.S. Armed Forces	Yes WW II
17. Specify married, never married, widowed, divorced	Married
18a. Name of present spouse	Kathleen G. Gable
18b. Present or last occupation of spouse	Housewife

PLACE OF DEATH

19a. Place of death—name of hospital	Hollywood Presbyterian Hospital
19b. Street address	1322 No. Vermont Ave
19c. City or town	Los Angeles
19d. County	Los Angeles
19e. Length of stay in county of death	30 Yrs
19f. Length of stay in California	30 Yrs

LAST USUAL RESIDENCE

20a. Last usual residence—street address	4525 Petit Ave
20c. City or town	Encino
20d. County	Los Angeles
20e. State	California
21a. Name of informant	Mrs. Kathleen G. Gable
21b. Address of informant	Same

PHYSICIAN'S OR CORONER'S CERTIFICATION

22a. Physician	11/16/60 — 11-6-60
22c. Physician or coroner signature	[signature] M.D.
22d. Address	6753 Hollywood Blvd.
22e. Date signed	11/17/60

FUNERAL DIRECTOR AND LOCAL REGISTRAR

23. Specify burial, entombment or cremation	Entombment
24. Date	11/19/60
25. Name of cemetery or crematory	Forest Lawn Memorial Park
26. Embalmer—signature	[signature]
27. Name of funeral director	Cunningham & O'Connor, L.A.
28. Date accepted for registration by local registrar	NOV 18 1960
29. Local registrar—signature	[signature], M.D.

CAUSE OF DEATH 4201

30. Cause of death. Part I. Death was caused by: Immediate cause (a): Coronary Thrombosis — 10 days (approximate interval between onset and death)

OPERATION AND AUTOPSY

INJURY INFORMATION

This is to certify that this document is a true copy of the official record filed with the Registrar-Recorder/County Clerk.

Beatriz Valdez
BEATRIZ VALDEZ
Registrar-Recorder/County Clerk

AUG 25 1995
19-398641

This copy not valid unless prepared on engraved border displaying the Seal and Signature of the Registrar-Recorder/County Clerk.

CERTIFICATION OF VITAL RECORD

COUNTY OF LOS ANGELES • REGISTRAR-RECORDER/COUNTY CLERK

STATE FILE NUMBER

CERTIFICATE OF DEATH

STATE OF CALIFORNIA—DEPARTMENT OF PUBLIC HEALTH

LOCAL REGISTRATION DISTRICT AND CERTIFICATE NUMBER 7053 11930

DECEDENT PERSONAL DATA	1a. NAME OF DECEASED—FIRST NAME: GRETCHEN	1b. MIDDLE NAME: IMOGENE	1c. LAST NAME: GAILING	2a. DATE OF DEATH: JUNE 18, 1961; 2b. HOUR: 12:15 A.M.
	3. SEX: Female; 4. COLOR OR RACE: Caucasian	5. BIRTHPLACE: Nebraska	6. DATE OF BIRTH: August 30, 1915	7. AGE: 45 YEARS
	8. NAME AND BIRTHPLACE OF FATHER: Chester Roy Hall, Nebraska		9. MAIDEN NAME AND BIRTHPLACE OF MOTHER: Lillian Snearl, Nebraska	10. CITIZEN OF WHAT COUNTRY: U.S.A.; 11. SOCIAL SECURITY NUMBER: 551-22-6518
	12. LAST OCCUPATION: Actress	13. NUMBER OF YEARS IN THIS OCCUPATION: 15	14. NAME OF LAST EMPLOYING COMPANY OR FIRM: Free Lance	15. KIND OF INDUSTRY OR BUSINESS: Motion Picture & Television
	16. IF DECEASED WAS EVER IN U.S. ARMED FORCES GIVE WAR OR DATES OF SERVICE: None	17. SPECIFY MARRIED, NEVER MARRIED, WIDOWED, DIVORCED: Married	18a. NAME OF PRESENT SPOUSE: Blaine LeRoy Gailing	18b. PRESENT OR LAST OCCUPATION OF SPOUSE: Asst Manager of Bank of America
PLACE OF DEATH	19a. PLACE OF DEATH—NAME OF HOSPITAL: U.C.L.A. Medical Center		19b. STREET ADDRESS: 10833 Le Conte Avenue; [X] INSIDE CITY CORPORATE LIMITS	
	19c. CITY OR TOWN: Los Angeles		19d. COUNTY: Los Angeles	19e. LENGTH OF STAY IN COUNTY OF DEATH: 28 YEARS; 19f. LENGTH OF STAY IN CALIFORNIA: 28 YEARS
LAST USUAL RESIDENCE	20a. LAST USUAL RESIDENCE—STREET ADDRESS: 3961 Weslin Avenue	20b. IF INSIDE CITY CORPORATE LIMITS: [X]		21a. NAME OF INFORMANT (IF OTHER THAN SPOUSE): - - -
	20c. CITY OR TOWN: Los Angeles 141	20d. COUNTY: Los Angeles	20e. STATE: California	21b. ADDRESS OF INFORMANT: - - -
PHYSICIAN'S OR CORONER'S CERTIFICATION	22a. PHYSICIAN: I HEREBY CERTIFY THAT DEATH OCCURRED AT THE HOUR, DATE AND PLACE STATED ABOVE FROM THE CAUSES STATED BELOW AND THAT I ATTENDED THE DECEASED FROM 6/18/61 TO 6/18/61 AND THAT I LAST SAW THE DECEASED ALIVE ON 6/18/61		22c. PHYSICIAN OR CORONER—SIGNATURE: [signature]	DEGREE OR TITLE: MD
	22b. CORONER: I HEREBY CERTIFY THAT DEATH OCCURRED AT THE HOUR, DATE AND PLACE STATED ABOVE FROM THE CAUSES STATED BELOW AND THAT I HAVE HELD AN (INVESTIGATION, AUTOPSY, INQUEST) ON THE REMAINS OF DECEASED AS REQUIRED BY LAW		22d. ADDRESS: UCLA Medical Center	22e. DATE SIGNED: 6/18/61
FUNERAL DIRECTOR AND LOCAL REGISTRAR	23. SPECIFY BURIAL, ENTOMBMENT OR CREMATION: Burial	24. DATE: June 21, 1961	25. NAME OF CEMETERY OR CREMATORY: Forest Lawn Hollywood Hills	26. EMBALMER—SIGNATURE: [signature]; LICENSE NUMBER: 2953
	27. NAME OF FUNERAL DIRECTOR: Forest Lawn Hollywood Hills	28. DATE ACCEPTED FOR REGISTRATION BY LOCAL REGISTRAR: JUN 20 1961	29. LOCAL REGISTRAR—SIGNATURE: George M. Uhl, M.D.	
CAUSE OF DEATH	30. CAUSE OF DEATH. PART I. DEATH WAS CAUSED BY: IMMEDIATE CAUSE (A): Cardio-respiratory failure			APPROXIMATE INTERVAL BETWEEN ONSET AND DEATH: 12 hrs
	CONDITIONS, IF ANY, WHICH GAVE RISE TO THE ABOVE CAUSE (A), STATING THE UNDERLYING CAUSE LAST: DUE TO (B): Extensive Carcinoma of Ovary			4 yrs
	DUE TO (C):			
	PART II. OTHER SIGNIFICANT CONDITIONS CONTRIBUTING TO DEATH BUT NOT RELATED TO THE TERMINAL DISEASE CONDITION GIVEN IN PART I (A)			
OPERATION AND AUTOPSY	31. OPERATION—CHECK ONE: [X] OPERATION PERFORMED—FINDINGS USED IN DETERMINING ABOVE STATED CAUSES OF DEATH		32. DATE OF OPERATION: 5/16/61	33. AUTOPSY—CHECK ONE: [X] NO AUTOPSY PERFORMED
INJURY INFORMATION	34a. SPECIFY ACCIDENT, SUICIDE OR HOMICIDE		34b. DESCRIBE HOW INJURY OCCURRED	
	35a. TIME OF INJURY: HOUR MONTH DAY YEAR			
	35b. INJURY OCCURRED: [ ] WHILE AT WORK [ ] NOT WHILE AT WORK	35c. PLACE OF INJURY	35d. CITY, TOWN, OR LOCATION; COUNTY; STATE	

REV. 1-1-58 FORM VS-11

This is to certify that this document is a true copy of the official record filed with the Registrar-Recorder/County Clerk.

Beatriz Valdez
BEATRIZ VALDEZ
Registrar-Recorder/County Clerk

AUG 10 1995
19-393981

This copy not valid unless prepared on engraved border displaying the Seal and Signature of the Registrar-Recorder/County Clerk.

American Bank Note Company ANY ALTERATION OR ERASURE VOIDS THIS CERTIFICATE

BOOK 1984 PAGE

CERTIFICATE OF DEATH 33 004686

STATE OF CALIFORNIA

STATE FILE NUMBER — LOCAL REGISTRATION DISTRICT AND CERTIFICATE NUMBER

DECEDENT PERSONAL DATA

1A. NAME OF DECEDENT—FIRST	1B. MIDDLE	1C. LAST	2A. DATE OF DEATH (MONTH, DAY, YEAR)	2B. HOUR
JANET	GAYNOR	GREGORY	September 14, 1984	0145

3. SEX	4. RACE/ETHNICITY	5. SPANISH/HISPANIC	6. DATE OF BIRTH	7. AGE	IF UNDER 1 YEAR MONTHS / DAYS	IF UNDER 24 HOURS HOURS / MINUTES
F	White/American	NO X	October 6, 1906	77 YEARS		

8. BIRTHPLACE OF DECEDENT (STATE OR FOREIGN COUNTRY)	9. NAME AND BIRTHPLACE OF FATHER	10. BIRTH NAME AND BIRTHPLACE OF MOTHER
Pennsylvania	Frank Gainor-Pennsylvania	Laura Unknown-Penn.

11. CITIZEN OF WHAT COUNTRY	12. SOCIAL SECURITY NUMBER	13. MARITAL STATUS	14. NAME OF SURVIVING SPOUSE (IF WIFE, ENTER BIRTH NAME)
U.S.A.	478-16-3354	Married	Paul Gregory

15. PRIMARY OCCUPATION	16. NUMBER OF YEARS THIS OCCUPATION	17. EMPLOYER (IF SELF-EMPLOYED, SO STATE)	18. KIND OF INDUSTRY OR BUSINESS
Actress	55 years	Self-Employed	Motion Pictures/Theatre

USUAL RESIDENCE

19A. USUAL RESIDENCE—STREET ADDRESS (STREET AND NUMBER OR LOCATION)	19B.	19C. CITY OR TOWN
SingingTrees Ranch 20th Ave. East of Mountain View	44502	Desert Hot Springs

19D. COUNTY	19E. STATE	20. NAME AND ADDRESS OF INFORMANT—RELATIONSHIP
Riverside	California	Paul Gregory-Husband P.O. Box 38 Palms Springs, CA 92263-0038

PLACE OF DEATH

21A. PLACE OF DEATH	21B. COUNTY
Desert Hospital	Riverside

21C. STREET ADDRESS (STREET AND NUMBER OR LOCATION)	21D. CITY OR TOWN
1150 N. Indian	Palm Springs

CAUSE OF DEATH

22. DEATH WAS CAUSED BY: (ENTER ONLY ONE CAUSE PER LINE FOR A, B, AND C)
IMMEDIATE CAUSE
(A) Pneumonia
CONDITIONS, IF ANY, WHICH GAVE RISE TO THE IMMEDIATE CAUSE, STATING THE UNDERLYING CAUSE LAST.
DUE TO, OR AS A CONSEQUENCE OF
(B) Suspect complications of trauma
DUE TO, OR AS A CONSEQUENCE OF
(C) 18:35 15 IX 84 [signature] M.D.

APPROXIMATE INTERVAL BETWEEN ONSET AND DEATH

24. WAS DEATH REPORTED TO CORONER? Yes
25. WAS BIOPSY PERFORMED? No
26. WAS AUTOPSY PERFORMED? Yes

23. OTHER SIGNIFICANT CONDITIONS—CONTRIBUTING TO DEATH BUT NOT RELATED TO CAUSE GIVEN IN 22A

27. WAS OPERATION PERFORMED FOR ANY CONDITION IN ITEMS 22 OR 23? TYPE OF OPERATION — DATE
yes

PHYSICIAN'S CERTIFICATION

28A. I CERTIFY THAT DEATH OCCURRED AT THE HOUR, DATE AND PLACE STATED FROM THE CAUSES STATED.
I ATTENDED DECEDENT SINCE (ENTER MO. DA. YR.) — I LAST SAW DECEDENT ALIVE (ENTER MO. DA. YR.)
28B. PHYSICIAN—SIGNATURE AND DEGREE OR TITLE — 28C. DATE SIGNED — 28D. PHYSICIAN'S LICENSE NUMBER
28E. TYPE PHYSICIAN'S NAME AND ADDRESS

INJURY INFORMATION

29. SPECIFY ACCIDENT, SUICIDE, ETC. — 30. PLACE OF INJURY — 31. INJURY AT WORK — 32A. DATE OF INJURY—MONTH, DAY, YEAR — 32B. HOUR
33. LOCATION (STREET AND NUMBER OR LOCATION AND CITY OR TOWN) — 34. DESCRIBE HOW INJURY OCCURRED (EVENTS WHICH RESULTED IN INJURY)

CORONER'S USE ONLY

35A. I CERTIFY THAT DEATH OCCURRED AT THE HOUR, DATE AND PLACE STATED FROM THE CAUSES STATED. AS REQUIRED BY LAW I HAVE HELD AN INVESTIGATION
Investigation
35B. William Jon Dykes, Coroner
By: [signature], Chief Deputy
35C. DATE SIGNED 9-15-84

36. DISPOSITION	37. DATE—MONTH, DAY, YEAR	38. NAME AND ADDRESS OF CEMETERY OR CREMATORY	39. EMBALMER'S LICENSE NUMBER AND SIGNATURE
Cremation	9-18-1984	Hollywood Cemetery 6000 Santa Monica Blvd.	6294 Haidel St. Charles

40A. NAME OF FUNERAL DIRECTOR (OR PERSON ACTING AS SUCH)	40B. LICENSE NO.	41. LOCAL REGISTRAR—SIGNATURE	42. DATE ACCEPTED BY LOCAL REGISTRAR
Gold Cross Mortuary	F-1303	Ronald P. Hattis, M.D.	SEP 18 1984

STATE REGISTRAR A. B. C. D. E. F.

VS-11 (7-83) — 87604-449 8-83 400M DUP OSP

STATE OF CALIFORNIA

CERTIFICATION OF VITAL RECORD

COUNTY OF LOS ANGELES • REGISTRAR-RECORDER/ COUNTY CLERK

STATE OF CALIFORNIA
DEPARTMENT OF PUBLIC HEALTH
VITAL STATISTICS
STANDARD CERTIFICATE OF DEATH

1. PLACE OF DEATH: DIST. NO. 1901

COUNTY OF Los Angeles

LOCAL REGISTERED NO. 563

CITY, TOWN OR RURAL DISTRICT OF Los Angeles

STREET AND NO. End of Tower Grove Drive

IF DEATH OCCURRED IN A HOSPITAL OR INSTITUTION, GIVE ITS NAME INSTEAD OF STREET AND NO.

2. FULL NAME JOHN GILBERT

RESIDENCE: NO. End of Tower Grove Drive ST. IF NON-RESIDENT, GIVE CITY OR TOWN, AND STATE

USUAL PLACE OF ABODE

3. SEX Male

4. COLOR OR RACE White

5. SINGLE, MARRIED, WIDOWED OR DIVORCED? (WRITE THE WORD) Divorced

5A. IF MARRIED, WIDOWED OR DIVORCED, NAME OF HUSBAND OR WIFE Virginia Briggs Gilbert

6. DATE OF BIRTH July 10 1897 (MONTH DAY YEAR)

7. AGE 38 YR. 5 MO. 30 DAYS. IF LESS THAN ONE DAY ___ HRS. ___ MIN.

OCCUPATION

8. TRADE, PROFESSION OR KIND OF WORK DONE AS SPINNER, SAWYER, BOOKKEEPER, ETC. Actor

9. INDUSTRY OR BUSINESS IN WHICH WORK DONE, AS SILKMILL, SAWMILL, BANK, ETC. Motion Picture

10. DATE DECEASED LAST WORKED AT THIS OCCUPATION (MO. AND YR.) 1/36

11. TOTAL YEARS SPENT IN THIS OCCUPATION 24

12. BIRTHPLACE (CITY OR TOWN) Logan

STATE OR COUNTRY Utah

FATHER

13. NAME John Pringle

14. BIRTHPLACE (CITY OR TOWN) Unknown

STATE OR COUNTRY Unknown

MOTHER

15. MAIDEN NAME Ida Apperley

16. BIRTHPLACE (CITY OR TOWN) Unknown

STATE OR COUNTRY Unknown

17. LENGTH OF RESIDENCE

A. CITY, TOWN OR RURAL DISTRICT OF DEATH 10 YRS. -- MOS. --- DAYS

B. IN CALIFORNIA 30 YRS. -- MOS. --- DAYS

C. IN U.S., IF OF FOREIGN BIRTH ___ YRS. ___ MOS. ___ DAYS

18. INFORMANT (SIGNATURE) Mr. Chas. A. Greene

ADDRESS 431 S. Camden Drive, B.H.

19. BURIAL, CREMATION OR REMOVAL (WRITE THE WORD) Entombment

PLACE Hollywood Receiving Vault DATE 1/13/36

20. EMBALMER LICENSE NO. 2218

SIGNATURE Ralph E. Dayton

FUNERAL DIRECTOR B. E. DAYTON, Inc.

ADDRESS Beverly Hills, California.

21. FILED JAN 13 1936 George Parrish M.D. LOCAL REGISTRAR

22. DATE OF DEATH January 9, 1936. (MONTH DAY YEAR)

23. MEDICAL CERTIFICATE OF DEATH

I HEREBY CERTIFY, THAT I ATTENDED DECEASED FROM 11-4-35 TO 1-9-36; THAT I LAST SAW HIM ALIVE ON 1-7-36 AND THAT DEATH OCCURRED ON THE ABOVE STATED DATE AT THE HOUR OF 7:50 a.M.

THE PRINCIPAL CAUSE OF DEATH AND RELATED CAUSES OF IMPORTANCE, IN ORDER OF ONSET, WERE AS FOLLOWS: DATE OF ONSET

Acute Myocarditis (Alcoholic) Dec 24-35

OTHER CONTRIBUTORY CAUSES OF IMPORTANCE:

Chronic alcoholism 1929

Arterio Sclerosis Genl. 1929

IF OPERATION, DATE OF no WAS THERE AN AUTOPSY? No

CONDITION FOR WHICH PERFORMED None

NAME LABORATORY TEST CONFIRMING DIAGNOSIS none.

24. CORONER'S CERTIFICATE OF DEATH

I HEREBY CERTIFY, THAT I TOOK CHARGE OF THE REMAINS DESCRIBED ABOVE, HELD AN ___ INQUEST, AUTOPSY OR INQUIRY THEREON, AND FROM SUCH ACTION FIND THAT SAID DECEASED CAME TO H___ DEATH ON THE DATE STATED ABOVE.

25. IF DEATH WAS DUE TO EXTERNAL CAUSES (VIOLENCE) FILL IN THE FOLLOWING:

ACCIDENT, SUICIDE OR HOMICIDE? ___ DATE OF INJURY ___

INJURED AT: CITY OR TOWN OF ___ COUNTY AND STATE OF ___

DID INJURY OCCUR IN HOME, INDUSTRY, OR PUBLIC PLACE? ___

MANNER OF INJURY ___

NATURE OF INJURY ___

26. IF DISEASE/INJURY RELATED TO OCCUPATION, SPECIFY no

27. SIGNATURE Leo J. Madsen M.D.

PHYSICIAN, AUTOPSY SURGEON

ADDRESS 718 Wilshire Blvd Santa Monica Calif

28. WHEN REQUIRED BY LAW ___ CORONER

COUNTY OF ___

This is to certify that this document is a true copy of the official record filed with the Registrar-Recorder/County Clerk.

Conny B. McCormack

CONNY B. McCORMACK
Registrar-Recorder/County Clerk

JUL 2 1998

19-418790

This copy not valid unless prepared on engraved border displaying the Seal and Signature of the Registrar-Recorder/County Clerk.

DE LA RUE

ANY ALTERATION OR ERASURE VOIDS THIS CERTIFICATE

39537009542

CERTIFICATE OF DEATH

STATE OF CALIFORNIA
USE BLACK INK ONLY/NO ERASURES, WHITEOUTS OR ALTERATIONS
VS-11 (REV. 7/93)

STATE FILE NUMBER — LOCAL REGISTRATION NUMBER

1. NAME OF DECEDENT—FIRST (GIVEN): CHARLES
2. MIDDLE: J
3. LAST (FAMILY): ALDRICH, JR
4. DATE OF BIRTH MM/DD/CCYY: 02/20/1906
5. AGE YRS.: 89
IF UNDER 1 YEAR: MONTHS / DAYS — IF UNDER 24 HOURS: HOURS / MINUTES
6. SEX: M
7. DATE OF DEATH MM/DD/CCYY: 06/30/1995
8. HOUR: 1815
9. STATE OF BIRTH: NY
10. SOCIAL SECURITY NO.: 568-10-6419
11. MILITARY SERVICE: 19 ___ TO 19___ ☐ NONE
12. MARITAL STATUS: WIDOWED
13. EDUCATION—YEARS COMPLETED: 12
14. RACE: WHITE
15. HISPANIC—SPECIFY: ☐ YES ☒ NO
16. USUAL EMPLOYER: SELF-EMPLOYED
17. OCCUPATION: ACTOR
18. KIND OF BUSINESS: ENTERTAINMENT
19. YEARS IN OCCUPATION: 70
20. RESIDENCE—STREET AND NUMBER OR LOCATION: 710 W 13th STREET #503
21. CITY: ESCONDIDO
22. COUNTY: SAN DIEGO
23. ZIP CODE: 92025
24. YRS IN COUNTY: 30
25. STATE OR FOREIGN COUNTRY: CA
26. NAME, RELATIONSHIP: MICHAEL BELL-DPOA
27. MAILING ADDRESS (STREET AND NUMBER OR RURAL ROUTE NUMBER, CITY OR TOWN, STATE, ZIP): 659 SUMMER VIEW CIRCLE ENCINITAS, CA 92024
28. NAME OF SURVIVING SPOUSE—FIRST: -
29. MIDDLE: -
30. LAST (MAIDEN NAME): -
31. NAME OF FATHER—FIRST: CHARLES
32. MIDDLE: J
33. LAST: ALDRICH
34. BIRTH STATE: NY
35. NAME OF MOTHER—FIRST: GLORIA
36. MIDDLE: -
37. LAST (MAIDEN): GORDON
38. BIRTH STATE: UNK
39. DATE MM/DD/CCYY: 07/11/1995
40. PLACE OF FINAL DISPOSITION: JUDY WORMSER 2365 E FRONTAGE ROAD TUBAC, AZ 85646
41. TYPE OF DISPOSITION(S): CR/TR/RES
42. SIGNATURE OF EMBALMER: NOT EMBALMED
43. LICENSE NO.: -
44. NAME OF FUNERAL DIRECTOR: NEPTUNE SOCIETY
45. LICENSE NO.: FD-1352
46. SIGNATURE OF LOCAL REGISTRAR: [signature]
47. DATE MM/DD/CCYY: 07/11/1995

101. PLACE OF DEATH: REDWOOD TERRACE CONVALESCENT
102. IF HOSPITAL, SPECIFY ONE: ☐ IP ☐ ER/OP ☐ DOA
103. FACILITY OTHER THAN HOSPITAL: ☒ CONV. HOSP. ☐ RES. ☐ OTHER
104. COUNTY: SAN DIEGO
105. STREET ADDRESS—STREET AND NUMBER OR LOCATION: 710 W 13th STREET
106. CITY: ESCONDIDO
107. DEATH WAS CAUSED BY: (ENTER ONLY ONE CAUSE PER LINE FOR A, B, C, AND D) — TIME INTERVAL BETWEEN ONSET AND DEATH
IMMEDIATE CAUSE (A): Cardio pulmonary arrest — 10 min
DUE TO (B): Lung Cancer — 4 mo
DUE TO (C):
DUE TO (D):
108. DEATH REPORTED TO CORONER: ☒ YES ☒ NO — REFERRAL NUMBER: 7-155
109. BIOPSY PERFORMED: ☐ YES ☒ NO
110. AUTOPSY PERFORMED: ☐ YES ☒ NO
111. USED IN DETERMINING CAUSE: ☐ YES ☒ NO
112. OTHER SIGNIFICANT CONDITIONS CONTRIBUTING TO DEATH BUT NOT RELATED TO CAUSE GIVEN IN 107
113. WAS OPERATION PERFORMED FOR ANY CONDITION IN ITEM 107 OR 112? IF YES, LIST TYPE OF OPERATION AND DATE.
114. I CERTIFY THAT TO THE BEST OF MY KNOWLEDGE DEATH OCCURRED AT THE HOUR, DATE AND PLACE STATED FROM THE CAUSES STATED.
DECEDENT ATTENDED SINCE MM/DD/CCYY: 090694 — DECEDENT LAST SEEN ALIVE MM/DD/CCYY: 060595
115. SIGNATURE AND TITLE OF CERTIFIER: [signature]
116. LICENSE NO.: A045129
117. DATE MM/DD/CCYY: 07/07/1995
118. TYPE ATTENDING PHYSICIAN'S NAME, MAILING ADDRESS + ZIP: JEFFREY YUSIM, MD 840 E LOS ANGELES DR VISTA, CA 92084
I CERTIFY THAT IN MY OPINION DEATH OCCURRED AT THE HOUR, DATE AND PLACE STATED FROM THE CAUSES STATED.
119. MANNER OF DEATH: ☐ NATURAL ☐ SUICIDE ☐ HOMICIDE ☐ ACCIDENT ☐ PENDING INVESTIGATION ☐ COULD NOT BE DETERMINED
120. INJURY AT WORK: ☐ YES ☐ NO
121. INJURY DATE MM/DD/CCYY
122. HOUR
123. PLACE OF INJURY
124. DESCRIBE HOW INJURY OCCURRED (EVENTS WHICH RESULTED IN INJURY)
125. LOCATION (STREET AND NUMBER OR LOCATION AND CITY AND ZIP CODE)
126. SIGNATURE OF CORONER OR DEPUTY CORONER
127. DATE MM/DD/CCYY
128. TYPED NAME, TITLE OF CORONER OR DEPUTY CORONER

A B C D E F G H — FAX AUTH. #: 9509199 — CENSUS TRACT

COUNTY OF SAN DIEGO - DEPARTMENT OF HEALTH SERVICES 3851 ROSECRANS ST. THIS IS TO CERTIFY THAT, IF BEARING THE OFFICIAL SEAL OF SAN DIEGO, DEPARTMENT OF HEALTH SERVICES, THIS IS A TRUE COPY OF THE ORIGINAL DOCUMENT FILED.
REQUIRED FEE PAID

[signature]
REGISTRAR OF VITAL RECORDS

DATE ISSUED: September 15, 1995

CERTIFICATION OF VITAL RECORD

COUNTY OF LOS ANGELES • REGISTRAR-RECORDER/COUNTY CLERK

CERTIFICATE OF DEATH

STATE OF CALIFORNIA—DEPARTMENT OF PUBLIC HEALTH

STATE FILE NUMBER — LOCAL REGISTRATION DISTRICT AND CERTIFICATE NUMBER: 7097-027916

DECEDENT PERSONAL DATA 8

- 1a. Name of deceased—first name: Elizabeth (aka Betty)
- 1b. Middle name: Ruth
- 1c. Last name: James Grable
- 2a. Date of death: July 2, 1973
- 2b. Hour: 5 P
- 3. Sex: Female
- 4. Color or race: Cauc
- 5. Birthplace: Mo.
- 6. Date of birth: Dec 18, 1916
- 7. Age (last birthday): 56 years
- 8. Name and birthplace of father: Conn Grable-Mo.
- 9. Maiden name and birthplace of mother: Lillian Hofmann-Mo.
- 10. Citizen of what country: U.S.A.
- 11. Social security number: 551-05-1544
- 12. Married, never married, widowed, divorced: Divorced
- 13. Name of surviving spouse:
- 14. Last occupation: Actress
- 15. Number of years in this occupation: 42
- 16. Name of last employing company or firm: Free Lance
- 17. Kind of industry or business: Stage Motion Pic. & TV

PLACE OF DEATH

- 18a. Place of death: St. Johns Hospital
- 18b. Street address: 1328 22nd St
- 18c. Inside city corporate limits: Yes
- 18d. City or town: Santa Monica
- 18e. County: Los Angeles
- 18f. Length of stay in county of death: 3 days
- 18g. Length of stay in California: 3 days

USUAL RESIDENCE

- 19a. Usual residence—street address: 164 Tropicana Rd
- 19b. Inside city corporate limits:
- 19c. City or town: Las Vegas
- 19d. County: Clark
- 19e. State: Nevada
- 20. Name and mailing address of informant: Victoria B Ivens, 2669 Hounds Chase, Troy Mich.

PHYSICIAN'S OR CORONER'S CERTIFICATION

- 21b. Physician: From 1947 to 7/2/73; last saw 7/1/73
- 21c. Signature: [signature]
- 21d. Address: 9804 Sunset Blvd
- 21e. Date signed: 7/3/73
- 21f. Physician's license number: AC9069

FUNERAL DIRECTOR AND LOCAL REGISTRAR

- 22a. Specify burial, entombment or cremation: Cremation
- 22b. Date: 7-5-73
- 23. Name of cemetery or crematory: Inglewood Mausoleum
- 24. Embalmer—signature, license number: Joseph E. Wiley 2561
- 25. Name of funeral director: Pierce Bros-Beverly Hills
- 26. If not certified by coroner, was this death reported to coroner: no
- 27. Local registrar signature: [signature]
- 28. Date accepted for registration: JUL 3 1973

MEDICAL AND HEALTH DATA — CAUSE OF DEATH 9

29. Part I. Death was caused by:

	Cause	Approximate interval between onset and death
(A) Immediate cause	Tumor Cachexia	6 mos
(B) Due to, or as a consequence of	CA of Lung (Cancer)	18 mos
(C) Due to, or as a consequence of	Visceral Metastases	6 mos

- 30. Part II. Other significant conditions:
- 31. Was operation or biopsy performed: yes
- 32a. Autopsy: No

INJURY INFORMATION 18

- 33. Specify accident, suicide or homicide:
- 34. Place of injury:
- 35. Injury at work:
- 36a. Date of injury:
- 36b. Hour:
- 37a. Place of injury:
- 37b. Distance from place of injury to usual residence:
- 38. Were laboratory tests done for drugs or toxic chemicals:
- 39. Were laboratory tests done for alcohol:
- 40. Describe how injury occurred:

STATE REGISTRAR A. B. C. D. E. F. X

REV. 1-1-68 FORM VS-11

This is to certify that this document is a true copy of the official record filed with the Registrar-Recorder/County Clerk.

Beatriz Valdez
BEATRIZ VALDEZ
Registrar-Recorder/County Clerk

AUG 16 1995
19-397411

This copy not valid unless prepared on engraved border displaying the Seal and Signature of the Registrar-Recorder/County Clerk.

American Bank Note Company

ANY ALTERATION OR ERASURE VOIDS THIS CERTIFICATE

CERTIFICATION OF VITAL RECORD

COUNTY OF LOS ANGELES • REGISTRAR-RECORDER/COUNTY CLERK

STATE OF CALIFORNIA
DEPARTMENT OF PUBLIC HEALTH
VITAL STATISTICS
STANDARD CERTIFICATE OF DEATH

37-039725

1. PLACE OF DEATH: DIST. NO. 1901
COUNTY OF LOS ANGELES
CITY, TOWN OR RURAL DISTRICT OF LOS ANGELES
STREET AND NO. GOOD SAM. HOSPITAL
LOCAL REGISTERED NO. 8965
(IF DEATH OCCURRED IN A HOSPITAL OR INSTITUTION, GIVE ITS NAME INSTEAD OF STREET AND NO.)

2. FULL NAME HARLEAN CARPENTER ALSO KNOWN AS "JEAN HARLOW"
RESIDENCE NO. 512 N. PALM DRIVE ST. (USUAL PLACE OF ABODE)
IF NON-RESIDENT, GIVE CITY OR TOWN, AND STATE BEVERLY HILLS CALIF.

3. SEX FEMALE
4. COLOR OR RACE CAUC
5. SINGLE, MARRIED, WIDOWED OR DIVORCED? (WRITE THE WORD) DIVORCED
5a. IF MARRIED, WIDOWED OR DIVORCED, NAME OF HUSBAND OR WIFE HAROLD ROSSEN
6. DATE OF BIRTH MARCH 3 1911 (MONTH, DAY, YEAR)
7. AGE 26 YR. 3 MO. 4 DAYS. IF LESS THAN ONE DAY ___ HRS. ___ MIN.
8. TRADE, PROFESSION OR KIND OF WORK DONE AS SPINNER, SAWYER, BOOKKEEPER, ETC. ACTRESS
9. INDUSTRY OR BUSINESS IN WHICH WORK WAS DONE AS SILK MILL, SAWMILL, BANK, ETC. SCREEN
10. DATE DECEASED LAST WORKED AT THIS OCCUPATION (MO. AND YR.) 6-37
11. TOTAL YEARS SPENT IN THIS OCCUPATION 8
12. BIRTHPLACE (CITY OR TOWN) KANSAS CITY
STATE OR COUNTRY MO

FATHER
13. NAME MONTCLAIR CARPENTER
14. BIRTHPLACE (CITY OR TOWN) UNKNOWN
STATE OR COUNTRY UNKNOWN

MOTHER
15. MAIDEN NAME JEAN HARLOW
16. BIRTHPLACE (CITY OR TOWN) DENVER
STATE OR COUNTRY COLO

17. LENGTH OF RESIDENCE
A. CITY, TOWN OR RURAL DISTRICT OF DEATH ___ YRS. 2 MOS. ___ DAYS
B. IN CALIFORNIA 10 YRS. ___ MOS. ___ DAYS
C. IN U.S., IF OF FOREIGN BIRTH ___ YRS. ___ MOS. ___ DAYS

18. INFORMANT (SIGNATURE) HOWARD STRICKLING
ADDRESS M G M STUDIOS
19. BURIAL, CREMATION OR REMOVAL? BURIAL
PLACE FOREST LAWN REC. VAULT DATE 6-9-37
20. EMBALMER LICENSE NO. 2350
SIGNATURE S. W. Lowry
FUNERAL DIRECTOR PIERCE BROS.
ADDRESS LOS ANGELES, CALIF.
21. FILED JUN 9 1937 George Parrish M.D. LOCAL REGISTRAR

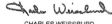

22. DATE OF DEATH JUNE 7 TH 1937 (MONTH, DAY, YEAR)

23. MEDICAL CERTIFICATE OF DEATH
I HEREBY CERTIFY, THAT I ATTENDED DECEASED FROM July 10, 1936 TO June 7, 1937; THAT I LAST SAW HER ALIVE ON June 7, 1937 AND THAT DEATH OCCURRED ON THE ABOVE STATED DATE AT THE HOUR OF 11:38 A. M.

24. CORONER'S CERTIFICATE OF DEATH
I HEREBY CERTIFY, THAT I TOOK CHARGE OF THE REMAINS DESCRIBED ABOVE, HELD AN ___ (INQUEST, AUTOPSY OR INQUIRY) THEREON, AND FROM SUCH ACTION FIND THAT SAID DECEASED CAME TO HER DEATH ON THE DATE STATED ABOVE.

THE PRINCIPAL CAUSE OF DEATH AND RELATED CAUSES OF IMPORTANCE, IN ORDER OF ONSET WERE AS FOLLOWS: DATE OF ONSET
Acute respiratory infection — May 1937
Acute nephritis — May 29, 1937
Uremia — June 4, 1937

OTHER CONTRIBUTORY CAUSES OF IMPORTANCE:

IF OPERATION, DATE OF ___ WAS THERE AN AUTOPSY? No
CONDITION FOR WHICH PERFORMED
NAME LABORATORY TEST CONFIRMING DIAGNOSIS Urine examinations repeated blood chemistry

25. IF DEATH WAS DUE TO EXTERNAL CAUSES (VIOLENCE) FILL IN THE FOLLOWING:
ACCIDENT, SUICIDE OR HOMICIDE? ___ DATE OF INJURY ___
INJURED AT: CITY OR TOWN OF ___ COUNTY AND STATE OF ___
DID INJURY OCCUR IN HOME, INDUSTRY, OR PUBLIC PLACE?
MANNER OF INJURY
NATURE OF INJURY
26. IF DISEASE/INJURY RELATED TO OCCUPATION, SPECIFY
27. SIGNATURE Leland Chapman M.D.
ADDRESS 1930 Wilshire Blvd, Los Angeles California
28. WHEN REQUIRED BY LAW ___ CORONER
COUNTY OF ___

This is to certify that this document is a true copy of the official record filed with the Registrar-Recorder/County Clerk.

Charles Weissburd
CHARLES WEISSBURD
Registrar-Recorder/County Clerk

19-1005811

This copy not valid unless prepared on engraved border displaying the Seal and Signature of the Registrar-Recorder/County Clerk.

American Bank Note Company

ANY ALTERATION OR ERASURE VOIDS THIS CERTIFICATE

STATE OF CALIFORNIA

CERTIFICATION OF VITAL RECORD

COUNTY OF LOS ANGELES • REGISTRAR-RECORDER/COUNTY CLERK

CERTIFICATE OF DEATH 3 200119050066

STATE OF CALIFORNIA — USE BLACK INK ONLY/NO ERASURES, WHITEOUTS OR ALTERATIONS — VS-11 (REV. 1/00)

STATE FILE NUMBER — LOCAL REGISTRATION NUMBER

DECEDENT PERSONAL DATA

1. NAME OF DECEDENT—FIRST (GIVEN): George
2. MIDDLE: –
3. LAST (FAMILY): Harrison
4. DATE OF BIRTH MM/DD/CCYY: 02/25/1943
5. AGE YRS.: 58
IF UNDER 1 YEAR: MONTHS / DAYS — IF UNDER 24 HOURS: HOURS / MINUTES
6. SEX: Male
7. DATE OF DEATH MM/DD/CCYY: 11/29/2001
8. HOUR: 1320
9. STATE OF BIRTH: Liverpool
10. SOCIAL SECURITY NO.: none
11. MILITARY SERVICE: ☐ YES ☒ NO ☐ UNK
12. MARITAL STATUS: Married
13. EDUCATION—YEARS COMPLETED: 12
14. RACE: Caucasian
15. HISPANIC—SPECIFY: ☐ YES ☒ NO
16. USUAL EMPLOYER: Self Employed
17. OCCUPATION: Musician
18. KIND OF BUSINESS: Music
19. YEARS IN OCCUPATION: 40

USUAL RESIDENCE

20. RESIDENCE—(STREET AND NUMBER OR LOCATION): Via Somaini #10
21. CITY: Lugano
22. COUNTY: –
23. ZIP CODE: 6900
24. YRS IN COUNTY: 1
25. STATE OR FOREIGN COUNTRY: Switzerland

INFORMANT

26. NAME, RELATIONSHIP: Olivia Harrison/Wife
27. MAILING ADDRESS (STREET AND NUMBER OR RURAL ROUTE NUMBER, CITY OR TOWN, STATE, ZIP): 1971 Coldwater Canyon, Beverly Hills, CA. 90210

SPOUSE AND PARENT INFORMATION

28. NAME OF SURVIVING SPOUSE—FIRST: Olivia
29. MIDDLE: Trinidad
30. LAST (MAIDEN NAME): Arias
31. NAME OF FATHER—FIRST: Harold
32. MIDDLE: Hargrove
33. LAST: Harrison
34. BIRTH STATE: Liverpool
35. NAME OF MOTHER—FIRST: Louise
36. MIDDLE: Ffrench
37. LAST (MAIDEN): Unknown
38. BIRTH STATE: Liverpool

DISPOSITION(S)

39. DATE MM/DD/CCYY: 11/30/2001
40. PLACE OF FINAL DISPOSITION: Res of Olivia Harrison 1971 Coldwater Canyon, Beverly Hills,CA. 90210

FUNERAL DIRECTOR AND LOCAL REGISTRAR

41. TYPE OF DISPOSITION(S): Cr/Res
42. SIGNATURE OF EMBALMER: ▶ Not Embalmed
43. LICENSE NO.: –
44. NAME OF FUNERAL DIRECTOR: Cremation Specialists of LA
45. LICENSE NO.: FD-1696
46. SIGNATURE OF LOCAL REGISTRAR: ▶ Fred Leaf
47. DATE MM/DD/CCYY: 11/29/2001

PLACE OF DEATH

101. PLACE OF DEATH: Residence
102. IF HOSPITAL, SPECIFY ONE: ☐ IP ☐ ER/OP ☐ DOA
103. FACILITY OTHER THAN HOSPITAL: ☐ CONV HOSP ☐ RES. CARE ☐ OTHER
104. COUNTY: Los Angeles
105. STREET ADDRESS—(STREET AND NUMBER OR LOCATION): 1971 Coldwater Canyon
106. CITY: Beverly Hills

1 of 2

CAUSE OF DEATH

107. DEATH WAS CAUSED BY: (ENTER ONLY ONE CAUSE PER LINE FOR A, B, C, AND D)

	Cause	Time interval between onset and death
IMMEDIATE CAUSE (A)	METASTATIC NON-SMALL CELL LUNG CANCER	9 MTHS
DUE TO (B)		
DUE TO (C)		
DUE TO (D)		

108. DEATH REPORTED TO CORONER: ☐ YES ☒ NO — REFERRAL NUMBER
109. BIOPSY PERFORMED: ☒ YES ☐ NO
110. AUTOPSY PERFORMED: ☐ YES ☒ NO
111. USED IN DETERMINING CAUSE: ☐ YES ☒ NO
112. OTHER SIGNIFICANT CONDITIONS CONTRIBUTING TO DEATH BUT NOT RELATED TO CAUSE GIVEN IN 107: HEAD AND NECK SQUAMOS CELL CARCINOMA
113. WAS OPERATION PERFORMED FOR ANY CONDITION IN ITEM 107 OR 112? IF YES, LIST TYPE OF OPERATION AND DATE: NONE

PHYSICIAN'S CERTIFICATION

114. I CERTIFY THAT TO THE BEST OF MY KNOWLEDGE DEATH OCCURRED AT THE HOUR, DATE AND PLACE STATED FROM THE CAUSES STATED. DECEDENT ATTENDED SINCE MM/DD/CCYY: 11/17/2001 — DECEDENT LAST SEEN ALIVE MM/DD/CCYY: 11/29/2001
115. SIGNATURE AND TITLE OF CERTIFIER: ▶ [signature]
116. LICENSE NO.: A49741
117. DATE MM/DD/CCYY: 11/29/2001
118. TYPE ATTENDING PHYSICIAN'S NAME, MAILING ADDRESS, ZIP: LEE S. ROSEN, MD 10945 LE CONTE AVE #2333 LOS ANGELES, CA 90095

CORONER'S USE ONLY

I CERTIFY THAT IN MY OPINION DEATH OCCURRED AT THE HOUR, DATE AND PLACE STATED FROM THE CAUSES STATED.
119. MANNER OF DEATH: ☐ NATURAL ☐ SUICIDE ☐ HOMICIDE ☐ ACCIDENT ☐ PENDING INVESTIGATION ☐ COULD NOT BE DETERMINED
120. INJURY AT WORK: ☐ YES ☐ NO
121. INJURY DATE MM/DD/CCYY
122. HOUR
123. PLACE OF INJURY
124. DESCRIBE HOW INJURY OCCURRED (EVENTS WHICH RESULTED IN INJURY)
125. LOCATION (STREET AND NUMBER OR LOCATION AND CITY, ZIP)
126. SIGNATURE OF CORONER OR DEPUTY CORONER ▶
127. DATE MM/DD/CCYY
128. TYPED NAME, TITLE OF CORONER OR DEPUTY CORONER

STATE REGISTRAR

A	B	C	D	E	F	G	H	FAX AUTH. #	CENSUS TRACT

This is to certify that this document is a true copy of the official record filed with the Registrar-Recorder/County Clerk.

Conny B. McCormack

CONNY B. McCORMACK
Registrar-Recorder/County Clerk

APR 17 2002
19-195939

This copy not valid unless prepared on engraved border displaying the Seal and Signature of the Registrar-Recorder/County Clerk.

ANY ALTERATION OR ERASURE VOIDS THIS CERTIFICATE

STATE OF CALIFORNIA
CERTIFICATION OF VITAL RECORD

COUNTY OF LOS ANGELES • REGISTRAR-RECORDER/COUNTY CLERK

AFFIDAVIT TO AMEND A RECORD 2
DEATHS AFTER 1-1994
NO ERASURES, WHITEOUTS, OR ALTERATIONS

STATE FILE NUMBER

02-002135
3 2001 19 050066
LOCAL REGISTRATION DISTRICT AND CERTIFICATE NUMBER

STATE/LOCAL REGISTRAR USE ONLY: 1. | 2. | 3.

PART I INFORMATION TO LOCATE RECORD—TYPE OR PRINT IN BLACK INK ONLY

NAME AS IT APPEARS ON RECORD	1. NAME—FIRST (GIVEN): George	2. MIDDLE: -	3. LAST (FAMILY): Harrison

ADDITIONAL INFORMATION TO LOCATE RECORD	4. SEX: Male	5. DATE OF EVENT—MM/DD/CCYY: 11/29/2001	6. CITY OF OCCURRENCE: Beverly Hills	7. COUNTY OF OCCURRENCE: Los Angeles
	8. FATHER'S NAME AS STATED ON ORIGINAL: Harold Hargrove Harrison		9. MOTHER'S NAME AS STATED ON ORIGINAL: Louise Ffrench Unknown	

PART II STATEMENT OF CORRECTIONS—NO ERASURES, WHITEOUTS, OR ALTERATIONS

LIST ONE ITEM PER LINE

10. CERTIFICATE ITEM NUMBER	11. INFORMATION AS IT APPEARS ON ORIGINAL RECORD	12. INFORMATION AS IT SHOULD APPEAR
27.	1971 Coldwater Canyon	Via Somaini #10
	Beverly Hills, CA 90201	Lugano SWITZERLAND 6900
40.	Res. of Olivia Harrison	Res. of Olivia Harrison
	1971 Coldwater Canyon	Via Somaini#10
	Beverly Hills, CA 90201	Lugano SWITZERLAND 6900
105.	1971 Coldwater Canyon 2 OF 2	9536 Heather Road
106.	Beverly Hills	Los Angeles

REASON FOR CORRECTION: 13. To correct discrepancies as listed on original death certificate.

AFFIDAVITS AND SIGNATURES: We, the undersigned, hereby certify under penalty of perjury that we have personal knowledge of the above facts and that the information given above is true and correct.

TWO PERSONS MUST SIGN THIS FORM — USE BLACK INK ONLY

14. SIGNATURE OF FIRST PERSON: [signature]	15. TITLE/RELATIONSHIP TO PERSON IN PART I: Consultant	16. DATE SIGNED—MM/DD/CCYY: 03/04/2002
17. AGE: Legal	18. ADDRESS (STREET, CITY, STATE, ZIP): 11684 Ventura Blvd., #440 Studio City, CA 91604	
19. SIGNATURE OF SECOND PERSON: [signature]	20. TITLE/RELATIONSHIP TO PERSON IN PART I: Consultant	21. DATE SIGNED—MM/DD/CCYY: 03/04/2002
22. AGE: Legal	23. ADDRESS (STREET, CITY, STATE, ZIP): 11684 Ventura Blvd., #440 Studio City, CA 91604	

S. Hawley

STATE/LOCAL REGISTRAR USE ONLY: 24. SIGNATURE OF STATE OR LOCAL REGISTRAR: OFFICE OF THE STATE REGISTRAR OF VITAL STATISTICS | 25. DATE ACCEPTED FOR REGISTRATION—MM/DD CCYY: 03/16/2002

STATE OF CALIFORNIA, DEPARTMENT OF HEALTH SERVICES, OFFICE OF STATE REGISTRAR VS 24(L) (Rev. 1/95)

This is to certify that this document is a true copy of the official record filed with the Registrar-Recorder/County Clerk.

Conny B. McCormack
CONNY B. McCORMACK
Registrar-Recorder/County Clerk

APR 17 2002
19-196067

This copy not valid unless prepared on engraved border displaying the Seal and Signature of the Registrar-Recorder/County Clerk.

MIDWEST BANK NOTE COMPANY
ANY ALTERATION OR ERASURE VOIDS THIS CERTIFICATE

STATE OF CALIFORNIA
CERTIFICATION OF VITAL RECORD

COUNTY OF LOS ANGELES • REGISTRAR-RECORDER/COUNTY CLERK

DISTRICT NO. 1901 REGISTRAR'S NO. 10577

1. FULL NAME WILLIAM SURREY HART

2. PLACE OF DEATH: (A) COUNTY Los Angeles
(B) CITY OR TOWN Los Angeles
(C) NAME OF HOSPITAL OR INSTITUTION California Hospital.
(D) LENGTH OF STAY: IN HOSPITAL OR INSTITUTION 19 days
IN THIS COMMUNITY 19 days IN CALIFORNIA 32 Yrs
(E) IF FOREIGN BORN, HOW LONG IN THE U. S. A.? YEARS

3. USUAL RESIDENCE OF DECEASED:
(A) STATE California
(B) COUNTY Los Angeles
(C) CITY OR TOWN Newhall
(D) STREET NO. Horse Shoe Ranch.

20. DATE OF DEATH: MONTH June DAY 23 YEAR 1946 HOUR 11 MINUTE 20 P.M.

3. (E) IF VETERAN, NAME OF WAR None
3. (F) SOCIAL SECURITY NO. None
4. SEX Male
5. COLOR OR RACE Caucasian
6. (A) SINGLE, MARRIED, WIDOWED OR DIVORCED Divorced
6. (B) NAME OF HUSBAND OR WIFE Winifred Westover Hart
6. (C) AGE OF HUSBAND OR WIFE IF ALIVE 46 YEARS
7. BIRTHDATE OF DECEASED December 6 1864
8. AGE 81 YRS. 6 MOS. 17 DAYS
9. BIRTHPLACE New Burgh New York
10. USUAL OCCUPATION Actor
11. INDUSTRY OR BUSINESS Motion Pictures
FATHER 12. NAME Nicholas Hart
13. BIRTHPLACE London England
MOTHER 14. MAIDEN NAME Unknown McCauley
15. BIRTHPLACE Ulster North Ireland
16. (A) INFORMANT William S.Hart Jr.
(B) ADDRESS 404 Georgina Avenue.Santa Monica
17. (A) Temporary Vault (B) DATE June 26 1946
(C) PLACE Cemetery
18. (A) EMBALMER'S SIGNATURE LICENSE NO. 1797
(B) FUNERAL DIRECTOR FOREST LAWN MEMORIAL-PARK ASSOCIATION, INC.
ADDRESS GLENDALE, CALIF.
19. JUN 26 1946 DATE FILED REGISTRAR

21. MEDICAL CERTIFICATE
I HEREBY CERTIFY, THAT I ATTENDED THE DECEASED FROM 6-12-1944 TO June 23 1946 THAT I LAST SAW HIM ALIVE ON June 23 1946 AND THAT DEATH OCCURRED ON THE DATE AND HOUR STATED ABOVE.
IMMEDIATE CAUSE OF DEATH Acute pyelonephritis Cystitis and Prostatitis
DUE TO Chronic suppurative prostatitis with calculi
OTHER CONDITIONS Arteriosclerosis general Aneurysm of abdominal aorta
OF AUTOPSY 6-24-46

22. CORONER'S CERTIFICATE
I HEREBY CERTIFY, THAT I HELD AN AUTOPSY, INQUEST OR INVESTIGATION ON THE REMAINS OF THE DECEASED AND FIND FROM SUCH ACTION THAT DECEASED CAME TO H DEATH ON THE DATE AND HOUR STATED ABOVE.

23. IF DEATH WAS DUE TO EXTERNAL CAUSES, FILL IN THE FOLLOWING:
(A) ACCIDENT, SUICIDE, OR HOMICIDE? (B) DATE OF INJURY
(C) WHERE DID INJURY OCCUR? CITY OR TOWN COUNTY STATE
(D) DID INJURY OCCUR IN OR ABOUT HOME, ON FARM, IN INDUSTRIAL PLACE, OR IN PUBLIC PLACE? WHILE AT WORK?
(E) MEANS OF INJURY

24. CORONER'S OR PHYSICIAN'S SIGNATURE B.H. Hagen M.D.
ADDRESS 1136 W 6 DATE 6/25/46

STATE OF CALIFORNIA DEPARTMENT OF PUBLIC HEALTH
CERTIFICATE OF DEATH
U. S. DEPT. OF COMMERCE BUREAU OF THE CENSUS

This is to certify that this document is a true copy of the official record filed with the Registrar-Recorder/County Clerk.

CONNY B. McCORMACK
Registrar-Recorder/County Clerk

NOV 28 2000
19-118082

This copy not valid unless prepared on engraved border displaying the Seal and Signature of the Registrar-Recorder/County Clerk.

ANY ALTERATION OR ERASURE VOIDS THIS CERTIFICATE

STATE OF CALIFORNIA
CERTIFICATION OF VITAL RECORD

COUNTY OF LOS ANGELES

DEPARTMENT OF HEALTH SERVICES

CERTIFICATE OF DEATH
STATE OF CALIFORNIA
USE BLACK INK ONLY/NO ERASURES, WHITEOUTS OR ALTERATIONS
VS-11 (REV. 7/97)

STATE FILE NUMBER | LOCAL REGISTRATION NUMBER

DECEDENT PERSONAL DATA	1. NAME OF DECEDENT—FIRST (GIVEN)	BRYNN
	2. MIDDLE	-
	3. LAST (FAMILY)	HARTMAN
	4. DATE OF BIRTH MM/DD/CCYY	04/11/1958
	5. AGE YRS.	40
	6. SEX	F
	7. DATE OF DEATH MM/DD/CCYY	05/28/1998
	8. HOUR	0709
	9. STATE OF BIRTH	MN
	10. SOCIAL SECURITY NO.	501-74-2911
	11. MILITARY SERVICE	[X] NO
	12. MARITAL STATUS	MARRIED/WIDOWED
	13. EDUCATION—YEARS COMPLETED	12
	14. RACE	WHITE
	15. HISPANIC—SPECIFY	[X] NO
	16. USUAL EMPLOYER	SELF EMPLOYED
	17. OCCUPATION	HOMEMAKER
	18. KIND OF BUSINESS	OWN HOME
	19. YEARS IN OCCUPATION	11
USUAL RESIDENCE	20. RESIDENCE—(STREET AND NUMBER OR LOCATION)	5065 ENCINO AVE.
	21. CITY	ENCINO
	22. COUNTY	LOS ANGELES
	23. ZIP CODE	91316
	24. YRS IN COUNTY	9
	25. STATE OR FOREIGN COUNTRY	CALIFORNIA
INFORMANT	26. NAME, RELATIONSHIP	GREGORY C. OMDAHL - BROTHER
	27. MAILING ADDRESS	1530 6th ST, FARGO ND 58103
SPOUSE AND PARENT INFORMATION	28. NAME OF SURVIVING SPOUSE—FIRST	PHILLIP
	29. MIDDLE	EDWARD
	30. LAST (MAIDEN NAME)	HARTMAN
	31. NAME OF FATHER—FIRST	DONALD
	32. MIDDLE	GENE
	33. LAST	OMDAHL
	34. BIRTH STATE	MN
	35. NAME OF MOTHER—FIRST	CONSTANCE
	36. MIDDLE	FAYE
	37. LAST (MAIDEN)	ARNOLD
	38. BIRTH STATE	MN
DISPOSITION(S)	39. DATE MM/DD/CCYY	06/03/1998
	40. PLACE OF FINAL DISPOSITION	PVT RES CONSTANCE F OMDAHL 110 NORA ST THIEF RIVER FALLS MN 56701
FUNERAL DIRECTOR AND LOCAL REGISTRAR	41. TYPE OF DISPOSITION(S)	CR/TR/RES
	42. SIGNATURE OF EMBALMER	NOT EMBALMED
	43. LICENSE NO.	-
	44. NAME OF FUNERAL DIRECTOR	FOREST LAWN MTY GLENDALE
	45. LICENSE NO.	FD 656
	46. SIGNATURE OF LOCAL REGISTRAR	[signature]
	47. DATE MM/DD/CCYY	06/02/1998
PLACE OF DEATH	101. PLACE OF DEATH	RESIDENCE BEDROOM
	102. IF HOSPITAL, SPECIFY ONE	IP / ER/OP / DOA
	103. FACILITY OTHER THAN HOSPITAL	CONV. HOSP. / RES. CARE / OTHER
	104. COUNTY	LOS ANGELES
	105. STREET ADDRESS	5065 ENCINO AVE.
	106. CITY	ENCINO
CAUSE OF DEATH	107. IMMEDIATE CAUSE (A)	GUNSHOT WOUND OF HEAD
	TIME INTERVAL BETWEEN ONSET AND DEATH	UNK
	DUE TO (B)	
	DUE TO (C)	
	DUE TO (D)	
	108. DEATH REPORTED TO CORONER	[X] YES; REFERRAL NUMBER 98-03786
	109. BIOPSY PERFORMED	[X] NO
	110. AUTOPSY PERFORMED	[X] YES
	111. USED IN DETERMINING CAUSE	[X] YES
	112. OTHER SIGNIFICANT CONDITIONS CONTRIBUTING TO DEATH BUT NOT RELATED TO CAUSE GIVEN IN 107	NONE
	113. WAS OPERATION PERFORMED FOR ANY CONDITION IN ITEM 107 OR 112? IF YES, LIST TYPE OF OPERATION AND DATE.	NO
PHYSICIAN'S CERTIFICATION	114. I CERTIFY THAT TO THE BEST OF MY KNOWLEDGE DEATH OCCURRED AT THE HOUR, DATE AND PLACE STATED FROM THE CAUSES STATED. DECEDENT ATTENDED SINCE MM/DD/CCYY; DECEDENT LAST SEEN ALIVE MM/DD/CCYY	
	115. SIGNATURE AND TITLE OF CERTIFIER	
	116. LICENSE NO.	
	117. DATE MM/DD/CCYY	
	118. TYPE ATTENDING PHYSICIAN'S NAME, MAILING ADDRESS, ZIP	
CORONER'S USE ONLY	I CERTIFY THAT IN MY OPINION DEATH OCCURRED AT THE HOUR, DATE AND PLACE STATED FROM THE CAUSES STATED. 119. MANNER OF DEATH	[X] SUICIDE
	120. INJURY AT WORK	[X] NO
	121. INJURY DATE MM/DD/CCYY	05/28/1998
	122. HOUR	0621
	123. PLACE OF INJURY	RESIDENCE BEDROOM
	124. DESCRIBE HOW INJURY OCCURRED	WITH REVOLVER
	125. LOCATION (STREET AND NUMBER OR LOCATION AND CITY, ZIP)	5065 ENCINO AVE., ENCINO 91316
	126. SIGNATURE OF CORONER OR DEPUTY CORONER	Maria C. Arreola
	127. DATE MM/DD/CCYY	06/02/1998
	128. TYPED NAME, TITLE OF CORONER OR DEPUTY CORONER	Deputy Coroner Maria C. Arreola
STATE REGISTRAR	A B C D E F G H	
	FAX AUTH. #	273/1698
	CENSUS TRACT	

0B0125191

This is a true certified copy of the record filed in the County of Los Angeles Department of Health Services if it bears the Registrar's signature in purple ink.

DATE ISSUED JUN 16 1998

Director of Health Service and Registrar

This copy not valid unless prepared on engraved border displaying seal and signature of Registrar.

DE LA RUE

ANY ALTERATION OR ERASURE VOIDS THIS CERTIFICATE

STATE OF CALIFORNIA
CERTIFICATION OF VITAL RECORD

COUNTY OF LOS ANGELES

DEPARTMENT OF HEALTH SERVICES

CERTIFICATE OF DEATH

STATE OF CALIFORNIA
USE BLACK INK ONLY/NO ERASURES, WHITEOUTS OR ALTERATIONS
VS-11 (REV. 7/97)

STATE FILE NUMBER — LOCAL REGISTRATION NUMBER

DECEDENT PERSONAL DATA

1. NAME OF DECEDENT—FIRST (GIVEN): PHILLIP
2. MIDDLE: EDWARD
3. LAST (FAMILY): HARTMAN
4. DATE OF BIRTH MM/DD/CCYY: 09/24/1948
5. AGE YRS.: 49
IF UNDER 1 YEAR: MONTHS, DAYS — IF UNDER 24 HOURS: HOURS, MINUTES
6. SEX: M
7. DATE OF DEATH MM/DD/CCYY: 05/28/1998 FND
8. HOUR: 0710
9. STATE OF BIRTH: CANADA
10. SOCIAL SECURITY NO.: 554-76-8086
11. MILITARY SERVICE: ☐ YES ☒ NO ☐ UNK
12. MARITAL STATUS: MARRIED/WIDOWED
13. EDUCATION—YEARS COMPLETED: 15
14. RACE: WHITE
15. HISPANIC—SPECIFY: ☐ YES ☒ NO
16. USUAL EMPLOYER: SELF EMPLOYED
17. OCCUPATION: ARTIST, WRITER, ACTOR
18. KIND OF BUSINESS: ENTERTAINMENT
19. YEARS IN OCCUPATION: 15

USUAL RESIDENCE

20. RESIDENCE—(STREET AND NUMBER OR LOCATION): 5065 ENCINO AVE
21. CITY: ENCINO
22. COUNTY: LOS ANGELES
23. ZIP CODE: 91316
24. YRS IN COUNTY: 38
25. STATE OR FOREIGN COUNTRY: CALIFORNIA

INFORMANT

26. NAME, RELATIONSHIP: GREGORY C. OMDAHL - BROTHER IN LAW
27. MAILING ADDRESS (STREET AND NUMBER OR RURAL ROUTE NUMBER, CITY OR TOWN, STATE, ZIP): 1530 6th STREET FARGO ND 58103

SPOUSE AND PARENT INFORMATION

28. NAME OF SURVIVING SPOUSE—FIRST: BRYNN
29. MIDDLE: -
30. LAST (MAIDEN NAME): OMDAHL
31. NAME OF FATHER—FIRST: RUPERT
32. MIDDLE: LOEBIG
33. LAST: HARTMANN
34. BIRTH STATE: CANADA
35. NAME OF MOTHER—FIRST: DORIS
36. MIDDLE: MARGERITE
37. LAST (MAIDEN): WARDEL
38. BIRTH STATE: CANADA

DISPOSITION(S)

39. DATE MM/DD/CCYY: 06/03/1998
40. PLACE OF FINAL DISPOSITION: PVT RES DORIS M. HARTMANN 21447 HIGHVALE TRAIL TOPANGA CA 90290

FUNERAL DIRECTOR AND LOCAL REGISTRAR

41. TYPE OF DISPOSITION(S): CR/RES
42. SIGNATURE OF EMBALMER: ▶ NOT EMBALMED
43. LICENSE NO.: -
44. NAME OF FUNERAL DIRECTOR: FOREST LAWN MTY GELNDALE
45. LICENSE NO.: FD 656
46. SIGNATURE OF LOCAL REGISTRAR: [signature]
47. DATE MM/DD/CCYY: 06/02/1998

PLACE OF DEATH

101. PLACE OF DEATH: RESIDENCE
102. IF HOSPITAL, SPECIFY ONE: ☐ IP ☐ ER/OP ☐ DOA
103. FACILITY OTHER THAN HOSPITAL: ☐ CONV. HOSP. ☐ RES. CARE ☐ OTHER
104. COUNTY: LOS ANGELES
105. STREET ADDRESS—(STREET AND NUMBER OR LOCATION): 5065 ENCINO AVE
106. CITY: ENCINO

CAUSE OF DEATH

107. DEATH WAS CAUSED BY: (ENTER ONLY ONE CAUSE PER LINE FOR A, B, C, AND D)
IMMEDIATE CAUSE (A): MULTIPLE GUNSHOT WOUNDS — TIME INTERVAL BETWEEN ONSET AND DEATH: RAPID
DUE TO (B):
DUE TO (C):
DUE TO (D):
108. DEATH REPORTED TO CORONER: ☒ YES ☐ NO — REFERRAL NUMBER: 98-03785
109. BIOPSY PERFORMED: ☐ YES ☒ NO
110. AUTOPSY PERFORMED: ☒ YES ☐ NO
111. USED IN DETERMINING CAUSE: ☒ YES ☐ NO
112. OTHER SIGNIFICANT CONDITIONS CONTRIBUTING TO DEATH BUT NOT RELATED TO CAUSE GIVEN IN 107: NONE
113. WAS OPERATION PERFORMED FOR ANY CONDITION IN ITEM 107 OR 112? IF YES, LIST TYPE OF OPERATION AND DATE.: NO

PHYSICIAN'S CERTIFICATION

114. I CERTIFY THAT TO THE BEST OF MY KNOWLEDGE DEATH OCCURRED AT THE HOUR, DATE AND PLACE STATED FROM THE CAUSES STATED. DECEDENT ATTENDED SINCE MM/DD/CCYY — DECEDENT LAST SEEN ALIVE MM/DD/CCYY
115. SIGNATURE AND TITLE OF CERTIFIER ▶
116. LICENSE NO.
117. DATE MM/DD/CCYY
118. TYPE ATTENDING PHYSICIAN'S NAME, MAILING ADDRESS, ZIP

CORONER'S USE ONLY

I CERTIFY THAT IN MY OPINION DEATH OCCURRED AT THE HOUR, DATE AND PLACE STATED FROM THE CAUSES STATED.
119. MANNER OF DEATH: ☐ NATURAL ☐ SUICIDE ☒ HOMICIDE ☐ ACCIDENT ☐ PENDING INVESTIGATION ☐ COULD NOT BE DETERMINED
120. INJURY AT WORK: ☐ YES ☒ NO
121. INJURY DATE MM/DD/CCYY: 05/28/1998
122. HOUR: UNK
123. PLACE OF INJURY: RESIDENCE/BEDROOM
124. DESCRIBE HOW INJURY OCCURRED (EVENTS WHICH RESULTED IN INJURY): WITH REVOLVER
125. LOCATION (STREET AND NUMBER OR LOCATION AND CITY, ZIP): 5065 ENCINO AVE., ENCINO 91316
126. SIGNATURE OF CORONER OR DEPUTY CORONER: ▶ Maria C Arreola
127. DATE MM/DD/CCYY: 06/02/1998
128. TYPED NAME, TITLE OF CORONER OR DEPUTY CORONER: DEPUTY CORONER Maria C. Arreola

STATE REGISTRAR: A B C D E F G H — FAX AUTH. #: 273/14182 — CENSUS TRACT

000125190

This is a true certified copy of the record filed in the County of Los Angeles Department of Health Services if it bears the Registrar's signature in purple ink.

[signature] DATE ISSUED JUN 16 1998

Director of Health Service and Registrar

This copy not valid unless prepared on engraved border displaying seal and signature of Registrar.

DE LA RUE

ANY ALTERATION OR ERASURE VOIDS THIS CERTIFICATE

CERTIFICATION OF VITAL RECORD

COUNTY OF LOS ANGELES • REGISTRAR-RECORDER/COUNTY CLERK

CERTIFICATE OF DEATH 0190-043691
STATE OF CALIFORNIA

STATE FILE NUMBER — LOCAL REGISTRATION DISTRICT AND CERTIFICATE NUMBER

DECEDENT PERSONAL DATA

1A. NAME OF DECEDENT—FIRST: Jon-Erik | 1B. MIDDLE: | 1C. LAST: Hexum | 2A. DATE OF DEATH (MONTH, DAY, YEAR): October 18, 1984 | 2B. HOUR: 1930

3. SEX: male | 4. RACE/ETHNICITY: cauc | 5. SPANISH/HISPANIC: NO xx | 6. DATE OF BIRTH: Jan 5 1957 | 7. AGE: 27 YEARS | IF UNDER 1 YEAR MONTHS DAYS | IF UNDER 24 HOURS HOURS MINUTES

8. BIRTHPLACE OF DECEDENT (STATE OR FOREIGN COUNTRY): New Jersey | 9. NAME AND BIRTHPLACE OF FATHER: Thorleif Hexum- Norway | 10. BIRTH NAME AND BIRTHPLACE OF MOTHER: Gretha Paulsen- Minn

11. CITIZEN OF WHAT COUNTRY: U.S.A. | 12. SOCIAL SECURITY NUMBER: 146 60 2855 | 13. MARITAL STATUS: never married | 14. NAME OF SURVIVING SPOUSE (IF WIFE, ENTER BIRTH NAME)

15. PRIMARY OCCUPATION: Actor | 16. NUMBER OF YEARS THIS OCCUPATION: 2 | 17. EMPLOYER (IF SELF-EMPLOYED, SO STATE): 20th Century Fox | 18. KIND OF INDUSTRY OR BUSINESS: Motion Picture and T.V.

USUAL RESIDENCE

19A. USUAL RESIDENCE—STREET ADDRESS (STREET AND NUMBER OR LOCATION): 2108 Kenwood Avenue | 19B. | 19C. CITY OR TOWN: Burbank

19D. COUNTY: Los Angeles | 19E. STATE: Calif | 20. NAME AND ADDRESS OF INFORMANT—RELATIONSHIP: Gretha Hexum (Mother) 14201 Foothill Blvd. Sylmar California 91342

PLACE OF DEATH

21A. PLACE OF DEATH: Beverly Hills Medical Center | 21B. COUNTY: Los Angeles

21C. STREET ADDRESS (STREET AND NUMBER OR LOCATION): 1177 S. Beverly Dr. | 21D. CITY OR TOWN: Los Angeles

CAUSE OF DEATH

22. DEATH WAS CAUSED BY: (ENTER ONLY ONE CAUSE PER LINE FOR A, B, AND C)
IMMEDIATE CAUSE (A) GUNSHOT WOUND OF HEAD
CONDITIONS, IF ANY, WHICH GAVE RISE TO THE IMMEDIATE CAUSE, STATING THE UNDERLYING CAUSE LAST.
DUE TO, OR AS A CONSEQUENCE OF (B)
DUE TO, OR AS A CONSEQUENCE OF (C)
APPROXIMATE INTERVAL BETWEEN ONSET AND DEATH

24. WAS DEATH REPORTED TO CORONER? 84-13291
25. WAS BIOPSY PERFORMED? No
26. WAS AUTOPSY PERFORMED? Yes

23. OTHER SIGNIFICANT CONDITIONS—CONTRIBUTING TO DEATH BUT NOT RELATED TO CAUSE GIVEN IN 22A
27. WAS OPERATION PERFORMED FOR ANY CONDITION IN ITEMS 22 OR 23? TYPE OF OPERATION: Craniotomy | DATE: 10-12-84

PHYSICIAN'S CERTIFICATION

28A. I CERTIFY THAT DEATH OCCURRED AT THE HOUR, DATE AND PLACE STATED FROM THE CAUSES STATED. I ATTENDED DECEDENT SINCE (ENTER MO. DA. YR.) | I LAST SAW DECEDENT ALIVE (ENTER MO. DA. YR.) | 28B. PHYSICIAN—SIGNATURE AND DEGREE OR TITLE | 28C. DATE SIGNED | 28D. PHYSICIAN'S LICENSE NUMBER | 28E. TYPE PHYSICIAN'S NAME AND ADDRESS

INJURY INFORMATION — CORONER'S USE ONLY

29. SPECIFY ACCIDENT, SUICIDE, ETC.: Accident | 30. PLACE OF INJURY: Movie Studio | 31. INJURY AT WORK: Yes | 32A. DATE OF INJURY—MONTH, DAY, YEAR: 10-12-84 | 32B. HOUR: 1710

33. LOCATION (STREET AND NUMBER OR LOCATION AND CITY OR TOWN): 10201 Pico Blvd - Los Angeles | 34. DESCRIBE HOW INJURY OCCURRED (EVENTS WHICH RESULTED IN INJURY): Accidental discharge of firearm

35A. I CERTIFY THAT DEATH OCCURRED AT THE HOUR, DATE AND PLACE STATED FROM THE CAUSES STATED. AS REQUIRED BY LAW I HAVE HELD AN INVESTIGATION | 35B. CORONER—SIGNATURE AND DEGREE OR TITLE: Deputy Coroner [signature] | 35C. DATE SIGNED: 10-30-84

36. DISPOSITION: Cremation | 37. DATE—MONTH, DAY, YEAR: 10-31-84 | 38. NAME AND ADDRESS OF CEMETERY OR CREMATORY: Grandview Crematory Glendale Calif | 39. EMBALMER'S LICENSE NUMBER AND SIGNATURE: not embalmed

40A. NAME OF FUNERAL DIRECTOR (OR PERSON ACTING AS SUCH): Westwood Village Mortuary | 40B. LICENSE NO.: 951 | 41. LOCAL REGISTRAR: [signature] | 42. DATE ACCEPTED BY LOCAL REGISTRAR: OCT 31 1984

STATE REGISTRAR: A. | B. | C. | D. | E. | F.

VS-11 (7-83) 9229 — 87604-449 8-83 400M DUP OSP

This is to certify that this document is a true copy of the official record filed with the Registrar-Recorder/County Clerk.

Beatriz Valdez
BEATRIZ VALDEZ
Registrar-Recorder/County Clerk

AUG 16 1995
19-397060

This copy not valid unless prepared on engraved border displaying the Seal and Signature of the Registrar-Recorder/County Clerk.

American Bank Note Company — ANY ALTERATION OR ERASURE VOIDS THIS CERTIFICATE

STATE OF CALIFORNIA
CERTIFICATION OF VITAL RECORD

COUNTY OF LOS ANGELES • REGISTRAR-RECORDER/ COUNTY CLERK

CERTIFICATE OF DEATH
STATE OF CALIFORNIA

0190-020098

DECEDENT PERSONAL DATA	1A. Name of decedent—First	Alfred
	1B. Middle	Joseph
	1C. Last	Hitchcock
	2A. Date of death	April 29, 1980
	2B. Hour	0917
	3. Sex	Male
	4. Race	White
	5. Ethnicity	
	6. Date of birth	August 13, 1899
	7. Age	80 years
	8. Birthplace of decedent	England
	9. Name and birthplace of father	William Hitchcock - England
	10. Birth name and birthplace of mother	Emma Whelan - England
	11. Citizen of what country	U.S.A.
	12. Social Security number	546-24-9858
	13. Marital status	Married
	14. Name of surviving spouse	Alma Reville
	15. Primary occupation	Producer Director
	16. Number of years this occupation	62
	17. Employer	Universal Studios
	18. Kind of industry or business	Motion Pictures
USUAL RESIDENCE	19A. Usual residence—street address	10957 Bellagio Rd.
	19C. City or town	Los Angeles
	19D. County	Los Angeles
	19E. State	California
	20. Name and address of informant—relationship	Patricia O'Connell Daughter, 20259 Aetna St., Woodland Hills, California 91367
PLACE OF DEATH	21A. Place of death	Residence
	21B. County	Los Angeles
	21C. Street address	10957 Bellagio Rd.
	21D. City or town	Los Angeles
CAUSE OF DEATH	22. Death was caused by: (A) Immediate cause	Terminal pneumonitis — 48 hrs
	(B) Due to	Chronic congestive heart failure — 5 yrs
	(C) Due to	Atherosclerotic heart disease — 10 yrs
	23. Other conditions contributing	Chronic Renal Insufficiency
	24. Was death reported to coroner?	NO
	25. Was biopsy performed?	NO
	26. Was autopsy performed?	NO
	27. Was operation performed	Scribner shunt-dialysis 3/29/80
PHYSICIAN'S CERTIFICATION	28A. Attended decedent since / last saw decedent alive	1/17/68 — 4/28/80
	28B. Physician signature	Walter A. Flieg MD
	28C. Date signed	4/29/80
	28D. Physician's license number	A-11992
	28E. Physician's name and address	Walter A. Flieg M.D., 9201 Sunset Blvd., L.A., Ca.
INJURY INFORMATION	29.–34.	
CORONER'S USE ONLY	35A.–35C.	24
	36. Disposition	Cremation
	37. Date	5-1-80
	38. Name and address of cemetery or crematory	Live Oak Crematory, Monrovia, Ca.
	39. Embalmer's license number and signature	NOT EMBALMED
	40. Name of funeral director	Gates, Kingsley, Gates, Price-Daniel
	41. Local registrar—signature	[signature] MD
	42. Date accepted by registrar	APR 30 1980
STATE REGISTRAR	A.–F.	

VS-11 (10.78)

01-3-1-7005

This is to certify that this document is a true copy of the official record filed with the Registrar-Recorder/County Clerk.

Conny B. McCormack
CONNY B. McCORMACK
Registrar-Recorder/County Clerk

SEP 4 1998
19-519015

This copy not valid unless prepared on engraved border displaying the Seal and Signature of the Registrar-Recorder/County Clerk.

ANY ALTERATION OR ERASURE VOIDS THIS CERTIFICATE

CERTIFICATION OF VITAL RECORD

COUNTY OF LOS ANGELES • REGISTRAR-RECORDER/COUNTY CLERK

CERTIFICATE OF DEATH
STATE OF CALIFORNIA

0190-052667

STATE FILE NUMBER — LOCAL REGISTRATION DISTRICT AND CERTIFICATE NUMBER

DECEDENT PERSONAL DATA

1A. Name of decedent—first	William
1B. Middle	Franklin
1C. Last	Holden
2A. Date of death (month, day, year)	Found Nov. 16, 1981
2B. Hour	1000
3. Sex	Male
4. Race	Cauc.
5. Ethnicity	
6. Date of birth	April 17, 1918
7. Age	63 years
8. Birthplace of decedent (state or foreign country)	Illinois
9. Name and birthplace of father	William F. Beedle - Illinois
10. Birth name and birthplace of mother	Mary Ball -- Illinois
11. Citizen of what country	U.S.A.
12. Social Security number	565-16-7734
13. Marital status	Divorced
14. Name of surviving spouse (if wife, enter birth name)	
15. Primary occupation	Actor
16. Number of years this occupation	40yrs.
17. Employer (if self-employed, so state)	Holden Prod., Inc.
18. Kind of industry or business	Motion Picture Prod.

USUAL RESIDENCE

19A. Usual residence—street address (street and number or location)	535 Ocean Avenue Apt. #43
19B.	
19C. City or town	Santa Monica
19D. County	Los Angeles
19E. State	Calif.
20. Name and address of informant—relationship	Mr. E.R. Comstock-Excutor, Tanner & Mainstin, 11620 Wilshire Blvd. #580, Los Angeles, Calif.

PLACE OF DEATH

21A. Place of death	Residence
21B. County	Los Angeles
21C. Street address (street and number or location)	535 Ocean Avenue Apt. #43
21D. City or town	Santa Monica

CAUSE OF DEATH

22. Death was caused by: (enter only one cause per line for A, B, and C)

Immediate cause (A) EXSANGUINATION

Conditions, if any, which gave rise to the immediate cause, stating the underlying cause last — due to, or as a consequence of (B) BLUNT LACERATION OF SCALP

Due to, or as a consequence of (C)

Approximate interval between onset and death

24. Was death reported to coroner? 81-14582

25. Was biopsy performed? NO

26. Was autopsy performed? YES

23. Other conditions contributing but not related to the immediate cause of death: FATTY METAMORPHOSIS OF LIVER

27. Was operation performed for any condition in items 22 or 23? Type of operation — Date: NO

PHYSICIAN'S CERTIFICATION

28A. I certify that death occurred at the hour, date and place stated from the causes stated. I attended decedent since (enter mo, da, yr) — I last saw decedent alive (enter mo, da, yr)

28B. Physician—signature and degree or title

28C. Date signed

28D. Physician's license number

28E. Type physician's name and address

INJURY INFORMATION — CORONER'S USE ONLY

29. Specify accident, suicide, etc.	ACCIDENT
30. Place of injury	RESIDENCE
31. Injury at work	NO
32A. Date of injury—month, day, year	UNK.
32B. Hour	UNK.
33. Location (street and number or location and city or town)	535 OCEAN AVE. APT. #43 SANTA MONICA
34. Describe how injury occurred (events which resulted in injury)	FALL TO FURNITURE
35A. I certify that death occurred at the hour, date and place stated from the causes stated. As required by law I have held an (inquest/investigation)	1104 N. MISSION RD. LOS ANGELES, CALIF. 90033
35B. Coroner—signature and degree	THOMAS T. NOGUCHI, M.D., CORONER — [signature], DEPUTY
35C. Date signed	11/19/81

36. Disposition	Cremation
37. Date—month, day, year	11/19/81
38. Name and address of cemetery or crematory	Angeles Abbey Crem.-1515 E. Compton, Compton, Calif.
39. Embalmer's license number and signature	Unembalmed
40. Name of funeral director (or person acting as such)	THE NEPTUNE SOCIETY
41. Local registrar—signature	[signature] MD
42. Date accepted by local registrar	NOV 19 1981

STATE REGISTRAR A. B. C. D. E. F.

VS-11 (10-78)

01-45-4-7005

This is to certify that this document is a true copy of the official record filed with the Registrar-Recorder/County Clerk.

FEB 12 1992

[signature]
CHARLES WEISSBURD
Registrar-Recorder/County Clerk

19-312717

This copy not valid unless prepared on engraved border displaying the Seal and Signature of the Registrar-Recorder/County Clerk.

THE GREAT SEAL OF THE STATE OF CALIFORNIA — EUREKA

REGISTRAR-RECORDER/COUNTY CLERK — COUNTY OF LOS ANGELES • CALIFORNIA

American Bank Note Company

ANY ALTERATION OR ERASURE VOIDS THIS CERTIFICATE

CERTIFICATION OF VITAL RECORD

COUNTY OF LOS ANGELES • REGISTRAR-RECORDER/COUNTY CLERK

Filed FEB 25 1966 RAY E. LEE, COUNTY RECORDER

STATE FILE NUMBER

CERTIFICATE OF DEATH

STATE OF CALIFORNIA—DEPARTMENT OF PUBLIC HEALTH

LOCAL REGISTRATION DISTRICT AND CERTIFICATE NUMBER 7097 004438

DECEDENT PERSONAL DATA

1a. NAME OF DECEASED—FIRST NAME: Elda Hedda | 1b. MIDDLE NAME: F | 1c. LAST NAME: Hopper AKA Hopper | 2a. DATE OF DEATH: Feb. 1, 1966 | 2b. HOUR: 10:30 A.M.

3. SEX: Female | 4. COLOR OR RACE: Cauc. | 5. BIRTHPLACE: Pennsylvania | 6. DATE OF BIRTH: June 2, 1890 | 7. AGE: 75 YEARS

8. NAME AND BIRTHPLACE OF FATHER: David Furry, Pennsylvania | 9. MAIDEN NAME AND BIRTHPLACE OF MOTHER: Margaret Miller, Penn. | 10. CITIZEN OF WHAT COUNTRY: U.S.A. | 11. SOCIAL SECURITY NUMBER: 550-07-1950

12. LAST OCCUPATION: Actress & Columist | 13. NUMBER OF YEARS IN THIS OCCUPATION: 57 | 14. NAME OF LAST EMPLOYING COMPANY OR FIRM: Hedda Hoppers Hol. | 15. KIND OF INDUSTRY OR BUSINESS: Acting & Newspaper

16. IF DECEASED WAS EVER IN U.S. ARMED FORCES GIVE WAR OR DATES OF SERVICE: No | 17. SPECIFY MARRIED, NEVER MARRIED, WIDOWED, DIVORCED: Widowed | 18a. NAME OF PRESENT SPOUSE: None | 18b. PRESENT OR LAST OCCUPATION OF SPOUSE: None

PLACE OF DEATH

19a. PLACE OF DEATH—NAME OF HOSPITAL: Cedars of Lebanon Hospital | 19b. STREET ADDRESS: 4833 Fountain Avenue | [X] INSIDE CITY CORPORATE LIMITS [ ] OUTSIDE CITY CORPORATE LIMITS

19c. CITY OR TOWN: Los Angeles | 19d. COUNTY: Los Angeles | 19e. LENGTH OF STAY IN COUNTY OF DEATH: 46 YEARS | 19f. LENGTH OF STAY IN CALIFORNIA: 46 YEARS

LAST USUAL RESIDENCE (WHERE DID DECEASED LIVE—IF IN INSTITUTION ENTER RESIDENCE BEFORE ADMISSION)

20a. LAST USUAL RESIDENCE—STREET ADDRESS: 1708 Tropical Avenue | 20b. IF INSIDE CITY CORPORATE LIMITS [X] CHECK HERE | IF OUTSIDE CITY CORPORATE LIMITS [ ] ON A FARM [ ] NOT ON A FARM | 21a. NAME OF INFORMANT (IF OTHER THAN SPOUSE): William Hopper

20c. CITY OR TOWN: Beverly Hills 7007 | 20d. COUNTY: Los Angeles | 20e. STATE: California | 21b. ADDRESS OF INFORMANT: 24358 Malibu Rd. Malibu

PHYSICIAN'S OR CORONER'S CERTIFICATION

22a. PHYSICIAN: I HEREBY CERTIFY THAT DEATH OCCURRED AT THE HOUR, DATE AND PLACE STATED ABOVE FROM THE CAUSES STATED BELOW AND THAT I ATTENDED THE DECEASED FROM 10-11-65 TO 2-1-66 AND THAT I LAST SAW THE DECEASED ALIVE ON 2-1-66

22b. CORONER: I HEREBY CERTIFY THAT DEATH OCCURRED AT THE HOUR, DATE AND PLACE STATED ABOVE FROM THE CAUSES STATED BELOW AND THAT I HAVE HELD AN ... ON THE REMAINS OF DECEASED AS REQUIRED BY LAW

22c. PHYSICIAN OR CORONER—SIGNATURE: S R Kemmamer | DEGREE OR TITLE: MD

22d. ADDRESS: 436 N Roxbury Beverly Hills | 22e. DATE SIGNED: 2-2-66.

FUNERAL DIRECTOR AND LOCAL REGISTRAR

23. SPECIFY BURIAL, ENTOMBMENT OR CREMATION: Cremation | 24. DATE: 2-5-66 | 25. NAME OF CEMETERY OR CREMATORY: Chapel of the Pines | 26. EMBALMER—SIGNATURE | LICENSE NUMBER: 4281

27. NAME OF FUNERAL DIRECTOR: Pierce Bros. Beverly Hills | 28. DATE ACCEPTED FOR REGISTRATION BY LOCAL REGISTRAR: FEB 3 - 1966 | 29. LOCAL REGISTRAR—SIGNATURE: [signature] MD

MEDICAL AND HEALTH DATA

CAUSE OF DEATH

30. CAUSE OF DEATH — ENTER ONLY ONE CAUSE PER LINE FOR (A), (B), AND (C)

PART I. DEATH WAS CAUSED BY: IMMEDIATE CAUSE (A): Acute Pulmonary Edema — 2 days

CONDITIONS, IF ANY, WHICH GAVE RISE TO THE ABOVE CAUSE (A) STATING THE UNDERLYING CAUSE LAST — DUE TO (B): Arteriosclerotic Heart Disease — 5 wks

DUE TO (C):

APPROXIMATE INTERVAL BETWEEN ONSET AND DEATH

PART II. OTHER SIGNIFICANT CONDITIONS CONTRIBUTING TO DEATH BUT NOT RELATED TO THE TERMINAL DISEASE CONDITION GIVEN IN PART I (A): Bilateral Bronchopneumonia

OPERATION AND AUTOPSY

31. OPERATION—CHECK ONE: [X] NO OPERATION PERFORMED [ ] OPERATION PERFORMED—FINDINGS USED IN DETERMINING ABOVE STATED CAUSES OF DEATH [ ] OPERATION PERFORMED—FINDINGS NOT USED IN DETERMINING ABOVE STATED CAUSES OF DEATH | 32. DATE OF OPERATION | 33. AUTOPSY—CHECK ONE: [X] NO AUTOPSY PERFORMED [ ] AUTOPSY PERFORMED—ABOVE FINDINGS USED IN DETERMINING ABOVE STATED CAUSES OF DEATH [ ] AUTOPSY PERFORMED—GROSS FINDINGS NOT USED IN DETERMINING ABOVE STATED CAUSES OF DEATH

INJURY INFORMATION

34a. SPECIFY ACCIDENT, SUICIDE OR HOMICIDE | 34b. DESCRIBE HOW INJURY OCCURRED

35a. TIME OF INJURY HOUR MONTH DAY YEAR M.

35b. INJURY OCCURRED [ ] WHILE AT WORK [ ] NOT WHILE AT WORK | 35c. PLACE OF INJURY | 35d. CITY, TOWN, OR LOCATION COUNTY STATE

This is to certify that this document is a true copy of the official record filed with the Registrar-Recorder/County Clerk.

Beatriz Valdez
BEATRIZ VALDEZ
Registrar-Recorder/County Clerk

AUG 1 1995

19-389278

This copy not valid unless prepared on engraved border displaying the Seal and Signature of the Registrar-Recorder/County Clerk.

American Bank Note Company

ANY ALTERATION OR ERASURE VOIDS THIS CERTIFICATE

BOOK 1970 PAGE 00797

CERTIFICATE OF DEATH

STATE FILE NUMBER — STATE OF CALIFORNIA—DEPARTMENT OF PUBLIC HEALTH — 3397 781 LOCAL REGISTRATION DISTRICT AND CERTIFICATE NUMBER

DECEDENT PERSONAL DATA

1a. Name of deceased—first name	William
1b. Middle name	De Wolf
1c. Last name	Hopper
2a. Date of death—month, day, year	March 6, 1970
2b. Hour	5:07 A. M
3. Sex	Male
4. Color or race	Caucasian
5. Birthplace (state or foreign country)	New York
6. Date of birth	January 26, 1915
7. Age (last birthday)	55 years
8. Name and birthplace of father	De Wolf Hopper-New York
9. Maiden name and birthplace of mother	Elda Fury- Penn.
10. Citizen of what country	U.S.A.
11. Social security number	565-16-5429
12. Married, never married, widowed, divorced (specify)	Married
13. Name of surviving spouse (if wife, enter maiden name)	Jeanette J. Ward
14. Last occupation	Actor
15. Number of years in this occupation	25
16. Name of last employing company or firm	20th Century Fox
17. Kind of industry or business	Motion Picture

PLACE OF DEATH

18a. Place of death—name of hospital or other in-patient facility	Desert Hospital
18b. Street address	1155 Via Miraleste
18c. Inside city corporate limits	Yes
18d. City or town	Palm Springs
18e. County	Riverside
18f. Length of stay in county of death	3 weeks
18g. Length of stay in California	40 years

USUAL RESIDENCE (if death occurred in institution, enter residence before admission)

19a. Usual residence—street address	8572 Joshua Lane
19b. Inside city corporate limits	No
19c. City or town	Yucca Valley
19d. County	San Bernardino
19e. State	California
20. Name and mailing address of informant	Eleanor K. Ward-Sister-in-law, 15632 E. Janine Dr. Whittier, Calif.

PHYSICIAN'S OR CORONER'S CERTIFICATION

21a. Coroner	
21b. Physician: attended the deceased from / to; last saw the deceased alive on	Feb. 14, 1970 / Mar. 6, 1970; Mar. 5, 1970
21c. Physician or coroner—signature and degree or title	Daniel E. Lapley MD
21d. Date signed	Mar. 6, 1970
21e. Address	1492 N. Palm Springs, Calif.
21f. Physician's California license number	A-16531

FUNERAL DIRECTOR AND LOCAL REGISTRAR

22a. Specify burial, entombment or cremation	Removal Cremation
22b. Date	March 10, 1970
23. Name of cemetery or crematory	Whittier, California Rose Hills Crematory
24. Embalmer—signature (if body embalmed) license number	Rex Spafford #4915
25. Name of funeral director (or person acting as such)	Whittier, California Rose Hills Mortuary
26. If not certified by coroner was this death reported to coroner	No
27. Local registrar—signature	[illegible signature]
28. Date accepted for registration by local registrar	MAR 10 1970

MEDICAL AND HEALTH DATA — CAUSE OF DEATH

29. Part I. Death was caused by: (enter only one cause per line for A, B, and C)

	Cause	Approximate interval between onset and death
Immediate cause (A)	Bilateral Bronchopneumonia	2 weeks
Due to, or as a consequence of (B)	Left Middle Cerebral Artery Thrombosis	3 weeks
Due to, or as a consequence of (C)		

30. Part II. Other significant conditions—contributing to death but not related to the immediate cause given in Part I: Coronary Arteriosclerosis

31. Was operation or biopsy performed for any condition in items 29 or 30? (specify operation and/or biopsy): No

32a. Autopsy (specify yes or no): Yes

32b. If yes, were findings considered in determining cause of death: Yes

INJURY INFORMATION

33. Specify accident, suicide or homicide —
34. Place of injury —
35. Injury at work —
36a. Date of injury —
36b. Hour —
37a. Place of injury —
37b. Distance from place of injury to usual residence — miles
38. Were laboratory tests done for drugs or toxic chemicals —
39. Were laboratory tests done for alcohol —
40. Describe how injury occurred —

STATE REGISTRAR A B C D E F

CERTIFICATION OF VITAL RECORD

COUNTY OF LOS ANGELES • REGISTRAR-RECORDER/COUNTY CLERK

1692

CERTIFICATE OF DEATH

STATE OF CALIFORNIA—DEPARTMENT OF PUBLIC HEALTH

STATE FILE NO. — REGISTRATION DISTRICT NO. 1979 — REGISTRAR'S NUMBER 28

DECEDENT PERSONAL DATA	1a. Name of deceased—first name	JEROME
	1b. Middle name	LESTER
	1c. Last name	HOWARD
	2a. Date of death	JANUARY 18, 1952
	2b. Hour	3:10 P.M.
	3. Sex	Male
	4. Color or race	Cauc.
	5. Married, never married, widowed, divorced	Married
	6. Date of birth	October 22, 1903
	7. Age (last birthday)	48 years
	8a. Usual occupation	Actor
	8b. Kind of business or industry	Stage and Screen
	9. Birthplace	New York
	10. Citizen of what country	United States of America
	11. Name and birthplace of father	Solomon Horwitz - Russia
	12. Maiden name and birthplace of mother	Jennie Horwitz - Russia
	13. Name of present spouse	Valerie Howard
	14. Was deceased ever in U.S. Armed Forces?	no / No
	15. Social Security number	563-12-6539
	16. Informant	Moe Howard
PLACE OF DEATH	17a. County	Los Angeles
	17b. City or town	San Gabriel (X outside corporate limits)
	17c. Length of stay in this city or town	1 Week
	17d. Full name of hospital or institution	Baldy View Sanitarium
	17e. Address	8101 Hill Drive
LAST USUAL RESIDENCE	18a. State	California
	18b. County	Los Angeles
	18c. City or town	Los Angeles (Van Nuys) (XX inside corporate limits)
	18d. Street or rural address	4524 Fulton Avenue
PHYSICIAN'S CERTIFICATION	19a. Physician: I hereby certify that death occurred at the hour, date and place stated above, from the causes stated below and that I attended the deceased from	1/7-1952 to 1/18-52 and that I last saw the deceased alive on 1/18-1952
	19c. Signature	N W Edwards MD
	19d. Address	112 W 9th Los Angeles 15 Cal
	19e. Date signed	1/18-1952
FUNERAL DIRECTOR AND REGISTRAR	20a. Burial, cremation or removal	Burial
	20b. Date	1-20-52
	20c. Cemetery or crematory	Home of Peace Memorial Park
	21. Signature of embalmer	John E. Moss — License number 3660
	22. Funeral director	Malinow and Simons, Los Angeles
	23. Date received by local registrar	JAN 19 1952
	24. Signature of local registrar	[illegible] By J. H. Gooch
CAUSE OF DEATH	25. Disease or condition directly leading to death (a)	Cerebral hemorrhage — 48 hrs
	Antecedent causes, due to (b)	Cerebral arterio sclerosis — 6 yrs
	Due to (c)	
OTHER SIGNIFICANT CONDITIONS	26. Conditions contributing to the death but not related to the disease or condition causing death	
OPERATIONS	27a. Date of operation	
	27b. Major findings of operation	
	28. Autopsy	No
DEATH DUE TO EXTERNAL VIOLENCE	29a–29f	

This is to certify that this document is a true copy of the official record filed with the Registrar-Recorder/County Clerk.

NOV 27 1995

19-080595

This copy not valid unless prepared on engraved border displaying the Seal of the Registrar-Recorder/County Clerk.

ANY ALTERATION OR ERASURE VOIDS THIS CERTIFICATE

CERTIFICATION OF VITAL RECORD

COUNTY OF LOS ANGELES • REGISTRAR-RECORDER/COUNTY CLERK

CERTIFICATE OF DEATH 0190-021956

STATE OF CALIFORNIA—DEPARTMENT OF HEALTH
OFFICE OF THE STATE REGISTRAR OF VITAL STATISTICS

STATE FILE NUMBER — LOCAL REGISTRATION DISTRICT AND CERTIFICATE NUMBER

DECEDENT PERSONAL DATA

- 1a. Name of deceased—first name: MOE
- 1b. Middle name:
- 1c. Last name: HOWARD
- 2a. Date of death—month day year: MAY 4, 1975
- 2b. Hour: 6:15 PM.
- 3. Sex: MALE
- 4. Color or race: CAUC.
- 5. Birthplace (state or foreign country): NEW YORK
- 6. Date of birth: JUNE 19,1897
- 7. Age (last birthday): 77 YEARS — If under 1 year: MONTHS / DAYS — If under 24 hours: HOURS / MINUTES
- 8. Name and birthplace of father: SOLOMON HORWITZ - RUSSIA
- 9. Maiden name and birthplace of mother: JENNIE (UNKNOWN) - RUSSIA
- 10. Citizen of what country: U.S.A.
- 11. Social security number: 563-12-6482
- 12. Married, never married, widowed, divorced (specify): MARRIED
- 13. Name of surviving spouse (if wife, enter maiden name): HELEN SCHOENBERGER
- 14. Last occupation: ACTOR
- 15. Number of years in this occupation: 50
- 16. Name of last employing company or firm (if self-employed, so state): COMEDY III PRODUCTIONS
- 17. Kind of industry or business: MOTION PICTURES

PLACE OF DEATH

- 18a. Place of death—name of hospital or other in-patient facility: HOLLYWOOD PRESBYTERIAN HOSPITAL
- 18b. Street address—(street and number or location): 1322 N. VERMONT AVENUE
- 18c. Inside city corporate limits (specify yes or no): YES
- 18d. City or town: LOS ANGELES
- 18e. County: LOS ANGELES
- 18f. Length of stay in county of death: 42 YEARS
- 18g. Length of stay in California: 42 YEARS

USUAL RESIDENCE (if death occurred in institution enter residence before admission)

- 19a. Usual residence—street address (street and number or location): 9061 THRASHER AVENUE
- 19b. Inside city corporate limits (specify yes or no): YES
- 19c. City or town: LOS ANGELES
- 19d. County: LOS ANGELES
- 19e. State: CALIFORNIA
- 20. Name and mailing address of informant: MR.NORMAN MAURER, 3100 CAVENDISH DR., LOS ANGELES, CALIF.90064

PHYSICIAN'S OR CORONER'S CERTIFICATION

- 21a. Coroner: I hereby certify that death occurred at the hour, date and place stated above from the causes stated below and that I have held an investigation or inquest.
- 21b. Physician: I hereby certify that death occurred at the hour, date and place stated above from the causes stated below and that I attended the deceased from 1/23/75 to 5/4/75 and last saw him alive 5/3/75
- 21c. Physician or coroner—signature and degree or title: S Sabulsky MD
- 21d. Date signed: 5/5/75
- 21e. Address: 1930 Wilshire
- 21f. Physician's California license number: C-2588

FUNERAL DIRECTOR AND LOCAL REGISTRAR

- 22a. Specify burial, entombment or cremation: ENTOMBMENT
- 22b. Date: 5/6/75
- 23. Name of cemetery or crematory: HILLSIDE MEMORIAL PARK
- 24. Embalmer—signature (if body embalmed) / License number: 6290
- 25. Name of funeral director (or person acting as such): GROMAN MORTUARY jmb
- 26. If not certified by coroner was this death reported to coroner (specify yes or no): No
- 27. Local registrar—signature
- 28. Date received for registration by local registrar: MAY 6 1975

MEDICAL AND HEALTH DATA — CAUSE OF DEATH

29. Part I. Death was caused by: (Enter only one cause per line for A, B, and C)

- Immediate cause (A): Cancer of Lung — Approximate interval between onset and death: 6 months
- Conditions, if any, which gave rise to the immediate cause (A), stating the underlying cause last: Due to, or as a consequence of (B)
- Due to, or as a consequence of (C)

30. Part II: Other significant conditions—contributing to death but not related to the immediate cause given in Part I(A)

- 31. Was operation or biopsy performed for any condition in items 29 or 30? (specify operation and/or biopsy): Biopsy
- 32a. Autopsy (specify yes or no): NO
- 32b. If yes were findings considered in determining cause of death? (specify yes or no)

INJURY INFORMATION

- 33. Specify accident, suicide or homicide
- 34. Place of injury (specify home, farm, factory, street, office building, etc.)
- 35. Injury at work (specify yes or no)
- 36a. Date of injury—month day year
- 36b. Hour M.
- 37a. Place of injury (street and number or location and city or town)
- 37b. Distance from place of injury to usual residence, item 19: MILES
- 38. Were laboratory tests done for drugs or toxic chemicals? (specify yes or no)
- 39. Were laboratory tests done for alcohol? (specify yes or no)
- 40. Describe how injury occurred (enter sequence of events which resulted in injury. Nature of injury should be entered in item 29)

10

STATE REGISTRAR A. B. C. D. E. F. 9-1-9

This is to certify that this document is a true copy of the official record filed with the Registrar-Recorder/County Clerk.

BEATRIZ VALDEZ
Registrar-Recorder/County Clerk

AUG 10 1995

19-389397

This copy not valid unless prepared on engraved border displaying the Seal and Signature of the Registrar-Recorder/County Clerk.

American Bank Note Company

ANY ALTERATION OR ERASURE VOIDS THIS CERTIFICATE

CERTIFICATION OF VITAL RECORD

COUNTY OF LOS ANGELES • REGISTRAR-RECORDER/COUNTY CLERK

20217

STATE FILE NO 55-101387

CERTIFICATE OF DEATH

STATE OF CALIFORNIA—DEPARTMENT OF PUBLIC HEALTH

REGISTRATION DISTRICT NO 7014 REGISTRAR'S NUMBER 16356

DECEDENT PERSONAL DATA

1a NAME OF DECEASED—FIRST NAME	SHEMP
1b MIDDLE NAME	-
1c LAST NAME	HOWARD
2a DATE OF DEATH—MONTH, DAY, YEAR	November 22, 1955
2b HOUR	11:00 PM
3 SEX	Male
4 COLOR OR RACE	Cauc.
5 SINGLE, MARRIED, NEVER MARRIED, WIDOWED, DIVORCED	Married
6 DATE OF BIRTH	March 4, 1895
7 AGE (LAST BIRTHDAY)	60
8a USUAL OCCUPATION	Actor
8b KIND OF BUSINESS OR INDUSTRY	Motion Pictures
9 BIRTHPLACE	New York
10 CITIZEN OF WHAT COUNTRY	U.S.A.
11 NAME AND BIRTHPLACE OF FATHER	Solomon Howard - Lithuania
12 MAIDEN NAME AND BIRTHPLACE OF MOTHER	Jennie Howard - Lithuania
13 NAME OF PRESENT SPOUSE (IF MARRIED)	Gertrude Howard
14 WAS DECEASED EVER IN U S ARMED FORCES?	yes
15 SOCIAL SECURITY NUMBER	Unknown
16 INFORMANT	Morton Howard

PLACE OF DEATH

17a COUNTY	Los Angeles
17b CITY OR TOWN	Burbank (inside corporate limits)
17c LENGTH OF STAY IN THIS CITY OR TOWN	Enroute
17d FULL NAME OF HOSPITAL OR INSTITUTION	St. Joseph Hospital
17e ADDRESS	501 S. Buena Vista Street

LAST USUAL RESIDENCE

18a STATE	California
18b COUNTY	Los Angeles
18c CITY OR TOWN	Los Angeles (No. Hollywood) (inside corporate limits)
18d STREET OR RURAL ADDRESS	10522 Riverside Drive

PHYSICIAN'S OR CORONER'S CERTIFICATION

19a PHYSICIAN — attended the deceased from	Mar 18, 1950 to Nov 8, 1955; last saw the deceased alive on Nov 8, 1955
19b SIGNATURE	H.H. Greene (H.H.Greene)
DEGREE OR TITLE	MD
19d ADDRESS	10137 Riverside Dr. North Hollywood
19e DATE SIGNED	11-23-55

FUNERAL DIRECTOR AND REGISTRAR

20a SPECIFY BURIAL, CREMATION OR REMOVAL	Entombment
20b DATE	Nov. 25, 1955
20c CEMETERY OR CREMATORY	Home of Peace Mausoleum
21 SIGNATURE OF EMBALMER / LICENSE NUMBER	John W. Fricker 3616
22 FUNERAL DIRECTOR	Malinow and Simons,
23 DATE RECEIVED BY LOCAL REGISTRAR	NOV 24 1955
24 SIGNATURE OF LOCAL REGISTRAR	[signature]

CAUSE OF DEATH

		Approximate interval between onset and death
25 DISEASE OR CONDITION DIRECTLY LEADING TO DEATH (a)	Acute Coronary Thrombosis	3 Minutes
ANTECEDENT CAUSES — DUE TO (b)	Hypertensive Heart Disease (see margin)	5 years
DUE TO (c)		
26 OTHER SIGNIFICANT CONDITIONS		
27a DATE OF OPERATION		
27b MAJOR FINDINGS OF OPERATION		
28 AUTOPSY	No	

DEATH DUE TO EXTERNAL VIOLENCE

29a SPECIFY ACCIDENT, SUICIDE OR HOMICIDE; 29b PLACE OF INJURY; 29c LOCATION (CITY OR TOWN, COUNTY, STATE); 29d TIME OF INJURY; 29e INJURY OCCURRED (WHILE AT WORK / NOT WHILE AT WORK); 29f HOW DID INJURY OCCUR? — [blank]

Margin note: MEDICAL AND HEALTH DATA 25b: Dr. states benign hypertension. NN 7053 11/29/55 5 cc Pd

This is to certify that this document is a true copy of the official record filed with the Registrar-Recorder/County Clerk.

DEC 22 1995

19-103386

This copy not valid unless prepared on engraved border displaying the Seal of the Registrar-Recorder/County Clerk.

ANY ALTERATION OR ERASURE VOIDS THIS CERTIFICATE

CERTIFICATION OF VITAL RECORD

COUNTY OF LOS ANGELES • REGISTRAR-RECORDER/COUNTY CLERK

CERTIFICATE OF DEATH
STATE OF CALIFORNIA

STATE FILE NUMBER — 3851904615 2 (LOCAL REGISTRATION DISTRICT AND CERTIFICATE NUMBER)

DECEDENT PERSONAL DATA

1A. Name of Decedent—First	ROCK
1B. Middle	
1C. Last	HUDSON
2A. Date of Death (Month, Day, Year)	Oct. 2, 1985
2B. Hour	0900
3. Sex	Male
4. Race/Ethnicity	White/American
5. Spanish/Hispanic	No
6. Date of Birth	Nov. 17, 1925
7. Age	59 Years
8. Birthplace of Decedent (State or Foreign Country)	Illinois
9. Name and Birthplace of Father	Roy Scherer - Illinois
10. Birth Name and Birthplace of Mother	Katherine Wood-Illinois
11A. Citizen of What Country	USA
11B. If Deceased Was Ever in Military, Give Dates of Service	1942 to 1945
12. Social Security Number	354-14-0316
13. Marital Status	Divorced
14. Name of Surviving Spouse (If Wife, Enter Birth Name)	
15. Primary Occupation	Actor
16. Number of Years This Occupation	35
17. Employer (If Self-Employed, So State)	Mammouth Films
18. Kind of Industry or Business	Motion Pictures

USUAL RESIDENCE

19A. Usual Residence—Street Address (Street and Number or Location)	9402 Beverly Crest Dr.
19C. City or Town	Beverly Hills
19D. County	Los Angeles
19E. State	Calif.
20. Name and Address of Informant—Relationship	Pre Need Memorial Records, 5423 Tujunga Ave., No. Hollywood, Calif. 91601

PLACE OF DEATH

21A. Place of Death	Residence
21B. County	Los Angeles
21C. Street Address (Street and Number or Location)	9402 Beverly Crest Dr.
21D. City or Town	Beverly Hills

CAUSE OF DEATH

22. Death was caused by: (Enter only one cause per line for A, B, and C)

Immediate cause / Conditions, if any, which gave rise to the immediate cause, stating the underlying cause last	Approximate interval between onset and death
(A) Cardio Respiratory Arrest	10 min
(B) Due to, or as a consequence of: Lymphoblastic lymphoma	4 mths
(C) Due to, or as a consequence of: Acquired Immune Deficiency Syndrome	16 mths

24. Was death reported to coroner? NO
25. Was biopsy performed? NO
26. Was autopsy performed? NO
23. Other significant conditions—contributing to death but not related to cause given in 22A:
27. Was operation performed for any condition in items 22 or 23? Type of operation: NO — Date:

PHYSICIAN'S CERTIFICATION

28A. I certify that death occurred at the hour, date and place stated from the causes stated.

Attended decedent since (Enter Mo. Da. Yr.)	7-1-75
Last saw decedent alive (Enter Mo. Da. Yr.)	10-1-85
28B. Physician—Signature and degree or title	S R Kennamer M.D.
28C. Date signed	10-2-85
28D. Physician's license number	A1805
28E. Type physician's name and address	S.R. Kennamer, M.D. 436 N. Roxbury Dr. Beverly Hills, Ca.

INJURY INFORMATION / CORONER'S USE ONLY

29. Specify accident, suicide, etc. 30. Place of injury 31. Injury at work 32A. Date of injury—Month, Day, Year 32B. Hour
33. Location (Street and number or location and city or town) 34. Describe how injury occurred (Events which resulted in injury)
35A. I certify that death occurred at the hour, date and place stated from the causes stated. As required by law I have held an (inquest-investigation) 35B. Coroner—Signature and degree or title 35C. Date signed

36. Disposition	Cremation
37. Date—Month, Day, Year	Oct. 2,1985
38. Name and Address of Cemetery or Crematory	Grand View Memorial Park Crematory, 1341 Glenwood Dr. Glendale, Ca.
39. Embalmer's License Number and Signature	Not Embalmed
40A. Name of Funeral Director (or Person Acting as Such)	Pierce-Hamrock-Reed Mortuary
40B. License No.	F 1227
41. Local Registrar—Signature	Robert S. Mate
42. Date Accepted by Local Registrar	OCT 02 1985

STATE REGISTRAR A. B. C. D. E. F.

VS-11 (1-85) 2001

This is to certify that this document is a true copy of the official record filed with the Registrar-Recorder/County Clerk.

Charles Weissburd
CHARLES WEISSBURD
Registrar-Recorder/County Clerk

FEB 05 1992
19-312849

This copy not valid unless prepared on engraved border displaying the Seal and Signature of the Registrar-Recorder/County Clerk.

American Bank Note Company

ANY ALTERATION OR ERASURE VOIDS THIS CERTIFICATE

STATE OF CALIFORNIA
CERTIFICATION OF VITAL RECORD

COUNTY OF LOS ANGELES
DEPARTMENT OF HEALTH SERVICES

CERTIFICATE OF DEATH
STATE OF CALIFORNIA
USE BLACK INK ONLY/NO ERASURES, WHITEOUTS OR ALTERATIONS
VS-11 (REV. 1/00)

STATE FILE NUMBER — LOCAL REGISTRATION NUMBER

DECEDENT PERSONAL DATA
- 1. NAME OF DECEDENT—FIRST (GIVEN): ROY
- 2. MIDDLE: MARSHALL
- 3. LAST (FAMILY): HUGGINS
- 4. DATE OF BIRTH MM/DD/CCYY: 07/18/1914
- 5. AGE YRS.: 87
- IF UNDER 1 YEAR: MONTHS / DAYS — IF UNDER 24 HOURS: HOURS / MINUTES
- 6. SEX: M
- 7. DATE OF DEATH MM/DD/CCYY: 04/03/2002
- 8. HOUR: 1703
- 9. STATE OF BIRTH: WA
- 10. SOCIAL SECURITY NO.: 565-16-9880
- 11. MILITARY SERVICE: ☐ YES ☒ NO ☐ UNK
- 12. MARITAL STATUS: MARRIED
- 13. EDUCATION—YEARS COMPLETED: 18
- 14. RACE: CAUCASIAN
- 15. HISPANIC—SPECIFY: ☐ YES ☒ NO
- 16. USUAL EMPLOYER: SELF EMPLOYED
- 17. OCCUPATION: WRITER/PRODUCER
- 18. KIND OF BUSINESS: TELEVISION
- 19. YEARS IN OCCUPATION: 45

USUAL RESIDENCE
- 20. RESIDENCE—(STREET AND NUMBER OR LOCATION): 1928 MANDEVILLE CANYON RD.
- 21. CITY: LOS ANGELES
- 22. COUNTY: LOS ANGELES
- 23. ZIP CODE: 90049
- 24. YRS IN COUNTY: 70
- 25. STATE OR FOREIGN COUNTRY: CA

INFORMANT
- 26. NAME, RELATIONSHIP: THOMAS ROY HUGGINS-SON
- 27. MAILING ADDRESS (STREET AND NUMBER OR RURAL ROUTE NUMBER, CITY OR TOWN, STATE, ZIP): 2356 PARNELL AVE. LOS ANGELES, CA. 90064

SPOUSE AND PARENT INFORMATION
- 28. NAME OF SURVIVING SPOUSE—FIRST: ADELE
- 29. MIDDLE: MARA
- 30. LAST (MAIDEN NAME): DELGADO
- 31. NAME OF FATHER—FIRST: EDWARD
- 32. MIDDLE: FRANCIS
- 33. LAST: HUGGINS
- 34. BIRTH STATE: WI
- 35. NAME OF MOTHER—FIRST: BELLE
- 36. MIDDLE: -
- 37. LAST (MAIDEN): CRAWFORD
- 38. BIRTH STATE: WI

DISPOSITION(S)
- 39. DATE MM/DD/CCYY: 04/10/2002
- 40. PLACE OF FINAL DISPOSITION: RES:ADELE HUGGINS 1928 MANDEVILLE CANYON RD. LOS ANGELES, CA. 90049

FUNERAL DIRECTOR AND LOCAL REGISTRAR
- 41. TYPE OF DISPOSITION(S): CR/RES
- 42. SIGNATURE OF EMBALMER: NOT EMBALMED
- 43. LICENSE NO.: -
- 44. NAME OF FUNERAL DIRECTOR: GATES KINGSLEY GATES MOELLER MURPHY
- 45. LICENSE NO.: FD-451
- 46. SIGNATURE OF LOCAL REGISTRAR: Fred Leaf MD
- 47. DATE MM/DD/CCYY: 04/09/2002

PLACE OF DEATH
- 101. PLACE OF DEATH: ST. JOHN'S HEALTH CENTER
- 102. IF HOSPITAL, SPECIFY ONE: ☒ IP ☐ ER/OP ☐ DOA
- 103. FACILITY OTHER THAN HOSPITAL: ☐ CONV. HOSP. ☐ RES. CARE ☐ OTHER
- 104. COUNTY: LOS ANGELES
- 105. STREET ADDRESS—(STREET AND NUMBER OR LOCATION): 1328 22nd ST.
- 106. CITY: SANTA MONICA

CAUSE OF DEATH

107. DEATH WAS CAUSED BY: (ENTER ONLY ONE CAUSE PER LINE FOR A, B, C, AND D)

	Cause	Time interval between onset and death
IMMEDIATE CAUSE (A)	RESPIRATORY FAILURE	2 DAYS
DUE TO (B)	PULMONARY FIBROSIS	5 YEARS
DUE TO (C)	PULMONARY OBSTRUCTIVE DISEASE	YEARS
DUE TO (D)		

- 108. DEATH REPORTED TO CORONER: ☐ YES ☒ NO — REFERRAL NUMBER
- 109. BIOPSY PERFORMED: ☐ YES ☒ NO
- 110. AUTOPSY PERFORMED: ☐ YES ☒ NO
- 111. USED IN DETERMINING CAUSE: ☐ YES ☐ NO
- 112. OTHER SIGNIFICANT CONDITIONS CONTRIBUTING TO DEATH BUT NOT RELATED TO CAUSE GIVEN IN 107: GASTROINTESTINAL HEMORRHAGE DUE TO ARTERIO-VENOUS MALFORMATIONS
- 113. WAS OPERATION PERFORMED FOR ANY CONDITION IN ITEM 107 OR 112? IF YES, LIST TYPE OF OPERATION AND DATE.: NO

PHYSICIAN'S CERTIFICATION
- 114. I CERTIFY THAT TO THE BEST OF MY KNOWLEDGE DEATH OCCURRED AT THE HOUR, DATE AND PLACE STATED FROM THE CAUSES STATED. DECEDENT ATTENDED SINCE MM/DD/CCYY: 03/01/1983 — DECEDENT LAST SEEN ALIVE MM/DD/CCYY: 04/03/2002
- 115. SIGNATURE AND TITLE OF CERTIFIER: William N. Katkov MD
- 116. LICENSE NO.: G-54468
- 117. DATE MM/DD/CCYY: 04/04/2002
- 118. TYPE ATTENDING PHYSICIAN'S NAME, MAILING ADDRESS, ZIP: WILLIAM N.KATKOV,MD. 2001 SANTA MONICA BLVD.SANTA MONICA CA.90404

5

CORONER'S USE ONLY
- I CERTIFY THAT IN MY OPINION DEATH OCCURRED AT THE HOUR, DATE AND PLACE STATED FROM THE CAUSES STATED.
- 119. MANNER OF DEATH: ☐ NATURAL ☐ SUICIDE ☐ HOMICIDE ☐ ACCIDENT ☐ PENDING INVESTIGATION ☐ COULD NOT BE DETERMINED
- 120. INJURY AT WORK: ☐ YES ☐ NO
- 121. INJURY DATE MM/DD/CCYY
- 122. HOUR
- 123. PLACE OF INJURY
- 124. DESCRIBE HOW INJURY OCCURRED (EVENTS WHICH RESULTED IN INJURY)
- 125. LOCATION (STREET AND NUMBER OR LOCATION AND CITY, ZIP)
- 126. SIGNATURE OF CORONER OR DEPUTY CORONER
- 127. DATE MM/DD/CCYY
- 128. TYPED NAME, TITLE OF CORONER OR DEPUTY CORONER

J449

STATE REGISTRAR: A B C D E F G H — FAX AUTH. # — CENSUS TRACT 090520405

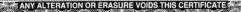

This is a true certified copy of the record filed in the County of Los Angeles Department of Health Services if it bears the Registrar's signature in purple ink.

DATE ISSUED
140 APR 15 2002

Fred Leaf
Director of Health Services and Registrar

THE GREAT SEAL OF THE STATE OF CALIFORNIA — EUREKA

This copy not valid unless prepared on engraved border displaying seal and signature of Registrar.

MIDWEST BANK NOTE COMPANY — ANY ALTERATION OR ERASURE VOIDS THIS CERTIFICATE

STATE OF CALIFORNIA

CERTIFICATION OF VITAL RECORD

COUNTY OF LOS ANGELES • REGISTRAR-RECORDER/COUNTY CLERK

CERTIFICATE OF DEATH
STATE OF CALIFORNIA
USE BLACK INK ONLY/NO ERASURES, WHITEOUTS OR ALTERATIONS
VS-11 (REV 11/94)

STATE FILE NUMBER — LOCAL REGISTRATION NUMBER: 3 199719 025730

DECEDENT PERSONAL DATA
1. NAME OF DECEDENT—FIRST (GIVEN): Richard
2. MIDDLE: Hanley
3. LAST (FAMILY): Jaeckel
4. DATE OF BIRTH MM/DD/CCYY: 10/10/1926
5. AGE YRS: 70
6. SEX: M
7. DATE OF DEATH MM/DD/CCYY: 06/14/1997
8. HOUR: 1925
9. STATE OF BIRTH: NY
10. SOCIAL SECURITY NO: 562-20-3323
11. MILITARY SERVICE: [ ] YES [X] NO
12. MARITAL STATUS: Married
13. EDUCATION—YEARS COMPLETED: 12
14. RACE: Caucasian
15. HISPANIC SPECIFY: [ ] YES [X] NO
16. USUAL EMPLOYER: Various Studios
17. OCCUPATION: Actor
18. KIND OF BUSINESS: Motion Pictures and Television
19. YEARS IN OCCUPATION: 54

USUAL RESIDENCE
20. RESIDENCE (STREET AND NUMBER OR LOCATION): 23388 Mulholland Dr.
21. CITY: Woodland Hills
22. COUNTY: Los Angeles
23. ZIP CODE: 91364
24. YRS IN COUNTY: 50
25. STATE OR FOREIGN COUNTRY: CA

INFORMANT
26. NAME, RELATIONSHIP: Barry Jaeckel – Son
27. MAILING ADDRESS (STREET AND NUMBER OR RURAL ROUTE NUMBER, CITY OR TOWN, STATE, ZIP): 321 Paseo Primavera, Palm Desert, CA 92260

SPOUSE AND PARENT INFORMATION
28. NAME OF SURVIVING SPOUSE—FIRST: Antionette
29. MIDDLE: Helen
30. LAST (MAIDEN NAME): Marches
31. NAME OF FATHER—FIRST: Unknown
32. MIDDLE: –
33. LAST: Jaeckel
34. BIRTH STATE: NY
35. NAME OF MOTHER—FIRST: Millicent
36. MIDDLE: –
37. LAST (MAIDEN): Unknown
38. BIRTH STATE: NY

DISPOSITION(S)
39. DATE MM/DD/CCYY: 06/20/1997
40. PLACE OF FINAL DISPOSITION: Scatter at sea three miles off the coast of Newport Beach, CA

FUNERAL DIRECTOR AND LOCAL REGISTRAR
41. TYPE OF DISPOSITION(S): CR/Scatter at sea
42. SIGNATURE OF EMBALMER: ▶ Not Embalmed
43. LICENSE NO.: –
44. NAME OF FUNERAL DIRECTOR: Pierce Brothers Cunningham O'Connor
45. LICENSE NO.: F-168
46. SIGNATURE OF LOCAL REGISTRAR: ▶ [signature]
47. DATE MM/DD/CCYY: 06/18/1997

PLACE OF DEATH
101. PLACE OF DEATH: Motion Picture Hospital
102. IF HOSPITAL, SPECIFY ONE: [ ] IP [ ] ER/OP [ ] DOA
103. FACILITY OTHER THAN HOSPITAL: [X] CONV HOSP [ ] RES. CARE [ ] OTHER
104. COUNTY: Los Angeles
105. STREET ADDRESS—STREET AND NUMBER OR LOCATION: 23388 Mulholland Dr.
106. CITY: Woodland Hills

CAUSE OF DEATH
107. DEATH WAS CAUSED BY: (ENTER ONLY ONE CAUSE PER LINE FOR A, B, C, AND D)
IMMEDIATE CAUSE (A) Multiple Myeloma — TIME INTERVAL BETWEEN ONSET AND DEATH: 6 Yrs
DUE TO (B)
DUE TO (C)
DUE TO (D)
108. DEATH REPORTED TO CORONER: [ ] YES [X] NO — REFERRAL NUMBER
109. BIOPSY PERFORMED: [ ] YES [X] NO
110. AUTOPSY PERFORMED: [ ] YES [X] NO
111. USED IN DETERMINING CAUSE: [ ] YES [ ] NO
112. OTHER SIGNIFICANT CONDITIONS CONTRIBUTING TO DEATH BUT NOT RELATED TO CAUSE GIVEN IN 107: Renal Failure
113. WAS OPERATION PERFORMED FOR ANY CONDITION IN ITEM 107 OR 112? IF YES, LIST TYPE OF OPERATION AND DATE: No

PHYSICIAN'S CERTIFICATION
114. I CERTIFY THAT TO THE BEST OF MY KNOWLEDGE DEATH OCCURRED AT THE HOUR, DATE AND PLACE STATED FROM THE CAUSES STATED.
DECEDENT ATTENDED SINCE MM/DD/CCYY: 06/13/1996
DECEDENT LAST SEEN ALIVE MM/DD/CCYY: 06/14/1997
115. SIGNATURE AND TITLE OF CERTIFIER: ▶ Janice Spinner MD
116. LICENSE NO.: G42727
117. DATE MM/DD/CCYY: 06/16/1997
118. TYPE ATTENDING PHYSICIAN'S NAME, MAILING ADDRESS, ZIP: Janice Spinner, MD: 23388 Mulholland Dr., Woodland Hills, CA 91364

CORONER'S USE ONLY
I CERTIFY THAT IN MY OPINION DEATH OCCURRED AT THE HOUR, DATE AND PLACE STATED FROM THE CAUSES STATED.
119. MANNER OF DEATH: [ ] NATURAL [ ] SUICIDE [ ] HOMICIDE [ ] ACCIDENT [ ] PENDING INVESTIGATION [ ] COULD NOT BE DETERMINED
120. INJURY AT WORK: [ ] YES [ ] NO
121. INJURY DATE MM/DD/CCYY
122. HOUR
123. PLACE OF INJURY
124. DESCRIBE HOW INJURY OCCURRED (EVENTS WHICH RESULTED IN INJURY)
125. LOCATION (STREET AND NUMBER OR LOCATION AND CITY, ZIP)
126. SIGNATURE OF CORONER OR DEPUTY CORONER ▶
127. DATE MM/DD/CCYY
128. TYPED NAME, TITLE OF CORONER OR DEPUTY CORONER

STATE REGISTRAR: A B C D E F G H — FAX AUTH. # — CENSUS TRACT

This is to certify that this document is a true copy of the official record filed with the Registrar-Recorder/County Clerk.

Conny B. McCormack

CONNY B. McCORMACK
Registrar-Recorder/County Clerk

OCT 30 1997

19-064097

This copy not valid unless prepared on engraved border displaying the Seal and Signature of the Registrar-Recorder/County Clerk.

American Bank Note Company — ANY ALTERATION OR ERASURE VOIDS THIS CERTIFICATE

STATE OF CALIFORNIA

CERTIFICATION OF VITAL RECORD

COUNTY OF LOS ANGELES • REGISTRAR-RECORDER/COUNTY CLERK

CERTIFICATE OF DEATH
STATE OF CALIFORNIA

STATE FILE NUMBER

LOCAL REGISTRATION DISTRICT AND CERTIFICATE NUMBER 0190-014098

DECEDENT PERSONAL DATA

1A. NAME OF DECEDENT—FIRST: David
1B. MIDDLE:
1C. LAST: Janssen
2A. DATE OF DEATH (MONTH, DAY, YEAR): FEBRUARY 13, 1980
2B. HOUR: 0555
3. SEX: Male
4. RACE: Cauc.
5. ETHNICITY:
6. DATE OF BIRTH: March 27, 1931
7. AGE: 48 YEARS
8. BIRTHPLACE OF DECEDENT (STATE OR FOREIGN COUNTRY): Nebraska
9. NAME AND BIRTHPLACE OF FATHER: Harold Edward Meyer, Nebraska
10. BIRTH NAME AND BIRTHPLACE OF MOTHER: Bernice Mae Graff, Nebraska
11. CITIZEN OF WHAT COUNTRY: USA
12. SOCIAL SECURITY NUMBER: 572-34-1786
13. MARITAL STATUS: Married
14. NAME OF SURVIVING SPOUSE (IF WIFE, ENTER BIRTH NAME): Darlyne Dani Swanson
15. PRIMARY OCCUPATION: Actor
16. NUMBER OF YEARS THIS OCCUPATION: 40
17. EMPLOYER (IF SELF-EMPLOYED, SO STATE): Tomorrow Entertainment
18. KIND OF INDUSTRY OR BUSINESS: Motion Pictures & T.V.

USUAL RESIDENCE

19A. USUAL RESIDENCE—STREET ADDRESS (STREET AND NUMBER OR LOCATION): 2220 Ave of the Stars
19B.
19C. CITY OR TOWN: Los Angeles
19D. COUNTY: Los Angeles
19E. STATE: California
20. NAME AND ADDRESS OF INFORMANT—RELATIONSHIP: Dani Janssen--wife, 2220 Ave of the Stars, Los Angeles, California

AMENDED 1 OF 2

PLACE OF DEATH

21A. PLACE OF DEATH: SANTA MONICA HOSPITAL
21B. COUNTY: LOS ANGELES
21C. STREET ADDRESS (STREET AND NUMBER OR LOCATION): 1225 15th. STREET
21D. CITY OR TOWN: SANTA MONICA

CAUSE OF DEATH

22. DEATH WAS CAUSED BY: (ENTER ONLY ONE CAUSE PER LINE FOR A, B, AND C)
IMMEDIATE CAUSE (A) DEFERRED
CONDITIONS, IF ANY, WHICH GAVE RISE TO THE IMMEDIATE CAUSE, STATING THE UNDERLYING CAUSE LAST
DUE TO, OR AS A CONSEQUENCE OF (B)
DUE TO, OR AS A CONSEQUENCE OF (C)
APPROXIMATE INTERVAL BETWEEN ONSET AND DEATH
24. WAS DEATH REPORTED TO CORONER? 80-2086
25. WAS BIOPSY PERFORMED?
26. WAS AUTOPSY PERFORMED? YES
23. OTHER CONDITIONS CONTRIBUTING BUT NOT RELATED TO THE IMMEDIATE CAUSE OF DEATH
27. WAS OPERATION PERFORMED FOR ANY CONDITION IN ITEMS 22 OR 23? TYPE OF OPERATION / DATE

PHYSICIAN'S CERTIFICATION

28A. I CERTIFY THAT DEATH OCCURRED AT THE HOUR, DATE AND PLACE STATED FROM THE CAUSES STATED. I ATTENDED DECEDENT SINCE (ENTER MO, DA, YR.) / I LAST SAW DECEDENT ALIVE (ENTER MO, DA, YR.)
28B. PHYSICIAN—SIGNATURE AND DEGREE OR TITLE
28C. DATE SIGNED
28D. PHYSICIAN'S LICENSE NUMBER
28E. TYPE PHYSICIAN'S NAME AND ADDRESS

INJURY INFORMATION

29. SPECIFY ACCIDENT, SUICIDE, ETC.
30. PLACE OF INJURY
31. INJURY AT WORK
32A. DATE OF INJURY—MONTH, DAY, YEAR
32B. HOUR
33. LOCATION (STREET AND NUMBER OR LOCATION AND CITY OR TOWN)
34. DESCRIBE HOW INJURY OCCURRED (EVENTS WHICH RESULTED IN INJURY)

9

CORONER'S USE ONLY

35A. I CERTIFY THAT DEATH OCCURRED AT THE HOUR, DATE AND PLACE STATED FROM THE CAUSES STATED. AS REQUIRED BY LAW I HAVE HELD AN INVESTIGATION
35B. CORONER—SIGNATURE AND DEGREE OR TITLE: 1104 N. MISSION RD. LOS ANGELES, CALIF. 90033 [signature] THOMAS T. NOGUCHI, CORONER, DEPUTY
35C. DATE SIGNED: 2-14-80

36. DISPOSITION: Entomb.
37. DATE—MONTH, DAY, YEAR: 2/17/80
38. NAME AND ADDRESS OF CEMETERY OR CREMATORY: Hillside Memorial Park, 6001 Centinela LA
39. EMBALMER'S LICENSE NUMBER AND SIGNATURE: 2350 [signature]
40. NAME OF FUNERAL DIRECTOR (OR PERSON ACTING AS SUCH): Groman Mortuary bb
41. LOCAL REGISTRAR—SIGNATURE: [signature]
42. DATE ACCEPTED BY LOCAL REGISTRAR: FEB 15 1980

STATE REGISTRAR A. B. C. D. E. F.

VS-11 (10-78)

1-3-4-0530

This is to certify that this document is a true copy of the official record filed with the Registrar-Recorder/County Clerk.

[signature]
CONNY B. McCORMACK
Registrar-Recorder/County Clerk

NOV 2 6 2000

19-116327

This copy not valid unless prepared on engraved border displaying the Seal and Signature of the Registrar-Recorder/County Clerk.

THE GREAT SEAL OF THE STATE OF CALIFORNIA
EUREKA

MIDWEST BANK NOTE COMPANY

ANY ALTERATION OR ERASURE VOIDS THIS CERTIFICATE

CERTIFICATION OF VITAL RECORD

COUNTY OF LOS ANGELES • REGISTRAR-RECORDER/COUNTY CLERK

CERTIFICATE OF DEATH
STATE OF CALIFORNIA

0190-024048

1A. Name of decedent—First	George
1B. Middle	Albert
1C. Last	Jessel
2A. Date of death	May 24, 1981
2B. Hour	2054
3. Sex	Male
4. Race	Cauc.
6. Date of birth	April 3, 1898
7. Age	83 years
8. Birthplace of decedent	New York
9. Name and birthplace of father	Joseph Jessel - Missouri
10. Birth name and birthplace of mother	Charlotte Schwartz - Unknown
11. Citizen of what country	U.S.A.
12. Social security number	559-10-8939
13. Marital status	Divorced
15. Primary occupation	Entertainer
16. Number of years this occupation	74
17. Employer	Self Employed
18. Kind of industry or business	Professional Entertainer
19A. Usual residence	7629 Lindley Ave.
19C. City or town	Reseda
19D. County	Los Angeles
19E. State	California
20. Name and address of informant—relationship	Jerilynn Jacobson - daughter, 5111 W. 51st St., Shawnee Mission, Kansas 66205
21A. Place of death	UCLA Medical Center
21B. County	Los Angeles
21C. Street address	10833 Le Conte Avenue
21D. City or town	Los Angeles
22. Death was caused by: (A) Immediate cause	Cardiorespiratory arrest — 2 hours
(B) Due to	atherosclerosis — approx. 20 years
(C)	
23. Other conditions contributing	RML lung syndrome
24. Was death reported to coroner?	no
25. Was biopsy performed?	yes
26. Was autopsy performed?	YES
27. Was operation performed	no
28A. Attended decedent since / Last saw decedent alive	21 Feb 81 / 5/24/81
28B. Physician signature	Alfred Sadler Jr. MD
28C. Date signed	5/24/81
28D. Physician's license number	G 4591
28E. Type physician's name and address	A Sadler Jr. MD, UCLA Med. Center, Los Angeles, CA 90024
36. Disposition	Entombment
37. Date	May 27, 1981
38. Name and address of cemetery	Hillside Memorial Park 6001 Centinela Ave. Los Angeles, CA
39. Embalmer's license number and signature	Not Embalmed
40. Name of funeral director	Hillside Memorial Park Mortuary
42. Date accepted by local registrar	MAY 27 1981

VS-11 (10-78)

This is to certify that this document is a true copy of the official record filed with the Registrar-Recorder/County Clerk.

CONNY B. McCORMACK
Registrar-Recorder/County Clerk

OCT 3 1996
19-386529

This copy not valid unless prepared on engraved border displaying the Seal and Signature of the Registrar-Recorder/County Clerk.

ANY ALTERATION OR ERASURE VOIDS THIS CERTIFICATE

STATE OF CALIFORNIA

CERTIFICATION OF VITAL RECORD

CITY AND COUNTY OF SAN FRANCISCO

REGISTRATION DISTRICT NO. 3801 REGISTRAR'S NUMBER 7574 **CERTIFICATE OF DEATH** STATE FILE NO.

DECEDENT PERSONAL DATA	1a. NAME OF DECEASED—FIRST NAME: ASA	1b. MIDDLE NAME: Also Known as Al Jolson	1c. LAST NAME: YOELSON	2a. DATE OF DEATH—MONTH, DAY, YEAR: October 23, 1950	2b. HOUR: 10:20 P.M.
	3. SEX: Male	4. COLOR OR RACE: White	5. MARRIED, NEVER MARRIED, WIDOWED, DIVORCED: Married	6. DATE OF BIRTH: May 26, 1886	7. AGE (LAST BIRTHDAY): 64 YEARS
	8a. USUAL OCCUPATION: Actor	8b. KIND OF BUSINESS OR INDUSTRY: Stage & Radio	9. BIRTHPLACE: [illegible]	10. CITIZEN OF WHAT COUNTRY? U.S.A.	
	11. NAME AND BIRTHPLACE OF FATHER: Morris Rubin Yoelson-Russia	12. MAIDEN NAME AND BIRTHPLACE OF MOTHER: Naomi Cantor - Russia		13. NAME OF SPOUSE (IF MARRIED): Erle Galbraith Jolson	
	14. WAS DECEASED EVER IN U.S. ARMED FORCES? Yes	Spanish American	15. SOCIAL SECURITY NUMBER: Unknown	16. INFORMANT: Harry Akst	
PLACE OF DEATH	17a. PLACE OF DEATH—CITY OR TOWN: San Francisco		17b. LENGTH OF STAY: 6 hours	17c. COUNTY: San Francisco	
	17d. FULL NAME AND ADDRESS OF HOSPITAL OR INSTITUTION: St. Francis Hotel - Room 1219 - Powell and Geary Sts.				
USUAL RESIDENCE	18a. STREET ADDRESS: 4875 Louise Avenue	18b. CITY OR TOWN: Encino		18c. COUNTY: Los Angeles	18d. STATE: California
CAUSE OF DEATH	19. I. DISEASE OR CONDITION DIRECTLY LEADING TO DEATH (A): Myocardial infarction				APPROXIMATE INTERVAL BETWEEN ONSET AND DEATH: 1 day
	ANTECEDENT CAUSES DUE TO (B): coronary sclerosis				?
	DUE TO (C)				
	19. II. OTHER SIGNIFICANT CONDITIONS				
OPERATIONS	20a. DATE OF OPERATION	20b. MAJOR FINDINGS OF OPERATION			21. AUTOPSY ☐ YES ☐ NO
DEATH DUE TO EXTERNAL VIOLENCE	22a. ACCIDENT SUICIDE HOMICIDE (SPECIFY)	22b. PLACE OF INJURY	22c. LOCATION CITY OR TOWN, COUNTY, STATE		
	22d. TIME OF INJURY	22e. INJURY OCCURRED ☐ WHILE AT WORK ☐ NOT WHILE AT WORK	22f. HOW DID INJURY OCCUR?		
PHYSICIAN'S OR CORONER'S CERTIFICATION	23a. CORONER'S: I HEREBY CERTIFY THAT I HAVE HELD AN ☐ AUTOPSY ☐ INQUEST, OR ☐ INVESTIGATION ON THE REMAINS OF THE DECEASED AND FIND THAT THE DECEASED CAME TO DEATH AT THE HOUR AND DATE STATED ABOVE.		23b. PHYSICIAN'S: I HEREBY CERTIFY THAT I ATTENDED THE DECEASED FROM 10/23 1950 TO 10/23 1950 THAT I LAST SAW THE DECEASED ALIVE ON 10/23 1950 AND THAT DEATH OCCURRED FROM THE CAUSES AND AT THE HOUR AND DATE STATED ABOVE		
	23c. SIGNATURE: [signature] M.D.		23d. ADDRESS: 384 Post, San Francisco		23e. DATE SIGNED: 10/24/50
FUNERAL DIRECTOR AND REGISTRAR	24a. ☐ BURIAL ☐ CREMATION ☒ REMOVAL	24b. DATE: 10/24/50	24c. CEMETERY OR CREMATORY: Los Angeles, California	25. SIGNATURE OF EMBALMER: [signature]	LICENSE NUMBER: 2906
	27. DATE RECEIVED BY LOCAL REGISTRAR: OCT 24 1950	28. SIGNATURE OF LOCAL REGISTRAR: [signature]		26. FUNERAL DIRECTOR: N. Gray & Co., 1545 Divisadero St.	

STATE OF CALIFORNIA — DEPARTMENT OF PUBLIC HEALTH

3802200345 **CERTIFIED COPY OF VITAL RECORDS**

STATE OF CALIFORNIA, CITY AND COUNTY OF SAN FRANCISCO

This is to certify that the image reproduced hereupon is a true copy of the record on file in the SAN FRANCISCO DEPARTMENT OF PUBLIC HEALTH as of the date issued.

DATE ISSUED 11/17/1998

Mitchell Katz, M.D.
Health Officer and Local Registrar

This copy is not valid unless prepared on an engraved border, displaying the date, seal and signature of the City and County Health Officer.

ANY ALTERATION OR ERASURE VOIDS THIS CERTIFICATE

1993

CERTIFICATE OF DEATH

STATE OF CALIFORNIA
USE BLACK INK ONLY

STATE FILE NUMBER

LOCAL REGISTRATION DISTRICT AND CERTIFICATE NUMBER: 39333001559

DECEDENT PERSONAL DATA

1A. NAME OF DECEDENT—FIRST (GIVEN): Ruby
1B. MIDDLE: Keeler
1C. LAST (FAMILY): Lowe
2A. DATE OF DEATH—MO, DAY, YR: February 28, 1993
2B. HOUR: 0040
3. SEX: Fe.
4. RACE: WHITE
5. HISPANIC—SPECIFY: YES ☐ NO ☒
6. DATE OF BIRTH—MO, DAY, YR: AUGUST 25, 1910
7. AGE IN YEARS: 82
IF UNDER 1 YEAR: MONTHS / DAYS
IF UNDER 24 HOURS: HOURS / MINUTES
8. STATE OF BIRTH: Nova Scotia
9. CITIZEN OF WHAT COUNTRY: U.S.A.
10A. FULL NAME OF FATHER: RALPH HECTOR
10B. STATE OF BIRTH: Nova Scotia
11A. FULL MAIDEN NAME OF MOTHER: ELNORA LEAHY
11B. STATE OF BIRTH: Nova Scotia
12. MILITARY SERVICE?: 19__ TO 19__ ☒ NONE
13. SOCIAL SECURITY NO.: 567-18-3100
14. MARITAL STATUS: WIDOWED
15. NAME OF SURVIVING SPOUSE (IF WIFE, ENTER MAIDEN NAME): NONE
16A. USUAL OCCUPATION: ACTRESS
16B. USUAL KIND OF BUSINESS OR INDUSTRY: FILM/ENTERTAINMENT
16C. USUAL EMPLOYER: SELF-EMPLOYED
16D. YEARS IN OCCUPATION: 50
17. EDUCATION—YEARS COMPLETED: 8

USUAL RESIDENCE

18A. RESIDENCE—STREET AND NUMBER OR LOCATION: 71-029 EARLY TIMES ROAD
18B. CITY: RANCHO MIRAGE
18C. ZIP CODE: 92270
18D. COUNTY: RIVERSIDE
18E. NUMBER OF YEARS IN THIS COUNTY: 12
18F. STATE OR FOREIGN COUNTRY: CALIFORNIA
20. NAME, RELATIONSHIP, MAILING ADDRESS AND ZIP CODE OF INFORMANT: JOHN LOWE -- SON, 330 N. SCREENLAND DR. #325, BURBANK, CA 91505

PLACE OF DEATH

19A. PLACE OF DEATH: Residence
19B. IF HOSPITAL, SPECIFY ONE: IP, ER/OP, DOA: - - -
19C. COUNTY: Riverside
19D. STREET ADDRESS—STREET AND NUMBER OR LOCATION: 71029 Early Times Road
19E. CITY: Rancho Mirage

CAUSE OF DEATH

21. DEATH WAS CAUSED BY: (ENTER ONLY ONE CAUSE PER LINE FOR A, B, AND C)
IMMEDIATE CAUSE (A): METASTATIC KIDNEY CANCER — TIME INTERVAL BETWEEN ONSET AND DEATH: MONTHS
DUE TO (B):
DUE TO (C):

1 OF 2

22. WAS DEATH REPORTED TO CORONER? ☒ YES REFERRAL NUMBER 93M0509 ☐ NO
23. WAS BIOPSY PERFORMED? ☒ YES ☐ NO
24A. WAS AUTOPSY PERFORMED? ☐ YES ☒ NO
24B. WAS IT USED IN DETERMINING CAUSE OF DEATH? ☐ YES ☐ NO
25. OTHER SIGNIFICANT CONDITIONS CONTRIBUTING TO DEATH BUT NOT RELATED TO CAUSE GIVEN IN 21: NONE
26. WAS OPERATION PERFORMED FOR ANY CONDITION IN ITEM 21 OR 25? IF YES, LIST TYPE OF OPERATION AND DATE.: NO

PHYSICIAN'S CERTIFICATION

I CERTIFY THAT TO THE BEST OF MY KNOWLEDGE DEATH OCCURRED AT THE HOUR, DATE AND PLACE STATED FROM THE CAUSES STATED.
27A. DECEDENT ATTENDED SINCE MONTH, DAY, YEAR: 12-7-92
DECEDENT LAST SEEN ALIVE MONTH, DAY, YEAR: 2-9-93
27B. SIGNATURE AND DEGREE OR TITLE OF CERTIFIER: [signature] MD
27C. CERTIFIER'S LICENSE NUMBER: G55873
27D. DATE SIGNED: 3-1-93
27E. TYPE ATTENDING PHYSICIAN'S NAME AND ADDRESS: R.POLKINGHORN,MD,39000 BOB HOPE DR.,RANCHO MIRAGE,CALIF

CORONER'S USE ONLY

I CERTIFY THAT IN MY OPINION DEATH OCCURRED AT THE HOUR, DATE AND PLACE STATED FROM THE CAUSES STATED.
28A. SIGNATURE AND TITLE OF CORONER OR DEPUTY CORONER
28B. DATE SIGNED
29. MANNER OF DEATH—specify one: natural, accident, suicide, homicide, pending investigation or could not be determined
30A. PLACE OF INJURY
30B. INJURY AT WORK ☐ YES ☐ NO
30C. DATE OF INJURY MONTH, DAY, YEAR
31. HOUR
32. LOCATION (STREET AND NUMBER OR LOCATION AND CITY)
33. DESCRIBE HOW INJURY OCCURRED (EVENTS WHICH RESULTED IN INJURY)

FUNERAL DIRECTOR AND LOCAL REGISTRAR

34A. DISPOSITION(S): BU
34B. PLACE OF FINAL DISPOSITION—NAME AND ADDRESS: Holy Sepulcher Cemetery, 7820 Santiago Canyon Rd., Orange, California
34C. DATE MO, DAY, YEAR: MAR.3,1993
35A. SIGNATURE OF EMBALMER: [signature]
35B. LICENSE NUMBER: 5856
36A. NAME OF FUNERAL DIRECTOR (OR PERSON ACTING AS SUCH): Palm Springs Mortuary
36B. LICENSE NO.: FD 1077
37. SIGNATURE OF LOCAL REGISTRAR: [signature]
38. REGISTRATION DATE: MAR.2,1993

STATE REGISTRAR

A. B. C. D. E. F.
CENSUS TRACT: 44902

VS-11 (REV. 3-91)

MAKE NO ERASURES, WHITEOUTS, OR OTHER ALTERATIONS

CERTIFICATION OF VITAL RECORD

COUNTY OF LOS ANGELES • REGISTRAR-RECORDER/COUNTY CLERK

CERTIFICATE OF DEATH

STATE OF CALIFORNIA—DEPARTMENT OF PUBLIC HEALTH

STATE FILE NUMBER

LOCAL REGISTRATION DISTRICT AND CERTIFICATE NUMBER 7053 26898

DECEDENT PERSONAL DATA

1A. NAME OF DECEASED—FIRST NAME: Percy | 1B. MIDDLE NAME: William | 1C. LAST NAME: Kilbride | 2A. DATE OF DEATH: December 11, 1964 | 2B. HOUR: 12:05A M

3. SEX: Male | 4. COLOR OR RACE: Cauc. | 5. BIRTHPLACE: California | 6. DATE OF BIRTH: July 16, 1888 | 7. AGE: 76 YEARS

8. NAME AND BIRTHPLACE OF FATHER: Owen Kilbride, Canada | 9. MAIDEN NAME AND BIRTHPLACE OF MOTHER: Elizabeth Kelly, Maryland | 10. CITIZEN OF WHAT COUNTRY: U.S.A. | 11. SOCIAL SECURITY NUMBER: 340-01-7082

12. LAST OCCUPATION: Actor | 13. NUMBER OF YEARS IN THIS OCCUPATION: 50 | 14. NAME OF LAST EMPLOYING COMPANY OR FIRM: Universal Studio | 15. KIND OF INDUSTRY OR BUSINESS: Movie

16. IF DECEASED WAS EVER IN U.S. ARMED FORCES GIVE WAR OR DATES OF SERVICE: WW I | 17. SPECIFY MARRIED, NEVER MARRIED, WIDOWED, DIVORCED: Never Married | 18A. NAME OF PRESENT SPOUSE: None | 18B. PRESENT OR LAST OCCUPATION OF SPOUSE: None

PLACE OF DEATH

19A. PLACE OF DEATH—NAME OF HOSPITAL: Chase Rest Home | 19B. STREET ADDRESS: 1032 W. 18th Street | INSIDE CITY CORPORATE LIMITS [X]

19C. CITY OR TOWN: Los Angeles | 19D. COUNTY: Los Angeles | 19E. LENGTH OF STAY IN COUNTY OF DEATH: 76 YEARS | 19F. LENGTH OF STAY IN CALIFORNIA: 76 YEARS

LAST USUAL RESIDENCE

20A. LAST USUAL RESIDENCE—STREET ADDRESS: 6650 Franklin Avenue | 20B. IF INSIDE CITY CORPORATE LIMITS: [X] CHECK HERE | 21A. NAME OF INFORMANT: Maude Crawley

20C. CITY OR TOWN: Hollywood (Los Angeles 4318) | 20D. COUNTY: Los Angeles | 20E. STATE: California | 21B. ADDRESS OF INFORMANT: 838 S. Grand Ave., L.A.

PHYSICIAN'S OR CORONER'S CERTIFICATION

22A. PHYSICIAN | 22B. CORONER: autopsy | 22C. PHYSICIAN OR CORONER—SIGNATURE: Theo. J. Curphey, M.D. Chief Medical Examiner-Coroner, By [signature] Deputy | 22D. ADDRESS: Hall of Justice, Los Angeles | 22E. DATE SIGNED: 2-4-65

FUNERAL DIRECTOR AND LOCAL REGISTRAR

23. SPECIFY BURIAL, ENTOMBMENT OR CREMATION: Cremation | 24. DATE: 12-14-64 | 25. NAME OF CEMETERY OR CREMATORY: Chapel of the Pines | 26. EMBALMER—SIGNATURE: [signature] LICENSE NUMBER 3730

27. NAME OF FUNERAL DIRECTOR: Armstrong Family | 28. DATE ACCEPTED FOR REGISTRATION BY LOCAL REGISTRAR: FEB - 9 1965 | 29. LOCAL REGISTRAR—SIGNATURE: [signature]

CAUSE OF DEATH

30. CAUSE OF DEATH. PART I. DEATH WAS CAUSED BY: IMMEDIATE CAUSE (A): HYPOSTATIC PNEUMONIA

DUE TO (B): CEREBRAL CONTUSION, SLIGHT

DUE TO (C):

PART II. OTHER SIGNIFICANT CONDITIONS CONTRIBUTING TO DEATH BUT NOT RELATED TO THE TERMINAL DISEASE CONDITION GIVEN IN PART I (A): ALZHEIMER'S DISEASE

OPERATION AND AUTOPSY

31. OPERATION—CHECK ONE: [X] OPERATION PERFORMED—FINDINGS USED IN DETERMINING ABOVE STATED CAUSES OF DEATH | 32. DATE OF OPERATION: 11/11/64 | 33. AUTOPSY—CHECK ONE: [X] AUTOPSY PERFORMED—GROSS FINDINGS USED IN DETERMINING ABOVE STATED CAUSES OF DEATH

INJURY INFORMATION

34A. SPECIFY ACCIDENT, SUICIDE OR HOMICIDE: Accident | 34B. DESCRIBE HOW INJURY OCCURRED: auto vs ped

35A. TIME OF INJURY: 9:10P M | MONTH 9 | DAY 21 | YEAR 64

35B. INJURY OCCURRED: [X] NOT WHILE AT WORK | 35C. PLACE OF INJURY: street | 35D. CITY, TOWN, OR LOCATION: Los Angeles | COUNTY: Los Angeles | STATE: Calif.

Margin notes: #11154 PERCY KILBRIDE; I. S. Woodard M.D.; FINAL 2/1/65; MEDICAL AND HEALTH DATA

This is to certify that this document is a true copy of the official record filed with the Registrar-Recorder/County Clerk.

Beatriz Valdez
BEATRIZ VALDEZ
Registrar-Recorder/County Clerk

AUG 25 1995

19-399111

This copy not valid unless prepared on engraved border displaying the Seal and Signature of the Registrar-Recorder/County Clerk.

ANY ALTERATION OR ERASURE VOIDS THIS CERTIFICATE

CERTIFICATION OF VITAL RECORD

COUNTY OF LOS ANGELES • REGISTRAR-RECORDER/COUNTY CLERK

CERTIFICATE OF DEATH
STATE OF CALIFORNIA

0190-011980
LOCAL REGISTRATION DISTRICT AND CERTIFICATE NUMBER

STATE FILE NUMBER

DECEDENT PERSONAL DATA

- 1A. NAME OF DECEDENT—FIRST: Victor
- 1B. MIDDLE: Arthur
- 1C. LAST: Kilian
- 2A. DATE OF DEATH (MONTH, DAY, YEAR): Found Mar. 11, 1979
- 2B. HOUR: 1325
- 3. SEX: male
- 4. RACE: cauc
- 5. ETHNICITY: not stated
- 6. DATE OF BIRTH: March 6 1891
- 7. AGE: 88 YEARS
- 8. BIRTHPLACE OF DECEDENT (STATE OR FOREIGN COUNTRY): New Jersey
- 9. NAME AND BIRTHPLACE OF FATHER: Henry (Heinrich) Kilian-Germany
- 10. BIRTH NAME AND BIRTHPLACE OF MOTHER: Josephine Sauer- Germany
- 11. CITIZEN OF WHAT COUNTRY: U.S.A.
- 12. SOCIAL SECURITY NUMBER: 560 18 3137
- 13. MARITAL STATUS: divorced
- 14. NAME OF SURVIVING SPOUSE (IF WIFE, ENTER BIRTH NAME): AMENDED 1 OF 2
- 15. PRIMARY OCCUPATION: Actor
- 16. NUMBER OF YEARS THIS OCCUPATION: 70
- 17. EMPLOYER (IF SELF-EMPLOYED, SO STATE): Free lance
- 18. KIND OF INDUSTRY OR BUSINESS: Actor

USUAL RESIDENCE

- 19A. USUAL RESIDENCE—STREET ADDRESS (STREET AND NUMBER OR LOCATION): 6500 Yucca St.
- 19B.
- 19C. CITY OR TOWN: Los Angeles
- 19D. COUNTY: Los Angeles
- 19E. STATE: Calif
- 20. NAME AND ADDRESS OF INFORMANT—RELATIONSHIP: Victor W.C.Kilian (Son) 4904 Tujunga Avenue North Hollywood Calif

PLACE OF DEATH

- 21A. PLACE OF DEATH: Home
- 21B. COUNTY: Los Angeles
- 21C. STREET ADDRESS (STREET AND NUMBER OR LOCATION): 6500 Yucca St.
- 21D. CITY OR TOWN: Los Angeles

CAUSE OF DEATH

22. DEATH WAS CAUSED BY: (ENTER ONLY ONE CAUSE PER LINE FOR A, B, AND C)
IMMEDIATE CAUSE
- (A) CRANIOCEREBRAL INJURIES
- DUE TO, OR AS A CONSEQUENCE OF (B) MULTIPLE BLUNT FORCE TRAUMA TO HEAD
- DUE TO, OR AS A CONSEQUENCE OF (C)

CONDITIONS, IF ANY, WHICH GAVE RISE TO THE IMMEDIATE CAUSE, STATING THE UNDERLYING CAUSE LAST.

APPROXIMATE INTERVAL BETWEEN ONSET AND DEATH

- 24. WAS DEATH REPORTED TO CORONER?: 79-3226
- 25. WAS BIOPSY PERFORMED?: No
- 26. WAS AUTOPSY PERFORMED?: Yes
- 23. OTHER CONDITIONS CONTRIBUTING BUT NOT RELATED TO THE IMMEDIATE CAUSE OF DEATH
- 27. WAS OPERATION PERFORMED FOR ANY CONDITION IN ITEMS 22 OR 23? TYPE OF OPERATION — DATE: No

PHYSICIAN'S CERTIFICATION

- 28A. I CERTIFY THAT DEATH OCCURRED AT THE HOUR, DATE AND PLACE STATED FROM THE CAUSES STATED. I ATTENDED DECEDENT SINCE (ENTER MO. DA. YR.) I LAST SAW DECEDENT ALIVE (ENTER MO. DA. YR.)
- 28B. PHYSICIAN—SIGNATURE AND DEGREE OR TITLE
- 28C. DATE SIGNED
- 28D. PHYSICIAN'S LICENSE NUMBER
- 28E. TYPE PHYSICIAN'S NAME AND ADDRESS

INJURY INFORMATION

- 29. SPECIFY ACCIDENT, SUICIDE, ETC.: Homicide
- 30. PLACE OF INJURY: Home
- 31. INJURY AT WORK: No
- 32A. DATE OF INJURY—MONTH, DAY, YEAR: Unknown
- 32B. HOUR: Unk.
- 33. LOCATION (STREET AND NUMBER OR LOCATION AND CITY OR TOWN): 6500 Yucca St - Los Angeles
- 34. DESCRIBE HOW INJURY OCCURRED (EVENTS WHICH RESULTED IN INJURY): As above

CORONER'S USE ONLY

- 35A. I CERTIFY THAT DEATH OCCURRED AT THE HOUR, DATE AND PLACE STATED FROM THE CAUSES STATED. AS REQUIRED BY LAW I HAVE HELD AN INVESTIGATION: 12
- 35B. CORONER—SIGNATURE AND DEGREE OR TITLE: ... NOGUCHI, M.D., CORONER ... LOS ANGELES, CALIF. [signature] DEPUTY
- 35C. DATE SIGNED: 3-14-79
- 36. DISPOSITION: Cremation
- 37. DATE—MONTH, DAY, YEAR: 3-16-79
- 38. NAME AND ADDRESS OF CEMETERY OR CREMATORY: Grandview Crematory Glendale Calif
- 39. EMBALMER'S LICENSE NUMBER AND SIGNATURE
- 40. NAME OF FUNERAL DIRECTOR (OR PERSON ACTING AS SUCH): Westwood Village Mortuary
- 41. LOCAL REGISTRAR—SIGNATURE: [signature]
- 42. DATE ACCEPTED BY LOCAL REGISTRAR: MAR 15 1979

STATE REGISTRAR A. B. C. D. E. F.

VS-11 (5-78)

01-9-41-7005

This is to certify that this document is a true copy of the official record filed with the Registrar-Recorder/County Clerk.

OCT 1 1996
19-381947

[signature]
CONNY B. McCORMACK
Registrar-Recorder/County Clerk

This copy not valid unless prepared on engraved border displaying the Seal and Signature of the Registrar-Recorder/County Clerk.

ANY ALTERATION OR ERASURE VOIDS THIS CERTIFICATE

1991

CERTIFICATE OF DEATH
STATE OF CALIFORNIA
USE BLACK INK ONLY

STATE FILE NUMBER

LOCAL REGISTRATION DISTRICT AND CERTIFICATE NUMBER: 39133000908

DECEDENT PERSONAL DATA

- 1A. NAME OF DECEDENT—FIRST (GIVEN): Nancy
- 1B. MIDDLE: Jane
- 1C. LAST (FAMILY): Kulp
- 2A. DATE OF DEATH—MO, DAY, YR: February 3, 1991
- 2B. HOUR: 0035
- 3. SEX: F
- 4. RACE: White
- 5. HISPANIC—SPECIFY: ☐ YES ☒ NO
- 6. DATE OF BIRTH—MO, DAY, YR: Aug. 28, 1921
- 7. AGE IN YEARS: 69 (IF UNDER 1 YEAR: MONTHS, DAYS; IF UNDER 24 HOURS: HOURS, MINUTES)
- 8. STATE OF BIRTH: PA
- 9. CITIZEN OF WHAT COUNTRY: U.S.A.
- 10A. FULL NAME OF FATHER: Unknown Kulp
- 10B. STATE OF BIRTH: Unk
- 11A. FULL MAIDEN NAME OF MOTHER: Unknown
- 11B. STATE OF BIRTH: Unk
- 12. MILITARY SERVICE?: 1942 TO 1944 ☐ NONE
- 13. SOCIAL SECURITY NO.: 267-24-3624
- 14. MARITAL STATUS: Widowed
- 15. NAME OF SURVIVING SPOUSE (IF WIFE, ENTER MAIDEN NAME): None
- 16A. USUAL OCCUPATION: Actress
- 16B. USUAL KIND OF BUSINESS OR INDUSTRY: Entertainment
- 16C. USUAL EMPLOYER: Self-Employed
- 16D. YEARS IN OCCUPATION: 50
- 17. EDUCATION—YEARS COMPLETED: 14

USUAL RESIDENCE

- 18A. RESIDENCE—STREET AND NUMBER OR LOCATION: #1 First Street
- 18B. CITY: Port Royal
- 18C. ZIP CODE: 17082
- 18D. COUNTY: Juanita
- 18E. NUMBER OF YEARS IN THIS COUNTY: 1
- 18F. STATE OR FOREIGN COUNTRY: PA
- 20. NAME, RELATIONSHIP, MAILING ADDRESS AND ZIP CODE OF INFORMANT: Joseph Baier - Friend, 377 West Bristo Road, Palm Springs, CA 92262

PLACE OF DEATH

- 19A. PLACE OF DEATH: A Residence
- 19B. IF HOSPITAL, SPECIFY ONE: IP, ER/OP, DOA: -
- 19C. COUNTY: Riverside
- 19D. STREET ADDRESS—STREET AND NUMBER OR LOCATION: 377 West Bristo Road
- 19E. CITY: Palm Springs

CAUSE OF DEATH

- 21. DEATH WAS CAUSED BY: (ENTER ONLY ONE CAUSE PER LINE FOR A, B, AND C)
  - IMMEDIATE CAUSE (A): METASTATIC LARYNGEAL CANCER — TIME INTERVAL BETWEEN ONSET AND DEATH: 2 yrs
  - DUE TO (B):
  - DUE TO (C):
- 22. WAS DEATH REPORTED TO CORONER?: ☒ YES — REFERRAL NUMBER 91M265 ☐ NO
- 23. WAS BIOPSY PERFORMED?: ☒ YES ☐ NO
- 24A. WAS AUTOPSY PERFORMED?: ☐ YES ☒ NO
- 24B. WAS IT USED IN DETERMINING CAUSE OF DEATH?: ☐ YES ☐ NO
- 25. OTHER SIGNIFICANT CONDITIONS CONTRIBUTING TO DEATH BUT NOT RELATED TO CAUSE GIVEN IN 21: NONE
- 26. WAS OPERATION PERFORMED FOR ANY CONDITION IN ITEM 21 OR 25? IF YES, LIST TYPE OF OPERATION AND DATE: NODE BIOPSY 12/16/90

PHYSICIAN'S CERTIFICATION

- I CERTIFY THAT TO THE BEST OF MY KNOWLEDGE DEATH OCCURRED AT THE HOUR, DATE AND PLACE STATED FROM THE CAUSES STATED.
- 27A. DECEDENT ATTENDED SINCE (MONTH, DAY, YEAR): 1/31/91
- DECEDENT LAST SEEN ALIVE (MONTH, DAY, YEAR): 1/31/91
- 27B. SIGNATURE AND DEGREE OR TITLE OF CERTIFIER: [signature] MD
- 27C. CERTIFIER'S LICENSE NUMBER: G49974
- 27D. DATE SIGNED: 2/4/91
- 27E. TYPE ATTENDING PHYSICIAN'S NAME AND ADDRESS: Gary A. Palmer, M.D., 1100 N. Palm Canyon Drive, #111, Palm Springs, CA 92262

CORONER'S USE ONLY

- I CERTIFY THAT IN MY OPINION DEATH OCCURRED AT THE HOUR, DATE AND PLACE STATED FROM THE CAUSES STATED.
- 28A. SIGNATURE AND TITLE OF CORONER OR DEPUTY CORONER:
- 28B. DATE SIGNED:
- 29. MANNER OF DEATH—specify one: natural, accident, suicide, homicide, pending investigation or could not be determined:
- 30A. PLACE OF INJURY:
- 30B. INJURY AT WORK: ☐ YES ☐ NO
- 30C. DATE OF INJURY MONTH, DAY, YEAR:
- 31. HOUR:
- 32. LOCATION (STREET AND NUMBER OR LOCATION AND CITY):
- 33. DESCRIBE HOW INJURY OCCURRED (EVENTS WHICH RESULTED IN INJURY):

FUNERAL DIRECTOR AND LOCAL REGISTRAR

- 34A. DISPOSITION(S): Cr/Res
- 34B. PLACE OF FINAL DISPOSITION—NAME AND ADDRESS: Residence, 377 West Bristo Road, Palm Springs, CA
- 34C. DATE MO, DAY, YEAR: 2/7/90
- 35A. SIGNATURE OF EMBALMER: Not embalmed
- 35B. LICENSE NUMBER: -
- 36A. NAME OF FUNERAL DIRECTOR (OR PERSON ACTING AS SUCH): Wiefels & Son, Palm Springs
- 36B. LICENSE NO.: 836
- 37. SIGNATURE OF LOCAL REGISTRAR: [signature] MD
- 38. REGISTRATION DATE: FEB 07 1991

STATE REGISTRAR

A. | B. | C. | D. | E. | F. | CENSUS TRACT

VS-11 (REV. 1-90) MAKE NO ERASURES, WHITEOUTS, OR OTHER ALTERATIONS

CERTIFICATION OF VITAL RECORD

COUNTY OF LOS ANGELES • REGISTRAR-RECORDER/COUNTY CLERK

CERTIFICATE OF DEATH
STATE OF CALIFORNIA

STATE FILE NUMBER — LOCAL REGISTRATION DISTRICT AND CERTIFICATE NUMBER: 0190-045104

DECEDENT PERSONAL DATA

- 1A. NAME OF DECEDENT—FIRST: Fernando
- 1B. MIDDLE: Alvaro
- 1C. LAST: Lamas
- 2A. DATE OF DEATH (MONTH, DAY, YEAR): October 8, 1982
- 2B. HOUR: 1448
- 3. SEX: Male
- 4. RACE: White
- 5. ETHNICITY:
- 6. DATE OF BIRTH: January 9, 1916
- 7. AGE: 66 YEARS — IF UNDER 1 YEAR: MONTHS / DAYS — IF UNDER 24 HOURS: HOURS / MINUTES
- 8. BIRTHPLACE OF DECEDENT (STATE OR FOREIGN COUNTRY): Argentina
- 9. NAME AND BIRTHPLACE OF FATHER: Ernesto Lamas - Argentina
- 10. BIRTH NAME AND BIRTHPLACE OF MOTHER: Maria Christina Fernandez Argentina
- 11. CITIZEN OF WHAT COUNTRY: U.S.A.
- 12. SOCIAL SECURITY NUMBER: 551-42-4087
- 13. MARITAL STATUS: Married
- 14. NAME OF SURVIVING SPOUSE (IF WIFE, ENTER BIRTH NAME): Esther Williams
- 15. PRIMARY OCCUPATION: Actor/Director
- 16. NUMBER OF YEARS THIS OCCUPATION: 32
- 17. EMPLOYER (IF SELF-EMPLOYED, SO STATE): Self
- 18. KIND OF INDUSTRY OR BUSINESS: Entertainment

USUAL RESIDENCE

- 19A. USUAL RESIDENCE—STREET ADDRESS (STREET AND NUMBER OR LOCATION): 9377 Readcrest Drive
- 19B.
- 19C. CITY OR TOWN: Beverly Hills
- 19D. COUNTY: Los Angeles
- 19E. STATE: California
- 20. NAME AND ADDRESS OF INFORMANT—RELATIONSHIP: Esther Williams Lamas, 9377 Readcrest Drive, Beverly Hills, California 90210

PLACE OF DEATH

- 21A. PLACE OF DEATH: UCLA Medical Center
- 21B. COUNTY: Los Angeles
- 21C. STREET ADDRESS (STREET AND NUMBER OR LOCATION): 10833 Le Conte Avenue
- 21D. CITY OR TOWN: Los Angeles

CAUSE OF DEATH

22. DEATH WAS CAUSED BY: (ENTER ONLY ONE CAUSE PER LINE FOR A, B, AND C)
IMMEDIATE CAUSE
CONDITIONS, IF ANY, WHICH GAVE RISE TO THE IMMEDIATE CAUSE, STATING THE UNDERLYING CAUSE LAST.

	Cause	Approximate interval between onset and death
(A)	Cardiopulmonary Arrest	10/8/82
(B) DUE TO, OR AS A CONSEQUENCE OF	Renal failure	3 days
(C) DUE TO, OR AS A CONSEQUENCE OF	Undifferentiated Carcinoma	4 wks

- 24. WAS DEATH REPORTED TO CORONER? no
- 25. WAS BIOPSY PERFORMED? yes
- 26. WAS AUTOPSY PERFORMED? yes
- 23. OTHER CONDITIONS CONTRIBUTING BUT NOT RELATED TO THE IMMEDIATE CAUSE OF DEATH: None
- 27. WAS OPERATION PERFORMED FOR ANY CONDITION IN ITEM 22 OR 23? TYPE OF OPERATION: Yes biopsy — DATE: 9/8/82

PHYSICIAN'S CERTIFICATION

- 28A. I CERTIFY THAT DEATH OCCURRED AT THE HOUR, DATE AND PLACE STATED FROM THE CAUSES STATED. I ATTENDED DECEDENT SINCE (ENTER MO, DA, YR): 9/28/82 — I LAST SAW DECEDENT ALIVE (ENTER MO, DA, YR): 10/8/82
- 28B. PHYSICIAN—SIGNATURE AND DEGREE OR TITLE: Steven Miles MD
- 28C. DATE SIGNED: 10/8/82
- 28D. PHYSICIAN'S LICENSE NUMBER: G48908
- 28E. TYPE PHYSICIAN'S NAME AND ADDRESS: Steven Miles, M.D., UCLA Medical Center, Los Angeles, CA 90024

INJURY INFORMATION

- 29. SPECIFY ACCIDENT, SUICIDE, ETC.
- 30. PLACE OF INJURY
- 31. INJURY AT WORK
- 32A. DATE OF INJURY—MONTH, DAY, YEAR
- 32B. HOUR
- 33. LOCATION (STREET AND NUMBER OR LOCATION AND CITY OR TOWN)
- 34. DESCRIBE HOW INJURY OCCURRED (EVENTS WHICH RESULTED IN INJURY)

CORONER'S USE ONLY

- 35A. I CERTIFY THAT DEATH OCCURRED AT THE HOUR, DATE AND PLACE STATED FROM THE CAUSES STATED. AS REQUIRED BY LAW I HAVE HELD AN (INQUEST-INVESTIGATION)
- 35B. CORONER—SIGNATURE AND DEGREE OR TITLE
- 35C. DATE SIGNED

- 36. DISPOSITION: Cremation
- 37. DATE—MONTH, DAY, YEAR: 10/13/82
- 38. NAME AND ADDRESS OF CEMETERY OR CREMATORY: Rosedale Crematory - Los Angeles, Calif.
- 39. EMBALMER'S LICENSE NUMBER AND SIGNATURE: Not Embalmed
- 40. NAME OF FUNERAL DIRECTOR (OR PERSON ACTING AS SUCH): Abbott & Hast Colonial Mansion 1255
- 41. LOCAL REGISTRAR—SIGNATURE: [signature]
- 42. DATE ACCEPTED BY LOCAL REGISTRAR: OCT 12 1982

STATE REGISTRAR: A. B. C. D. E. F.

VS-11 (10-78)

This is to certify that this document is a true copy of the official record filed with the Registrar-Recorder/County Clerk.

Beatriz Valdez
BEATRIZ VALDEZ
Registrar-Recorder/County Clerk

AUG 15 1995

19-397058

This copy not valid unless prepared on engraved border displaying the Seal and Signature of the Registrar-Recorder/County Clerk.

American Bank Note Company

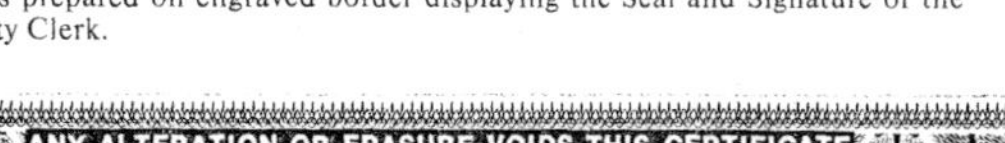

CERTIFICATE OF DEATH

STATE OF CALIFORNIA
USE BLACK INK ONLY/NO ERASURES, WHITEOUTS OR ALTERATIONS
VS-11 (REV. 7/93)

STATE FILE NUMBER — LOCAL REGISTRATION NUMBER

DECEDENT PERSONAL DATA

1. NAME OF DECEDENT—FIRST (GIVEN): DOROTHY
2. MIDDLE: LAMOUR
3. LAST (FAMILY): HOWARD
4. DATE OF BIRTH MM/DD/CCYY: 12/10/1914
5. AGE YRS.: 81
IF UNDER 1 YEAR (MONTHS, DAYS) / IF UNDER 24 HOURS (HOURS, MINUTES):
6. SEX: F
7. DATE OF DEATH MM/DD/CCYY: 09/21/1996
8. HOUR: 2047
9. STATE OF BIRTH: LA
10. SOCIAL SECURITY NO.: 564-18-1759
11. MILITARY SERVICE: 19__ TO 19__ [X] NONE
12. MARITAL STATUS: WIDOWED
13. EDUCATION—YEARS COMPLETED: UNK
14. RACE: CAUCASIAN
15. HISPANIC—SPECIFY: [ ] YES [X] NO
16. USUAL EMPLOYER: SELF EMPLOYED
17. OCCUPATION: ACTRESS
18. KIND OF BUSINESS: ENTERTAINMENT
19. YEARS IN OCCUPATION: 64

USUAL RESIDENCE

20. RESIDENCE—STREET AND NUMBER OR LOCATION: 5309 GOODLAND AVE
21. CITY: NORTH HOLLYWOOD
22. COUNTY: LOS ANGELES
23. ZIP CODE: 91602
24. YRS IN COUNTY: 67
25. STATE OR FOREIGN COUNTRY: CA

INFORMANT

26. NAME, RELATIONSHIP: DONNA MATSOOK, EXECUTOR
27. MAILING ADDRESS (STREET AND NUMBER OR RURAL ROUTE NUMBER, CITY OR TOWN, STATE, ZIP): 5309 GOODLAND AVE NORTH HOLLYWOOD,CA 91607

SPOUSE AND PARENT INFORMATION

28. NAME OF SURVIVING SPOUSE—FIRST: -
29. MIDDLE: -
30. LAST (MAIDEN NAME): -
31. NAME OF FATHER—FIRST: JOHN
32. MIDDLE: -
33. LAST: SLATON
34. BIRTH STATE: LA
35. NAME OF MOTHER—FIRST: CARMEN
36. MIDDLE: -
37. LAST (MAIDEN): LA PORTE
38. BIRTH STATE: LA

DISPOSITION(S)

39. DATE MM/DD/CCYY: 09/25/1996
40. PLACE OF FINAL DISPOSITION: FOREST LAWN MEMORIAL PARK,LOS ANGELES,CA 90068

FUNERAL DIRECTOR AND LOCAL REGISTRAR

41. TYPE OF DISPOSITION(S): BURIAL
42. SIGNATURE OF EMBALMER: ▶ Sonia Caldera
43. LICENSE NO.: 7661
44. NAME OF FUNERAL DIRECTOR: FOREST LAWN HOLLYWOOD HILLS
45. LICENSE NO.: F 904
46. SIGNATURE OF LOCAL REGISTRAR: ▶ Mark [illegible] 4
47. DATE MM/DD/CCYY: 09/25/1996

PLACE OF DEATH

101. PLACE OF DEATH: ST. VINCENT MED CENTER
102. IF HOSPITAL, SPECIFY ONE: [X] IP [ ] ER/OP [ ] DOA
103. FACILITY OTHER THAN HOSPITAL: [ ] CONV. HOSP. [ ] RES. [ ] OTHER
104. COUNTY: LOS ANGELES
105. STREET ADDRESS—STREET AND NUMBER OR LOCATION: 2131 W. 3rd ST.
106. CITY: LOS ANGELES

CAUSE OF DEATH

107. DEATH WAS CAUSED BY: (ENTER ONLY ONE CAUSE PER LINE FOR A, B, C, AND D) — TIME INTERVAL BETWEEN ONSET AND DEATH

	Cause	Time interval
IMMEDIATE CAUSE (A)	cardiac arrest	minutes
DUE TO (B)	intestinal infarction	hours
DUE TO (C)	mesenteric thrombosis	hours
DUE TO (D)	generalized arteriosclerosis	years

108. DEATH REPORTED TO CORONER: [ ] YES [✓] NO — REFERRAL NUMBER
109. BIOPSY PERFORMED: [ ] YES [✓] NO
110. AUTOPSY PERFORMED: [ ] YES [✓] NO
111. USED IN DETERMINING CAUSE: [ ] YES [ ] NO
112. OTHER SIGNIFICANT CONDITIONS CONTRIBUTING TO DEATH BUT NOT RELATED TO CAUSE GIVEN IN 107: None
113. WAS OPERATION PERFORMED FOR ANY CONDITION IN ITEM 107 OR 112? IF YES, LIST TYPE OF OPERATION AND DATE. No

PHYSICIAN'S CERTIFICATION

114. I CERTIFY THAT TO THE BEST OF MY KNOWLEDGE DEATH OCCURRED AT THE HOUR, DATE AND PLACE STATED FROM THE CAUSES STATED.
DECEDENT ATTENDED SINCE MM/DD/CCYY: 10/18/94
DECEDENT LAST SEEN ALIVE MM/DD/CCYY: 9/21/96
115. SIGNATURE AND TITLE OF CERTIFIER: ▶ F. Lieberman MD
116. LICENSE NO.: G8711
117. DATE MM/DD/CCYY: 9/23/96
118. TYPE ATTENDING PHYSICIAN'S NAME, MAILING ADDRESS + ZIP: FRED LIEBERMAN,M.D., 201 S. ALVARADO ST,LOS ANGELES.CA90057

CORONER'S USE ONLY

10

I CERTIFY THAT IN MY OPINION DEATH OCCURRED AT THE HOUR, DATE AND PLACE STATED FROM THE CAUSES STATED.
119. MANNER OF DEATH: [ ] NATURAL [ ] SUICIDE [ ] HOMICIDE [ ] ACCIDENT [ ] PENDING INVESTIGATION [ ] COULD NOT BE DETERMINED
120. INJURY AT WORK: [ ] YES [ ] NO
121. INJURY DATE MM/DD/CCYY
122. HOUR
123. PLACE OF INJURY
124. DESCRIBE HOW INJURY OCCURRED (EVENTS WHICH RESULTED IN INJURY)
125. LOCATION (STREET AND NUMBER OR LOCATION AND CITY AND ZIP CODE)
126. SIGNATURE OF CORONER OR DEPUTY CORONER ▶
127. DATE MM/DD/CCYY
128. TYPED NAME, TITLE OF CORONER OR DEPUTY CORONER

4409

STATE REGISTRAR

A B C D E F G H — FAX AUTH. #: 273/45360 — CENSUS TRACT

CERTIFICATE OF DEATH

STATE OF CALIFORNIA
USE BLACK INK ONLY/NO ERASURES, WHITEOUTS OR ALTERATIONS
VS-11 (REV. 7/93)

STATE FILE NUMBER — LOCAL REGISTRATION NUMBER

DECEDENT PERSONAL DATA

1. NAME OF DECEDENT—FIRST (GIVEN): BURTON
2. MIDDLE: STEPHEN
3. LAST (FAMILY): LANCASTER
4. DATE OF BIRTH MM/DD/CCYY: 11/02/1913
5. AGE YRS.: 80
IF UNDER 1 YEAR: MONTHS / DAYS — IF UNDER 24 HOURS: HOURS / MINUTES
6. SEX: MALE
7. DATE OF DEATH MM/DD/CCYY: 10/20/1994
8. HOUR: 2120
9. STATE OF BIRTH: NY
10. SOCIAL SECURITY NO.: 052-14-1561
11. MILITARY SERVICE: 19 43 TO 19 45 ☐ NONE
12. MARITAL STATUS: MARRIED
13. EDUCATION—YEARS COMPLETED: 14
14. RACE: CAUCASIAN
15. HISPANIC—SPECIFY: ☐ YES ☒ NO
16. USUAL EMPLOYER: VARIOUS
17. OCCUPATION: ACTOR
18. KIND OF BUSINESS: MOTION PICTURES
19. YEARS IN OCCUPATION: 48

USUAL RESIDENCE

20. RESIDENCE—STREET AND NUMBER OR LOCATION: 2220 AVENUE OF THE STARS
21. CITY: LOS ANGELES
22. COUNTY: LOS ANGELES
23. ZIP CODE: 90067
24. YRS IN COUNTY: 80
25. STATE OR FOREIGN COUNTRY: CALIFORNIA

INFORMANT

26. NAME, RELATIONSHIP: SUSAN J. LANCASTER WIFE
27. MAILING ADDRESS (STREET AND NUMBER OR RURAL ROUTE NUMBER, CITY OR TOWN, STATE, ZIP): 2220 AVENUE OF THE STARS LOS ANGELES, CALIFORNIA 90067

SPOUSE AND PARENT INFORMATION

28. NAME OF SURVIVING SPOUSE—FIRST: SUSAN
29. MIDDLE: JUNE
30. LAST (MAIDEN NAME): MARTIN
31. NAME OF FATHER—FIRST: JAMES
32. MIDDLE: STEPHEN
33. LAST: LANCASTER
34. BIRTH STATE: NY
35. NAME OF MOTHER—FIRST: ELIZABETH
36. MIDDLE: -
37. LAST (MAIDEN): ROBERTS
38. BIRTH STATE: NY

DISPOSITION(S)

39. DATE MM/DD/CCYY: 10/25/1994
40. PLACE OF FINAL DISPOSITION: RES:SUSAN JUNE LANCASTER, 2220 AVENUE OF THE STARS, LOS ANGELES, CA 90067

FUNERAL DIRECTOR AND LOCAL REGISTRAR

41. TYPE OF DISPOSITION(S): CR/RES
42. SIGNATURE OF EMBALMER: ▶ NOT EMBALMED
43. LICENSE NO.: -
44. NAME OF FUNERAL DIRECTOR: PIERCE BROTHERS CUNNINGHAM & O'CONNOR
45. LICENSE NO.: FD-8
46. SIGNATURE OF LOCAL REGISTRAR: ▶ Robert C. Mato Re
47. DATE MM/DD/CCYY: 10/24/1994

PLACE OF DEATH

101. PLACE OF DEATH: RESIDENCE
102. IF HOSPITAL, SPECIFY ONE: ☐ IP ☐ ER/OP ☐ DOA
103. FACILITY OTHER THAN HOSPITAL: ☐ CONV. HOSP. ☒ RES. ☐ OTHER
104. COUNTY: LOS ANGELES
105. STREET ADDRESS—STREET AND NUMBER OR LOCATION: 2220 AVENUE OF THE STARS
106. CITY: LOS ANGELES

CAUSE OF DEATH

107. DEATH WAS CAUSED BY: (ENTER ONLY ONE CAUSE PER LINE FOR A, B, C, AND D)

		TIME INTERVAL BETWEEN ONSET AND DEATH
IMMEDIATE CAUSE (A)	ATHEROSCLEROTIC CORONARY ARTERY DISEASE	15 YEARS
DUE TO (B)		
DUE TO (C)		
DUE TO (D)		

108. DEATH REPORTED TO CORONER: ☐ YES ☒ NO — REFERRAL NUMBER
109. BIOPSY PERFORMED: ☐ YES ☒ NO
110. AUTOPSY PERFORMED: ☐ YES ☒ NO
111. USED IN DETERMINING CAUSE: ☐ YES ☒ NO

112. OTHER SIGNIFICANT CONDITIONS CONTRIBUTING TO DEATH BUT NOT RELATED TO CAUSE GIVEN IN 107: CEREBROVASCULAR ARTERY DISEASE

113. WAS OPERATION PERFORMED FOR ANY CONDITION IN ITEM 107 OR 112? IF YES, LIST TYPE OF OPERATION AND DATE. CORONARY ARTERY BYPASS 1983

PHYSICIAN'S CERTIFICATION

114. I CERTIFY THAT TO THE BEST OF MY KNOWLEDGE DEATH OCCURRED AT THE HOUR, DATE AND PLACE STATED FROM THE CAUSES STATED.
DECEDENT ATTENDED SINCE MM/DD/CCYY: 11/01/1990
DECEDENT LAST SEEN ALIVE MM/DD/CCYY: 10/16/1994
115. SIGNATURE AND TITLE OF CERTIFIER: ▶ [signature] MD
116. LICENSE NO.: G033330
117. DATE MM/DD/CCYY: 10/21/1994
118. TYPE ATTENDING PHYSICIAN'S NAME, MAILING ADDRESS + ZIP: PHILLIP S. FRANKEL, M.D. 301 N. PRAIRIE AVE., INGLEWOOD, CA 90301

CORONER'S USE ONLY

I CERTIFY THAT IN MY OPINION DEATH OCCURRED AT THE HOUR, DATE AND PLACE STATED FROM THE CAUSES STATED.
119. MANNER OF DEATH: ☐ NATURAL ☐ SUICIDE ☐ HOMICIDE ☐ ACCIDENT ☐ PENDING INVESTIGATION ☐ COULD NOT BE DETERMINED
120. INJURY AT WORK: ☐ YES ☐ NO
121. INJURY DATE MM/DD/CCYY
122. HOUR
123. PLACE OF INJURY
124. DESCRIBE HOW INJURY OCCURRED (EVENTS WHICH RESULTED IN INJURY)
125. LOCATION (STREET AND NUMBER OR LOCATION AND CITY AND ZIP CODE)
126. SIGNATURE OF CORONER OR DEPUTY CORONER ▶
127. DATE MM/DD/CCYY
128. TYPED NAME, TITLE OF CORONER OR DEPUTY CORONER

STATE REGISTRAR

A	B	C	D	E	F	G	H	FAX AUTH. #	CENSUS TRACT

CERTIFICATE OF DEATH
STATE OF CALIFORNIA
USE BLACK INK ONLY

STATE FILE NUMBER — LOCAL REGISTRATION DISTRICT AND CERTIFICATE NUMBER

DECEDENT PERSONAL DATA

1A. NAME OF DECEDENT—FIRST (GIVEN)	1B. MIDDLE	1C. LAST (FAMILY)	2A. DATE OF DEATH—MO, DAY, YR	2B. HOUR	3. SEX
MICHAEL	- - -	LANDON	JULY 1, 1991	1310	MALE

4. RACE	5. HISPANIC—SPECIFY	6. DATE OF BIRTH—MO, DAY, YR	7. AGE IN YEARS	IF UNDER 1 YEAR (MONTHS / DAYS)	IF UNDER 24 HOURS (HOURS / MINUTES)
CAUCASIAN	YES [ ] XX NO	OCTOBER 31, 1936	54		

8. STATE OF BIRTH	9. CITIZEN OF WHAT COUNTRY	10A. FULL NAME OF FATHER	10B. STATE OF BIRTH	11A. FULL MAIDEN NAME OF MOTHER	11B. STATE OF BIRTH
NY	U.S.A.	ELI OROWITZ	PA	PEGGY O'NEIL	NY

12. MILITARY SERVICE?	13. SOCIAL SECURITY NO.	14. MARITAL STATUS	15. NAME OF SURVIVING SPOUSE (IF WIFE, ENTER MAIDEN NAME)
19 ___ TO 19 ___ [X] NONE	152-28-1500	MARRIED	CINDY CLERICO

16A. USUAL OCCUPATION	16B. USUAL KIND OF BUSINESS OR INDUSTRY	16C. USUAL EMPLOYER	16D. YEARS IN OCCUPATION	17. EDUCATION—YEARS COMPLETED
ACTOR PRODUCER & DIRECTOR	ENTERTAINMENT	LYNN PRODUCTIONS	36	13

USUAL RESIDENCE

18A. RESIDENCE—STREET AND NUMBER OR LOCATION	18B. CITY	18C. ZIP CODE
5820 BONSALL DRIVE	MALIBU	90265

18D. COUNTY	18E. NUMBER OF YEARS IN THIS COUNTY	18F. STATE OR FOREIGN COUNTRY	20. NAME, RELATIONSHIP, MAILING ADDRESS AND ZIP CODE OF INFORMANT
LOS ANGELES	10	CALIFORNIA	CINDY LANDON - WIFE, 5820 BONSALL DRIVE, MALIBU, CALIFORNIA 90265

PLACE OF DEATH

19A. PLACE OF DEATH	19B. IF HOSPITAL, SPECIFY ONE: IP, ER/OP, DOA	19C. COUNTY
RESIDENCE	- - -	LOS ANGELES

19D. STREET ADDRESS—STREET AND NUMBER OR LOCATION	19E. CITY
5820 BONSALL DRIVE	MALIBU

CAUSE OF DEATH

21. DEATH WAS CAUSED BY: (ENTER ONLY ONE CAUSE PER LINE FOR A, B, AND C)

		TIME INTERVAL BETWEEN ONSET AND DEATH
IMMEDIATE CAUSE (A)	Metastatic Pancreatic Cancer	3 months
DUE TO (B)		
DUE TO (C)		

22. WAS DEATH REPORTED TO CORONER? REFERRAL NUMBER — [ ] YES [X] NO
23. WAS BIOPSY PERFORMED? — [ ] YES [X] NO
24A. WAS AUTOPSY PERFORMED? — [ ] YES [X] NO
24B. WAS IT USED IN DETERMINING CAUSE OF DEATH? — [ ] YES [ ] NO

25. OTHER SIGNIFICANT CONDITIONS CONTRIBUTING TO DEATH BUT NOT RELATED TO CAUSE GIVEN IN 21: NONE
26. WAS OPERATION PERFORMED FOR ANY CONDITION IN ITEM 21 OR 25? IF YES, LIST TYPE OF OPERATION AND DATE.: NO

PHYSICIAN'S CERTIFICATION

I CERTIFY THAT TO THE BEST OF MY KNOWLEDGE DEATH OCCURRED AT THE HOUR, DATE AND PLACE STATED FROM THE CAUSES STATED.

27A. DECEDENT ATTENDED SINCE (MONTH, DAY, YEAR)	DECEDENT LAST SEEN ALIVE (MONTH, DAY, YEAR)	27B. SIGNATURE AND DEGREE OR TITLE OF CERTIFIER	27C. CERTIFIER'S LICENSE NUMBER	27D. DATE SIGNED
4/8/91	6/29/91	[signature]	G-22745	7/2/91

27E. TYPE ATTENDING PHYSICIAN'S NAME AND ADDRESS: BARRY E. ROSENBLOOM, M.D. 8635 WEST 3RD STREET, #1165 LOS ANGELES, CALIFORNIA 90048

CORONER'S USE ONLY

I CERTIFY THAT IN MY OPINION DEATH OCCURRED AT THE HOUR, DATE AND PLACE STATED FROM THE CAUSES STATED.

28A. SIGNATURE AND TITLE OF CORONER OR DEPUTY CORONER — 28B. DATE SIGNED

29. MANNER OF DEATH—specify one: natural, accident suicide, homicide, pending investigation or could not be determined — 30A. PLACE OF INJURY — 30B. INJURY AT WORK [ ] YES [ ] NO — 30C. DATE OF INJURY MONTH, DAY, YEAR — 31. HOUR

32. LOCATION (STREET AND NUMBER OR LOCATION AND CITY) — 33. DESCRIBE HOW INJURY OCCURRED (EVENTS WHICH RESULTED IN INJURY)

FUNERAL DIRECTOR AND LOCAL REGISTRAR

34A. DISPOSITION(S)	34B. PLACE OF FINAL DISPOSITION—NAME AND ADDRESS	34C. DATE MO, DAY, YEAR	35A. SIGNATURE OF EMBALMER	35B. LICENSE NUMBER
CR/RES	LANDON RESIDENCE, 5820 BONSALL DRIVE MALIBU, CALIFORNIA 90265	07/02/1991	NOT EMBALMED	NONE

36A. NAME OF FUNERAL DIRECTOR (OR PERSON ACTING AS SUCH)	36B. LICENSE NO.	37. SIGNATURE OF LOCAL REGISTRAR	38. REGISTRATION DATE
MALINOW AND SILVERMAN MORTUARY	FD-487	[signature]	JUL 02 1991

30

STATE REGISTRAR A. B. C. D. E. F. CENSUS TRACT

VS-11 (REV. 1-90) 15 79 MAKE NO ERASURES, WHITEOUTS, OR OTHER ALTERATIONS 01-9-1-7005

THIS IS A TRUE CERTIFIED COPY OF THE RECORD FILED IN THE COUNTY OF LOS ANGELES DEPARTMENT OF HEALTH SERVICES IF IT BEARS THIS SEAL IN PURPLE INK.

JUL 17 1991

39

Director of Health Services and Registrar

CERTIFICATION OF VITAL RECORD

COUNTY OF LOS ANGELES • REGISTRAR-RECORDER/COUNTY CLERK

CERTIFICATE OF DEATH
STATE OF CALIFORNIA

STATE FILE NUMBER — LOCAL REGISTRATION DISTRICT AND CERTIFICATE NUMBER: -059631

DECEDENT PERSONAL DATA

1A. NAME OF DECEDENT—FIRST: Peter
1B. MIDDLE: Sydney
1C. LAST: Lawford
2A. DATE OF DEATH (MONTH, DAY, YEAR): Dec 24 1984
2B. HOUR: 0850
3. SEX: male
4. RACE/ETHNICITY: cauc
5. SPANISH/HISPANIC: NO
6. DATE OF BIRTH: Sept 7 1923
7. AGE: 61 YEARS
8. BIRTHPLACE OF DECEDENT (STATE OR FOREIGN COUNTRY): England
9. NAME AND BIRTHPLACE OF FATHER: General Sir Sydney Lawford- England
10. BIRTH NAME AND BIRTHPLACE OF MOTHER: Lady Mae Bunny- England
11. CITIZEN OF WHAT COUNTRY: U.S.A.
12. SOCIAL SECURITY NUMBER: 554 16 4546
13. MARITAL STATUS: married
14. NAME OF SURVIVING SPOUSE (IF WIFE, ENTER BIRTH NAME): Patricia Seaton
15. PRIMARY OCCUPATION: Actor
16. NUMBER OF YEARS THIS OCCUPATION: 40
17. EMPLOYER (IF SELF-EMPLOYED, SO STATE): Self
18. KIND OF INDUSTRY OR BUSINESS: Entertainment

USUAL RESIDENCE

19A. USUAL RESIDENCE—STREET ADDRESS (STREET AND NUMBER OR LOCATION): 1275 N Havenhurst Dr
19B.
19C. CITY OR TOWN: Los Angeles
19D. COUNTY: Los Angeles
19E. STATE: Calif
20. NAME AND ADDRESS OF INFORMANT—RELATIONSHIP: Patricia Seaton Lawford (Wife) same address 90046

PLACE OF DEATH

21A. PLACE OF DEATH: Cedars Sinai Hospital
21B. COUNTY: Los Angeles
21C. STREET ADDRESS (STREET AND NUMBER OR LOCATION): 8700 Beverly Blve
21D. CITY OR TOWN: Los Angeles

CAUSE OF DEATH

22. DEATH WAS CAUSED BY: (ENTER ONLY ONE CAUSE PER LINE FOR A, B, AND C)
IMMEDIATE CAUSE (A): MEDULLARY FAILURE — APPROXIMATE INTERVAL BETWEEN ONSET AND DEATH: 24 HRS
CONDITIONS, IF ANY, WHICH GAVE RISE TO THE IMMEDIATE CAUSE, STATING THE UNDERLYING CAUSE LAST.
DUE TO, OR AS A CONSEQUENCE OF (B): HEPATO-RENAL SYNDROME — 1 WK
DUE TO, OR AS A CONSEQUENCE OF (C): CIRRHOSIS of LIVER — 5 YRS
24. WAS DEATH REPORTED TO CORONER?: NO
25. WAS BIOPSY PERFORMED?: NO
26. WAS AUTOPSY PERFORMED?: NO
23. OTHER SIGNIFICANT CONDITIONS—CONTRIBUTING TO DEATH BUT NOT RELATED TO CAUSE GIVEN IN 22A: COAGULOPATHY
27. WAS OPERATION PERFORMED FOR ANY CONDITION IN ITEMS 22 OR 23? TYPE OF OPERATION: NONE — DATE

PHYSICIAN'S CERTIFICATION

28A. I CERTIFY THAT DEATH OCCURRED AT THE HOUR, DATE AND PLACE STATED FROM THE CAUSES STATED.
I ATTENDED DECEDENT SINCE (ENTER MO. DA. YR.): Aug 1984
I LAST SAW DECEDENT ALIVE (ENTER MO. DA. YR.): 12/24/84
28B. PHYSICIAN—SIGNATURE AND DEGREE OR TITLE: Harold J Strick MD
28C. DATE SIGNED: 12/24/84
28D. PHYSICIAN'S LICENSE NUMBER: A27599
28E. TYPE PHYSICIAN'S NAME AND ADDRESS: HAROLD J. STRICK 9201 SUNSET LA 90069

INJURY INFORMATION

29. SPECIFY ACCIDENT, SUICIDE, ETC.
30. PLACE OF INJURY
31. INJURY AT WORK
32A. DATE OF INJURY—MONTH, DAY, YEAR
32B. HOUR
33. LOCATION (STREET AND NUMBER OR LOCATION AND CITY OR TOWN)
34. DESCRIBE HOW INJURY OCCURRED (EVENTS WHICH RESULTED IN INJURY)

CORONER'S USE ONLY

35A. I CERTIFY THAT DEATH OCCURRED AT THE HOUR, DATE AND PLACE STATED FROM THE CAUSES STATED. AS REQUIRED BY LAW I HAVE HELD AN (INQUEST-INVESTIGATION)
35B. CORONER—SIGNATURE AND DEGREE OR TITLE
35C. DATE SIGNED

36. DISPOSITION: Cremation
37. DATE—MONTH, DAY, YEAR: 12-25-84
38. NAME AND ADDRESS OF CEMETERY OR CREMATORY: Grandview Crematory Glendale Calif
39. EMBALMER'S LICENSE NUMBER AND SIGNATURE: 5595 William R Pierce 5595
40A. NAME OF FUNERAL DIRECTOR (OR PERSON ACTING AS SUCH): Westwood Village Mortuary
40B. LICENSE NO.: 951
41. LOCAL REGISTRAR—SIGNATURE: [signature]
42. DATE ACCEPTED BY LOCAL REGISTRAR: DEC 25 1984

STATE REGISTRAR: A. B. C. D. E. F.

VS-11 (7-83) 5712 01-12/9-1-0555

This is to certify that this document is a true copy of the official record filed with the Registrar-Recorder/County Clerk.

Beatriz Valdez
BEATRIZ VALDEZ
Registrar-Recorder/County Clerk

AUG 16 1995
19-397061

This copy not valid unless prepared on engraved border displaying the Seal and Signature of the Registrar-Recorder/County Clerk.

American Bank Note Company

CERTIFICATION OF VITAL RECORD

COUNTY OF LOS ANGELES • REGISTRAR-RECORDER/COUNTY CLERK

STATE FILE NUMBER

CERTIFICATE OF DEATH

STATE OF CALIFORNIA—DEPARTMENT OF PUBLIC HEALTH

LOCAL REGISTRATION DISTRICT AND CERTIFICATE NUMBER 7097-017987

DECEDENT PERSONAL DATA

1a. NAME OF DECEASED—FIRST NAME: AKA Rose Gypsy
1b. MIDDLE NAME: AKA Louise Rose
1c. LAST NAME: AKA Hovick Lee AKA deDiego
2a. DATE OF DEATH—MONTH, DAY, YEAR: April 26, 1970
2b. HOUR: 7:00PM
3. SEX: Female
4. COLOR OR RACE: Cauc.
5. BIRTHPLACE (STATE OR FOREIGN COUNTRY): Washington
6. DATE OF BIRTH: January 9, 1914
7. AGE (LAST BIRTHDAY): 56 YEARS
8. NAME AND BIRTHPLACE OF FATHER: John O. Hovick UNKNOWN
9. MAIDEN NAME AND BIRTHPLACE OF MOTHER: Rose Thompson No. Dakota
10. CITIZEN OF WHAT COUNTRY: U.S.A.
11. SOCIAL SECURITY NUMBER: 084-07-1990
12. MARRIED, NEVER MARRIED, WIDOWED, DIVORCED (SPECIFY): Divorced
13. NAME OF SURVIVING SPOUSE (IF WIFE, ENTER MAIDEN NAME): None
14. LAST OCCUPATION: Actress
15. NUMBER OF YEARS IN THIS OCCUPATION: 52
16. NAME OF LAST EMPLOYING COMPANY OR FIRM (IF SELF EMPLOYED, SO STATE): Self Employed
17. KIND OF INDUSTRY OR BUSINESS: Motion Pictures

PLACE OF DEATH

18a. PLACE OF DEATH—NAME OF HOSPITAL OR OTHER IN-PATIENT FACILITY: University of California @ Los Angeles-Medical Center
18b. STREET ADDRESS: 10833 Le Conte
18c. INSIDE CITY CORPORATE LIMITS (SPECIFY YES OR NO): yes
18d. CITY OR TOWN: West Los Angeles
18e. COUNTY: Los Angeles
18f. LENGTH OF STAY IN COUNTY OF DEATH: 8 YEARS
18g. LENGTH OF STAY IN CALIFORNIA: 8 YEARS

USUAL RESIDENCE (IF DEATH OCCURRED IN INSTITUTION, ENTER RESIDENCE BEFORE ADMISSION)

19a. USUAL RESIDENCE—STREET ADDRESS: 1240 Cerrocrest Dr.
19b. INSIDE CITY CORPORATE LIMITS (SPECIFY YES OR NO): yes
19c. CITY OR TOWN: Beverly Hills
19d. COUNTY: Los Angeles
19e. STATE: California
20. NAME AND MAILING ADDRESS OF INFORMANT: Erik Kirkland SAME

PHYSICIAN'S OR CORONER'S CERTIFICATION

21a. CORONER: I HEREBY CERTIFY THAT DEATH OCCURRED AT THE HOUR, DATE AND PLACE STATED ABOVE FROM THE CAUSES STATED BELOW AND THAT I HAVE HELD AN INVESTIGATION OR INQUEST
21b. PHYSICIAN: I HEREBY CERTIFY THAT DEATH OCCURRED AT THE HOUR, DATE AND PLACE STATED ABOVE FROM THE CAUSES STATED BELOW AND THAT I ATTENDED THE DECEASED FROM: Oct. 25 69 TO: April 26 70 AND LAST SAW THE DECEASED ALIVE ON: April 26 70
21c. PHYSICIAN OR CORONER—SIGNATURE AND DEGREE OR TITLE: [signature]
21d. DATE SIGNED: 4-28-70
21e. ADDRESS: SAUL L. FOX, M.D. 435 NORTH BEDFORD DRIVE BEVERLY HILLS, CALIFORNIA
21f. PHYSICIAN'S CALIFORNIA LICENSE NUMBER: G-67

FUNERAL DIRECTOR AND LOCAL REGISTRAR

22a. SPECIFY BURIAL, ENTOMBMENT OR CREMATION: Cremation
22b. DATE: 4-29-70
23. NAME OF CEMETERY OR CREMATORY: Chapel of the Pines
24. EMBALMER—SIGNATURE (IF BODY EMBALMED) LICENSE NUMBER: No Embalming
25. NAME OF FUNERAL DIRECTOR (OR PERSON ACTING AS SUCH): PIERCE BROTHERS-BEVERLY HILLS
26. IF NOT CERTIFIED BY CORONER, WAS THIS DEATH REPORTED TO CORONER? (SPECIFY YES OR NO): no
27. LOCAL REGISTRAR—SIGNATURE: [signature] MD
28. DATE ACCEPTED FOR REGISTRATION: APR 29 1970

MEDICAL AND HEALTH DATA — CAUSE OF DEATH

29. PART I. DEATH WAS CAUSED BY: ENTER ONLY ONE CAUSE PER LINE FOR A, B, AND C

		APPROXIMATE INTERVAL BETWEEN ONSET AND DEATH
IMMEDIATE CAUSE (A)	Acute Congestive Heart Failure & shock	6 hrs.
DUE TO, OR AS A CONSEQUENCE OF (B)	Cancer of lung, Bronchogenic	6 mos.
DUE TO, OR AS A CONSEQUENCE OF (C)	Atrial Fibrillation	6 hrs.

CONDITIONS, IF ANY, WHICH GAVE RISE TO THE IMMEDIATE CAUSE (A), STATING THE UNDERLYING CAUSE LAST.

30. PART II: OTHER SIGNIFICANT CONDITIONS—CONTRIBUTING TO DEATH BUT NOT RELATED TO THE IMMEDIATE CAUSE GIVEN IN PART I:
31. WAS OPERATION OR BIOPSY PERFORMED FOR ANY CONDITION IN ITEMS 29 OR 30? (SPECIFY TYPE OF OPERATION AND/OR BIOPSY): YES
32a. AUTOPSY (SPECIFY YES OR NO): yes
32b. IF YES WERE FINDINGS CONSIDERED IN DETERMINING CAUSE OF DEATH? (SPECIFY YES OR NO): yes

INJURY INFORMATION

33. SPECIFY ACCIDENT, SUICIDE OR HOMICIDE
34. PLACE OF INJURY (SPECIFY HOME, FARM, FACTORY, STREET, OFFICE BUILDING, ETC.)
35. INJURY AT WORK (SPECIFY YES OR NO)
36a. DATE OF INJURY—MONTH, DAY, YEAR
36b. HOUR
37a. PLACE OF INJURY (STREET AND NUMBER OR LOCATION AND CITY OR TOWN)
37b. DISTANCE FROM PLACE OF INJURY TO USUAL RESIDENCE, ITEM 19. MILES
38. WERE LABORATORY TESTS DONE FOR DRUGS OR TOXIC CHEMICALS (SPECIFY YES OR NO)
39. WERE LABORATORY TESTS DONE FOR ALCOHOL? (SPECIFY YES OR NO)
40. DESCRIBE HOW INJURY OCCURRED (ENTER SEQUENCE OF EVENTS WHICH RESULTED IN INJURY. NATURE OF INJURY SHOULD BE ENTERED IN ITEM 29)

STATE REGISTRAR A. B. C. D. E. F.

REV. 1-1-68 Form VS-11

This is to certify that this document is a true copy of the official record filed with the Registrar-Recorder/County Clerk.

Beatriz Valdez
BEATRIZ VALDEZ
Registrar-Recorder/County Clerk

AUG 10 1995

19-388002

This copy not valid unless prepared on engraved border displaying the Seal and Signature of the Registrar-Recorder/County Clerk.

THE GREAT SEAL OF THE STATE OF CALIFORNIA — EUREKA

REGISTRAR-RECORDER/COUNTY CLERK — COUNTY OF LOS ANGELES, CALIFORNIA

American Bank Note Company

ANY ALTERATION OR ERASURE VOIDS THIS CERTIFICATE

BOOK 1987 PAGE

CERTIFICATE OF DEATH 38 000766
STATE OF CALIFORNIA

STATE FILE NUMBER — LOCAL REGISTRATION DISTRICT AND CERTIFICATE NUMBER

DECEDENT PERSONAL DATA

1A. NAME OF DECEDENT—FIRST: | 1B. MIDDLE: | 1C. LAST: LIBERACE | 2A. DATE OF DEATH (MONTH, DAY, YEAR): February 4, 1987 | 2B. HOUR: 1405

3. SEX: Male | 4. RACE/ETHNICITY: Polish-White/Italian | 5. SPANISH/HISPANIC: NO ☒ | 6. DATE OF BIRTH: May 16, 1919 | 7. AGE: 67 YEARS | IF UNDER 1 YEAR MONTHS / DAYS | IF UNDER 24 HOURS HOURS / MINUTES

8. BIRTHPLACE OF DECEDENT (STATE OR FOREIGN COUNTRY): Wisconsin | 9. NAME AND BIRTHPLACE OF FATHER: Salvatore Liberace - Italy | 10. BIRTH NAME AND BIRTHPLACE OF MOTHER: Frances Zuchowski - Wisconsin

11A. CITIZEN OF WHAT COUNTRY: USA | 11B. IF DECEASED WAS EVER IN MILITARY GIVE DATES OF SERVICE: 19__ TO 19__ | 12. SOCIAL SECURITY NUMBER: 472-14-4916 | 13. MARITAL STATUS: Never Married | 14. NAME OF SURVIVING SPOUSE (IF WIFE, ENTER BIRTH NAME):

15. PRIMARY OCCUPATION: Entertainer/Pianist | 16. NUMBER OF YEARS THIS OCCUPATION: 42 | 17. EMPLOYER (IF SELF-EMPLOYED, SO STATE): Self-employed | 18. KIND OF INDUSTRY OR BUSINESS: Entertainment

1 OF 2

USUAL RESIDENCE

19A. USUAL RESIDENCE—STREET ADDRESS (STREET AND NUMBER OR LOCATION): 4982 Shirley Street | 19B. | 19C. CITY OR TOWN: Las Vegas

19D. COUNTY: Clark | 19E. STATE: Nevada | 20. NAME AND ADDRESS OF INFORMANT—RELATIONSHIP: Mr. Joel R. Strote, executor & truste[e] 280 South Beverly Drive Beverly Hills, California 90212

PLACE OF DEATH

21A. PLACE OF DEATH: Residence | 21B. COUNTY: Riverside

21C. STREET ADDRESS (STREET AND NUMBER OR LOCATION): 226 Alejo Road | 21D. CITY OR TOWN: Palm Springs

CAUSE OF DEATH

22. DEATH WAS CAUSED BY: (ENTER ONLY ONE CAUSE PER LINE FOR A, B, AND C)
IMMEDIATE CAUSE (A) Pending
CONDITIONS, IF ANY, WHICH GAVE RISE TO THE IMMEDIATE CAUSE, STATING THE UNDERLYING CAUSE LAST.
DUE TO, OR AS A CONSEQUENCE OF (B)
DUE TO, OR AS A CONSEQUENCE OF (C) 19:55, 6 II 87 F. Rose [signature]

APPROXIMATE INTERVAL BETWEEN ONSET AND DEATH

24. WAS DEATH REPORTED TO CORONER? Yes 60121
25. WAS BIOPSY PERFORMED? No
26. WAS AUTOPSY PERFORMED? Yes

23. OTHER SIGNIFICANT CONDITIONS—CONTRIBUTING TO DEATH, BUT NOT RELATED TO CAUSE GIVEN IN 22A | 27. WAS OPERATION PERFORMED FOR ANY CONDITION IN ITEMS 22 OR 23? TYPE OF OPERATION | DATE

PHYSICIAN'S CERTIFICATION

28A. I CERTIFY THAT DEATH OCCURRED AT THE HOUR, DATE AND PLACE STATED FROM THE CAUSES STATED. I ATTENDED DECEDENT SINCE (ENTER MO. DA. YR.) | I LAST SAW DECEDENT ALIVE (ENTER MO. DA. YR.) | 28B. PHYSICIAN—SIGNATURE AND DEGREE OR TITLE | 28C. DATE SIGNED | 28D. PHYSICIAN'S LICENSE NUMBER
28E. TYPE PHYSICIAN'S NAME AND ADDRESS

INJURY INFORMATION

29. SPECIFY ACCIDENT, SUICIDE, ETC.: Pending | 30. PLACE OF INJURY | 31. INJURY AT WORK | 32A. DATE OF INJURY—MONTH, DAY, YEAR | 32B. HOUR
33. LOCATION (STREET AND NUMBER OR LOCATION AND CITY OR TOWN) | 34. DESCRIBE HOW INJURY OCCURRED (EVENTS WHICH RESULTED IN INJURY)

CORONER'S USE ONLY

35A. I CERTIFY THAT DEATH OCCURRED AT THE HOUR, DATE AND PLACE STATED FROM THE CAUSES STATED. AS REQUIRED BY LAW I HAVE HELD AN (INQUEST-INVESTIGATION): Investigation | 35B. CORONER—SIGNATURE AND DEGREE OR TITLE: Raymond L. Carrillo, Coroner By: Nancy Strauss, Deputy | 35C. DATE SIGNED: 02-06-87

36. DISPOSITION: Entombment | 37. DATE—MONTH, DAY, YEAR: February 7, 1987 | 38. NAME AND ADDRESS OF CEMETERY OR CREMATORY: Forest Lawn Memorial- Park, 6300 Forest Lawn Drive, Los Angeles, Ca | 39. EMBALMER'S LICENSE NUMBER AND SIGNATURE: 7621 [signature]

40A. NAME OF FUNERAL DIRECTOR (OR PERSON ACTING AS SUCH): Forest Lawn Hollywood Hills Mty | 40B. LICENSE NO.: F-904 | 41. LOCAL REGISTRAR—SIGNATURE: [signature] | 42. DATE ACCEPTED BY LOCAL REGISTRAR: February 6, 1987

STATE REGISTRAR: A. | B. | C. | D. | E. | F.

VS-11 (1-85)

AMENDMENT

BOOK 1987 PAGE

THIS FORM MUST BE COMPLETED IN BLACK INK
AMENDMENT OF MEDICAL AND HEALTH SECTION DATA—DEATH

INSTRUCTIONS ON REVERSE

STATE CERTIFICATE NUMBER — LOCAL REGISTRATION DISTRICT AND CERTIFICATE NUMBER: 33 000764

IDENTIFICATION OF THE RECORD

1a FIRST NAME — 1b MIDDLE NAME — 1c LAST NAME: Liberace

2 PLACE OF OCCURRENCE—CITY OR COUNTY: Palm Springs

3 DATE OF EVENT: February 4, 1987

ORIGINALLY REPORTED INFORMATION

INFORMATION AS REPORTED ON THE ORIGINALLY REGISTERED CERTIFICATE

22. DEATH WAS CAUSED BY: (ENTER ONLY ONE CAUSE PER LINE FOR A, B, AND C)
IMMEDIATE CAUSE
(A) Pending
DUE TO OR AS A CONSEQUENCE OF
(B)
DUE TO OR AS A CONSEQUENCE OF
19:55, 6 II 87
(C) F. Rene Modglin, M.D. /s/

CONDITIONS IF ANY, WHICH GAVE RISE TO THE IMMEDIATE CAUSE, STATING THE UNDERLYING CAUSE LAST

APPROXIMATE INTERVAL BETWEEN ONSET AND DEATH

24. WAS DEATH REPORTED TO CORONER? Yes 60121
25. WAS BIOPSY PERFORMED? No
26. WAS AUTOPSY PERFORMED? Yes

2 OF 2

23. OTHER CONDITIONS CONTRIBUTING BUT NOT RELATED TO THE IMMEDIATE CAUSE OF DEATH
27. WAS OPERATION PERFORMED FOR ANY CONDITION IN ITEMS 22 OR 23? OPERATION / DATE
29. SPECIFY ACCIDENT SUICIDE ETC.
30. PLACE OF INJURY
31. INJURY AT WORK
32A. DATE OF INJURY MONTH DAY YEAR
32B. HOUR
33. LOCATION (STREET AND NUMBER OR LOCATION AND CITY OR TOWN)
34. DESCRIBE HOW INJURY OCCURRED (EVENTS WHICH RESULTED IN INJURY)

INFORMATION AS IT SHOULD BE STATED ON THE ORIGINALLY REGISTERED CERTIFICATE

INFORMATION AS IT SHOULD BE STATED ON THE ORIGINALLY REGISTERED CERTIFICATE

22. DEATH WAS CAUSED BY: (ENTER ONLY ONE CAUSE PER LINE FOR A, B, AND C)
IMMEDIATE CAUSE
(A) Cytomegalic Virus Pneumonia — wks./mos.
DUE TO OR AS A CONSEQUENCE OF
(B) Human Immunodeficiency Viral Disease — mos./yrs.
DUE TO OR AS A CONSEQUENCE OF
(C)

CONDITIONS IF ANY, WHICH GAVE RISE TO THE IMMEDIATE CAUSE, STATING THE UNDERLYING CAUSE LAST

APPROXIMATE INTERVAL BETWEEN ONSET AND DEATH

24. WAS DEATH REPORTED TO CORONER? Yes 60121
25. WAS BIOPSY PERFORMED? No
26. WAS AUTOPSY PERFORMED? Yes

23. OTHER CONDITIONS CONTRIBUTING BUT NOT RELATED TO THE IMMEDIATE CAUSE OF DEATH: Pulmonary heart disease; calcific mitral valvulitis
27. WAS OPERATION PERFORMED FOR ANY CONDITION IN ITEMS 22 OR 23? OPERATION / DATE: None
29. SPECIFY ACCIDENT SUICIDE ETC.: Natural
30. PLACE OF INJURY
31. INJURY AT WORK
32A. DATE OF INJURY MONTH DAY YEAR
32B. HOUR
33. LOCATION (STREET AND NUMBER OR LOCATION AND CITY OR TOWN)
34. DESCRIBE HOW INJURY OCCURRED (EVENTS WHICH RESULTED IN INJURY)

DECLARATION OF CERTIFYING PHYSICIAN OR CORONER

4. I, THE CERTIFYING PHYSICIAN OR CORONER HAVING PERSONAL KNOWLEDGE OF SUPPLEMENTAL INFORMATION WHICH MODIFIES THE INFORMATION ORIGINALLY REPORTED DECLARE UNDER PENALTY OF PERJURY THAT THE ABOVE INFORMATION IS TRUE AND CORRECT TO THE BEST OF MY KNOWLEDGE

5a SIGNATURE OF PHYSICIAN OR CORONER: R. L. Carrillo, Coroner by: Nancy Traver
5b DATE SIGNED: 02-09-87
6a NAME OF PHYSICIAN OR CORONER (PRINT OR TYPE): R. L. Carrillo, Coroner by: Nancy Traver
6b DEGREE OR TITLE: Deputy
6c ADDRESS—STREET CITY STATE: 46-209 Oasis St., RM 410, Indio, CA 92201

REGISTRAR'S OFFICE

7a OFFICE OF STATE OR LOCAL REGISTRAR
7b DATE ACCEPTED: FEB 10 1987

STATE OF CALIFORNIA, DEPARTMENT OF HEALTH SERVICES, OFFICE OF THE STATE REGISTRAR OF VITAL STATISTICS

STATE OF CALIFORNIA
CERTIFICATION OF VITAL RECORD

COUNTY OF LOS ANGELES
DEPARTMENT OF HEALTH SERVICES

CERTIFICATE OF DEATH
STATE OF CALIFORNIA
USE BLACK INK ONLY/NO ERASURES, WHITEOUTS OR ALTERATIONS
VS-11 (REV. 11/96)

STATE FILE NUMBER — LOCAL REGISTRATION NUMBER

DECEDENT PERSONAL DATA
1. NAME OF DECEDENT—FIRST (GIVEN): AUDRA
2. MIDDLE: MARIE
3. LAST (FAMILY): LINDLEY
4. DATE OF BIRTH MM/DD/CCYY: 09/24/1918
5. AGE YRS.: 79
6. SEX: F
7. DATE OF DEATH MM/DD/CCYY: 10/16/1997
8. HOUR: 1425
9. STATE OF BIRTH: CA
10. SOCIAL SECURITY NO.: 562-14-9438
11. MILITARY SERVICE: YES [ ] NO [X]
12. MARITAL STATUS: DIVORCED
13. EDUCATION—YEARS COMPLETED: 12
14. RACE: CAUCASIAN
15. HISPANIC—SPECIFY: YES [ ] NO [X]
16. USUAL EMPLOYER: SELF EMPLOYED
17. OCCUPATION: ACTRESS
18. KIND OF BUSINESS: ENTERTAINMENT
19. YEARS IN OCCUPATION: 65

USUAL RESIDENCE
20. RESIDENCE—STREET AND NUMBER OR LOCATION: 200 NO. SWALL
21. CITY: BEVERLY HILLS
22. COUNTY: LOS ANGELES
23. ZIP CODE: 90211
24. YRS IN COUNTY: 20
25. STATE OR FOREIGN COUNTRY: CA

INFORMANT
26. NAME, RELATIONSHIP: ELIZABETH BLALOCK, DAUGHTER
27. MAILING ADDRESS (STREET AND NUMBER OR RURAL ROUTE NUMBER, CITY OR TOWN, STATE, ZIP): 495 EL BOSQUE, LAGUNA BEACH, CA. 92651

SPOUSE AND PARENT INFORMATION
28. NAME OF SURVIVING SPOUSE—FIRST: -
29. MIDDLE: -
30. LAST (MAIDEN NAME): -
31. NAME OF FATHER—FIRST: HERBERT
32. MIDDLE: -
33. LAST: LINDLEY
34. BIRTH STATE: IOWA
35. NAME OF MOTHER—FIRST: BESSIE
36. MIDDLE: -
37. LAST (MAIDEN): FISHER
38. BIRTH STATE: CO

DISPOSITION(S)
39. DATE MM/DD/CCYY: 10/21/1997
40. PLACE OF FINAL DISPOSITION: WOODLAWN CEMETERY 1847 14th ST., SANTA MONICA, CA. 90404

FUNERAL DIRECTOR AND LOCAL REGISTRAR
41. TYPE OF DISPOSITION(S): CR/BU
42. SIGNATURE OF EMBALMER: NOT EMBALMED
43. LICENSE NO.: -
44. NAME OF FUNERAL DIRECTOR: FOREST LAWN HOLLYWOOD HILLS
45. LICENSE NO.: F 904
46. SIGNATURE OF LOCAL REGISTRAR: [signature]
47. DATE MM/DD/CCYY: 10/20/1997

PLACE OF DEATH
101. PLACE OF DEATH: Cedars Sinai Med Ctr
102. IF HOSPITAL, SPECIFY ONE: IP [X] ER/OP [ ] DOA [ ]
103. FACILITY OTHER THAN HOSPITAL: CONV. HOSP. [ ] RES. CARE [ ] OTHER [ ]
104. COUNTY: Los Angeles
105. STREET ADDRESS—STREET AND NUMBER OR LOCATION: 8700 Beverly Blvd
106. CITY: Los Angeles

CAUSE OF DEATH
107. DEATH WAS CAUSED BY: (ENTER ONLY ONE CAUSE PER LINE FOR A, B, C, AND D)

	Cause	Time interval between onset and death
IMMEDIATE CAUSE (A)	Acute myelogenous Leukemia	4 mos
DUE TO (B)	Myelodysplasia	3 yrs
DUE TO (C)		
DUE TO (D)		

108. DEATH REPORTED TO CORONER: YES [ ] NO [X] — REFERRAL NUMBER
109. BIOPSY PERFORMED: YES [ ] NO [X]
110. AUTOPSY PERFORMED: YES [ ] NO [X]
111. USED IN DETERMINING CAUSE: YES [ ] NO [X]
112. OTHER SIGNIFICANT CONDITIONS CONTRIBUTING TO DEATH BUT NOT RELATED TO CAUSE GIVEN IN 107: None
113. WAS OPERATION PERFORMED FOR ANY CONDITION IN ITEM 107 OR 112? IF YES, LIST TYPE OF OPERATION AND DATE: None

PHYSICIAN'S CERTIFICATION
114. I CERTIFY THAT TO THE BEST OF MY KNOWLEDGE DEATH OCCURRED AT THE HOUR, DATE AND PLACE STATED FROM THE CAUSES STATED.
DECEDENT ATTENDED SINCE MM/DD/CCYY: 05/01/1995
DECEDENT LAST SEEN ALIVE MM/DD/CCYY: 10/15/1997
115. SIGNATURE AND TITLE OF CERTIFIER: [signature]
116. LICENSE NO.: G53431
117. DATE MM/DD/CCYY: 10/17/97
118. TYPE ATTENDING PHYSICIAN'S NAME, MAILING ADDRESS, ZIP: Solomon Hamburg,MD 8635 W 3rd St,#665,LA,CA 90048

CORONER'S USE ONLY
I CERTIFY THAT IN MY OPINION DEATH OCCURRED AT THE HOUR, DATE AND PLACE STATED FROM THE CAUSES STATED.
119. MANNER OF DEATH: NATURAL [ ] SUICIDE [ ] HOMICIDE [ ] ACCIDENT [ ] PENDING INVESTIGATION [ ] COULD NOT BE DETERMINED [ ]
120. INJURY AT WORK: YES [ ] NO [ ]
121. INJURY DATE MM/DD/CCYY
122. HOUR
123. PLACE OF INJURY
124. DESCRIBE HOW INJURY OCCURRED (EVENTS WHICH RESULTED IN INJURY)
125. LOCATION (STREET AND NUMBER OR LOCATION AND CITY, ZIP)
126. SIGNATURE OF CORONER OR DEPUTY CORONER
127. DATE MM/DD/CCYY
128. TYPED NAME, TITLE OF CORONER OR DEPUTY CORONER

STATE REGISTRAR
A B C D E F G H
FAX AUTH. #: 273/8329
CENSUS TRACT

090048011

This is a true certified copy of the record filed in the County of Los Angeles Department of Health Services if it bears the Registrar's signature in purple ink.

[signature] DATE ISSUED NOV 07 1997

Director of Health Services and Registrar

This copy not valid unless prepared on engraved border displaying seal and signature of Registrar.

MIDWEST BANK NOTE COMPANY
ANY ALTERATION OR ERASURE VOIDS THIS CERTIFICATE

CERTIFICATION OF VITAL RECORD

COUNTY OF LOS ANGELES • REGISTRAR-RECORDER/COUNTY CLERK

STATE FILE NO.

CERTIFICATE OF DEATH

STATE OF CALIFORNIA—DEPARTMENT OF PUBLIC HEALTH

REGISTRATION DISTRICT NO. 7051 REGISTRAR'S NUMBER 15906

DECEDENT PERSONAL DATA (TYPE OR PRINT NAME)

1a. NAME OF DECEASED—FIRST NAME: BELA | 1b. MIDDLE NAME: | 1c. LAST NAME: LUGOSI | 2a. DATE OF DEATH—MONTH DAY YEAR: August 16, 1956 | 2b. HOUR: 6:45 P. M.

3. SEX: Male | 4. COLOR OR RACE: Cauc. | 5. SPECIFY MARRIED, NEVER MARRIED, WIDOWED, DIVORCED: Married | 6. DATE OF BIRTH: October 20, 1882 | 7. AGE (LAST BIRTHDAY): 73 YEARS | IF UNDER 1 YEAR: MONTHS DAYS | IF UNDER 24 HOURS: HOURS MINUTES

8a. USUAL OCCUPATION (GIVE KIND OF WORK DONE DURING MOST OF WORKING LIFE, EVEN IF RETIRED): Actor | 8b. KIND OF BUSINESS OR INDUSTRY: Stage & Screen | 9. BIRTHPLACE (STATE OR FOREIGN COUNTRY): Hungary | 10. CITIZEN OF WHAT COUNTRY: U.S.A.

11. NAME AND BIRTHPLACE OF FATHER: Stephan Blasko, Hungary | 12. MAIDEN NAME AND BIRTHPLACE OF MOTHER: Paula de Vojnich, Hungary | 13. NAME OF PRESENT SPOUSE (IF MARRIED): Hope Lugosi

14. WAS DECEASED EVER IN U.S. ARMED FORCES? SPECIFY YES, NO, UNKNOWN: No | IF YES, GIVE WAR OR DATES OF SERVICE: | 15. SOCIAL SECURITY NUMBER: 568-01-2643 | 16. INFORMANT: Bela Lugosi, Jr., son

PLACE OF DEATH

17a. COUNTY: Los Angeles | 17b. CITY OR TOWN: Los Angeles | OUTSIDE CORPORATE LIMITS / INSIDE CORPORATE LIMITS: [X] inside | 17c. LENGTH OF STAY IN THIS CITY OR TOWN: 30 years

17d. FULL NAME OF HOSPITAL OR INSTITUTION: | 17e. ADDRESS (IF NOT IN HOSPITAL OR INSTITUTION GIVE STREET OR RURAL ADDRESS OR LOCATION. DO NOT USE P.O. BOX NUMBERS): 5620 Harold Way

LAST USUAL RESIDENCE (WHERE DECEASED LIVED. IF INSTITUTION, RESIDENCE BEFORE ADMISSION)

18a. STATE: California | 18b. COUNTY: Los Angeles | 18c. CITY OR TOWN: Los Angeles | OUTSIDE CORPORATE LIMITS / INSIDE CORPORATE LIMITS: [X] inside | 18d. STREET OR RURAL ADDRESS (DO NOT USE P.O. BOX NUMBERS): 5620 Harold Way

PHYSICIAN'S OR CORONER'S CERTIFICATION

19a. CORONER: I HEREBY CERTIFY THAT DEATH OCCURRED AT THE HOUR, DATE AND PLACE STATED ABOVE FROM THE CAUSES STATED BELOW AND THAT I HAVE HELD AN autopsy ON THE REMAINS OF DECEASED AS REQUIRED BY LAW. ... STANLEY, CORONER

19b. PHYSICIAN: I HEREBY CERTIFY THAT DEATH OCCURRED AT THE HOUR, DATE AND PLACE STATED ABOVE FROM THE CAUSES STATED BELOW AND THAT I ATTENDED THE DECEASED FROM ___ TO ___ AND THAT I LAST SAW THE DECEASED ALIVE ON ___

19c. SIGNATURE: BY Harold Wise DEPUTY | DEGREE OR TITLE | 19d. ADDRESS: HALL OF JUSTICE, LOS ANGELES | 19e. DATE SIGNED: 8-30-56

FUNERAL DIRECTOR AND REGISTRAR

20a. SPECIFY BURIAL, CREMATION OR REMOVAL: Burial | 20b. DATE: 8-18-56 | 20c. CEMETERY OR CREMATORY: Holy Cross Cemetery | 21. SIGNATURE OF EMBALMER: Manuel M. Garcia | LICENSE NUMBER: 4289

22. FUNERAL DIRECTOR: Utter-McKinley Mortuaries, 6240 Hollywood Boulevard | 23. DATE RECEIVED BY LOCAL REGISTRAR: 9-4-56 | 24. SIGNATURE OF LOCAL REGISTRAR: George M. Uhl, M.D.

CAUSE OF DEATH (ENTER ONLY ONE CAUSE PER LINE FOR (A), (B) AND (C).)

THIS DOES NOT MEAN THE MODE OF DYING SUCH AS HEART FAILURE, ASTHENIA, ETC. IT MEANS THE DISEASE, INJURY OR COMPLICATIONS WHICH CAUSED DEATH.

25. DISEASE OR CONDITION DIRECTLY LEADING TO DEATH (A): Coronary Occlusion with Myocardial

ANTECEDENT CAUSES — MORBID CONDITIONS, IF ANY, GIVING RISE TO THE ABOVE CAUSE (A) STATING THE UNDERLYING CAUSE LAST — DUE TO (B): ~~XXXXX~~ Fibrosis.

DUE TO (C):

APPROXIMATE INTERVAL BETWEEN ONSET AND DEATH

OTHER SIGNIFICANT CONDITIONS

26. CONDITIONS CONTRIBUTING TO THE DEATH BUT NOT RELATED TO THE DISEASE OR CONDITION CAUSING DEATH:

OPERATIONS

27a. DATE OF OPERATION | 27b. MAJOR FINDINGS OF OPERATION | 28. AUTOPSY: [X] YES [ ] NO

DEATH DUE TO EXTERNAL VIOLENCE

29a. SPECIFY ACCIDENT, SUICIDE OR HOMICIDE | 29b. PLACE OF INJURY (E.G., IN OR ABOUT HOME, FARM, FACTORY, STREET, OFFICE BUILDING) | 29c. LOCATION: CITY OR TOWN, COUNTY, STATE

29d. TIME OF INJURY: MONTH DAY YEAR HOUR M. | 29e. INJURY OCCURRED: [ ] WHILE AT WORK [ ] NOT WHILE AT WORK | 29f. HOW DID INJURY OCCUR?

REV. 1-1-55. FORM R69-11

MEDICAL AND HEALTH DATA 16164 Bela LUGOSI 8-29-56

This is to certify that this document is a true copy of the official record filed with the Registrar-Recorder/County Clerk.

Beatriz Valdez
BEATRIZ VALDEZ
Registrar-Recorder/County Clerk

AUG 24 1995
19-000078

This copy not valid unless prepared on engraved border displaying the Seal and Signature of the Registrar-Recorder/County Clerk.

THE GREAT SEAL OF THE STATE OF CALIFORNIA

REGISTRAR-RECORDER/COUNTY CLERK • COUNTY OF LOS ANGELES CALIFORNIA

BANKNOTE CORPORATION OF AMERICA

ANY ALTERATION OR ERASURE VOIDS THIS CERTIFICATE

CERTIFICATE OF DEATH

STATE OF CALIFORNIA
USE BLACK INK ONLY/NO ERASURES, WHITEOUTS OR ALTERATIONS
VS-11 (REV. 7/93)

STATE FILE NUMBER | LOCAL REGISTRATION NUMBER

DECEDENT PERSONAL DATA

1. NAME OF DECEDENT—FIRST (GIVEN): Ida
2. MIDDLE: -
3. LAST (FAMILY): Lupino
4. DATE OF BIRTH MM/DD/CCYY: 02/04/1918
5. AGE YRS.: 77
IF UNDER 1 YEAR: MONTHS / DAYS; IF UNDER 24 HOURS: HOURS / MINUTES
6. SEX: F
7. DATE OF DEATH MM/DD/CCYY: 08/03/1995
8. HOUR: 2210
9. STATE OF BIRTH: ENGLAND
10. SOCIAL SECURITY NO.: 560-14-6294
11. MILITARY SERVICE: 19__ TO 19__ [X] NONE
12. MARITAL STATUS: DIVORCED
13. EDUCATION—YEARS COMPLETED: 12
14. RACE: CAUCASIAN
15. HISPANIC—SPECIFY: [ ] YES [X] NO
16. USUAL EMPLOYER: SELF EMPLOYED
17. OCCUPATION: ACTRESS,WRITER,DIRECTOR,PRODUCER
18. KIND OF BUSINESS: FILM/MOTION PICTURE
19. YEARS IN OCCUPATION: 45

USUAL RESIDENCE

20. RESIDENCE—STREET AND NUMBER OR LOCATION: 1807 PARKSIDE
21. CITY: BURBANK
22. COUNTY: LOS ANGELES
23. ZIP CODE: 91506
24. YRS IN COUNTY: 62
25. STATE OR FOREIGN COUNTRY: CALIFORNIA

INFORMANT

26. NAME, RELATIONSHIP: MARY ANN ANDERSON, CONSERVATOR
27. MAILING ADDRESS (STREET AND NUMBER OR RURAL ROUTE NUMBER, CITY OR TOWN, STATE, ZIP): 535 S.ORCHARD DR., BURBANK, CA. 91506

SPOUSE AND PARENT INFORMATION

28. NAME OF SURVIVING SPOUSE—FIRST: -
29. MIDDLE: -
30. LAST (MAIDEN NAME): -
31. NAME OF FATHER—FIRST: STANLEY
32. MIDDLE: -
33. LAST: LUPINO
34. BIRTH STATE: ENGLAND
35. NAME OF MOTHER—FIRST: CONSTANCE
36. MIDDLE: -
37. LAST (MAIDEN): O'SHAY
38. BIRTH STATE: ENGLAND

DISPOSITION(S)

39. DATE MM/DD/CCYY: 08/10/1995
40. PLACE OF FINAL DISPOSITION: RES: MARY ANN ANDERSON, 535 S. ORCHARD DR.,BURBANK, CA. 91506

FUNERAL DIRECTOR AND LOCAL REGISTRAR

41. TYPE OF DISPOSITION(S): CR/RES
42. SIGNATURE OF EMBALMER: ▶ NOT EMBALMED
43. LICENSE NO.: -
44. NAME OF FUNERAL DIRECTOR: FOREST LAWN HOLLYWOOD HILLS
45. LICENSE NO.: F 904
46. SIGNATURE OF LOCAL REGISTRAR: ▶ Robert C. Kaster
47. DATE MM/DD/CCYY: 08/09/1995

PLACE OF DEATH

101. PLACE OF DEATH: Residence
102. IF HOSPITAL, SPECIFY ONE: [ ] IP [ ] ER/OP [ ] DOA
103. FACILITY OTHER THAN HOSPITAL: [ ] CONV. HOSP. [X] RES. [ ] OTHER
104. COUNTY: Los Angeles
105. STREET ADDRESS—STREET AND NUMBER OR LOCATION: 1807 PARKSIDE
106. CITY: BURBANK

CAUSE OF DEATH

107. DEATH WAS CAUSED BY: (ENTER ONLY ONE CAUSE PER LINE FOR A, B, C, AND D)

		TIME INTERVAL BETWEEN ONSET AND DEATH
IMMEDIATE CAUSE (A)	Bronchopneumonia	24 hrs
DUE TO (B)	Metastatic Colon Cancer	mos
DUE TO (C)		
DUE TO (D)		

108. DEATH REPORTED TO CORONER: [ ] YES [X] NO — REFERRAL NUMBER
109. BIOPSY PERFORMED: [ ] YES [X] NO
110. AUTOPSY PERFORMED: [ ] YES [X] NO
111. USED IN DETERMINING CAUSE: [ ] YES [X] NO
112. OTHER SIGNIFICANT CONDITIONS CONTRIBUTING TO DEATH BUT NOT RELATED TO CAUSE GIVEN IN 107: No
113. WAS OPERATION PERFORMED FOR ANY CONDITION IN ITEM 107 OR 112? IF YES, LIST TYPE OF OPERATION AND DATE.: No

PHYSICIAN'S CERTIFICATION

114. I CERTIFY THAT TO THE BEST OF MY KNOWLEDGE DEATH OCCURRED AT THE HOUR, DATE AND PLACE STATED FROM THE CAUSES STATED.
DECEDENT ATTENDED SINCE MM/DD/CCYY: 07/06/1994
DECEDENT LAST SEEN ALIVE MM/DD/CCYY: 07/25/1995
115. SIGNATURE AND TITLE OF CERTIFIER: ▶ Lee Parsons MD
116. LICENSE NO.: G14208
117. DATE MM/DD/CCYY: 08/04/1995
118. TYPE ATTENDING PHYSICIAN'S NAME, MAILING ADDRESS + ZIP: Lee L. Parsons,MD 348 E. Olive, Burbank, CA 91502

CORONER'S USE ONLY

I CERTIFY THAT IN MY OPINION DEATH OCCURRED AT THE HOUR, DATE AND PLACE STATED FROM THE CAUSES STATED.
119. MANNER OF DEATH: [ ] NATURAL [ ] SUICIDE [ ] HOMICIDE [ ] ACCIDENT [ ] PENDING INVESTIGATION [ ] COULD NOT BE DETERMINED
120. INJURY AT WORK: [ ] YES [ ] NO
121. INJURY DATE MM/DD/CCYY
122. HOUR
123. PLACE OF INJURY
124. DESCRIBE HOW INJURY OCCURRED (EVENTS WHICH RESULTED IN INJURY)
125. LOCATION (STREET AND NUMBER OR LOCATION AND CITY AND ZIP CODE)
126. SIGNATURE OF CORONER OR DEPUTY CORONER ▶
127. DATE MM/DD/CCYY
128. TYPED NAME, TITLE OF CORONER OR DEPUTY CORONER

12

STATE REGISTRAR

A	B	C	D	E	F	G	H	FAX AUTH. #	CENSUS TRACT
								273/1786	

1534

07-7-1-7006

STATE OF CALIFORNIA

CERTIFICATION OF VITAL RECORD

COUNTY OF LOS ANGELES • REGISTRAR-RECORDER/COUNTY CLERK

CERTIFICATE OF DEATH
STATE OF CALIFORNIA

0190-001620

STATE FILE NUMBER — LOCAL REGISTRATION DISTRICT AND CERTIFICATE NUMBER

DECEDENT PERSONAL DATA

- 1A. NAME OF DECEDENT—FIRST: Paul
- 1B. MIDDLE: Edward
- 1C. LAST: Lynde
- 2A. DATE OF DEATH (MONTH, DAY, YEAR): Found: January 11, 1982
- 2B. HOUR: 0238
- 3. SEX: Male
- 4. RACE: Caucasian
- 5. ETHNICITY: not stated
- 6. DATE OF BIRTH: June 13, 1926
- 7. AGE: 55 YEARS
- 8. BIRTHPLACE OF DECEDENT (STATE OR FOREIGN COUNTRY): Ohio
- 9. NAME AND BIRTHPLACE OF FATHER: Hoy Lynde., Ohio
- 10. BIRTH NAME AND BIRTHPLACE OF MOTHER: Sylvia Doup, Ohio
- 11. CITIZEN OF WHAT COUNTRY: United States
- 12. SOCIAL SECURITY NUMBER: 300-20-0191
- 13. MARITAL STATUS: Never Married
- 14. NAME OF SURVIVING SPOUSE (IF WIFE, ENTER BIRTH NAME): -
- 15. PRIMARY OCCUPATION: Actor
- 16. NUMBER OF YEARS THIS OCCUPATION: 35
- 17. EMPLOYER (IF SELF-EMPLOYED, SO STATE): Self
- 18. KIND OF INDUSTRY OR BUSINESS: Motion Pictures - T.V.

USUAL RESIDENCE

- 19A. USUAL RESIDENCE—STREET ADDRESS (STREET AND NUMBER OR LOCATION): 509 No. Palm
- 19B.
- 19C. CITY OR TOWN: Beverly Hills
- 19D. COUNTY: Los Angeles
- 19E. STATE: California
- 20. NAME AND ADDRESS OF INFORMANT—RELATIONSHIP: Helen Lynde - Sister, 757 Ocean Avenue # 211, Santa Monica, California

PLACE OF DEATH

- 21A. PLACE OF DEATH: Residence
- 21B. COUNTY: Los Angeles
- 21C. STREET ADDRESS (STREET AND NUMBER OR LOCATION): 509 No. Palm Drive
- 21D. CITY OR TOWN: Beverly Hills

CAUSE OF DEATH

22. DEATH WAS CAUSED BY: (ENTER ONLY ONE CAUSE PER LINE FOR A, B, AND C)

IMMEDIATE CAUSE (A) ACUTE MYOCARDIAL INFARCT

CONDITIONS, IF ANY, WHICH GAVE RISE TO THE IMMEDIATE CAUSE, STATING THE UNDERLYING CAUSE LAST

DUE TO, OR AS A CONSEQUENCE OF (B) ARTERIOSCLEROTIC CORONARY ARTERY DISEASE

DUE TO, OR AS A CONSEQUENCE OF (C)

APPROXIMATE INTERVAL BETWEEN ONSET AND DEATH

- 24. WAS DEATH REPORTED TO CORONER? 82-484
- 25. WAS BIOPSY PERFORMED? NO
- 26. WAS AUTOPSY PERFORMED? YES
- 23. OTHER CONDITIONS CONTRIBUTING BUT NOT RELATED TO THE IMMEDIATE CAUSE OF DEATH: PULMONARY EMPHYSEMA
- 27. WAS OPERATION PERFORMED FOR ANY CONDITION IN ITEMS 22 OR 23? TYPE OF OPERATION — DATE: NO

PHYSICIAN'S CERTIFICATION

- 28A. I CERTIFY THAT DEATH OCCURRED AT THE HOUR, DATE AND PLACE STATED FROM THE CAUSES STATED. I ATTENDED DECEDENT SINCE (ENTER MO. DA. YR.) | I LAST SAW DECEDENT ALIVE (ENTER MO. DA. YR.)
- 28B. PHYSICIAN—SIGNATURE AND DEGREE OR TITLE
- 28C. DATE SIGNED
- 28D. PHYSICIAN'S LICENSE NUMBER
- 28E. TYPE PHYSICIAN'S NAME AND ADDRESS

INJURY INFORMATION

- 29. SPECIFY ACCIDENT, SUICIDE, ETC.
- 30. PLACE OF INJURY
- 31. INJURY AT WORK
- 32A. DATE OF INJURY—MONTH, DAY, YEAR
- 32B. HOUR
- 33. LOCATION (STREET AND NUMBER OR LOCATION AND CITY OR TOWN)
- 34. DESCRIBE HOW INJURY OCCURRED (EVENTS WHICH RESULTED IN INJURY)

CORONER'S USE ONLY

18

- 35A. I CERTIFY THAT DEATH OCCURRED AT THE HOUR, DATE AND PLACE STATED FROM THE CAUSES STATED. AS REQUIRED BY LAW I HAVE HELD AN INVESTIGATION
- 35B. CORONER—SIGNATURE AND DEGREE OR TITLE: THOMAS T. NOGUCHI, M.D. CORONER, ... N. MISSION RD. LOS ANGELES, CALIF. [signature] DEPUTY
- 35C. DATE SIGNED: 1-12-82
- 36. DISPOSITION: Cremation
- 37. DATE—MONTH, DAY, YEAR: 15 Jan 81
- 38. NAME AND ADDRESS OF CEMETERY OR CREMATORY: Grandview Crematory, Glendale, Calif.
- 39. EMBALMER'S LICENSE NUMBER AND SIGNATURE: Not Embalmed
- 40. NAME OF FUNERAL DIRECTOR (OR PERSON ACTING AS SUCH): Westwood Village Mortuary
- 41. LOCAL REGISTRAR—SIGNATURE: [signature]
- 42. DATE ACCEPTED BY LOCAL REGISTRAR: JAN 14 1982

STATE REGISTRAR: A. B. C. D. E. F.

VS-11 (10-78)

This is to certify that this document is a true copy of the official record filed with the Registrar-Recorder/County Clerk.

CONNY B. McCORMACK
Registrar-Recorder/County Clerk

19-557856

This copy not valid unless prepared on engraved border displaying the Seal and Signature of the Registrar-Recorder/County Clerk.

ANY ALTERATION OR ERASURE VOIDS THIS CERTIFICATE

CERTIFICATION OF VITAL RECORD

COUNTY OF LOS ANGELES • REGISTRAR-RECORDER/COUNTY CLERK

CERTIFICATE OF DEATH
STATE OF CALIFORNIA
USE BLACK INK ONLY

STATE FILE NUMBER — LOCAL REGISTRATION DISTRICT AND CERTIFICATE NUMBER: 39119046583

DECEDENT PERSONAL DATA

1A. NAME OF DECEDENT—FIRST (GIVEN): FREDERICK
1B. MIDDLE: M.
1C. LAST (FAMILY): MacMURRAY
2A. DATE OF DEATH—MO, DAY, YR: NOVEMBER 5, 1991
2B. HOUR: 1045
3. SEX: M
4. RACE: CAUCASIAN
5. HISPANIC—SPECIFY: ☐ YES ☒ NO
6. DATE OF BIRTH—MO, DAY, YR: AUGUST 30, 1908
7. AGE IN YEARS: 83 — IF UNDER 1 YEAR: MONTHS, DAYS — IF UNDER 24 HOURS: HOURS, MINUTES
8. STATE OF BIRTH: IL
9. CITIZEN OF WHAT COUNTRY: USA
10A. FULL NAME OF FATHER: FREDERICK MacMURRAY
10B. STATE OF BIRTH: IL
11A. FULL MAIDEN NAME OF MOTHER: MALETA MARTIN
11B. STATE OF BIRTH: WI
12. MILITARY SERVICE: 19__ TO 19__ ☒ NONE
13. SOCIAL SECURITY NO.: 564-09-2582
14. MARITAL STATUS: MARRIED
15. NAME OF SURVIVING SPOUSE (IF WIFE, ENTER MAIDEN NAME): JUNE HAVER
16A. USUAL OCCUPATION: ACTOR
16B. USUAL KIND OF BUSINESS OR INDUSTRY: MOTION PICS., TV, THEATER
16C. USUAL EMPLOYER: SELF-EMPLOYED
16D. YEARS IN OCCUPATION: 60
17. EDUCATION—YEARS COMPLETED: 14

USUAL RESIDENCE

18A. RESIDENCE—STREET AND NUMBER OR LOCATION: 485 HALVERN DRIVE
18B. CITY: LOS ANGELES
18C. ZIP CODE: 90049
18D. COUNTY: LOS ANGELES
18E. NUMBER OF YEARS IN THIS COUNTY: 37
18F. STATE OR FOREIGN COUNTRY: CALIFORNIA
20. NAME, RELATIONSHIP, MAILING ADDRESS AND ZIP CODE OF INFORMANT: JUNE HAVER MacMURRAY - WIFE, 485 HALVERN DRIVE, LOS ANGELES, CA 90049

PLACE OF DEATH

19A. PLACE OF DEATH: ST. JOHN'S HOSPITAL
19B. IF HOSPITAL, SPECIFY ONE: IP, ER/OP, DOA: IP
19C. COUNTY: LOS ANGELES
19D. STREET ADDRESS—STREET AND NUMBER OR LOCATION: 1328 22ND STREET
19E. CITY: SANTA MONICA

CAUSE OF DEATH

21. DEATH WAS CAUSED BY: (ENTER ONLY ONE CAUSE PER LINE FOR A, B, AND C) — TIME INTERVAL BETWEEN ONSET AND DEATH
IMMEDIATE CAUSE (A) PULMONARY EDEMA — 2 HOURS
DUE TO (B) SEPSIS SYNDROME — 2 days
DUE TO (C) URINARY TRACT INFECTION — 2 days
22. WAS DEATH REPORTED TO CORONER? REFERRAL NUMBER ☐ YES ☒ NO
23. WAS BIOPSY PERFORMED? ☐ YES ☒ NO
24A. WAS AUTOPSY PERFORMED? ☐ YES ☒ NO
24B. WAS IT USED IN DETERMINING CAUSE OF DEATH? ☐ YES ☒ NO
25. OTHER SIGNIFICANT CONDITIONS CONTRIBUTING TO DEATH BUT NOT RELATED TO CAUSE GIVEN IN 21: LYMPHOCYTIC LEUKEMIA.
26. WAS OPERATION PERFORMED FOR ANY CONDITION IN ITEM 21 OR 25? IF YES, LIST TYPE OF OPERATION AND DATE: NO

PHYSICIAN'S CERTIFICATION

I CERTIFY THAT TO THE BEST OF MY KNOWLEDGE DEATH OCCURRED AT THE HOUR, DATE AND PLACE STATED FROM THE CAUSES STATED.
27A. DECEDENT ATTENDED SINCE MONTH, DAY, YEAR: 9/4/91 — DECEDENT LAST SEEN ALIVE MONTH, DAY, YEAR: 11/5/91
27B. SIGNATURE AND DEGREE OR TITLE OF CERTIFIER: [signature] MD
27C. CERTIFIER'S LICENSE NUMBER: A41221
27D. DATE SIGNED: 11/5/91
27E. TYPE ATTENDING PHYSICIAN'S NAME AND ADDRESS: LOUIS E. SCADUTO, MD 2001 SANTA MONICA BLVD. #560W SANTA MONICA, CA 90404

CORONER'S USE ONLY

I CERTIFY THAT IN MY OPINION DEATH OCCURRED AT THE HOUR, DATE AND PLACE STATED FROM THE CAUSES STATED.
28A. SIGNATURE AND TITLE OF CORONER OR DEPUTY CORONER
28B. DATE SIGNED
29. MANNER OF DEATH—specify one: natural, accident, suicide, homicide, pending investigation or could not be determined
30A. PLACE OF INJURY
30B. INJURY AT WORK ☐ YES ☐ NO
30C. DATE OF INJURY MONTH, DAY, YEAR
31. HOUR
32. LOCATION (STREET AND NUMBER OR LOCATION AND CITY)
33. DESCRIBE HOW INJURY OCCURRED (EVENTS WHICH RESULTED IN INJURY)

FUNERAL DIRECTOR AND LOCAL REGISTRAR

34A. DISPOSITION(S): CR/RES
34B. PLACE OF FINAL DISPOSITION—NAME AND ADDRESS: RESIDENCE: 485 HALVERN DRIVE LOS ANGELES, CA 90049
34C. DATE MO, DAY, YEAR: 11-6-91
35A. SIGNATURE OF EMBALMER: NOT EMBALMED
35B. LICENSE NUMBER: NONE
36A. NAME OF FUNERAL DIRECTOR (OR PERSON ACTING AS SUCH): GATES, KINGSLEY & GATES, SM
36B. LICENSE NO.: FD-451
37. SIGNATURE OF LOCAL REGISTRAR: Robert C. [signature]
38. REGISTRATION DATE: NOV 06 1991

150 STATE REGISTRAR — A. B. C. D. E. F. CENSUS TRACT

VS-11 (REV. 3-91) 5990 MAKE NO ERASURES, WHITEOUTS, OR OTHER ALTERATIONS

This is to certify that this document is a true copy of the official record filed with the Registrar-Recorder/County Clerk.

[signature]
CHARLES WEISSBURD
Registrar-Recorder/County Clerk

JAN 22 1992
19-298624

This copy not valid unless prepared on engraved border displaying the Seal and Signature of the Registrar-Recorder/County Clerk.

THE GREAT SEAL OF THE STATE OF CALIFORNIA — REGISTRAR-RECORDER/COUNTY CLERK • COUNTY OF LOS ANGELES • CALIFORNIA

American Bank Note Company

ANY ALTERATION OR ERASURE VOIDS THIS CERTIFICATE

CERTIFICATION OF VITAL RECORD

COUNTY OF RIVERSIDE

RIVERSIDE, CALIFORNIA

CERTIFICATE OF DEATH
STATE OF CALIFORNIA
USE BLACK INK ONLY/NO ERASURES, WHITEOUTS OR ALTERATIONS
VS-11 (REV. 7/93)

39633001013

STATE FILE NUMBER — LOCAL REGISTRATION NUMBER

DECEDENT PERSONAL DATA

1. NAME OF DECEDENT—FIRST (GIVEN): GUY
2. MIDDLE: -
3. LAST (FAMILY): MADISON
4. DATE OF BIRTH MM/DD/CCYY: 01/19/1922
5. AGE YRS.: 74
IF UNDER 1 YEAR: MONTHS | DAYS — IF UNDER 24 HOURS: HOURS | MINUTES
6. SEX: M
7. DATE OF DEATH MM/DD/CCYY: 02/06/1996
8. HOUR: 0757
9. STATE OF BIRTH: CA
10. SOCIAL SECURITY NO.: 558-28-9505
11. MILITARY SERVICE: 19__ TO 19__ NONE
12. MARITAL STATUS: DIV.
13. EDUCATION—YEARS COMPLETED: 12
14. RACE: WHITE
15. HISPANIC—SPECIFY: YES ___ [X] NO
16. USUAL EMPLOYER: SCREEN ACTORS BUILD
17. OCCUPATION: ACTOR
18. KIND OF BUSINESS: MOVIE INDUSTRY
19. YEARS IN OCCUPATION: 50

1OF2

USUAL RESIDENCE

20. RESIDENCE—STREET AND NUMBER OR LOCATION: 50210 ASPEN DR.
21. CITY: MORONGO VALLEY
22. COUNTY: SAN BERNARDINO
23. ZIP CODE: 92256
24. YRS IN COUNTY: 8
25. STATE OR FOREIGN COUNTRY: CA

INFORMANT

26. NAME, RELATIONSHIP: BRIDGET KAROL - DAUGHTER
27. MAILING ADDRESS (STREET AND NUMBER OR RURAL ROUTE NUMBER, CITY OR TOWN, STATE, ZIP): 51110 CHEYENNE TRAIL, MORONGO VALLEY, CA 92256

SPOUSE AND PARENT INFORMATION

28. NAME OF SURVIVING SPOUSE—FIRST: -
29. MIDDLE: -
30. LAST (MAIDEN NAME): -
31. NAME OF FATHER—FIRST: BENJAMIN
32. MIDDLE: -
33. LAST: MOSELEY
34. BIRTH STATE: MO
35. NAME OF MOTHER—FIRST: MARY
36. MIDDLE: JANE
37. LAST (MAIDEN): HOLDER
38. BIRTH STATE: MO

DISPOSITION(S)

39. DATE MM/DD/CCYY: 02/12/1996
40. PLACE OF FINAL DISPOSITION: PALM SPRINGS MAUSOLEUM, 69901 E. RAMON RD., CATHEDRAL CITY, CA 92234

FUNERAL DIRECTOR AND LOCAL REGISTRAR

41. TYPE OF DISPOSITION(S): BU
42. SIGNATURE OF EMBALMER: David McKnight
43. LICENSE NO.: 7371
44. NAME OF FUNERAL DIRECTOR: PALM SPRINGS MORT., CATHEDRAL CITY
45. LICENSE NO.: FD 1513
46. SIGNATURE OF LOCAL REGISTRAR: Bradley P. Gilbert M.D.
47. DATE MM/DD/CCYY: 02/07/1996

PLACE OF DEATH

101. PLACE OF DEATH: DESERT HOSPITAL HOSPICE
102. IF HOSPITAL, SPECIFY ONE: IP / ER/OP / DOA
103. FACILITY OTHER THAN HOSPITAL: CONV. HOSP. / RES. / [X] OTHER
104. COUNTY: RIVERSIDE
105. STREET ADDRESS—STREET AND NUMBER OR LOCATION: 1150 N. INDIAN CANYON DR.
106. CITY: PALM SPRINGS

CAUSE OF DEATH

107. DEATH WAS CAUSED BY: (ENTER ONLY ONE CAUSE PER LINE FOR A, B, C, AND D)

		Cause	Time interval between onset and death
IMMEDIATE CAUSE	(A)	RESPIRATORY ARREST	MINUTES
DUE TO	(B)	END-STAGE EMPHYSEMA	YEARS
DUE TO	(C)	SMOKING HISTORY	YEARS
DUE TO	(D)		

108. DEATH REPORTED TO CORONER: YES [X] NO — REFERRAL NUMBER
109. BIOPSY PERFORMED: YES [X] NO
110. AUTOPSY PERFORMED: YES [X] NO
111. USED IN DETERMINING CAUSE: YES NO
112. OTHER SIGNIFICANT CONDITIONS CONTRIBUTING TO DEATH BUT NOT RELATED TO CAUSE GIVEN IN 107: CANCER PROSTATE
113. WAS OPERATION PERFORMED FOR ANY CONDITION IN ITEM 107 OR 112? IF YES, LIST TYPE OF OPERATION AND DATE.: NO

PHYSICIAN'S CERTIFICATION

114. I CERTIFY THAT TO THE BEST OF MY KNOWLEDGE DEATH OCCURRED AT THE HOUR, DATE AND PLACE STATED FROM THE CAUSES STATED.
DECEDENT ATTENDED SINCE MM/DD/CCYY: 01/11/1992 — DECEDENT LAST SEEN ALIVE MM/DD/CCYY: 02/05/1996
115. SIGNATURE AND TITLE OF CERTIFIER: David Neumann
116. LICENSE NO.: G027957
117. DATE MM/DD/CCYY: 02/06/1996
118. TYPE ATTENDING PHYSICIAN'S NAME, MAILING ADDRESS, ZIP: DAVID L. NEUMANN, M.D., 555 TACHEVAH, 3W-103, PALM SPRINGS, CA 92262

CORONER'S USE ONLY

I CERTIFY THAT IN MY OPINION DEATH OCCURRED AT THE HOUR, DATE AND PLACE STATED FROM THE CAUSES STATED.
119. MANNER OF DEATH: NATURAL / SUICIDE / HOMICIDE / ACCIDENT / PENDING INVESTIGATION / COULD NOT BE DETERMINED
120. INJURY AT WORK: YES / NO
121. INJURY DATE MM/DD/CCYY
122. HOUR
123. PLACE OF INJURY
124. DESCRIBE HOW INJURY OCCURRED (EVENTS WHICH RESULTED IN INJURY)
125. LOCATION (STREET AND NUMBER OR LOCATION AND CITY AND ZIP CODE)
126. SIGNATURE OF CORONER OR DEPUTY CORONER
127. DATE MM/DD/CCYY
128. TYPED NAME, TITLE OF CORONER OR DEPUTY CORONER

663806

STATE REGISTRAR: A B C D E F G H — FAX AUTH. #: 263762 — CENSUS TRACT

CERTIFIED COPY OF VITAL RECORDS

STATE OF CALIFORNIA }
COUNTY OF RIVERSIDE } ss

DATE ISSUED 10/08/1996

This is a true and exact reproduction of the document officially registered and placed on file in the office of County of Riverside, Department of Health.

Herbert A. Giese Jr. MD. MPH.
Herbert A. Giese Jr., M.D. M.P.H.
Local Registrar
RIVERSIDE COUNTY, CALIFORNIA

THE GREAT SEAL OF THE STATE OF CALIFORNIA — EUREKA

DEPARTMENT OF HEALTH — REGISTRAR OF VITAL STATISTICS — COUNTY OF RIVERSIDE

This copy not valid unless prepared on engraved border displaying seal and signature of Registrar.

American Bank Note Company

ANY ALTERATION OR ERASURE VOIDS THIS CERTIFICATE

CERTIFICATION OF VITAL RECORD

COUNTY OF RIVERSIDE

RIVERSIDE, CALIFORNIA

AFFIDAVIT TO AMEND A RECORD

STATE FILE NUMBER

☐ BIRTH ☒ DEATH ☐ FETAL DEATH

39633001013

LOCAL REGISTRATION DISTRICT AND CERTIFICATE NUMBER

NO ERASURES, WHITEOUTS, OR ALTERATIONS

STATE/LOCAL REGISTRAR USE ONLY	1.	2.	3.

PART I INFORMATION TO LOCATE RECORD—TYPE OR PRINT IN BLACK INK ONLY

NAME AS IT APPEARS ON RECORD	1. NAME—FIRST (GIVEN) GUY	2. MIDDLE -	3. LAST (FAMILY) MADISON
ADDITIONAL INFORMATION TO LOCATE RECORD	4. SEX M; 5. DATE OF EVENT—MM/DD/CCYY 02/06/1996	6. CITY OF OCCURRENCE PALM SPRINGS	7. COUNTY OF OCCURRENCE RIVERSIDE
	8. FATHER'S NAME AS STATED ON ORIGINAL BENJAMIN - MOSELEY	9. MOTHER'S NAME AS STATED ON ORIGINAL MARY JANE HOLDER	

PART II STATEMENT OF CORRECTIONS—NO ERASURES, WHITEOUTS, OR ALTERATIONS 2OF2

LIST ONE ITEM PER LINE

10. CERTIFICATE ITEM NUMBER	11. INFORMATION AS IT APPEARS ON ORIGINAL RECORD	12. INFORMATION AS IT SHOULD APPEAR
1,2,3	GUY - MADISON	GUY - MADISON
		AKA - ROBERT OZELL MOSELEY

REASON FOR CORRECTION 13. TO ADD TO RECORDS

AFFIDAVITS AND SIGNATURES

We, the undersigned, hereby certify under penalty of perjury that we have personal knowledge of the above facts and that the information given above is true and correct.

TWO PERSONS MUST SIGN THIS FORM

USE BLACK INK ONLY

14. SIGNATURE OF FIRST PERSON	15. TITLE/RELATIONSHIP TO PERSON IN PART I	16. DATE SIGNED—MM/DD/CCYY
Betty Stephens	MORTUARY PERSONNEL	02/07/1996
17. AGE LEGAL	18. ADDRESS (STREET, CITY, STATE, ZIP) 69 855 E. RAMON RD., CATHEDRAL CITY, CA 92234	
19. SIGNATURE OF SECOND PERSON	20. TITLE/RELATIONSHIP TO PERSON IN PART I	21. DATE SIGNED—MM/DD/CCYY
Karen Druner	MORTUARY PERSONNEL	02/07/1996
22. AGE LEGAL	23. ADDRESS (STREET, CITY, STATE, ZIP) 69 855 E. RAMON RD., CATHEDRAL CITY, CA 92234	

STATE/LOCAL REGISTRAR USE ONLY	24. SIGNATURE OF STATE OR LOCAL REGISTRAR Bradley P. Gilbert M.D CR	25. DATE ACCEPTED FOR REGISTRATION—MM/DD CCYY 02/07/1996

663805

STATE OF CALIFORNIA, DEPARTMENT OF HEALTH SERVICES, OFFICE OF STATE REGISTRAR 93 24420 VS 24 (Rev. 1/94)

CERTIFIED COPY OF VITAL RECORDS

STATE OF CALIFORNIA
COUNTY OF RIVERSIDE } SS DATE ISSUED 10 / 08 / 1996

This is a true and exact reproduction of the document officially registered and placed on file in the office of County of Riverside, Department of Health.

Herbert A. Giese Jr., M.D. M.P.H.
Local Registrar
RIVERSIDE COUNTY, CALIFORNIA

THE GREAT SEAL OF THE STATE OF CALIFORNIA EUREKA

DEPARTMENT OF HEALTH REGISTRAR OF VITAL STATISTICS COUNTY OF RIVERSIDE

This copy not valid unless prepared on engraved border displaying seal and signature of Registrar.

American Bank Note Company

ANY ALTERATION OR ERASURE VOIDS THIS CERTIFICATE

CERTIFICATION OF VITAL RECORD

COUNTY OF LOS ANGELES • REGISTRAR-RECORDER/COUNTY CLERK

CERTIFICATE OF DEATH 0190-017136

STATE OF CALIFORNIA—DEPARTMENT OF HEALTH
OFFICE OF THE STATE REGISTRAR OF VITAL STATISTICS

STATE FILE NUMBER — LOCAL REGISTRATION DISTRICT AND CERTIFICATE NUMBER

DECEDENT PERSONAL DATA

1a. NAME OF DECEASED—FIRST NAME: Mary Marjorie
1b. MIDDLE NAME: Tomlinson
1c. LAST NAME: Krebs AKA Main
2a. DATE OF DEATH—MONTH DAY YEAR: APRIL 10, 1975
2b. HOUR: 6:20 A M
3. SEX: Female
4. COLOR OR RACE: Caucasian
5. BIRTHPLACE (STATE OR FOREIGN COUNTRY): Indiana
6. DATE OF BIRTH: February 24, 1890
7. AGE (LAST BIRTHDAY): 85 YEARS — IF UNDER 1 YEAR / IF UNDER 24 HOURS
8. NAME AND BIRTHPLACE OF FATHER: Samuel J. Tomlinson - Indiana
9. MAIDEN NAME AND BIRTHPLACE OF MOTHER: Mary McGaughey- Indiana
10. CITIZEN OF WHAT COUNTRY: United States
11. SOCIAL SECURITY NUMBER: 110-10-0846
12. MARRIED, NEVER MARRIED, WIDOWED, DIVORCED (SPECIFY): Widowed
13. NAME OF SURVIVING SPOUSE (IF WIFE, ENTER MAIDEN NAME): ---
14. LAST OCCUPATION: Actress
15. NUMBER OF YEARS IN THIS OCCUPATION: 41
16. NAME OF LAST EMPLOYING COMPANY OR FIRM (IF SELF-EMPLOYED, SO STATE): Self Employed
17. KIND OF INDUSTRY OR BUSINESS: Motion Pictures

PLACE OF DEATH

18a. PLACE OF DEATH—NAME OF HOSPITAL OR OTHER IN-PATIENT FACILITY: St. Vincents Hospital
18b. STREET ADDRESS—(STREET AND NUMBER OR LOCATION): 2131 West 3rd. Street
18c. INSIDE CITY CORPORATE LIMITS (SPECIFY YES OR NO): Yes
18d. CITY OR TOWN: Los Angeles
18e. COUNTY: Los Angeles
18f. LENGTH OF STAY IN COUNTY OF DEATH: 38 YEARS
18g. LENGTH OF STAY IN CALIFORNIA: 38 YEARS

USUAL RESIDENCE (IF DEATH OCCURRED IN INSTITUTION, ENTER RESIDENCE BEFORE ADMISSION)

19a. USUAL RESIDENCE—STREET ADDRESS (STREET AND NUMBER OR LOCATION): 3066 Patricia Avenue
19b. INSIDE CITY CORPORATE LIMITS (SPECIFY YES OR NO): Yes
19c. CITY OR TOWN: Los Angeles
19d. COUNTY: Los Angeles
19e. STATE: California
20. NAME AND MAILING ADDRESS OF INFORMANT: Miss. Frances M. Nelson, P.O. Box 54410 Terminal Annex, Los Angeles, California

PHYSICIAN'S OR CORONER'S CERTIFICATION

21a. CORONER: I HEREBY CERTIFY THAT DEATH OCCURRED AT THE HOUR, DATE AND PLACE STATED ABOVE FROM THE CAUSES STATED BELOW AND THAT I HAVE HELD AN INQUEST OR INVESTIGATION ON THE REMAINS OF DECEASED AS REQUIRED BY LAW
21b. PHYSICIAN: I HEREBY CERTIFY THAT DEATH OCCURRED AT THE HOUR, DATE AND PLACE STATED ABOVE FROM THE CAUSES STATED BELOW AND THAT I ATTENDED THE DECEASED FROM 1956 TO 4-10-75 AND LAST SAW HIM/HER ALIVE 4-9-75
21c. PHYSICIAN OR CORONER—SIGNATURE AND DEGREE OR TITLE: ACT Lakin MD
21d. DATE SIGNED: 4-10-75
21e. ADDRESS: 1930 Wilshire, L.A.
21f. PHYSICIAN'S CALIFORNIA LICENSE NUMBER: C-11728

FUNERAL DIRECTOR AND LOCAL REGISTRAR

22a. SPECIFY BURIAL, ENTOMBMENT OR CREMATION: Burial
22b. DATE: 4-14-1975
23. NAME OF CEMETERY OR CREMATORY: FOREST LAWN MEMORIAL-PARK
24. EMBALMER—SIGNATURE (IF BODY EMBALMED) LICENSE NUMBER: Frederick B. Macdonald
25. NAME OF FUNERAL DIRECTOR (OR PERSON ACTING AS SUCH): Forest Lawn Hollywood Hills Mortuary
26. IF NOT CERTIFIED BY CORONER, WAS THIS DEATH REPORTED TO CORONER (SPECIFY YES OR NO): No
27. LOCAL REGISTRAR—SIGNATURE: [signature]
28. DATE RECEIVED FOR REGISTRATION BY LOCAL REGISTRAR: APR 14 1975

MEDICAL AND HEALTH DATA

CAUSE OF DEATH

29. PART I. DEATH WAS CAUSED BY: ENTER ONLY ONE CAUSE PER LINE FOR A, B, AND C
IMMEDIATE CAUSE (A) Adenocarcinoma of recto-sigmoid colon. — APPROXIMATE INTERVAL BETWEEN ONSET AND DEATH: 9 mos.
CONDITIONS, IF ANY, WHICH GAVE RISE TO THE IMMEDIATE CAUSE (A), STATING THE UNDERLYING CAUSE LAST — DUE TO, OR AS A CONSEQUENCE OF (B)
DUE TO, OR AS A CONSEQUENCE OF (C)
30. PART II. OTHER SIGNIFICANT CONDITIONS—CONTRIBUTING TO DEATH BUT NOT RELATED TO THE IMMEDIATE CAUSE GIVEN IN PART I: Arteriosclerotic Heart Disease, Diabetes Mellitus.
31. WAS OPERATION OR BIOPSY PERFORMED FOR ANY CONDITION IN ITEMS 29 OR 30? (SPECIFY OPERATION AND/OR BIOPSY): BIOPSY
32a. AUTOPSY (SPECIFY YES OR NO): NO
32b. IF YES, WERE FINDINGS CONSIDERED IN DETERMINING CAUSE OF DEATH? (SPECIFY YES OR NO)

INJURY INFORMATION

33. SPECIFY ACCIDENT, SUICIDE OR HOMICIDE
34. PLACE OF INJURY (SPECIFY HOME, FARM, FACTORY, STREET, OFFICE BUILDING, ETC.)
35. INJURY AT WORK (SPECIFY YES OR NO)
36a. DATE OF INJURY—MONTH, DAY, YEAR
36b. HOUR
37a. PLACE OF INJURY (STREET AND NUMBER OR LOCATION AND CITY OR TOWN)
37b. DISTANCE FROM PLACE OF INJURY TO USUAL RESIDENCE (ITEM 19) MILES
38. WERE LABORATORY TESTS DONE FOR DRUGS OR TOXIC CHEMICALS? (SPECIFY YES OR NO)
39. WERE LABORATORY TESTS DONE FOR ALCOHOL? (SPECIFY YES OR NO)
40. DESCRIBE HOW INJURY OCCURRED (ENTER SEQUENCE OF EVENTS WHICH RESULTED IN INJURY. NATURE OF INJURY SHOULD BE ENTERED IN ITEM 29)

6

STATE REGISTRAR A. B. C. D. E. F. 9-1-9

This is to certify that this document is a true copy of the official record filed with the Registrar-Recorder/County Clerk.

OCT 02 1995

19-033427

This copy not valid unless prepared on engraved border displaying the Seal of the Registrar-Recorder/County Clerk.

BANKNOTE CORPORATION OF AMERICA

ANY ALTERATION OR ERASURE VOIDS THIS CERTIFICATE

CERTIFICATE OF DEATH

STATE OF CALIFORNIA
USE BLACK INK ONLY/NO ERASURES, WHITEOUTS OR ALTERATIONS
VS-11 (REV. 7/93)

STATE FILE NUMBER — LOCAL REGISTRATION NUMBER

DECEDENT PERSONAL DATA

1. NAME OF DECEDENT—FIRST (GIVEN)	2. MIDDLE	3. LAST (FAMILY)
DEAN	PAUL	MARTIN

4. DATE OF BIRTH MM/DD/CCYY	5. AGE YRS.	IF UNDER 1 YEAR (MONTHS / DAYS)	IF UNDER 24 HOURS (HOURS / MINUTES)	6. SEX	7. DATE OF DEATH MM/DD/CCYY	8. HOUR
06/07/1917	78			M	12/25/1995	0330

9. STATE OF BIRTH	10. SOCIAL SECURITY NO.	11. MILITARY SERVICE	12. MARITAL STATUS	13. EDUCATION—YEARS COMPLETED
OHIO	268-16-9502	19 __ TO 19 __ ☐ NONE	DIVORCED	12

14. RACE	15. HISPANIC—SPECIFY	16. USUAL EMPLOYER
CAUCASIAN	☐ YES ☒ NO	SELF EMPLOYED

17. OCCUPATION	18. KIND OF BUSINESS	19. YEARS IN OCCUPATION
ACTOR	ENTERTAINMENT	55

USUAL RESIDENCE

20. RESIDENCE—STREET AND NUMBER OR LOCATION: 511 N. MAPLE DRIVE

21. CITY	22. COUNTY	23. ZIP CODE	24. YRS IN COUNTY	25. STATE OR FOREIGN COUNTRY
BEVERLY HILLS	LOS ANGELES	90210	50	CA

INFORMANT

26. NAME, RELATIONSHIP	27. MAILING ADDRESS (STREET AND NUMBER OR RURAL ROUTE NUMBER, CITY OR TOWN, STATE, ZIP)
MORT LLOYD VINER - FRIEND	8942 WILSHIRE BLVD. BEVERLY HILLS,CA 90211

SPOUSE AND PARENT INFORMATION

28. NAME OF SURVIVING SPOUSE—FIRST	29. MIDDLE	30. LAST (MAIDEN NAME)	
-	-	-	
31. NAME OF FATHER—FIRST	**32. MIDDLE**	**33. LAST**	**34. BIRTH STATE**
GUY	-	CROCETTI	ITALY
35. NAME OF MOTHER—FIRST	**36. MIDDLE**	**37. LAST (MAIDEN)**	**38. BIRTH STATE**
ANGELA	-	BARR	OHIO

DISPOSITION(S)

39. DATE MM/DD/CCYY	40. PLACE OF FINAL DISPOSITION
12/29/1995	WESTWOOD MEMORIAL PARK, 1218 GLENDON AVENUE LOS ANGELES, CA 90024

FUNERAL DIRECTOR AND LOCAL REGISTRAR

41. TYPE OF DISPOSITION(S)	42. SIGNATURE OF EMBALMER	43. LICENSE NO.
BURIAL	▶ William Lee Abel	7981

44. NAME OF FUNERAL DIRECTOR	45. LICENSE NO.	46. SIGNATURE OF LOCAL REGISTRAR	47. DATE MM/DD/CCYY
PIERCE BROS.WESTWOOD VILLAGE	F-951	▶ Robert [illegible]	12/27/1995

PLACE OF DEATH

101. PLACE OF DEATH	102. IF HOSPITAL, SPECIFY ONE	103. FACILITY OTHER THAN HOSPITAL	104. COUNTY
RESIDENCE	☐ IP ☐ ER/OP ☐ DOA	☐ CONV. HOSP. ☒ RES. ☐ OTHER	LOS ANGELES

105. STREET ADDRESS—STREET AND NUMBER OR LOCATION	106. CITY
511 N. MAPLE DRIVE	BEVERLY HILLS

CAUSE OF DEATH

107. DEATH WAS CAUSED BY: (ENTER ONLY ONE CAUSE PER LINE FOR A, B, C, AND D)

		TIME INTERVAL BETWEEN ONSET AND DEATH
IMMEDIATE CAUSE (A)	RESPIRATORY ARREST	IMMED.
DUE TO (B)	LUNG CANCER	YEARS
DUE TO (C)		
DUE TO (D)		

108. DEATH REPORTED TO CORONER: ☐ YES ☒ NO — REFERRAL NUMBER
109. BIOPSY PERFORMED: ☐ YES ☒ NO
110. AUTOPSY PERFORMED: ☐ YES ☒ NO
111. USED IN DETERMINING CAUSE: ☐ YES ☐ NO

112. OTHER SIGNIFICANT CONDITIONS CONTRIBUTING TO DEATH BUT NOT RELATED TO CAUSE GIVEN IN 107: RIGHT HEART FAILURE

113. WAS OPERATION PERFORMED FOR ANY CONDITION IN ITEM 107 OR 112? IF YES, LIST TYPE OF OPERATION AND DATE: NO

PHYSICIAN'S CERTIFICATION

114. I CERTIFY THAT TO THE BEST OF MY KNOWLEDGE DEATH OCCURRED AT THE HOUR, DATE AND PLACE STATED FROM THE CAUSES STATED.

DECEDENT ATTENDED SINCE MM/DD/CCYY	DECEDENT LAST SEEN ALIVE MM/DD/CCYY	115. SIGNATURE AND TITLE OF CERTIFIER	116. LICENSE NO.	117. DATE MM/DD/CCYY
12/16/1995	12/21/1995	▶ [signature]	645920	12/25/1995

118. TYPE ATTENDING PHYSICIAN'S NAME, MAILING ADDRESS + ZIP: REED WILSON,M.D.435 N.ROXBURY DR.,BEVERLY HILLS,CA 90210

CORONER'S USE ONLY

I CERTIFY THAT IN MY OPINION DEATH OCCURRED AT THE HOUR, DATE AND PLACE STATED FROM THE CAUSES STATED.

119. MANNER OF DEATH: ☐ NATURAL ☐ SUICIDE ☐ HOMICIDE ☐ ACCIDENT ☐ PENDING INVESTIGATION ☐ COULD NOT BE DETERMINED

120. INJURY AT WORK	121. INJURY DATE MM/DD/CCYY	122. HOUR	123. PLACE OF INJURY
☐ YES ☐ NO			

124. DESCRIBE HOW INJURY OCCURRED (EVENTS WHICH RESULTED IN INJURY)

125. LOCATION (STREET AND NUMBER OR LOCATION AND CITY AND ZIP CODE)

126. SIGNATURE OF CORONER OR DEPUTY CORONER	127. DATE MM/DD/CCYY	128. TYPED NAME, TITLE OF CORONER OR DEPUTY CORONER
▶		

STATE	A	B	C	D	E	F	G	H	FAX AUTH. #	CENSUS TRACT

BOOK 1987 PAGE

CERTIFICATE OF DEATH
STATE OF CALIFORNIA

STATE FILE NUMBER — LOCAL REGISTRATION DISTRICT AND CERTIFICATE NUMBER: 38 002371

DECEDENT PERSONAL DATA

Field	Entry
1A. Name of Decedent—First	DEAN
1B. Middle	PAUL
1C. Last	MARTIN, Jr.
2A. Date of Death (Month, Day, Year)	MARCH 21, 1987
2B. Hour	1351
3. Sex	MALE
4. Race/Ethnicity	Caucasian
5. Spanish/Hispanic	NO X
6. Date of Birth	November 17,1951
7. Age	35 YEARS
If under 1 year: Months / Days	
If under 24 hours: Hours / Minutes	
8. Birthplace of Decedent (State or Foreign Country)	Los Angeles,Calif.
9. Name and Birthplace of Father	Dean Paul Martin Sr. - Ohio
10. Birth Name and Birthplace of Mother	Jeanne Bieggar - Florida
11A. Citizen of What Country	U.S.A.
11B. If Deceased Was Ever in Military Give Dates of Service	19 N/A TO 19 N/A
12. Social Security Number	545-76-3469
13. Marital Status	Divorced
14. Name of Surviving Spouse (If wife, enter birth name)	- - -
15. Primary Occupation	Actor
16. Number of Years This Occupation	Ten
17. Employer (If self-employed, so state)	Freelance
18. Kind of Industry or Business	Entertainment

USUAL RESIDENCE

Field	Entry
19A. Usual Residence—Street Address (Street and Number or Location)	10634 Holman
19B.	
19C. City or Town	Los Angeles
19D. County	Los Angeles
19E. State	California
20. Name and Address of Informant—Relationship	Jack Bieggar - Uncle 2324 Alta Drive Las Vegas, Nevada 89102

PLACE OF DEATH

Field	Entry
21A. Place of Death	MOUNTAINS
21B. County	RIVERSIDE
21C. Street Address (Street and Number or Location)	WOOD CANYON/SAN BERNARDINO MTNS
21D. City or Town	BANNING

CAUSE OF DEATH

22. Death was caused by: (Enter only one cause per line for A, B, and C)

	Cause	Approximate Interval Between Onset and Death
Immediate Cause (A)	MULTIPLE TRAUMATIC INJURIES	MINS
Due to, or as a consequence of (B)	BLUNT FORCE TRAUMA	MINS
Due to, or as a consequence of (C)		

Conditions, if any, which gave rise to the immediate cause, stating the underlying cause last.

Field	Entry
24. Was Death Reported to Coroner?	YES 60568
25. Was Biopsy Performed?	NO
26. Was Autopsy Performed?	YES
23. Other Significant Conditions—Contributing to Death but Not Related to Cause Given in 22A	NONE
27. Was Operation Performed for Any Condition in Items 22 or 23? Type of Operation / Date	NO

PHYSICIAN'S CERTIFICATION

Field	Entry
28A. I certify that death occurred at the hour, date and place stated from the causes stated. I Attended Decedent Since (Enter Mo. Da. Yr.) / I Last Saw Decedent Alive (Enter Mo. Da. Yr.)	
28B. Physician—Signature and Degree or Title	
28C. Date Signed	
28D. Physician's License Number	
28E. Type Physician's Name and Address	

INJURY INFORMATION

Field	Entry
29. Specify Accident, Suicide, etc.	ACCIDENT
30. Place of Injury	MOUNTAIN
31. Injury at Work	YES
32A. Date of Injury—Month, Day, Year	MARCH 21, 1987
32B. Hour	1351
33. Location (Street and Number or Location and City or Town)	WOOD CANYON, SAN BERNARDINO MOUNTAINS BANNING
34. Describe How Injury Occurred (Events which resulted in injury)	PILOT OF MILITARY JET THAT CRASHED INTO MOUNTAIN

CORONER'S USE ONLY

Field	Entry
35A. I certify that death occurred at the hour, date and place stated from the causes stated. As required by law I have held an (inquest-investigation)	
35B. Coroner—Signature and Degree or Title	R.L. CARRILLO CORONER BY: [signature] DEPUTY
35C. Date Signed	3-28-87

Field	Entry
36. Disposition	Burial
37. Date—Month, Day, Year	April 17,1987
38. Name and Address of Cemetery or Crematory	Los Angeles National Cemetery 950 South Sepulveda - Los Angeles,Ca.
39. Embalmer's License Number and Signature	Not Embalmed
40A. Name of Funeral Director (or Person Acting as Such)	Pierce Brothers Westwood Village
40B. License No.	F-951
41. Local Registrar—Signature	[signature]
42. Date Accepted by Local Registrar	April 16,1987

STATE REGISTRAR

A.	B.	C.	D.	E.	F.

VS-11 (1-85)

STATE OF CALIFORNIA

CERTIFICATION OF VITAL RECORD

COUNTY OF LOS ANGELES • REGISTRAR-RECORDER/COUNTY CLERK

CERTIFICATE OF DEATH 3 2000 19 028255

STATE OF CALIFORNIA
USE BLACK INK ONLY/NO ERASURES, WHITEOUTS OR ALTERATIONS
VS-11 (REV. 1/00)

STATE FILE NUMBER — LOCAL REGISTRATION NUMBER

DECEDENT PERSONAL DATA	1. Name of decedent—First (Given)	Walter
	2. Middle	-
	3. Last (Family)	Matthau
	4. Date of birth MM/DD/CCYY	10/01/1920
	5. Age yrs.	79
	6. Sex	M
	7. Date of death MM/DD/CCYY	07/01/2000
	8. Hour	0142
	9. State of birth	NY
	10. Social security no.	065-03-9840
	11. Military service	[x] Yes [ ] No [ ] Unk
	12. Marital status	Married
	13. Education—years completed	16
	14. Race	White
	15. Hispanic—specify	[ ] Yes [x] No
	16. Usual employer	Self-Employed
	17. Occupation	Actor
	18. Kind of business	Entertainment
	19. Years in occupation	63
USUAL RESIDENCE	20. Residence—(street and number or location)	278 Toyopa Dr.
	21. City	Pacific Palisades
	22. County	Los Angeles
	23. Zip code	90272
	24. Yrs in county	40
	25. State or foreign country	California
INFORMANT	26. Name, relationship	Carol Matthau - Wife
	27. Mailing address	278 Toyopa Dr., Pacific Palisades, CA 90272
SPOUSE AND PARENT INFORMATION	28. Name of surviving spouse—First	Carol
	29. Middle	Grace
	30. Last (maiden name)	Marcus
	31. Name of father—First	Milton
	32. Middle	-
	33. Last	Matthow
	34. Birth state	Russia
	35. Name of mother—First	Rose
	36. Middle	-
	37. Last (maiden)	Baraltsky
	38. Birth state	Lithuania
DISPOSITION(S)	39. Date MM/DD/CCYY	07/02/2000
	40. Place of final disposition	Pierce Brothers Westwood Village Memorial Park, 1218 Glendon Av., Los Angeles, CA 90024
FUNERAL DIRECTOR AND LOCAL REGISTRAR	41. Type of disposition(s)	BU
	42. Signature of embalmer	Not Embalmed
	43. License no.	-
	44. Name of funeral director	Pierce Brothers Westwood Village Mort.
	45. License no.	FD-951
	46. Signature of local registrar	[signature]
	47. Date MM/DD/CCYY	07/02/2000
PLACE OF DEATH	101. Place of death	St. John's Hospital
	102. If hospital, specify one	[ ] IP [x] ER/OP [ ] DOA
	103. Facility other than hospital	[ ] Conv. Hosp. [ ] Res. Care [ ] Other
	104. County	Los Angeles
	105. Street address	1328 22nd St.
	106. City	Santa Monica
CAUSE OF DEATH	107. Immediate cause (A)	Cardiac Arrest — Minutes
	Due to (B)	Atherosclerotic Heart Disease — Years
	Due to (C)	
	Due to (D)	
	108. Death reported to coroner	[ ] Yes [x] No
	109. Biopsy performed	[ ] Yes [x] No
	110. Autopsy performed	[ ] Yes [x] No
	111. Used in determining cause	[ ] Yes [ ] No
	112. Other significant conditions contributing to death but not related to cause given in 107	End Stage Renal Disease, Atrial Fibrillation
	113. Was operation performed for any condition in item 107 or 112?	No
PHYSICIAN'S CERTIFICATION	114. Decedent attended since MM/DD/CCYY	12/09/1996
	Decedent last seen alive MM/DD/CCYY	06/25/2000
	115. Signature and title of certifier	Neil Parker, MD [signature]
	116. License no.	G04294
	117. Date MM/DD/CCYY	07/01/2000
	118. Type attending physician's name, mailing address, zip	Neil Parker, M.D., 200 UCLA Medical Plaza, Los Angeles, CA 90095
CORONER'S USE ONLY	119. Manner of death	[ ] Natural [ ] Suicide [ ] Homicide [ ] Accident [ ] Pending investigation [ ] Could not be determined
	120. Injury at work	[ ] Yes [ ] No
	121. Injury date MM/DD/CCYY	
	122. Hour	
	123. Place of injury	
	124. Describe how injury occurred	
	125. Location	
	126. Signature of coroner or deputy coroner	
	127. Date MM/DD/CCYY	
	128. Typed name, title of coroner or deputy coroner	

STATE A B C D E F G H FAX AUTH. # CENSUS TRACT

This is to certify that this document is a true copy of the official record filed with the Registrar-Recorder/County Clerk.

Conny B. McCormack

CONNY B. McCORMACK
Registrar-Recorder/County Clerk

NOV 29 2000

19-135760

This copy not valid unless prepared on engraved border displaying the Seal and Signature of the Registrar-Recorder/County Clerk.

ANY ALTERATION OR ERASURE VOIDS THIS CERTIFICATE

STATE OF CALIFORNIA

CERTIFICATION OF VITAL RECORD

COUNTY OF SAN DIEGO

GREGORY J. SMITH

ASSESSOR/RECORDER/COUNTY CLERK

CERTIFICATE OF DEATH 3 199937 011806

STATE OF CALIFORNIA

USE BLACK INK ONLY/NO ERASURES, WHITEOUTS OR ALTERATIONS

VS-11 (REV. 7/97)

STATE FILE NUMBER — LOCAL REGISTRATION NUMBER

0585

DECEDENT PERSONAL DATA

1. NAME OF DECEDENT—FIRST (GIVEN): Victor
2. MIDDLE: John Joseph
3. LAST (FAMILY): Mature
4. DATE OF BIRTH MM/DD/CCYY: 01/29/1913
5. AGE YRS.: 86 — IF UNDER 1 YEAR: MONTHS, DAYS — IF UNDER 24 HOURS: HOURS, MINUTES
6. SEX: M
7. DATE OF DEATH MM/DD/CCYY: 08/04/1999
8. HOUR: 2145
9. STATE OF BIRTH: KY
10. SOCIAL SECURITY NO.: 570-18-0630
11. MILITARY SERVICE: [X] YES [ ] NO [ ] UNK
12. MARITAL STATUS: Married
13. EDUCATION—YEARS COMPLETED: 14
14. RACE: White
15. HISPANIC—SPECIFY: [ ] YES [X] NO
16. USUAL EMPLOYER: 20th Century Fox
17. OCCUPATION: Actor
18. KIND OF BUSINESS: Entertainment
19. YEARS IN OCCUPATION: 50

USUAL RESIDENCE

20. RESIDENCE—(STREET AND NUMBER OR LOCATION): 1001 La Pluma Court
21. CITY: San Marcos
22. COUNTY: San Diego
23. ZIP CODE: 92069
24. YRS IN COUNTY: 46
25. STATE OR FOREIGN COUNTRY: CA

INFORMANT

26. NAME, RELATIONSHIP: Loretta G Mature - WIFE
27. MAILING ADDRESS (STREET AND NUMBER OR RURAL ROUTE NUMBER, CITY OR TOWN, STATE, ZIP): P.O.Box 706 Rancho Santa Fe CA 92067

SPOUSE AND PARENT INFORMATION

28. NAME OF SURVIVING SPOUSE—FIRST: Loretta
29. MIDDLE: G
30. LAST (MAIDEN NAME): Sebena
31. NAME OF FATHER—FIRST: Marcel
32. MIDDLE: -
33. LAST: Mature
34. BIRTH STATE: AUSTRIA
35. NAME OF MOTHER—FIRST: UNK
36. MIDDLE: UNK
37. LAST (MAIDEN): UNK
38. BIRTH STATE: IN

DISPOSITION(S)

39. DATE MM/DD/CCYY: 08/09/1999
40. PLACE OF FINAL DISPOSITION: St Michael's Cemetery, Louisville KY

FUNERAL DIRECTOR AND LOCAL REGISTRAR

41. TYPE OF DISPOSITION(S): TR/BU
42. SIGNATURE OF EMBALMER: [signature]
43. LICENSE NO.: 7010
44. NAME OF FUNERAL DIRECTOR: Encinitas Mortuary
45. LICENSE NO: FD857
46. SIGNATURE OF LOCAL REGISTRAR: [signature] MA
47. DATE MM/DD/CCYY: 08/06/1999

PLACE OF DEATH

101. PLACE OF DEATH: Own Residence
102. IF HOSPITAL, SPECIFY ONE: [ ] IP [ ] ER/OP [ ] DOA
103. FACILITY OTHER THAN HOSPITAL: [ ] CONV. HOSP [ ] RES. CARE [ ] OTHER
104. COUNTY: San Diego
105. STREET ADDRESS—(STREET AND NUMBER OR LOCATION): 1001 La Pluma Court
106. CITY: San Marcos

CAUSE OF DEATH

107. DEATH WAS CAUSED BY: (ENTER ONLY ONE CAUSE PER LINE FOR A, B, C, AND D)

IMMEDIATE CAUSE (A) Myelodysplasia — TIME INTERVAL BETWEEN ONSET AND DEATH: 5 yrs

DUE TO (B)

DUE TO (C)

DUE TO (D)

108. DEATH REPORTED TO CORONER: [X] YES [ ] NO — REFERRAL NUMBER: 8-108
109. BIOPSY PERFORMED: [X] YES [ ] NO
110. AUTOPSY PERFORMED: [ ] YES [X] NO
111. USED IN DETERMINING CAUSE: [ ] YES [ ] NO
112. OTHER SIGNIFICANT CONDITIONS CONTRIBUTING TO DEATH BUT NOT RELATED TO CAUSE GIVEN IN 107: Atrial Fibrillation
113. WAS OPERATION PERFORMED FOR ANY CONDITION IN ITEM 107 OR 112? IF YES, LIST TYPE OF OPERATION AND DATE.: No

PHYSICIAN'S CERTIFICATION

114. I CERTIFY THAT TO THE BEST OF MY KNOWLEDGE DEATH OCCURRED AT THE HOUR, DATE AND PLACE STATED FROM THE CAUSES STATED. DECEDENT ATTENDED SINCE MM/DD/CCYY: 06/30/1999 — DECEDENT LAST SEEN ALIVE MM/DD/CCYY: 07/18/1999
115. SIGNATURE AND TITLE OF CERTIFIER: [signature] MD
116. LICENSE NO.: G035680
117. DATE MM/DD/CCYY: 08/06/1999
118. TYPE ATTENDING PHYSICIAN'S NAME, MAILING ADDRESS, ZIP: Michael Kosty, M.D. 10666 N Torrey Pines Rd La Jolla CA 92037

CORONER'S USE ONLY

I CERTIFY THAT IN MY OPINION DEATH OCCURRED AT THE HOUR, DATE AND PLACE STATED FROM THE CAUSES STATED.

119. MANNER OF DEATH: [ ] NATURAL [ ] SUICIDE [ ] HOMICIDE [ ] ACCIDENT [ ] PENDING INVESTIGATION [ ] COULD NOT BE DETERMINED
120. INJURY AT WORK: [ ] YES [ ] NO
121. INJURY DATE MM/DD/CCYY
122. HOUR
123. PLACE OF INJURY
124. DESCRIBE HOW INJURY OCCURRED (EVENTS WHICH RESULTED IN INJURY)
125. LOCATION (STREET AND NUMBER OR LOCATION AND CITY, ZIP)
126. SIGNATURE OF CORONER OR DEPUTY CORONER
127. DATE MM/DD/CCYY
128. TYPED NAME, TITLE OF CORONER OR DEPUTY CORONER

STATE REGISTRAR

A B C D E F G H — FAX AUTH. # 9912066 — CENSUS TRACT

EL CAMINO MORTUARY

188867

THE NOBLEST MOTIVE IS THE PUBLIC GOOD — COUNTY OF SAN DIEGO — MDCCCLI

MIDWEST BANK NOTE COMPANY

ANY ALTERATION OR ERASURE VOIDS THIS CERTIFICATE

CERTIFICATION OF VITAL RECORD

COUNTY OF LOS ANGELES • REGISTRAR-RECORDER/COUNTY CLERK

CERTIFICATE OF DEATH

STATE OF CALIFORNIA—DEPARTMENT OF PUBLIC HEALTH

STATE FILE No. | REGISTRATION DISTRICT NO. 1901 | REGISTRAR'S NUMBER 17862

DECEDENT PERSONAL DATA

- 1a. NAME OF DECEASED—FIRST NAME: HATTIE
- 1b. MIDDLE NAME:
- 1c. LAST NAME: MC DANIEL
- 2a. DATE OF DEATH: Oct. 26, 1952
- 2b. HOUR: 12:30 P
- 3. SEX: Female
- 4. COLOR OR RACE: Negro
- 5. SPECIFY MARRIED, NEVER MARRIED, WIDOWED, DIVORCED: Divorced
- 6. DATE OF BIRTH: June 10, 1895
- 7. AGE (LAST BIRTHDAY): 57 YEARS
- 8a. USUAL OCCUPATION: Actress
- 8b. KIND OF BUSINESS OR INDUSTRY: Screen & Radio
- 9. BIRTHPLACE: Wichita, Kansas
- 10. CITIZEN OF WHAT COUNTRY: U.S.A.
- 11. NAME AND BIRTHPLACE OF FATHER: Henry McDaniel-Virginia
- 12. MAIDEN NAME AND BIRTHPLACE OF MOTHER: Susan Holbert-Tennessee
- 13. NAME OF PRESENT SPOUSE (IF MARRIED):
- 14. WAS DECEASED EVER IN U.S. ARMED FORCES? No
- 15. SOCIAL SECURITY NUMBER: 564-14-5218
- 16. INFORMANT: Samuel McDaniel

PLACE OF DEATH

- 17a. COUNTY: Los Angeles
- 17b. CITY OR TOWN: Los Angeles (X INSIDE CORPORATE LIMITS)
- 17c. LENGTH OF STAY IN THIS CITY OR TOWN: 21 yrs
- 17d. FULL NAME OF HOSPITAL OR INSTITUTION: Motion Picture Home & Hospital
- 17e. ADDRESS: 23430 Ventura Blvd

LAST USUAL RESIDENCE

- 18a. STATE: California
- 18b. COUNTY: Los Angeles
- 18c. CITY OR TOWN: Los Angeles (X INSIDE CORPORATE LIMITS)
- 18d. STREET OR RURAL ADDRESS: 3341 Country Club Drive

PHYSICIAN'S OR CORONER'S CERTIFICATION

- 19a. CORONER:
- 19b. PHYSICIAN: I hereby certify that death occurred at the hour, date and place stated above from the causes stated below, and that I attended the deceased from 8/7/52 to 10/26/52 and that I last saw the deceased alive on 10/26/52
- 19c. SIGNATURE: Arthur L. [illegible], M.D.
- 19d. ADDRESS: 23430 Ventura Blvd. Woodland Hills, Calif
- 19e. DATE SIGNED: 10/26/52

FUNERAL DIRECTOR AND REGISTRAR

- 20a. SPECIFY BURIAL, CREMATION OR REMOVAL: Burial
- 20b. DATE: 11-1-1952
- 20c. CEMETERY OR CREMATORY: Rosedale Cemetery
- 21. SIGNATURE OF EMBALMER: [illegible] LICENSE NUMBER 3316
- 22. FUNERAL DIRECTOR: Angelus Funeral Home, 1030 E. Jefferson Blvd
- 23. DATE RECEIVED BY LOCAL REGISTRAR: OCT 28 1952
- 24. SIGNATURE OF LOCAL REGISTRAR: [illegible]

MEDICAL AND HEALTH DATA

- CAUSE OF DEATH — 25. DISEASE OR CONDITION DIRECTLY LEADING TO DEATH (A): Adenocarcinoma of breast with metastasis — APPROXIMATE INTERVAL BETWEEN ONSET AND DEATH: 3 yrs
- ANTECEDENT CAUSES: DUE TO (B): — DUE TO (C):
- 26. OTHER SIGNIFICANT CONDITIONS:
- 27a. DATE OF OPERATION:
- 27b. MAJOR FINDINGS OF OPERATION:
- 28. AUTOPSY: YES / X NO
- DEATH DUE TO EXTERNAL VIOLENCE: 29a–29f (blank)

REV. 1-1-52 FORM BBS 11

This is to certify that this document is a true copy of the official record filed with the Registrar-Recorder/County Clerk.

OCT 4 1996

19-386817

Conny B. McCormack
CONNY B. McCORMACK
Registrar-Recorder/County Clerk

This copy not valid unless prepared on engraved border displaying the Seal and Signature of the Registrar-Recorder/County Clerk.

ANY ALTERATION OR ERASURE VOIDS THIS CERTIFICATE

CERTIFICATE OF DEATH

STATE OF CALIFORNIA
USE BLACK INK ONLY/NO ERASURES, WHITEOUTS OR ALTERATIONS
VS-11 (REV. 7/93)

STATE FILE NUMBER — LOCAL REGISTRATION NUMBER

DECEDENT PERSONAL DATA

1. NAME OF DECEDENT—FIRST (GIVEN)	2. MIDDLE	3. LAST (FAMILY)
AUDREY	COTTER	SIX

4. DATE OF BIRTH MM/DD/CCYY	5. AGE YRS.	IF UNDER 1 YEAR MONTHS / DAYS	IF UNDER 24 HOURS HOURS / MINUTES	6. SEX	7. DATE OF DEATH MM/DD/CCYY	8. HOUR
02/08/1926	69			F	02/03/1996	2050

9. STATE OF BIRTH	10. SOCIAL SECURITY NO.	11. MILITARY SERVICE	12. MARITAL STATUS	13. EDUCATION—YEARS COMPLETED
CHINA	119-18-7120	19 __ TO 19 __ ☐ NONE	WIDOWED	16

14. RACE	15. HISPANIC—SPECIFY	16. USUAL EMPLOYER
CAUCASIAN	☐ YES [X] NO	SELF

17. OCCUPATION	18. KIND OF BUSINESS	19. YEARS IN OCCUPATION
ACTRESS	TELEVISION	45

USUAL RESIDENCE

20. RESIDENCE—STREET AND NUMBER OR LOCATION: 350 TROUSDALE PLACE

21. CITY	22. COUNTY	23. ZIP CODE	24. YRS IN COUNTY	25. STATE OR FOREIGN COUNTRY
BEVERLY HILLS	LOS ANGELES	90210	38	CALIFORNIA

INFORMANT

26. NAME, RELATIONSHIP	27. MAILING ADDRESS (STREET AND NUMBER OR RURAL ROUTE NUMBER, CITY OR TOWN, STATE, ZIP)
WILLIAM C. ALLEN - EXECUTOR	4432 LIBBIT AVE.,ENCINO,CA. 91436

SPOUSE AND PARENT INFORMATION

28. NAME OF SURVIVING SPOUSE—FIRST	29. MIDDLE	30. LAST (MAIDEN NAME)	
-	-	-	
31. NAME OF FATHER—FIRST	**32. MIDDLE**	**33. LAST**	**34. BIRTH STATE**
FRANCIS	MEADOWS	COTTER	UNKNOWN
35. NAME OF MOTHER—FIRST	**36. MIDDLE**	**37. LAST (MAIDEN)**	**38. BIRTH STATE**
IDA	MILLER	TAYLOR	UNKNOWN

DISPOSITION(S)

39. DATE MM/DD/CCYY	40. PLACE OF FINAL DISPOSITION
02/07/1996	HOLY CROSS CEMETERY,5835 W. SLAUSON AVE.,CULVER CITY,CA. 90230

FUNERAL DIRECTOR AND LOCAL REGISTRAR

41. TYPE OF DISPOSITION(S)	42. SIGNATURE OF EMBALMER		43. LICENSE NO.
BU	▶ Kenneth Schenk		5799
44. NAME OF FUNERAL DIRECTOR	**45. LICENSE NO.**	**46. SIGNATURE OF LOCAL REGISTRAR**	**47. DATE MM/DD/CCYY**
CALLANAN MORTUARY	F-86	▶ Robert C. Hatz ES	02/07/1996

PLACE OF DEATH

101. PLACE OF DEATH	102. IF HOSPITAL, SPECIFY ONE:	103. FACILITY OTHER THAN HOSPITAL:	104. COUNTY
CEDARS SINAI MEDICAL CENTER	[X] IP ☐ ER/OP ☐ DOA	☐ CONV. HOSP. ☐ RES. ☐ OTHER	LOS ANGELES

105. STREET ADDRESS—STREET AND NUMBER OR LOCATION	106. CITY
8700 BEVERLY BLVD.	LOS ANGELES

CAUSE OF DEATH

107. DEATH WAS CAUSED BY: (ENTER ONLY ONE CAUSE PER LINE FOR A, B, C, AND D)

		TIME INTERVAL BETWEEN ONSET AND DEATH
IMMEDIATE CAUSE (A)	LUNG CARCINOMA	1 YEAR
DUE TO (B)		
DUE TO (C)		
DUE TO (D)		

108. DEATH REPORTED TO CORONER: ☐ YES [X] NO — REFERRAL NUMBER

109. BIOPSY PERFORMED: [X] YES ☐ NO

110. AUTOPSY PERFORMED: ☐ YES [X] NO

111. USED IN DETERMINING CAUSE: ☐ YES [X] NO

112. OTHER SIGNIFICANT CONDITIONS CONTRIBUTING TO DEATH BUT NOT RELATED TO CAUSE GIVEN IN 107

NONE

113. WAS OPERATION PERFORMED FOR ANY CONDITION IN ITEM 107 OR 112? IF YES, LIST TYPE OF OPERATION AND DATE.

LUNG BIOPSY 05/02/1995

PHYSICIAN'S CERTIFICATION

114. I CERTIFY THAT TO THE BEST OF MY KNOWLEDGE DEATH OCCURRED AT THE HOUR, DATE AND PLACE STATED FROM THE CAUSES STATED.

DECEDENT ATTENDED SINCE MM/DD/CCYY	DECEDENT LAST SEEN ALIVE MM/DD/CCYY	115. SIGNATURE AND TITLE OF CERTIFIER	116. LICENSE NO.	117. DATE MM/DD/CCYY
11/03/1986	02/02/1996	▶ Stephen Corday MD	G 31116	02/05/1996

118. TYPE ATTENDING PHYSICIAN'S NAME, MAILING ADDRESS + ZIP: STEPHEN CORDAY, M.D.,8635 W. THIRD ST.,#790,LOS ANGELES,CA. 90048

CORONER'S USE ONLY

24

1629

I CERTIFY THAT IN MY OPINION DEATH OCCURRED AT THE HOUR, DATE AND PLACE STATED FROM THE CAUSES STATED.

119. MANNER OF DEATH: ☐ NATURAL ☐ SUICIDE ☐ HOMICIDE ☐ ACCIDENT ☐ PENDING INVESTIGATION ☐ COULD NOT BE DETERMINED

120. INJURY AT WORK	121. INJURY DATE MM/DD/CCYY	122. HOUR	123. PLACE OF INJURY
☐ YES ☐ NO			

124. DESCRIBE HOW INJURY OCCURRED (EVENTS WHICH RESULTED IN INJURY)

125. LOCATION (STREET AND NUMBER OR LOCATION AND CITY AND ZIP CODE)

126. SIGNATURE OF CORONER OR DEPUTY CORONER	127. DATE MM/DD/CCYY	128. TYPED NAME, TITLE OF CORONER OR DEPUTY CORONER
▶		

STATE REGISTRAR

A	B	C	D	E	F	G	H	FAX AUTH. #	CENSUS TRACT

CERTIFICATION OF VITAL RECORD

COUNTY OF LOS ANGELES • REGISTRAR-RECORDER/COUNTY CLERK

CERTIFICATE OF DEATH

STATE OF CALIFORNIA—DEPARTMENT OF HEALTH
OFFICE OF THE STATE REGISTRAR OF VITAL STATISTICS

STATE FILE NUMBER

LOCAL REGISTRATION DISTRICT AND CERTIFICATE NUMBER: 0190-006196

DECEDENT PERSONAL DATA

Field	Entry
1a. Name of deceased—first name	Salvatore
1b. Middle name	
1c. Last name	Mineo
2a. Date of death—month, day, year	2-12-76
2b. Hour	2155 hrs.
3. Sex	Male
4. Color or race	Caucasian
5. Birthplace (state or foreign country)	New York
6. Date of birth	Jan. 10,1939
7. Age (last birthday)	37 years
8. Name and birthplace of father	Salvatore Mineo, Sicily
9. Maiden name and birthplace of mother	Josephine Alvisi, Unknown.
10. Citizen of what country	U.S.A.
11. Social security number	134-36-4678
12. Married, never married, widowed, divorced (specify)	Never Married
13. Name of surviving spouse (if wife, enter maiden name)	None
14. Last occupation	Actor
15. Number of years in this occupation	20
16. Name of last employing company or firm (if self employed so state)	Self Employed
17. Kind of industry or business	Movies, T.V. Theatre

PLACE OF DEATH

Field	Entry
18a. Place of death—name of hospital or other in-patient facility	
18b. Street address—(street and number, or location)	rear of 8567 Holloway Drive
18c. Inside city corporate limits (specify yes or no)	yes
18d. City or town	West Los Angeles
18e. County	Los Angeles
18f. Length of stay in county of death	20 years
18g. Length of stay in California	20 years

USUAL RESIDENCE (if death occurred in institution, enter residence before admission)

Field	Entry
19a. Usual residence—street address (street and number or location)	8569 Holloway Drive
19b. Inside city corporate limits (specify yes or no)	Yes
19c. City or town	West Los Angeles
19d. County	Los Angeles
19e. State	California
20. Name and mailing address of informant	Mrs. Josephine Mineo, 83 West Street, Harrison, New York 10528

PHYSICIAN'S OR CORONER'S CERTIFICATION

Field	Entry
21a. Coroner: I hereby certify that death occurred at the hour, date and place stated above from the causes stated below and that I have held an	Investigation (investigation or inquest)
21b. Physician: I hereby certify that death occurred at the hour, date, and place stated above from the causes stated below and that I attended the deceased from / to / and last saw the deceased alive on	
21c. Physician or coroner—signature and degree or title	Thomas T. Noguchi, M.D., Coroner; Roy D. Smith, Deputy
21d. Date signed	2-13-76
21e. Address	1104 N. Mission Rd. Los Angeles, Calif. 90033
21f. Physician's California license number	

FUNERAL DIRECTOR AND LOCAL REGISTRAR

Field	Entry
22a. Specify burial, entombment or cremation	Burial
22b. Date	Feb.17,1976
23. Name of cemetery or crematory	Gate of Heaven, Mamaroneck N.Y.
24. Embalmer—signature (if body embalmed) license number	J. C. Mitten 4550
25. Name of funeral director (or person acting as such)	O'Neill Funeral Home
26. If not certified by coroner was this death reported to coroner? (specify yes or no)	
27. Local registrar—signature	[signature]
28. Date received for registration by local registrar	FEB 14 1976

MEDICAL AND HEALTH DATA — CAUSE OF DEATH

29. Part I. Death was caused by: (enter only one cause per line for A, B, and C)

	Cause	Approximate interval between onset and death
Immediate cause (A)	MASSIVE HEMORRHAGE.	
Due to, or as a consequence of (B)	STAB WOUND TO CHEST, PERFORATING THE HEART.	
Due to, or as a consequence of (C)		

Conditions, if any, which gave rise to the immediate cause (A), stating the underlying cause last.

Field	Entry
30. Part II: Other significant conditions—contributing to death but not related to the immediate cause given in Part I	
31. Was operation or biopsy performed for any condition in items 29 or 30? (specify type of operation and date of biopsy)	No
32a. Autopsy (specify yes or no)	Yes
32b. If yes were findings considered in determining cause of death? (specify yes or no)	Yes

INJURY INFORMATION

Field	Entry
33. Specify accident, suicide or homicide	Homicide
34. Place of injury (specify home, farm, factory, street, office building, etc.)	alley
35. Injury at work (specify yes or no)	No
36a. Date of injury—month, day, year	2-12-76
36b. Hour	2130 hrs.
37a. Place of injury (street and number or location and city or town)	rear of 8567 Holloway Drive/West Los Angeles
37b. Distance from place of injury to usual residence (in miles)	0 miles
38. Were laboratory tests done for drugs or toxic chemicals? (specify yes or no)	Yes
39. Were laboratory tests done for alcohol? (specify yes or no)	Yes
40. Describe how injury occurred (enter sequence of events which resulted in injury; nature of injury should be entered in item 29)	As above, by unknown person(s).

5

STATE REGISTRAR

A.	B.	C.	D.	E.	F.
					01-9-4-

This is to certify that this document is a true copy of the official record filed with the Registrar-Recorder/County Clerk.

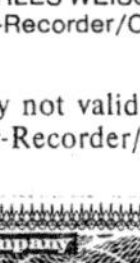

CHARLES WEISSBURD
Registrar-Recorder/County Clerk

FEB 12 1992
19-312722

This copy not valid unless prepared on engraved border displaying the Seal and Signature of the Registrar-Recorder/County Clerk.

ANY ALTERATION OR ERASURE VOIDS THIS CERTIFICATE

STATE OF CALIFORNIA
CERTIFICATION OF VITAL RECORD

SANTA BARBARA COUNTY
HEALTH CARE SERVICES

CERTIFICATE OF DEATH
STATE OF CALIFORNIA
USE BLACK INK ONLY/NO ERASURES, WHITEOUTS OR ALTERATIONS
VS-11 (REV. 11/96)

STATE FILE NUMBER

3-97-42-001363
LOCAL REGISTRATION NUMBER

DECEDENT PERSONAL DATA

1. NAME OF DECEDENT—FIRST (GIVEN): ROBERT
2. MIDDLE: CHARLES
3. LAST (FAMILY): MITCHUM
4. DATE OF BIRTH MM/DD/CCYY: 08/06/1917
5. AGE YRS: 79
6. SEX: M
7. DATE OF DEATH MM/DD/CCYY: 07/01/1997
8. HOUR: FND 0700
9. STATE OF BIRTH: CT
10. SOCIAL SECURITY NO.: 555-26-5421
11. MILITARY SERVICE: [X] YES [ ] NO
12. MARITAL STATUS: MARRIED
13. EDUCATION—YEARS COMPLETED: UNKNOWN
14. RACE: WHITE
15. HISPANIC—SPECIFY: [ ] YES [X] NO
16. USUAL EMPLOYER: SELF
17. OCCUPATION: ACTOR
18. KIND OF BUSINESS: MOTION PICTURE/TELEVISION
19. YEARS IN OCCUPATION: 40

USUAL RESIDENCE

20. RESIDENCE—STREET AND NUMBER OR LOCATION: 860 SAN YSIDRO ROAD
21. CITY: MONTECITO
22. COUNTY: SANTA BARBARA
23. ZIP CODE: 993108
24. YRS IN COUNTY: 20
25. STATE OR FOREIGN COUNTRY: CA

INFORMANT

26. NAME, RELATIONSHIP: NEPTUNE SOCIETY FUNERAL HOME
27. MAILING ADDRESS: 16 W. MISSION ST., SANTA BARBARA CA 93101

SPOUSE AND PARENT INFORMATION

28. NAME OF SURVIVING SPOUSE—FIRST: DOROTHY
29. MIDDLE: -
30. LAST (MAIDEN NAME): SPENCE

1 of 2

31. NAME OF FATHER—FIRST: JAMES
32. MIDDLE: THOMAS
33. LAST: MITCHUM
34. BIRTH STATE: SC
35. NAME OF MOTHER—FIRST: ANNE
36. MIDDLE: -
37. LAST (MAIDEN): GUNDERSON
38. BIRTH STATE: NORWAY

DISPOSITION(S)

39. DATE MM/DD/CCYY: 07/09/1997
40. PLACE OF FINAL DISPOSITION: BURIAL AT SEA- 3 MI OFF SANTA BARBARA CHANNEL-SANTA BARBARA CA

FUNERAL DIRECTOR AND LOCAL REGISTRAR

41. TYPE OF DISPOSITION(S): Burial at sea.
42. SIGNATURE OF EMBALMER: NOT EMBALMED
43. LICENSE NO.: -
44. NAME OF FUNERAL DIRECTOR: NEPTUNE SOCIETY OF S.B.
45. LICENSE NO.: FD 1309
46. SIGNATURE OF LOCAL REGISTRAR: [signature]
47. DATE MM/DD/CCYY: 07/02/1997

PLACE OF DEATH

101. PLACE OF DEATH: RESIDENCE
102. IF HOSPITAL, SPECIFY ONE: [ ] IP [ ] ER/OP [ ] DOA
103. FACILITY OTHER THAN HOSPITAL: [ ] CONV. HOSP. [X] RES. CARE [ ] OTHER
104. COUNTY: SANTA BARBARA
105. STREET ADDRESS—STREET AND NUMBER OR LOCATION: 860 SAN YSIDRO ROAD
106. CITY: MONTECITO

CAUSE OF DEATH

107. DEATH WAS CAUSED BY: (ENTER ONLY ONE CAUSE PER LINE FOR A, B, C, AND D)

	Cause	Time interval between onset and death
IMMEDIATE CAUSE (A)	RESPIRATORY ARREST	MINS
DUE TO (B)	EMPHYSEMA	YRS
DUE TO (C)	-	
DUE TO (D)	-	

108. DEATH REPORTED TO CORONER: [ ] YES [X] NO — REFERRAL NUMBER
109. BIOPSY PERFORMED: [X] YES [ ] NO
110. AUTOPSY PERFORMED: [ ] YES [X] NO
111. USED IN DETERMINING CAUSE: [ ] YES [X] NO
112. OTHER SIGNIFICANT CONDITIONS CONTRIBUTING TO DEATH BUT NOT RELATED TO CAUSE GIVEN IN 107: LUNG CANCER
113. WAS OPERATION PERFORMED FOR ANY CONDITION IN ITEM 107 OR 112? IF YES, LIST TYPE OF OPERATION AND DATE: NO

PHYSICIAN'S CERTIFICATION

114. I CERTIFY THAT TO THE BEST OF MY KNOWLEDGE DEATH OCCURRED AT THE HOUR, DATE AND PLACE STATED FROM THE CAUSES STATED. DECEDENT ATTENDED SINCE MM/DD/CCYY: 06/03/1997 — DECEDENT LAST SEEN ALIVE MM/DD/CCYY: 06/30/1997
115. SIGNATURE AND TITLE OF CERTIFIER: Thomas H. Weisenburger
116. LICENSE NO.: A 023859
117. DATE MM/DD/CCYY: 07/02/1997
118. TYPE ATTENDING PHYSICIAN'S NAME, MAILING ADDRESS, ZIP: THOMAS H. WEISENBURGER, MD. 300 W.PUEBLO ST.SANTA BARBARA CA 93105

CORONER'S USE ONLY

I CERTIFY THAT IN MY OPINION DEATH OCCURRED AT THE HOUR, DATE AND PLACE STATED FROM THE CAUSES STATED.
119. MANNER OF DEATH: [ ] NATURAL [ ] SUICIDE [ ] HOMICIDE [ ] ACCIDENT [ ] PENDING INVESTIGATION [ ] COULD NOT BE DETERMINED
120. INJURY AT WORK: [ ] YES [ ] NO
121. INJURY DATE MM/DD/CCYY
122. HOUR
123. PLACE OF INJURY
124. DESCRIBE HOW INJURY OCCURRED (EVENTS WHICH RESULTED IN INJURY)
125. LOCATION (STREET AND NUMBER OR LOCATION AND CITY, ZIP)
126. SIGNATURE OF CORONER OR DEPUTY CORONER
127. DATE MM/DD/CCYY
128. TYPED NAME, TITLE OF CORONER OR DEPUTY CORONER

STATE REGISTRAR

A	B	C	D	E	F	G	H	FAX AUTH. #	CENSUS TRACT

42536

CERTIFIED COPY OF VITAL RECORDS

STATE OF CALIFORNIA
COUNTY OF SANTA BARBARA } SS DATE ISSUED 09/19/1997

This is a true and exact reproduction of the document officially registered and placed on file in the office of the Registrar, Health Care Services, County of Santa Barbara, California.

HEALTH OFFICER
HEALTH CARE SERVICES
COUNTY OF SANTA BARBARA, CALIFORNIA

This copy not valid unless prepared on engraved border displaying seal and signature of Registrar.

MIDWEST BANK NOTE COMPANY
ANY ALTERATION OR ERASURE VOIDS THIS CERTIFICATE

CERTIFICATION OF VITAL RECORD

COUNTY OF LOS ANGELES • REGISTRAR-RECORDER/COUNTY CLERK

State File Number 62-096657 CERTIFICATE OF DEATH STATE OF CALIFORNIA—DEPARTMENT OF PUBLIC HEALTH Local Registration District and Certificate Number 7053 17716

FINAL 8/27/62 MARILYN MONROE. NOGUCHI M.D. 81128

DECEDENT PERSONAL DATA

1a. Name of Deceased—First Name: Marilyn 1b. Middle Name: 1c. Last Name: Monroe 2a. Date of Death: August 5, 1962 2b. Hour: 3:40 A.

3. Sex: Female 4. Color or Race: Cauc. 5. Birthplace: Los Angeles, Calif. 6. Date of Birth: June 1, 1926 7. Age: 36 years

8. Name and Birthplace of Father: unk unk. 9. Maiden Name and Birthplace of Mother: Gladys Pearl Baker - Mexico 10. Citizen of What Country: United States 11. Social Security Number: 563-32-0764

12. Last Occupation: Actress 13. Number of years in this occupation: 20 14. Name of Last Employing Company or Firm: 20th Century-fox 15. Kind of Industry or Business: Motion Pictures

16. If Deceased Was Ever in U.S. Armed Forces: none 17. Specify Married, Never Married, Widowed, Divorced: Divorced 18a. Name of Present Spouse: 18b. Present or Last Occupation of Spouse:

PLACE OF DEATH

19a. Place of Death—Name of Hospital: 19b. Street Address: 12305 -5th Helena Drive

19c. City or Town: Los Angeles 19d. County: Los Angeles 19e. Length of Stay in County of Death: 36 years 19f. Length of Stay in California: 36 years

LAST USUAL RESIDENCE

20a. Last Usual Residence—Street Address: 12305 -5th Helena Drive 21a. Name of Informant: Mrs. Inez C. Melson

20c. City or Town: Los Angeles 20d. County: Los Angeles 20e. State: Calif. 21b. Address of Informant: 9110 Sunset Blvd.

PHYSICIAN'S OR CORONER'S CERTIFICATION

22a. Physician: 22c. Physician or Coroner Signature: Theo J. Curphey M.D., Coroner By Lionel Grandison Deputy

22b. Coroner: autopsy 22d. Address: HALL OF JUSTICE LOS ANGELES 22e. Date Signed: 8-28-62

FUNERAL DIRECTOR AND LOCAL REGISTRAR

23. Specify Burial, Entombment or Cremation: Entombment 24. Date: Aug. 8, 1962 25. Name of Cemetery or Crematory: Westwood Memorial Park 26. Embalmer—Signature: Charles Maylord

27. Name of Funeral Director: Westwood Village Mortuary 28. Date Accepted for Registration by Local Registrar: SEP 12 1962 29. Local Registrar—Signature: George M. Uhl, M.D.

CAUSE OF DEATH

30. Cause of Death Part I. Death was caused by: Immediate Cause (a) ACUTE BARBITURATE POISONING

Due to (b) INGESTION OF OVERDOSE

Due to (c)

Part II. Other significant conditions contributing to death but not related to the terminal disease condition given in Part I (a)

OPERATION AND AUTOPSY

31. Operation—Check One 32. Date of Operation 33. Autopsy—Check One

INJURY INFORMATION

34a. Specify Accident, Suicide or Homicide: Probable Suicide 34b. Describe How Injury Occurred: As Above

35a. Time of Injury: Prior to 3:40 A. 8-5-62

35b. Injury Occurred 35c. Place of Injury: Home 35d. City, Town or Location: Los Angeles County: L.A. State: Calif.

This is to certify that this document is a true copy of the official record filed with the Registrar-Recorder/County Clerk.

Charles Weissburd

CHARLES WEISSBURD
Registrar-Recorder/County Clerk

AUG 08 1991

19-132088

This copy not valid unless prepared on engraved border displaying the Seal and Signature of the Registrar-Recorder/County Clerk.

American Bank Note Company

ANY ALTERATION OR ERASURE VOIDS THIS CERTIFICATE

STATE OF CALIFORNIA
CERTIFICATION OF VITAL RECORD

COUNTY OF LOS ANGELES
DEPARTMENT OF HEALTH SERVICES

CERTIFICATE OF DEATH
STATE OF CALIFORNIA
USE BLACK INK ONLY/NO ERASURES, WHITEOUTS OR ALTERATIONS
VS-11 (REV. 7/97)

STATE FILE NUMBER
3 1999 19 054785
LOCAL REGISTRATION NUMBER

DECEDENT PERSONAL DATA
1. NAME OF DECEDENT—FIRST (GIVEN): JACK
2. MIDDLE: CARLSON
3. LAST (FAMILY): MOORE
4. DATE OF BIRTH MM/DD/CCYY: 09/14/1914
5. AGE YRS.: 85
IF UNDER 1 YEAR: MONTHS | DAYS
IF UNDER 24 HOURS: HOURS | MINUTES
6. SEX: MALE
7. DATE OF DEATH MM/DD/CCYY: 12/28/1999
8. HOUR: 0919
9. STATE OF BIRTH: ILLINOIS
10. SOCIAL SECURITY NO.: 114-12-2692
11. MILITARY SERVICE: [X] YES [ ] NO [ ] UNK
12. MARITAL STATUS: MARRIED
13. EDUCATION—YEARS COMPLETED: 11
14. RACE: WHITE
15. HISPANIC—SPECIFY: [ ] YES [X] NO
16. USUAL EMPLOYER: SELF EMPLOYED
17. OCCUPATION: ACTOR
18. KIND OF BUSINESS: ENTERTAINMENT
19. YEARS IN OCCUPATION: 47

USUAL RESIDENCE
20. RESIDENCE—(STREET AND NUMBER OR LOCATION): 4720 PARK OLIVO
21. CITY: CALABASAS
22. COUNTY: LOS ANGELES
23. ZIP CODE: 91302
24. YRS IN COUNTY: 61
25. STATE OR FOREIGN COUNTRY: CALIFORNIA

INFORMANT
26. NAME, RELATIONSHIP: DAWN A. MOORE - DAUGHTER
27. MAILING ADDRESS (STREET AND NUMBER OR RURAL ROUTE NUMBER, CITY OR TOWN, STATE, ZIP): 3158 OAKSHIRE DR. LOS ANGELES,CA. 90068

SPOUSE AND PARENT INFORMATION
28. NAME OF SURVIVING SPOUSE—FIRST: CLARITA
29. MIDDLE: -
30. LAST (MAIDEN NAME): PETRONE
31. NAME OF FATHER—FIRST: SPRAGUE
32. MIDDLE: -
33. LAST: MOORE
34. BIRTH STATE: NY
35. NAME OF MOTHER—FIRST: THERESA
36. MIDDLE: V.
37. LAST (MAIDEN): FISHER
38. BIRTH STATE: IL

DISPOSITION(S)
39. DATE MM/DD/CCYY: 12/31/1999
40. PLACE OF FINAL DISPOSITION: FOREST LAWN MEM. PARK 1712 S. GLENDALE AVE., GLENDALE,CA. 91205

FUNERAL DIRECTOR AND LOCAL REGISTRAR
41. TYPE OF DISPOSITION(S): BURIAL
42. SIGNATURE OF EMBALMER: ▶ [signature]
43. LICENSE NO.: 5641
44. NAME OF FUNERAL DIRECTOR: FOREST LAWN MTY GLENDALE
45. LICENSE NO.: FD-656
46. SIGNATURE OF LOCAL REGISTRAR: ▶ [signature]
47. DATE MM/DD/CCYY: 12/30/1999

PLACE OF DEATH
101. PLACE OF DEATH: WEST HILLS REGIONAL MED.CTR.
102. IF HOSPITAL, SPECIFY ONE: [ ] IP [X] ER/OP [ ] DOA
103. FACILITY OTHER THAN HOSPITAL: [ ] CONV. HOSP. [ ] RES. CARE [ ] OTHER
104. COUNTY: LOS ANGELES
105. STREET ADDRESS—(STREET AND NUMBER OR LOCATION): 7300 MEDICAL CENTER DRIVE
106. CITY: CHATSWORTH

CAUSE OF DEATH
107. DEATH WAS CAUSED BY: (ENTER ONLY ONE CAUSE PER LINE FOR A, B, C, AND D) — TIME INTERVAL BETWEEN ONSET AND DEATH
IMMEDIATE CAUSE (A) MYOCARDIAL INFARCTION — UNKNOWN
DUE TO (B) ARTERIOSCLEROTIC CARDIOVASCULAR DISEASE — YEARS
DUE TO (C)
DUE TO (D)
108. DEATH REPORTED TO CORONER: [X] YES [ ] NO — REFERRAL NUMBER 99-09036
109. BIOPSY PERFORMED: [ ] YES [X] NO
110. AUTOPSY PERFORMED: [ ] YES [X] NO
111. USED IN DETERMINING CAUSE: [ ] YES [ ] NO
112. OTHER SIGNIFICANT CONDITIONS CONTRIBUTING TO DEATH BUT NOT RELATED TO CAUSE GIVEN IN 107: NONE
113. WAS OPERATION PERFORMED FOR ANY CONDITION IN ITEM 107 OR 112? IF YES, LIST TYPE OF OPERATION AND DATE.: NO

PHYSICIAN'S CERTIFICATION
114. I CERTIFY THAT TO THE BEST OF MY KNOWLEDGE DEATH OCCURRED AT THE HOUR, DATE AND PLACE STATED FROM THE CAUSES STATED. DECEDENT ATTENDED SINCE MM/DD/CCYY | DECEDENT LAST SEEN ALIVE MM/DD/CCYY
115. SIGNATURE AND TITLE OF CERTIFIER ▶
116. LICENSE NO.
117. DATE MM/DD/CCYY
118. TYPE ATTENDING PHYSICIAN'S NAME, MAILING ADDRESS, ZIP

CORONER'S USE ONLY
25
I CERTIFY THAT IN MY OPINION DEATH OCCURRED AT THE HOUR, DATE AND PLACE STATED FROM THE CAUSES STATED.
119. MANNER OF DEATH: [X] NATURAL [ ] SUICIDE [ ] HOMICIDE [ ] ACCIDENT [ ] PENDING INVESTIGATION [ ] COULD NOT BE DETERMINED
120. INJURY AT WORK: [ ] YES [ ] NO
121. INJURY DATE MM/DD/CCYY
122. HOUR
123. PLACE OF INJURY
124. DESCRIBE HOW INJURY OCCURRED (EVENTS WHICH RESULTED IN INJURY)
125. LOCATION (STREET AND NUMBER OR LOCATION AND CITY, ZIP)
126. SIGNATURE OF CORONER OR DEPUTY CORONER: ▶ Mari Saiz
127. DATE MM/DD/CCYY: 12/30/1999
128. TYPED NAME, TITLE OF CORONER OR DEPUTY CORONER: Mario Saiz, Dep. Coroner

STATE REGISTRAR
A | B | C | D | E | F | G | H
FAX AUTH. #: 273/4627
CENSUS TRACT: 090312774

This is a true certified copy of the record filed in the County of Los Angeles Department of Health Services if it bears the Registrar's signature in purple ink.

DATE ISSUED FEB 23 2000

Director of Health Services and Registrar

This copy not valid unless prepared on engraved border displaying seal and signature of Registrar.

THE GREAT SEAL OF THE STATE OF CALIFORNIA — EUREKA

LOS ANGELES COUNTY — REGISTRAR OF VITAL STATISTICS — STATE OF CALIFORNIA

MIDWEST BANK NOTE COMPANY

ANY ALTERATION OR ERASURE VOIDS THIS CERTIFICATE

CERTIFICATION OF VITAL RECORD

COUNTY OF LOS ANGELES • REGISTRAR-RECORDER/COUNTY CLERK

CERTIFICATE OF DEATH
STATE OF CALIFORNIA

STATE FILE NUMBER — LOCAL REGISTRATION DISTRICT AND CERTIFICATE NUMBER: 0190-033704

DECEDENT PERSONAL DATA

1A. NAME OF DECEDENT—FIRST	1B. MIDDLE	1C. LAST	2A. DATE OF DEATH (MONTH, DAY, YEAR)	2B. HOUR
Vic		Morrow	JULY 23, 1982	0230

3. SEX	4. RACE	5. ETHNICITY	6. DATE OF BIRTH	7. AGE	IF UNDER 1 YEAR (MONTHS, DAYS)	IF UNDER 24 HOURS (HOURS, MINUTES)
Male	Cauc.		February 14, 1929	53 YEARS		

8. BIRTHPLACE OF DECEDENT (STATE OR FOREIGN COUNTRY)	9. NAME AND BIRTHPLACE OF FATHER	10. BIRTH NAME AND BIRTHPLACE OF MOTHER
New York	Harry Morrow, Russia	Jean Kress, Russia

11. CITIZEN OF WHAT COUNTRY	12. SOCIAL SECURITY NUMBER	13. MARITAL STATUS	14. NAME OF SURVIVING SPOUSE (IF WIFE, ENTER BIRTH NAME)
USA	113-20-0386	Divorced	

15. PRIMARY OCCUPATION	16. NUMBER OF YEARS THIS OCCUPATION	17. EMPLOYER (IF SELF-EMPLOYED, SO STATE)	18. KIND OF INDUSTRY OR BUSINESS
Actor	35	Self Employed	Entertainment

USUAL RESIDENCE

19A. USUAL RESIDENCE—STREET ADDRESS (STREET AND NUMBER OR LOCATION)	19B.	19C. CITY OR TOWN
3913 Ventura Canyon Ave.		Sherman Oaks

19D. COUNTY	19E. STATE	20. NAME AND ADDRESS OF INFORMANT—RELATIONSHIP
Los Angeles	California	Carrie Morrow daughter, 1850 Outpost Dr., Hollywood, California 90068

PLACE OF DEATH

21A. PLACE OF DEATH	21B. COUNTY
INDIAN DUNES PARK	LOS ANGELES

21C. STREET ADDRESS (STREET AND NUMBER OR LOCATION)	21D. CITY OR TOWN
HENRY MAYO DRIVE, CASTAIC	CASTAIC

CAUSE OF DEATH

22. DEATH WAS CAUSED BY: (ENTER ONLY ONE CAUSE PER LINE FOR A, B, AND C)
IMMEDIATE CAUSE
(A) ROTOR BLADE INJURY TO HEAD/NECK/SHOULDERS
CONDITIONS, IF ANY, WHICH GAVE RISE TO THE IMMEDIATE CAUSE, STATING THE UNDERLYING CAUSE LAST
DUE TO, OR AS A CONSEQUENCE OF (B)
DUE TO, OR AS A CONSEQUENCE OF (C)
APPROXIMATE INTERVAL BETWEEN ONSET AND DEATH

24. WAS DEATH REPORTED TO CORONER? 82-9217
25. WAS BIOPSY PERFORMED? NO
26. WAS AUTOPSY PERFORMED? YES

23. OTHER CONDITIONS CONTRIBUTING BUT NOT RELATED TO THE IMMEDIATE CAUSE OF DEATH
27. WAS OPERATION PERFORMED FOR ANY CONDITION IN ITEMS 22 OR 23? TYPE OF OPERATION — DATE: NO

PHYSICIAN'S CERTIFICATION

28A. I CERTIFY THAT DEATH OCCURRED AT THE HOUR, DATE AND PLACE STATED FROM THE CAUSES STATED. I ATTENDED DECEDENT SINCE (ENTER MO. DA. YR.) | I LAST SAW DECEDENT ALIVE (ENTER MO. DA. YR.)
28B. PHYSICIAN—SIGNATURE AND DEGREE OR TITLE
28C. DATE SIGNED
28D. PHYSICIAN'S LICENSE NUMBER
28E. TYPE PHYSICIAN'S NAME AND ADDRESS

INJURY INFORMATION

29. SPECIFY ACCIDENT, SUICIDE, ETC.	30. PLACE OF INJURY	31. INJURY AT WORK	32A. DATE OF INJURY—MONTH, DAY, YEAR	32B. HOUR
ACCIDENT	INDIAN DUNES PARK	YES	7/23/82	0215

33. LOCATION (STREET AND NUMBER OR LOCATION AND CITY OR TOWN)	34. DESCRIBE HOW INJURY OCCURRED (EVENTS WHICH RESULTED IN INJURY)
HENRY MAYO DRIVE, CASTAIC	HIT BY CRASHING HELICOPTER

CORONER'S USE ONLY 15

35A. I CERTIFY THAT DEATH OCCURRED AT THE HOUR, DATE AND PLACE STATED FROM THE CAUSES STATED. AS REQUIRED BY LAW I HAVE HELD AN (INQUEST-INVESTIGATION)
35B. CORONER—SIGNATURE AND DEGREE OR TITLE: DEPUTY CORONER [signature]
35C. DATE SIGNED: 7/24/82

36. DISPOSITION	37. DATE—MONTH, DAY, YEAR	38. NAME AND ADDRESS OF CEMETERY OR CREMATORY	39. EMBALMER'S LICENSE NUMBER AND SIGNATURE
Burial	7/25/82	Hillside Memorial Park, 6001 Centinela Ave. Los Angeles, Calif.	Not Embalmed

40. NAME OF FUNERAL DIRECTOR (OR PERSON ACTING AS SUCH)	41. LOCAL REGISTRAR—SIGNATURE	42. DATE ACCEPTED BY LOCAL REGISTRAR
Hillside Memorial Park Mortuary 1358	[signature]	JUL 25 1982

STATE REGISTRAR: A. B. C. D. E. F.

VS-11 (10-78) 01-7-4-7007

This is to certify that this document is a true copy of the official record filed with the Registrar-Recorder/County Clerk.

Beatriz Valdez
BEATRIZ VALDEZ
Registrar-Recorder/County Clerk

AUG 16 1985
19-397057

This copy not valid unless prepared on engraved border displaying the Seal and Signature of the Registrar-Recorder/County Clerk.

American Bank Note Company

ANY ALTERATION OR ERASURE VOIDS THIS CERTIFICATE

CERTIFICATION OF VITAL RECORD

COUNTY OF ORANGE

DEPARTMENT OF PUBLIC HEALTH
1719 W. 17TH STREET SANTA ANA, CALIFORNIA 92706

3-94-30-011519

CERTIFICATE OF DEATH
STATE OF CALIFORNIA

DECEDENT PERSONAL DATA
1. Name of Decedent—First (Given): HARRIET | 2. Middle: HILLIARD | 3. Last (Family): NELSON
4. Date of Birth: 07/18/1909 | 5. Age Yrs.: 85 | 6. Sex: F | 7. Date of Death: 10/02/1994 | 8. Hour: 1425
9. State of Birth: IA | 10. Social Security No.: 568-03-4616 | 11. Military Service: None | 12. Marital Status: WIDOWED | 13. Education—Years Completed: 12
14. Race: CAUCASIAN | 15. Hispanic: No | 16. Usual Employer: CASA BLANCA PRODUCTIONS
17. Occupation: ACTRESS | 18. Kind of Business: ENTERTAINMENT | 19. Years in Occupation: 82

USUAL RESIDENCE
20. Residence: 16 LAGUNITA
21. City: LAGUNA BEACH | 22. County: ORANGE | 23. Zip Code: 92651 | 24. Yrs in County: 14 | 25. State or Foreign Country: CA

INFORMANT
26. Name, Relationship: DAVID O. NELSON-SON | 27. Mailing Address: 4179 VALLEY MEADOW ROAD, ENCINO, CA 91316

SPOUSE AND PARENT INFORMATION
28. Name of Surviving Spouse—First: - | 29. Middle: - | 30. Last (Maiden Name): -
31. Name of Father—First: LEROY | 32. Middle: - | 33. Last: SNYDER | 34. Birth State: IA
35. Name of Mother—First: HAZEL | 36. Middle: - | 37. Last (Maiden): MC NUTT | 38. Birth State: IA

FUNERAL DIRECTOR AND LOCAL REGISTRAR
39. Disposition Date: 10/06/1994 | 40. Place of Final Disposition: FOREST LAWN MEM. PARK, 6300 FOREST LAWN DR. LOS ANGELES, CA 90068
41. Type of Disposition(s): CR/BU | 42. Signature of Embalmer: NOT EMBALMED | 43. License No: -
44. Name of Funeral Director: FOREST LAWN HOLLYWOOD HILLS | 45. License No.: FD-904 | 46. Signature of Local Registrar: [signature] | 47. Date: 10/04/1994

PLACE OF DEATH
101. Place of Death: RESIDENCE | 104. County: ORANGE
105. Street Address: 16 LAGUNITA | 106. City: LAGUNA BEACH

CAUSE OF DEATH
107. Death was caused by:
Immediate Cause (A) CARDIORESPIRATORY FAILURE — MINS.
Due to (B) ASHD — YEARS
Due to (C) HYPERTENSION — YEARS
Due to (D)
108. Death reported to coroner: Yes — Referral Number 94-06095-VA
109. Biopsy performed: No
110. Autopsy performed: No
111. Used in determining cause:
112. Other significant conditions contributing to death but not related to cause given in 107: COPD
113. Was operation performed for any condition in item 107 or 112?: NO

PHYSICIAN'S CERTIFICATION
114. Decedent attended since: 08/30/1994 | Decedent last seen alive: 09/30/1994
115. Signature and Title of Certifier: Maya B Kaura, MD. | 116. License No: C41651 | 117. Date: 10/04/1994
118. Type attending physician's name, mailing address, zip: MAYA B. KAURA, MD, 24953 PASEO DE VALENCIA, LAG. HILLS, CA92653

CORONER'S USE ONLY
119. Manner of Death: Natural / Suicide / Homicide / Accident / Pending Investigation / Could not be determined
120. Injury at work | 121. Injury date | 122. Hour | 123. Place of injury
124. Describe how injury occurred
125. Location
126. Signature of Coroner or Deputy Coroner | 127. Date | 128. Typed name, title of coroner or deputy coroner

STATE REGISTRAR A B C D E F G H FAX AUTH # 0153 CENSUS TRACT

CERTIFIED COPY OF VITAL RECORDS

51259

STATE OF CALIFORNIA
COUNTY OF ORANGE } SS

DATE ISSUED JUL 25 1995

This is a true and exact reproduction of the document officially registered and placed on file in the VITAL RECORDS SECTION, ORANGE COUNTY DEPARTMENT OF PUBLIC HEALTH.

HUGH F. STALLWORTH, M.D.
COUNTY HEALTH OFFICER
REGISTRAR OF VITAL STATISTICS

This copy not valid unless prepared on engraved border displaying seal and signature of Registrar.

ANY ALTERATION OR ERASURE VOIDS THIS CERTIFICATE

CERTIFICATION OF VITAL RECORD

COUNTY OF LOS ANGELES • REGISTRAR-RECORDER/COUNTY CLERK

CERTIFICATE OF DEATH 0190-025678

STATE OF CALIFORNIA—DEPARTMENT OF HEALTH
OFFICE OF THE STATE REGISTRAR OF VITAL STATISTICS

DECEDENT PERSONAL DATA	1A. Name of deceased—first name	OSWALD OZZIE
	1B. Middle name	GEORGE
	1C. Last name	NELSON AKA NELSON
	2A. Date of death	June 3, 1975
	2B. Hour	4:30 A. M.
	3. Sex	Male
	4. Color or race	Caucasian
	5. Birthplace	New Jersey
	6. Date of birth	March 20, 1906
	7. Age	69 years
	8. Name and birthplace of father	George W. Nelson - New Jersey
	9. Maiden name and birthplace of mother	Ethel I. Orr - New York
	10. Citizen of what country	United States
	11. Social security number	560-26-1534
	12. Married, never married, widowed, divorced	Married
	13. Name of surviving spouse	Harriet Hilliard
	14. Last occupation	Producer Director
	15. Number of years in this occupation	40
	16. Name of last employing company or firm	Self Employed
	17. Kind of industry or business	Movies, Radio, T.V.
PLACE OF DEATH	18A. Place of death	
	18B. Street address	1822 Camino Palmero
	18C. Inside city corporate limits	Yes
	18D. City or town	Hollywood
	18E. County	Los Angeles
	18F. Length of stay in county of death	34 years
	18G. Length of stay in California	34 years
USUAL RESIDENCE	19A. Usual residence	1822 Camino Palmero
	19B. Inside city corporate limits	Yes
	19C. City or town	Hollywood
	19D. County	Los Angeles
	19E. State	California
	20. Name and mailing address of informant	Mrs. Harriett Nelson, Wife, 1822 Camino Palmero, Hollywood, California 90046
PHYSICIAN'S OR CORONER'S CERTIFICATION	21A. Coroner	
	21B. Physician: from / to / last saw	1-31-67 / 6-1-75 / 6-1-75
	21C. Physician or coroner	Marvin Calmenson M.D.
	21D. Date signed	6-3-75
	21E. Address	4911 Van Nuys Blvd Van Nuys
	21F. License number	C 8783
FUNERAL DIRECTOR AND LOCAL REGISTRAR	22A. Specify burial, entombment or cremation	Cremation
	22B. Date	6-6-1975
	23. Name of cemetery or crematory	FOREST LAWN MEMORIAL-PARK
	24. Embalmer—signature, license number	Robert P Haggerty #5249
	25. Funeral director	Forest Lawn Hollywood Hills Mortuary
	26. If not certified by coroner, was this death reported to coroner?	No
	27. Local registrar—signature	[signature]
	28. Date received for registration	JUN 6 1975
CAUSE OF DEATH	29. Part I. (A) Immediate cause	cardiac failure
	(B) Due to	neoplastic intestinal obstruction c inanition — 3 wk
	(C) Due to	Metastatic adenocarcinoma (colon) — 8 yr.
	30. Part II. Other significant conditions	Colon resection for carcinoma 1-31-67
	31. Was operation or biopsy performed	Operation + Biopsy
	32A. Autopsy	No
INJURY INFORMATION	33–40	
		15
STATE REGISTRAR	F.	9-1-9

This is to certify that this document is a true copy of the official record filed with the Registrar-Recorder/County Clerk.

Beatriz Valdez
BEATRIZ VALDEZ
Registrar-Recorder/County Clerk

AUG 10 1995
19-389398

This copy not valid unless prepared on engraved border displaying the Seal and Signature of the Registrar-Recorder/County Clerk.

American Bank Note Company
ANY ALTERATION OR ERASURE VOIDS THIS CERTIFICATE

CERTIFICATION OF VITAL RECORD

COUNTY OF LOS ANGELES • REGISTRAR-RECORDER/COUNTY CLERK

CERTIFICATE OF DEATH 38519046540
STATE OF CALIFORNIA

STATE FILE NUMBER — LOCAL REGISTRATION DISTRICT AND CERTIFICATE NUMBER

DECEDENT PERSONAL DATA

1A. NAME OF DECEDENT—FIRST: Lloyd | 1B. MIDDLE: Benedict | 1C. LAST: Nolan | 2A. DATE OF DEATH (MONTH, DAY, YEAR): September 27, 1985 | 2B. HOUR: 0755

3. SEX: Male | 4. RACE/ETHNICITY: Caucasian | 5. SPANISH/HISPANIC: NO X | 6. DATE OF BIRTH: August 11, 1902 | 7. AGE: 83 YEARS | IF UNDER 1 YEAR: MONTHS, DAYS | IF UNDER 24 HOURS: HOURS, MINUTES

8. BIRTHPLACE OF DECEDENT (STATE OR FOREIGN COUNTRY): California | 9. NAME AND BIRTHPLACE OF FATHER: James Charles Nolan, Ireland | 10. BIRTH NAME AND BIRTHPLACE OF MOTHER: Margaret E. Shea, Calif.

11A. CITIZEN OF WHAT COUNTRY: U.S.A. | 11B. IF DECEASED WAS EVER IN MILITARY GIVE DATES OF SERVICE: 19 NA TO 19 NA | 12. SOCIAL SECURITY NUMBER: 562-09-7117 | 13. MARITAL STATUS: Married | 14. NAME OF SURVIVING SPOUSE (IF WIFE, ENTER BIRTH NAME): Virginia Dabney

15. PRIMARY OCCUPATION: Actor | 16. NUMBER OF YEARS THIS OCCUPATION: 60 | 17. EMPLOYER (IF SELF-EMPLOYED, SO STATE): Free Lance | 18. KIND OF INDUSTRY OR BUSINESS: Motion Picture/T.V.

USUAL RESIDENCE

19A. USUAL RESIDENCE—STREET ADDRESS (STREET AND NUMBER OR LOCATION): 11411 Ayrshire Road | 19B. | 19C. CITY OR TOWN: Los Angeles

19D. COUNTY: Los Angeles | 19E. STATE: California | 20. NAME AND ADDRESS OF INFORMANT—RELATIONSHIP: Virginia F. Nolan - wife, Same as 19a (90049)

PLACE OF DEATH

21A. PLACE OF DEATH: Residence | 21B. COUNTY: Los Angeles

21C. STREET ADDRESS (STREET AND NUMBER OR LOCATION): 11411 Ayrshire Road | 21D. CITY OR TOWN: Los Angeles

CAUSE OF DEATH

22. DEATH WAS CAUSED BY: (ENTER ONLY ONE CAUSE PER LINE FOR A, B, AND C)

IMMEDIATE CAUSE (A): Respiratory Arrest — APPROXIMATE INTERVAL BETWEEN ONSET AND DEATH: Acute

CONDITIONS, IF ANY, WHICH GAVE RISE TO THE IMMEDIATE CAUSE, STATING THE UNDERLYING CAUSE LAST. DUE TO, OR AS A CONSEQUENCE OF (B): Carcinoma of Lung — 3 mo.

DUE TO, OR AS A CONSEQUENCE OF (C):

24. WAS DEATH REPORTED TO CORONER? NO | 25. WAS BIOPSY PERFORMED? Yes | 26. WAS AUTOPSY PERFORMED? NO

23. OTHER SIGNIFICANT CONDITIONS—CONTRIBUTING TO DEATH BUT NOT RELATED TO CAUSE GIVEN IN 22A: Anemia - Sideroblastic - Refractory | 27. WAS OPERATION PERFORMED FOR ANY CONDITION IN ITEMS 22 OR 23? TYPE OF OPERATION: Mediastinoscopy-Biopsy | DATE: Aug-85

PHYSICIAN'S CERTIFICATION

28A. I CERTIFY THAT DEATH OCCURRED AT THE HOUR, DATE AND PLACE STATED FROM THE CAUSES STATED. I ATTENDED DECEDENT SINCE (ENTER MO. DA. YR.): May 16 1984 | I LAST SAW DECEDENT ALIVE (ENTER MO. DA. YR.): 9-26-85 | 28B. PHYSICIAN—SIGNATURE AND DEGREE OR TITLE: [signature] | 28C. DATE SIGNED: 9-27-85 | 28D. PHYSICIAN'S LICENSE NUMBER: C-29672

28E. TYPE PHYSICIAN'S NAME AND ADDRESS: Norman S. Bobes M.D. 434 San Vicente Blvd Los Angeles Calif

INJURY INFORMATION

29. SPECIFY ACCIDENT, SUICIDE, ETC. | 30. PLACE OF INJURY | 31. INJURY AT WORK | 32A. DATE OF INJURY—MONTH, DAY, YEAR | 32B. HOUR

33. LOCATION (STREET AND NUMBER OR LOCATION AND CITY OR TOWN) | 34. DESCRIBE HOW INJURY OCCURRED (EVENTS WHICH RESULTED IN INJURY)

CORONER'S USE ONLY

35A. I CERTIFY THAT DEATH OCCURRED AT THE HOUR, DATE AND PLACE STATED FROM THE CAUSES STATED. AS REQUIRED BY LAW I HAVE HELD AN (INQUEST-INVESTIGATION) | 35B. CORONER—SIGNATURE AND DEGREE OR TITLE | 35C. DATE SIGNED

36. DISPOSITION: Cremation | 37. DATE—MONTH, DAY, YEAR: 10-1-85 | 38. NAME AND ADDRESS OF CEMETERY OR CREMATORY: Grandview Crematory, Glendale, Ca. | 39. EMBALMER'S LICENSE NUMBER AND SIGNATURE: Not Embalmed

40A. NAME OF FUNERAL DIRECTOR (OR PERSON ACTING AS SUCH): Westwood Village Mortuary | 40B. LICENSE NO.: 951 | 41. LOCAL REGISTRAR—SIGNATURE: [signature] | 42. DATE ACCEPTED BY LOCAL REGISTRAR: OCT 1 1985

STATE REGISTRAR: A. | B. | C. | D. | E. | F.

VS-11(1-85) 162.9 01-9-1-7005

This is to certify that this document is a true copy of the official record filed with the Registrar-Recorder/County Clerk.

Beatriz Valdez
BEATRIZ VALDEZ
Registrar-Recorder/County Clerk

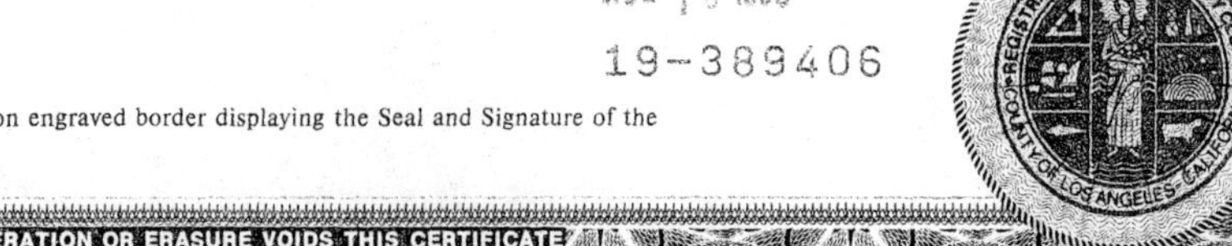

This copy not valid unless prepared on engraved border displaying the Seal and Signature of the Registrar-Recorder/County Clerk.

American Bank Note Company

ANY ALTERATION OR ERASURE VOIDS THIS CERTIFICATE

CERTIFICATION OF VITAL RECORD

COUNTY OF LOS ANGELES • REGISTRAR-RECORDER/COUNTY CLERK

Filed DEC 13, 1968 RAY E. LEE, COUNTY RECORDER

CERTIFICATE OF DEATH

7097-047537

STATE OF CALIFORNIA—DEPARTMENT OF PUBLIC HEALTH

DECEDENT PERSONAL DATA

1A Name of deceased—first name	Ramon
1B Middle name	
1C Last name	Novarro
2A Date of death	OCT. 31, 1968
2B Hour	8:30A.M.
3 Sex	Male
4 Color or race	White
5 Birthplace	Mexico
6 Date of birth	February 6, 1899
7 Age	69 years
8 Name and birthplace of father	Mariano N. Samaniego, Mexico
9 Maiden name and birthplace of mother	Leonor Gavilan, Mexico
10 Citizen of what country	United States
11 Social security number	550 14 3900
12 Married, never married, widowed, divorced	Never Married
13 Name of surviving spouse	None
14 Last occupation	Actor
15 Number of years in this occupation	50 Yrs.
16 Name of last employing company or firm	Metro Goldwyn Studios
17 Kind of industry or business	Motion Pictures

PLACE OF DEATH

18A Place of death—name of hospital or other in-patient facility	
18B Street address	3110 Laurel Canyon Blvd.
18C Inside city corporate limits	Yes
18D City or town	Los Angeles
18E County	Los Angeles
18F Length of stay in county of death	51 Yrs.
18G Length of stay in California	51 Yrs.

USUAL RESIDENCE

19A Usual residence—street address	3110 Laurel Canyon Blvd.
19B Inside city corporate limits	Yes
19C City or town	Los Angeles
19D County	Los Angeles
19E State	California
20 Name and mailing address of informant	Eduardo J. Samaniego (Bro.) 826 So. Third Ave Los Angeles, California 90005

PHYSICIAN'S OR CORONER'S CERTIFICATION

21A Coroner	Investigation
21B Physician	
21C Physician or coroner—signature and degree or title	Thomas T. Noguchi, M.D. Coroner; By: [signature] Deputy
21D Date signed	11-22-68
21E Address	Hall of Justice, Los Angeles

FUNERAL DIRECTOR AND LOCAL REGISTRAR

22A Specify burial, entombment or cremation	Burial
22B Date	11/4/68
23 Name of cemetery or crematory	Calvary Cemetery
24 Embalmer—signature / license number	[signature] 3317
25 Name of funeral director	Cunningham & O'Connor, L.A.
26 If not certified by coroner was this death reported to coroner?	
27 Local registrar—signature	[signature]
28 Date accepted for registration	NOV 27 1968

CAUSE OF DEATH

29 PART I. DEATH WAS CAUSED BY:

- IMMEDIATE CAUSE (A) **Suffocation.**
- DUE TO, OR AS A CONSEQUENCE OF (B) **Aspiration of blood.**
- DUE TO, OR AS A CONSEQUENCE OF (C) **Multiple traumatic injuries of face, nose and mouth.**

30 PART II. OTHER SIGNIFICANT CONDITIONS:

31 Was operation or biopsy performed	no
32A Autopsy	yes
32B If yes were findings considered in determining cause of death	yes

INJURY INFORMATION

33 Specify accident, suicide or homicide	HOMICIDE
34 Place of injury	HOME
35 Injury at work	NO
36A Date of injury	10-31-68
36B Hour	prior to 8:30 A.M.
37A Place of injury	3110 LAURAL CANYON BLVD. STUDIO CITY
37B Distance from place of injury to usual residence	0 miles
38 Were laboratory tests done for drugs or toxic chemicals	no
39 Were laboratory tests done for alcohol	yes
40 Describe how injury occurred	BEATING

STATE REGISTRAR: A. B. C. D. E. F. 1434

REV. 1-1-68 Form VS-11

This is to certify that this document is a true copy of the official record filed with the Registrar-Recorder/County Clerk.

[signature]
BEATRIZ VALDEZ
Registrar-Recorder/County Clerk

AUG 16 1995

19-397405

This copy not valid unless prepared on engraved border displaying the Seal and Signature of the Registrar-Recorder/County Clerk.

American Bank Note Company

ANY ALTERATION OR ERASURE VOIDS THIS CERTIFICATE

CERTIFICATION OF VITAL RECORD

COUNTY OF LOS ANGELES • REGISTRAR-RECORDER/COUNTY CLERK

CERTIFICATE OF DEATH
STATE OF CALIFORNIA

Local Registration District and Certificate Number: 0190-047940

DECEDENT PERSONAL DATA

1A. Name of Decedent—First: PAT
1B. Middle:
1C. Last: O'BRIEN
2A. Date of Death (Month, Day, Year): OCTOBER 15,1983
2B. Hour: 0459
3. Sex: Male
4. Race: White
5. Ethnicity:
6. Date of Birth: November 11,1899
7. Age: 83 Years
8. Birthplace of Decedent (State or Foreign Country): Wisconsin
9. Name and Birthplace of Father: William J.O'Brien,New York
10. Birth Name and Birthplace of Mother: Margaret McGovern,Ireland
11. Citizen of What Country: USA
12. Social Security Number: 565-01-1777
13. Marital Status: Married
14. Name of Surviving Spouse (If Wife, Enter Birth Name): Eloise Taylor
15. Primary Occupation: Actor
16. Number of Years This Occupation: 67
17. Employer (If Self-Employed, So State): Self Employed
18. Kind of Industry or Business: Entertainment

USUAL RESIDENCE

19A. Usual Residence—Street Address (Street and Number or Location): 466 No.Carmelina Ave.
19B.
19C. City or Town: Los Angeles
19D. County: Los Angeles
19E. State: California
20. Name and Address of Informant—Relationship: Eloise T.O'Brien Wife, 466 No.Carmelina Ave., Los Angeles,Calif. 90049

PLACE OF DEATH

21A. Place of Death: St.John's Hospital
21B. County: Los Angeles
21C. Street Address (Street and Number or Location): 1328 22nd Street
21D. City or Town: Santa Monica

CAUSE OF DEATH

22. Death was caused by: (Enter only one cause per line for A, B, and C)

		Approximate interval between onset and death
Immediate cause	(A) Cardiac Arrest	1 hr.
Due to, or as a consequence of	(B) Arteriosclerotic Heart Disease Pacemaker	15 yrs.
Due to, or as a consequence of	(C) Probable acute coronary occlusion	1 hr.

Conditions, if any, which gave rise to the immediate cause, stating the underlying cause last.

24. Was death reported to coroner? No
25. Was biopsy performed? No
26. Was autopsy performed? No
23. Other conditions contributing but not related to the immediate cause of death: Post-op 2 days - Prostatectomy
27. Was operation performed for any condition in items 22 or 23? Type of operation: Prostatectomy Date: 10/12/83

PHYSICIAN'S CERTIFICATION

28A. I certify that death occurred at the hour, date and place stated from the causes stated. I attended decedent since (Enter Mo, Da, Yr.): 1970. I last saw decedent alive (Enter Mo, Da, Yr.): 10/15/83
28B. Physician—Signature and Degree or Title: [signature] MD
28C. Date Signed: 10/17/83
28D. Physician's License Number: A05069
28E. Type Physician's Name and Address: Robert Kositchek,MD 2080 Century Park East,Los Angeles,Calif.90067

INJURY INFORMATION — CORONER'S USE ONLY

29. Specify accident, suicide, etc.
30. Place of injury
31. Injury at work
32A. Date of injury—month, day, year
32B. Hour
33. Location (Street and number or location and city or town)
34. Describe how injury occurred (Events which resulted in injury)
35A. I certify that death occurred at the hour, date and place stated from the causes stated. As required by law I have held an (Inquest-Investigation)
35B. Coroner—Signature and degree or title
35C. Date signed

36. Disposition: Burial
37. Date—Month, Day, Year: 10-19-83
38. Name and Address of Cemetery or Crematory: HOLY CROSS CEMETERY 5835 W.Slauson Ave.Culver City,Ca.
39. Embalmer's License Number and Signature: 5799 [signature]
40. Name of Funeral Director (or Person Acting as Such): THE CALLANAN MORTUARY F-86
41. Local Registrar—Signature: [signature]
42. Date Accepted by Local Registrar: OCT 18 1983

State Registrar: A. B. C. D. E. F.

VS-11 (10-78) 4/10   01-3-1-0756

This is to certify that this document is a true copy of the official record filed with the Registrar-Recorder/County Clerk.

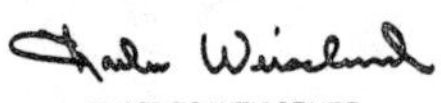

CHARLES WEISSBURD
Registrar-Recorder/County Clerk

FEB 05 1992
19-312851

This copy not valid unless prepared on engraved border displaying the Seal and Signature of the Registrar-Recorder/County Clerk.

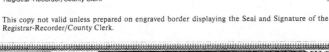

American Bank Note Company

ANY ALTERATION OR ERASURE VOIDS THIS CERTIFICATE

STATE OF CALIFORNIA
CERTIFICATION OF VITAL RECORD

COUNTY OF LOS ANGELES
DEPARTMENT OF HEALTH SERVICES

CERTIFICATE OF DEATH
STATE OF CALIFORNIA
USE BLACK INK ONLY/NO ERASURES, WHITEOUTS OR ALTERATIONS
VS-11 (REV. 1/00)

STATE FILE NUMBER — LOCAL REGISTRATION NUMBER

DECEDENT PERSONAL DATA
1. NAME OF DECEDENT—FIRST (GIVEN): JOHN
2. MIDDLE: CARROLL
3. LAST (FAMILY): O'CONNOR
4. DATE OF BIRTH MM/DD/CCYY: 08/02/1924
5. AGE YRS.: 76 — IF UNDER 1 YEAR: MONTHS / DAYS — IF UNDER 24 HOURS: HOURS / MINUTES
6. SEX: M
7. DATE OF DEATH MM/DD/CCYY: 06/21/2001
8. HOUR: 1520
9. STATE OF BIRTH: NY
10. SOCIAL SECURITY NO.: 129-14-6989
11. MILITARY SERVICE: ☐ YES ☒ NO ☐ UNK
12. MARITAL STATUS: MARRIED
13. EDUCATION—YEARS COMPLETED: 17
14. RACE: CAUC
15. HISPANIC—SPECIFY: ☐ YES ☒ NO
16. USUAL EMPLOYER: SELF EMPLOYED
17. OCCUPATION: WRITER/ACTOR/PRODUCER
18. KIND OF BUSINESS: TELEVISION/STAGE/MOTION PICTURE
19. YEARS IN OCCUPATION: 51

USUAL RESIDENCE
20. RESIDENCE—(STREET AND NUMBER OR LOCATION): 201 TILDEN AVE.
21. CITY: LOS ANGELES
22. COUNTY: LOS ANGELES
23. ZIP CODE: 90049
24. YRS IN COUNTY: 40
25. STATE OR FOREIGN COUNTRY: CA

INFORMANT
26. NAME, RELATIONSHIP: NANCY O'CONNOR - WIFE
27. MAILING ADDRESS (STREET AND NUMBER OR RURAL ROUTE NUMBER, CITY OR TOWN, STATE, ZIP): 201 TILDEN AVE. LOS ANGELES, CA. 90049

SPOUSE AND PARENT INFORMATION
28. NAME OF SURVIVING SPOUSE—FIRST: NANCY
29. MIDDLE: KATHLEEN
30. LAST (MAIDEN NAME): FIELDS
31. NAME OF FATHER—FIRST: EDWARD
32. MIDDLE: -
33. LAST: O'CONNOR
34. BIRTH STATE: NY
35. NAME OF MOTHER—FIRST: ELISE
36. MIDDLE: -
37. LAST (MAIDEN): O'CONNOR
38. BIRTH STATE: NY

DISPOSITION(S)
39. DATE MM/DD/CCYY: 06/28/2001
40. PLACE OF FINAL DISPOSITION: WESTWOOD VILLAGE MEMORIAL PARK 1218 GLENDON AVE. LOS ANGELES,CA.90024

FUNERAL DIRECTOR AND LOCAL REGISTRAR
41. TYPE OF DISPOSITION(S): CR/BU
42. SIGNATURE OF EMBALMER: ▶ Eric P. Solter
43. LICENSE NO.: 8514
44. NAME OF FUNERAL DIRECTOR: GATES KINGSLEY GATES MOELLER MURPHY
45. LICENSE NO.: FD451
46. SIGNATURE OF LOCAL REGISTRAR: ▶ [signature]
47. DATE MM/DD/CCYY: 06/26/2001

PLACE OF DEATH
101. PLACE OF DEATH: BROTMAN MEDICAL CENTER
102. IF HOSPITAL, SPECIFY ONE: ☐ IP ☒ ER/OP ☐ DOA
103. FACILITY OTHER THAN HOSPITAL: ☐ CONV. HOSP. ☐ RES. CARE ☐ OTHER
104. COUNTY: LOS ANGELES
105. STREET ADDRESS—(STREET AND NUMBER OR LOCATION): 3828 DELMAS TERRACE
106. CITY: CULVER CITY

CAUSE OF DEATH
107. DEATH WAS CAUSED BY: (ENTER ONLY ONE CAUSE PER LINE FOR A, B, C, AND D) — TIME INTERVAL BETWEEN ONSET AND DEATH

		Cause	Time interval
IMMEDIATE CAUSE	(A)	CARDIAC ARREST	1hour
DUE TO	(B)	ACUTE MYOCARDIAL INFARCTION	2hours
DUE TO	(C)	ARTERIOSCLEROTIC HEART DISEASE	14years
DUE TO	(D)		

108. DEATH REPORTED TO CORONER: ☐ YES ☒ NO — REFERRAL NUMBER
109. BIOPSY PERFORMED: ☐ YES ☒ NO
110. AUTOPSY PERFORMED: ☐ YES ☒ NO
111. USED IN DETERMINING CAUSE: ☐ YES ☐ NO
112. OTHER SIGNIFICANT CONDITIONS CONTRIBUTING TO DEATH BUT NOT RELATED TO CAUSE GIVEN IN 107: DIABETES MELLITUS
113. WAS OPERATION PERFORMED FOR ANY CONDITION IN ITEM 107 OR 112? IF YES, LIST TYPE OF OPERATION AND DATE.: NO

PHYSICIAN'S CERTIFICATION
114. I CERTIFY THAT TO THE BEST OF MY KNOWLEDGE DEATH OCCURRED AT THE HOUR, DATE AND PLACE STATED FROM THE CAUSES STATED.
DECEDENT ATTENDED SINCE MM/DD/CCYY: 06/21/2001 — DECEDENT LAST SEEN ALIVE MM/DD/CCYY: 06/21/2001
115. SIGNATURE AND TITLE OF CERTIFIER: ▶ Michael B. Kamiel MD
116. LICENSE NO.: G24597
117. DATE MM/DD/CCYY: 06/25/2001
118. TYPE ATTENDING PHYSICIAN'S NAME, MAILING ADDRESS, ZIP: MICHAEL B.KAMIEL,MD. 3831 HUGHES AVE. CULVER CITY,CA.90232

CORONER'S USE ONLY
I CERTIFY THAT IN MY OPINION DEATH OCCURRED AT THE HOUR, DATE AND PLACE STATED FROM THE CAUSES STATED.
119. MANNER OF DEATH: ☐ NATURAL ☐ SUICIDE ☐ HOMICIDE ☐ ACCIDENT ☐ PENDING INVESTIGATION ☐ COULD NOT BE DETERMINED
120. INJURY AT WORK: ☐ YES ☐ NO
121. INJURY DATE MM/DD/CCYY
122. HOUR
123. PLACE OF INJURY
124. DESCRIBE HOW INJURY OCCURRED (EVENTS WHICH RESULTED IN INJURY)
125. LOCATION (STREET AND NUMBER OR LOCATION AND CITY, ZIP)
126. SIGNATURE OF CORONER OR DEPUTY CORONER ▶
127. DATE MM/DD/CCYY
128. TYPED NAME, TITLE OF CORONER OR DEPUTY CORONER

090444559

STATE REGISTRAR: A B C D E F G H — FAX AUTH. # — CENSUS TRACT

This is a true certified copy of the record filed in the County of Los Angeles Department of Health Services if it bears the Registrar's signature in purple ink.

Jonathan E Fielding MD — DATE ISSUED 033 JUL 03 2001
Director of Health Services and Registrar

This copy not valid unless prepared on engraved border displaying seal and signature of Registrar.

THE GREAT SEAL OF THE STATE OF CALIFORNIA — EUREKA
LOS ANGELES COUNTY — REGISTRAR OF VITAL STATISTICS — STATE OF CALIFORNIA

MIDWEST BANK NOTE COMPANY — ANY ALTERATION OR ERASURE VOIDS THIS CERTIFICATE

CERTIFICATE OF DEATH
STATE OF CALIFORNIA

STATE FILE NUMBER

38837 001478
LOCAL REGISTRATION DISTRICT AND CERTIFICATE NUMBER

DECEDENT PERSONAL DATA

1A. NAME OF DECEDENT—FIRST: Heather | 1B. MIDDLE: Michelle | 1C. LAST: O'Rourke
2A. DATE OF DEATH (MONTH, DAY, YEAR): February 1, 1988 | 2B. HOUR: 1443
3. SEX: Female | 4. RACE/ETHNICITY: Caucasian | 5. SPANISH/HISPANIC: NO
6. DATE OF BIRTH: December 27, 1975 | 7. AGE: 12 YEARS | IF UNDER 1 YEAR: MONTHS, DAYS | IF UNDER 24 HOURS: HOURS, MINUTES
8. BIRTHPLACE OF DECEDENT (STATE OR FOREIGN COUNTRY): California
9. NAME AND BIRTHPLACE OF FATHER: Michael O'Rourke CA.
10. BIRTH NAME AND BIRTHPLACE OF MOTHER: Kathleen Rasmussen WI.
11A. CITIZEN OF WHAT COUNTRY: USA
11B. IF DECEASED WAS EVER IN MILITARY GIVE DATES OF SERVICE: 19 NO TO 19 NO
12. SOCIAL SECURITY NUMBER: 569-53-4073
13. MARITAL STATUS: Never Married
14. NAME OF SURVIVING SPOUSE (IF WIFE, ENTER BIRTH NAME): --------

1347

15. PRIMARY OCCUPATION: Actress
16. NUMBER OF YEARS THIS OCCUPATION: 7
17. EMPLOYER (IF SELF-EMPLOYED, SO STATE): MGM Studios
18. KIND OF INDUSTRY OR BUSINESS: Movie

USUAL RESIDENCE

19A. USUAL RESIDENCE—STREET ADDRESS (STREET AND NUMBER OR LOCATION): 9727 Channel Rd.
19B.
19C. CITY OR TOWN: Lakeside
19D. COUNTY: San Diego
19E. STATE: California
20. NAME AND ADDRESS OF INFORMANT—RELATIONSHIP: Kathleen O'Rourke Peele Mother, 9727 Channel Rd. Lakeside, Ca. 92040

PLACE OF DEATH

21A. PLACE OF DEATH: Childrens Hospital
21B. COUNTY: San Diego
21C. STREET ADDRESS (STREET AND NUMBER OR LOCATION): 8001 Frost St.
21D. CITY OR TOWN: San Diego

CAUSE OF DEATH

4279
5609

22. DEATH WAS CAUSED BY: (ENTER ONLY ONE CAUSE PER LINE FOR A, B, AND C)

IMMEDIATE CAUSE (A) Cardio-Respiratory Arrest — APPROXIMATE INTERVAL BETWEEN ONSET AND DEATH: 30min

CONDITIONS, IF ANY, WHICH GAVE RISE TO THE IMMEDIATE CAUSE, STATING THE UNDERLYING CAUSE LAST.

DUE TO, OR AS A CONSEQUENCE OF (B) Suspected Septic Shock — 6hrs

DUE TO, OR AS A CONSEQUENCE OF (C) Acute Bowel obstruction — 36hrs

24. WAS DEATH REPORTED TO CORONER? Yes 2-012
25. WAS BIOPSY PERFORMED? Yes
26. WAS AUTOPSY PERFORMED? No

95

23. OTHER SIGNIFICANT CONDITIONS—CONTRIBUTING TO DEATH BUT NOT RELATED TO CAUSE GIVEN IN 22A: stenosis of small intestine
27. WAS OPERATION PERFORMED FOR ANY CONDITION IN ITEMS 22 OR 23? TYPE OF OPERATION: Bowel Resection Exploratory Laparotomy — DATE 2/1/88

PHYSICIAN'S CERTIFICATION

28A. I CERTIFY THAT DEATH OCCURRED AT THE HOUR, DATE AND PLACE STATED FROM THE CAUSES STATED.
I ATTENDED DECEDENT SINCE (ENTER MO. DA. YR.): 2/1/88 | I LAST SAW DECEDENT ALIVE (ENTER MO. DA. YR.): 2/1/88
28B. PHYSICIAN—SIGNATURE AND DEGREE OR TITLE: H. Michael Worthen
28C. DATE SIGNED: 2/2/88
28D. PHYSICIAN'S LICENSE NUMBER: G047955
28E. TYPE PHYSICIAN'S NAME AND ADDRESS: H. Michael Worthen, M.D. 8001 Frost Street San Diego, CA 92123

INJURY INFORMATION

29. SPECIFY ACCIDENT, SUICIDE, ETC. | 30. PLACE OF INJURY | 31. INJURY AT WORK | 32A. DATE OF INJURY—MONTH, DAY, YEAR | 32B. HOUR
33. LOCATION (STREET AND NUMBER OR LOCATION AND CITY OR TOWN) | 34. DESCRIBE HOW INJURY OCCURRED (EVENTS WHICH RESULTED IN INJURY)

CORONER'S USE ONLY

35A. I CERTIFY THAT DEATH OCCURRED AT THE HOUR, DATE AND PLACE STATED FROM THE CAUSES STATED. AS REQUIRED BY LAW I HAVE HELD AN (INQUEST-INVESTIGATION)
35B. CORONER—SIGNATURE AND DEGREE OR TITLE | 35C. DATE SIGNED

36. DISPOSITION: Entombment
37. DATE—MONTH, DAY, YEAR: Feb. 5, 1988
38. NAME AND ADDRESS OF CEMETERY OR CREMATORY: Westwood Memorial Park 1218 Glendon Ave. Los Angeles, Ca.
39. EMBALMER'S LICENSE NUMBER AND SIGNATURE: 6984 Claudia Lautatjung by Teddy Brodt Atty in Fact
40A. NAME OF FUNERAL DIRECTOR (OR PERSON ACTING AS SUCH): Lakeside-Santee Funeral Chapel
40B. LICENSE NO.: F-997
41. LOCAL REGISTRAR—SIGNATURE: Donald G. Ramras, M.D. jw
42. DATE ACCEPTED BY LOCAL REGISTRAR: FEB 03 1988

STATE REGISTRAR: A. | B. | C. | D. | E. | F.

VS-11 (1-88)

This is a true certified copy of the record if it bears the seal, imprinted in purple ink, of the Recorder. JUL 06 1995

Recorder/County Clerk
San Diego County, California

RECORDER / COUNTY CLERK · SAN DIEGO COUNTY, CA

CERTIFICATION OF VITAL RECORD

COUNTY OF LOS ANGELES • REGISTRAR-RECORDER/COUNTY CLERK

James S. Allison, Registrar-Recorder

Filed 12-29-72

CERTIFICATE OF DEATH

7097-049444

STATE FILE NUMBER — STATE OF CALIFORNIA—DEPARTMENT OF PUBLIC HEALTH — LOCAL REGISTRATION DISTRICT AND CERTIFICATE NUMBER

DECEDENT PERSONAL DATA

1a. Name of deceased—first name	Louella
1b. Middle name	Parsons
1c. Last name	Martin
2a. Date of death	12-9-72
2b. Hour	2:30 p. m
3. Sex	Female
4. Color or race	Cauc.
5. Birthplace	Illinois
6. Date of birth	8-6-1881
7. Age	91 years
8. Name and birthplace of father	Joshua Oettinger — unknown
9. Maiden name and birthplace of mother	Helen Ida Wilcox — unknown
10. Citizen of what country	U.S.A.
11. Social security number	548-05-9358 A
12. Married, never married, widowed, divorced	Widowed
13. Name of surviving spouse	---
14. Last occupation	Columnist
15. Number of years in this occupation	53
16. Name of last employing company or firm	L.A. Herald Examiner
17. Kind of industry or business	Publishing

PLACE OF DEATH

18a. Place of death—name of hospital	Berkley East Conv. Hospital
18b. Street address	2021 Arizona Street
18c. Inside city corporate limits	yes
18d. City or town	Santa Monica
18e. County	Los Angeles
18f. Length of stay in county of death	46 years
18g. Length of stay in California	47 years

USUAL RESIDENCE

19a. Usual residence—street address	2253 Coldwater Canyon Road
19b. Inside city corporate limits	yes
19c. City or town	Beverly Hills
19d. County	Los Angeles
19e. State	California
20. Name and mailing address of informant	Miss Harriet Parsons, 2253 Coldwater Canyon Road, Beverly Hills, California

PHYSICIAN'S OR CORONER'S CERTIFICATION

21b. Physician — from / to / and last saw	7-1-60 / 12-9-72 / 12-7-72
21c. Physician or coroner—signature	[signature] MD
21d. Date signed	12-11-72
21e. Address	436 N Roxbury Dr. Beverly Hills
21f. Physician's license number	G1805

FUNERAL DIRECTOR AND LOCAL REGISTRAR

22a. Specify burial, entombment or cremation	Burial
22b. Date	12-13-72
23. Name of cemetery or crematory	Holy Cross Cemetery
24. Embalmer—signature, license number	Charles E. Meeks 3118
25. Name of funeral director	Pierce Brothers Bev. Hills
26. If not certified by coroner was this death reported to coroner	no
27. Local registrar—signature	[signature] MD
28. Date accepted for registration by local registrar	DEC 12 1972

CAUSE OF DEATH

		Approximate interval between onset and death
29. Part I. (A) Immediate cause	Cerebro Vascular Accident	30 MIN.
(B) Due to, or as a consequence of	Generalized Arteriosclerosis	10 YRS
(C) Due to, or as a consequence of		
30. Part II. Other significant conditions		
31. Was operation or biopsy performed	NO	
32a. Autopsy	NO	

INJURY INFORMATION

33. Specify accident, suicide or homicide — 34. Place of injury — 35. Injury at work — 36a. Date of injury — 36b. Hour — 37a. Place of injury — 37b. Distance from place of injury to usual residence — 38. Were laboratory tests done for drugs or toxic chemicals — 39. Were laboratory tests done for alcohol — 40. Describe how injury occurred

STATE REGISTRAR A. B. C. D. E. F.

This is to certify that this document is a true copy of the official record filed with the Registrar-Recorder/County Clerk.

SEP 13 1995

19-015906

This copy not valid unless prepared on engraved border displaying the Seal of the Registrar-Recorder/County Clerk.

ANY ALTERATION OR ERASURE VOIDS THIS CERTIFICATE

CERTIFICATE OF DEATH

STATE OF CALIFORNIA
USE BLACK INK ONLY/NO ERASURES, WHITEOUTS OR ALTERATIONS
VS-11 (REV. 7/93)

STATE FILE NUMBER | LOCAL REGISTRATION NUMBER

DECEDENT PERSONAL DATA

1. NAME OF DECEDENT—FIRST (GIVEN)	2. MIDDLE	3. LAST (FAMILY)
GEORGE	WILLIAM	PEPPARD

4. DATE OF BIRTH MM/DD/CCYY	5. AGE YRS.	IF UNDER 1 YEAR: MONTHS / DAYS	IF UNDER 24 HOURS: HOURS / MINUTES	6. SEX	7. DATE OF DEATH MM/DD/CCYY	8. HOUR
10/01/1928	65			M	05/08/1994	1900

9. STATE OF BIRTH	10. SOCIAL SECURITY NO.	11. MILITARY SERVICE	12. MARITAL STATUS	13. EDUCATION —YEARS COMPLETED
MICHIGAN	382-24-6744	1945 TO 1946 ☐ NONE	MARRIED	16

14. RACE	15. HISPANIC—SPECIFY	16. USUAL EMPLOYER
CAUCASIAN	☐ YES [X] NO	SELF EMPLOYED

17. OCCUPATION	18. KIND OF BUSINESS	19. YEARS IN OCCUPATION
ACTOR/DIRECTOR	MOTION PICTURE	45

USUAL RESIDENCE

20. RESIDENCE—STREET AND NUMBER OR LOCATION: 321 S. BEVERLY DR., SUITE M

21. CITY	22. COUNTY	23. ZIP CODE	24. YRS IN COUNTY	25. STATE OR FOREIGN COUNTRY
BEVERLY HILLS	LOS ANGELES	90212	33	CALIFORNIA

INFORMANT

26. NAME, RELATIONSHIP	27. MAILING ADDRESS (STREET AND NUMBER OR RURAL ROUTE NUMBER, CITY OR TOWN, STATE, ZIP)
LAURA PEPPARD, WIFE	321 S. BEVERLY DR., SUITE M, BEVERLY HILLS, CA. 90212

SPOUSE AND PARENT INFORMATION

28. NAME OF SURVIVING SPOUSE—FIRST	29. MIDDLE	30. LAST (MAIDEN NAME)	
LAURA	-	TAYLOR	
31. NAME OF FATHER—FIRST	**32. MIDDLE**	**33. LAST**	**34. BIRTH STATE**
GEORGE	-	PEPPARD	CANADA
35. NAME OF MOTHER—FIRST	**36. MIDDLE**	**37. LAST (MAIDEN)**	**38. BIRTH STATE**
VERNELLE	-	ROHR	OHIO

DISPOSITION(S)

39. DATE MM/DD/CCYY	40. PLACE OF FINAL DISPOSITION
05/12/1994	NORTH VIEW CEMETERY, DEARBORN, MICHIGAN

FUNERAL DIRECTOR AND LOCAL REGISTRAR

41. TYPE OF DISPOSITION(S)	42. SIGNATURE OF EMBALMER	43. LICENSE NO.
TR/BU	Elizabeth Derrick	7435
44. NAME OF FUNERAL DIRECTOR	**45. LICENSE NO.**	**46. SIGNATURE OF LOCAL REGISTRAR**	**47. DATE MM/DD/CCYY**
FOREST LAWN HOLLYWOOD HILLS	F 904	[signature]	05/12/1994

PLACE OF DEATH

101. PLACE OF DEATH	102. IF HOSPITAL, SPECIFY ONE	103. FACILITY OTHER THAN HOSPITAL	104. COUNTY
UCLA MEDICAL CENTER	[X] IP ☐ ER/OP ☐ DOA	☐ CONV. HOSP. ☐ RES. ☐ OTHER	LOS ANGELES

105. STREET ADDRESS—STREET AND NUMBER OR LOCATION	106. CITY
10833 LE CONTE AVE.	LOS ANGELES

CAUSE OF DEATH

107. DEATH WAS CAUSED BY: (ENTER ONLY ONE CAUSE PER LINE FOR A, B, C, AND D)

		TIME INTERVAL BETWEEN ONSET AND DEATH
IMMEDIATE CAUSE	(A) RESPIRATORY FAILURE	MINS.
DUE TO	(B) LEUKEMIA	MONTHS
DUE TO	(C)	
DUE TO	(D)	

108. DEATH REPORTED TO CORONER: ☐ YES [X] NO — REFERRAL NUMBER
109. BIOPSY PERFORMED: [X] YES ☐ NO
110. AUTOPSY PERFORMED: ☐ YES [X] NO
111. USED IN DETERMINING CAUSE: ☐ YES ☐ NO

112. OTHER SIGNIFICANT CONDITIONS CONTRIBUTING TO DEATH BUT NOT RELATED TO CAUSE GIVEN IN 107: NONE

113. WAS OPERATION PERFORMED FOR ANY CONDITION IN ITEM 107 OR 112? IF YES, LIST TYPE OF OPERATION AND DATE. NO

PHYSICIAN'S CERTIFICATION

114. I CERTIFY THAT TO THE BEST OF MY KNOWLEDGE DEATH OCCURRED AT THE HOUR, DATE AND PLACE STATED FROM THE CAUSES STATED.

DECEDENT ATTENDED SINCE MM/DD/CCYY	DECEDENT LAST SEEN ALIVE MM/DD/CCYY	115. SIGNATURE AND TITLE OF CERTIFIER	116. LICENSE NO.	117. DATE MM/DD/CCYY
09/02/1993	05/08/1994	[signature] MD	G55562	05/10/1994

118. TYPE ATTENDING PHYSICIAN'S NAME, MAILING ADDRESS + ZIP: ROBERT B. SHPINER, MD, 100 UCLA MEDICAL PLAZA, LOS ANGELES, CA. 90024

CORONER'S USE ONLY

I CERTIFY THAT IN MY OPINION DEATH OCCURRED AT THE HOUR, DATE AND PLACE STATED FROM THE CAUSES STATED.

119. MANNER OF DEATH: ☐ NATURAL ☐ SUICIDE ☐ HOMICIDE ☐ ACCIDENT ☐ PENDING INVESTIGATION ☐ COULD NOT BE DETERMINED

120. INJURY AT WORK: ☐ YES ☐ NO | 121. INJURY DATE MM/DD/CCYY | 122. HOUR | 123. PLACE OF INJURY

124. DESCRIBE HOW INJURY OCCURRED (EVENTS WHICH RESULTED IN INJURY)

125. LOCATION (STREET AND NUMBER OR LOCATION AND CITY AND ZIP CODE)

126. SIGNATURE OF CORONER OR DEPUTY CORONER | 127. DATE MM/DD/CCYY | 128. TYPED NAME, TITLE OF CORONER OR DEPUTY CORONER

STATE REGISTRAR

A	B	C	D	E	F	G	H	FAX AUTH. #	CENSUS TRACT

CERTIFICATE OF DEATH

STATE OF CALIFORNIA
USE BLACK INK ONLY

STATE FILE NUMBER | LOCAL REGISTRATION DISTRICT AND CERTIFICATE NUMBER

DECEDENT PERSONAL DATA

1A. NAME OF DECEDENT—FIRST (GIVEN)	1B. MIDDLE	1C. LAST (FAMILY)	2A. DATE OF DEATH—MO, DAY, YR	2B. HOUR	3. SEX
RIVER	JUDE	PHOENIX	10/31/1993	0151	M

4. RACE	5. HISPANIC—SPECIFY	6. DATE OF BIRTH—MO, DAY, YR	7. AGE IN YEARS	IF UNDER 1 YEAR: MONTHS / DAYS	IF UNDER 24 HOURS: HOURS / MINUTES
Caucasian	YES ☐ NO ☒	08/23/1970	23		

8. STATE OF BIRTH	9. CITIZEN OF WHAT COUNTRY	10A. FULL NAME OF FATHER	10B. STATE OF BIRTH	11A. FULL MAIDEN NAME OF MOTHER	11B. STATE OF BIRTH
OR	USA	John Lee Phoenix	MO	Arlyn Dunetz	NY

12. MILITARY SERVICE	13. SOCIAL SECURITY NO.	14. MARITAL STATUS	15. NAME OF SURVIVING SPOUSE (IF WIFE, ENTER MAIDEN NAME)
19 __ TO 19 __ ☒ NONE	571-61-9058	Never Marr.	None

16A. USUAL OCCUPATION	16B. USUAL KIND OF BUSINESS OR INDUSTRY	16C. USUAL EMPLOYER	16D. YEARS IN OCCUPATION	17. EDUCATION—YEARS COMPLETED
Actor	Entertainment	Self-employed	15	12

USUAL RESIDENCE

18A. RESIDENCE—STREET AND NUMBER OR LOCATION	18B. CITY	18C. ZIP CODE
3232 S. W. 35th Boulevard	Gainesville	32608

18D. COUNTY	18E. NUMBER OF YEARS IN THIS COUNTY	18F. STATE OR FOREIGN COUNTRY	20. NAME, RELATIONSHIP, MAILING ADDRESS AND ZIP CODE OF INFORMANT
Alachua	6	Florida	George Siewierski, Friend 3232 S. W. 35th Boulevard Gainesville, FL 32608

PLACE OF DEATH

19A. PLACE OF DEATH	19B. IF HOSPITAL, SPECIFY ONE: IP, ER/OP, DOA	19C. COUNTY
Cedars-Sinai Medical Center	ER/OP	Los Angeles

19D. STREET ADDRESS—STREET AND NUMBER OR LOCATION	19E. CITY
8700 Beverly Blvd.	Los Angeles

CAUSE OF DEATH

21. DEATH WAS CAUSED BY: (ENTER ONLY ONE CAUSE PER LINE FOR A, B, AND C) — TIME INTERVAL BETWEEN ONSET AND DEATH

IMMEDIATE CAUSE (A) Deferred

DUE TO (B)

DUE TO (C)

1 OF 2

22. WAS DEATH REPORTED TO CORONER ☒ YES REFERRAL NUMBER 93-10011 ☐ NO

23. WAS BIOPSY PERFORMED ☐ YES ☐ NO

24A. WAS AUTOPSY PERFORMED ☒ YES ☐ NO

24B. WAS IT USED IN DETERMINING CAUSE OF DEATH ☐ YES ☐ NO

25. OTHER SIGNIFICANT CONDITIONS CONTRIBUTING TO DEATH BUT NOT RELATED TO CAUSE GIVEN IN 21

26. WAS OPERATION PERFORMED FOR ANY CONDITION IN ITEM 21 OR 25. IF YES, LIST TYPE OF OPERATION AND DATE.

PHYSICIAN'S CERTIFICATION

I CERTIFY THAT TO THE BEST OF MY KNOWLEDGE DEATH OCCURRED AT THE HOUR, DATE AND PLACE STATED FROM THE CAUSES STATED.

27A. DECEDENT ATTENDED SINCE MONTH, DAY, YEAR | DECEDENT LAST SEEN ALIVE MONTH, DAY, YEAR

27B. SIGNATURE AND DEGREE OR TITLE OF CERTIFIER | 27C. CERTIFIER'S LICENSE NUMBER | 27D. DATE SIGNED

27E. TYPE ATTENDING PHYSICIAN'S NAME AND ADDRESS

CORONER'S USE ONLY

I CERTIFY THAT IN MY OPINION DEATH OCCURRED AT THE HOUR, DATE AND PLACE STATED FROM THE CAUSES STATED.

28A. SIGNATURE AND TITLE OF CORONER OR DEPUTY CORONER: Deputy Coroner [signature]

28B. DATE SIGNED: 11/01/1993

29. MANNER OF DEATH—specify one: natural, accident, suicide, homicide, pending investigation or could not be determined: Pending Investigation

30A. PLACE OF INJURY | 30B. INJURY AT WORK ☐ YES ☐ NO | 30C. DATE OF INJURY MONTH, DAY, YEAR | 31. HOUR

32. LOCATION (STREET AND NUMBER OR LOCATION AND CITY) | 33. DESCRIBE HOW INJURY OCCURRED (EVENTS WHICH RESULTED IN INJURY)

FUNERAL DIRECTOR AND LOCAL REGISTRAR

34A. DISPOSITION(S)	34B. PLACE OF FINAL DISPOSITION—NAME AND ADDRESS	34C. DATE MO, DAY, YR.	35A. SIGNATURE OF EMBALMER	35B. LICENSE NO.
TR/BU	GAINESVILLE CITY CEMETERY GAINESVILLE, FLORIDA	11/02/1993	Elizabeth Derrick	7435

36A. NAME OF FUNERAL DIRECTOR (OR PERSON ACTING AS SUCH)	36B. LICENSE NO.	37. SIGNATURE OF LOCAL REGISTRAR	38. REGISTRATION DATE
Forest Lawn Hollywood Hills	F 904	[signature]	NOV 0 2 1993

STATE REGISTRAR

A. | B. | C. | D. | E. | F. | CENSUS TRACT

VS-11 (REV. 7-92) MAKE NO ERASURES, WHITEOUTS, OR OTHER ALTERATIONS 01-10-4-0556

THIS IS A TRUE CERTIFIED COPY OF THE RECORD FILED IN THE COUNTY OF LOS ANGELES DEPARTMENT OF HEALTH SERVICES IF IT BEARS THIS SEAL IN PURPLE INK.

LOS ANGELES COUNTY · STATE OF CALIFORNIA

NOV 1 9 1993

60

Director of Health Services and Registrar

AMENDMENT OF MEDICAL AND HEALTH DATA—DEATH

STATE FILE NUMBER | USE BLACK INK ONLY—NO ERASURES, WHITEOUT, OR ALTERATIONS | LOCAL REGISTRATION DISTRICT AND CERTIFICATE NUMBER

STATE/LOCAL REGISTRAR USE ONLY	1A.	1B.	1C.	

TYPE OR PRINT IN BLACK INK ONLY

PART I INFORMATION TO LOCATE RECORD	1A. NAME—FIRST (GIVEN) River	1B. MIDDLE Jude	1C. LAST (FAMILY) Phoenix	2. SEX M
	3. DATE OF EVENT—MONTH, DAY, YEAR 10/31/1993	4A. CITY OF OCCURRENCE Los Angeles	4B. COUNTY OF OCCURRENCE Los Angeles	

PART II — INFORMATION AS IT APPEARS ON RECORD

21. DEATH WAS CAUSED BY: (ENTER ONLY ONE CAUSE PER LINE FOR A, B, AND C)
IMMEDIATE CAUSE (A) Deferred
DUE TO (B)
DUE TO (C)
TIME BETWEEN ONSET & DEATH

22. WAS DEATH REPORTED TO CORONER? [X] YES [ ] NO — REFERRAL NUMBER 93-10011
23. WAS BIOPSY PERFORMED? [ ] YES [ ] NO
24A. WAS AUTOPSY PERFORMED? [X] YES [ ] NO
24B. WAS IT USED IN DETERMINING CAUSE OF DEATH? [ ] YES [ ] NO
25. OTHER SIGNIFICANT CONDITIONS CONTRIBUTING TO DEATH BUT NOT RELATED TO CAUSE GIVEN IN 21
26. WAS OPERATION PERFORMED FOR ANY CONDITION IN ITEM 21 or 25? IF YES, LIST TYPE OF OPERATION AND DATE.
29. MANNER OF DEATH—SPECIFY ONE: NATURAL, ACCIDENT, SUICIDE, HOMICIDE, PENDING INVESTIGATION OR COULD NOT BE DETERMINED: Pending Investigation
30A. PLACE OF INJURY
30B. INJURY AT WORK [ ] YES [ ] NO
30C. DATE OF INJURY—MONTH, DAY, YEAR
31. HOUR
32. LOCATION (STREET AND NUMBER OR LOCATION AND CITY)
33. DESCRIBE HOW INJURY OCCURRED (EVENTS WHICH RESULTED IN INJURY)

PART III — INFORMATION AS IT SHOULD APPEAR

21. DEATH WAS CAUSED BY: (ENTER ONLY ONE CAUSE PER LINE FOR A, B, AND C)
IMMEDIATE CAUSE (A) Acute Multiple Drug Intoxication — TIME BETWEEN ONSET & DEATH: Unk.
DUE TO (B)
DUE TO (C)

2 OF 2

22. WAS DEATH REPORTED TO CORONER? [X] YES [ ] NO — REFERRAL NUMBER 93-10011
23. WAS BIOPSY PERFORMED? [ ] YES [X] NO
24A. WAS AUTOPSY PERFORMED? [X] YES [ ] NO
24B. WAS IT USED IN DETERMINING CAUSE OF DEATH? [X] YES [ ] NO
25. OTHER SIGNIFICANT CONDITIONS CONTRIBUTING TO DEATH BUT NOT RELATED TO CAUSE GIVEN IN 21: None
26. WAS OPERATION PERFORMED FOR ANY CONDITION IN ITEM 21 or 25? IF YES, LIST TYPE OF OPERATION AND DATE.: No
29. MANNER OF DEATH—SPECIFY ONE: NATURAL, ACCIDENT, SUICIDE, HOMICIDE, PENDING INVESTIGATION OR COULD NOT BE DETERMINED: Accident
30A. PLACE OF INJURY: Night Club
30B. INJURY AT WORK [ ] YES [X] NO
30C. DATE OF INJURY—MONTH, DAY, YEAR: Unknown
31. HOUR: Unk
32. LOCATION (STREET AND NUMBER OR LOCATION AND CITY): 8860 Sunset Blvd., West Hollywood
33. DESCRIBE HOW INJURY OCCURRED (EVENTS WHICH RESULTED IN INJURY): Intake Of Drugs

DECLARATION OF CERTIFYING PHYSICIAN OR CORONER

I HEREBY DECLARE UNDER PENALTY OF PERJURY THAT THE ABOVE INFORMATION IS TRUE AND CORRECT TO THE BEST OF MY KNOWLEDGE.

6A. SIGNATURE OF CERTIFYING PHYSICIAN OR CORONER	6B. DATE SIGNED	6C. TYPED OR PRINTED NAME AND DEGREE/TITLE OF CERTIFIER		
▶ Christopher Rogers	11-16-93	Christopher Rogers, M.D. DME		
7A. ADDRESS—STREET AND NUMBER		7B. CITY	7C. STATE	7D. ZIP CODE
1104 N. Mission Rd.		Los Angeles	CA.	90033

STATE/LOCAL REGISTRAR USE ONLY	8A. OFFICE OF STATE REGISTRAR OR SIGNATURE OF LOCAL REGISTRAR	8B. DATE ACCEPTED FOR REGISTRATION
	▶ Robert C. Gates	NOV 19 1993

STATE OF CALIFORNIA, DEPARTMENT OF HEALTH SERVICES, OFFICE OF STATE REGISTRAR — VS 24B (REV. 7/91)

THIS IS A TRUE CERTIFIED COPY OF THE RECORD FILED IN THE COUNTY OF LOS ANGELES DEPARTMENT OF HEALTH SERVICES IF IT BEARS THIS SEAL IN PURPLE INK.

NOV 19 1993

60

Director of Health Services and Registrar

CERTIFICATION OF VITAL RECORD

COUNTY OF LOS ANGELES • REGISTRAR-RECORDER/COUNTY CLERK

CERTIFICATE OF DEATH
STATE OF CALIFORNIA

STATE FILE NUMBER — LOCAL REGISTRATION DISTRICT AND CERTIFICATE NUMBER: 0190-024392

DECEDENT PERSONAL DATA

1A. NAME OF DECEDENT—FIRST: MARY | 1B. MIDDLE: PICKFORD | 1C. LAST: ROGERS | 2A. DATE OF DEATH (MONTH, DAY, YEAR): May 29, 1979 | 2B. HOUR: 1400

3. SEX: Female | 4. RACE: White | 5. ETHNICITY | 6. DATE OF BIRTH: APRIL 9, 1894 | 7. AGE: 85 YEARS | IF UNDER 1 YEAR: MONTHS, DAYS | IF UNDER 24 HOURS: HOURS, MINUTES

8. BIRTHPLACE OF DECEDENT (STATE OR FOREIGN COUNTRY): CANADA | 9. NAME AND BIRTHPLACE OF FATHER: JOHN SMITH CANADA | 10. BIRTH NAME AND BIRTHPLACE OF MOTHER: CHARLOTTE HENNESSEY CANADA

11. CITIZEN OF WHAT COUNTRY: U.S.A. | 12. SOCIAL SECURITY NUMBER: 564-26-9446 | 13. MARITAL STATUS: MARRIED | 14. NAME OF SURVIVING SPOUSE (IF WIFE, ENTER BIRTH NAME): BUDDY ROGERS

15. PRIMARY OCCUPATION: PRODUCER | 16. NUMBER OF YEARS THIS OCCUPATION: 50 | 17. EMPLOYER (IF SELF-EMPLOYED, SO STATE): SELF EMPLOYED | 18. KIND OF INDUSTRY OR BUSINESS: MOTION PICTURE

USUAL RESIDENCE

19A. USUAL RESIDENCE—STREET ADDRESS (STREET AND NUMBER OR LOCATION): 1143 Summit Drive | 19B. | 19C. CITY OR TOWN: Beverly Hills

19D. COUNTY: Los Angeles | 19E. STATE: California | 20. NAME AND ADDRESS OF INFORMANT—RELATIONSHIP: CHARLES BUDDY ROGERS, 1143 Summit Drive, Beverly Hills, Calif. 90210

PLACE OF DEATH

21A. PLACE OF DEATH: Santa Monica Hospital | 21B. COUNTY: Los Angeles

21C. STREET ADDRESS (STREET AND NUMBER OR LOCATION): 1225 15th Street | 21D. CITY OR TOWN: Santa Monica

CAUSE OF DEATH

22. DEATH WAS CAUSED BY: (ENTER ONLY ONE CAUSE PER LINE FOR A, B, AND C)

IMMEDIATE CAUSE (A) Cerebro vascular hemorrhage — 4 days

CONDITIONS, IF ANY, WHICH GAVE RISE TO THE IMMEDIATE CAUSE, STATING THE UNDERLYING CAUSE LAST

DUE TO, OR AS A CONSEQUENCE OF (B) Chronic arterio sclerotic heart disease — 6 years

DUE TO, OR AS A CONSEQUENCE OF (C) Chronic myocarditis — 7 "

APPROXIMATE INTERVAL BETWEEN ONSET AND DEATH

24. WAS DEATH REPORTED TO CORONER? no | 25. WAS BIOPSY PERFORMED? no | 26. WAS AUTOPSY PERFORMED? no

23. OTHER CONDITIONS CONTRIBUTING BUT NOT RELATED TO THE IMMEDIATE CAUSE OF DEATH: — | 27. WAS OPERATION PERFORMED FOR ANY CONDITION IN ITEMS 22 OR 23: TYPE OF OPERATION: no | DATE

PHYSICIAN'S CERTIFICATION

28A. I CERTIFY THAT DEATH OCCURRED AT THE HOUR, DATE AND PLACE STATED FROM THE CAUSES STATED. I ATTENDED DECEDENT SINCE (ENTER MO, DA, YR): 2-3-1942 | I LAST SAW DECEDENT ALIVE (ENTER MO, DA, YR): 5-29-79 | 28B. PHYSICIAN—SIGNATURE AND DEGREE OR TITLE: [signature] | 28C. DATE SIGNED: 5-30-79 | 28D. PHYSICIAN'S LICENSE NUMBER: 407327

28E. TYPE PHYSICIAN'S NAME AND ADDRESS: Lester V. Laurion M.D. 9615 Brighton Way Beverly Hills, Ca.

INJURY INFORMATION — CORONER'S USE ONLY

29. SPECIFY ACCIDENT, SUICIDE, ETC.: — | 30. PLACE OF INJURY: — | 31. INJURY AT WORK: — | 32A. DATE OF INJURY—MONTH, DAY, YEAR: — | 32B. HOUR

33. LOCATION (STREET AND NUMBER OR LOCATION AND CITY OR TOWN) | 34. DESCRIBE HOW INJURY OCCURRED (EVENTS WHICH RESULTED IN INJURY)

35A. I CERTIFY THAT DEATH OCCURRED AT THE HOUR, DATE AND PLACE STATED FROM THE CAUSES STATED. AS REQUIRED BY LAW I HAVE HELD AN (INQUEST-INVESTIGATION) | 35B. CORONER—SIGNATURE AND DEGREE OR TITLE | 35C. DATE SIGNED

36. DISPOSITION: CREMATION | 37. DATE—MONTH, DAY, YEAR: 5-31-79 | 38. NAME AND ADDRESS OF CEMETERY OR CREMATORY: LIVE OAK CREMATORY MONROVIA, CALIF. | 39. EMBALMER'S LICENSE NUMBER AND SIGNATURE: NOT EMBALMED

40. NAME OF FUNERAL DIRECTOR (OR PERSON ACTING AS SUCH): GATES, KINGSLEY & GATES SM | 41. LOCAL REGISTRAR—SIGNATURE: [signature] | 42. DATE ACCEPTED BY LOCAL REGISTRAR: MAY 30 1979

STATE REGISTRAR: A. | B. | C. | D. | E. | F.

VS-11 (10-78) — 01-3-1-0687

This is to certify that this document is a true copy of the official record filed with the Registrar-Recorder/County Clerk.

Beatriz Valdez
BEATRIZ VALDEZ
Registrar-Recorder/County Clerk

AUG 18 1995
19-397055

This copy not valid unless prepared on engraved border displaying the Seal and Signature of the Registrar-Recorder/County Clerk.

American Bank Note Company — ANY ALTERATION OR ERASURE VOIDS THIS CERTIFICATE

CERTIFICATION OF VITAL RECORD

COUNTY OF LOS ANGELES • REGISTRAR-RECORDER/COUNTY CLERK

CERTIFICATE OF DEATH

STATE OF CALIFORNIA—DEPARTMENT OF HEALTH
OFFICE OF THE STATE REGISTRAR OF VITAL STATISTICS

STATE FILE NUMBER

0190-003330

LOCAL REGISTRATION DISTRICT AND CERTIFICATE NUMBER

DECEDENT PERSONAL DATA

1a. NAME OF DECEASED—FIRST NAME: FREDDIE | 1b. MIDDLE NAME: | 1c. LAST NAME: PRINZE | 2a. DATE OF DEATH—MONTH DAY YEAR: January 29, 1977 | 2b. HOUR: 1300 hours

3. SEX: Male | 4. COLOR OR RACE: Caucasian | 5. BIRTHPLACE (STATE OR FOREIGN COUNTRY): New York | 6. DATE OF BIRTH: June 22, 1954 | 7. AGE (LAST BIRTHDAY): 22 YEARS | IF UNDER 1 YEAR | IF UNDER 24 HOURS

8. NAME AND BIRTHPLACE OF FATHER: Edward Karl Pruetzel, Germany | 9. MAIDEN NAME AND BIRTHPLACE OF MOTHER: Maria G. Graniela, Puerto Rico

10. CITIZEN OF WHAT COUNTRY: United States | 11. SOCIAL SECURITY NUMBER: 077-44-4340 | 12. MARRIED, NEVER MARRIED, WIDOWED, DIVORCED (SPECIFY): Married | 13. NAME OF SURVIVING SPOUSE (IF WIFE ENTER MAIDEN NAME): Kathy Cochran

14. LAST OCCUPATION: Actor | 15. NUMBER OF YEARS IN THIS OCCUPATION: 2½ | 16. NAME OF LAST EMPLOYING COMPANY OR FIRM (IF SELF EMPLOYED, SO STATE): Hunga Rican Productions, Inc. | 17. KIND OF INDUSTRY OR BUSINESS: Movies and Television

PLACE OF DEATH

18a. PLACE OF DEATH—NAME OF HOSPITAL OR OTHER IN PATIENT FACILITY: U.C.L.A. Medical Center | 18b. STREET ADDRESS—(STREET AND NUMBER, OR LOCATION): 10833 LeConte Avenue | 18c. INSIDE CITY CORPORATE LIMITS (SPECIFY YES OR NO): Yes

18d. CITY OR TOWN: West Los Angeles | 18e. COUNTY: Los Angeles | 18f. LENGTH OF STAY IN COUNTY OF DEATH: 2½ YEARS | 18g. LENGTH OF STAY IN CALIFORNIA: 2½ YEARS

USUAL RESIDENCE (IF DEATH OCCURRED IN INSTITUTION, ENTER RESIDENCE BEFORE ADMISSION)

19a. USUAL RESIDENCE—STREET ADDRESS (STREET AND NUMBER OR LOCATION): 10300 Wilshire Boulevard | 19b. INSIDE CITY CORPORATE LIMITS (SPECIFY YES OR NO): Yes | 20. NAME AND MAILING ADDRESS OF INFORMANT: Mrs. Kathy Prinze, 2837 LaCastano Drive, Hollywood, California 90046

19c. CITY OR TOWN: Los Angeles | 19d. COUNTY: Los Angeles | 19e. STATE: California

PHYSICIAN'S OR CORONER'S CERTIFICATION

21a. CORONER: I HEREBY CERTIFY THAT DEATH OCCURRED AT THE HOUR DATE AND PLACE STATED ABOVE FROM THE CAUSES STATED BELOW AND THAT I HAVE HELD AN INVESTIGATION OR INQUEST: Investigation | 21b. PHYSICIAN: I HEREBY CERTIFY THAT DEATH OCCURRED AT THE HOUR, DATE, AND PLACE STATED ABOVE FROM THE CAUSES STATED BELOW AND THAT I ATTENDED THE DECEASED FROM ... TO ... AND LAST SAW THE DECEASED ... | 21c. PHYSICIAN OR CORONER SIGNATURE: THOMAS T. NOGUCHI, M.D., CORONER, Roy D. Smith, DEPUTY | 21d. DATE SIGNED: 1-30-77

21e. ADDRESS: 1104 N. MISSION RD., LOS ANGELES, CALIF. 90033 | 21f. PHYSICIAN'S CALIFORNIA LICENSE NUMBER

FUNERAL DIRECTOR AND LOCAL REGISTRAR

22a. SPECIFY BURIAL, ENTOMBMENT OR CREMATION: Burial | 22b. DATE: 1-31-77 | 23. NAME OF CEMETERY OR CREMATORY: FOREST LAWN MEMORIAL-PARK | 24. EMBALMER—SIGNATURE (IF BODY EMBALMED) LICENSE NUMBER: #6707

25. NAME OF FUNERAL DIRECTOR (OR PERSON ACTING AS SUCH): Forest Lawn Hollywood Hills Mortuary | 26. IF NOT CERTIFIED BY CORONER, WAS THIS DEATH REPORTED TO CORONER? (SPECIFY YES OR NO) | 27. LOCAL REGISTRAR—SIGNATURE | 28. DATE RECEIVED FOR REGISTRATION BY LOCAL REGISTRAR: JAN 31 1977

MEDICAL AND HEALTH DATA — CAUSE OF DEATH

29. PART I. DEATH WAS CAUSED BY: ENTER ONLY ONE CAUSE PER LINE FOR A, B, AND C

IMMEDIATE CAUSE (A) GUNSHOT WOUND THROUGH HEAD.

CONDITIONS, IF ANY, WHICH GAVE RISE TO THE IMMEDIATE CAUSE (A), STATING THE UNDERLYING CAUSE LAST. DUE TO, OR AS A CONSEQUENCE OF (B)

DUE TO, OR AS A CONSEQUENCE OF (C)

APPROXIMATE INTERVAL BETWEEN ONSET AND DEATH

30. PART II: OTHER SIGNIFICANT CONDITIONS—CONTRIBUTING TO DEATH BUT NOT RELATED TO THE IMMEDIATE CAUSE GIVEN IN PART I | 31. WAS OPERATION OR BIOPSY PERFORMED FOR ANY CONDITION IN ITEMS 29 OR 30? (SPECIFY TYPE OF OPERATION AND/OR BIOPSY): Operation | 32a. AUTOPSY (SPECIFY YES OR NO): yes | 32b. IF YES, WERE FINDINGS CONSIDERED IN DETERMINING CAUSE OF DEATH? (SPECIFY YES OR NO): yes

INJURY INFORMATION

33. SPECIFY ACCIDENT, SUICIDE OR HOMICIDE: suicide | 34. PLACE OF INJURY (SPECIFY HOME, FARM, FACTORY, OFFICE BUILDING, ETC.): apartment | 35. INJURY AT WORK (SPECIFY YES OR NO): no | 36a. DATE OF INJURY—MONTH, DAY, YEAR: 1-28-77 | 36b. HOUR: 0330 hrs.

37a. PLACE OF INJURY (STREET AND NUMBER OR LOCATION AND CITY OR TOWN): 10300 Wilshire Blvd. #216 -West Los Angeles | 37b. DISTANCE FROM PLACE OF INJURY TO USUAL RESIDENCE, ITEM 19: 0 MILES | 38. WERE LABORATORY TESTS DONE FOR DRUGS OR TOXIC CHEMICALS (SPECIFY YES OR NO): yes | 39. WERE LABORATORY TESTS DONE FOR ALCOHOL? (SPECIFY YES OR NO): yes

12

40. DESCRIBE HOW INJURY OCCURRED (ENTER SEQUENCE OF EVENTS WHICH RESULTED IN INJURY. NATURE OF INJURY SHOULD BE ENTERED IN ITEM 29): As above, with .38 calibre revolver.

STATE REGISTRAR A. | B. | C. | D. | E. | F. 01-9-4-0796

This is to certify that this document is a true copy of the official record filed with the Registrar-Recorder/County Clerk.

CHARLES WEISSBURD
Registrar-Recorder/County Clerk

FEB 12 1992

19-312721

This copy not valid unless prepared on engraved border displaying the Seal and Signature of the Registrar-Recorder/County Clerk.

ANY ALTERATION OR ERASURE VOIDS THIS CERTIFICATE

CERTIFICATION OF VITAL RECORD

COUNTY OF LOS ANGELES • REGISTRAR-RECORDER/COUNTY CLERK

CERTIFICATE OF DEATH
STATE OF CALIFORNIA
USE BLACK INK ONLY

STATE FILE NUMBER | LOCAL REGISTRATION DISTRICT AND CERTIFICATE NUMBER: 38919025184

DECEDENT PERSONAL DATA

1A. NAME OF DECEDENT—FIRST (GIVEN): GILDA
1B. MIDDLE: SUSAN
1C. LAST (FAMILY): RADNER - WILDER
2A. DATE OF DEATH—MONTH, DAY, YEAR: MAY 20, 1989
2B. HOUR: 0620
3. SEX: FEMALE
4. RACE: CAUCASIAN
5. SPANISH/HISPANIC: ☐ YES ___ SPECIFY XX NO
6. DATE OF BIRTH—MONTH, DAY, YEAR: JUNE 28, 1946
7. AGE IN YEARS: 42 | IF UNDER 1 YEAR: MONTHS / DAYS | IF UNDER 24 HOURS: HOURS / MINUTES
8. STATE OF BIRTH: MICH.
9. CITIZEN OF WHAT COUNTRY: USA
10A. FULL NAME OF FATHER: HERMAN RADNER
10B. STATE OF BIRTH: RUSSIA
11A. FULL MAIDEN NAME OF MOTHER: HENRIETTA DWORKIN
11B. STATE OF BIRTH: RUSSIA
12. MILITARY SERVICE? 19__ TO 19__ XX NONE
13. SOCIAL SECURITY NUMBER: 371 46 2861
14. MARITAL STATUS: MARRIED
15. NAME OF SURVIVING SPOUSE (IF WIFE, ENTER MAIDEN NAME): GENE WILDER
16A. USUAL OCCUPATION: ACTRESS/WRITER
16B. USUAL KIND OF BUSINESS OR INDUSTRY: ENTERTAINMENT
16C. USUAL EMPLOYER: SELF-EMPLOYED
16D. YEARS IN USUAL OCCUPATION: 15
17. NUMBER OF HIGHEST GRADE COMPLETED (1-12 OR COLLEGE 13-17+): 14

USUAL RESIDENCE

18A. RESIDENCE—STREET AND NUMBER OR LOCATION: 476 SCOFIELDTOWN ROAD
18B. CITY: STAMFORD
18C. ZIP CODE: 06903
18D. COUNTY: FAIRFIELD
18E. NUMBER OF YEARS IN THIS COUNTY: 8
18F. STATE OR FOREIGN COUNTRY: CONNECTICUT
20. NAME, RELATIONSHIP, MAILING ADDRESS AND ZIP CODE OF INFORMANT: GENE WILDER-HUSBAND, 476 SCOFIELDTOWN ROAD, STAMFORD, CONNECTICUT. 06903

PLACE OF DEATH

19A. PLACE OF DEATH: CEDARS SINAI MEDICAL CTR
19B. IF HOSPITAL, SPECIFY ONE: IP
19C. COUNTY: LOS ANGELES
19D. STREET ADDRESS—STREET AND NUMBER OR LOCATION: 8700 BEVERLY BOULEVARD
19E. CITY: LOS ANGELES
22. WAS DEATH REPORTED TO CORONER? ☐ YES X NO

CAUSE OF DEATH

21. DEATH WAS CAUSED BY: (ENTER ONLY ONE CAUSE PER LINE FOR A, B, AND C)
IMMEDIATE CAUSE (A) OVARIAN CARCINOMA, METASTATIC — TIME INTERVAL BETWEEN ONSET AND DEATH: 2½ YRS
DUE TO (B)
DUE TO (C)
1 of 2
23. WAS BIOPSY PERFORMED? X YES ☐ NO
24A. WAS AUTOPSY PERFORMED? ☐ YES X NO
24B. IF YES, WAS IT USED IN DETERMINING CAUSE OF DEATH? X YES ☐ NO
25. OTHER SIGNIFICANT CONDITIONS CONTRIBUTING TO DEATH BUT NOT RELATED TO CAUSE GIVEN IN 21: NONE
26. WAS OPERATION PERFORMED FOR ANY CONDITION IN ITEM 21 OR 25? NO

PHYSICIAN'S CERTIFICATION

I CERTIFY THAT DEATH OCCURRED AT THE HOUR, DATE AND PLACE STATED FROM THE CAUSES STATED.
27A. DECEDENT ATTENDED SINCE: JANUARY 8, 1989 | DECEDENT LAST SEEN ALIVE: MAY 20, 1989
27B. SIGNATURE AND DEGREE OR TITLE OF PHYSICIAN: Edward J. Feldman
27C. PHYSICIAN'S LICENSE NUMBER: C032700
27D. DATE SIGNED: 5/22/89
27E. TYPE ATTENDING PHYSICIAN'S NAME AND ADDRESS: EDWARD J. FELDMAN, MD 8635 W.3RD. ST. #960-W LOS ANGELES, CALIF. 90048

CORONER'S USE ONLY

I CERTIFY THAT DEATH OCCURRED AT THE HOUR, DATE AND PLACE STATED FROM THE CAUSES STATED.
28A. SIGNATURE OF CORONER OR DEPUTY CORONER
28B. DATE SIGNED
29. MANNER OF DEATH—specify one: natural, accident, suicide, homicide, pending investigation or could not be determined
30A. PLACE OF INJURY
30B. INJURY AT WORK ☐ YES ☐ NO
30C. DATE OF INJURY MONTH, DAY, YEAR
31. HOUR
32. LOCATION (STREET AND NUMBER OR LOCATION AND CITY)
33. DESCRIBE HOW INJURY OCCURRED (EVENTS WHICH RESULTED IN INJURY)

FUNERAL DIRECTOR AND LOCAL REGISTRAR

34A. DISPOSITION: TR/BU
34B. PLACE OF FINAL DISPOSITION: LONG RIDGE UNION CEMETERY STAMFORD, FAIRFIELD CO, CT
34C. DATE OF DISPOSITION MONTH, DAY, YEAR: MAY 24, 1989
35A. SIGNATURE OF EMBALMER: [signature]
35B. LICENSE NUMBER: 7658
36A. NAME OF FUNERAL DIRECTOR (OR PERSON ACTING AS SUCH): PIERCE BROS. WESTWOOD VILLAGE
36B. LICENSE NO.: F-951
37. SIGNATURE OF LOCAL REGISTRAR: [signature] L.R.
38. REGISTRATION DATE: MAY 22 1989

20 STATE REGISTRAR: A. B. C. D. E. F. CENSUS TRACT

VS-11 (REV. 1-89) MAKE NO ERASURES, WHITEOUTS, OR OTHER ALTERATIONS

This is to certify that this document is a true copy of the official record filed with the Registrar-Recorder/County Clerk.

Charles Weissburd
CHARLES WEISSBURD
Registrar-Recorder/County Clerk

FEB 12 1992
19-312707

This copy not valid unless prepared on engraved border displaying the Seal and Signature of the Registrar-Recorder/County Clerk.

THE GREAT SEAL OF THE STATE OF CALIFORNIA — EUREKA

REGISTRAR-RECORDER/COUNTY CLERK — COUNTY OF LOS ANGELES, CALIFORNIA

American Bank Note Company

ANY ALTERATION OR ERASURE VOIDS THIS CERTIFICATE

CERTIFICATION OF VITAL RECORD

COUNTY OF LOS ANGELES • REGISTRAR-RECORDER/COUNTY CLERK

AFFIDAVIT TO AMEND A RECORD

89 14204
38919025184
LOCAL REGISTRATION DISTRICT AND CERTIFICATE NUMBER

89-109171
STATE FILE NUMBER

☐ BIRTH ☒ DEATH ☐ FETAL DEATH

PART I INFORMATION ON ORIGINAL CERTIFICATE

2 of 2

TYPE OR PRINT IN BLACK INK ONLY

1A. NAME—FIRST (GIVEN)	1B. MIDDLE	1C. LAST (FAMILY)
GILDA	SUSAN	RADNER-WILDER

2. SEX	3. DATE OF EVENT—MONTH, DAY, YEAR	4A. CITY OF OCCURRENCE	4B. COUNTY OF OCCURRENCE
F	May 20, 1989	LOS ANGELES	LOS ANGELES

5. FULL NAME OF FATHER	6. FULL MAIDEN NAME OF MOTHER
HERMAN RADNER	HENRIETTA DWORKIN

PART II STATEMENT OF CORRECTIONS

LIST ONE ITEM PER LINE

7. CERTIFICATE ITEM NUMBER	8A. INCORRECT INFORMATION ON ORIGINAL CERTIFICATE	8B. INFORMATION AS IT SHOULD BE STATED
18A	476 SCOFIELDTOWN ROAD	10930 CHALON ROAD
18B	STAMFORD	LOS ANGELES
18C	06903	90077
18D	FAIRFIELD	LOS ANGELES
18E	8	2
18F	CONNECTICUT	CALIFORNIA
20	GENE WILDER - HUSBAND	GENE WILDER - HUSBAND
	476 SCOFIELD TOWN ROAD, STAMFORD, CT.	10930 CHALON ROAD, LOS ANGELES, CA

REASON FOR CORRECTION: 9. Decendent was residing in Los Angeles for approximately two years prior to her death.

PART III SUPPORTING AFFIDAVITS

FIRST SUPPORTING AFFIDAVIT

I hereby certify under penalty of perjury that I have personal knowledge of the above facts and that the information given above is true and correct.

10A. SIGNATURE OF PERSON COMPLETING THE AFFIDAVIT	10B. TITLE OR RELATIONSHIP TO PERSON IN ITEM 1	10C. DATE SIGNED
[signature]	Executor of Estate	11/8/89

10D. AGE OF PERSON COMPLETING THE AFFIDAVIT	10E. ADDRESS OF PERSON COMPLETING THE AFFIDAVIT (STREET, CITY, STATE, ZIP)
53	605 Third Avenue, New York, New York 10158

SECOND SUPPORTING AFFIDAVIT

I hereby certify under penalty of perjury that I have personal knowledge of the above facts and that the information given above is true and correct.

11A. SIGNATURE OF PERSON COMPLETING THE AFFIDAVIT	11B. TITLE OR RELATIONSHIP TO PERSON IN ITEM 1	11C. DATE SIGNED
[signature]	Attorney for Decedent	11/10/89

11D. AGE OF PERSON COMPLETING THE AFFIDAVIT	11E. ADDRESS OF PERSON COMPLETING THE AFFIDAVIT (STREET, CITY, STATE, ZIP)
FORTY SEVEN (47)	2029 Century Park East, Suite 1690, Los Angeles, CA 90067

STATE/LOCAL REGISTRAR USE ONLY

12. OFFICE OF STATE OR LOCAL REGISTRAR	13. DATE ACCEPTED FOR REGISTRATION
Office of State Registrar of Vital Statistics	NOV 29 1989

STATE OF CALIFORNIA, DEPARTMENT OF HEALTH SERVICES, OFFICE OF STATE REGISTRAR — VS 24 (REV. 1/88)

This is to certify that this document is a true copy of the official record filed with the Registrar-Recorder/County Clerk.

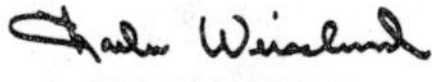

CHARLES WEISSBURD
Registrar-Recorder/County Clerk

19-312787

This copy not valid unless prepared on engraved border displaying the Seal and Signature of the Registrar-Recorder/County Clerk.

American Bank Note Company

ANY ALTERATION OR ERASURE VOIDS THIS CERTIFICATE

CERTIFICATE OF DEATH

STATE OF CALIFORNIA
USE BLACK INK ONLY/NO ERASURES, WHITEOUTS OR ALTERATIONS
VS-11 (REV. 7/93)

STATE FILE NUMBER 3 1994 15 — LOCAL REGISTRATION NUMBER 0927

DECEDENT PERSONAL DATA

1. NAME OF DECEDENT—FIRST (GIVEN)	2. MIDDLE	3. LAST (FAMILY)
Norman	Jay	Rambo

4. DATE OF BIRTH MM/DD/CCYY	5. AGE YRS.	IF UNDER 1 YEAR MONTHS / DAYS	IF UNDER 24 HOURS HOURS / MINUTES	6. SEX	7. DATE OF DEATH MM/DD/CCYY	8. HOUR
11/13/1941	52			M	03/21/1994	1630

9. STATE OF BIRTH	10. SOCIAL SECURITY NO.	11. MILITARY SERVICE	12. MARITAL STATUS	13. EDUCATION —YEARS COMPLETED
CA	551-56-3360	19 __ TO 19 __ [X] NONE	Never Married	12

14. RACE	15. HISPANIC—SPECIFY	16. USUAL EMPLOYER
Caucasian	[ ] YES [X] NO	Self-employed

17. OCCUPATION	18. KIND OF BUSINESS	19. YEARS IN OCCUPATION
Actor	Television Entertainment	35

USUAL RESIDENCE

20. RESIDENCE—STREET AND NUMBER OR LOCATION: 120 White Rock Avenue

21. CITY	22. COUNTY	23. ZIP CODE	24. YRS IN COUNTY	25. STATE OR FOREIGN COUNTRY
Earlimart	Tulare	93219	3	California

INFORMANT

26. NAME, RELATIONSHIP	27. MAILING ADDRESS (STREET AND NUMBER OR RURAL ROUTE NUMBER, CITY OR TOWN, STATE, ZIP)
Beatrice Rambo (mother)	120 White Rock Avenue Earlimart, CA 93219

SPOUSE AND PARENT INFORMATION

28. NAME OF SURVIVING SPOUSE—FIRST	29. MIDDLE	30. LAST (MAIDEN NAME)	
---	---	---	
31. NAME OF FATHER—FIRST	**32. MIDDLE**	**33. LAST**	**34. BIRTH STATE**
William	Lester	Rambo	MO
35. NAME OF MOTHER—FIRST	**36. MIDDLE**	**37. LAST (MAIDEN)**	**38. BIRTH STATE**
Beatrice	Ann	Rossi	CA

DISPOSITION(S)

39. DATE MM/DD/CCYY	40. PLACE OF FINAL DISPOSITION
03/25/1994	North Kern Cemetery District Delano, California

FUNERAL DIRECTOR AND LOCAL REGISTRAR

41. TYPE OF DISPOSITION(S)	42. SIGNATURE OF EMBALMER	43. LICENSE NO.
BURIAL	Dewey Stafford	5287

44. NAME OF FUNERAL DIRECTOR	45. LICENSE NO.	46. SIGNATURE OF LOCAL REGISTRAR	47. DATE MM/DD/CCYY
Delano Mortuary	FD 520	B. Jinadu, M.D.	03/24/1994

PLACE OF DEATH

101. PLACE OF DEATH	102. IF HOSPITAL, SPECIFY ONE	103. FACILITY OTHER THAN HOSPITAL	104. COUNTY
Delano Reg. Med. Center	[ ] IP [X] ER/OP [ ] DOA	[ ] CONV. HOSP. [ ] RES. [ ] OTHER	Kern

105. STREET ADDRESS—STREET AND NUMBER OR LOCATION	106. CITY
1401 Garces Highway	Delano

CAUSE OF DEATH

107. DEATH WAS CAUSED BY: (ENTER ONLY ONE CAUSE PER LINE FOR A, B, C, AND D)

	Cause	TIME INTERVAL BETWEEN ONSET AND DEATH
IMMEDIATE CAUSE (A)	RESPIRATORY ARREST	4 HRS
DUE TO (B)	DESSEMINATED KAPOSI SARCOMA	3 YRS
DUE TO (C)	ACQUIRED IMMUNODEFFICECY SYNDROME	3 YRS.
DUE TO (D)		

108. DEATH REPORTED TO CORONER: [X] YES [✓] NO — REFERRAL NUMBER C-0411-94
109. BIOPSY PERFORMED: [ ] YES [✓] NO
110. AUTOPSY PERFORMED: [ ] YES [✓] NO
111. USED IN DETERMINING CAUSE: [ ] YES [✓] NO

112. OTHER SIGNIFICANT CONDITIONS CONTRIBUTING TO DEATH BUT NOT RELATED TO CAUSE GIVEN IN 107: WASTING SYNDROME

113. WAS OPERATION PERFORMED FOR ANY CONDITION IN ITEM 107 OR 112? IF YES, LIST TYPE OF OPERATION AND DATE. NO.

PHYSICIAN'S CERTIFICATION

114. I CERTIFY THAT TO THE BEST OF MY KNOWLEDGE DEATH OCCURRED AT THE HOUR, DATE AND PLACE STATED FROM THE CAUSES STATED.

DECEDENT ATTENDED SINCE MM/DD/CCYY	DECEDENT LAST SEEN ALIVE MM/DD/CCYY	115. SIGNATURE AND TITLE OF CERTIFIER	116. LICENSE NO.	117. DATE MM/DD/CCYY
1/13/94	2/28/94	N Amin	A34159	3/22/94

118. TYPE ATTENDING PHYSICIAN'S NAME, MAILING ADDRESS + ZIP: Navin Amin, M.D., 2201 Mt. Vernon Ave, Bakersfield, CA 93306

CORONER'S USE ONLY

I CERTIFY THAT IN MY OPINION DEATH OCCURRED AT THE HOUR, DATE AND PLACE STATED FROM THE CAUSES STATED.

119. MANNER OF DEATH: [ ] NATURAL [ ] SUICIDE [ ] HOMICIDE [ ] ACCIDENT [ ] PENDING INVESTIGATION [ ] COULD NOT BE DETERMINED

120. INJURY AT WORK: [ ] YES [ ] NO — 121. INJURY DATE MM/DD/CCYY — 122. HOUR — 123. PLACE OF INJURY

124. DESCRIBE HOW INJURY OCCURRED (EVENTS WHICH RESULTED IN INJURY)

125. LOCATION (STREET AND NUMBER OR LOCATION AND CITY AND ZIP CODE)

126. SIGNATURE OF CORONER OR DEPUTY CORONER — 127. DATE MM/DD/CCYY — 128. TYPED NAME, TITLE OF CORONER OR DEPUTY CORONER

STATE REGISTRAR

A	B	C	D	E	F	G	H	FAX AUTH. #	CENSUS TRACT
		0429							99

CERTIFICATION OF VITAL RECORD

COUNTY OF LOS ANGELES • REGISTRAR-RECORDER/COUNTY CLERK

STATE FILE NUMBER

CERTIFICATE OF DEATH

STATE OF CALIFORNIA—DEPARTMENT OF PUBLIC HEALTH

LOCAL REGISTRATION DISTRICT AND CERTIFICATE NUMBER 7097-008945

FILED MAR 8 1967 RAY E. LEE COUNTY RECORDER

Orman R. Rambo #67-1385

H. Spear, M.D.

Final 2-28-67

DECEDENT PERSONAL DATA

1a. Name of deceased—first name	Orman
1b. Middle name	Ray
1c. Last name	Rambo
2a. Date of death—month, day, year	FEB. 5, 1967
2b. Hour	Approx. 7:45 P.M.
3. Sex	Male
4. Color or race	White
5. Birthplace (state or foreign country)	California
6. Date of birth	Nov. 13-1941
7. Age (last birthday)	25 years
8. Name and birthplace of father	William Lester Rambo-Missouri
9. Maiden name and birthplace of mother	Beatrice Rossi-Arkansas
10. Citizen of what country	United States
11. Social Security number	551-56-3361
12. Last occupation	Actor
13. Number of years in this occupation	1 Yr.
14. Name of last employing company or firm	Universal International
15. Kind of industry or business	Acting
16. If deceased was ever in U.S. armed forces, give war or dates of service	No
17. Specify married, never married, widowed, divorced	Single
18a. Name of present spouse	None
18b. Present or last occupation of spouse	None

PLACE OF DEATH 1901

19a. Place of death—name of hospital	
19b. Street address	Vista & Franklin Ave.
19c. City or town	Hollywood
19d. County	Los Angeles
19e. Length of stay in county of death	5 years
19f. Length of stay in California	Life

LAST USUAL RESIDENCE

20a. Last usual residence—street address	1965 Outpost Circle Dr.
20b. If inside city corporate limits	[X] Check here
20c. City or town	Los Angeles
20d. County	L.A.
20e. State	California
21a. Name of informant (if other than spouse)	William L. Rambo
21b. Address of informant	Rt. 1 Box 225 A.

PHYSICIAN'S OR CORONER'S CERTIFICATION

22a. Physician	
22b. Coroner	Autopsy
22c. Physician or coroner signature	B. Weinstein, Deputy, Theodore J. Curphey, M.D. Coroner
22d. Address	HALL OF JUSTICE, LOS ANGELES
22e. Date signed	3-1-67

FUNERAL DIRECTOR AND LOCAL REGISTRAR

23. Specify burial, entombment or cremation	Burial
24. Date	Feb. 9-1967
25. Name of cemetery or crematory	Delano Cemetery
26. Embalmer—signature, license number	J. V. Gallagher 4718
27. Name of funeral director	Delano Mortuary
28. Date accepted for registration by local registrar	MAR 2 1967
29. Local registrar—signature	[signature]

CAUSE OF DEATH

30. Cause of death. Part I. Death was caused by: Immediate cause (A) EXTENSIVE THERMAL BURNS OF ENTIRE BODY

Due to (B)

Due to (C)

Part II: Other significant conditions contributing to death but not related to the terminal disease condition given in Part I (A)

OPERATION AND AUTOPSY

31. Operation—check one: [X] No operation performed
32. Date of operation
33. Autopsy—check one: [X] Autopsy performed—gross findings used in determining above stated causes of death

INJURY INFORMATION

34a. Specify accident, suicide or homicide	ACCIDENT
34b. Describe how injury occurred	AUTO VS. AUTO AND BURST INTO FLAMES AS A RESULT OF COLLISION. (DRIVER)
35a. Time of injury (hour, month, day, year)	7:45 P.M. 2 5 67
35b. Injury occurred	[X] Not while at work
35c. Place of injury	STREET
35d. City, town, or location; county; state	LOS ANGELES, LA, CALIF.

This is to certify that this document is a true copy of the official record filed with the Registrar-Recorder/County Clerk.

OCT 4 1995

19-024558

This copy not valid unless prepared on engraved border displaying the Seal of the Registrar-Recorder/County Clerk.

ANY ALTERATION OR ERASURE VOIDS THIS CERTIFICATE

39419045636

CERTIFICATE OF DEATH

STATE OF CALIFORNIA

USE BLACK INK ONLY/NO ERASURES, WHITEOUTS OR ALTERATIONS

VS-11 (REV. 7/93)

STATE FILE NUMBER — LOCAL REGISTRATION NUMBER

DECEDENT PERSONAL DATA

Field	Entry
1. NAME OF DECEDENT—FIRST (GIVEN)	MARTHA
2. MIDDLE	-
3. LAST (FAMILY)	RAYE
4. DATE OF BIRTH MM/DD/CCYY	08/27/1916
5. AGE YRS.	78
IF UNDER 1 YEAR: MONTHS / DAYS	
IF UNDER 24 HOURS: HOURS / MINUTES	
6. SEX	F
7. DATE OF DEATH MM/DD/CCYY	10/19/1994
8. HOUR	1345
9. STATE OF BIRTH	MONTANA
10. SOCIAL SECURITY NO.	563-18-1774
11. MILITARY SERVICE	19 42 TO 19 73 ☐ NONE
12. MARITAL STATUS	MARRIED
13. EDUCATION —YEARS COMPLETED	12
14. RACE	CAUCASIAN
15. HISPANIC—SPECIFY	☐ YES ☒ NO
16. USUAL EMPLOYER	SELF-EMPLOYED
17. OCCUPATION	ENTERTAINER
18. KIND OF BUSINESS	THEATER/FILM/TELEVISION
19. YEARS IN OCCUPATION	74

USUAL RESIDENCE

Field	Entry
20. RESIDENCE—STREET AND NUMBER OR LOCATION	1153 ROSCOMARE ROAD
21. CITY	LOS ANGELES
22. COUNTY	LOS ANGELES
23. ZIP CODE	90077
24. YRS IN COUNTY	31
25. STATE OR FOREIGN COUNTRY	CALIFORNIA

INFORMANT

Field	Entry
26. NAME, RELATIONSHIP	MARK HARRIS - HUSBAND
27. MAILING ADDRESS (STREET AND NUMBER OR RURAL ROUTE NUMBER, CITY OR TOWN, STATE, ZIP)	1153 ROSCOMARE ROAD, LOS ANGELES, CA 90077

SPOUSE AND PARENT INFORMATION

Field	Entry
28. NAME OF SURVIVING SPOUSE—FIRST	MARK
29. MIDDLE	S.
30. LAST (MAIDEN NAME)	HARRIS
31. NAME OF FATHER—FIRST	PETER
32. MIDDLE	-
33. LAST	REED
34. BIRTH STATE	IRELAND
35. NAME OF MOTHER—FIRST	MAYBELLE
36. MIDDLE	-
37. LAST (MAIDEN)	HOOPER
38. BIRTH STATE	WISCONSIN

DISPOSITION(S)

Field	Entry
39. DATE MM/DD/CCYY	10/23/1994
40. PLACE OF FINAL DISPOSITION	FORT BRAGG NATIONAL CEMETERY, FORT BRAGG, NORTH CAROLINA

FUNERAL DIRECTOR AND LOCAL REGISTRAR

Field	Entry
41. TYPE OF DISPOSITION(S)	TR/BU
42. SIGNATURE OF EMBALMER	▶ William R. Pierce
43. LICENSE NO.	5595
44. NAME OF FUNERAL DIRECTOR	PIERCE BROS. WESTWOOD VILLAGE MORT.
45. LICENSE NO.	F-951
46. SIGNATURE OF LOCAL REGISTRAR	▶ [signature]
47. DATE MM/DD/CCYY	10/20/1994

PLACE OF DEATH

Field	Entry
101. PLACE OF DEATH	CEDARS SINAI MED. CENTER
102. IF HOSPITAL, SPECIFY ONE:	☒ IP ☐ ER/OP ☐ DOA
103. FACILITY OTHER THAN HOSPITAL:	☐ CONV. HOSP. ☐ RES. ☐ OTHER
104. COUNTY	LOS ANGELES
105. STREET ADDRESS—STREET AND NUMBER OR LOCATION	8700 BEVERLY BLVD.
106. CITY	LOS ANGELES

CAUSE OF DEATH

107. DEATH WAS CAUSED BY: (ENTER ONLY ONE CAUSE PER LINE FOR A, B, C, AND D)

	Cause	Time interval between onset and death
IMMEDIATE CAUSE (A)	ASPIRATION PNEUMONIA	2 DAYS
DUE TO (B)	MULTI CEREBRAL INFARCTION	3 YRS
DUE TO (C)	ARTERIOSCLEROSIS	YRS
DUE TO (D)		

Field	Entry
108. DEATH REPORTED TO CORONER	☒ YES ☐ NO — REFERRAL NUMBER 94-56113
109. BIOPSY PERFORMED	☒ YES ☐ NO
110. AUTOPSY PERFORMED	☐ YES ☒ NO
111. USED IN DETERMINING CAUSE	☐ YES ☐ NO
112. OTHER SIGNIFICANT CONDITIONS CONTRIBUTING TO DEATH BUT NOT RELATED TO CAUSE GIVEN IN 107	NO
113. WAS OPERATION PERFORMED FOR ANY CONDITION IN ITEM 107 OR 112? IF YES, LIST TYPE OF OPERATION AND DATE.	BILATERAL BELOW KNEE AMPUTATION 10/1993

18F

PHYSICIAN'S CERTIFICATION

Field	Entry
114. I CERTIFY THAT TO THE BEST OF MY KNOWLEDGE DEATH OCCURRED AT THE HOUR, DATE AND PLACE STATED FROM THE CAUSES STATED. DECEDENT ATTENDED SINCE MM/DD/CCYY	11/01/1993
DECEDENT LAST SEEN ALIVE MM/DD/CCYY	10/19/1994
115. SIGNATURE AND TITLE OF CERTIFIER	▶ Gilbert D. Callis MD
116. LICENSE NO.	C-24147
117. DATE MM/DD/CCYY	10/20/1994
118. TYPE ATTENDING PHYSICIAN'S NAME, MAILING ADDRESS + ZIP	GILBERT D. CALLIS, M.D. 444 SO. SAN VICENTE BLVD. #600, L.A.,CA 90048

CORONER'S USE ONLY

I CERTIFY THAT IN MY OPINION DEATH OCCURRED AT THE HOUR, DATE AND PLACE STATED FROM THE CAUSES STATED.

Field	Entry
119. MANNER OF DEATH	☐ NATURAL ☐ SUICIDE ☐ HOMICIDE ☐ ACCIDENT ☐ PENDING INVESTIGATION ☐ COULD NOT BE DETERMINED
120. INJURY AT WORK	☐ YES ☐ NO
121. INJURY DATE MM/DD/CCYY	
122. HOUR	
123. PLACE OF INJURY	
124. DESCRIBE HOW INJURY OCCURRED (EVENTS WHICH RESULTED IN INJURY)	
125. LOCATION (STREET AND NUMBER OR LOCATION AND CITY AND ZIP CODE)	
126. SIGNATURE OF CORONER OR DEPUTY CORONER	▶
127. DATE MM/DD/CCYY	
128. TYPED NAME, TITLE OF CORONER OR DEPUTY CORONER	

STATE REGISTRAR

A	B	C	D	E	F	G	H	FAX AUTH. #	CENSUS TRACT

4319 — 019-1-0555

CERTIFICATION OF VITAL RECORD

COUNTY OF LOS ANGELES • REGISTRAR-RECORDER/COUNTY CLERK

CERTIFICATE OF DEATH

STATE OF CALIFORNIA DEPARTMENT OF PUBLIC HEALTH

STATE FILE NUMBER

LOCAL REGISTRATION DISTRICT AND CERTIFICATE NUMBER 7053 12335

DECEDENT PERSONAL DATA

1A. NAME OF DECEASED—FIRST NAME: George aka: George | 1B. MIDDLE NAME: Lescher | 1C. LAST NAME: BESSOLO REEVES | 2A. DATE OF DEATH: 6-16-59 | 2B. HOUR: 1:20 A.M.

3. SEX: Male | 4. COLOR OR RACE: Caucasian | 5. BIRTHPLACE: Kentucky | 6. DATE OF BIRTH: January 6, 1914 | 7. AGE: 45 YEARS

8. NAME AND BIRTHPLACE OF FATHER: Frank Joseph Bessolo, Calif. | 9. MAIDEN NAME AND BIRTHPLACE OF MOTHER: Helen Lescher, Illinois | 10. CITIZEN OF WHAT COUNTRY: U. S. A. | 11. SOCIAL SECURITY NUMBER: 542-28-8600

12. LAST OCCUPATION: Actor | 13. NUMBER OF YEARS IN THIS OCCUPATION: 20 | 14. NAME OF LAST EMPLOYING COMPANY OR FIRM: Superman Inc. | 15. KIND OF INDUSTRY OR BUSINESS: Television & Motion Picture

16. IF DECEASED WAS EVER IN U.S. ARMED FORCES GIVE WAR OR DATES OF SERVICE: W. W. II | 17. SPECIFY MARRIED, NEVER MARRIED, WIDOWED, DIVORCED: Divorced | 18A. NAME OF PRESENT SPOUSE: — | 18B. PRESENT OR LAST OCCUPATION OF SPOUSE:

PLACE OF DEATH

19A. PLACE OF DEATH—NAME OF HOSPITAL: | 19B. STREET ADDRESS: 1579 Benedict Canyon Drive | [X] INSIDE CITY CORPORATE LIMITS | [ ] OUTSIDE CITY CORPORATE LIMITS

19C. CITY OR TOWN: Los Angeles | 19D. COUNTY: Los Angeles | 19E. LENGTH OF STAY IN COUNTY OF DEATH: 14 YEARS | 19F. LENGTH OF STAY IN CALIFORNIA: 14 YEARS

LAST USUAL RESIDENCE (WHERE DID DECEASED LIVE—IF IN INSTITUTION ENTER RESIDENCE BEFORE ADMISSION)

20A. LAST USUAL RESIDENCE—STREET ADDRESS: 1579 Benedict Canyon Drive | 20B. IF INSIDE CITY CORPORATE LIMITS: X | 21A. NAME OF INFORMANT (IF OTHER THAN SPOUSE): Helen L. Bessolo

20C. CITY OR TOWN: Los Angeles | 20D. COUNTY: Los Angeles | 20E. STATE: California | 21B. ADDRESS OF INFORMANT: 1447 N. Michigan Avenue, Pasadena, California

PHYSICIAN'S OR CORONER'S CERTIFICATION

22A. PHYSICIAN: I HEREBY CERTIFY THAT DEATH OCCURRED AT THE HOUR, DATE AND PLACE STATED ABOVE FROM THE CAUSES STATED BELOW AND THAT I ATTENDED THE DECEASED FROM ___ TO ___ AND THAT I LAST SAW THE DECEASED ALIVE ON ___

22C. PHYSICIAN OR CORONER—SIGNATURE: Theo. J. Curphey, M. D. Coroner By [signature] Deputy

22B. CORONER: I HEREBY CERTIFY THAT DEATH OCCURRED AT THE HOUR, DATE AND PLACE STATED ABOVE FROM THE CAUSES STATED BELOW AND THAT I HAVE HELD AN autopsy ON THE REMAINS OF DECEASED AS REQUIRED BY LAW | 22D. ADDRESS: HALL OF JUSTICE, LOS ANGELES | 22E. DATE SIGNED: 6-30-59

FUNERAL DIRECTOR AND LOCAL REGISTRAR

23. SPECIFY BURIAL, ENTOMBMENT OR CREMATION: Entombment | 24. DATE: July 1, 1959 | 25. NAME OF CEMETERY OR CREMATORY: Woodlawn Mausoleum | 26. EMBALMER—SIGNATURE: George C. Bouskill Jr. | LICENSE NUMBER: 4598

27. NAME OF FUNERAL DIRECTOR: Gates, Kingsley & Gates WW | 28. DATE ACCEPTED FOR REGISTRATION BY LOCAL REGISTRAR: JUL 3 1959 | 29. LOCAL REGISTRAR—SIGNATURE: George M. Uhl, M.D.

CAUSE OF DEATH

30. CAUSE OF DEATH — ENTER ONLY ONE CAUSE PER LINE FOR (A), (B) AND (C)

PART I. DEATH WAS CAUSED BY IMMEDIATE CAUSE (A): GUNSHOT WOUND OF HEAD

CONDITIONS, IF ANY, WHICH GAVE RISE TO THE ABOVE CAUSE (A) STATING THE UNDERLYING CAUSE LAST: DUE TO (B): | DUE TO (C):

APPROXIMATE INTERVAL BETWEEN ONSET AND DEATH

PART II. OTHER SIGNIFICANT CONDITIONS CONTRIBUTING TO DEATH BUT NOT RELATED TO THE TERMINAL DISEASE CONDITION GIVEN IN PART I (A)

OPERATION AND AUTOPSY

31. OPERATION—CHECK ONE: [ ] NO OPERATION PERFORMED [ ] OPERATION PERFORMED—FINDINGS USED IN DETERMINING ABOVE STATED CAUSES OF DEATH [ ] OPERATION PERFORMED—FINDINGS NOT USED IN DETERMINING ABOVE STATED CAUSES OF DEATH | 32. DATE OF OPERATION | 33. AUTOPSY—CHECK ONE: [ ] NO AUTOPSY PERFORMED [X] AUTOPSY PERFORMED—GROSS FINDINGS USED IN DETERMINING ABOVE STATED CAUSES OF DEATH [ ] AUTOPSY PERFORMED—GROSS FINDINGS NOT USED IN DETERMINING ABOVE STATED CAUSES OF DEATH

INJURY INFORMATION

34A. SPECIFY ACCIDENT, SUICIDE OR HOMICIDE: Suicide | 34B. DESCRIBE HOW INJURY OCCURRED: as above

35A. TIME OF INJURY: HOUR PRIOR TO 1:20 A.M. MONTH, DAY, YEAR 6-16-59

35B. INJURY OCCURRED: [ ] WHILE AT WORK [X] NOT WHILE AT WORK | 35C. PLACE OF INJURY: HOME | 35D. CITY, TOWN OR LOCATION: LOS ANGELES | COUNTY: LA | STATE: CALIF.

REEVES, George #41526 Pending 6-22

This is to certify that this document is a true copy of the official record filed with the Registrar-Recorder/County Clerk.

[signature]
CHARLES WEISSBURD
Registrar-Recorder/County Clerk

FEB 12 1992

19-310136

This copy not valid unless prepared on engraved border displaying the Seal and Signature of the Registrar-Recorder/County Clerk.

American Bank Note Company

ANY ALTERATION OR ERASURE VOIDS THIS CERTIFICATE

CERTIFICATION OF VITAL RECORD

COUNTY OF LOS ANGELES • REGISTRAR-RECORDER/COUNTY CLERK

CERTIFICATE OF DEATH
STATE OF CALIFORNIA
USE BLACK INK ONLY

39119027116

STATE FILE NUMBER — LOCAL REGISTRATION DISTRICT AND CERTIFICATE NUMBER

DECEDENT PERSONAL DATA

1A. NAME OF DECEDENT—FIRST (GIVEN): LEE
1B. MIDDLE: REMICK
1C. LAST (FAMILY): GOWANS
2A. DATE OF DEATH—MO, DAY, YR: JULY 2, 1991
2B. HOUR: 0515
3. SEX: FEMALE
4. RACE: CAUCASIAN
5. HISPANIC—SPECIFY: [ ] YES [X] NO
6. DATE OF BIRTH—MO, DAY, YR: DECEMBER 14, 1935
7. AGE IN YEARS: 55
IF UNDER 1 YEAR: MONTHS / DAYS — IF UNDER 24 HOURS: HOURS / MINUTES
8. STATE OF BIRTH: MASS.
9. CITIZEN OF WHAT COUNTRY: USA
10A. FULL NAME OF FATHER: FRANCIS EDWIN REMICK
10B. STATE OF BIRTH: MASS.
11A. FULL MAIDEN NAME OF MOTHER: MARGARET WALDO
11B. STATE OF BIRTH: NY
12. MILITARY SERVICE: 19__ TO 19__ [X] NONE
13. SOCIAL SECURITY NO.: 079-28-6011
14. MARITAL STATUS: MARRIED
15. NAME OF SURVIVING SPOUSE (IF WIFE, ENTER MAIDEN NAME): WILLIAM RORY GOWANS
16A. USUAL OCCUPATION: ACTRESS
16B. USUAL KIND OF BUSINESS OR INDUSTRY: FILM/TV
16C. USUAL EMPLOYER: SELF
16D. YEARS IN OCCUPATION: 38
17. EDUCATION—YEARS COMPLETED: 12

USUAL RESIDENCE

18A. RESIDENCE—STREET AND NUMBER OR LOCATION: 570 NORTH BUNDY DRIVE
18B. CITY: LOS ANGELES
18C. ZIP CODE: 90049
18D. COUNTY: LOS ANGELES
18E. NUMBER OF YEARS IN THIS COUNTY: 10
18F. STATE OR FOREIGN COUNTRY: CALIFORNIA
20. NAME, RELATIONSHIP, MAILING ADDRESS AND ZIP CODE OF INFORMANT: KATE COLLERAN SULLIVAN (DAUGHTER) 407 PARK AVE. SOUTH #4B NEW YORK, NY 10016

PLACE OF DEATH

19A. PLACE OF DEATH: RESIDENCE
19B. IF HOSPITAL, SPECIFY ONE: IP, ER/OP, DOA: —
19C. COUNTY: LOS ANGELES
19D. STREET ADDRESS—STREET AND NUMBER OR LOCATION: 570 N. BUNDY DRIVE
19E. CITY: LOS ANGELES

CAUSE OF DEATH

21. DEATH WAS CAUSED BY: (ENTER ONLY ONE CAUSE PER LINE FOR A, B, AND C)

	Cause	Time interval between onset and death
IMMEDIATE CAUSE (A)	Brain metastases	2 yr
DUE TO (B)	Right hypernephroma	2¼ yr
DUE TO (C)		

22. WAS DEATH REPORTED TO CORONER? REFERRAL NUMBER: [ ] YES [✓] NO
23. WAS BIOPSY PERFORMED? [✓] YES [ ] NO
24A. WAS AUTOPSY PERFORMED? [ ] YES [✓] NO
24B. WAS IT USED IN DETERMINING CAUSE OF DEATH? [ ] YES [✓] NO
25. OTHER SIGNIFICANT CONDITIONS CONTRIBUTING TO DEATH BUT NOT RELATED TO CAUSE GIVEN IN 21: Pulmonary metastases
26. WAS OPERATION PERFORMED FOR ANY CONDITION IN ITEM 21 OR 25? IF YES, LIST TYPE OF OPERATION AND DATE: Right nephrectomy 7/21/89

PHYSICIAN'S CERTIFICATION

I CERTIFY THAT TO THE BEST OF MY KNOWLEDGE DEATH OCCURRED AT THE HOUR, DATE AND PLACE STATED FROM THE CAUSES STATED.
27A. DECEDENT ATTENDED SINCE MONTH, DAY, YEAR: 4-3-89 — DECEDENT LAST SEEN ALIVE MONTH, DAY, YEAR: 6-30-91
27B. SIGNATURE AND DEGREE OR TITLE OF CERTIFIER: Avrum Bluming, MD
27C. CERTIFIER'S LICENSE NUMBER: G15859
27D. DATE SIGNED: 7/3/91
27E. TYPE ATTENDING PHYSICIAN'S NAME AND ADDRESS: AVRUM Z. BLUMING, MD 16311 VENTURA BLVD. #780. ENCINO, CA 91439

CORONER'S USE ONLY

I CERTIFY THAT IN MY OPINION DEATH OCCURRED AT THE HOUR, DATE AND PLACE STATED FROM THE CAUSES STATED.
28A. SIGNATURE AND TITLE OF CORONER OR DEPUTY CORONER
28B. DATE SIGNED
29. MANNER OF DEATH—specify one: natural, accident, suicide, homicide, pending investigation or could not be determined
30A. PLACE OF INJURY
30B. INJURY AT WORK [ ] YES [ ] NO
30C. DATE OF INJURY MONTH, DAY, YEAR
31. HOUR
32. LOCATION (STREET AND NUMBER OR LOCATION AND CITY)
33. DESCRIBE HOW INJURY OCCURRED (EVENTS WHICH RESULTED IN INJURY)

FUNERAL DIRECTOR AND LOCAL REGISTRAR

34A. DISPOSITION(S): CR/RES
34B. PLACE OF FINAL DISPOSITION—NAME AND ADDRESS: RESIDENCE: 570 NORTH BUNDY DRIVE LOS ANGELES, CA 90049
34C. DATE MO, DAY, YEAR: JULY 5, 1991
35A. SIGNATURE OF EMBALMER: NOT EMBALMED
35B. LICENSE NUMBER: NONE
36A. NAME OF FUNERAL DIRECTOR (OR PERSON ACTING AS SUCH): PIERCE BROS. WESTWOOD VILLAGE
36B. LICENSE NO.: F-951
37. SIGNATURE OF LOCAL REGISTRAR: Robert C. [illegible]
38. REGISTRATION DATE: JUL 03 1991

STATE REGISTRAR

A. B. C. D. E. F. CENSUS TRACT

VS-11 (REV 1-90) — MAKE NO ERASURES, WHITEOUTS, OR OTHER ALTERATIONS

This is to certify that this document is a true copy of the official record filed with the Registrar-Recorder/County Clerk.

JAN 22 1992

19-298650

CHARLES WEISSBURD
Registrar-Recorder/County Clerk

This copy not valid unless prepared on engraved border displaying the Seal and Signature of the Registrar-Recorder/County Clerk.

ANY ALTERATION OR ERASURE VOIDS THIS CERTIFICATE

STATE OF CALIFORNIA
CERTIFICATION OF VITAL RECORD

COUNTY OF LOS ANGELES • REGISTRAR-RECORDER/ COUNTY CLERK

Filed 2-13-73 James S. Allison Registrar-Recorder

CERTIFICATE OF DEATH

STATE FILE NUMBER — STATE OF CALIFORNIA—DEPARTMENT OF PUBLIC HEALTH — LOCAL REGISTRATION DISTRICT AND CERTIFICATE NUMBER 7097-005279

DECEDENT PERSONAL DATA

1a. NAME OF DECEASED—FIRST NAME	1b. MIDDLE NAME	1c. LAST NAME	2a. DATE OF DEATH—MONTH, DAY, YEAR	2b. HOUR
Edward	G.	Robinson	January 26, 1973	7:00 P M

3. SEX	4. COLOR OR RACE	5. BIRTHPLACE (STATE OR FOREIGN COUNTRY)	6. DATE OF BIRTH	7. AGE (LAST BIRTHDAY)	IF UNDER 1 YEAR	IF UNDER 24 HOURS
Male	Cauc.	Rumania	Dec. 12, 1893	79 YEARS		

8. NAME AND BIRTHPLACE OF FATHER	9. MAIDEN NAME AND BIRTHPLACE OF MOTHER
Shia Moshe Goldenberg, Rumania	Sara Gittel (Unknown) Rumania

10. CITIZEN OF WHAT COUNTRY	11. SOCIAL SECURITY NUMBER	12. MARRIED, NEVER MARRIED, WIDOWED, DIVORCED (SPECIFY)	13. NAME OF SURVIVING SPOUSE (IF WIFE, ENTER MAIDEN NAME)
USA	124-01-0380	Married	Jane Bodenheimer

14. LAST OCCUPATION	15. NUMBER OF YEARS IN THIS OCCUPATION	16. NAME OF LAST EMPLOYING COMPANY OR FIRM	17. KIND OF INDUSTRY OR BUSINESS
Actor	50	Self Employed	Motion Pictures

PLACE OF DEATH

18a. PLACE OF DEATH—NAME OF HOSPITAL OR OTHER IN-PATIENT FACILITY	18b. STREET ADDRESS—(STREET AND NUMBER, OR LOCATION)	18c. INSIDE CITY CORPORATE LIMITS (SPECIFY YES OR NO)
Mt. Sinai Hospital	8720 Beverly Blvd.	yes

18d. CITY OR TOWN	18e. COUNTY	18f. LENGTH OF STAY IN COUNTY OF DEATH	18g. LENGTH OF STAY IN CALIFORNIA
Los Angeles	Los Angeles	35 YEARS	35 YEARS

USUAL RESIDENCE (IF DEATH OCCURRED IN INSTITUTION, ENTER RESIDENCE BEFORE ADMISSION)

19a. USUAL RESIDENCE—STREET ADDRESS (STREET AND NUMBER OR LOCATION)	19b. INSIDE CITY CORPORATE LIMITS (SPECIFY YES OR NO)	20. NAME AND MAILING ADDRESS OF INFORMANT
910 N. Rexford Dr.	yes	Jack Karp

19c. CITY OR TOWN	19d. COUNTY	19e. STATE	
Beverly Hills	Los Angeles	California	1140 Laurel Way, Bev. Hills

PHYSICIAN'S OR CORONER'S CERTIFICATION

21a. CORONER	21b. PHYSICIAN: FROM	TO	LAST SAW HIM ALIVE	21c. PHYSICIAN OR CORONER—SIGNATURE AND DEGREE OR TITLE	21d. DATE SIGNED
	12-29-72	1-26-73	1-26-73	W G Mosher, MD	1-27-73
				21e. ADDRESS: 8733 Beverly Blvd	21f. PHYSICIAN'S CALIFORNIA LICENSE NUMBER: G 22248

FUNERAL DIRECTOR AND LOCAL REGISTRAR

22a. SPECIFY BURIAL, ENTOMBMENT OR CREMATION	22b. DATE	23. NAME OF CEMETERY OR CREMATORY	24. EMBALMER—SIGNATURE (IF BODY EMBALMED) LICENSE NUMBER
Entombment	Removal 1/28/73	Beth El Cemetery Brooklyn, New York	David George Rice #5229

25. NAME OF FUNERAL DIRECTOR (OR PERSON ACTING AS SUCH)	26. IF NOT CERTIFIED BY CORONER, WAS DEATH REPORTED TO CORONER?	27. LOCAL REGISTRAR—SIGNATURE	28. DATE ACCEPTED FOR REGISTRATION BY LOCAL REGISTRAR
Groman Mortuary bb	No	[illegible]	JAN 28 1973

MEDICAL AND HEALTH DATA — CAUSE OF DEATH

29. PART I. DEATH WAS CAUSED BY: ENTER ONLY ONE CAUSE PER LINE FOR A, B, AND C

		APPROXIMATE INTERVAL BETWEEN ONSET AND DEATH
IMMEDIATE CAUSE (A)	METASTATIC CARCINOMA of BLADDER	1 YR.
CONDITIONS, IF ANY, WHICH GAVE RISE TO THE IMMEDIATE CAUSE (A), STATING THE UNDERLYING CAUSE LAST. DUE TO, OR AS A CONSEQUENCE OF (B)		
DUE TO, OR AS A CONSEQUENCE OF (C)		

30. PART II: OTHER SIGNIFICANT CONDITIONS	31. WAS OPERATION OR BIOPSY PERFORMED?	32a. AUTOPSY	32b. IF YES, WERE FINDINGS CONSIDERED IN DETERMINING CAUSE OF DEATH?
	Biopsy	YES	YES

INJURY INFORMATION

33. SPECIFY ACCIDENT, SUICIDE OR HOMICIDE	34. PLACE OF INJURY	35. INJURY AT WORK	36a. DATE OF INJURY	36b. HOUR
				M.

37a. PLACE OF INJURY (STREET AND NUMBER OR LOCATION AND CITY OR TOWN)	37b. DISTANCE FROM PLACE OF INJURY TO USUAL RESIDENCE	38. WERE LABORATORY TESTS DONE FOR DRUGS OR TOXIC CHEMICALS	39. WERE LABORATORY TESTS DONE FOR ALCOHOL
	MILES		

40. DESCRIBE HOW INJURY OCCURRED

STATE REGISTRAR	A.	B.	C.	D.	E.	F.

This is to certify that this document is a true copy of the official record filed with the Registrar-Recorder/County Clerk.

Conny B. McCormack

CONNY B. McCORMACK
Registrar-Recorder/County Clerk

SEP 4 1998
19-518624

This copy not valid unless prepared on engraved border displaying the Seal and Signature of the Registrar-Recorder/County Clerk.

ANY ALTERATION OR ERASURE VOIDS THIS CERTIFICATE

CERTIFICATION OF VITAL RECORD

COUNTY OF RIVERSIDE

RIVERSIDE, CALIFORNIA 39533003396

CERTIFICATE OF DEATH
STATE OF CALIFORNIA
USE BLACK INK ONLY/NO ERASURES, WHITEOUTS OR ALTERATIONS
VS-11 (REV. 7/93)

STATE FILE NUMBER — LOCAL REGISTRATION NUMBER

DECEDENT PERSONAL DATA

1. NAME OF DECEDENT—FIRST (GIVEN): GINGER
2. MIDDLE: -
3. LAST (FAMILY): ROGERS
4. DATE OF BIRTH MM/DD/CCYY: 07/16/1911
5. AGE YRS.: 83
IF UNDER 1 YEAR: MONTHS / DAYS — IF UNDER 24 HOURS: HOURS / MINUTES
6. SEX: F
7. DATE OF DEATH MM/DD/CCYY: 04/25/1995
8. HOUR: 0710
9. STATE OF BIRTH: MO
10. SOCIAL SECURITY NO.: 551-09-3106
11. MILITARY SERVICE: 19__ TO 19__ [X] NONE
12. MARITAL STATUS: DIVORCED
13. EDUCATION—YEARS COMPLETED: 12
14. RACE: WHITE
15. HISPANIC—SPECIFY: [ ] YES ____ [X] NO
16. USUAL EMPLOYER: SELF EMPLOYED
17. OCCUPATION: ENTERTAINER
18. KIND OF BUSINESS: MOTION PICTURE INDUSTRY
19. YEARS IN OCCUPATION: 50

01

1OF3

USUAL RESIDENCE

20. RESIDENCE—STREET AND NUMBER OR LOCATION: 4460 PIONEER ROAD
21. CITY: MEDFORD
22. COUNTY: JACKSON
23. ZIP CODE: 97501
24. YRS IN COUNTY: 24
25. STATE OR FOREIGN COUNTRY: OREGON

INFORMANT

26. NAME, RELATIONSHIP: PAUL BECKER, EXECUTOR
27. MAILING ADDRESS (STREET AND NUMBER OR RURAL ROUTE NUMBER, CITY OR TOWN, STATE, ZIP): 975 OLD FERRY RD, SHADY COVE, OR 97539

SPOUSE AND PARENT INFORMATION

28. NAME OF SURVIVING SPOUSE—FIRST: -
29. MIDDLE: -
30. LAST (MAIDEN NAME): -
31. NAME OF FATHER—FIRST: WILLIAM
32. MIDDLE: -
33. LAST: McMATH
34. BIRTH STATE: USA-UNK
35. NAME OF MOTHER—FIRST: LELA
36. MIDDLE: -
37. LAST (MAIDEN): OWENS
38. BIRTH STATE: IA

DISPOSITION(S)

39. DATE MM/DD/CCYY: 04/28/1995
40. PLACE OF FINAL DISPOSITION: OAKWOOD MEMORIAL PARK, 22601 LASSEN, CHATSWORTH, CA 91311

FUNERAL DIRECTOR AND LOCAL REGISTRAR

41. TYPE OF DISPOSITION(S): CR/BU
42. SIGNATURE OF EMBALMER: David Mc Knight
43. LICENSE NO.: E7371
44. NAME OF FUNERAL DIRECTOR: PALM SPRINGS MORT. CATHEDRAL CITY
45. LICENSE NO.: FD 1513
46. SIGNATURE OF LOCAL REGISTRAR: Bradley P. Gilbert MD
47. DATE MM/DD/CCYY: 04/28/1995

PLACE OF DEATH

26

44902

101. PLACE OF DEATH: RESIDENCE
102. IF HOSPITAL, SPECIFY ONE: [ ] IP [ ] ER/OP [ ] DOA
103. FACILITY OTHER THAN HOSPITAL: [ ] CONV. HOSP. [X] RES. [ ] OTHER
104. COUNTY: RIVERSIDE
105. STREET ADDRESS—STREET AND NUMBER OR LOCATION: 40 230 CLUB VIEW DRIVE
106. CITY: RANCHO MIRAGE

CAUSE OF DEATH

107. DEATH WAS CAUSED BY: (ENTER ONLY ONE CAUSE PER LINE FOR A, B, C, AND D)
IMMEDIATE CAUSE (A): PENDING
DUE TO (B)
DUE TO (C)
DUE TO (D)
TIME INTERVAL BETWEEN ONSET AND DEATH
108. DEATH REPORTED TO CORONER: [X] YES [ ] NO — REFERRAL NUMBER: 95-2118
109. BIOPSY PERFORMED: [ ] YES [X] NO
110. AUTOPSY PERFORMED: [X] YES [ ] NO
111. USED IN DETERMINING CAUSE: [X] YES [ ] NO
112. OTHER SIGNIFICANT CONDITIONS CONTRIBUTING TO DEATH BUT NOT RELATED TO CAUSE GIVEN IN 107
113. WAS OPERATION PERFORMED FOR ANY CONDITION IN ITEM 107 OR 112? IF YES, LIST TYPE OF OPERATION AND DATE.

PHYSICIAN'S CERTIFICATION

114. I CERTIFY THAT TO THE BEST OF MY KNOWLEDGE DEATH OCCURRED AT THE HOUR, DATE AND PLACE STATED FROM THE CAUSES STATED. DECEDENT ATTENDED SINCE MM/DD/CCYY — DECEDENT LAST SEEN ALIVE MM/DD/CCYY
115. SIGNATURE AND TITLE OF CERTIFIER
116. LICENSE NO.
117. DATE MM/DD/CCYY
118. TYPE ATTENDING PHYSICIAN'S NAME, MAILING ADDRESS + ZIP

CORONER'S USE ONLY

I CERTIFY THAT IN MY OPINION DEATH OCCURRED AT THE HOUR, DATE AND PLACE STATED FROM THE CAUSES STATED.
119. MANNER OF DEATH: [ ] NATURAL [ ] SUICIDE [ ] HOMICIDE [ ] ACCIDENT [X] PENDING INVESTIGATION [ ] COULD NOT BE DETERMINED
120. INJURY AT WORK: [ ] YES [ ] NO
121. INJURY DATE MM/DD/CCYY
122. HOUR
123. PLACE OF INJURY
124. DESCRIBE HOW INJURY OCCURRED (EVENTS WHICH RESULTED IN INJURY)
125. LOCATION (STREET AND NUMBER OR LOCATION AND CITY AND ZIP CODE)
126. SIGNATURE OF CORONER OR DEPUTY CORONER: William R. Broman Jr.
127. DATE MM/DD/CCYY: 04/28/1995
128. TYPED NAME, TITLE OF CORONER OR DEPUTY CORONER: WILLIAM R. BROMAN JR. DEPUTY CORONER

STATE REGISTRAR A B C D E F G H FAX AUTH. # CENSUS TRACT

563588

CERTIFIED COPY OF VITAL RECORDS

STATE OF CALIFORNIA } ss
COUNTY OF RIVERSIDE }

DATE ISSUED 06/20/1995

This is a true and exact reproduction of the document officially registered and placed on file in the office of County of Riverside, Department of Health.

Bradley P. Gilbert M.D
Director, Health Services
Local Registrar
RIVERSIDE COUNTY, CALIFORNIA

THE GREAT SEAL OF THE STATE OF CALIFORNIA — EUREKA

DEPARTMENT OF HEALTH — REGISTRAR OF VITAL STATISTICS — COUNTY OF RIVERSIDE

This copy not valid unless prepared on engraved border displaying seal and signature of Registrar.

American Bank Note Company

ANY ALTERATION OR ERASURE VOIDS THIS CERTIFICATE

CERTIFICATION OF VITAL RECORD

COUNTY OF RIVERSIDE

RIVERSIDE, CALIFORNIA

AMENDMENT OF MEDICAL AND HEALTH DATA—DEATH

STATE FILE NUMBER — USE BLACK INK ONLY—NO ERASURES, WHITEOUT, OR ALTERATIONS — 39533003396 LOCAL REGISTRATION DISTRICT AND CERTIFICATE NUMBER

STATE/LOCAL REGISTRAR USE ONLY: 1 | 2 | 3

TYPE OR PRINT IN BLACK INK ONLY

PART I — INFORMATION TO LOCATE RECORD

1. NAME—FIRST (GIVEN)	2. MIDDLE	3. LAST (FAMILY)	4. SEX
GINGER	-	ROGERS	F
5. DATE OF EVENT—MM/DD/CCYY	6. CITY OF OCCURENCE	7. COUNTY OF OCCURRENCE	
04/25/1995	RANCHO MIRAGE	RIVERSIDE	

PART II — INFORMATION AS IT APPEARS ON RECORD

3 OF 3

107. DEATH WAS CAUSED BY ENTER ONLY ONE CAUSE PER LINE FOR A, B, C, AND D) — TIME INTERVAL BETWEEN ONSET AND DEATH

IMMEDIATE CAUSE (A) PENDING

(B)

(C)

DUE TO (D)

108. DEATH REPORTED TO CORONER [X] YES [ ] NO — REFERRAL NUMBER 95-2118

109. BIOPSY PERFORMED [ ] YES [X] NO

110. AUTOPSY PERFORMED [X] YES [ ] NO

111. USED IN DETERMINING CAUSE [X] YES [ ] NO

112. OTHER SIGNIFICANT CONDITIONS CONTRIBUTING TO DEATH BUT NOT RELATED TO CAUSE GIVEN IN 107

113. WAS OPERATION PERFORMED FOR ANY CONDITION IN ITEM 107 or 112? IF YES, LIST TYPE OF OPERATION AND DATE.

119. MANNER OF DEATH [ ] NATURAL [ ] SUICIDE [ ] HOMICIDE [ ] ACCIDENT [X] PENDING INVESTIGATION [ ] COULD NOT BE DETERMINED

120. INJURY AT WORK [ ] YES [ ] NO — 121. INJURY DATE—MM / DD / CCYY — 122. HOUR — 123. PLACE OF INJURY

124. DESCRIBE HOW INJURY OCCURED (EVENTS WHICH RESULTED IN INJURY)

125. LOCATION (STREET AND NUMBER OR LOCATION AND CITY AND ZIP CODE)

PART III — INFORMATION AS IT SHOULD APPEAR

107. DEATH WAS CAUSED BY ENTER ONLY ONE CAUSE PER LINE FOR A, B, C, AND D) — TIME INTERVAL BETWEEN ONSET AND DEATH

IMMEDIATE CAUSE (A) ACUTE MYOCARDIAL INFARCTION — MINS.

(B) ATHEROSCLEROTIC CARDIOVASCULAR DISEASE — YRS.

(C)

DUE TO (D)

108. DEATH REPORTED TO CORONER [X] YES [ ] NO — REFERRAL NUMBER 95-2118

109. BIOPSY PERFORMED [ ] YES [X] NO

110. AUTOPSY PERFORMED [X] YES [ ] NO

111. USED IN DETERMINING CAUSE [X] YES [ ] NO

112. OTHER SIGNIFICANT CONDITIONS CONTRIBUTING TO DEATH BUT NOT RELATED TO CAUSE GIVEN IN 107

NONE

113. WAS OPERATION PERFORMED FOR ANY CONDITION IN ITEM 107 or 112? IF YES, LIST TYPE OF OPERATION AND DATE.

NO

119. MANNER OF DEATH [X] NATURAL [ ] SUICIDE [ ] HOMICIDE [ ] ACCIDENT [ ] PENDING INVESTIGATION [ ] COULD NOT BE DETERMINED

120. INJURY AT WORK [ ] YES [ ] NO — 121. INJURY DATE—MM / DD / CCYY — 122. HOUR — 123. PLACE OF INJURY

124. DESCRIBE HOW INJURY OCCURRED (EVENTS WHICH RESULTED IN INJURY)

125. LOCATION (STREET AND NUMBER OR LOCATION AND CITY AND ZIP CODE)

DECLARATION OF CERTIFYING PHYSICIAN OR CORONER

I HEREBY DECLARE UNDER PENALTY OF PERJURY THAT THE ABOVE INFORMATION IS TRUE AND CORRECT TO THE BEST OF MY KNOWLEDGE.

8. SIGNATURE OF CERTIFYING PHYSICIAN OR CORONER	9. DATE SIGNED—MM/DD/CCYY	10. TYPED OR PRINTED NAME AND DEGREE/TITLE OF CERTIFIER	
Phillip Sandoval	05/09/1995	PHILLIP SANDOVAL, DEPUTY	
11. ADDRESS—STREET AND NUMBER	12. CITY	13. STATE	14. ZIP CODE
79-733 COUNTRY CLUB DRIVE, SUITE A	BERMUDA DUNES	CA	92201

STATE/LOCAL REGISTRAR USE ONLY: 15. OFFICE OF STATE REGISTRAR OR SIGNATURE OF LOCAL REGISTRAR — OFFICE OF THE STATE REGISTRAR OF VITAL STATISTICS — 16. DATE ACCEPTED FOR REGISTRATION—MM/DD/CCYY — JUN 0 9 1995

STATE OF CALIFORNIA, DEPARTMENT OF HEALTH SERVICES, OFFICE OF STATE REGISTRAR — VS-24 B (1/94) 93 24457

563606

CERTIFIED COPY OF VITAL RECORDS

STATE OF CALIFORNIA }
COUNTY OF RIVERSIDE } ss

DATE ISSUED

This is a true and exact reproduction of the document officially registered and placed on file in the office of County of Riverside, Department of Health. 06/20/1995

Bradley P. Gilbert M.D.
Director, Health Services
Local Registrar
RIVERSIDE COUNTY, CALIFORNIA

This copy not valid unless prepared on engraved border displaying seal and signature of Registrar.

THE GREAT SEAL OF THE STATE OF CALIFORNIA — EUREKA

DEPARTMENT OF HEALTH — REGISTRAR OF VITAL STATISTICS — COUNTY OF RIVERSIDE

American Bank Note Company — ANY ALTERATION OR ERASURE VOIDS THIS CERTIFICATE

STATE OF CALIFORNIA
CERTIFICATION OF VITAL RECORD

COUNTY of SAN BERNARDINO

DEPARTMENT OF PUBLIC HEALTH
351 MT. VIEW AVENUE, SAN BERNARDINO, CALIFORNIA 92415-0010

CERTIFICATE OF DEATH

STATE OF CALIFORNIA
USE BLACK INK ONLY/NO ERASURES, WHITEOUTS OR ALTERATIONS
VS-11 (REV. 7/97)

STATE FILE NUMBER

LOCAL REGISTRATION NUMBER: 3 1998 36005985

DECEDENT PERSONAL DATA

1. NAME OF DECEDENT—FIRST (GIVEN): Roy
2. MIDDLE: –
3. LAST (FAMILY): Rogers
4. DATE OF BIRTH MM/DD/CCYY: 11/05/1911
5. AGE YRS.: 86
IF UNDER 1 YEAR: MONTHS / DAYS; IF UNDER 24 HOURS: HOURS / MINUTES
6. SEX: Male
7. DATE OF DEATH MM/DD/CCYY: 07/06/1998
8. HOUR: 0415
9. STATE OF BIRTH: OH
10. SOCIAL SECURITY NO.: 570-16-5174
11. MILITARY SERVICE: ☐ YES ☒ NO ☐ UNK
12. MARITAL STATUS: Married
13. EDUCATION—YEARS COMPLETED: 10
14. RACE: White
15. HISPANIC—SPECIFY: ☐ YES ☒ NO
16. USUAL EMPLOYER: Self Employed
17. OCCUPATION: Entertainer
18. KIND OF BUSINESS: Entertainment
19. YEARS IN OCCUPATION: 65

USUAL RESIDENCE

20. RESIDENCE—(STREET AND NUMBER OR LOCATION): 19838 Tomahawk Rd.
21. CITY: Apple Valley
22. COUNTY: San Bernardino
23. ZIP CODE: 92307
24. YRS IN COUNTY: 32
25. STATE OR FOREIGN COUNTRY: CA

INFORMANT

26. NAME, RELATIONSHIP: Roy Rogers Jr. Son
27. MAILING ADDRESS (STREET AND NUMBER OR RURAL ROUTE NUMBER, CITY OR TOWN, STATE, ZIP): 15050 Seneca Rd., Victorville, CA 92392

SPOUSE AND PARENT INFORMATION

28. NAME OF SURVIVING SPOUSE—FIRST: Dale
29. MIDDLE: Evans
30. LAST (MAIDEN NAME): Smith
31. NAME OF FATHER—FIRST: Andrew
32. MIDDLE: Erlin
33. LAST: Slye –
34. BIRTH STATE: OH
35. NAME OF MOTHER—FIRST: Mattie
36. MIDDLE: Martha
37. LAST (MAIDEN): Womack
38. BIRTH STATE: KY

DISPOSITION(S)

39. DATE MM/DD/CCYY: 07/11/1998
40. PLACE OF FINAL DISPOSITION: Sunset Hills Memorial Park, 24000 Waalew Rd., Apple Valley, CA 92307

FUNERAL DIRECTOR AND LOCAL REGISTRAR

41. TYPE OF DISPOSITION(S): BU
42. SIGNATURE OF EMBALMER: ▶ [signature]
43. LICENSE NO.: 7504
44. NAME OF FUNERAL DIRECTOR: Sunset Hills Mortuary
45. LICENSE NO.: FD1640
46. SIGNATURE OF LOCAL REGISTRAR: ▶ [signature] MD
47. DATE MM/DD/CCYY: 07/09/1998

PLACE OF DEATH

101. PLACE OF DEATH: At Home
102. IF HOSPITAL, SPECIFY ONE: ☐ IP ☐ ER/OP ☐ DOA
103. FACILITY OTHER THAN HOSPITAL: ☐ CONV. HOSP. ☐ RES. CARE ☐ OTHER
104. COUNTY: San Bernardino
105. STREET ADDRESS—STREET AND NUMBER OR LOCATION: 19838 Tomahawk Rd.
106. CITY: Apple Valley

CAUSE OF DEATH

107. DEATH WAS CAUSED BY: (ENTER ONLY ONE CAUSE PER LINE FOR A, B, C, AND D)

		TIME INTERVAL BETWEEN ONSET AND DEATH
IMMEDIATE CAUSE	(A) Congestive heart failure	Yrs.
DUE TO	(B) Arteriosclerotic heart disease	Yrs.
DUE TO	(C)	
DUE TO	(D)	

108. DEATH REPORTED TO CORONER: ☒ YES ☐ NO — REFERRAL NUMBER: 98-4143LM
109. BIOPSY PERFORMED: ☐ YES ☒ NO
110. AUTOPSY PERFORMED: ☐ YES ☒ NO
111. USED IN DETERMINING CAUSE: ☐ YES ☐ NO
112. OTHER SIGNIFICANT CONDITIONS CONTRIBUTING TO DEATH BUT NOT RELATED TO CAUSE GIVEN IN 107: Chronic Obstructive Pulmonary Disease, Renal Insufficency
113. WAS OPERATION PERFORMED FOR ANY CONDITION IN ITEM 107 OR 112? IF YES, LIST TYPE OF OPERATION AND DATE: Coronary Artery Bypass Surgery – 09/--/1976

PHYSICIAN'S CERTIFICATION

114. I CERTIFY THAT TO THE BEST OF MY KNOWLEDGE DEATH OCCURRED AT THE HOUR, DATE AND PLACE STATED FROM THE CAUSES STATED.
DECEDENT ATTENDED SINCE MM/DD/CCYY: 06/26/1998
DECEDENT LAST SEEN ALIVE MM/DD/CCYY: 06/26/1998
115. SIGNATURE AND TITLE OF CERTIFIER: ▶ [signature]
116. LICENSE NO.: C17924
117. DATE MM/DD/CCYY: 07/09/1998
118. TYPE ATTENDING PHYSICIAN'S NAME, MAILING ADDRESS, ZIP: Jack Brokken, MD, 17450 Main St., Hesperia, CA 92345

CORONER'S USE ONLY

I CERTIFY THAT IN MY OPINION DEATH OCCURRED AT THE HOUR, DATE AND PLACE STATED FROM THE CAUSES STATED.
119. MANNER OF DEATH: ☐ NATURAL ☐ SUICIDE ☐ HOMICIDE ☐ ACCIDENT ☐ PENDING INVESTIGATION ☐ COULD NOT BE DETERMINED
120. INJURY AT WORK: ☐ YES ☐ NO
121. INJURY DATE MM/DD/CCYY
122. HOUR
123. PLACE OF INJURY
124. DESCRIBE HOW INJURY OCCURRED (EVENTS WHICH RESULTED IN INJURY)
125. LOCATION (STREET AND NUMBER OR LOCATION AND CITY, ZIP)
126. SIGNATURE OF CORONER OR DEPUTY CORONER ▶
127. DATE MM/DD/CCYY
128. TYPED NAME, TITLE OF CORONER OR DEPUTY CORONER

STATE REGISTRAR	A 10-7-13	B	C	D	E	F	G	H	FAX AUTH. # 4055873	CENSUS TRACT 09706

878007

CERTIFIED COPY OF VITAL RECORDS

STATE OF CALIFORNIA
COUNTY OF SAN BERNARDINO } SS

DATE ISSUED 08 / 19 / 1998

This is a true and exact reproduction of the document officially registered and placed on file in the VITAL RECORDS SECTION, SAN BERNARDINO DEPARTMENT OF PUBLIC HEALTH.

THOMAS J. PRENDERGAST, M.D.
COUNTY HEALTH OFFICER
REGISTRAR OF VITAL STATISTICS

THE GREAT SEAL OF THE STATE OF CALIFORNIA — EUREKA

DEPARTMENT OF PUBLIC HEALTH — COUNTY OF SAN BERNARDINO

This copy not valid unless prepared on engraved border displaying seal and signature of Registrar.

MIDWEST BANK NOTE COMPANY

ANY ALTERATION OR ERASURE VOIDS THIS CERTIFICATE

CERTIFICATE OF DEATH

STATE OF CALIFORNIA
USE BLACK INK ONLY/NO ERASURES, WHITEOUTS OR ALTERATIONS
VS-11 (REV. 7/93)

STATE FILE NUMBER | LOCAL REGISTRATION NUMBER

DECEDENT PERSONAL DATA

1. NAME OF DECEDENT—FIRST (GIVEN)	2. MIDDLE	3. LAST (FAMILY)
CESAR	JULIO	ROMERO JR

4. DATE OF BIRTH MM/DD/CCYY	5. AGE YRS.	IF UNDER 1 YEAR MONTHS / DAYS	IF UNDER 24 HOURS HOURS / MINUTES	6. SEX	7. DATE OF DEATH MM/DD/CCYY	8. HOUR
02/15/1907	86			M	01/01/1994	2110

9. STATE OF BIRTH	10. SOCIAL SECURITY NO.	11. MILITARY SERVICE	12. MARITAL STATUS	13. EDUCATION—YEARS COMPLETED
NY	546-01-7235	19 42 TO 19 45 ☐ NONE	NEVER MARRIED	16

14. RACE	15. HISPANIC—SPECIFY	16. USUAL EMPLOYER
WHITE	[X] YES CUBAN ☐ NO	SELF EMPLOYED

17. OCCUPATION	18. KIND OF BUSINESS	19. YEARS IN OCCUPATION
ACTOR	MOTION PICTURES	60

USUAL RESIDENCE

20. RESIDENCE—STREET AND NUMBER OR LOCATION: 12115 SAN VICENTE BLVD.

21. CITY	22. COUNTY	23. ZIP CODE	24. YRS IN COUNTY	25. STATE OR FOREIGN COUNTRY
LOS ANGELES	LOS ANGELES	90049	52	CALIFORNIA

INFORMANT

26. NAME, RELATIONSHIP	27. MAILING ADDRESS (STREET AND NUMBER OR RURAL ROUTE NUMBER, CITY OR TOWN, STATE, ZIP)
MARTI M. ROMERO - NIECE	9400 LA TIJERA BLVD. #4104-LOS ANGELES, CA. 90045

SPOUSE AND PARENT INFORMATION

28. NAME OF SURVIVING SPOUSE—FIRST	29. MIDDLE	30. LAST (MAIDEN NAME)	
-	-	-	
31. NAME OF FATHER—FIRST	**32. MIDDLE**	**33. LAST**	**34. BIRTH STATE**
CESAR	JULIO	ROMERO SR	SPAIN
35. NAME OF MOTHER—FIRST	**36. MIDDLE**	**37. LAST (MAIDEN)**	**38. BIRTH STATE**
MARIA	M.	MARTI	NY

DISPOSITION(S)

39. DATE MM/DD/CCYY	40. PLACE OF FINAL DISPOSITION
01/06/1994	INGLEWOOD CEMETERY MORTUARY

FUNERAL DIRECTOR AND LOCAL REGISTRAR

41. TYPE OF DISPOSITION(S)	42. SIGNATURE OF EMBALMER	43. LICENSE NO.
CR/BU	▶ NOT EMBALMED	NONE

44. NAME OF FUNERAL DIRECTOR	45. LICENSE NO.	46. SIGNATURE OF LOCAL REGISTRAR	47. DATE MM/DD/CCYY
INGLEWOOD CEMETERY MORTUARY	F-1101	▶ Robert C. Mateo Jr.	01/06/1994

PLACE OF DEATH

101. PLACE OF DEATH	102. IF HOSPITAL, SPECIFY ONE:	103. FACILITY OTHER THAN HOSPITAL:	104. COUNTY
ST. JOHN'S HOSP.	[X] IP ☐ ER/OP ☐ DOA	☐ CONV. HOSP. ☐ RES. ☐ OTHER	LOS ANGELES

105. STREET ADDRESS—STREET AND NUMBER OR LOCATION	106. CITY
1328 22ND ST.	SANTA MONICA

CAUSE OF DEATH

107. DEATH WAS CAUSED BY: (ENTER ONLY ONE CAUSE PER LINE FOR A, B, C, AND D)

		TIME INTERVAL BETWEEN ONSET AND DEATH
IMMEDIATE CAUSE (A)	CARDIORESPIRATORY ARREST	5MIN
DUE TO (B)	PULMONARY EMBOLUS	5MIN
DUE TO (C)	THROMBOPHLEBITIS - RT. LEG	2DAYS
DUE TO (D)	BRONCHITIS	1WK

108. DEATH REPORTED TO CORONER: ☐ YES [X] NO — REFERRAL NUMBER

109. BIOPSY PERFORMED: ☐ YES [X] NO

110. AUTOPSY PERFORMED: ☐ YES [X] NO

111. USED IN DETERMINING CAUSE: ☐ YES [X] NO

112. OTHER SIGNIFICANT CONDITIONS CONTRIBUTING TO DEATH BUT NOT RELATED TO CAUSE GIVEN IN 107: NONE

113. WAS OPERATION PERFORMED FOR ANY CONDITION IN ITEM 107 OR 112? IF YES, LIST TYPE OF OPERATION AND DATE.: NO

PHYSICIAN'S CERTIFICATION

114. I CERTIFY THAT TO THE BEST OF MY KNOWLEDGE DEATH OCCURRED AT THE HOUR, DATE AND PLACE STATED FROM THE CAUSES STATED.

DECEDENT ATTENDED SINCE MM/DD/CCYY	DECEDENT LAST SEEN ALIVE MM/DD/CCYY
10/16/1992	12/31/1993

115. SIGNATURE AND TITLE OF CERTIFIER	116. LICENSE NO.	117. DATE MM/DD/CCYY
▶ David Stein, M.D.	G29578	01/03/1994

118. TYPE ATTENDING PHYSICIAN'S NAME, MAILING ADDRESS + ZIP: DAVID STEIN MD. 2001 SANTA MONICA BLVD.-SANTA MONICA, CA #680W 90404

CORONER'S USE ONLY

13/F

I CERTIFY THAT IN MY OPINION DEATH OCCURRED AT THE HOUR, DATE AND PLACE STATED FROM THE CAUSES STATED.

119. MANNER OF DEATH: ☐ NATURAL ☐ SUICIDE ☐ HOMICIDE ☐ ACCIDENT ☐ PENDING INVESTIGATION ☐ COULD NOT BE DETERMINED

120. INJURY AT WORK	121. INJURY DATE MM/DD/CCYY	122. HOUR	123. PLACE OF INJURY
☐ YES ☐ NO			

124. DESCRIBE HOW INJURY OCCURRED (EVENTS WHICH RESULTED IN INJURY)

125. LOCATION (STREET AND NUMBER OR LOCATION AND CITY AND ZIP CODE)

126. SIGNATURE OF CORONER OR DEPUTY CORONER	127. DATE MM/DD/CCYY	128. TYPED NAME, TITLE OF CORONER OR DEPUTY CORONER
▶		

STATE REGISTRAR

A	B	C	D	E	F	G	H	FAX AUTH. #	CENSUS TRACT

03 0756

CERTIFICATION OF VITAL RECORD

COUNTY OF LOS ANGELES • REGISTRAR-RECORDER/COUNTY CLERK

CERTIFICATE OF DEATH

STATE OF CALIFORNIA—DEPARTMENT OF PUBLIC HEALTH

STATE FILE NUMBER — LOCAL REGISTRATION DISTRICT AND CERTIFICATE NUMBER: 7097-053119

DECEDENT PERSONAL DATA

1a. NAME OF DECEASED—FIRST NAME: CHARLES
1b. MIDDLE NAME: SHERMAN
1c. LAST NAME: RUGGLES
2a. DATE OF DEATH—MONTH, DAY, YEAR: DECEMBER 23, 1970
2b. HOUR: 4:10A M
3. SEX: Male
4. COLOR OR RACE: Caucasian
5. BIRTHPLACE (STATE OR FOREIGN COUNTRY): California
6. DATE OF BIRTH: February 8, 1886
7. AGE (LAST BIRTHDAY): 84 YEARS — IF UNDER 1 YEAR: MONTHS, DAYS — IF UNDER 24 HOURS: HOURS, MINUTES
8. NAME AND BIRTHPLACE OF FATHER: Charles Ruggles- Unknown
9. MAIDEN NAME AND BIRTHPLACE OF MOTHER: Unknown- Unknown
10. CITIZEN OF WHAT COUNTRY: U.S.A.
11. SOCIAL SECURITY NUMBER: Unknown
12. MARRIED, NEVER MARRIED, WIDOWED, DIVORCED (SPECIFY): Married
13. NAME OF SURVIVING SPOUSE (IF WIFE, ENTER MAIDEN NAME): Marion Shields
14. LAST OCCUPATION: Actor
15. NUMBER OF YEARS IN THIS OCCUPATION: 65 Yrs.
16. NAME OF LAST EMPLOYING COMPANY OR FIRM (IF SELF EMPLOYED, SO STATE): Self Employed
17. KIND OF INDUSTRY OR BUSINESS: Motion Pictures

PLACE OF DEATH

18a. PLACE OF DEATH—NAME OF HOSPITAL OR OTHER IN-PATIENT FACILITY: St. John's Hospital
18b. STREET ADDRESS—(STREET AND NUMBER, OR LOCATION): 1328 22nd. Street
18c. INSIDE CITY CORPORATE LIMITS (SPECIFY YES OR NO): Yes
18d. CITY OR TOWN: Santa Monica
18e. COUNTY: Los Angeles
18f. LENGTH OF STAY IN COUNTY OF DEATH: 65 YEARS
18g. LENGTH OF STAY IN CALIFORNIA: 65 YEARS

USUAL RESIDENCE (IF DEATH OCCURRED IN INSTITUTION, ENTER RESIDENCE BEFORE ADMISSION)

19a. USUAL RESIDENCE—STREET ADDRESS (STREET AND NUMBER OR LOCATION): 1129 North Amalfi Drive
19b. INSIDE CITY CORPORATE LIMITS (SPECIFY YES OR NO): Yes
19c. CITY OR TOWN: Pacific Palisades
19d. COUNTY: Los Angeles
19e. STATE: California
20. NAME AND MAILING ADDRESS OF INFORMANT: Marion Ruggles- Wife, Same

PHYSICIAN'S OR CORONER'S CERTIFICATION

21a. CORONER: I HEREBY CERTIFY THAT DEATH OCCURRED AT THE HOUR, DATE AND PLACE STATED ABOVE FROM THE CAUSES STATED BELOW AND THAT I HAVE HELD AN INVESTIGATION OR INQUEST ON THE REMAINS OF DECEASED AS REQUIRED BY LAW
21b. PHYSICIAN: I HEREBY CERTIFY THAT DEATH OCCURRED AT THE HOUR, DATE AND PLACE STATED ABOVE FROM THE CAUSES STATED BELOW AND THAT I ATTENDED THE DECEASED FROM 5/17/68 TO 12/23/70 AND LAST SAW THE DECEASED ALIVE ON 12/22/70
21c. PHYSICIAN OR CORONER—SIGNATURE AND DEGREE OR TITLE: Q. E. Fredericks, M.D.
21d. DATE SIGNED: 12/23/70
21e. ADDRESS: 11600 Wilshire Boulevard Los Angeles Calif.
21f. PHYSICIAN'S CALIFORNIA LICENSE NUMBER: G5302

FUNERAL DIRECTOR AND LOCAL REGISTRAR

22a. SPECIFY BURIAL, ENTOMBMENT OR CREMATION: Burial
22b. DATE: 12-26-70
23. NAME OF CEMETERY OR CREMATORY: FOREST LAWN MEMORIAL-PARK ASSN. GLENDALE, CALIFORNIA
24. EMBALMER—SIGNATURE (IF BODY EMBALMED): Gary L. Neal — LICENSE NUMBER: 4206
25. NAME OF FUNERAL DIRECTOR (OR PERSON ACTING AS SUCH): FOREST LAWN MEMORIAL-PARK ASSN. GLENDALE, CALIFORNIA
26. IF NOT CERTIFIED BY CORONER, WAS THIS DEATH REPORTED TO CORONER? (SPECIFY YES OR NO): no
27. LOCAL REGISTRAR—SIGNATURE: G.A. Heidbreder MD my
28. DATE ACCEPTED FOR REGISTRATION BY LOCAL REGISTRAR: DEC 2 6 1970

CAUSE OF DEATH (MEDICAL AND HEALTH DATA)

29. PART I. DEATH WAS CAUSED BY: ENTER ONLY ONE CAUSE PER LINE FOR A, B, AND C
IMMEDIATE CAUSE (A) Carcinoma of colon — APPROXIMATE INTERVAL BETWEEN ONSET AND DEATH: 4 mons
CONDITIONS, IF ANY, WHICH GAVE RISE TO THE IMMEDIATE CAUSE (A), STATING THE UNDERLYING CAUSE LAST: DUE TO, OR AS A CONSEQUENCE OF (B) — DUE TO, OR AS A CONSEQUENCE OF (C)
30. PART II: OTHER SIGNIFICANT CONDITIONS—CONTRIBUTING TO DEATH BUT NOT RELATED TO THE IMMEDIATE CAUSE GIVEN IN PART I
31. WAS OPERATION OR BIOPSY PERFORMED FOR ANY CONDITION IN ITEMS 29 OR 30? (SPECIFY OPERATION AND/OR BIOPSY): operation
32a. AUTOPSY (SPECIFY YES OR NO): No
32b. IF YES WERE FINDINGS CONSIDERED IN DETERMINING CAUSE OF DEATH (SPECIFY YES OR NO)

INJURY INFORMATION

33. SPECIFY ACCIDENT, SUICIDE OR HOMICIDE
34. PLACE OF INJURY (SPECIFY HOME, FARM, FACTORY, STREET, OFFICE BUILDING, ETC.)
35. INJURY AT WORK (SPECIFY YES OR NO)
36a. DATE OF INJURY—MONTH, DAY, YEAR
36b. HOUR
37a. PLACE OF INJURY (STREET AND NUMBER OR LOCATION AND CITY OR TOWN)
37b. DISTANCE FROM PLACE OF INJURY TO USUAL RESIDENCE (ITEM 19) MILES
38. WERE LABORATORY TESTS DONE FOR DRUGS OR TOXIC CHEMICALS (SPECIFY YES OR NO)
39. WERE LABORATORY TESTS DONE FOR ALCOHOL? (SPECIFY YES OR NO)
40. DESCRIBE HOW INJURY OCCURRED (ENTER SEQUENCE OF EVENTS WHICH RESULTED IN INJURY. NATURE OF INJURY SHOULD BE ENTERED IN ITEM 29)

STATE REGISTRAR A. B. C. D. E. F. 2624

REV 1-1-68 Form VS-11

This is to certify that this document is a true copy of the official record filed with the Registrar-Recorder/County Clerk.

Beatriz Valdez
BEATRIZ VALDEZ
Registrar-Recorder/County Clerk

AUG 1 1995
19-389300

This copy not valid unless prepared on engraved border displaying the Seal and Signature of the Registrar-Recorder/County Clerk.

THE GREAT SEAL OF THE STATE OF CALIFORNIA — EUREKA

REGISTRAR-RECORDER/COUNTY CLERK — COUNTY OF LOS ANGELES • CALIFORNIA

American Bank Note Company

ANY ALTERATION OR ERASURE VOIDS THIS CERTIFICATE

CERTIFICATION OF VITAL RECORD

COUNTY OF LOS ANGELES • REGISTRAR-RECORDER/COUNTY CLERK

STATE FILE NUMBER

CERTIFICATE OF DEATH

STATE OF CALIFORNIA—DEPARTMENT OF PUBLIC HEALTH

LOCAL REGISTRATION DISTRICT AND CERTIFICATE NUMBER 7053 17744

DECEDENT PERSONAL DATA

1a. NAME OF DECEASED—FIRST NAME: Gail | 1b. MIDDLE NAME: Russell | 1c. LAST NAME: Moseley | 2a. DATE OF DEATH—MONTH, DAY, YEAR: August 27,1961 | 2b. HOUR: 1:00 A M.

3. SEX: Female | 4. COLOR OR RACE: Cauc | 5. BIRTHPLACE (STATE OR FOREIGN COUNTRY): Chicago,Illinois | 6. DATE OF BIRTH: September 21,1925 | 7. AGE (LAST BIRTHDAY): 35 YEARS | IF UNDER 1 YEAR | IF UNDER 24 HOURS

8. NAME AND BIRTHPLACE OF FATHER: Geo.H.Russell- Illinois | 9. MAIDEN NAME AND BIRTHPLACE OF MOTHER: Gladys Barnet- Illinois | 10. CITIZEN OF WHAT COUNTRY: United States | 11. SOCIAL SECURITY NUMBER: 566-24-5320

12. LAST OCCUPATION: Actress | 13. NUMBER OF YEARS IN THIS OCCUPATION: 18 | 14. NAME OF LAST EMPLOYING COMPANY OR FIRM (IF SELF-EMPLOYED, SO STATE): Associated Producers,Inc. | 15. KIND OF INDUSTRY OR BUSINESS: Movies- Television

16. IF DECEASED WAS EVER IN U.S. ARMED FORCES, GIVE WAR OR DATES OF SERVICE: none | 17. SPECIFY MARRIED, NEVER MARRIED, WIDOWED, DIVORCED: Divorced | 18a. NAME OF PRESENT SPOUSE | 18b. PRESENT OR LAST OCCUPATION OF SPOUSE

PLACE OF DEATH

19a. PLACE OF DEATH—NAME OF HOSPITAL | 19b. STREET ADDRESS—(GIVE STREET OR RURAL ADDRESS OR LOCATION. DO NOT USE P.O. BOX NUMBERS): 1436 Bentley Ave. | INSIDE CITY CORPORATE LIMITS [X] | OUTSIDE CITY CORPORATE LIMITS

19c. CITY OR TOWN: Los Angeles | 19d. COUNTY: Los Angeles | 19e. LENGTH OF STAY IN COUNTY OF DEATH: 23 YEARS | 19f. LENGTH OF STAY IN CALIFORNIA: 23 YEARS

LAST USUAL RESIDENCE (WHERE DID DECEASED LIVE—IF IN INSTITUTION ENTER RESIDENCE BEFORE ADMISSION)

20a. LAST USUAL RESIDENCE—STREET ADDRESS (GIVE STREET OR RURAL ADDRESS OR LOCATION. DO NOT USE P.O. BOX NUMBERS): 1436 Bentley Ave. | 20b. IF INSIDE CITY CORPORATE LIMITS CHECK HERE [X] | IF OUTSIDE CITY CORPORATE LIMITS CHECK ONE: ON A FARM / NOT ON A FARM | 21a. NAME OF INFORMANT (IF OTHER THAN SPOUSE): George H. Russell,Jr.

20c. CITY OR TOWN: Los Angeles 1652 | 20d. COUNTY: Los Angeles | 20e. STATE: California | 21b. ADDRESS OF INFORMANT: 1308 No.Martel Ave.L.A.46

PHYSICIAN'S OR CORONER'S CERTIFICATION

22a. PHYSICIAN: I HEREBY CERTIFY THAT DEATH OCCURRED AT THE HOUR, DATE AND PLACE STATED ABOVE FROM THE CAUSES STATED BELOW AND THAT I ATTENDED THE DECEASED FROM ___ TO ___ AND THAT I LAST SAW THE DECEASED ALIVE ON ___

22c. PHYSICIAN OR CORONER—SIGNATURE: Theodore J. Curphey, M.D., Coroner — L. J. Malins, Deputy | DEGREE OR TITLE

22b. CORONER: I HEREBY CERTIFY THAT DEATH OCCURRED AT THE HOUR, DATE AND PLACE STATED ABOVE FROM THE CAUSES STATED BELOW AND THAT I HAVE HELD AN autopsy (INVESTIGATION, AUTOPSY, INQUEST) ON THE REMAINS OF DECEASED AS REQUIRED BY LAW | 22d. ADDRESS: HALL OF JUSTICE, LOS ANGELES | 22e. DATE SIGNED: 9-6-61

FUNERAL DIRECTOR AND LOCAL REGISTRAR

23. SPECIFY BURIAL, ENTOMBMENT OR CREMATION: Burial | 24. DATE: Aug.29,1961 | 25. NAME OF CEMETERY OR CREMATORY: Valhalla Memorial Park | 26. EMBALMER—SIGNATURE (IF BODY EMBALMED): J. C. Cisneros | LICENSE NUMBER: 1943

27. NAME OF FUNERAL DIRECTOR (OR PERSON ACTING AS SUCH): Westwood Village Mortuary | 28. DATE ACCEPTED FOR REGISTRATION BY LOCAL REGISTRAR: SEP 1 3 1961 | 29. LOCAL REGISTRAR—SIGNATURE: George M. Uhl, M.D.

MEDICAL AND HEALTH DATA — CAUSE OF DEATH

30. CAUSE OF DEATH — ENTER ONLY ONE CAUSE PER LINE FOR (A), (B), AND (C)

PART I. DEATH WAS CAUSED BY: IMMEDIATE CAUSE (A) FATTY LIVER, SEVERE

CONDITIONS, IF ANY, WHICH GAVE RISE TO THE ABOVE CAUSE (A) STATING THE UNDERLYING CAUSE LAST. DUE TO (B) ACUTE AND CHRONIC ALCOHOLISM

DUE TO (C)

APPROXIMATE INTERVAL BETWEEN ONSET AND DEATH

PART II: OTHER SIGNIFICANT CONDITIONS CONTRIBUTING TO DEATH BUT NOT RELATED TO THE TERMINAL DISEASE CONDITION GIVEN IN PART I (A): TERMINAL ASPIRATION STOMACH CONTENTS

OPERATION AND AUTOPSY

31. OPERATION—CHECK ONE: [X] NO OPERATION PERFORMED / OPERATION PERFORMED—FINDINGS USED IN DETERMINING ABOVE STATED CAUSES OF DEATH / OPERATION PERFORMED—FINDINGS NOT USED IN DETERMINING ABOVE STATED CAUSES OF DEATH | 32. DATE OF OPERATION | 33. AUTOPSY—CHECK ONE: NO AUTOPSY PERFORMED / [X] AUTOPSY PERFORMED—GROSS FINDINGS USED IN DETERMINING ABOVE STATED CAUSES OF DEATH / AUTOPSY PERFORMED—GROSS FINDINGS NOT USED IN DETERMINING ABOVE STATED CAUSES OF DEATH

INJURY INFORMATION

34a. SPECIFY ACCIDENT, SUICIDE OR HOMICIDE | 34b. DESCRIBE HOW INJURY OCCURRED

35a. TIME OF INJURY: HOUR MONTH DAY YEAR M.

35b. INJURY OCCURRED: WHILE AT WORK / NOT WHILE AT WORK | 35c. PLACE OF INJURY (E.G. IN OR ABOUT HOME, FARM, FACTORY, STREET, OFFICE BUILDING) | 35d. CITY, TOWN, OR LOCATION | COUNTY | STATE

Rev. 1-1-58 Form VS-11

(Margin annotations:) GAIL RUSSELL MOSELEY #69403 — 8-29-61 MORRISON M.D. (final 9-6-61) — Pending

This is to certify that this document is a true copy of the official record filed with the Registrar-Recorder/County Clerk.

Conny B. McCormack
CONNY B. McCORMACK
Registrar-Recorder/County Clerk

SEP 20 1996
19-376816

This copy not valid unless prepared on engraved border displaying the Seal and Signature of the Registrar-Recorder/County Clerk.

THE GREAT SEAL OF THE STATE OF CALIFORNIA

REGISTRAR-RECORDER/COUNTY CLERK • COUNTY OF LOS ANGELES • CALIFORNIA

AMERICAN BANKNOTE CORPORATION OF AMERICA

ANY ALTERATION OR ERASURE VOIDS THIS CERTIFICATE

CERTIFICATION OF VITAL RECORD

COUNTY OF LOS ANGELES • REGISTRAR-RECORDER/COUNTY CLERK

CERTIFICATE OF DEATH

STATE FILE NUMBER — STATE OF CALIFORNIA—DEPARTMENT OF PUBLIC HEALTH — LOCAL REGISTRATION DISTRICT AND CERTIFICATE NUMBER: 0190-053029

DECEDENT PERSONAL DATA

- 1a. NAME OF DECEASED—FIRST NAME: Rosalind
- 1b. MIDDLE NAME: Russell
- 1c. LAST NAME: Brisson
- 2a. DATE OF DEATH—MONTH DAY YEAR: November 28, 1976
- 2b. HOUR: 10:10 A.M.
- 3. SEX: Female
- 4. COLOR OR RACE: Caucasian
- 5. BIRTHPLACE (STATE OR FOREIGN COUNTRY): Connecticut
- 6. DATE OF BIRTH: June 4, 1907
- 7. AGE (LAST BIRTHDAY): 69 YEARS — IF UNDER 1 YEAR — IF UNDER 24 HOURS
- 8. NAME AND BIRTHPLACE OF FATHER: James E. Russell ; Connecticut
- 9. MAIDEN NAME AND BIRTHPLACE OF MOTHER: Clara McKnight; Connecticut
- 10. CITIZEN OF WHAT COUNTRY: United States
- 11. SOCIAL SECURITY NUMBER: 573-05-8861
- 12. MARRIED, NEVER MARRIED, WIDOWED, DIVORCED (SPECIFY): Married
- 13. NAME OF SURVIVING SPOUSE (IF WIFE ENTER MAIDEN NAME): Frederick Brisson
- 14. LAST OCCUPATION: Actress
- 15. NUMBER OF YEARS IN THIS OCCUPATION: 45
- 16. NAME OF LAST EMPLOYING COMPANY OR FIRM (IF SELF EMPLOYED, SO STATE): Self-Employed
- 17. KIND OF INDUSTRY OR BUSINESS: Entertainment

PLACE OF DEATH

- 18a. PLACE OF DEATH—NAME OF HOSPITAL OR OTHER IN-PATIENT FACILITY:
- 18b. STREET ADDRESS—(STREET AND NUMBER, OR LOCATION): 706 No. Beverly Drive
- 18c. INSIDE CITY CORPORATE LIMITS (SPECIFY YES OR NO): yes
- 18d. CITY OR TOWN: Beverly Hills
- 18e. COUNTY: Los Angeles
- 18f. LENGTH OF STAY IN COUNTY OF DEATH: 41 YEARS
- 18g. LENGTH OF STAY IN CALIFORNIA: 41 YEARS

USUAL RESIDENCE (IF DEATH OCCURRED IN INSTITUTION, ENTER RESIDENCE BEFORE ADMISSION)

- 19a. USUAL RESIDENCE—STREET ADDRESS (STREET AND NUMBER OR LOCATION): 706 No. Beverly Drive
- 19b. INSIDE CITY CORPORATE LIMITS (SPECIFY YES OR NO): yes
- 19c. CITY OR TOWN: Beverly Hills
- 19d. COUNTY: Los Angeles
- 19e. STATE: California
- 20. NAME AND MAILING ADDRESS OF INFORMANT: Mr. Frederick Brisson, 706 No. Beverly Drive, Beverly Hills, Calif.

PHYSICIAN'S OR CORONER'S CERTIFICATION

- 21a. CORONER:
- 21b. PHYSICIAN: I HEREBY CERTIFY THAT DEATH OCCURRED AT THE HOUR, DATE, AND PLACE STATED ABOVE FROM THE CAUSES STATED BELOW AND THAT I ATTENDED THE DECEASED FROM 11-1-75 TO 11-28-76 AND LAST SAW THE DECEASED ALIVE ON 11-28-76
- 21c. PHYSICIAN OR CORONER—SIGNATURE AND DEGREE OR TITLE: Martin J. Cline
- 21d. DATE SIGNED: 11-29-76
- 21e. ADDRESS: UCLA Los Angeles
- 21f. PHYSICIAN'S CALIFORNIA LICENSE NUMBER: G8637

FUNERAL DIRECTOR AND LOCAL REGISTRAR

- 22a. SPECIFY BURIAL, ENTOMBMENT OR CREMATION: Burial
- 22b. DATE: 12-1-76
- 23. NAME OF CEMETERY OR CREMATORY: Holy Cross Cemetery
- 24. EMBALMER—SIGNATURE (IF BODY EMBALMED) LICENSE NUMBER: Paul A. Thomas 6061
- 25. NAME OF FUNERAL DIRECTOR (OR PERSON ACTING AS SUCH): Cunningham & O'Connor Hollywood
- 26. IF NOT CERTIFIED BY CORONER, WAS THIS DEATH REPORTED TO CORONER? (SPECIFY YES OR NO): No
- 27. LOCAL REGISTRAR—SIGNATURE: [signature]
- 28. DATE ACCEPTED FOR REGISTRATION BY LOCAL REGISTRAR: NOV 30 1976

MEDICAL AND HEALTH DATA — CAUSE OF DEATH

29. PART I. DEATH WAS CAUSED BY: ENTER ONLY ONE CAUSE PER LINE FOR A, B, AND C

	Cause	Approximate interval between onset and death
(A) IMMEDIATE CAUSE	Intestinal obstruction	10 days
(B) DUE TO, OR AS A CONSEQUENCE OF	Carcinoma of the breast	15 years
(C) DUE TO, OR AS A CONSEQUENCE OF		

CONDITIONS, IF ANY, WHICH GAVE RISE TO THE IMMEDIATE CAUSE (A), STATING THE UNDERLYING CAUSE LAST.

- 30. PART II: OTHER SIGNIFICANT CONDITIONS—CONTRIBUTING TO DEATH BUT NOT RELATED TO THE IMMEDIATE CAUSE GIVEN IN PART I: Rheumatoid arthritis
- 31. WAS OPERATION OR BIOPSY PERFORMED FOR ANY CONDITION IN ITEMS 29 OR 30? (SPECIFY TYPE OF OPERATION AND/OR BIOPSY): no
- 32a. AUTOPSY (SPECIFY YES OR NO): no
- 32b. IF YES, WERE FINDINGS CONSIDERED IN DETERMINING CAUSE OF DEATH? (SPECIFY YES OR NO):

INJURY INFORMATION

- 33. SPECIFY ACCIDENT, SUICIDE OR HOMICIDE:
- 34. PLACE OF INJURY (SPECIFY HOME, FARM, FACTORY, STREET, OFFICE BUILDING, ETC.):
- 35. INJURY AT WORK (SPECIFY YES OR NO):
- 36a. DATE OF INJURY—MONTH DAY YEAR:
- 36b. HOUR: M.
- 37a. PLACE OF INJURY (STREET AND NUMBER OR LOCATION AND CITY OR TOWN):
- 37b. DISTANCE FROM PLACE OF INJURY TO USUAL RESIDENCE, ITEM 19: MILES
- 38. WERE LABORATORY TESTS DONE FOR DRUGS OR TOXIC CHEMICALS? (SPECIFY YES OR NO):
- 39. WERE LABORATORY TESTS DONE FOR ALCOHOL? (SPECIFY YES OR NO):
- 40. DESCRIBE HOW INJURY OCCURRED (ENTER SEQUENCE OF EVENTS WHICH RESULTED IN INJURY. NATURE OF INJURY SHOULD BE ENTERED IN ITEM 29)

STATE REGISTRAR: A. B. C. D. E. F. 01-8-1

REV 1-1-69 FORM VS-11

This is to certify that this document is a true copy of the official record filed with the Registrar-Recorder/County Clerk.

Beatriz Valdez
BEATRIZ VALDEZ
Registrar-Recorder/County Clerk

AUG 10 1995
19-389399

This copy not valid unless prepared on engraved border displaying the Seal and Signature of the Registrar-Recorder/County Clerk.

American Bank Note Company

ANY ALTERATION OR ERASURE VOIDS THIS CERTIFICATE

CERTIFICATION OF VITAL RECORD

COUNTY OF LOS ANGELES • REGISTRAR-RECORDER/COUNTY CLERK

CERTIFICATE OF DEATH 7097-018305

STATE OF CALIFORNIA—DEPARTMENT OF PUBLIC HEALTH

DECEDENT PERSONAL DATA	1a. Name of deceased—first name	Irene
	1c. Last name	Ryan
	2a. Date of death	April 26, 1973
	2b. Hour	7:15 P.M.
	3. Sex	Female
	4. Color or race	Cauc.
	5. Birthplace	Texas
	6. Date of birth	October 17, 1902
	7. Age	70 years
	8. Name and birthplace of father	James M. Noblitt - North Carolina
	9. Maiden name and birthplace of mother	Catherine McSharry - Ireland
	10. Citizen of what country	U.S.A.
	11. Social security number	112-09-8976
	12. Married, never married, widowed, divorced	Divorced
	13. Name of surviving spouse	
	14. Last occupation	Actress
	15. Number of years in this occupation	59
	16. Name of last employing company or firm	Pippin Company
	17. Kind of industry or business	Theatrical
PLACE OF DEATH	18a. Place of death	St. John's Hospital
	18b. Street address	1328 22nd Street
	18c. Inside city corporate limits	Yes
	18d. City or town	Santa Monica
	18e. County	Los Angeles
	18f. Length of stay in county of death	30 years
	18g. Length of stay in California	30 years
USUAL RESIDENCE	19a. Usual residence	107 Esparta Way
	19b. Inside city corporate limits	Yes
	19c. City or town	Santa Monica
	19d. County	Los Angeles
	19e. State	California
	20. Name and mailing address of informant	Ralph Handley, 13063 Ventura Blvd., Studio City, Ca. 91604
PHYSICIAN'S OR CORONER'S CERTIFICATION	21b. Physician: from / to / last saw	Sept 8 1961 / 26 Apr 73 / 26 Apr 73
	21c. Signature and degree or title	Ray [illegible] M.D.
	21d. Date signed	30 Apr 73
	21e. Address	2200 [illegible] Santa Monica Ca
	21f. Physician's California license number	C-8611
FUNERAL DIRECTOR AND LOCAL REGISTRAR	22a. Specify burial, entombment or cremation	Entombment
	22b. Date	May 1, 1973
	23. Name of cemetery or crematory	Woodlawn Mausoleum
	24. Embalmer—signature, license number	Andrew P. Smith 5429
	25. Name of funeral director	Gates, Kingsley & Gates SM
	26. If not certified by coroner, was this death reported to coroner?	No
	27. Local registrar—signature	[illegible]
	28. Date accepted for registration by local registrar	MAY 1 1973
CAUSE OF DEATH	29. Part I. (A) Immediate cause	Glioblastoma — 3 mo.
	(B) Due to, or as a consequence of	Arteriosclerotic Heart Disease — 1 mo.
	(C) Due to, or as a consequence of	
	30. Part II. Other significant conditions	Arteriosclerosis
	31. Was operation or biopsy performed?	Craniotomy
	32a. Autopsy	Yes
	32b. If yes, were findings considered in determining cause of death	Yes
INJURY INFORMATION	33–40	
STATE REGISTRAR	A.–F.	

This is to certify that this document is a true copy of the official record filed with the Registrar-Recorder/County Clerk.

Beatriz Valdez
BEATRIZ VALDEZ
Registrar-Recorder/County Clerk

SEP 05 1995
19-000329

This copy not valid unless prepared on engraved border displaying the Seal and Signature of the Registrar-Recorder/County Clerk.

ANY ALTERATION OR ERASURE VOIDS THIS CERTIFICATE

STATE OF CALIFORNIA
CERTIFICATION OF VITAL RECORD

COUNTY OF VENTURA

VENTURA, CALIFORNIA

CERTIFICATE OF DEATH

STATE OF CALIFORNIA
USE BLACK INK ONLY/NO ERASURES, WHITEOUTS OR ALTERATIONS
VS-11 (REV. 7/97)

STATE FILE NUMBER —— LOCAL REGISTRATION NUMBER 3 1999 56 003078

DECEDENT PERSONAL DATA

1. NAME OF DECEDENT—FIRST (GIVEN): George
2. MIDDLE: C.
3. LAST (FAMILY): SCOTT
4. DATE OF BIRTH MM/DD/CCYY: 10/18/1927
5. AGE YRS.: 71
IF UNDER 1 YEAR (MONTHS / DAYS) — IF UNDER 24 HOURS (HOURS / MINUTES)
6. SEX: M
7. DATE OF DEATH MM/DD/CCYY: FND. 09/22/1999
8. HOUR: 1457
9. STATE OF BIRTH: VA
10. SOCIAL SECURITY NO.: 382-20-3422
11. MILITARY SERVICE: [X] YES [ ] NO [ ] UNK
12. MARITAL STATUS: Married
13. EDUCATION—YEARS COMPLETED: 16
14. RACE: Caucasian
15. HISPANIC—SPECIFY: [ ] YES [X] NO
16. USUAL EMPLOYER: Self
17. OCCUPATION: Actor
18. KIND OF BUSINESS: Entertainment
19. YEARS IN OCCUPATION: 45

USUAL RESIDENCE

20. RESIDENCE—(STREET AND NUMBER OR LOCATION): 2679 Lakewood Pl.
21. CITY: Westlake Village
22. COUNTY: Ventura
23. ZIP CODE: 91361
24. YRS IN COUNTY: 2
25. STATE OR FOREIGN COUNTRY: CA

INFORMANT

26. NAME, RELATIONSHIP: Matthew Scott - Son
27. MAILING ADDRESS (STREET AND NUMBER OR RURAL ROUTE NUMBER, CITY OR TOWN, STATE, ZIP): 6550 Sunset Blvd. Los Angeles CA 90028

SPOUSE AND PARENT INFORMATION

28. NAME OF SURVIVING SPOUSE—FIRST: Trish
29. MIDDLE: -
30. LAST (MAIDEN NAME): Van Devere
31. NAME OF FATHER—FIRST: George
32. MIDDLE: D.
33. LAST: Scott
34. BIRTH STATE: VA
35. NAME OF MOTHER—FIRST: Helena
36. MIDDLE: Agnes
37. LAST (MAIDEN): Slemp
38. BIRTH STATE: VA

DISPOSITION(S)

39. DATE MM/DD/CCYY: 10/01/1999
40. PLACE OF FINAL DISPOSITION: Pierce Brothers Westwood Village Memorial Park, Los Angeles, CA

FUNERAL DIRECTOR AND LOCAL REGISTRAR

41. TYPE OF DISPOSITION(S): BU
42. SIGNATURE OF EMBALMER: ▶ [signature]
43. LICENSE NO.: 8474
44. NAME OF FUNERAL DIRECTOR: P.B. Griffin - Thousand Oaks
45. LICENSE NO.: FD-1055
46. SIGNATURE OF LOCAL REGISTRAR: ▶ [signature]
47. DATE MM/DD/CCYY: 09/30/1999

PLACE OF DEATH

101. PLACE OF DEATH: Residence
102. IF HOSPITAL, SPECIFY ONE: [ ] IP [ ] ER/OP [ ] DOA
103. FACILITY OTHER THAN HOSPITAL: [ ] CONV. HOSP. [ ] RES. CARE [ ] OTHER
104. COUNTY: Ventura
105. STREET ADDRESS—(STREET AND NUMBER OR LOCATION): 2679 Lakewood Place
106. CITY: Westlake Village

CAUSE OF DEATH

107. DEATH WAS CAUSED BY: (ENTER ONLY ONE CAUSE PER LINE FOR A, B, C, AND D) — TIME INTERVAL BETWEEN ONSET AND DEATH
IMMEDIATE CAUSE (A) RUPTURED ABDOMINAL AORTIC ANEURYSM
DUE TO (B)
DUE TO (C)
DUE TO (D)
108. DEATH REPORTED TO CORONER: [X] YES [ ] NO — REFERRAL NUMBER 1797-99
109. BIOPSY PERFORMED: [ ] YES [X] NO
110. AUTOPSY PERFORMED: [X] YES [ ] NO
111. USED IN DETERMINING CAUSE: [X] YES [ ] NO
112. OTHER SIGNIFICANT CONDITIONS CONTRIBUTING TO DEATH BUT NOT RELATED TO CAUSE GIVEN IN 107: Atherosclerotic cardiovascular disease, hypertension
113. WAS OPERATION PERFORMED FOR ANY CONDITION IN ITEM 107 OR 112? IF YES, LIST TYPE OF OPERATION AND DATE: Coronary angioplasty, unknown

PHYSICIAN'S CERTIFICATION

114. I CERTIFY THAT TO THE BEST OF MY KNOWLEDGE DEATH OCCURRED AT THE HOUR, DATE AND PLACE STATED FROM THE CAUSES STATED. DECEDENT ATTENDED SINCE MM/DD/CCYY — DECEDENT LAST SEEN ALIVE MM/DD/CCYY
115. SIGNATURE AND TITLE OF CERTIFIER ▶
116. LICENSE NO.
117. DATE MM/DD/CCYY
118. TYPE ATTENDING PHYSICIAN'S NAME, MAILING ADDRESS, ZIP

CORONER'S USE ONLY

I CERTIFY THAT IN MY OPINION DEATH OCCURRED AT THE HOUR, DATE AND PLACE STATED FROM THE CAUSES STATED.
119. MANNER OF DEATH: [X] NATURAL [ ] SUICIDE [ ] HOMICIDE [ ] ACCIDENT [ ] PENDING INVESTIGATION [ ] COULD NOT BE DETERMINED
120. INJURY AT WORK: [ ] YES [ ] NO
121. INJURY DATE MM/DD/CCYY
122. HOUR
123. PLACE OF INJURY
124. DESCRIBE HOW INJURY OCCURRED (EVENTS WHICH RESULTED IN INJURY)
125. LOCATION (STREET AND NUMBER OR LOCATION AND CITY, ZIP)
126. SIGNATURE OF CORONER OR DEPUTY CORONER: ▶ [signature]
127. DATE MM/DD/CCYY: 09/23/1999
128. TYPED NAME, TITLE OF CORONER OR DEPUTY CORONER: JANICE G. FRANK, M.D. ASSISTANT MEDICAL EXAMINER

STATE REGISTRAR: A B C D E F G H — FAX AUTH. # — CENSUS TRACT

339336

CERTIFIED COPY OF VITAL RECORDS

STATE OF CALIFORNIA
COUNTY OF VENTURA } SS

DATE ISSUED 10/01/1999

This is a true and exact reproduction of the document officially registered and placed on file in the Vital Records Section, Ventura County Public Health Department, if it bears the date of issue in red ink.

HEALTH OFFICER
VENTURA COUNTY, CALIFORNIA

This copy not valid unless prepared on engraved border displaying seal and signature of Registrar.

MIDWEST BANK NOTE COMPANY

ANY ALTERATION OR ERASURE VOIDS THIS CERTIFICATE

CERTIFICATE OF DEATH

STATE OF CALIFORNIA
USE BLACK INK ONLY/NO ERASURES, WHITEOUTS OR ALTERATIONS
VS-11 (REV. 7/93)

STATE FILE NUMBER | LOCAL REGISTRATION NUMBER

DECEDENT PERSONAL DATA

1. NAME OF DECEDENT—FIRST (GIVEN): Dinah
2. MIDDLE: -
3. LAST (FAMILY): Shore
4. DATE OF BIRTH MM/DD/CCYY: 03/01/1916
5. AGE YRS.: 77
IF UNDER 1 YEAR: MONTHS | DAYS — IF UNDER 24 HOURS: HOURS | MINUTES
6. SEX: F
7. DATE OF DEATH MM/DD/CCYY: 02/24/1994
8. HOUR: 0220
9. STATE OF BIRTH: TN
10. SOCIAL SECURITY NO.: 409-14-1954
11. MILITARY SERVICE: 19 ___ TO 19 ___ [x] NONE
12. MARITAL STATUS: divorced
13. EDUCATION—YEARS COMPLETED: 16
14. RACE: White
15. HISPANIC—SPECIFY: [ ] YES ___ [x] NO
16. USUAL EMPLOYER: various
17. OCCUPATION: Singer
18. KIND OF BUSINESS: Entertainment
19. YEARS IN OCCUPATION: 50

USUAL RESIDENCE

20. RESIDENCE—STREET AND NUMBER OR LOCATION: 916 N. Oxford Way
21. CITY: Beverly Hills
22. COUNTY: Los Angeles
23. ZIP CODE: 90210
24. YRS IN COUNTY: 50
25. STATE OR FOREIGN COUNTRY: California

INFORMANT

26. NAME, RELATIONSHIP: Murray Niedorf, Friend
27. MAILING ADDRESS (STREET AND NUMBER OR RURAL ROUTE NUMBER, CITY OR TOWN, STATE, ZIP): 9720 Wilshire Blvd., Beverly Hills, CA 90210

SPOUSE AND PARENT INFORMATION

28. NAME OF SURVIVING SPOUSE—FIRST: -
29. MIDDLE: -
30. LAST (MAIDEN NAME): -
31. NAME OF FATHER—FIRST: Salamon
32. MIDDLE: -
33. LAST: Shore
34. BIRTH STATE: USSR
35. NAME OF MOTHER—FIRST: Anna
36. MIDDLE: -
37. LAST (MAIDEN): Stein
38. BIRTH STATE: USSR

DISPOSITION(S)

39. DATE MM/DD/CCYY: 02/25/1994
40. PLACE OF FINAL DISPOSITION: Hillside Memorial Park 6001 Centinela Av. Los Angeles, CA 90045

FUNERAL DIRECTOR AND LOCAL REGISTRAR

41. TYPE OF DISPOSITION(S): CR/BU/RES
42. SIGNATURE OF EMBALMER: ▶ Not Embalmed
43. LICENSE NO.: -
44. NAME OF FUNERAL DIRECTOR: Hillside Mortuary
45. LICENSE NO.: FD1358
46. SIGNATURE OF LOCAL REGISTRAR: ▶ [signature]
47. DATE MM/DD/CCYY: 02/24/1994

PLACE OF DEATH

101. PLACE OF DEATH: Residence
102. IF HOSPITAL, SPECIFY ONE: [ ] IP [ ] ER/OP [ ] DOA
103. FACILITY OTHER THAN HOSPITAL: [ ] CONV. HOSP. [x] RES. [ ] OTHER
104. COUNTY: Los Angeles
105. STREET ADDRESS—STREET AND NUMBER OR LOCATION: 916 N. Oxford Way
106. CITY: Beverly Hills

CAUSE OF DEATH

107. DEATH WAS CAUSED BY: (ENTER ONLY ONE CAUSE PER LINE FOR A, B, C, AND D)

		Cause	Time interval between onset and death
IMMEDIATE CAUSE	(A)	Cachexia	2 weeks
DUE TO	(B)	Metastasis	1 year
DUE TO	(C)	Carcinoma of ovary	1 year
DUE TO	(D)		

108. DEATH REPORTED TO CORONER: [ ] YES [x] NO — REFERRAL NUMBER
109. BIOPSY PERFORMED: [x] YES [ ] NO
110. AUTOPSY PERFORMED: [ ] YES [x] NO
111. USED IN DETERMINING CAUSE: [ ] YES [x] NO
112. OTHER SIGNIFICANT CONDITIONS CONTRIBUTING TO DEATH BUT NOT RELATED TO CAUSE GIVEN IN 107: None
113. WAS OPERATION PERFORMED FOR ANY CONDITION IN ITEM 107 OR 112? IF YES, LIST TYPE OF OPERATION AND DATE.: Exploratory laparotomy 03/--/1993

PHYSICIAN'S CERTIFICATION

114. I CERTIFY THAT TO THE BEST OF MY KNOWLEDGE DEATH OCCURRED AT THE HOUR, DATE AND PLACE STATED FROM THE CAUSES STATED.
DECEDENT ATTENDED SINCE MM/DD/CCYY: 06/07/1979
DECEDENT LAST SEEN ALIVE MM/DD/CCYY: 02/23/1994
115. SIGNATURE AND TITLE OF CERTIFIER: ▶ [signature]
116. LICENSE NO.: G11662
117. DATE MM/DD/CCYY: 02/24/1994
118. TYPE ATTENDING PHYSICIAN'S NAME, MAILING ADDRESS + ZIP: James R. Blake, MD-1301 - 20th St., Santa Monica, CA 90404

CORONER'S USE ONLY

I CERTIFY THAT IN MY OPINION DEATH OCCURRED AT THE HOUR, DATE AND PLACE STATED FROM THE CAUSES STATED.
119. MANNER OF DEATH: [ ] NATURAL [ ] SUICIDE [ ] HOMICIDE [ ] ACCIDENT [ ] PENDING INVESTIGATION [ ] COULD NOT BE DETERMINED
120. INJURY AT WORK: [ ] YES [ ] NO
121. INJURY DATE MM/DD/CCYY
122. HOUR
123. PLACE OF INJURY
124. DESCRIBE HOW INJURY OCCURRED (EVENTS WHICH RESULTED IN INJURY)
125. LOCATION (STREET AND NUMBER OR LOCATION AND CITY AND ZIP CODE)
126. SIGNATURE OF CORONER OR DEPUTY CORONER ▶
127. DATE MM/DD/CCYY
128. TYPED NAME, TITLE OF CORONER OR DEPUTY CORONER

STATE REGISTRAR

A | B | C | D | E | F | G | H | FAX AUTH. # | CENSUS TRACT

CERTIFICATION OF VITAL RECORD

COUNTY OF LOS ANGELES • REGISTRAR-RECORDER/COUNTY CLERK

CERTIFICATE OF DEATH
STATE OF CALIFORNIA

0190-010646

STATE FILE NUMBER — LOCAL REGISTRATION DISTRICT AND CERTIFICATE NUMBER

DECEDENT PERSONAL DATA

1A. NAME OF DECEDENT—FIRST	1B. MIDDLE	1C. LAST	2A. DATE OF DEATH (MONTH, DAY, YEAR)	2B. HOUR
JAY		SILVERHEELS	March 5, 1980	0400

3. SEX	4. RACE	5. ETHNICITY	6. DATE OF BIRTH	7. AGE
Male	White	Mohawk Indian	May 26,1912	67 YEARS

8. BIRTHPLACE OF DECEDENT (STATE OR FOREIGN COUNTRY): Canada
9. NAME AND BIRTHPLACE OF FATHER: George A. Smith - Canada
10. BIRTH NAME AND BIRTHPLACE OF MOTHER: Unknown - Unknown
11. CITIZEN OF WHAT COUNTRY: Canada
12. SOCIAL SECURITY NUMBER: 134-05-0806
13. MARITAL STATUS: Married
14. NAME OF SURVIVING SPOUSE (IF WIFE, ENTER BIRTH NAME): Mary Di Roma
15. PRIMARY OCCUPATION: Actor
16. NUMBER OF YEARS THIS OCCUPATION: 41
17. EMPLOYER (IF SELF-EMPLOYED, SO STATE): Various Motion Picture Studios
18. KIND OF INDUSTRY OR BUSINESS: Motion Picture&T.V.

USUAL RESIDENCE

19A. USUAL RESIDENCE—STREET ADDRESS (STREET AND NUMBER OR LOCATION): 20345 Enadia Way
19B.
19C. CITY OR TOWN: Canoga Park
19D. COUNTY: Los Angeles
19E. STATE: California
20. NAME AND ADDRESS OF INFORMANT—RELATIONSHIP: Mrs. Mary Silverheels- Wife, 20345 Enadia Way, Canoga Park, California 91306

PLACE OF DEATH

21A. PLACE OF DEATH: Motion Picture and TV Hospital
21B. COUNTY: Los Angeles
21C. STREET ADDRESS (STREET AND NUMBER OR LOCATION): 23450 Calabasas Road
21D. CITY OR TOWN: Woodland Hills

CAUSE OF DEATH

22. DEATH WAS CAUSED BY: (ENTER ONLY ONE CAUSE PER LINE FOR A, B, AND C)

	Cause	Approximate interval between onset and death
IMMEDIATE CAUSE (A)	Terminal bronchopneumonia	7 days
DUE TO, OR AS A CONSEQUENCE OF (B)	Arteriosclerotic heart disease	6 years
DUE TO, OR AS A CONSEQUENCE OF (C)		

CONDITIONS, IF ANY, WHICH GAVE RISE TO THE IMMEDIATE CAUSE, STATING THE UNDERLYING CAUSE LAST.

24. WAS DEATH REPORTED TO CORONER? no
25. WAS BIOPSY PERFORMED? no
26. WAS AUTOPSY PERFORMED? no
23. OTHER CONDITIONS CONTRIBUTING BUT NOT RELATED TO THE IMMEDIATE CAUSE OF DEATH: Chronic brain damage due to cerebral embolization
27. WAS OPERATION PERFORMED FOR ANY CONDITION IN ITEMS 22 OR 23? TYPE OF OPERATION / DATE: no

PHYSICIAN'S CERTIFICATION

28A. I CERTIFY THAT DEATH OCCURRED AT THE HOUR, DATE AND PLACE STATED FROM THE CAUSES STATED. I ATTENDED DECEDENT SINCE (ENTER MO, DA, YR): October 15, 1979 — I LAST SAW DECEDENT ALIVE (ENTER MO, DA, YR): March 4, 1980
28B. PHYSICIAN—SIGNATURE AND DEGREE OR TITLE: [signature] M.D.
28C. DATE SIGNED: March 5, 1980
28D. PHYSICIAN'S LICENSE NUMBER: A09619
28E. TYPE PHYSICIAN'S NAME AND ADDRESS: Otto Lange,M.D.,23450 Calabasas Rd.,Woodland Hills,California 91364

INJURY INFORMATION

29. SPECIFY ACCIDENT, SUICIDE, ETC.
30. PLACE OF INJURY
31. INJURY AT WORK
32A. DATE OF INJURY—MONTH, DAY, YEAR
32B. HOUR
33. LOCATION (STREET AND NUMBER OR LOCATION AND CITY OR TOWN)
34. DESCRIBE HOW INJURY OCCURRED (EVENTS WHICH RESULTED IN INJURY)

CORONER'S USE ONLY

35A. I CERTIFY THAT DEATH OCCURRED AT THE HOUR, DATE AND PLACE STATED FROM THE CAUSES STATED. AS REQUIRED BY LAW I HAVE HELD AN (INQUEST-INVESTIGATION)
35B. CORONER—SIGNATURE AND DEGREE OF TITLE
35C. DATE SIGNED

36. DISPOSITION	37. DATE—MONTH, DAY, YEAR	38. NAME AND ADDRESS OF CEMETERY OR CREMATORY	39. EMBALMER'S LICENSE NUMBER AND SIGNATURE
Cremation	March 10,1980	Chapel of the Pines-Los Angeles, California	Not Embalmed

40. NAME OF FUNERAL DIRECTOR (OR PERSON ACTING AS SUCH): Pierce Brothers Hollywood
41. LOCAL REGISTRAR—SIGNATURE: [signature]
42. DATE ACCEPTED BY LOCAL REGISTRAR: MAR 7 1980

STATE REGISTRAR: A. B. C. D. E. F.

VS-11 (10-78)

08-3-1-0552

This is to certify that this document is a true copy of the official record filed with the Registrar-Recorder/County Clerk.

OCT 3 1996
19-386527

CONNY B. McCORMACK
Registrar-Recorder/County Clerk

This copy not valid unless prepared on engraved border displaying the Seal and Signature of the Registrar-Recorder/County Clerk.

BANKNOTE CORPORATION OF AMERICA

ANY ALTERATION OR ERASURE VOIDS THIS CERTIFICATE

STATE OF CALIFORNIA
CERTIFICATION OF VITAL RECORD

COUNTY OF LOS ANGELES
DEPARTMENT OF HEALTH SERVICES

CERTIFICATE OF DEATH
STATE OF CALIFORNIA
USE BLACK INK ONLY/NO ERASURES, WHITEOUTS OR ALTERATIONS
VS-11 (REV. 7/97)

STATE FILE NUMBER — LOCAL REGISTRATION NUMBER

DECEDENT PERSONAL DATA

1. NAME OF DECEDENT—FIRST (GIVEN)	2. MIDDLE	3. LAST (FAMILY)
Francis	Albert	Sinatra

4. DATE OF BIRTH MM/DD/CCYY	5. AGE YRS.	IF UNDER 1 YEAR (MONTHS, DAYS)	IF UNDER 24 HOURS (HOURS, MINUTES)	6. SEX	7. DATE OF DEATH MM/DD/CCYY	8. HOUR
12/12/1915	82			Male	05/14/1998	2250

9. STATE OF BIRTH	10. SOCIAL SECURITY NO.	11. MILITARY SERVICE	12. MARITAL STATUS	13. EDUCATION—YEARS COMPLETED
New Jersey	138-16-0442	☐ YES ☒ NO ☐ UNK	Married	12

14. RACE	15. HISPANIC—SPECIFY	16. USUAL EMPLOYER
Caucasian	☐ YES ☒ NO	Self-employed

17. OCCUPATION	18. KIND OF BUSINESS	19. YEARS IN OCCUPATION
Entertainer	Entertainment	65

USUAL RESIDENCE

20. RESIDENCE—(STREET AND NUMBER OR LOCATION): 915 North Foothill Road

21. CITY	22. COUNTY	23. ZIP CODE	24. YRS IN COUNTY	25. STATE OR FOREIGN COUNTRY
Beverly Hills	Los Angeles	90210	40	California

INFORMANT

26. NAME, RELATIONSHIP	27. MAILING ADDRESS (STREET AND NUMBER OR RURAL ROUTE NUMBER, CITY OR TOWN, STATE, ZIP)
Barbara Sinatra - Wife	915 North Foothill Road , Beverly Hills, CA 90210

SPOUSE AND PARENT INFORMATION

28. NAME OF SURVIVING SPOUSE—FIRST	29. MIDDLE	30. LAST (MAIDEN NAME)	
Barbara	Ann	Blakeley	
31. NAME OF FATHER—FIRST	**32. MIDDLE**	**33. LAST**	**34. BIRTH STATE**
Martin	Anthony	Sinatra	Italy
35. NAME OF MOTHER—FIRST	**36. MIDDLE**	**37. LAST (MAIDEN)**	**38. BIRTH STATE**
Natalie	-	Garavanti	Italy

DISPOSITION(S)

39. DATE MM/DD/CCYY	40. PLACE OF FINAL DISPOSITION
05/20/1998	Desert Memorial Park Cemetery,69920 Ramon Rd.,Cathedral City, CA 92234

FUNERAL DIRECTOR AND LOCAL REGISTRAR

41. TYPE OF DISPOSITION(S)	42. SIGNATURE OF EMBALMER	43. LICENSE NO.
Burial	▶ [signature]	7516
44. NAME OF FUNERAL DIRECTOR	**45. LICENSE NO. / 46. SIGNATURE OF LOCAL REGISTRAR**	**47. DATE MM/DD/CCYY**
McCormick Mortuary	FD 292 ▶ [signature]	05/18/1998

PLACE OF DEATH

101. PLACE OF DEATH	102. IF HOSPITAL, SPECIFY ONE	103. FACILITY OTHER THAN HOSPITAL	104. COUNTY
Cedars-Sinai Medical Cntr	☐ IP ☒ ER/OP ☐ DOA	☐ CONV. HOSP. ☐ RES. CARE ☐ OTHER	Los Angeles

105. STREET ADDRESS—(STREET AND NUMBER OR LOCATION)	106. CITY
8700 Beverly Boulevard	Los Angeles

CAUSE OF DEATH

107. DEATH WAS CAUSED BY: (ENTER ONLY ONE CAUSE PER LINE FOR A, B, C, AND D)

	Cause	TIME INTERVAL BETWEEN ONSET AND DEATH
IMMEDIATE CAUSE (A)	Cardiorespiratory Arrest	30 Mins
DUE TO (B)	Acute Myocardial Infarction	2 Hrs
DUE TO (C)	Coronary Atherosclerosis	10 Yrs
DUE TO (D)		

108. DEATH REPORTED TO CORONER: ☐ YES ☒ NO — REFERRAL NUMBER
109. BIOPSY PERFORMED: ☐ YES ☒ NO
110. AUTOPSY PERFORMED: ☐ YES ☒ NO
111. USED IN DETERMINING CAUSE: ☐ YES ☒ NO

112. OTHER SIGNIFICANT CONDITIONS CONTRIBUTING TO DEATH BUT NOT RELATED TO CAUSE GIVEN IN 107: None

113. WAS OPERATION PERFORMED FOR ANY CONDITION IN ITEM 107 OR 112? IF YES, LIST TYPE OF OPERATION AND DATE: None

PHYSICIAN'S CERTIFICATION

114. I CERTIFY THAT TO THE BEST OF MY KNOWLEDGE DEATH OCCURRED AT THE HOUR, DATE AND PLACE STATED FROM THE CAUSES STATED.

DECEDENT ATTENDED SINCE MM/DD/CCYY	DECEDENT LAST SEEN ALIVE MM/DD/CCYY	115. SIGNATURE AND TITLE OF CERTIFIER	116. LICENSE NO.	117. DATE MM/DD/CCYY
06/30/1993	05/14/1998	▶ [signature] MD	G31651	05/15/1998

118. TYPE ATTENDING PHYSICIAN'S NAME, MAILING ADDRESS, ZIP: Jeffrey Helfenstein,MD.,436 N.Roxbury,Beverly Hills,CA90210

CORONER'S USE ONLY

I CERTIFY THAT IN MY OPINION DEATH OCCURRED AT THE HOUR, DATE AND PLACE STATED FROM THE CAUSES STATED.

119. MANNER OF DEATH: ☐ NATURAL ☐ SUICIDE ☐ HOMICIDE ☐ ACCIDENT ☐ PENDING INVESTIGATION ☐ COULD NOT BE DETERMINED

120. INJURY AT WORK ☐ YES ☐ NO | 121. INJURY DATE MM/DD/CCYY | 122. HOUR | 123. PLACE OF INJURY

124. DESCRIBE HOW INJURY OCCURRED (EVENTS WHICH RESULTED IN INJURY)

125. LOCATION (STREET AND NUMBER OR LOCATION AND CITY, ZIP)

126. SIGNATURE OF CORONER OR DEPUTY CORONER	127. DATE MM/DD/CCYY	128. TYPED NAME, TITLE OF CORONER OR DEPUTY CORONER
▶		

STATE REGISTRAR

A	B	C	D	E	F	G	H	FAX AUTH. #	CENSUS TRACT

090092671

This is a true certified copy of the record filed in the County of Los Angeles Department of Health Services if it bears the Registrar's signature in purple ink.

DATE ISSUED MAY 27 1998

Director of Health Services and Registrar

This copy not valid unless prepared on engraved border displaying seal and signature of Registrar.

THE GREAT SEAL OF THE STATE OF CALIFORNIA — EUREKA

LOS ANGELES COUNTY — REGISTRAR OF VITAL STATISTICS — STATE OF CALIFORNIA

MIDWEST BANK NOTE COMPANY

ANY ALTERATION OR ERASURE VOIDS THIS CERTIFICATE

CERTIFICATION OF VITAL RECORD

COUNTY OF LOS ANGELES • REGISTRAR-RECORDER/COUNTY CLERK

CERTIFICATE OF DEATH
STATE OF CALIFORNIA
USE BLACK INK ONLY

STATE FILE NUMBER

39019005675
LOCAL REGISTRATION DISTRICT AND CERTIFICATE NUMBER

DECEDENT PERSONAL DATA

1A. NAME OF DECEDENT—FIRST (GIVEN): BARBARA
1B. MIDDLE: CATHERINE
1C. LAST (FAMILY): STANWYCK
2A. DATE OF DEATH—MO, DAY, YR: JAN. 20, 1990
2B. HOUR: 1659
3. SEX: FEM.
4. RACE: WHITE
5. SPANISH/HISPANIC—SPECIFY: YES [ ] NO [X]
6. DATE OF BIRTH—MO, DAY, YR: JULY 16, 1907
7. AGE IN YEARS: 82
IF UNDER 1 YEAR: MONTHS / DAYS
IF UNDER 24 HOURS: HOURS / MINUTES
8. STATE OF BIRTH: NY
9. CITIZEN OF WHAT COUNTRY: USA
10A. FULL NAME OF FATHER: BYRON STEVENS
10B. STATE OF BIRTH: MA
11A. FULL MAIDEN NAME OF MOTHER: CATHERINE McFEE
11B. STATE OF BIRTH: NOVA SCOTIA
12. MILITARY SERVICE? 19__ TO 19__ [X] NONE
13. SOCIAL SECURITY NO.: 568-12-2985
14. MARITAL STATUS: DIVORCED
15. NAME OF SURVIVING SPOUSE (IF WIFE, ENTER MAIDEN NAME): ---
16A. USUAL OCCUPATION: ACTRESS
16B. USUAL KIND OF BUSINESS OR INDUSTRY: ACTING
16C. USUAL EMPLOYER: SELF-EMPLOYED
16D. YEARS IN OCCUPATION: 60
17. EDUCATION—YEARS COMPLETED: 12

USUAL RESIDENCE

18A. RESIDENCE—STREET AND NUMBER OR LOCATION: 1055 LOMA VISTA DR.
18B. CITY: BEVERLY HILLS
18C. ZIP CODE: 90210
18D. COUNTY: LOS ANGELES
18E. NUMBER OF YEARS IN THIS COUNTY: 51
18F. STATE OR FOREIGN COUNTRY: CA
20. NAME, RELATIONSHIP, MAILING ADDRESS AND ZIP CODE OF INFORMANT: EUGENE F. VASLETT - NEPHEW, 9 PORTO BELLO DR., SAN RAFAEL, CA 94901

PLACE OF DEATH

19A. PLACE OF DEATH: ST. JOHN'S HOSPITAL
19B. IF HOSPITAL, SPECIFY ONE: IP, ER/OP, DOA: IP
19C. COUNTY: LOS ANGELES
19D. STREET ADDRESS—STREET AND NUMBER OR LOCATION: 1328 22ND ST.
19E. CITY: SANTA MONICA

CAUSE OF DEATH

21. DEATH WAS CAUSED BY: (ENTER ONLY ONE CAUSE PER LINE FOR A, B, AND C)

	Cause	Time interval between onset and death
IMMEDIATE CAUSE (A)	Pneumonia	5 days
DUE TO (B)	Chronic Obstructive Lung Disease	7 years
DUE TO (C)	Emphysema	20 years

22. WAS DEATH REPORTED TO CORONER? REFERRAL NUMBER: YES [ ] NO [X]
23. WAS BIOPSY PERFORMED? YES [ ] NO [X]
24A. WAS AUTOPSY PERFORMED? YES [ ] NO [X]
24B. WAS IT USED IN DETERMINING CAUSE OF DEATH? YES [ ] NO [X]
25. OTHER SIGNIFICANT CONDITIONS CONTRIBUTING TO DEATH BUT NOT RELATED TO CAUSE GIVEN IN 21: Arteriosclerotic Heart Disease with myocardial infarct
26. WAS OPERATION PERFORMED FOR ANY CONDITION IN ITEM 21 OR 25? IF YES, LIST TYPE OF OPERATION AND DATE: Bronchoscopy 1/19/90

PHYSICIAN'S CERTIFICATION

I CERTIFY THAT TO THE BEST OF MY KNOWLEDGE DEATH OCCURRED AT THE HOUR, DATE AND PLACE STATED FROM THE CAUSES STATED.
27A. DECEDENT ATTENDED SINCE MONTH, DAY, YEAR: 12/21/71
DECEDENT LAST SEEN ALIVE MONTH, DAY, YEAR: 1/20/90
27B. SIGNATURE AND DEGREE OF TITLE OF PHYSICIAN: [signature] MD
27C. PHYSICIAN'S LICENSE NUMBER: A09069
27D. DATE SIGNED: 1/22/90
27E. TYPE ATTENDING PHYSICIAN'S NAME AND ADDRESS: ROBERT KOSITCHEK, M.D., 9675 BRIGHTON WAY, #380 BEVERLY HILLS, CA

CORONER'S USE ONLY

I CERTIFY THAT IN MY OPINION DEATH OCCURRED AT THE HOUR, DATE AND PLACE STATED FROM THE CAUSES STATED.
28A. SIGNATURE AND TITLE OF CORONER OR DEPUTY CORONER:
28B. DATE SIGNED
29. MANNER OF DEATH—specify one: natural, accident, suicide, homicide, pending investigation or could not be determined
30A. PLACE OF INJURY
30B. INJURY AT WORK: YES [ ] NO [ ]
30C. DATE OF INJURY MONTH, DAY, YEAR
31. HOUR
32. LOCATION (STREET AND NUMBER OR LOCATION AND CITY)
33. DESCRIBE HOW INJURY OCCURRED (EVENTS WHICH RESULTED IN INJURY)

FUNERAL DIRECTOR AND LOCAL REGISTRAR

34A. DISPOSITION(S): CR/RES
34B. PLACE OF FINAL DISPOSITION—NAME AND ADDRESS: 9 PORTO BELLO DR. SAN RAFAEL, CA 94901
34C. DATE MO, DAY, YEAR: JAN. 25, 1990
35A. SIGNATURE OF EMBALMER: NOT EMBALMED
35B. LICENSE NUMBER: ——
36A. NAME OF FUNERAL DIRECTOR (OR PERSON ACTING AS SUCH): GATES, KINGSLEY & GATES SM
36B. LICENSE NO.: F451
37. SIGNATURE OF LOCAL REGISTRAR: [signature]
38. REGISTRATION DATE: JAN 22 1990

STATE REGISTRAR: A. B. C. D. E. F. CENSUS TRACT

15

VS-11 (REV. 3-89) 492 MAKE NO ERASURES, WHITEOUTS, OR OTHER ALTERATIONS 01-9-1-0756

This is to certify that this document is a true copy of the official record filed with the Registrar-Recorder/County Clerk.

[signature]
CHARLES WEISSBURD
Registrar-Recorder/County Clerk

FEB 05 1992
19-312834

This copy not valid unless prepared on engraved border displaying the Seal and Signature of the Registrar-Recorder/County Clerk.

THE GREAT SEAL OF THE STATE OF CALIFORNIA

REGISTRAR-RECORDER/COUNTY CLERK • COUNTY OF LOS ANGELES, CALIFORNIA

American Bank Note Company

ANY ALTERATION OR ERASURE VOIDS THIS CERTIFICATE

STATE OF CALIFORNIA
CERTIFICATION OF VITAL RECORD

COUNTY OF LOS ANGELES

DEPARTMENT OF HEALTH SERVICES

CERTIFICATE OF DEATH
STATE OF CALIFORNIA
USE BLACK INK ONLY/NO ERASURES, WHITEOUTS OR ALTERATIONS
VS-11 (REV. 1/00)

STATE FILE NUMBER — LOCAL REGISTRATION NUMBER

DECEDENT PERSONAL DATA

1. NAME OF DECEDENT—FIRST (GIVEN): CRAIG
2. MIDDLE: -
3. LAST (FAMILY): STEVENS
4. DATE OF BIRTH MM/DD/CCYY: 07/08/1918
5. AGE YRS.: 81
IF UNDER 1 YEAR: MONTHS / DAYS — IF UNDER 24 HOURS: HOURS / MINUTES
6. SEX: MALE
7. DATE OF DEATH MM/DD/CCYY: 05/10/2000
8. HOUR: 0155
9. STATE OF BIRTH: MISSOURI
10. SOCIAL SECURITY NO.: 545-14-3791
11. MILITARY SERVICE: ☐ YES ☐ NO ☒ UNK
12. MARITAL STATUS: WIDOWER
13. EDUCATION—YEARS COMPLETED: 14
14. RACE: CAUCASIAN
15. HISPANIC—SPECIFY: ☐ YES ☒ NO
16. USUAL EMPLOYER: SELF EMPLOYED
17. OCCUPATION: ACTOR
18. KIND OF BUSINESS: ENTERTAINMENT
19. YEARS IN OCCUPATION: 60

USUAL RESIDENCE

20. RESIDENCE—(STREET AND NUMBER OR LOCATION): 1308 N. FLORES STREET
21. CITY: LOS ANGELES
22. COUNTY: LOS ANGELES
23. ZIP CODE: 90069
24. YRS IN COUNTY: 60
25. STATE OR FOREIGN COUNTRY: CALIFORNIA

INFORMANT

26. NAME, RELATIONSHIP: LARRY DRESSLER - BUSINESS MANAGER
27. MAILING ADDRESS (STREET AND NUMBER OR RURAL ROUTE NUMBER, CITY OR TOWN, STATE, ZIP): 10390 SANTA MONICA BLVD. #360, L.A., CA. 90025

SPOUSE AND PARENT INFORMATION

28. NAME OF SURVIVING SPOUSE—FIRST: -
29. MIDDLE: -
30. LAST (MAIDEN NAME): -
31. NAME OF FATHER—FIRST: GAIL
32. MIDDLE: -
33. LAST: STEVENS
34. BIRTH STATE: MISSOURI
35. NAME OF MOTHER—FIRST: MARIE
36. MIDDLE: -
37. LAST (MAIDEN): HUGHES
38. BIRTH STATE: MISSOURI

DISPOSITION(S)

39. DATE MM/DD/CCYY: 05/23/2000
40. PLACE OF FINAL DISPOSITION: AT SEA OFF THE COAST OF LOS ANGELES COUNTY

FUNERAL DIRECTOR AND LOCAL REGISTRAR

41. TYPE OF DISPOSITION(S): CR/SEA
42. SIGNATURE OF EMBALMER: ▶ NOT EMBALMED
43. LICENSE NO.: -
44. NAME OF FUNERAL DIRECTOR: NEPTUNE SOCIETY - BURBANK
45. LICENSE NO.: FD-1359
46. SIGNATURE OF LOCAL REGISTRAR: [signature]
47. DATE MM/DD/CCYY: 05/19/2000

PLACE OF DEATH

101. PLACE OF DEATH: CEDARS-SINAI MEDICAL CTR
102. IF HOSPITAL, SPECIFY ONE: ☒ IP ☐ ER/OP ☐ DOA
103. FACILITY OTHER THAN HOSPITAL: ☐ CONV. HOSP. ☐ RES. CARE ☐ OTHER
104. COUNTY: LOS ANGELES
105. STREET ADDRESS—(STREET AND NUMBER OR LOCATION): 8700 BEVERLY BLVD.
106. CITY: LOS ANGELES

CAUSE OF DEATH

107. DEATH WAS CAUSED BY: (ENTER ONLY ONE CAUSE PER LINE FOR A, B, C, AND D)
IMMEDIATE CAUSE (A) MALIGNANT LYMPHOMA — TIME INTERVAL BETWEEN ONSET AND DEATH: 3 MTHS
DUE TO (B)
DUE TO (C)
DUE TO (D)
108. DEATH REPORTED TO CORONER: ☐ YES ☒ NO — REFERRAL NUMBER
109. BIOPSY PERFORMED: ☒ YES ☐ NO
110. AUTOPSY PERFORMED: ☐ YES ☒ NO
111. USED IN DETERMINING CAUSE: ☐ YES ☐ NO
112. OTHER SIGNIFICANT CONDITIONS CONTRIBUTING TO DEATH BUT NOT RELATED TO CAUSE GIVEN IN 107: PNEUMONIA
113. WAS OPERATION PERFORMED FOR ANY CONDITION IN ITEM 107 OR 112? IF YES, LIST TYPE OF OPERATION AND DATE: NO

PHYSICIAN'S CERTIFICATION

114. I CERTIFY THAT TO THE BEST OF MY KNOWLEDGE DEATH OCCURRED AT THE HOUR, DATE AND PLACE STATED FROM THE CAUSES STATED.
DECEDENT ATTENDED SINCE MM/DD/CCYY: 02/08/2000 — DECEDENT LAST SEEN ALIVE MM/DD/CCYY: 05/09/2000
115. SIGNATURE AND TITLE OF CERTIFIER: ▶ [signature]
116. LICENSE NO.: G048876
117. DATE MM/DD/CCYY: 05/17/2000
118. TYPE ATTENDING PHYSICIAN'S NAME, MAILING ADDRESS, ZIP: ROBERT DECKER, MD,8635 W. 3RD STREET, LOS ANGELES, CA. 90048

CORONER'S USE ONLY

I CERTIFY THAT IN MY OPINION DEATH OCCURRED AT THE HOUR, DATE AND PLACE STATED FROM THE CAUSES STATED.
119. MANNER OF DEATH: ☐ NATURAL ☐ SUICIDE ☐ HOMICIDE ☐ ACCIDENT ☐ PENDING INVESTIGATION ☐ COULD NOT BE DETERMINED
120. INJURED AT WORK: ☐ YES ☐ NO
121. INJURY DATE MM/DD/CCYY
122. HOUR
123. PLACE OF INJURY
124. DESCRIBE HOW INJURY OCCURRED (EVENTS WHICH RESULTED IN INJURY)
125. LOCATION (STREET AND NUMBER OR LOCATION AND CITY, ZIP)
126. SIGNATURE OF CORONER OR DEPUTY CORONER ▶
127. DATE MM/DD/CCYY
128. TYPED NAME, TITLE OF CORONER OR DEPUTY CORONER

STATE REGISTRAR

A B C D E F G H — FAX AUTH. #: 195/122911 — CENSUS TRACT

090336545

This is a true certified copy of the record filed in the County of Los Angeles Department of Health Services if it bears the Registrar's signature in purple ink.

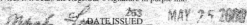

DATE ISSUED MAY 25 2000

Director of Health Services and Registrar

This copy not valid unless prepared on engraved border displaying seal and signature of Registrar.

MIDWEST BANK NOTE COMPANY
ANY ALTERATION OR ERASURE VOIDS THIS CERTIFICATE

STATE OF CALIFORNIA

CERTIFICATION OF VITAL RECORD

COUNTY OF LOS ANGELES • REGISTRAR-RECORDER/COUNTY CLERK

CERTIFICATE OF DEATH
STATE OF CALIFORNIA
USE BLACK INK ONLY/NO ERASURES, WHITEOUTS OR ALTERATIONS
VS-11 (REV 11/96)

STATE FILE NUMBER

3 199719028195
LOCAL REGISTRATION NUMBER

DECEDENT PERSONAL DATA

1. NAME OF DECEDENT—FIRST (GIVEN)	2. MIDDLE	3. LAST (FAMILY)
JAMES	MAITLAND	STEWART

4. DATE OF BIRTH MM/DD/CCYY	5. AGE YRS	IF UNDER 1 YEAR (MONTHS / DAYS)	IF UNDER 24 HOURS (HOURS / MINUTES)	6. SEX	7. DATE OF DEATH MM/DD/CCYY	8. HOUR
05/20/1908	89			MALE	07/02/1997	1105

9. STATE OF BIRTH	10. SOCIAL SECURITY NO	11. MILITARY SERVICE	12. MARITAL STATUS	13. EDUCATION—YEARS COMPLETED
PA	573-05-8879	[X] YES [ ] NO	WIDOWED	16

14. RACE	15. HISPANIC—SPECIFY	16. USUAL EMPLOYER
CAUC.	[ ] YES [X] NO	SELF EMPLOYED

17. OCCUPATION	18. KIND OF BUSINESS	19. YEARS IN OCCUPATION
ACTOR	ENTERTAINMENT	62

USUAL RESIDENCE

20. RESIDENCE—STREET AND NUMBER OR LOCATION: 918 N ROXBURY DRIVE

21. CITY	22. COUNTY	23. ZIP CODE	24. YRS IN COUNTY	25. STATE OR FOREIGN COUNTRY
BEVERLY HILLS	LOS ANGELES	90210	58	CALIFORNIA

INFORMANT

26. NAME, RELATIONSHIP	27. MAILING ADDRESS (STREET AND NUMBER OR RURAL ROUTE NUMBER, CITY OR TOWN, STATE, ZIP)
MICHAEL McLEAN - SON	4744 N 56th STREET, PHOENIX AZ 85018

SPOUSE AND PARENT INFORMATION

28. NAME OF SURVIVING SPOUSE—FIRST	29. MIDDLE	30. LAST (MAIDEN NAME)	
-	-	-	
31. NAME OF FATHER—FIRST	**32. MIDDLE**	**33. LAST**	**34. BIRTH STATE**
ALEXANDER	MAITLAND	STEWART	PA
35. NAME OF MOTHER—FIRST	**36. MIDDLE**	**37. LAST (MAIDEN)**	**38. BIRTH STATE**
ELIZABETH	RUTH	JACKSON	PA

DISPOSITION(S)

39. DATE MM/DD/CCYY	40. PLACE OF FINAL DISPOSITION
07/07/1997	FOREST LAWN MEM. PARK 1712 S GLENDALE AVE, GLENDALE CA 91205

FUNERAL DIRECTOR AND LOCAL REGISTRAR

41. TYPE OF DISPOSITION(S)	42. SIGNATURE OF EMBALMER	43. LICENSE NO.
BURIAL	▶ John W Riley	5641
44. NAME OF FUNERAL DIRECTOR	**45. LICENSE NO. / 46. SIGNATURE OF LOCAL REGISTRAR**	**47. DATE MM/DD/CCYY**
FOREST LAWN MTY GLENDALE	FD 656 ▶ [signature]	07/07/1997

PLACE OF DEATH

101. PLACE OF DEATH	102. IF HOSPITAL, SPECIFY ONE	103. FACILITY OTHER THAN HOSPITAL	104. COUNTY
RESIDENCE	[ ] IP [ ] ER/OP [ ] DOA	[ ] CONV. HOSP [ ] RES. CARE [ ] OTHER	LOS ANGELES

105. STREET ADDRESS—STREET AND NUMBER OR LOCATION	106. CITY
918 N. ROXBURY DRIVE	BEVERLY HILLS

CAUSE OF DEATH

107. DEATH WAS CAUSED BY: (ENTER ONLY ONE CAUSE PER LINE FOR A, B, C, AND D)

	Cause	TIME INTERVAL BETWEEN ONSET AND DEATH
IMMEDIATE CAUSE (A)	CARDIAC ARREST	MINS
DUE TO (B)	PULMONARY EMBOLUS	7 HOURS
DUE TO (C)	RIGHT LEG THROMBOSIS	7DAYS
DUE TO (D)		

108. DEATH REPORTED TO CORONER: [ ] YES [X] NO — REFERRAL NUMBER
109. BIOPSY PERFORMED: [ ] YES [X] NO
110. AUTOPSY PERFORMED: [ ] YES [X] NO
111. USED IN DETERMINING CAUSE: [ ] YES [ ] NO

112. OTHER SIGNIFICANT CONDITIONS CONTRIBUTING TO DEATH BUT NOT RELATED TO CAUSE GIVEN IN 107: NONE

113. WAS OPERATION PERFORMED FOR ANY CONDITION IN ITEM 107 OR 112? IF YES, LIST TYPE OF OPERATION AND DATE: NONE

PHYSICIAN'S CERTIFICATION

114. I CERTIFY THAT TO THE BEST OF MY KNOWLEDGE DEATH OCCURRED AT THE HOUR, DATE AND PLACE STATED FROM THE CAUSES STATED.
DECEDENT ATTENDED SINCE MM/DD/CCYY: 03/--/1990
DECEDENT LAST SEEN ALIVE MM/DD/CCYY: 07/02/1997

115. SIGNATURE AND TITLE OF CERTIFIER	116. LICENSE NO.	117. DATE MM/DD/CCYY
▶ Terry Schaack	A43132	07/02/1997

118. TYPE ATTENDING PHYSICIAN'S NAME, MAILING ADDRESS, ZIP: TERRY SCHAACK,MD 9675 BRIGHTON WAY #290 BEVERLY HILLS,CA 90210

CORONER'S USE ONLY

I CERTIFY THAT IN MY OPINION DEATH OCCURRED AT THE HOUR, DATE AND PLACE STATED FROM THE CAUSES STATED.

119. MANNER OF DEATH: [ ] NATURAL [ ] SUICIDE [ ] HOMICIDE [ ] ACCIDENT [ ] PENDING INVESTIGATION [ ] COULD NOT BE DETERMINED

120. INJURY AT WORK [ ] YES [ ] NO | 121. INJURY DATE MM/DD/CCYY | 122. HOUR | 123. PLACE OF INJURY

124. DESCRIBE HOW INJURY OCCURRED (EVENTS WHICH RESULTED IN INJURY)

125. LOCATION (STREET AND NUMBER OR LOCATION AND CITY, ZIP)

126. SIGNATURE OF CORONER OR DEPUTY CORONER ▶ | 127. DATE MM/DD/CCYY | 128. TYPED NAME, TITLE OF CORONER OR DEPUTY CORONER

STATE REGISTRAR

A	B	C	D	E	F	G	H	FAX AUTH. #	CENSUS TRACT
								273/6860	

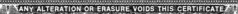

This is to certify that this document is a true copy of the official record filed with the Registrar-Recorder/County Clerk.

Conny B. McCormack

CONNY B. McCORMACK
Registrar-Recorder/County Clerk

OCT 30 1997

19-064102

This copy not valid unless prepared on engraved border displaying the Seal and Signature of the Registrar-Recorder/County Clerk.

American Bank Note Company

ANY ALTERATION OR ERASURE VOIDS THIS CERTIFICATE

STATE OF CALIFORNIA

CERTIFICATION OF VITAL RECORD

COUNTY OF SAN DIEGO

GREGORY J. SMITH

ASSESSOR/RECORDER/COUNTY CLERK

80-000406

CERTIFICATE OF DEATH
STATE OF CALIFORNIA

8009

06184

STATE FILE NUMBER

LOCAL REGISTRATION DISTRICT AND CERTIFICATE NUMBER

DECEDENT PERSONAL DATA

1A. NAME OF DECEDENT—FIRST	1B. MIDDLE	1C. LAST	2A. DATE OF DEATH (MONTH, DAY, YEAR)	2B. HOUR
HUGH	MILBURN	STONE	June 12, 1980	0800

3. SEX	4. RACE	5. ETHNICITY	6. DATE OF BIRTH	7. AGE
Male	White	9	July 5, 1904	75 YEARS

8. BIRTHPLACE OF DECEDENT (STATE OR FOREIGN COUNTRY)	9. NAME AND BIRTHPLACE OF FATHER	10. BIRTH NAME AND BIRTHPLACE OF MOTHER
Kansas	Herbert M. Stone - Kansas	Laura Belfield - Kansas

11. CITIZEN OF WHAT COUNTRY	12. SOCIAL SECURITY NUMBER	13. MARITAL STATUS	14. NAME OF SURVIVING SPOUSE (IF WIFE, ENTER BIRTH NAME)
U.S.A.	110-12-7732	Married	Jane Garrison

15. PRIMARY OCCUPATION	16. NUMBER OF YEARS THIS OCCUPATION	17. EMPLOYER (IF SELF-EMPLOYED, SO STATE)	18. KIND OF INDUSTRY OR BUSINESS
Actor	55	CBS	Television & Motion Pictures

USUAL RESIDENCE

19A. USUAL RESIDENCE—STREET ADDRESS (STREET AND NUMBER OR LOCATION)	19B.	19C. CITY OR TOWN
Stoneridge On La Sencilla	9-1-47	Rancho Santa Fe

19D. COUNTY	19E. STATE	20. NAME AND ADDRESS OF INFORMANT—RELATIONSHIP
San Diego	California	Jane Stone - Wife P O Box 1617 Rancho Santa Fe, Ca 92067

PLACE OF DEATH

21A. PLACE OF DEATH	21B. COUNTY
Scripps Memorial Hospital	San Diego

21C. STREET ADDRESS (STREET AND NUMBER OR LOCATION)	21D. CITY OR TOWN
9888 Genesee Avenue	La Jolla

CAUSE OF DEATH

427.0
414.0

22. DEATH WAS CAUSED BY: (ENTER ONLY ONE CAUSE PER LINE FOR A, B, AND C)

	Cause	Approximate interval between onset and death
IMMEDIATE CAUSE (A)	Congestive heart failure	2 yrs
DUE TO, OR AS A CONSEQUENCE OF (B)	Mitral regurgitation, severe LV dysfunction	9 years
DUE TO, OR AS A CONSEQUENCE OF (C)	arteriosclerotic heart disease	15 yrs

CONDITIONS, IF ANY, WHICH GAVE RISE TO THE IMMEDIATE CAUSE, STATING THE UNDERLYING CAUSE LAST

24. WAS DEATH REPORTED TO CORONER? NO
25. WAS BIOPSY PERFORMED? NO
26. WAS AUTOPSY PERFORMED? YES

23. OTHER CONDITIONS CONTRIBUTING BUT NOT RELATED TO THE IMMEDIATE CAUSE OF DEATH

27. WAS OPERATION PERFORMED FOR ANY CONDITION IN ITEMS 22 OR 23? YES — TYPE OF OPERATION: Double Coronary Bypass — DATE: 1971

PHYSICIAN'S CERTIFICATION

28A. I CERTIFY THAT DEATH OCCURRED AT THE HOUR, DATE AND PLACE STATED FROM THE CAUSES STATED.

I ATTENDED DECEDENT SINCE (ENTER MO. DA. YR.)	I LAST SAW DECEDENT ALIVE (ENTER MO. DA. YR.)	28B. PHYSICIAN—SIGNATURE AND DEGREE OF TITLE	28C. DATE SIGNED	28D. PHYSICIAN'S LICENSE NUMBER
12-8-75	6-11-80	Frederic Shean MD	6-12-80	A22204

28E. TYPE PHYSICIAN'S NAME AND ADDRESS: Frederic C. Shean, M.D. 9844 Genesee Ave. Suite #400, La Jolla, CA

INJURY INFORMATION

29. SPECIFY ACCIDENT, SUICIDE, ETC. — 30. PLACE OF INJURY — 31. INJURY AT WORK — 32A. DATE OF INJURY—MONTH, DAY, YEAR — 32B. HOUR

33. LOCATION (STREET AND NUMBER OR LOCATION AND CITY OR TOWN) — 34. DESCRIBE HOW INJURY OCCURRED (EVENTS WHICH RESULTED IN INJURY)

CORONER'S USE ONLY

35A. I CERTIFY THAT DEATH OCCURRED AT THE HOUR, DATE AND PLACE STATED FROM THE CAUSES STATED, AS REQUIRED BY LAW I HAVE HELD AN (INQUEST-INVESTIGATION) — 35B. CORONER—SIGNATURE AND DEGREE OR TITLE — 35C. DATE SIGNED

36. DISPOSITION	37. DATE—MONTH, DAY, YEAR	38. NAME AND ADDRESS OF CEMETERY OR CREMATORY	39. EMBALMER'S LICENSE NUMBER AND SIGNATURE
Burial	6-16-80	El Camino Memorial Park, San Diego, Ca.	4190 Robert McAllister

40. NAME OF FUNERAL DIRECTOR (OR PERSON ACTING AS SUCH)	41. LOCAL REGISTRAR—SIGNATURE	42. DATE ACCEPTED BY LOCAL REGISTRAR
El Camino Mortuary	Donald G. Ramras, M.D.	JUN 13 1980

STATE REGISTRAR	A.	B.	C.	D.	E.	F.
	1	X	2		4140	

VS-11 (10-78)

473897

This is a true certified copy of the record if it bears the seal, imprinted in purple ink, of the Recorder. JAN 08 2001

Recorder/County Clerk
San Diego County, California

THE GREAT SEAL OF THE STATE OF CALIFORNIA — EUREKA

MIDWEST BANK NOTE COMPANY

ANY ALTERATION OR ERASURE VOIDS THIS CERTIFICATE

CERTIFICATION OF VITAL RECORD

COUNTY OF LOS ANGELES • REGISTRAR-RECORDER/COUNTY CLERK

CERTIFICATE OF DEATH
STATE OF CALIFORNIA

0190-037291

STATE FILE NUMBER — LOCAL REGISTRATION DISTRICT AND CERTIFICATE NUMBER

DECEDENT PERSONAL DATA

1A. NAME OF DECEDENT—FIRST: Dorothy
1B. MIDDLE: Ruth
1C. LAST: aka Stratten Hoogstraten
2A. DATE OF DEATH (MONTH, DAY, YEAR): Found August 14, 1980
2B. HOUR: 2345
3. SEX: Female
4. RACE: Cauc.
5. ETHNICITY: not stated
6. DATE OF BIRTH: February 28, 1960
7. AGE: 20 YEARS
8. BIRTHPLACE OF DECEDENT (STATE OR FOREIGN COUNTRY): Canada
9. NAME AND BIRTHPLACE OF FATHER: Simon Hoogstraten, Holland
10. BIRTH NAME AND BIRTHPLACE OF MOTHER: Peternella Fuchs, Holland
11. CITIZEN OF WHAT COUNTRY: Canada
12. SOCIAL SECURITY NUMBER: 626-18-9849
13. MARITAL STATUS: Married
14. NAME OF SURVIVING SPOUSE (IF WIFE, ENTER BIRTH NAME): Paul Snider
15. PRIMARY OCCUPATION: Actress - Model
16. NUMBER OF YEARS THIS OCCUPATION: 3
17. EMPLOYER (IF SELF-EMPLOYED, SO STATE): Free Lance
18. KIND OF INDUSTRY OR BUSINESS: Acting - Modeling

USUAL RESIDENCE

19A. USUAL RESIDENCE—STREET ADDRESS (STREET AND NUMBER OR LOCATION): 262 1/2 So. Spalding
19C. CITY OR TOWN: Beverly Hills
19D. COUNTY: Los Angeles
19E. STATE: California
20. NAME AND ADDRESS OF INFORMANT—RELATIONSHIP: L. Wayne Alexander - Attorney, 9255 Sunset Blvd., Los Angeles, California

PLACE OF DEATH

21A. PLACE OF DEATH: Private Residence
21B. COUNTY: Los Angeles
21C. STREET ADDRESS (STREET AND NUMBER OR LOCATION): 10881 W. Clarkson Rd.
21D. CITY OR TOWN: W.Los Angeles

CAUSE OF DEATH

22. DEATH WAS CAUSED BY: (ENTER ONLY ONE CAUSE PER LINE FOR A, B, AND C)
IMMEDIATE CAUSE (A) GUNSHOT WOUND OF HEAD
24. WAS DEATH REPORTED TO CORONER?: 80-10485
25. WAS BIOPSY PERFORMED?: No
26. WAS AUTOPSY PERFORMED?: Yes
27. WAS OPERATION PERFORMED FOR ANY CONDITION IN ITEMS 22 OR 23?: No

INJURY INFORMATION

29. SPECIFY ACCIDENT, SUICIDE, ETC.: Homicide
30. PLACE OF INJURY: Private Residence
31. INJURY AT WORK: No
32A. DATE OF INJURY—MONTH, DAY, YEAR: Unknown
32B. HOUR: Unk.
33. LOCATION (STREET AND NUMBER OR LOCATION AND CITY OR TOWN): 10881 W. Clarkson Rd - W.Los Angeles
34. DESCRIBE HOW INJURY OCCURRED: As above
35B. CORONER: 1104 N. MISSION RD. LOS ANGELES, CALIF. 90033 — THOMAS T. NOGUCHI, M.D., CORONER — DEPUTY — 8-19-80

CORONER'S USE ONLY: 10

36. DISPOSITION: Cremation
37. DATE—MONTH, DAY, YEAR: 8-19-80
38. NAME AND ADDRESS OF CEMETERY OR CREMATORY: Westwood Memorial Park
39. EMBALMER'S LICENSE NUMBER AND SIGNATURE: not embalmed
40. NAME OF FUNERAL DIRECTOR (OR PERSON ACTING AS SUCH): Westwood Village Mortuary
42. DATE ACCEPTED BY LOCAL REGISTRAR: AUG 19 1980

VS-11 (10-78)

01-9-4-7007

This is to certify that this document is a true copy of the official record filed with the Registrar-Recorder/County Clerk.

CHARLES WEISSBURD
Registrar-Recorder/County Clerk

JAN 22 1992
19-298710

This copy not valid unless prepared on engraved border displaying the Seal and Sigature of the Registrar-Recorder/County Clerk.

American Bank Note Company

ANY ALTERATION OR ERASURE VOIDS THIS CERTIFICATE

STATE OF CALIFORNIA

CERTIFICATION OF VITAL RECORD

COUNTY OF LOS ANGELES • REGISTRAR-RECORDER/COUNTY CLERK

CERTIFICATE OF DEATH

STATE FILE NUMBER — STATE OF CALIFORNIA—DEPARTMENT OF PUBLIC HEALTH — LOCAL REGISTRATION DISTRICT AND CERTIFICATE NUMBER: 7097-049961

DECEDENT PERSONAL DATA

- 1a. Name of deceased—first name: Sharon
- 1b. Middle name: Tate
- 1c. Last name: Polanski
- 2a. Date of death: AUG. 9, 1969
- 2b. Hour: FOUND 9:10 A.M.
- 3. Sex: Female
- 4. Color or race: Caucasian
- 5. Birthplace: Texas
- 6. Date of birth: January 24, 1943
- 7. Age: 26 years
- 8. Name and birthplace of father: Paul Tate; Texas
- 9. Maiden name and birthplace of mother: Doris Willett; Texas
- 10. Citizen of what country: U.S.A.
- 11. Social security number: 452-74-4733
- 12. Married, never married, widowed, divorced: Married
- 13. Name of surviving spouse: Roman Polanski
- 14. Last occupation: Actress
- 15. Number of years in this occupation: 7
- 16. Name of last employing company or firm: 20th Century Fox Studio
- 17. Kind of industry or business: Motion Pictures

AMENDED 1 of 2

PLACE OF DEATH

- 18a. Place of death—name of hospital or other in-patient facility:
- 18b. Street address: 10050 Cielo Drive
- 18c. Inside city corporate limits: Yes
- 18d. City or town: Los Angeles
- 18e. County: Los Angeles
- 18f. Length of stay in county of death: 6 years
- 18g. Length of stay in California: 6 years

USUAL RESIDENCE

- 19a. Usual residence: 10050 Cielo Drive
- 19b. Inside city corporate limits: Yes
- 19c. City or town: Los Angeles
- 19d. County: Los Angeles
- 19e. State: California
- 20. Name and mailing address of informant: Victor Lownes, # 1 Connaught Square, London, W 2, England

PHYSICIAN'S OR CORONER'S CERTIFICATION

- 21a. Coroner: INVESTIGATION
- 21c. Physician or coroner—signature: Coroner By: [signature] Deputy
- 21d. Date signed: 8-10-69
- 21e. Address: Hall of Justice, Los Angeles

FUNERAL DIRECTOR AND LOCAL REGISTRAR

- 22a. Specify burial, entombment or cremation: Burial
- 22b. Date: Aug. 13, 1969
- 23. Name of cemetery or crematory: Holy Cross Cemetery
- 24. Embalmer—signature: [signature] License number 3455
- 25. Name of funeral director: Cunningham & O'Connor Hollywood
- 27. Local registrar—signature: [signature] MD
- 28. Date accepted for registration by local registrar: AUG 12 1969

MEDICAL AND HEALTH DATA — CAUSE OF DEATH

- 29. Part I. Death was caused by: Immediate cause (A) DEFERRED
- 30. Part II. Other significant conditions:
- 31. Was operation or biopsy performed: NO
- 32a. Autopsy: YES

INJURY INFORMATION

- 33. Specify accident, suicide or homicide:
- 34. Place of injury:
- 35. Injury at work:
- 36a. Date of injury:
- 36b. Hour:
- 37a. Place of injury:
- 40. Describe how injury occurred:

STATE REGISTRAR A B C D E F

REV. 1-1-68 Form VS-11

This is to certify that this document is a true copy of the official record filed with the Registrar-Recorder/County Clerk.

[signature]

CONNY B. McCORMACK
Registrar-Recorder/County Clerk

MAY 14 2002

19-254016

This copy not valid unless prepared on engraved border displaying the Seal and Signature of the Registrar-Recorder/County Clerk.

ANY ALTERATION OR ERASURE VOIDS THIS CERTIFICATE

STATE OF CALIFORNIA
CERTIFICATION OF VITAL RECORD

COUNTY OF LOS ANGELES • REGISTRAR-RECORDER/COUNTY CLERK

69 10080

AMENDMENT OF MEDICAL AND HEALTH SECTION DATA—DEATH

(INSTRUCTIONS ON REVERSE)

STATE CERTIFICATE NUMBER — LOCAL REGISTRATION DISTRICT AND CERTIFICATE NUMBER: 7097 49961

2 of 2

IDENTIFICATION OF THE RECORD

1a. FIRST NAME	1b. MIDDLE NAME	1c. LAST NAME
SHARON	TATE	POLANSKI

2. PLACE OF OCCURRENCE—CITY OR COUNTY	3. DATE OF EVENT	4. DATE ORIGINAL FILED
LOS ANGELES,	Aug. 9, 1969 Found	8-12-69

ORIGINALLY REPORTED INFORMATION

INFORMATION AS REPORTED ON THE ORIGINALLY REGISTERED CERTIFICATE

29. PART I. DEATH WAS CAUSED BY: ENTER ONLY ONE CAUSE PER LINE FOR A, B, AND C
IMMEDIATE CAUSE (A) Deferred
CONDITIONS, IF ANY, WHICH GAVE RISE TO THE IMMEDIATE CAUSE (A), STATING THE UNDERLYING CAUSE LAST: DUE TO, OR AS A CONSEQUENCE OF (B); DUE TO, OR AS A CONSEQUENCE OF (C)
APPROXIMATE INTERVAL BETWEEN ONSET AND DEATH

30. PART II. OTHER SIGNIFICANT CONDITIONS
31. WAS OPERATION OR BIOPSY PERFORMED: NO
32a. AUTOPSY: YES
32b.

33. SPECIFY ACCIDENT, SUICIDE OR HOMICIDE — 34. PLACE OF INJURY — 35. INJURY AT WORK — 36a. DATE OF INJURY — 36b. HOUR

37a. PLACE OF INJURY (STREET AND NUMBER OR LOCATION AND CITY OR TOWN) — 37b. DISTANCE FROM PLACE OF INJURY TO USUAL RESIDENCE — 38. WERE LABORATORY TESTS DONE FOR DRUGS OR TOXIC CHEMICALS — 39. WERE LABORATORY TESTS DONE FOR ALCOHOL

40. DESCRIBE HOW INJURY OCCURRED

INFORMATION AS IT SHOULD BE STATED ON THE ORIGINALLY REGISTERED CERTIFICATE

INFORMATION AS IT SHOULD BE STATED ON THE ORIGINALLY REGISTERED CERTIFICATE

29. PART I. DEATH WAS CAUSED BY: ENTER ONLY ONE CAUSE PER LINE FOR A, B, AND C
IMMEDIATE CAUSE (A) Multiple stab wounds of chest and back
(B) penetrating heart, lungs and liver causing massive hemorrhage.
DUE TO, OR AS A CONSEQUENCE OF (C)

30. PART II. OTHER SIGNIFICANT CONDITIONS
31. WAS OPERATION OR BIOPSY PERFORMED: NO
32a. AUTOPSY: YES
32b. YES

33. SPECIFY ACCIDENT, SUICIDE OR HOMICIDE	34. PLACE OF INJURY	35. INJURY AT WORK	36a. DATE OF INJURY	36b. HOUR
HOMICIDE	HOME	NO	prior 8-9-69	9:00 A.M.

37a. PLACE OF INJURY	37b. DISTANCE FROM PLACE OF INJURY TO USUAL RESIDENCE	38. LABORATORY TESTS FOR DRUGS OR TOXIC CHEMICALS	39. LABORATORY TESTS FOR ALCOHOL
10050 Cielo Dr., W. L.A.	0 MILES	YES	YES

40. DESCRIBE HOW INJURY OCCURRED: AS ABOVE

DECLARATION OF CERTIFYING PHYSICIAN OR CORONER

5. I, THE CERTIFYING PHYSICIAN OR CORONER HAVING PERSONAL KNOWLEDGE OF SUPPLEMENTAL INFORMATION WHICH MODIFIES THE INFORMATION ORIGINALLY REPORTED, DECLARE UNDER PENALTY OF PERJURY THAT THE ABOVE INFORMATION IS TRUE AND CORRECT TO THE BEST OF MY KNOWLEDGE.

6a. SIGNATURE OF PHYSICIAN OR CORONER: Thomas T. Noguchi M.D.
6b. DATE SIGNED: 12-3-69
7a. NAME OF PHYSICIAN OR CORONER (PRINT OR TYPE): THOMAS T. NOGUCHI M.D., CHIEF MEDICAL EXAMINER-CORONER
7b. DEGREE OR TITLE
7c. ADDRESS: HALL OF JUSTICE, LOS ANGELES, CALIF.

REGISTRAR'S OFFICE

8a. OFFICE OF STATE OR LOCAL REGISTRAR: [signature] M.D.
8b. DATE ACCEPTED: DEC - 4 1969

STATE OF CALIFORNIA, DEPARTMENT OF PUBLIC HEALTH, BUREAU OF VITAL STATISTICS (REV. 1-1-69) FORM VS 24B

This is to certify that this document is a true copy of the official record filed with the Registrar-Recorder/County Clerk.

Conny B. McCormack
CONNY B. McCORMACK
Registrar-Recorder/County Clerk

MAY 14 2002
19-253200

This copy not valid unless prepared on engraved border displaying the Seal and Signature of the Registrar-Recorder/County Clerk.

THE GREAT SEAL OF THE STATE OF CALIFORNIA — EUREKA
COUNTY OF LOS ANGELES CALIFORNIA

MIDWEST BANK NOTE COMPANY
ANY ALTERATION OR ERASURE VOIDS THIS CERTIFICATE

CERTIFICATION OF VITAL RECORD

COUNTY OF LOS ANGELES • REGISTRAR-RECORDER/COUNTY CLERK

Filed 6-20-69 RAY E. LEE, COUNTY RECORDER

CERTIFICATE OF DEATH

STATE OF CALIFORNIA—DEPARTMENT OF PUBLIC HEALTH

STATE FILE NUMBER

LOCAL REGISTRATION DISTRICT AND CERTIFICATE NUMBER: 7097-024675

DECEDENT PERSONAL DATA 8

1a. NAME OF DECEASED—FIRST NAME: ROBERT
1b. MIDDLE NAME:
1c. LAST NAME: TAYLOR
2a. DATE OF DEATH—MONTH, DAY, YEAR: JUNE 8 1969
2b. HOUR: 10.30 A M
3. SEX: Male
4. COLOR OR RACE: Caucasian
5. BIRTHPLACE (STATE OR FOREIGN COUNTRY): Nebraska
6. DATE OF BIRTH: August 5, 1911
7. AGE (LAST BIRTHDAY): 57 YEARS
8. NAME AND BIRTHPLACE OF FATHER: Spangler A. Brugh-Nebraska
9. MAIDEN NAME AND BIRTHPLACE OF MOTHER: Ruth A. Stanhope-Nebraska
10. CITIZEN OF WHAT COUNTRY: U.S.A.
11. SOCIAL SECURITY NUMBER: 569-18-9194
12. MARRIED, NEVER MARRIED, WIDOWED, DIVORCED (SPECIFY): Married
13. NAME OF SURVIVING SPOUSE (IF WIFE, ENTER MAIDEN NAME): Ursula Thiess
14. LAST OCCUPATION: Actor
15. NUMBER OF YEARS IN THIS OCCUPATION: 37
16. NAME OF LAST EMPLOYING COMPANY OR FIRM (IF SELF EMPLOYED SO STATE): McCann Erickson Inc.
17. KIND OF INDUSTRY OR BUSINESS: Entertainment

PLACE OF DEATH

18a. PLACE OF DEATH—NAME OF HOSPITAL OR OTHER IN-PATIENT FACILITY: St. John's Hospital
18b. STREET ADDRESS—(STREET AND NUMBER, OR LOCATION): 1328 22nd Street
18c. INSIDE CITY CORPORATE LIMITS (SPECIFY YES OR NO): yes
18d. CITY OR TOWN: Santa Monica
18e. COUNTY: Los Angeles
18f. LENGTH OF STAY IN COUNTY OF DEATH: 37 YEARS
18g. LENGTH OF STAY IN CALIFORNIA: 37 YEARS

USUAL RESIDENCE (IF DEATH OCCURRED IN INSTITUTION, ENTER RESIDENCE BEFORE ADMISSION)

19a. USUAL RESIDENCE—STREET ADDRESS (STREET AND NUMBER OR LOCATION): 3099 Mandeville Canyon Road
19b. INSIDE CITY CORPORATE LIMITS (SPECIFY YES OR NO): yes
19c. CITY OR TOWN: West Los Angeles
19d. COUNTY: Los Angeles
19e. STATE: California
20. NAME AND MAILING ADDRESS OF INFORMANT: S.A. Mac Sween-Business Manager, 6363 Wilshire Boulevard, Los Angeles, California

PHYSICIAN'S OR CORONER'S CERTIFICATION

21a. CORONER: I HEREBY CERTIFY THAT DEATH OCCURRED AT THE HOUR, DATE AND PLACE STATED ABOVE FROM THE CAUSES STATED BELOW AND THAT I HAVE HELD AN INVESTIGATION OR INQUEST ON THE REMAINS OF DECEASED AS REQUIRED BY LAW
21b. PHYSICIAN: I HEREBY CERTIFY THAT DEATH OCCURRED AT THE HOUR, DATE AND PLACE STATED ABOVE FROM THE CAUSES STATED BELOW AND THAT I ATTENDED THE DECEASED FROM 1950 TO 6-7-69 AND LAST SAW THE DECEASED ALIVE ON 6-7-69
21c. PHYSICIAN OR CORONER—SIGNATURE AND DEGREE OR TITLE: M. Burstona MD
21d. DATE SIGNED: 6/9/69
21e. ADDRESS: 2021 S. Monica Blvd Santa Monica
21f. PHYSICIAN'S CALIFORNIA LICENSE NUMBER: A-08509

FUNERAL DIRECTOR AND LOCAL REGISTRAR

22a. SPECIFY BURIAL, ENTOMBMENT OR CREMATION: Cremation
22b. DATE: 6-11-69
23. NAME OF CEMETERY OR CREMATORY: Forest Lawn Memorial Park
24. EMBALMER—SIGNATURE (IF BODY EMBALMED) LICENSE NUMBER: Wayne A. Bowman 4365
25. NAME OF FUNERAL DIRECTOR (OR PERSON ACTING AS SUCH): FOREST LAWN MEMORIAL-PARK ASS'N. GLENDALE, CALIFORNIA
26. IF NOT CERTIFIED BY CORONER, WAS THIS DEATH REPORTED TO CORONER? (SPECIFY YES OR NO):
27. LOCAL REGISTRAR—SIGNATURE: [signature] MD
28. DATE ACCEPTED FOR REGISTRATION BY LOCAL REGISTRAR: JUN 11 1969

MEDICAL AND HEALTH DATA

CAUSE OF DEATH 9

29. PART I. DEATH WAS CAUSED BY: ENTER ONLY ONE CAUSE PER LINE FOR A, B, AND C
IMMEDIATE CAUSE (A) Lung Cancer — APPROXIMATE INTERVAL BETWEEN ONSET AND DEATH: 10 mo.
CONDITIONS, IF ANY, WHICH GAVE RISE TO THE IMMEDIATE CAUSE (A), STATING THE UNDERLYING CAUSE LAST: DUE TO, OR AS A CONSEQUENCE OF (B)
DUE TO, OR AS A CONSEQUENCE OF (C)
30. PART II: OTHER SIGNIFICANT CONDITIONS—CONTRIBUTING TO DEATH BUT NOT RELATED TO THE IMMEDIATE CAUSE GIVEN IN PART I:
31. WAS OPERATION OR BIOPSY PERFORMED FOR ANY CONDITION IN ITEMS 29 OR 30? (SPECIFY OPERATION AND/OR BIOPSY): YES
32a. AUTOPSY (SPECIFY YES OR NO): No
32b. IF YES WERE FINDINGS CONSIDERED IN DETERMINING CAUSE OF DEATH? (SPECIFY YES OR NO):

INJURY INFORMATION 12

33. SPECIFY ACCIDENT, SUICIDE OR HOMICIDE:
34. PLACE OF INJURY (SPECIFY HOME, FARM, FACTORY, STREET, OFFICE BUILDING, ETC.):
35. INJURY AT WORK (SPECIFY YES OR NO):
36a. DATE OF INJURY—MONTH, DAY, YEAR:
36b. HOUR: M
37a. PLACE OF INJURY (STREET AND NUMBER OR LOCATION AND CITY OR TOWN):
37b. DISTANCE FROM PLACE OF INJURY TO USUAL RESIDENCE, ITEM 19: MILES
38. WERE LABORATORY TESTS DONE FOR DRUGS OR TOXIC CHEMICALS? (SPECIFY YES OR NO):
39. WERE LABORATORY TESTS DONE FOR ALCOHOL? (SPECIFY YES OR NO):
40. DESCRIBE HOW INJURY OCCURRED (ENTER SEQUENCE OF EVENTS WHICH RESULTED IN INJURY. NATURE OF INJURY SHOULD BE ENTERED IN ITEM 29)

STATE REGISTRAR A. B. C. D. E. F. 2624

REV. 1-1-68 FORM VS-11

This is to certify that this document is a true copy of the official record filed with the Registrar-Recorder/County Clerk.

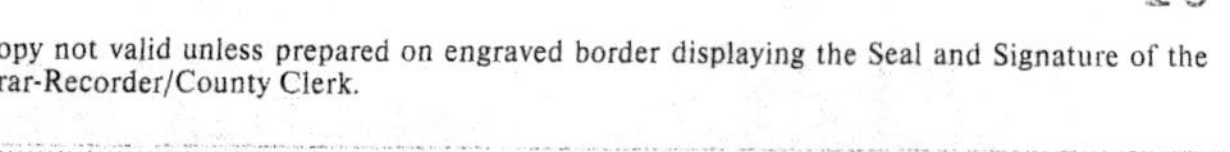

BEATRIZ VALDEZ
Registrar-Recorder/County Clerk

AUG 10 1995

19-389290

This copy not valid unless prepared on engraved border displaying the Seal and Signature of the Registrar-Recorder/County Clerk.

American Bank Note Company

ANY ALTERATION OR ERASURE VOIDS THIS CERTIFICATE

STATE OF CALIFORNIA

CERTIFICATION OF VITAL RECORD

COUNTY OF LOS ANGELES • REGISTRAR-RECORDER/COUNTY CLERK

CERTIFICATE OF DEATH
STATE OF CALIFORNIA
USE BLACK INK ONLY

39119005294

STATE FILE NUMBER — LOCAL REGISTRATION DISTRICT AND CERTIFICATE NUMBER

DECEDENT PERSONAL DATA

1A. NAME OF DECEDENT—FIRST (GIVEN): DANNY
1B. MIDDLE: —
1C. LAST (FAMILY): THOMAS
2A. DATE OF DEATH—MO, DAY, YR: FEBRUARY 6, 1991
2B. HOUR: 0130
3. SEX: MALE
4. RACE: CAUCASIAN
5. HISPANIC—SPECIFY: YES [ ] NO [X]
6. DATE OF BIRTH—MO, DAY, YR: JANUARY 6, 1912
7. AGE IN YEARS: 79 — IF UNDER 1 YEAR: MONTHS, DAYS — IF UNDER 24 HOURS: HOURS, MINUTES
8. STATE OF BIRTH: MICH.
9. CITIZEN OF WHAT COUNTRY: USA
10A. FULL NAME OF FATHER: CHARLES JACOBS
10B. STATE OF BIRTH: LEBANON
11A. FULL MAIDEN NAME OF MOTHER: MARGARET SIMON
11B. STATE OF BIRTH: LEBANON
12. MILITARY SERVICE?: 19__ TO 19__ [X] NONE
13. SOCIAL SECURITY NO.: 374-10-1559
14. MARITAL STATUS: MARRIED
15. NAME OF SURVIVING SPOUSE (IF WIFE, ENTER MAIDEN NAME): ROSE MARIE CASSANITI
1 OF 2
16A. USUAL OCCUPATION: ENTERTAINER
16B. USUAL KIND OF BUSINESS OR INDUSTRY: TELEVISION AND MOTION PICTURE
16C. USUAL EMPLOYER: SELF-EMPLOYED
16D. YEARS IN OCCUPATION: 60
17. EDUCATION—YEARS COMPLETED: 12

USUAL RESIDENCE

18A. RESIDENCE—STREET AND NUMBER OR LOCATION: 1187 HILLCREST ROAD
18B. CITY: BEVERLY HILLS
18C. ZIP CODE: 90210
18D. COUNTY: LOS ANGELES
18E. NUMBER OF YEARS IN THIS COUNTY: 47
18F. STATE OR FOREIGN COUNTRY: CALIFORNIA
20. NAME, RELATIONSHIP, MAILING ADDRESS AND ZIP CODE OF INFORMANT: MRS. ROSE MARIE THOMAS-WIFE, 1187 HILLCREST ROAD, BEVERLY HILLS, CA. 90210

PLACE OF DEATH

19A. PLACE OF DEATH: RESIDENCE
19B. IF HOSPITAL, SPECIFY ONE: IP, ER/OP, DOA: ----
19C. COUNTY: LOS ANGELES
19D. STREET ADDRESS—STREET AND NUMBER OR LOCATION: 1187 HILLCREST ROAD
19E. CITY: BEVERLY HILLS

CAUSE OF DEATH

21. DEATH WAS CAUSED BY: (ENTER ONLY ONE CAUSE PER LINE FOR A, B, AND C) — TIME INTERVAL BETWEEN ONSET AND DEATH
IMMEDIATE CAUSE (A) Cardio respiratory arrest — 40 min
DUE TO (B) Acute pulmonary edema — 90 min
DUE TO (C) Acute myocardial infarction — 2 hrs
22. WAS DEATH REPORTED TO CORONER? YES [ ] NO [X] REFERRAL NUMBER
23. WAS BIOPSY PERFORMED? YES [ ] NO [X]
24A. WAS AUTOPSY PERFORMED? YES [ ] NO [X]
24B. WAS IT USED IN DETERMINING CAUSE OF DEATH? YES [ ] NO [ ]
25. OTHER SIGNIFICANT CONDITIONS CONTRIBUTING TO DEATH BUT NOT RELATED TO CAUSE GIVEN IN 21: Hypertension cardiac arrhythmia
26. WAS OPERATION PERFORMED FOR ANY CONDITION IN ITEM 21 OR 25? IF YES, LIST TYPE OF OPERATION AND DATE: NO

PHYSICIAN'S CERTIFICATION

I CERTIFY THAT TO THE BEST OF MY KNOWLEDGE DEATH OCCURRED AT THE HOUR, DATE AND PLACE STATED FROM THE CAUSES STATED.
27A. DECEDENT ATTENDED SINCE MONTH, DAY, YEAR: 3-8-84 — DECEDENT LAST SEEN ALIVE MONTH, DAY, YEAR: 2-6-91
27B. SIGNATURE AND DEGREE OR TITLE OF CERTIFIER: [signature]
27C. CERTIFIER'S LICENSE NUMBER: G16910
27D. DATE SIGNED: 2-6-91
27E. TYPE ATTENDING PHYSICIAN'S NAME AND ADDRESS: DR. CHARLES KIVOWITZ 435 NORTH ROXBURY DR. #300 BEVERLY HILLS, CA

CORONER'S USE ONLY

I CERTIFY THAT IN MY OPINION DEATH OCCURRED AT THE HOUR, DATE AND PLACE STATED FROM THE CAUSES STATED.
28A. SIGNATURE AND TITLE OF CORONER OR DEPUTY CORONER
28B. DATE SIGNED
29. MANNER OF DEATH—specify one: natural, accident, suicide, homicide, pending investigation or could not be determined
30A. PLACE OF INJURY
30B. INJURY AT WORK: YES [ ] NO [ ]
30C. DATE OF INJURY MONTH, DAY, YEAR
31. HOUR
32. LOCATION (STREET AND NUMBER OR LOCATION AND CITY)
33. DESCRIBE HOW INJURY OCCURRED (EVENTS WHICH RESULTED IN INJURY)

FUNERAL DIRECTOR AND LOCAL REGISTRAR

34A. DISPOSITION(S): TR/BU
34B. PLACE OF FINAL DISPOSITION—NAME AND ADDRESS: ST. JUDE HOSPITAL MEMPHIS, TENN.
34C. DATE MO, DAY, YEAR: FEB. 10, 1991
35A. SIGNATURE OF EMBALMER: James E. Austin
35B. LICENSE NUMBER: 4350
36A. NAME OF FUNERAL DIRECTOR (OR PERSON ACTING AS SUCH): PIERCE BROTHERS CUNNINGHAM O'CONNOR UTTER MCKINLEY
36B. LICENSE NO.: F-168
37. SIGNATURE OF LOCAL REGISTRAR: Robert C. [signature]
38. REGISTRATION DATE: FEB 8 1991

STATE REGISTRAR A. B. C. D. E. F. CENSUS TRACT

This is to certify that this document is a true copy of the official record filed with the Registrar-Recorder/County Clerk.

Conny B. McCormack

CONNY B. McCORMACK
Registrar-Recorder/County Clerk

This copy not valid unless prepared on engraved border displaying the Seal and Signature of the Registrar-Recorder/County Clerk.

ANY ALTERATION OR ERASURE VOIDS THIS CERTIFICATE

CERTIFICATION OF VITAL RECORD

COUNTY OF LOS ANGELES • REGISTRAR-RECORDER/COUNTY CLERK

STATE OF CALIFORNIA
DEPARTMENT OF PUBLIC HEALTH
VITAL STATISTICS
STANDARD CERTIFICATE OF DEATH

1. PLACE OF DEATH: DIST. NO. 1901 LOCAL REGISTERED NO. 15708
COUNTY OF Los Angeles
CITY, TOWN OR RURAL DISTRICT OF Los Angeles STREET AND NO. 17531 Posetano Road
2. FULL NAME Thelma Alice Todd Di Cicco
RESIDENCE: NO. 17576 Roosevelt Highway

3. SEX Female 4. COLOR OR RACE Cauc 5. SINGLE, MARRIED, WIDOWED OR DIVORCED Divorced
5a. IF MARRIED, WIDOWED OR DIVORCED, NAME OF HUSBAND OR WIFE Pasquale Di Cicco
6. DATE OF BIRTH July 29 1906
7. AGE 29 YR. 4 MO. 17 DAYS
8. TRADE, PROFESSION OR KIND OF WORK DONE Motion Picture
9. INDUSTRY OR BUSINESS IN WHICH WORK WAS DONE Actress
10. DATE DECEASED LAST WORKED AT THIS OCCUPATION 12 1935 11. TOTAL YEARS SPENT IN THIS OCCUPATION 9
12. BIRTHPLACE Lawrence STATE OR COUNTRY Massachusetts
13. NAME (FATHER) John Shaw Todd
14. BIRTHPLACE Unknown STATE OR COUNTRY Ireland
15. MAIDEN NAME (MOTHER) Alice Elizabeth Edwards
16. BIRTHPLACE Inverness STATE OR COUNTRY Quebec - Canada
17. LENGTH OF RESIDENCE: A. CITY, TOWN OR RURAL DISTRICT OF DEATH 2 YRS. B. IN CALIFORNIA 9 YRS. C. IN U.S., IF OF FOREIGN BIRTH
18. INFORMANT Harvey H. Priester ADDRESS 6853 Camrose Dr.
19. BURIAL, CREMATION OR REMOVAL Cremation PLACE Forest Lawn Crem. DATE 12-19-35
20. EMBALMER LICENSE NO. 282 SIGNATURE E. Bullington
FUNERAL DIRECTOR Pierce Bros. ADDRESS Los Angeles, California
21. FILED DEC 19 1935 George Parrish M.D. REGISTRAR

22. DATE OF DEATH found Dec 16 1935
23. MEDICAL CERTIFICATE OF DEATH
24. CORONER'S CERTIFICATE OF DEATH: I HEREBY CERTIFY, THAT I TOOK CHARGE OF THE REMAINS DESCRIBED ABOVE, HELD AN Inquest Autopsy THEREON, AND FROM SUCH ACTION FIND THAT SAID DECEASED CAME TO H. DEATH ON THE DATE STATED ABOVE.
THE PRINCIPAL CAUSE OF DEATH AND RELATED CAUSES OF IMPORTANCE, IN ORDER OF ONSET, WERE AS FOLLOWS: Carbon monoxide poisoning
OTHER CONTRIBUTORY CAUSES OF IMPORTANCE:
IF OPERATION, DATE OF ... WAS THERE AN AUTOPSY? Yes
NAME LABORATORY TEST CONFIRMING DIAGNOSIS Anal for CO Chemical Test for Alcohol
25. IF DEATH WAS DUE TO EXTERNAL CAUSES (VIOLENCE) FILL IN THE FOLLOWING: ACCIDENT, SUICIDE OR HOMICIDE? Accident DATE OF INJURY 12/15/35
INJURED AT: CITY OR TOWN OF Los Angeles COUNTY AND STATE OF Los Angeles
DID INJURY OCCUR IN HOME, INDUSTRY, OR PUBLIC PLACE? Garage, private
MANNER OF INJURY Inhaled gas from motor car
NATURE OF INJURY Carbon monoxide poisoning
26. IF DISEASE/INJURY RELATED TO OCCUPATION, SPECIFY
27. SIGNATURE A. F. Wagner M.D. ADDRESS Coroner's Office Los Angeles
28. WHEN REQUIRED BY LAW Frank A. Nance CORONER COUNTY OF Los Angeles

This is to certify that this document is a true copy of the official record filed with the Registrar-Recorder/County Clerk.

NOV 27 1995
19-080597

This copy not valid unless prepared on engraved border displaying the Seal of the Registrar-Recorder/County Clerk.

ANY ALTERATION OR ERASURE VOIDS THIS CERTIFICATE

STATE OF CALIFORNIA

CERTIFICATION OF VITAL RECORD

COUNTY OF LOS ANGELES • REGISTRAR-RECORDER/COUNTY CLERK

CERTIFICATE OF DEATH
STATE OF CALIFORNIA
USE BLACK INK ONLY/NO ERASURES, WHITEOUTS OR ALTERATIONS
VS-11 (REV. 7/97)

STATE FILE NUMBER — LOCAL REGISTRATION NUMBER: 3 199919 024252

DECEDENT PERSONAL DATA

1. NAME OF DECEDENT—FIRST (GIVEN): Melvin
2. MIDDLE: Howard
3. LAST (FAMILY): Torme
4. DATE OF BIRTH MM/DD/CCYY: 09/13/1925
5. AGE YRS: 73
6. SEX: M
7. DATE OF DEATH MM/DD/CCYY: 06/05/1999
8. HOUR: 0143
9. STATE OF BIRTH: Illinois
10. SOCIAL SECURITY NO.: 321-14-9958
11. MILITARY SERVICE: [X] YES [ ] NO [ ] UNK
12. MARITAL STATUS: Married
13. EDUCATION—YEARS COMPLETED: 12
14. RACE: Caucasian
15. HISPANIC—SPECIFY: [ ] YES [X] NO
16. USUAL EMPLOYER: Self Employed
17. OCCUPATION: Entertainer
18. KIND OF BUSINESS: Entertainment
19. YEARS IN OCCUPATION: 69

USUAL RESIDENCE

20. RESIDENCE—(STREET AND NUMBER OR LOCATION): 1734 Coldwater Canyon Drive
21. CITY: Beverly Hills
22. COUNTY: Los Angeles
23. ZIP CODE: 90210
24. YRS IN COUNTY: 17
25. STATE OR FOREIGN COUNTRY: California

INFORMANT

26. NAME, RELATIONSHIP: Ali Torme - Wife
27. MAILING ADDRESS (STREET AND NUMBER OR RURAL ROUTE NUMBER, CITY OR TOWN, STATE, ZIP): 1734 Coldwater Canyon Drive, Beverly Hills, CA 90210

SPOUSE AND PARENT INFORMATION

28. NAME OF SURVIVING SPOUSE—FIRST: Ali
29. MIDDLE: Kay
30. LAST (MAIDEN NAME): Severson
31. NAME OF FATHER—FIRST: William
32. MIDDLE: David
33. LAST: Torme
34. BIRTH STATE: Russia
35. NAME OF MOTHER—FIRST: Sara
36. MIDDLE: Betty
37. LAST (MAIDEN): Sopkin
38. BIRTH STATE: New York

DISPOSITION(S)

39. DATE MM/DD/CCYY: 06/08/1999
40. PLACE OF FINAL DISPOSITION: Westwood Memorial Park 1218 Glendon Ave. Los Angeles, CA 90024

FUNERAL DIRECTOR AND LOCAL REGISTRAR

41. TYPE OF DISPOSITION(S): Burial
42. SIGNATURE OF EMBALMER: Not Embalmed
43. LICENSE NO.: -
44. NAME OF FUNERAL DIRECTOR: Pierce Bros. Westwood Village
45. LICENSE NO.: FD 859
46. SIGNATURE OF LOCAL REGISTRAR: [signature]
47. DATE MM/DD/CCYY: 06/07/1999 SN

PLACE OF DEATH

101. PLACE OF DEATH: UCLA Medical Center
102. IF HOSPITAL, SPECIFY ONE: [ ] IP [X] ER/OP [ ] DOA
103. FACILITY OTHER THAN HOSPITAL: [ ] CONV. HOSP. [ ] RES. CARE [ ] OTHER
104. COUNTY: Los Angeles
105. STREET ADDRESS—STREET AND NUMBER OR LOCATION: 10833 Le Conte Ave.
106. CITY: Los Angeles

CAUSE OF DEATH

107. DEATH WAS CAUSED BY: (ENTER ONLY ONE CAUSE PER LINE FOR A, B, C, AND D)

	Cause	Time interval between onset and death
IMMEDIATE CAUSE (A)	Cardiopulmonary Arrest	5 Mins.
DUE TO (B)	Congestive Heart Failure	5 Yrs.
DUE TO (C)	Coronary Heart Disease	5 Yrs.
DUE TO (D)	Diabetes Mellitus	13 Yrs.

108. DEATH REPORTED TO CORONER: [X] YES [ ] NO — REFERRAL NUMBER: 99-55455
109. BIOPSY PERFORMED: [ ] YES [X] NO
110. AUTOPSY PERFORMED: [ ] YES [X] NO
111. USED IN DETERMINING CAUSE: [ ] YES [ ] NO
112. OTHER SIGNIFICANT CONDITIONS CONTRIBUTING TO DEATH BUT NOT RELATED TO CAUSE GIVEN IN 107: Stroke
113. WAS OPERATION PERFORMED FOR ANY CONDITION IN ITEM 107 OR 112? IF YES, LIST TYPE OF OPERATION AND DATE: No

PHYSICIAN'S CERTIFICATION

114. I CERTIFY THAT TO THE BEST OF MY KNOWLEDGE DEATH OCCURRED AT THE HOUR, DATE AND PLACE STATED FROM THE CAUSES STATED. DECEDENT ATTENDED SINCE MM/DD/CCYY: 09/12/1997 — DECEDENT LAST SEEN ALIVE MM/DD/CCYY: 02/07/1999
115. SIGNATURE AND TITLE OF CERTIFIER: [signature] M.D.
116. LICENSE NO.: G 50929
117. DATE MM/DD/CCYY: 06/07/1999
118. TYPE ATTENDING PHYSICIAN'S NAME, MAILING ADDRESS, ZIP: Dennis Evangelatos, MD. 100 UCLA MED Plaza, #490 Los Angeles, CA 90095

CORONER'S USE ONLY

I CERTIFY THAT IN MY OPINION DEATH OCCURRED AT THE HOUR, DATE AND PLACE STATED FROM THE CAUSES STATED
119. MANNER OF DEATH: [ ] NATURAL [ ] SUICIDE [ ] HOMICIDE [ ] ACCIDENT [ ] PENDING INVESTIGATION [ ] COULD NOT BE DETERMINED
120. INJURY AT WORK: [ ] YES [ ] NO
121. INJURY DATE MM/DD/CCYY:
122. HOUR:
123. PLACE OF INJURY:
124. DESCRIBE HOW INJURY OCCURRED (EVENTS WHICH RESULTED IN INJURY):
125. LOCATION (STREET AND NUMBER OR LOCATION AND CITY, ZIP):
126. SIGNATURE OF CORONER OR DEPUTY CORONER:
127. DATE MM/DD/CCYY:
128. TYPED NAME, TITLE OF CORONER OR DEPUTY CORONER:

STATE REGISTRAR: A B C D E F G H — FAX AUTH. #: 849-14352 — CENSUS TRACT

This is to certify that this document is a true copy of the official record filed with the Registrar-Recorder/County Clerk.

[signature]
CONNY B. McCORMACK
Registrar-Recorder/County Clerk

OCT 04 2001
19-673784

This copy not valid unless prepared on engraved border displaying the Seal and Signature of the Registrar-Recorder/County Clerk.

MIDWEST BANK NOTE COMPANY

ANY ALTERATION OR ERASURE VOIDS THIS CERTIFICATE

CERTIFICATION OF VITAL RECORD

COUNTY OF LOS ANGELES • REGISTRAR-RECORDER/COUNTY CLERK

FILED JUN 30 1967 RAY E LEE COUNTY RECORDER

CERTIFICATE OF DEATH

STATE OF CALIFORNIA—DEPARTMENT OF PUBLIC HEALTH

STATE FILE NUMBER

LOCAL REGISTRATION DISTRICT AND CERTIFICATE NUMBER 7097-023587

DECEDENT PERSONAL DATA

1a. NAME OF DECEASED—FIRST NAME: Spencer
1b. MIDDLE NAME: B.
1c. LAST NAME: Tracy
2a. DATE OF DEATH—MONTH, DAY, YEAR: June 10, 1967
2b. HOUR: 6:00 A.M.
3. SEX: Male
4. COLOR OR RACE: White
5. BIRTHPLACE (STATE OR FOREIGN COUNTRY): Wisconsin
6. DATE OF BIRTH: April 5, 1900
7. AGE (LAST BIRTHDAY): 67 YEARS
8. NAME AND BIRTHPLACE OF FATHER: John E. Tracy; Illinois
9. MAIDEN NAME AND BIRTHPLACE OF MOTHER: Carrie Brown; Illinois
10. CITIZEN OF WHAT COUNTRY: U.S.A.
11. SOCIAL SECURITY NUMBER: 573-05-9213
12. LAST OCCUPATION: Actor
13. NUMBER OF YEARS IN THIS OCCUPATION: 46
14. NAME OF LAST EMPLOYING COMPANY OR FIRM: Columbia Pictures
15. KIND OF INDUSTRY OR BUSINESS: Motion Pictures
16. IF DECEASED WAS EVER IN U.S. ARMED FORCES GIVE WAR OR DATES OF SERVICE: Yes; World War I
17. SPECIFY MARRIED, NEVER MARRIED, WIDOWED, DIVORCED: Married
18a. NAME OF PRESENT SPOUSE: Louise T. Tracy
18b. PRESENT OR LAST OCCUPATION OF SPOUSE: Housewife

PLACE OF DEATH

19a. PLACE OF DEATH—NAME OF HOSPITAL:
19b. STREET ADDRESS: 9191 St. Ives Drive
19c. CITY OR TOWN: Los Angeles
19d. COUNTY: Los Angeles
19e. LENGTH OF STAY IN COUNTY OF DEATH: 37 YEARS
19f. LENGTH OF STAY IN CALIFORNIA: 37 YEARS

1943

LAST USUAL RESIDENCE

20a. LAST USUAL RESIDENCE—STREET ADDRESS: 9191 St. Ives Drive
20b. IF INSIDE CITY CORPORATE LIMITS: [X] CHECK HERE
20c. CITY OR TOWN: Los Angeles
20d. COUNTY: Los Angeles
20e. STATE: California
21a. NAME OF INFORMANT (IF OTHER THAN SPOUSE): Louise T. Tracy (wife)
21b. ADDRESS OF INFORMANT: 1158 Tower Road Beverly Hills, California

PHYSICIAN'S OR CORONER'S CERTIFICATION

22a. PHYSICIAN: I HEREBY CERTIFY THAT DEATH OCCURRED AT THE HOUR, DATE AND PLACE STATED ABOVE, FROM THE CAUSES STATED BELOW AND THAT I ATTENDED THE DECEASED FROM 9/1/64 TO 6/10/67 AND THAT I LAST SAW THE DECEASED ALIVE ON 6/9/67
22b. CORONER: I HEREBY CERTIFY THAT DEATH OCCURRED AT THE HOUR, DATE AND PLACE STATED ABOVE FROM THE CAUSES STATED BELOW AND THAT I HAVE HELD AN ______ ON THE REMAINS OF DECEASED AS REQUIRED BY LAW.
22c. PHYSICIAN OR CORONER—SIGNATURE: [signature] M.D.
22d. ADDRESS: 9730 Wilshire Blvd. Beverly Hills Calif.
22e. DATE SIGNED: 6/10/67

FUNERAL DIRECTOR AND LOCAL REGISTRAR

23. SPECIFY BURIAL, ENTOMBMENT OR CREMATION: Burial
24. DATE: 6/12/67
25. NAME OF CEMETERY OR CREMATORY: Forest Lawn Cemetery; Glendale, California
26. EMBALMER—SIGNATURE: [signature] LICENSE NUMBER 2929
27. NAME OF FUNERAL DIRECTOR: Cunningham & O'Connor, Holly.
28. DATE ACCEPTED FOR REGISTRATION BY LOCAL REGISTRAR: JUN 10 1967
29. LOCAL REGISTRAR—SIGNATURE: [signature]

MEDICAL AND HEALTH DATA

CAUSE OF DEATH

30. CAUSE OF DEATH
PART I. DEATH WAS CAUSED BY: ENTER ONLY ONE CAUSE PER LINE FOR (A), (B), AND (C)
IMMEDIATE CAUSE (A): Cardiac arrest — Immediate
CONDITIONS, IF ANY, WHICH GAVE RISE TO THE ABOVE CAUSE (A) STATING THE UNDERLYING CAUSE LAST. DUE TO (B): Hypertensive and coronary heart disease — 7+ yrs
DUE TO (C):
APPROXIMATE INTERVAL BETWEEN ONSET AND DEATH
PART II. OTHER SIGNIFICANT CONDITIONS CONTRIBUTING TO DEATH BUT NOT RELATED TO THE TERMINAL DISEASE CONDITION GIVEN IN PART I (A): 1) Diabetes mellitus 2) Myocardial infarction, old

OPERATION AND AUTOPSY

31. OPERATION—CHECK ONE: [X] NO OPERATION PERFORMED
32. DATE OF OPERATION:
33. AUTOPSY—CHECK ONE: [X] NO AUTOPSY PERFORMED

INJURY INFORMATION

34a. SPECIFY ACCIDENT, SUICIDE OR HOMICIDE
34b. DESCRIBE HOW INJURY OCCURRED
35a. TIME OF INJURY: HOUR MONTH DAY YEAR
35b. INJURY OCCURRED: WHILE AT WORK / NOT WHILE AT WORK
35c. PLACE OF INJURY
35d. CITY, TOWN, OR LOCATION COUNTY STATE

This is to certify that this document is a true copy of the official record filed with the Registrar-Recorder/County Clerk.

Beatriz Valdez
BEATRIZ VALDEZ
Registrar-Recorder/County Clerk

AUG 10 1995

19-389284

This copy not valid unless prepared on engraved border displaying the Seal and Signature of the Registrar-Recorder/County Clerk.

ANY ALTERATION OR ERASURE VOIDS THIS CERTIFICATE

CERTIFICATE OF DEATH

STATE OF CALIFORNIA
USE BLACK INK ONLY/NO ERASURES, WHITEOUTS OR ALTERATIONS
VS-11 (REV. 7/93)

STATE FILE NUMBER — LOCAL REGISTRATION NUMBER

DECEDENT PERSONAL DATA

1. Name of Decedent—First (Given): Lana
2. Middle: -
3. Last (Family): Turner
4. Date of Birth MM/DD/CCYY: 02/08/1921
5. Age Yrs.: 74
If under 1 year: Months / Days — If under 24 hours: Hours / Minutes
6. Sex: Female
7. Date of Death MM/DD/CCYY: 06/29/1995
8. Hour: 2022
9. State of Birth: ID
10. Social Security No.: 567-18-3907
11. Military Service: 19___ to 19___ [x] None
12. Marital Status: Divorced
13. Education—Years Completed: 12
14. Race: Caucasian
15. Hispanic—Specify: [ ] Yes ___ [x] No
16. Usual Employer: Self Employed
17. Occupation: Actress
18. Kind of Business: Motion Pictures
19. Years in Occupation: 60

USUAL RESIDENCE

20. Residence—Street and Number or Location: 2170 Century Park East #2006
21. City: Century City
22. County: Los Angeles
23. Zip Code: 90067
24. Yrs in County: 60
25. State or Foreign Country: California

INFORMANT

26. Name, Relationship: Cheryl Crane (Daughter)
27. Mailing Address (Street and Number or Rural Route Number, City or Town, State, Zip): 906 N. Doheny Drive #410, Los Angeles, CA 90069

SPOUSE AND PARENT INFORMATION

28. Name of Surviving Spouse—First: -
29. Middle: -
30. Last (Maiden Name): -
31. Name of Father—First: Virgil
32. Middle: -
33. Last: Turner
34. Birth State: Alabama
35. Name of Mother—First: Mildred
36. Middle: F.
37. Last (Maiden): Cowan
38. Birth State: Arkansas

DISPOSITION(S)

39. Date MM/DD/CCYY: 06/30/1995
40. Place of Final Disposition: Residence Cheryl Crane 906 N. Doheny Drive #410, Los Angeles, CA 90069

FUNERAL DIRECTOR AND LOCAL REGISTRAR

41. Type of Disposition(s): CR/RES
42. Signature of Embalmer: ▶ Not Embalmed
43. License No.: -
44. Name of Funeral Director: McCormick Mortuary
45. License No.: FD 292
46. Signature of Local Registrar: ▶ [signature]
47. Date MM/DD/CCYY: 06/30/1995

PLACE OF DEATH

101. Place of Death: Residence
102. If Hospital, Specify One: [ ] IP [ ] ER/OP [ ] DOA
103. Facility Other Than Hospital: [ ] Conv. Hosp. [x] Res. [ ] Other
104. County: Los Angeles
105. Street Address—Street and Number or Location: 2170 Century Park East #2006
106. City: Century City

CAUSE OF DEATH

107. Death was caused by: (Enter only one cause per line for A, B, C, and D)

		Time Interval Between Onset and Death
Immediate Cause (A)	Cancer of Nasopharynx	3 Years
Due to (B)		
Due to (C)		
Due to (D)		

108. Death Reported to Coroner: [ ] Yes [x] No — Referral Number
109. Biopsy Performed: [ ] Yes [x] No
110. Autopsy Performed: [ ] Yes [x] No
111. Used in Determining Cause: [ ] Yes [ ] No
112. Other significant conditions contributing to death but not related to cause given in 107: None
113. Was operation performed for any condition in item 107 or 112? If yes, list type of operation and date: No

PHYSICIAN'S CERTIFICATION

114. I certify that to the best of my knowledge death occurred at the hour, date and place stated from the causes stated.
Decedent Attended Since MM/DD/CCYY: 07/21/1994
Decedent Last Seen Alive MM/DD/CCYY: 06/30/1995
115. Signature and Title of Certifier: ▶ [signature] MD
116. License No.: G 22248
117. Date MM/DD/CCYY: 06/30/1995
118. Type Attending Physician's Name, Mailing Address + Zip: M.Van Scoy-Mosher MD,8631 W.Third St.Los Angeles,CA 90048

CORONER'S USE ONLY

I certify that in my opinion death occurred at the hour, date and place stated from the causes stated.
119. Manner of Death: [ ] Natural [ ] Suicide [ ] Homicide [ ] Accident [ ] Pending Investigation [ ] Could Not Be Determined
120. Injury at Work: [ ] Yes [ ] No
121. Injury Date MM/DD/CCYY
122. Hour
123. Place of Injury
124. Describe how injury occurred (events which resulted in injury)
125. Location (street and number or location and city and zip code)
126. Signature of Coroner or Deputy Coroner ▶
127. Date MM/DD/CCYY
128. Typed Name, Title of Coroner or Deputy Coroner

10

STATE REGISTRAR

A	B	C	D	E	F	G	H	FAX AUTH. #	CENSUS TRACT

STATE OF CALIFORNIA
CERTIFICATION OF VITAL RECORD

COUNTY OF VENTURA

VENTURA, CALIFORNIA

CERTIFICATE OF DEATH
STATE OF CALIFORNIA
USE BLACK INK ONLY/NO ERASURES, WHITEOUTS OR ALTERATIONS
VS-11 (REV. 1/00)

STATE FILE NUMBER

3 200256 001402
LOCAL REGISTRATION NUMBER

DECEDENT PERSONAL DATA

1. NAME OF DECEDENT—FIRST (GIVEN): ROBERT
2. MIDDLE: MICHAEL
3. LAST (FAMILY): URICH
4. DATE OF BIRTH MM/DD/CCYY: 12/19/1946
5. AGE YRS.: 55
IF UNDER 1 YEAR (MONTHS, DAYS) / IF UNDER 24 HOURS (HOURS, MINUTES)
6. SEX: M
7. DATE OF DEATH MM/DD/CCYY: 04/16/2002
8. HOUR: 0115
9. STATE OF BIRTH: Ohio
10. SOCIAL SECURITY NO.: 283-44-8292
11. MILITARY SERVICE: [ ] YES [X] NO [ ] UNK
12. MARITAL STATUS: Married
13. EDUCATION—YEARS COMPLETED: 18
14. RACE: Caucasian
15. HISPANIC—SPECIFY: [ ] YES [X] NO
16. USUAL EMPLOYER: Self-Employed
17. OCCUPATION: Actor
18. KIND OF BUSINESS: Entertainment
19. YEARS IN OCCUPATION: 25

USUAL RESIDENCE

20. RESIDENCE—(STREET AND NUMBER OR LOCATION): 2899 Agoura Road
21. CITY: Westlake Village
22. COUNTY: Ventura
23. ZIP CODE: 91361
24. YRS IN COUNTY: 2
25. STATE OR FOREIGN COUNTRY: California

INFORMANT

26. NAME, RELATIONSHIP: Heather Urich - Wife
27. MAILING ADDRESS (STREET AND NUMBER OR RURAL ROUTE NUMBER, CITY OR TOWN, STATE, ZIP): 2899 Agoura Road, Westlake Village, CA 91361

SPOUSE AND PARENT INFORMATION

28. NAME OF SURVIVING SPOUSE—FIRST: Heather
29. MIDDLE: Margaret
30. LAST (MAIDEN NAME): Menzies
31. NAME OF FATHER—FIRST: John
32. MIDDLE: Paul
33. LAST: Urich
34. BIRTH STATE: Ohio
35. NAME OF MOTHER—FIRST: Cecelia
36. MIDDLE: Monica
37. LAST (MAIDEN): Halpate
38. BIRTH STATE: Ohio

DISPOSITION(S)

39. DATE MM/DD/CCYY: 04/22/2002
40. PLACE OF FINAL DISPOSITION: RES/Heather Urich 2899 Agoura Road, Westlake Village, CA 91361

FUNERAL DIRECTOR AND LOCAL REGISTRAR

41. TYPE OF DISPOSITION(S): CR/RES
42. SIGNATURE OF EMBALMER: ▶ Not Embalmed
43. LICENSE NO.: -
44. NAME OF FUNERAL DIRECTOR: Pierce Brothers Valley Oaks Mortuary
45. LICENSE NO.: FD 1344
46. SIGNATURE OF LOCAL REGISTRAR: ▶ Robert M Levin MD
47. DATE MM/DD/CCYY: 04/17/2002

PLACE OF DEATH

101. PLACE OF DEATH: Los Robles Regional Medical Center
102. IF HOSPITAL, SPECIFY ONE: [X] IP [ ] ER/OP [ ] DOA
103. FACILITY OTHER THAN HOSPITAL: [ ] CONV. HOSP. [ ] RES. CARE [ ] OTHER
104. COUNTY: Ventura
105. STREET ADDRESS—(STREET AND NUMBER OR LOCATION): 215 W. Janss Road
106. CITY: Thousand Oaks

CAUSE OF DEATH

107. DEATH WAS CAUSED BY: (ENTER ONLY ONE CAUSE PER LINE FOR A, B, C, AND D)

	Cause	Time interval between onset and death
IMMEDIATE CAUSE (A)	Cardiopulmonary Arrest	minutes
DUE TO (B)	Multisystem Failure	2 days
DUE TO (C)	Metastatic Sarcoma	5 yrs
DUE TO (D)		

108. DEATH REPORTED TO CORONER: [ ] YES [X] NO — REFERRAL NUMBER
109. BIOPSY PERFORMED: [ ] YES [X] NO
110. AUTOPSY PERFORMED: [ ] YES [X] NO
111. USED IN DETERMINING CAUSE: [ ] YES [X] NO
112. OTHER SIGNIFICANT CONDITIONS CONTRIBUTING TO DEATH BUT NOT RELATED TO CAUSE GIVEN IN 107: None
113. WAS OPERATION PERFORMED FOR ANY CONDITION IN ITEM 107 OR 112? IF YES, LIST TYPE OF OPERATION AND DATE.: No

PHYSICIAN'S CERTIFICATION

114. I CERTIFY THAT TO THE BEST OF MY KNOWLEDGE DEATH OCCURRED AT THE HOUR, DATE AND PLACE STATED FROM THE CAUSES STATED.
DECEDENT ATTENDED SINCE MM/DD/CCYY: 04/13/2002
DECEDENT LAST SEEN ALIVE MM/DD/CCYY: 04/16/2002
115. SIGNATURE AND TITLE OF CERTIFIER: ▶ [signature]
116. LICENSE NO.: A 49628
117. DATE MM/DD/CCYY: 04/16/2002
118. TYPE ATTENDING PHYSICIAN'S NAME, MAILING ADDRESS, ZIP: Anil Daya MD 1240 Westlake Blvd. Westlake Village, CA 91361

CORONER'S USE ONLY

I CERTIFY THAT IN MY OPINION DEATH OCCURRED AT THE HOUR, DATE AND PLACE STATED FROM THE CAUSES STATED.
119. MANNER OF DEATH: [ ] NATURAL [ ] SUICIDE [ ] HOMICIDE [ ] ACCIDENT [ ] PENDING INVESTIGATION [ ] COULD NOT BE DETERMINED
120. INJURY AT WORK: [ ] YES [ ] NO
121. INJURY DATE MM/DD/CCYY
122. HOUR
123. PLACE OF INJURY
124. DESCRIBE HOW INJURY OCCURRED (EVENTS WHICH RESULTED IN INJURY)
125. LOCATION (STREET AND NUMBER OR LOCATION AND CITY, ZIP)
126. SIGNATURE OF CORONER OR DEPUTY CORONER ▶
127. DATE MM/DD/CCYY
128. TYPED NAME, TITLE OF CORONER OR DEPUTY CORONER

STATE REGISTRAR

A B C D E F G H
FAX AUTH. #: 41237
CENSUS TRACT

474402

CERTIFIED COPY OF VITAL RECORDS

STATE OF CALIFORNIA } SS
COUNTY OF VENTURA

DATE ISSUED 04/22/2002

This is a true and exact reproduction of the document officially registered and placed on file in the Vital Records Section, Ventura County Public Health Department, if it bears the date of issue in red ink.

Robert M Levin MD
HEALTH OFFICER
VENTURA COUNTY, CALIFORNIA

This copy not valid unless prepared on engraved border displaying seal and signature of Registrar.

MIDWEST BANK NOTE COMPANY

ANY ALTERATION OR ERASURE VOIDS THIS CERTIFICATE

CERTIFICATION OF VITAL RECORD

COUNTY OF MARIN

SAN RAFAEL, CALIFORNIA

90

CERTIFICATE OF DEATH

STATE OF CALIFORNIA

2100 864

LOCAL REGISTRATION DISTRICT AND CERTIFICATE NUMBER

STATE FILE NUMBER

DECEDENT PERSONAL DATA

1A. Name of decedent—first	VIVIAN
1B. Middle	ROBERTA
1C. Last	DODDS
2A. Date of death	Aug. 17, 1979
2B. Hour	
3. Sex	Female
4. Race	White
5. Ethnicity	American
6. Date of birth	July 26, 1915
7. Age	64 years
8. Birthplace of decedent	Kansas
9. Name and birthplace of father	Robert Jones, Kansas
10. Birth name and birthplace of mother	Mae Ragan, Kansas
11. Citizen of what country	USA
12. Social security number	110-09-0642
13. Marital status	Married
14. Name of surviving spouse	John R. Dodds
15. Primary occupation	Actress
16. Number of years this occupation	30
17. Employer	Various
18. Kind of industry or business	Acting

USUAL RESIDENCE

19A. Usual residence—street address	88 Beach Rd.
19B.	
19C. City or town	Belvedere
19D. County	Marin
19E. State	Ca.
20. Name and address of informant—relationship	John R. Dodds, 88 Beach Rd., Belvedere, Ca. 94920 — Husband

PLACE OF DEATH

21A. Place of death	88 Beach Rd. (Home)
21B. County	Marin
21C. Street address	88 Beach Rd.
21D. City or town	Belvedere

CAUSE OF DEATH

22. DEATH WAS CAUSED BY: (ENTER ONLY ONE CAUSE PER LINE FOR A, B, AND C)

	Cause	Approximate interval between onset and death
Immediate cause (A)	Cardiorespiratory Arrest	minutes
Due to, or as a consequence of (B)	Metastatic Carcinoma	
Due to, or as a consequence of (C)		

23. Other conditions contributing but not related to the immediate cause of death	
24. Was death reported to coroner?	yes
25. Was biopsy performed?	yes
26. Was autopsy performed?	No
27. Was operation performed for any condition in items 22 or 23? Type of operation / Date	

PHYSICIAN'S CERTIFICATION

28A. I certify that death occurred at the hour, date and place stated from the causes stated. I attended decedent since / I last saw decedent alive	1977 / 2yrs. — 8-12-79
28B. Physician—signature and degree or title	E B Seaman, MD
28C. Date signed	8-17-79
28D. Physician's license number	G3266
28E. Type physician's name and address	E. Seaman 11 Prof Center Pkwy, San Rafael 94903

INJURY INFORMATION

29. Specify accident, suicide, etc.	
30. Place of injury	
31. Injury at work	
32A. Date of injury	
32B. Hour	
33. Location	
34. Describe how injury occurred	

CORONER'S USE ONLY

35A. I certify that death occurred at the hour, date and place stated from the causes stated. As required by law I have held an (inquest-investigation)	
35B. Coroner—signature and degree or title	
35C. Date signed	

36. Disposition	Cremation
37. Date	8/20/79
38. Name and address of cemetery or crematory	Bahia Crematory, Novato
39. Embalmer's license number and signature	Not Embalmed
40. Name of funeral director (or person acting as such)	Neptune Society
41. Local registrar—signature	Theodore D. Hiatt M.D. L.M.
42. Date accepted by local registrar	8-17-79

STATE REGISTRAR A. B. C. D. E. F.

VS-11 (10-78)

1an

52867

CERTIFIED COPY OF VITAL RECORDS

STATE OF CALIFORNIA
COUNTY OF MARIN } SS.

DATE ISSUED AUG 24 1995

Joan C. Thayer

MARIN COUNTY ASSESSOR-RECORDER
MARIN COUNTY, CALIFORNIA

This is a true and exact reproduction of the document officially registered and placed on file in the Vital Records Section, Marin County Assessor Recorder's Office.

This copy not valid unless prepared on engraved border displaying seal and signature of Registrar.

THE GREAT SEAL OF THE STATE OF CALIFORNIA

RECORDERS OFFICE MARIN COUNTY CALIFORNIA

ANY ALTERATION OR ERASURE VOIDS THIS CERTIFICATE

CERTIFICATION OF VITAL RECORD

COUNTY OF LOS ANGELES • REGISTRAR-RECORDER/COUNTY CLERK

CERTIFICATE OF DEATH
STATE OF CALIFORNIA

STATE FILE NUMBER

LOCAL REGISTRATION DISTRICT AND CERTIFICATE NUMBER: 0190-011119

DECEDENT PERSONAL DATA

1A. NAME OF DECEDENT—FIRST: Charles
1B. MIDDLE:
1C. LAST: Wagenheim
2A. DATE OF DEATH (MONTH, DAY, YEAR): 3-6-79
2B. HOUR: 1807 hrs.
3. SEX: male
4. RACE: cauc
5. ETHNICITY: not stated
6. DATE OF BIRTH: Feb 21 1896
7. AGE: 83 YEARS — IF UNDER 1 YEAR: MONTHS, DAYS — IF UNDER 24 HOURS: HOURS, MINUTES
8. BIRTHPLACE OF DECEDENT (STATE OR FOREIGN COUNTRY): New Jersey
9. NAME AND BIRTHPLACE OF FATHER: Abraham Wagenheim- Unknown
10. BIRTH NAME AND BIRTHPLACE OF MOTHER: Frieda Polansky-unknown
11. CITIZEN OF WHAT COUNTRY: U.S.A.
12. SOCIAL SECURITY NUMBER: 084 03 2264
13. MARITAL STATUS: married
14. NAME OF SURVIVING SPOUSE (IF WIFE, ENTER BIRTH NAME): Lillian Engel
15. PRIMARY OCCUPATION: Actor
16. NUMBER OF YEARS THIS OCCUPATION: 60
17. EMPLOYER (IF SELF-EMPLOYED, SO STATE): Free Lance
18. KIND OF INDUSTRY OR BUSINESS: Entertainment

USUAL RESIDENCE

19A. USUAL RESIDENCE—STREET ADDRESS (STREET AND NUMBER OR LOCATION): 8078 Fareholm Dr.
19B.
19C. CITY OR TOWN: Los Angeles
19D. COUNTY: Los Angeles
19E. STATE: Calif
20. NAME AND ADDRESS OF INFORMANT—RELATIONSHIP: Allen Remes (Friend) 315 S Beverly Dr. Beverly Hills Calif

PLACE OF DEATH

21A. PLACE OF DEATH: 8078 Fareholm Dr. (Residence)
21B. COUNTY: Los Angeles
21C. STREET ADDRESS (STREET AND NUMBER OR LOCATION): 8078 Fareholm Dr
21D. CITY OR TOWN: Los Angeles

CAUSE OF DEATH

22. DEATH WAS CAUSED BY: (ENTER ONLY ONE CAUSE PER LINE FOR A, B, AND C)
IMMEDIATE CAUSE (A) MULTIPLE TRAUMATIC INJURIES.
CONDITIONS, IF ANY, WHICH GAVE RISE TO THE IMMEDIATE CAUSE, STATING THE UNDERLYING CAUSE LAST.
DUE TO, OR AS A CONSEQUENCE OF (B)
DUE TO, OR AS A CONSEQUENCE OF (C)
APPROXIMATE INTERVAL BETWEEN ONSET AND DEATH
24. WAS DEATH REPORTED TO CORONER? 79-3008
25. WAS BIOPSY PERFORMED? no
26. WAS AUTOPSY PERFORMED? yes
23. OTHER CONDITIONS CONTRIBUTING BUT NOT RELATED TO THE IMMEDIATE CAUSE OF DEATH
27. WAS OPERATION PERFORMED FOR ANY CONDITION IN ITEMS 22 OR 23? TYPE OF OPERATION DATE no

PHYSICIAN'S CERTIFICATION

28A. I CERTIFY THAT DEATH OCCURRED AT THE HOUR, DATE AND PLACE STATED FROM THE CAUSES STATED. I ATTENDED DECEDENT SINCE (ENTER NO, DA, YR.) I LAST SAW DECEDENT ALIVE (ENTER NO, DA, YR.)
28B. PHYSICIAN—SIGNATURE AND DEGREE OR TITLE
28C. DATE SIGNED
28D. PHYSICIAN'S LICENSE NUMBER
28E. TYPE PHYSICIAN'S NAME AND ADDRESS

INJURY INFORMATION

29. SPECIFY ACCIDENT, SUICIDE, ETC.: homicide
30. PLACE OF INJURY: residence
31. INJURY AT WORK: no
32A. DATE OF INJURY—MONTH, DAY, YEAR: 3-6-79
32B. HOUR: 1757 hrs.
33. LOCATION (STREET AND NUMBER OR LOCATION AND CITY OR TOWN): 8078 Fareholm Drive - Los Angeles
34. DESCRIBE HOW INJURY OCCURRED (EVENTS WHICH RESULTED IN INJURY): As above.

CORONER'S USE ONLY

35A. I CERTIFY THAT DEATH OCCURRED AT THE HOUR, DATE AND PLACE STATED FROM THE CAUSES STATED. AS REQUIRED BY LAW I HAVE HELD AN INVESTIGATION. 1104 N. MISSION RD. LOS ANGELES, CALIF. 90033
35B. CORONER—SIGNATURE AND DEGREE OR TITLE: THOMAS T. NOGUCHI, M.D., CORONER [signature] DEPUTY
35C. DATE SIGNED: 3-16-79

36. DISPOSITION: Cremation
37. DATE—MONTH, DAY, YEAR: 3-16-79
38. NAME AND ADDRESS OF CEMETERY OR CREMATORY: Grandview Crematory Glendale Calif
39. EMBALMER'S LICENSE NUMBER AND SIGNATURE: 5587 Armando Cordova
40. NAME OF FUNERAL DIRECTOR (OR PERSON ACTING AS SUCH): Westwood Village Mortuary
41. LOCAL REGISTRAR—SIGNATURE: [signature]
42. DATE ACCEPTED BY LOCAL REGISTRAR: MAR 16 1979

STATE REGISTRAR: A. B. C. D. E. F.

VS-11 (5-78)

01-9-4-7005

This is to certify that this document is a true copy of the official record filed with the Registrar-Recorder/County Clerk.

Conny B. McCormack
CONNY B. McCORMACK
Registrar-Recorder/County Clerk

OCT 1 1996
19-381945

This copy not valid unless prepared on engraved border displaying the Seal and Signature of the Registrar-Recorder/County Clerk.

ANY ALTERATION OR ERASURE VOIDS THIS CERTIFICATE

CERTIFICATION OF VITAL RECORD

COUNTY OF LOS ANGELES • REGISTRAR-RECORDER/COUNTY CLERK

CERTIFICATE OF DEATH

STATE OF CALIFORNIA—DEPARTMENT OF HEALTH
OFFICE OF THE STATE REGISTRAR OF VITAL STATISTICS

STATE FILE NUMBER

LOCAL REGISTRATION DISTRICT AND CERTIFICATE NUMBER: 0190-037589

DECEDENT PERSONAL DATA

1a. Name of deceased—first name	ETHEL
1b. Middle name	- - -
1c. Last name	WATERS
2a. Date of death—month, day, year	SEPTEMBER 1, 1977
2b. Hour	7:45A M.
3. Sex	Female
4. Color or race	Negro
5. Birthplace (state or foreign country)	Pennsylvania
6. Date of birth	October 31, 1896
7. Age (last birthday)	80 years
8. Name and birthplace of father	John Waters - Pennsylvania
9. Maiden name and birthplace of mother	Louise Anderson - Pennsylvaria
10. Citizen of what country	USA
11. Social security number	116-01-1303
12. Married, never married, widowed, divorced (specify)	divorced
13. Name of surviving spouse (if wife, enter maiden name)	- - -
14. Last occupation	Entertainer Singer -
15. Number of years in this occupation	65
16. Name of last employing company or firm (if self employed, so state)	Self employed
17. Kind of industry or business	entertainment

PLACE OF DEATH

18a. Place of death—name of hospital or other in-patient facility	
18b. Street address—(street and number, or location)	10511 Keokuk Avenue
18c. Inside city corporate limits (specify yes or no)	Yes
18d. City or town	Chatsworth
18e. County	Los Angeles
18f. Length of stay in county of death	37 years
18g. Length of stay in California	37 years

USUAL RESIDENCE (if death occurred in institution, enter residence before admission)

19a. Usual residence—street address (street and number or location)	10511 Keokuk
19b. Inside city corporate limits (specify yes or no)	yes
19c. City or town	Chatsworth
19d. County	Los Angeles
19e. State	California
20. Name and mailing address of informant	Miss Twila Knaack - Friend, 1730 Rogers Place, Burbank, California 91504

PHYSICIAN'S OR CORONER'S CERTIFICATION

21a. Coroner	
21b. Physician: from / to / last saw the decedent alive	4/3/77 / 8/31/77 / 8/4/77
21c. Physician or coroner—signature and degree or title	[signature]
21d. Date signed	9/1/77
21e. Address	22101 Sherman Place, Canoga Park, CA
21f. Physician's California license number	G-26721

FUNERAL DIRECTOR AND LOCAL REGISTRAR

22a. Specify burial, entombment or cremation	Burial
22b. Date	9/6/77
23. Name of cemetery or crematory	FOREST LAWN MEMORIAL-PARK ASSN. GLENDALE, CALIFORNIA
24. Embalmer—signature (if body embalmed), license number	[signature] 4365
25. Name of funeral director (or person acting as such)	FOREST LAWN MEMORIAL-PARK ASSN. GLENDALE, CALIFORNIA
26. If not certified by coroner was this death reported to coroner?	yes 77-10519
27. Local registrar—signature	[signature]
28. Date received for registration by local registrar	SEP 6 1977

CAUSE OF DEATH

29. PART I. DEATH WAS CAUSED BY: (ENTER ONLY ONE CAUSE PER LINE FOR A, B, AND C)

	Cause	Approximate interval between onset and death
Immediate cause (A)	Renal failure	1 month
Due to, or as a consequence of (B)	Metastatic Endometrial Carcinoma	4 year
Due to, or as a consequence of (C)		

Conditions, if any, which gave rise to the immediate cause (A), stating the underlying cause last.

30. PART II: Other significant conditions—contributing to death but not related to the immediate cause given in Part I: Congestive Heart Failure

31. Was operation or biopsy performed for any condition in items 29 or 30? No

32a. Autopsy (specify yes or no): No

32b. If yes, were findings considered in determining cause of death?

INJURY INFORMATION

33. Specify accident, suicide or homicide
34. Place of injury
35. Injury at work
36a. Date of injury
36b. Hour
37a. Place of injury (street and number or location and city or town)
37b. Distance from place of injury to usual residence
38. Were laboratory tests done for drugs or toxic chemicals?
39. Were laboratory tests done for alcohol?
40. Describe how injury occurred

STATE REGISTRAR

A. B. C. D. E. F. 04-8-1-7555

This is to certify that this document is a true copy of the official record filed with the Registrar-Recorder/County Clerk.

Conny B. McCormack
CONNY B. McCORMACK
Registrar-Recorder/County Clerk

OCT 3 1996
19-386522

This copy not valid unless prepared on engraved border displaying the Seal and Signature of the Registrar-Recorder/County Clerk.

ANY ALTERATION OR ERASURE VOIDS THIS CERTIFICATE

CERTIFICATION OF VITAL RECORD

COUNTY OF LOS ANGELES • REGISTRAR-RECORDER/COUNTY CLERK

CERTIFICATE OF DEATH
STATE OF CALIFORNIA

0190-026841

DECEDENT PERSONAL DATA

- 1A. Name of decedent—first: ~~Marion~~ John
- 1B. Middle: Robert
- 1C. Last: Morrison Wayne
- 2A. Date of death: June 11, 1979 6-11-79
- 2B. Hour: 1770
- 3. Sex: Male
- 4. Race: White
- 5. Ethnicity: American
- 6. Date of birth: May 26, 1907
- 7. Age: 72 years
- 8. Birthplace of decedent: Winterset, Iowa
- 9. Name and birthplace of father: Clyde Morrison, Illinois
- 10. Birth name and birthplace of mother: Mary A. Brown, Nebraska
- 11. Citizen of what country: United States
- 12. Social security number: 561-01-2534
- 13. Marital status: Married
- 14. Name of surviving spouse: Pilar Pallete
- 15. Primary occupation: Actor
- 16. Number of years this occupation: 50
- 17. Employer: Batjac Productions, Inc.
- 18. Kind of industry or business: Motion Pictures

USUAL RESIDENCE

- 19A. Usual residence—street address: 2686 Bay Shore Dr.
- 19C. City or town: Newport Beach
- 19D. County: Orange
- 19E. State: California
- 20. Name and address of informant—relationship: Michael A. Wayne – Son, 9570 Wilshire Blvd. – Suite 400, Beverly Hills, California 90212

PLACE OF DEATH

- 21A. Place of death: UCLA Hospital
- 21B. County: Los Angeles
- 21C. Street address: 10833 Le Conte Avenue
- 21D. City or town: Los Angeles

CAUSE OF DEATH

22. Death was caused by: (Enter only one cause per line for A, B, and C)

Immediate cause		Approximate interval between onset and death
(A)	Respiratory arrest	5 min
(B)	Gastric Cancer	5 mos
(C)		8 mon

- 24. Was death reported to coroner: no
- 25. Was biopsy performed: yes
- 26. Was autopsy performed: no
- 23. Other conditions contributing but not related to the immediate cause of death:
- 27. Was operation performed for any condition in items 22 or 23: Explor lap for obstruction — Date: May 2, 1979

PHYSICIAN'S CERTIFICATION

- 28A. I certify that death occurred at the hour, date and place stated from the causes stated. I attended decedent since: May 2, 1979. I last saw decedent alive: June 11, 1979
- 28B. Physician—signature and degree or title: Janet Salmonson, M.D.
- 28C. Date signed: 6/11/79
- 28D. Physician's license number: G35161
- 28E. Type physician's name and address: Janet Salmonson, M.D., 10833 LeConte Ave, Los Angeles, Ca.

INJURY INFORMATION

- 29. Specify accident, suicide, etc.
- 30. Place of injury
- 31. Injury at work
- 32A. Date of injury—month, day, year
- 32B. Hour
- 33. Location (street and number or location and city or town)
- 34. Describe how injury occurred (events which resulted in injury)

CORONER'S USE ONLY

- 35A. I certify that death occurred at the hour, date and place stated from the causes stated. As required by law I have held an (inquest-investigation)
- 35B. Coroner—signature and degree or title
- 35C. Date signed

- 36. Disposition: Burial
- 37. Date: 6-15-1979
- 38. Name and address of cemetery or crematory: Pacific View Memorial Park, Newport Beach, Ca.
- 39. Embalmer's license number and signature: 6744
- 40. Name of funeral director: O'Connor Laguna Hills Mortuary
- 41. Local registrar—signature
- 42. Date accepted by local registrar: JUN 15 1979

STATE REGISTRAR A. B. C. D. E. F.

VS-11 (10-78)

01-8-1-[illegible]

This is to certify that this document is a true copy of the official record filed with the Registrar-Recorder/County Clerk.

Charles Weissburd
CHARLES WEISSBURD
Registrar-Recorder/County Clerk

FEB 03 1992

19-308523

This copy not valid unless prepared on engraved border displaying the Seal and Signature of the Registrar-Recorder/County Clerk.

American Bank Note Company

ANY ALTERATION OR ERASURE VOIDS THIS CERTIFICATE

CERTIFICATION OF VITAL RECORD

COUNTY OF LOS ANGELES • REGISTRAR-RECORDER/COUNTY CLERK

FILED NOV 10 1966 RAY E LEE COUNTY RECORDER

STATE FILE NUMBER

CERTIFICATE OF DEATH

STATE OF CALIFORNIA—DEPARTMENT OF PUBLIC HEALTH

LOCAL REGISTRATION DISTRICT AND CERTIFICATE NUMBER 7097-042481

DECEDENT PERSONAL DATA

1a. NAME OF DECEASED—FIRST NAME: Clifton
1b. MIDDLE NAME:
1c. LAST NAME: Webb
2a. DATE OF DEATH: Oct. 13, 1966
2b. HOUR: 8:57 P.M.
3. SEX: male
4. COLOR OR RACE: cauc
5. BIRTHPLACE: Indiana
6. DATE OF BIRTH: Nov 19, 1889
7. AGE: 76 YEARS
8. NAME AND BIRTHPLACE OF FATHER: Jacob Hollenbeck- unknown
9. MAIDEN NAME AND BIRTHPLACE OF MOTHER: Mabelle Parmelee- Ill
10. CITIZEN OF WHAT COUNTRY: U.S.A.
11. SOCIAL SECURITY NUMBER: 066-16-1815
12. LAST OCCUPATION: Actor
13. NUMBER OF YEARS IN THIS OCCUPATION: 69 yrs
14. NAME OF LAST EMPLOYING COMPANY OR FIRM: Free Lance -
15. KIND OF INDUSTRY OR BUSINESS: Radio, Stage and Motion Pictures
16. IF DECEASED WAS EVER IN U.S. ARMED FORCES GIVE WAR OR DATES OF SERVICE: no
17. SPECIFY MARRIED, NEVER MARRIED, WIDOWED, DIVORCED: never married
18a. NAME OF PRESENT SPOUSE:
18b. PRESENT OR LAST OCCUPATION OF SPOUSE:

PLACE OF DEATH

19a. PLACE OF DEATH—NAME OF HOSPITAL:
19b. STREET ADDRESS: 1005 No. Rexford Drive [X] INSIDE CITY CORPORATE LIMITS [ ] OUTSIDE CITY CORPORATE LIMITS
19c. CITY OR TOWN: Beverly Hills
19d. COUNTY: Los Angeles
19e. LENGTH OF STAY IN COUNTY OF DEATH: 19 YEARS
19f. LENGTH OF STAY IN CALIFORNIA: 19 YEARS

LAST USUAL RESIDENCE

20a. LAST USUAL RESIDENCE—STREET ADDRESS: 1005 N. Rexford Drive
20b. IF INSIDE CITY CORPORATE LIMITS: [X] CHECK HERE; IF OUTSIDE CITY CORPORATE LIMITS: [ ] ON A FARM [ ] NOT ON A FARM
20c. CITY OR TOWN: Beverly Hills 7006
20d. COUNTY: Los Angeles
20e. STATE: Calif
21a. NAME OF INFORMANT: Helen Matthews
21b. ADDRESS OF INFORMANT: 1131 Larrabee St. Los Angeles, California

PHYSICIAN'S OR CORONER'S CERTIFICATION

22a. PHYSICIAN: I HEREBY CERTIFY THAT DEATH OCCURRED AT THE HOUR, DATE AND PLACE STATED ABOVE FROM THE CAUSES STATED BELOW AND THAT I ATTENDED THE DECEASED FROM 6/8/58 TO 10/13/66 AND THAT I LAST SAW THE DECEASED ALIVE ON 10/12/66
22b. CORONER: I HEREBY CERTIFY THAT DEATH OCCURRED AT THE HOUR, DATE AND PLACE STATED ABOVE FROM THE CAUSES STATED BELOW AND THAT I HAVE HELD AN INVESTIGATION AUTOPSY INQUEST ON THE REMAINS OF DECEASED AS REQUIRED BY LAW
22c. PHYSICIAN OR CORONER—SIGNATURE: [signature] DEGREE OR TITLE: MD
22d. ADDRESS: 431 No. Roxbury Dr. B.H.
22e. DATE SIGNED: 10-14-66

FUNERAL DIRECTOR AND LOCAL REGISTRAR

23. SPECIFY BURIAL, ENTOMBMENT OR CREMATION: entombment
24. DATE: 10-18-66
25. NAME OF CEMETERY OR CREMATORY: Hollywood Mausoleum
26. EMBALMER—SIGNATURE: [signature] Paul A. Willis LICENSE NUMBER: 4948
27. NAME OF FUNERAL DIRECTOR: Pierce Bros. Beverly Hills
28. DATE ACCEPTED FOR REGISTRATION BY LOCAL REGISTRAR: OCT 15 1966
29. LOCAL REGISTRAR—SIGNATURE: [signature] MD

MEDICAL AND HEALTH DATA

CAUSE OF DEATH

30. CAUSE OF DEATH. ENTER ONLY ONE CAUSE PER LINE FOR (A), (B), AND (C)

PART I. DEATH WAS CAUSED BY:		APPROXIMATE INTERVAL BETWEEN ONSET AND DEATH
IMMEDIATE CAUSE (A)	Acute Congestive Heart Failure	12 hrs
CONDITIONS, IF ANY, WHICH GAVE RISE TO THE ABOVE CAUSE (A) STATING THE UNDERLYING CAUSE LAST. DUE TO (B)	Chronic Heart Failure	2 yrs
DUE TO (C)	Atherosclerotic Heart Disease	6+ yrs

PART II: OTHER SIGNIFICANT CONDITIONS CONTRIBUTING TO DEATH BUT NOT RELATED TO THE TERMINAL DISEASE CONDITION GIVEN IN PART I (A)

OPERATION AND AUTOPSY

31. OPERATION—CHECK ONE: [X] NO OPERATION PERFORMED [ ] OPERATION PERFORMED—FINDINGS USED IN DETERMINING ABOVE STATED CAUSES OF DEATH [ ] OPERATION PERFORMED—FINDINGS NOT USED IN DETERMINING ABOVE STATED CAUSES OF DEATH
32. DATE OF OPERATION:
33. AUTOPSY—CHECK ONE: [X] NO AUTOPSY PERFORMED [ ] AUTOPSY PERFORMED—GROSS FINDINGS USED IN DETERMINING ABOVE STATED CAUSES OF DEATH [ ] AUTOPSY PERFORMED—GROSS FINDINGS NOT USED IN DETERMINING ABOVE STATED CAUSES OF DEATH

INJURY INFORMATION

34a. SPECIFY ACCIDENT, SUICIDE OR HOMICIDE
34b. DESCRIBE HOW INJURY OCCURRED
35a. TIME OF INJURY: HOUR M. MONTH DAY YEAR
35b. INJURY OCCURRED: [ ] WHILE AT WORK [ ] NOT WHILE AT WORK
35c. PLACE OF INJURY
35d. CITY, TOWN, OR LOCATION COUNTY STATE

Rev 1-1-58 Form VS-11

This is to certify that this document is a true copy of the official record filed with the Registrar-Recorder/County Clerk.

Beatriz Valdez
BEATRIZ VALDEZ
Registrar-Recorder/County Clerk

AUG 10 1995

19-389287

This copy not valid unless prepared on engraved border displaying the Seal and Signature of the Registrar-Recorder/County Clerk.

THE GREAT SEAL OF THE STATE OF CALIFORNIA · EUREKA

REGISTRAR-RECORDER/COUNTY CLERK · COUNTY OF LOS ANGELES · CALIFORNIA

American Bank Note Company

ANY ALTERATION OR ERASURE VOIDS THIS CERTIFICATE

STATE OF CALIFORNIA

CERTIFICATION OF VITAL RECORD

COUNTY OF LOS ANGELES • REGISTRAR-RECORDER/COUNTY CLERK

CERTIFICATE OF DEATH
STATE OF CALIFORNIA

0190-058248

STATE FILE NUMBER — LOCAL REGISTRATION DISTRICT AND CERTIFICATE NUMBER

DECEDENT PERSONAL DATA

1A. NAME OF DECEDENT—FIRST: JACK
1B. MIDDLE:
1C. LAST: WEBB
2A. DATE OF DEATH (MONTH, DAY, YEAR): December 23, 1982
2B. HOUR: 0323
3. SEX: Male
4. RACE: Caucasian
5. ETHNICITY:
6. DATE OF BIRTH: April 2, 1920
7. AGE: 62 YEARS
8. BIRTHPLACE OF DECEDENT (STATE OR FOREIGN COUNTRY): California
9. NAME AND BIRTHPLACE OF FATHER: Samuel Webb - Idaho
10. BIRTH NAME AND BIRTHPLACE OF MOTHER: Margaret Smith - Idaho
11. CITIZEN OF WHAT COUNTRY: U.S.A.
12. SOCIAL SECURITY NUMBER: 570-14-8385
13. MARITAL STATUS: Married
14. NAME OF SURVIVING SPOUSE (IF WIFE, ENTER BIRTH NAME): Opal Wright
15. PRIMARY OCCUPATION: T. V. Producer
16. NUMBER OF YEARS THIS OCCUPATION: 30
17. EMPLOYER (IF SELF-EMPLOYED, SO STATE): Self-employed
18. KIND OF INDUSTRY OR BUSINESS: Entertainment

USUAL RESIDENCE

19A. USUAL RESIDENCE—STREET ADDRESS (STREET AND NUMBER OR LOCATION): 9255 Doheny Road, Apt. 2604
19B.
19C. CITY OR TOWN: Los Angeles
19D. COUNTY: Los Angeles
19E. STATE: California
20. NAME AND ADDRESS OF INFORMANT—RELATIONSHIP: Mrs. Opal Webb, wife, 9255 Doheny Road Apt 2604, Los Angeles, California 90069

PLACE OF DEATH

21A. PLACE OF DEATH: 9255 Doheny Road (residence)
21B. COUNTY: Los Angeles
21C. STREET ADDRESS (STREET AND NUMBER OR LOCATION): 9255 Doheny Road, Apt. 2604
21D. CITY OR TOWN: Los Angeles

CAUSE OF DEATH

22. DEATH WAS CAUSED BY: (ENTER ONLY ONE CAUSE PER LINE FOR A, B, AND C)
IMMEDIATE CAUSE (A) Occlusive Coronary Artery Disease
DUE TO, OR AS A CONSEQUENCE OF (B) Arteriosclerotic Cardiovascular Disease
DUE TO, OR AS A CONSEQUENCE OF (C)
CONDITIONS, IF ANY, WHICH GAVE RISE TO THE IMMEDIATE CAUSE, STATING THE UNDERLYING CAUSE LAST.
APPROXIMATE INTERVAL BETWEEN ONSET AND DEATH
24. WAS DEATH REPORTED TO CORONER? 82-16164
25. WAS BIOPSY PERFORMED? No
26. WAS AUTOPSY PERFORMED? Yes
23. OTHER CONDITIONS CONTRIBUTING BUT NOT RELATED TO THE IMMEDIATE CAUSE OF DEATH
27. WAS OPERATION PERFORMED FOR ANY CONDITION IN ITEMS 22 OR 23? TYPE OF OPERATION: No DATE

PHYSICIAN'S CERTIFICATION

28A. I CERTIFY THAT DEATH OCCURRED AT THE HOUR, DATE AND PLACE STATED FROM THE CAUSES STATED. I ATTENDED DECEDENT SINCE (ENTER MO. DA. YR.) I LAST SAW DECEDENT ALIVE (ENTER MO. DA. YR.)
28B. PHYSICIAN—SIGNATURE AND DEGREE OR TITLE
28C. DATE SIGNED
28D. PHYSICIAN'S LICENSE NUMBER
28E. TYPE PHYSICIAN'S NAME AND ADDRESS

INJURY INFORMATION

29. SPECIFY ACCIDENT, SUICIDE, ETC.
30. PLACE OF INJURY
31. INJURY AT WORK
32A. DATE OF INJURY—MONTH, DAY, YEAR
32B. HOUR
33. LOCATION (STREET AND NUMBER OR LOCATION AND CITY OR TOWN)
34. DESCRIBE HOW INJURY OCCURRED (EVENTS WHICH RESULTED IN INJURY)

CORONER'S USE ONLY 30

35A. I CERTIFY THAT DEATH OCCURRED AT THE HOUR, DATE AND PLACE STATED FROM THE CAUSES STATED. AS REQUIRED BY LAW I HAVE HELD AN INVESTIGATION
35B. CORONER—SIGNATURE AND DEGREE OR TITLE: Deputy Coroner W.L. Shuster
35C. DATE SIGNED: 12-23-82

36. DISPOSITION: Burial
37. DATE—MONTH, DAY, YEAR: Dec.28,1982
38. NAME AND ADDRESS OF CEMETERY OR CREMATORY: Forest Lawn Memorial Park, 6300 Forest Lawn Dr., Los Angeles, Ca. N
39. EMBALMER'S LICENSE NUMBER AND SIGNATURE: 6397 John Alfred Green
40. NAME OF FUNERAL DIRECTOR (OR PERSON ACTING AS SUCH): Forest Lawn-Hollywood Hills Mty
41. LOCAL REGISTRAR
42. DATE ACCEPTED BY LOCAL REGISTRAR: DEC 28 1982

STATE REGISTRAR A. B. C. D. E. F.

VS-11 (10-78) 4292

This is to certify that this document is a true copy of the official record filed with the Registrar-Recorder/County Clerk.

CONNY B. McCORMACK
Registrar-Recorder/County Clerk

APR 10 2000
19-557849

This copy not valid unless prepared on engraved border displaying the Seal and Signature of the Registrar-Recorder/County Clerk.

ANY ALTERATION OR ERASURE VOIDS THIS CERTIFICATE

CERTIFICATION OF VITAL RECORD

COUNTY OF LOS ANGELES • REGISTRAR-RECORDER/COUNTY CLERK

CERTIFICATE OF DEATH 38519048749
STATE OF CALIFORNIA

STATE FILE NUMBER — LOCAL REGISTRATION DISTRICT AND CERTIFICATE NUMBER

DECEDENT PERSONAL DATA

1A. NAME OF DECEDENT—FIRST: GEORGE | 1B. MIDDLE: ORSON | 1C. LAST: WELLES
2A. DATE OF DEATH (MONTH, DAY, YEAR): October 10, 1985 | 2B. HOUR: 0430
3. SEX: Male | 4. RACE/ETHNICITY: White | 5. SPANISH/HISPANIC: NO ☒ | 6. DATE OF BIRTH: May 6, 1915
7. AGE: 70 YEARS | IF UNDER 1 YEAR: MONTHS / DAYS | IF UNDER 24 HOURS: HOURS / MINUTES
8. BIRTHPLACE OF DECEDENT (STATE OR FOREIGN COUNTRY): Wisconsin
9. NAME AND BIRTHPLACE OF FATHER: Richard Head Welles-Unknown
10. BIRTH NAME AND BIRTHPLACE OF MOTHER: Beatrice Ives-Unknown
11A. CITIZEN OF WHAT COUNTRY: U.S.A.
11B. IF DECEASED WAS EVER IN MILITARY GIVE DATES OF SERVICE: 19__ TO 19__
12. SOCIAL SECURITY NUMBER: 119-07-5431
13. MARITAL STATUS: Married
14. NAME OF SURVIVING SPOUSE (IF WIFE, ENTER BIRTH NAME): Paola Mori
15. PRIMARY OCCUPATION: Director
16. NUMBER OF YEARS THIS OCCUPATION: 50
17. EMPLOYER (IF SELF-EMPLOYED, SO STATE): Self-employed
18. KIND OF INDUSTRY OR BUSINESS: Motion Pictures

USUAL RESIDENCE

19A. USUAL RESIDENCE—STREET ADDRESS (STREET AND NUMBER OR LOCATION): 3189 Montecito Drive | 19B.
19C. CITY OR TOWN: Las Vegas
19D. COUNTY: Clark
19E. STATE: Nevada
20. NAME AND ADDRESS OF INFORMANT—RELATIONSHIP: Paola Mori Welles-Wife, 3189 Montecito Drive, Las Vegas, Nevada 89120

PLACE OF DEATH

21A. PLACE OF DEATH: Residence
21B. COUNTY: Los Angeles
21C. STREET ADDRESS (STREET AND NUMBER OR LOCATION): 1717 N. Stanley Avenue
21D. CITY OR TOWN: Los Angeles

CAUSE OF DEATH

22. DEATH WAS CAUSED BY: (ENTER ONLY ONE CAUSE PER LINE FOR A, B, AND C)

	Cause	Approximate interval between onset and death
IMMEDIATE CAUSE (A)	Cardio Pulmonary Collapse	1 hour
DUE TO, OR AS A CONSEQUENCE OF (B)	Ventricular Tachacardia	10 min
DUE TO, OR AS A CONSEQUENCE OF (C)	Atrial Fibrillation	5 yrs

CONDITIONS, IF ANY, WHICH GAVE RISE TO THE IMMEDIATE CAUSE, STATING THE UNDERLYING CAUSE LAST.

24. WAS DEATH REPORTED TO CORONER? No
25. WAS BIOPSY PERFORMED? No
26. WAS AUTOPSY PERFORMED? No
23. OTHER SIGNIFICANT CONDITIONS—CONTRIBUTING TO DEATH BUT NOT RELATED TO CAUSE GIVEN IN 22A: Diabetes, Chronic Phlebitis
27. WAS OPERATION PERFORMED FOR ANY CONDITION IN ITEMS 22 OR 23? TYPE OF OPERATION: No — DATE

PHYSICIAN'S CERTIFICATION

28A. I CERTIFY THAT DEATH OCCURRED AT THE HOUR, DATE AND PLACE STATED FROM THE CAUSES STATED.
I ATTENDED DECEDENT SINCE (ENTER MO, DA, YR): 9/25/80 | I LAST SAW DECEDENT ALIVE (ENTER MO, DA, YR): 9/24/85
28B. PHYSICIAN—SIGNATURE AND DEGREE OR TITLE: Thomas J. Dailey MD
28C. DATE SIGNED: 10/10/85
28D. PHYSICIAN'S LICENSE NUMBER: A27939
28E. TYPE PHYSICIAN'S NAME AND ADDRESS: Thomas J. Dailey, 6272 DeLongpre Ave., Hollywood, Ca.

INJURY INFORMATION

29. SPECIFY ACCIDENT, SUICIDE, ETC. | 30. PLACE OF INJURY | 31. INJURY AT WORK | 32A. DATE OF INJURY—MONTH, DAY, YEAR | 32B. HOUR
33. LOCATION (STREET AND NUMBER OR LOCATION AND CITY OR TOWN) | 34. DESCRIBE HOW INJURY OCCURRED (EVENTS WHICH RESULTED IN INJURY)

CORONER'S USE ONLY

35A. I CERTIFY THAT DEATH OCCURRED AT THE HOUR, DATE AND PLACE STATED FROM THE CAUSES STATED. AS REQUIRED BY LAW I HAVE HELD AN (INQUEST-INVESTIGATION) | 35B. CORONER—SIGNATURE AND DEGREE OR TITLE | 35C. DATE SIGNED

36. DISPOSITION: Cremation
37. DATE—MONTH, DAY, YEAR: Oct. 13, 1985
38. NAME AND ADDRESS OF CEMETERY OR CREMATORY: Chapel of the Pines, Los Angeles, Ca.
39. EMBALMER'S LICENSE NUMBER AND SIGNATURE: Not Embalmed
40A. NAME OF FUNERAL DIRECTOR (OR PERSON ACTING AS SUCH): Pierce Brothers Cunningham & O'Connor-Hollywood
40B. LICENSE NO.: F-168
41. LOCAL REGISTRAR—SIGNATURE: Robert S. Mate LK
42. DATE ACCEPTED BY LOCAL REGISTRAR: OCT 11 1985

STATE REGISTRAR: A. | B. | C. | D. | E. | F.

VS-11 (1-85) 4273

01-9-1-0007

This is to certify that this document is a true copy of the official record filed with the Registrar-Recorder/County Clerk.

Beatriz Valdez
BEATRIZ VALDEZ
Registrar-Recorder/County Clerk

AUG 24 1995
19-000169

This copy not valid unless prepared on engraved border displaying the Seal and Signature of the Registrar-Recorder/County Clerk.

THE GREAT SEAL OF THE STATE OF CALIFORNIA — EUREKA

REGISTRAR-RECORDER/COUNTY CLERK — COUNTY OF LOS ANGELES • CALIFORNIA

BANKNOTE CORPORATION OF AMERICA

ANY ALTERATION OR ERASURE VOIDS THIS CERTIFICATE

CERTIFICATION OF VITAL RECORD

COUNTY OF LOS ANGELES • REGISTRAR-RECORDER/COUNTY CLERK

CERTIFICATE OF DEATH
STATE OF CALIFORNIA

0190-053423

STATE FILE NUMBER — LOCAL REGISTRATION DISTRICT AND CERTIFICATE NUMBER

DECEDENT PERSONAL DATA

1A. NAME OF DECEDENT—FIRST: MAE
1B. MIDDLE:
1C. LAST: WEST
2A. DATE OF DEATH (MONTH, DAY, YEAR): NOVEMBER 22, 1980
2B. HOUR: 1030
3. SEX: Female
4. RACE: White
5. ETHNICITY: American
6. DATE OF BIRTH: August 17, 1893
7. AGE: 87 YEARS
8. BIRTHPLACE OF DECEDENT (STATE OR FOREIGN COUNTRY): New York
9. NAME AND BIRTHPLACE OF FATHER: John West - New York
10. BIRTH NAME AND BIRTHPLACE OF MOTHER: Mathilda Doelger- Germany
11. CITIZEN OF WHAT COUNTRY: United States
12. SOCIAL SECURITY NUMBER: 568-12-5001
13. MARITAL STATUS: Divorced
14. NAME OF SURVIVING SPOUSE (IF WIFE, ENTER BIRTH NAME):
15. PRIMARY OCCUPATION: Actress
16. NUMBER OF YEARS THIS OCCUPATION: 86
17. EMPLOYER (IF SELF-EMPLOYED, SO STATE): Self-em loyed
18. KIND OF INDUSTRY OR BUSINESS: Entertainment

USUAL RESIDENCE

19A. USUAL RESIDENCE—STREET ADDRESS (STREET AND NUMBER OR LOCATION): 570 North Rossmore
19B.
19C. CITY OR TOWN: Hollywood
19D. COUNTY: Los Angeles
19E. STATE: California
20. NAME AND ADDRESS OF INFORMANT—RELATIONSHIP: Mr. Paul Novak, executor, 570 North Rossmore, Hollywood, California 90004

PLACE OF DEATH

21A. PLACE OF DEATH: Residence
21B. COUNTY: los Angeles
21C. STREET ADDRESS (STREET AND NUMBER OR LOCATION): 570 N.Rossmore
21D. CITY OR TOWN: Hollywood

CAUSE OF DEATH

22. DEATH WAS CAUSED BY: (ENTER ONLY ONE CAUSE PER LINE FOR A, B, AND C)
IMMEDIATE CAUSE (A) Cerebral thrombosis — APPROXIMATE INTERVAL BETWEEN ONSET AND DEATH: 3 mo.
CONDITIONS, IF ANY, WHICH GAVE RISE TO THE IMMEDIATE CAUSE, STATING THE UNDERLYING CAUSE LAST. DUE TO, OR AS A CONSEQUENCE OF (B)
DUE TO, OR AS A CONSEQUENCE OF (C)
24. WAS DEATH REPORTED TO CORONER? no
25. WAS BIOPSY PERFORMED? no
26. WAS AUTOPSY PERFORMED? no
23. OTHER CONDITIONS CONTRIBUTING BUT NOT RELATED TO THE IMMEDIATE CAUSE OF DEATH: Diabetes mellitus
27. WAS OPERATION PERFORMED FOR ANY CONDITION IN ITEMS 22 OR 23? TYPE OF OPERATION: no DATE

PHYSICIAN'S CERTIFICATION

28A. I CERTIFY THAT DEATH OCCURRED AT THE HOUR, DATE AND PLACE STATED FROM THE CAUSES STATED. I ATTENDED DECEDENT SINCE: 3-7-67 I LAST SAW DECEDENT ALIVE: 11-22-80
28B. PHYSICIAN—SIGNATURE AND DEGREE OR TITLE: John M Masson MD
28C. DATE SIGNED: 11-24-80
28D. PHYSICIAN'S LICENSE NUMBER: A09788
28E. TYPE PHYSICIAN'S NAME AND ADDRESS: JOHN M. MASSON, M.D., 133 So. Lasky Dr, Beverly Hills 90213

16 INJURY INFORMATION

29. SPECIFY ACCIDENT, SUICIDE, ETC.
30. PLACE OF INJURY
31. INJURY AT WORK
32A. DATE OF INJURY—MONTH, DAY, YEAR
32B. HOUR
33. LOCATION (STREET AND NUMBER OR LOCATION AND CITY OR TOWN)
34. DESCRIBE HOW INJURY OCCURRED (EVENTS WHICH RESULTED IN INJURY)

CORONER'S USE ONLY

35A. I CERTIFY THAT DEATH OCCURRED AT THE HOUR, DATE AND PLACE STATED FROM THE CAUSES STATED. AS REQUIRED BY LAW I HAVE HELD AN (INQUEST-INVESTIGATION)
35B. CORONER—SIGNATURE AND DEGREE OR TITLE
35C. DATE SIGNED

36. DISPOSITION: Entombment
37. DATE—MONTH, DAY, YEAR: Shipped Nov 25, 1980
38. NAME AND ADDRESS OF CEMETERY OR CREMATORY: Cypress Hills Abbey, 833 Jamaica Avenue, Brooklyn, New York
39. EMBALMER'S LICENSE NUMBER AND SIGNATURE: 6707 [signature]
40. NAME OF FUNERAL DIRECTOR (OR PERSON ACTING AS SUCH): FOREST LAWN MORTUARY HOLLYWOOD HILLS
41. LOCAL REGISTRAR—SIGNATURE: [signature]
42. DATE ACCEPTED BY LOCAL REGISTRAR: NOV 25 1980

STATE REGISTRAR A. B. C. D. E. F.

VS-11 (10-78)

01-9-1-7005

This is to certify that this document is a true copy of the official record filed with the Registrar-Recorder/County Clerk.

Beatriz Valdez
BEATRIZ VALDEZ
Registrar-Recorder/County Clerk

AUG 10 1995

19-389404

This copy not valid unless prepared on engraved border displaying the Seal and Signature of the Registrar-Recorder/County Clerk.

American Bank Note Company

ANY ALTERATION OR ERASURE VOIDS THIS CERTIFICATE

CERTIFICATE OF DEATH

STATE OF CALIFORNIA
USE BLACK INK ONLY/NO ERASURES, WHITEOUTS OR ALTERATIONS
VS-11 (REV. 7/93)

STATE FILE NUMBER | LOCAL REGISTRATION NUMBER

DECEDENT PERSONAL DATA

1. NAME OF DECEDENT—FIRST (GIVEN): MARY | 2. MIDDLE: ISABELLA | 3. LAST (FAMILY): WICKES
4. DATE OF BIRTH MM/DD/CCYY: 06/13/1916 | 5. AGE YRS.: 79 | IF UNDER 1 YEAR: MONTHS, DAYS | IF UNDER 24 HOURS: HOURS, MINUTES | 6. SEX: FEMALE | 7. DATE OF DEATH MM/DD/CCYY: 10/22/1995 | 8. HOUR: 1905
9. STATE OF BIRTH: MO | 10. SOCIAL SECURITY NO.: 066-07-1012 | 11. MILITARY SERVICE: 19__ TO 19__ [X] NONE | 12. MARITAL STATUS: NEVER MARRIED | 13. EDUCATION—YEARS COMPLETED: 18
14. RACE: CAUCASIAN | 15. HISPANIC—SPECIFY: [ ] YES [X] NO | 16. USUAL EMPLOYER: FREE LANCE
17. OCCUPATION: ACTRESS | 18. KIND OF BUSINESS: MOTION PICTURE | 19. YEARS IN OCCUPATION: 69

USUAL RESIDENCE

20. RESIDENCE—STREET AND NUMBER OR LOCATION: 2160 CENTURY PARK EAST
21. CITY: LOS ANGELES | 22. COUNTY: LOS ANGELES | 23. ZIP CODE: 90067 | 24. YRS IN COUNTY: 45 | 25. STATE OR FOREIGN COUNTRY: CALIFORNIA

INFORMANT

26. NAME, RELATIONSHIP: M. GREGORY RICHARDS - EXECUTOR | 27. MAILING ADDRESS (STREET AND NUMBER OR RURAL ROUTE NUMBER, CITY OR TOWN, STATE, ZIP): P.O. BOX 16414 BEVERLY HILLS, CA 90209

SPOUSE AND PARENT INFORMATION

28. NAME OF SURVIVING SPOUSE—FIRST: - | 29. MIDDLE: - | 30. LAST (MAIDEN NAME): -
31. NAME OF FATHER—FIRST: FRANK | 32. MIDDLE: A. | 33. LAST: WICKENHAUSER | 34. BIRTH STATE: MO
35. NAME OF MOTHER—FIRST: A. | 36. MIDDLE: ISABELLE | 37. LAST (MAIDEN): SHANNON | 38. BIRTH STATE: IL

DISPOSITION(S)

39. DATE MM/DD/CCYY: 10/31/1995 | 40. PLACE OF FINAL DISPOSITION: SHILOH CEMETERY, SHILOH, IL, ST. CLAIR COUNTY

FUNERAL DIRECTOR AND LOCAL REGISTRAR

41. TYPE OF DISPOSITION(S): CR/TR/BU | 42. SIGNATURE OF EMBALMER: ▶ Kristen Deem | 43. LICENSE NO.: 8265
44. NAME OF FUNERAL DIRECTOR: PIERCE BROS. WESTWOOD VILLAGE | 45. LICENSE NO.: F-951 | 46. SIGNATURE OF LOCAL REGISTRAR: ▶ Robert C. Hate | 47. DATE MM/DD/CCYY: 10/27/1995

PLACE OF DEATH

101. PLACE OF DEATH: UCLA MEDICAL CENTER | 102. IF HOSPITAL, SPECIFY ONE: [X] IP [ ] ER/OP [ ] DOA | 103. FACILITY OTHER THAN HOSPITAL: [ ] CONV. HOSP. [ ] RES. [ ] OTHER | 104. COUNTY: Los Angeles
105. STREET ADDRESS—STREET AND NUMBER OR LOCATION: 10833 LeConte Avenue | 106. CITY: Los Angeles

CAUSE OF DEATH

107. DEATH WAS CAUSED BY: (ENTER ONLY ONE CAUSE PER LINE FOR A, B, C, AND D)

		TIME INTERVAL BETWEEN ONSET AND DEATH
IMMEDIATE CAUSE (A)	ACUTE RENAL FAILURE	days
DUE TO (B)	MASSIVE GASTROINTESTINAL BLEED	days
DUE TO (C)	SEVERE HYPOTENSION	weeks
DUE TO (D)	ISCHEMIC CARDIOMYOPATHY	months

108. DEATH REPORTED TO CORONER: [ ] YES [X] NO — REFERRAL NUMBER
109. BIOPSY PERFORMED: [ ] YES [X] NO
110. AUTOPSY PERFORMED: [ ] YES [X] NO
111. USED IN DETERMINING CAUSE: [ ] YES [ ] NO

112. OTHER SIGNIFICANT CONDITIONS CONTRIBUTING TO DEATH BUT NOT RELATED TO CAUSE GIVEN IN 107: Myocardial Infarction, Breast Cancer, Peptic Ulcer, Anemia

113. WAS OPERATION PERFORMED FOR ANY CONDITION IN ITEM 107 OR 112? IF YES, LIST TYPE OF OPERATION AND DATE. No

PHYSICIAN'S CERTIFICATION

114. I CERTIFY THAT TO THE BEST OF MY KNOWLEDGE DEATH OCCURRED AT THE HOUR, DATE AND PLACE STATED FROM THE CAUSES STATED.
DECEDENT ATTENDED SINCE MM/DD/CCYY: 10/03/1995 | DECEDENT LAST SEEN ALIVE MM/DD/CCYY: 10/22/1995
115. SIGNATURE AND TITLE OF CERTIFIER: ▶ [signature] | 116. LICENSE NO.: C11739 | 117. DATE MM/DD/CCYY: 10/22/1995
118. TYPE ATTENDING PHYSICIAN'S NAME, MAILING ADDRESS + ZIP: Steven J. Tucker, M.D., 10833 LeConte Ave, L.A. CA 90095

CORONER'S USE ONLY

I CERTIFY THAT IN MY OPINION DEATH OCCURRED AT THE HOUR, DATE AND PLACE STATED FROM THE CAUSES STATED.
119. MANNER OF DEATH: [ ] NATURAL [ ] SUICIDE [ ] HOMICIDE [ ] ACCIDENT [ ] PENDING INVESTIGATION [ ] COULD NOT BE DETERMINED
120. INJURY AT WORK: [ ] YES [ ] NO | 121. INJURY DATE MM/DD/CCYY | 122. HOUR | 123. PLACE OF INJURY
124. DESCRIBE HOW INJURY OCCURRED (EVENTS WHICH RESULTED IN INJURY)
125. LOCATION (STREET AND NUMBER OR LOCATION AND CITY AND ZIP CODE)
126. SIGNATURE OF CORONER OR DEPUTY CORONER ▶ | 127. DATE MM/DD/CCYY | 128. TYPED NAME, TITLE OF CORONER OR DEPUTY CORONER

STATE | A | B | C | D | E | F | G | H | FAX AUTH. # | CENSUS TRACT

STATE OF CALIFORNIA

CERTIFICATION OF VITAL RECORD

COUNTY OF LOS ANGELES

DEPARTMENT OF HEALTH SERVICES

CERTIFICATE OF DEATH

STATE OF CALIFORNIA

USE BLACK INK ONLY/NO ERASURES, WHITEOUTS OR ALTERATIONS

VS-11 (REV. 1/00)

STATE FILE NUMBER — LOCAL REGISTRATION NUMBER

DECEDENT PERSONAL DATA

1. NAME OF DECEDENT—FIRST (GIVEN): BILLY
2. MIDDLE: -
3. LAST (FAMILY): WILDER
4. DATE OF BIRTH MM/DD/CCYY: 06/22/1906
5. AGE YRS.: 95
6. SEX: M
7. DATE OF DEATH MM/DD/CCYY: 03/27/2002
8. HOUR: 2300
9. STATE OF BIRTH: AUSTRIA
10. SOCIAL SECURITY NO.: 551-05-1953
11. MILITARY SERVICE: [ ] YES [X] NO [ ] UNK
12. MARITAL STATUS: MARRIED
13. EDUCATION—YEARS COMPLETED: 12
14. RACE: CAUCASIAN
15. HISPANIC—SPECIFY: [ ] YES [X] NO
16. USUAL EMPLOYER: SELF EMPLOYED
17. OCCUPATION: WRITER/DIRECTOR
18. KIND OF BUSINESS: ENTERTAINMENT
19. YEARS IN OCCUPATION: 70

USUAL RESIDENCE

20. RESIDENCE—(STREET AND NUMBER OR LOCATION): 10375 WILSHIRE BLVD. #12-F
21. CITY: LOS ANGELES
22. COUNTY: LOS ANGELES
23. ZIP CODE: 90024
24. YRS IN COUNTY: 64
25. STATE OR FOREIGN COUNTRY: CA

INFORMANT

26. NAME, RELATIONSHIP: AUDREY L. WILDER - WIFE
27. MAILING ADDRESS (STREET AND NUMBER OR RURAL ROUTE NUMBER, CITY OR TOWN, STATE, ZIP): 10375 WILSHIRE BLVD. #12-F LOS ANGELES,CA.90024

SPOUSE AND PARENT INFORMATION

28. NAME OF SURVIVING SPOUSE—FIRST: AUDREY
29. MIDDLE: LORRAINE
30. LAST (MAIDEN NAME): YOUNG
31. NAME OF FATHER—FIRST: MAX
32. MIDDLE: -
33. LAST: WILDER
34. BIRTH STATE: AUSTRIA
35. NAME OF MOTHER—FIRST: EUGENIA
36. MIDDLE: -
37. LAST (MAIDEN): BALDINGER
38. BIRTH STATE: AUSTRIA

DISPOSITION(S)

39. DATE MM/DD/CCYY: 04/03/2002
40. PLACE OF FINAL DISPOSITION: WESTWOOD VILLAGE MEMORIAL PARK 1218 GLENDON AVE. LOS ANGELES,CA.90024

FUNERAL DIRECTOR AND LOCAL REGISTRAR

41. TYPE OF DISPOSITION(S): CR/BU
42. SIGNATURE OF EMBALMER: NOT EMBALMED
43. LICENSE NO.: -
44. NAME OF FUNERAL DIRECTOR: PIERCE BROS. WESTWOOD
45. LICENSE NO.: FD-951
46. SIGNATURE OF LOCAL REGISTRAR: Fred Leaf
47. DATE MM/DD/CCYY: 04/02/2002

PLACE OF DEATH

101. PLACE OF DEATH: RESIDENCE
102. IF HOSPITAL, SPECIFY ONE: [ ] IP [ ] ER/OP [ ] DOA
103. FACILITY OTHER THAN HOSPITAL: [ ] CONV. HOSP. [ ] RES. CARE [ ] OTHER
104. COUNTY: LOS ANGELES
105. STREET ADDRESS—(STREET AND NUMBER OR LOCATION): 10375 WILSHIRE BLVD. #12-F
106. CITY: LOS ANGELES

CAUSE OF DEATH

107. DEATH WAS CAUSED BY: (ENTER ONLY ONE CAUSE PER LINE FOR A, B, C, AND D)

	Cause	Time interval between onset and death
IMMEDIATE CAUSE (A)	RESPIRATORY FAILURE	1hour
DUE TO (B)	PNEUMONIA	9days
DUE TO (C)		
DUE TO (D)		

108. DEATH REPORTED TO CORONER: [ ] YES [X] NO — REFERRAL NUMBER
109. BIOPSY PERFORMED: [ ] YES [X] NO
110. AUTOPSY PERFORMED: [ ] YES [X] NO
111. USED IN DETERMINING CAUSE: [ ] YES [ ] NO
112. OTHER SIGNIFICANT CONDITIONS CONTRIBUTING TO DEATH BUT NOT RELATED TO CAUSE GIVEN IN 107: CORONARY ARTERY DISEASE, IRON DEFICIENCY ANEMIA, RENAL INSUFFICIENCY
113. WAS OPERATION PERFORMED FOR ANY CONDITION IN ITEM 107 OR 112? IF YES, LIST TYPE OF OPERATION AND DATE: NO

PHYSICIAN'S CERTIFICATION

114. I CERTIFY THAT TO THE BEST OF MY KNOWLEDGE DEATH OCCURRED AT THE HOUR, DATE AND PLACE STATED FROM THE CAUSES STATED. DECEDENT ATTENDED SINCE MM/DD/CCYY: 08/31/1998 — DECEDENT LAST SEEN ALIVE MM/DD/CCYY: 03/19/2002
115. SIGNATURE AND TITLE OF CERTIFIER: Harley R. Liker M.D.
116. LICENSE NO.: G079084
117. DATE MM/DD/CCYY: 04/01/2002
118. TYPE ATTENDING PHYSICIAN'S NAME, MAILING ADDRESS, ZIP: HARLEY R.LIKER,MD.435 N.BEDFORD DR. BEVERLY HILLS,CA.90210

CORONER'S USE ONLY

I CERTIFY THAT IN MY OPINION DEATH OCCURRED AT THE HOUR, DATE AND PLACE STATED FROM THE CAUSES STATED.

119. MANNER OF DEATH: [ ] NATURAL [ ] SUICIDE [ ] HOMICIDE [ ] ACCIDENT [ ] PENDING INVESTIGATION [ ] COULD NOT BE DETERMINED
120. INJURY AT WORK: [ ] YES [ ] NO
121. INJURY DATE MM/DD/CCYY
122. HOUR
123. PLACE OF INJURY
124. DESCRIBE HOW INJURY OCCURRED (EVENTS WHICH RESULTED IN INJURY)
125. LOCATION (STREET AND NUMBER OR LOCATION AND CITY, ZIP)
126. SIGNATURE OF CORONER OR DEPUTY CORONER
127. DATE MM/DD/CCYY
128. TYPED NAME, TITLE OF CORONER OR DEPUTY CORONER

10 — 1789

STATE REGISTRAR: A B C D E F G H — FAX AUTH. # — CENSUS TRACT

090495253

This is a true certified copy of the record filed in the County of Los Angeles Department of Health Services if it bears the Registrar's signature in purple ink.

Fred Leaf

DATE ISSUED 140 APR 08 2002

Director of Health Services and Registrar

This copy not valid unless prepared on engraved border displaying seal and signature of Registrar.

ANY ALTERATION OR ERASURE VOIDS THIS CERTIFICATE

STATE OF CALIFORNIA

CERTIFICATION OF VITAL RECORD

COUNTY OF LOS ANGELES • REGISTRAR-RECORDER/COUNTY CLERK

CERTIFICATE OF DEATH 7097-007797

STATE OF CALIFORNIA—DEPARTMENT OF PUBLIC HEALTH

DECEDENT PERSONAL DATA	1a. NAME OF DECEASED—FIRST NAME: Walter	1c. LAST NAME: Winchell	2a. DATE OF DEATH: FEB. 20, 1972 — 2b. HOUR: 0600 hrs
	3. SEX: male — 4. COLOR OR RACE: cauc	5. BIRTHPLACE: New York — 6. DATE OF BIRTH: April 7 1897	7. AGE: 74 YEARS
	8. NAME AND BIRTHPLACE OF FATHER: unknown -unknown	9. MAIDEN NAME AND BIRTHPLACE OF MOTHER: Jeanette Baker -unknown	
	10. CITIZEN OF WHAT COUNTRY: U.S.A — 11. SOCIAL SECURITY NUMBER: 116-10-8769	12. MARRIED, NEVER MARRIED, WIDOWED, DIVORCED: widowed	13. NAME OF SURVIVING SPOUSE
	14. LAST OCCUPATION: Newscaster — 15. NUMBER OF YEARS IN THIS OCCUPATION: 30	16. NAME OF LAST EMPLOYING COMPANY OR FIRM: (unknown)	17. KIND OF INDUSTRY OR BUSINESS: Newscasting
PLACE OF DEATH	18a. PLACE OF DEATH: U.C.L.A Medical Center	18b. STREET ADDRESS: 10877 LeConte St	18c. yes
	18c. CITY OR TOWN: West Los Angeles	18d. COUNTY: Los Angeles	18e. 1 YEARS — 18f. 1
USUAL RESIDENCE	19a. USUAL RESIDENCE—STREET ADDRESS: 7257 Hollywood Blvd	19b. INSIDE CITY CORPORATE LIMITS: yes	20. NAME AND MAILING ADDRESS OF INFORMANT: Wanda Winchell, Same
	19c. CITY OR TOWN: Hollywood — 19d. COUNTY: Los Angeles	19e. STATE: California	
PHYSICIAN'S OR CORONER'S CERTIFICATION	21a. CORONER — 21b. PHYSICIAN: FROM 11/4/71 2/20/72 AND 2/19/72	21c. PHYSICIAN OR CORONER: [signature] MD — 21e. ADDRESS: UCLA Medical Center	21d. DATE SIGNED: 2/20/72
FUNERAL DIRECTOR AND LOCAL REGISTRAR	22a. burial — 22b. shipped 2-20 1972	23. NAME OF CEMETERY OR CREMATORY: Greenwood Cemetery, Phoenix, Arizona	24. EMBALMER—SIGNATURE: [signature]
	25. NAME OF FUNERAL DIRECTOR: Westwood Village Mortuary	27. LOCAL REGISTRAR—SIGNATURE: [signature] MD	28. FEB 20 1972
CAUSE OF DEATH	29. PART I. DEATH WAS CAUSED BY: (A) Cardiac Arrest		
	DUE TO, OR AS A CONSEQUENCE OF: (B) Acidosis + Cachexia		2wks
	DUE TO, OR AS A CONSEQUENCE OF: (C) Metastatic Carcinoma of Prostate		19 mos
	30. PART II. OTHER SIGNIFICANT CONDITIONS: MONILIAL ESOPHAGITIS	31. Prostate Biopsy 1970	32. No
INJURY INFORMATION	33. SPECIFY ACCIDENT, SUICIDE OR HOMICIDE	34. PLACE OF INJURY — 35. INJURY AT WORK	36a. DAYS OF INJURY — 36b. HOUR
	37a. PLACE OF INJURY	37b.	38. 39.
	40. DESCRIBE HOW INJURY OCCURRED		
STATE REGISTRAR	A. B. C.	D.	E.

This is to certify that this document is a true copy of the official record filed with the Registrar-Recorder/County Clerk.

Conny B. McCormack

CONNY B. McCORMACK
Registrar-Recorder/County Clerk

JAN 4 2001

19-797900

This copy not valid unless prepared on engraved border displaying the Seal and Signature of the Registrar-Recorder/County Clerk.

ANY ALTERATION OR ERASURE VOIDS THIS CERTIFICATE

CERTIFICATION OF VITAL RECORD

COUNTY OF LOS ANGELES • REGISTRAR-RECORDER/COUNTY CLERK

CERTIFICATE OF DEATH
STATE OF CALIFORNIA

STATE FILE NUMBER — LOCAL REGISTRATION DISTRICT AND CERTIFICATE NUMBER: 0190-053765

DECEDENT PERSONAL DATA

1A. NAME OF DECEDENT—FIRST: NATALIE
1B. MIDDLE: WOOD
1C. LAST: WAGNER
2A. DATE OF DEATH (MONTH, DAY, YEAR): Found Nov. 29, 1981
2B. HOUR: 0744
3. SEX: Female
4. RACE: Cauc.
5. ETHNICITY: not-stated
6. DATE OF BIRTH: July 20, 1938
7. AGE: 43 YEARS
8. BIRTHPLACE OF DECEDENT (STATE OR FOREIGN COUNTRY): California
9. NAME AND BIRTHPLACE OF FATHER: Nicholas S. Gurdin - Russia
10. BIRTH NAME AND BIRTHPLACE OF MOTHER: Maria Zudilova - Russia
11. CITIZEN OF WHAT COUNTRY: U.S.A.
12. SOCIAL SECURITY NUMBER: 565-30-7855
13. MARITAL STATUS: Married
14. NAME OF SURVIVING SPOUSE (IF WIFE, ENTER BIRTH NAME): Robert Wagner
15. PRIMARY OCCUPATION: Actress
16. NUMBER OF YEARS THIS OCCUPATION: 38
17. EMPLOYER (IF SELF-EMPLOYED, SO STATE): Self-Employed
18. KIND OF INDUSTRY OR BUSINESS: Motion Pictures

USUAL RESIDENCE

19A. USUAL RESIDENCE—STREET ADDRESS (STREET AND NUMBER OR LOCATION): 603 No. Canon Drive
19B.
19C. CITY OR TOWN: Beverly Hills
19D. COUNTY: Los Angeles
19E. STATE: California
20. NAME AND ADDRESS OF INFORMANT—RELATIONSHIP: Robert Wagner - husband, 603 No. Canon Drive, Beverly Hills, Calif. 90210

PLACE OF DEATH

21A. PLACE OF DEATH: Pacific Ocean
21B. COUNTY: Los Angeles
21C. STREET ADDRESS (STREET AND NUMBER OR LOCATION): Isthmus of Catalina Island
21D. CITY OR TOWN: Catalina Island

CAUSE OF DEATH

22. DEATH WAS CAUSED BY: (ENTER ONLY ONE CAUSE PER LINE FOR A, B, AND C)
IMMEDIATE CAUSE (A) DROWNING
CONDITIONS, IF ANY, WHICH GAVE RISE TO THE IMMEDIATE CAUSE, STATING THE UNDERLYING CAUSE LAST: DUE TO, OR AS A CONSEQUENCE OF (B) — DUE TO, OR AS A CONSEQUENCE OF (C)
APPROXIMATE INTERVAL BETWEEN ONSET AND DEATH
24. WAS DEATH REPORTED TO CORONER? 81-15167
25. WAS BIOPSY PERFORMED? No
26. WAS AUTOPSY PERFORMED? Yes
23. OTHER CONDITIONS CONTRIBUTING BUT NOT RELATED TO THE IMMEDIATE CAUSE OF DEATH
27. WAS OPERATION PERFORMED FOR ANY CONDITION IN ITEMS 22 OR 23? TYPE OF OPERATION — DATE: No

PHYSICIAN'S CERTIFICATION

28A. I CERTIFY THAT DEATH OCCURRED AT THE HOUR, DATE AND PLACE STATED FROM THE CAUSES STATED. I ATTENDED DECEDENT SINCE (ENTER MO, DA, YR.) | I LAST SAW DECEDENT ALIVE (ENTER MO, DA, YR.)
28B. PHYSICIAN—SIGNATURE AND DEGREE OR TITLE
28C. DATE SIGNED
28D. PHYSICIAN'S LICENSE NUMBER
28E. TYPE PHYSICIAN'S NAME AND ADDRESS

INJURY INFORMATION — CORONER'S USE ONLY

29. SPECIFY ACCIDENT, SUICIDE, ETC.: Accident
30. PLACE OF INJURY: Ocean
31. INJURY AT WORK: No
32A. DATE OF INJURY—MONTH, DAY, YEAR: Unknown
32B. HOUR: Unk.
33. LOCATION (STREET AND NUMBER OR LOCATION AND CITY OR TOWN): Isthmus of Catalina Island - Catalina Island
34. DESCRIBE HOW INJURY OCCURRED (EVENTS WHICH RESULTED IN INJURY): As above
35A. I CERTIFY THAT DEATH OCCURRED AT THE HOUR, DATE AND PLACE STATED FROM THE CAUSES STATED. AS REQUIRED BY LAW I HAVE HELD AN INVESTIGATION
35B. CORONER—SIGNATURE AND DEGREE: THOMAS T. NOGUCHI, M.D., CORONER, 1104 N. MISSION RD., LOS ANGELES, CALIF. 90033 — DEPUTY
35C. DATE SIGNED: 12-1-81

36. DISPOSITION: Burial
37. DATE—MONTH, DAY, YEAR: Dec. 2, 1981
38. NAME AND ADDRESS OF CEMETERY OR CREMATORY: Westwood Memorial Park, 1218 Glendon Ave., L.A., Calif.
39. EMBALMER'S LICENSE NUMBER AND SIGNATURE: 5595
40. NAME OF FUNERAL DIRECTOR (OR PERSON ACTING AS SUCH): Westwood Village Mortuary
41. LOCAL REGISTRAR—SIGNATURE: R.R.
42. DATE ACCEPTED BY LOCAL REGISTRAR: DEC 02 1981

STATE REGISTRAR: A. B. C. D. E. F.

12 VS-11 (10-78) 01-7-4-7007

This is to certify that this document is a true copy of the official record filed with the Registrar-Recorder/County Clerk.

CHARLES WEISSBURD
Registrar-Recorder/County Clerk

DEC 23 1991

19-275395

This copy not valid unless prepared on engraved border displaying the Seal and Signature of the Registrar-Recorder/County Clerk.

American Bank Note Company

STATE OF CALIFORNIA
CERTIFICATION OF VITAL RECORD

COUNTY OF LOS ANGELES
DEPARTMENT OF HEALTH SERVICES

CERTIFICATE OF DEATH

STATE OF CALIFORNIA
USE BLACK INK ONLY/NO ERASURES, WHITEOUTS OR ALTERATIONS
VS-11 (REV. 1/00)

STATE FILE NUMBER — LOCAL REGISTRATION NUMBER

DECEDENT PERSONAL DATA
1. NAME OF DECEDENT—FIRST (GIVEN): LORETTA
2. MIDDLE: Y.
3. LAST (FAMILY): LOUIS
4. DATE OF BIRTH MM/DD/CCYY: 01/06/1913
5. AGE YRS.: 87
IF UNDER 1 YEAR: MONTHS, DAYS; IF UNDER 24 HOURS: HOURS, MINUTES
6. SEX: F
7. DATE OF DEATH MM/DD/CCYY: 08/12/2000
8. HOUR: 0240
9. STATE OF BIRTH: UTAH
10. SOCIAL SECURITY NO.: 564-18-4791
11. MILITARY SERVICE: YES / [X] NO / UNK
12. MARITAL STATUS: WIDOWED
13. EDUCATION—YEARS COMPLETED: 12
14. RACE: CAUCASIAN
15. HISPANIC—SPECIFY: YES / [X] NO
16. USUAL EMPLOYER: SELF-EMPLOYED
17. OCCUPATION: ACTRESS
18. KIND OF BUSINESS: MOTION PICTURES & TELEVISION
19. YEARS IN OCCUPATION: 75

USUAL RESIDENCE
20. RESIDENCE—(STREET AND NUMBER OR LOCATION): 1075 MANZANITA
21. CITY: PALM SPRINGS
22. COUNTY: RIVERSIDE
23. ZIP CODE: 92262
24. YRS IN COUNTY: 8
25. STATE OR FOREIGN COUNTRY: CA

INFORMANT
26. NAME, RELATIONSHIP: JUDY LEWIS, DAUGHTER
27. MAILING ADDRESS (STREET AND NUMBER OR RURAL ROUTE NUMBER, CITY OR TOWN, STATE, ZIP): 8400 DE LONGPRE AVE. #215, LOS ANGELES, CA 90069

SPOUSE AND PARENT INFORMATION
28. NAME OF SURVIVING SPOUSE—FIRST: -
29. MIDDLE:
30. LAST (MAIDEN NAME): -
31. NAME OF FATHER—FIRST: JOHN
32. MIDDLE: EARL
33. LAST: YOUNG
34. BIRTH STATE: UTAH
35. NAME OF MOTHER—FIRST: GLADYS
36. MIDDLE: -
37. LAST (MAIDEN): ROYAL
38. BIRTH STATE: CA

DISPOSITION(S)
39. DATE MM/DD/CCYY: 08/17/2000
40. PLACE OF FINAL DISPOSITION: HOLY CROSS CEMETERY 5835 W. SLAUSON AVE., CULVER CITY, CA

FUNERAL DIRECTOR AND LOCAL REGISTRAR
41. TYPE OF DISPOSITION(S): CR/BU
42. SIGNATURE OF EMBALMER: David L. Fox
43. LICENSE NO.: 5761
44. NAME OF FUNERAL DIRECTOR: PALM SPRINGS MORTUARY
45. LICENSE NO.: FD1513
46. SIGNATURE OF LOCAL REGISTRAR: [signature]
47. DATE MM/DD/CCYY: 08/17/2000

PLACE OF DEATH
101. PLACE OF DEATH: RESIDENCE
102. IF HOSPITAL, SPECIFY ONE: IP / ER/OP / DOA
103. FACILITY OTHER THAN HOSPITAL: CONV. HOSP. / RES. CARE / OTHER
104. COUNTY: LOS ANGELES
105. STREET ADDRESS—(STREET AND NUMBER OR LOCATION): 1423 ORIOLE DRIVE
106. CITY: LOS ANGELES

CAUSE OF DEATH
107. DEATH WAS CAUSED BY: (ENTER ONLY ONE CAUSE PER LINE FOR A, B, C, AND D)
IMMEDIATE CAUSE (A): OVARIAN CANCER — TIME INTERVAL BETWEEN ONSET AND DEATH: 6 MOS
DUE TO (B):
DUE TO (C):
DUE TO (D):
108. DEATH REPORTED TO CORONER: YES / [X] NO — REFERRAL NUMBER
109. BIOPSY PERFORMED: [X] YES / NO
110. AUTOPSY PERFORMED: YES / [X] NO
111. USED IN DETERMINING CAUSE: YES / NO
112. OTHER SIGNIFICANT CONDITIONS CONTRIBUTING TO DEATH BUT NOT RELATED TO CAUSE GIVEN IN 107: CHRONIC OBSTRUCTIVE LUNG DISEASE
113. WAS OPERATION PERFORMED FOR ANY CONDITION IN ITEM 107 OR 112? IF YES, LIST TYPE OF OPERATION AND DATE: LAPAROTOMY, OMENTECTOMY, COLOSTOMY, EXCISION BIOPSY 07/03/2000

PHYSICIAN'S CERTIFICATION
114. I CERTIFY THAT TO THE BEST OF MY KNOWLEDGE DEATH OCCURRED AT THE HOUR, DATE AND PLACE STATED FROM THE CAUSES STATED.
DECEDENT ATTENDED SINCE MM/DD/CCYY: 06/30/2000
DECEDENT LAST SEEN ALIVE MM/DD/CCYY: 08/07/2000
115. SIGNATURE AND TITLE OF CERTIFIER: [signature] MD
116. LICENSE NO.: A13943
117. DATE MM/DD/CCYY: 08/15/2000
118. TYPE ATTENDING PHYSICIAN'S NAME, MAILING ADDRESS, ZIP: EDWIN W. BUTLER, M.D., 2121 WILSHIRE BL., STE.#101, SANTA MONICA, CA 90403

CORONER'S USE ONLY
I CERTIFY THAT IN MY OPINION DEATH OCCURRED AT THE HOUR, DATE AND PLACE STATED FROM THE CAUSES STATED.
119. MANNER OF DEATH: NATURAL / SUICIDE / HOMICIDE / ACCIDENT / PENDING INVESTIGATION / COULD NOT BE DETERMINED
120. INJURY AT WORK: YES / NO
121. INJURY DATE MM/DD/CCYY
122. HOUR
123. PLACE OF INJURY
124. DESCRIBE HOW INJURY OCCURRED (EVENTS WHICH RESULTED IN INJURY)
125. LOCATION (STREET AND NUMBER OR LOCATION AND CITY, ZIP)
126. SIGNATURE OF CORONER OR DEPUTY CORONER
127. DATE MM/DD/CCYY
128. TYPED NAME, TITLE OF CORONER OR DEPUTY CORONER

STATE REGISTRAR
A B C D E F G H — FAX AUTH. # — CENSUS TRACT

090362304

This is a true certified copy of the record filed in the County of Los Angeles Department of Health Services if it bears the Registrar's signature in purple ink.

DATE ISSUED SEP 13 2000

Director of Health Services and Registrar

This copy not valid unless prepared on engraved border displaying seal and signature of Registrar.

THE GREAT SEAL OF THE STATE OF CALIFORNIA — EUREKA

LOS ANGELES COUNTY — REGISTRAR OF VITAL STATISTICS — STATE OF CALIFORNIA

MIDWEST BANK NOTE COMPANY

ANY ALTERATION OR ERASURE VOIDS THIS CERTIFICATE

STATE OF CALIFORNIA
CERTIFICATION OF VITAL RECORD

COUNTY OF LOS ANGELES

DEPARTMENT OF HEALTH SERVICES

CERTIFICATE OF DEATH
STATE OF CALIFORNIA
USE BLACK INK ONLY/NO ERASURES, WHITEOUTS OR ALTERATIONS
VS-11 (REV. 7/97)

STATE FILE NUMBER — LOCAL REGISTRATION NUMBER 3 199819030656

DECEDENT PERSONAL DATA

1. NAME OF DECEDENT—FIRST (GIVEN): ROBERT	2. MIDDLE: GEORGE	3. LAST (FAMILY): YOUNG
4. DATE OF BIRTH MM/DD/CCYY: 02/22/1907	5. AGE YRS.: 91	IF UNDER 1 YEAR: MONTHS / DAYS; IF UNDER 24 HOURS: HOURS / MINUTES
6. SEX: MALE	7. DATE OF DEATH MM/DD/CCYY: 07/21/1998	8. HOUR: 2110
9. STATE OF BIRTH: IL	10. SOCIAL SECURITY NO.: 548-05-5990	11. MILITARY SERVICE: YES / [X] NO / UNK
12. MARITAL STATUS: WIDOWED	13. EDUCATION—YEARS COMPLETED: 12	
14. RACE: CAUC.	15. HISPANIC—SPECIFY: YES / [X] NO	16. USUAL EMPLOYER: SELF EMPLOYED
17. OCCUPATION: ACTOR	18. KIND OF BUSINESS: ENTERTAINMENT	19. YEARS IN OCCUPATION: 73

USUAL RESIDENCE

20. RESIDENCE—(STREET AND NUMBER OR LOCATION): 31589 SADDLETREE DRIVE		
21. CITY: WESTLAKE VILLAGE	22. COUNTY: LOS ANGELES	23. ZIP CODE: 91361
24. YRS IN COUNTY: 79	25. STATE OR FOREIGN COUNTRY: CA	

INFORMANT

26. NAME, RELATIONSHIP: BETTY LOU GLEASON - DAUGHTER
27. MAILING ADDRESS (STREET AND NUMBER OR RURAL ROUTE NUMBER, CITY OR TOWN, STATE, ZIP): 7228 N RED LEDGE DRIVE PARADISE VALLEY AZ 85253

SPOUSE AND PARENT INFORMATION

28. NAME OF SURVIVING SPOUSE—FIRST: -	29. MIDDLE: -	30. LAST (MAIDEN NAME): -	
31. NAME OF FATHER—FIRST: THOMAS	32. MIDDLE: E.	33. LAST: YOUNG	34. BIRTH STATE: IRELAND
35. NAME OF MOTHER—FIRST: MARGARET	36. MIDDLE: CARIN	37. LAST (MAIDEN): FIFE	38. BIRTH STATE: SCOTLAND

DISPOSITION(S)

39. DATE MM/DD/CCYY: 07/27/1998
40. PLACE OF FINAL DISPOSITION: FOREST LAWN MEM. PARK 1712 S GLENDALE AVE, GLENDALE CA 91205

FUNERAL DIRECTOR AND LOCAL REGISTRAR

41. TYPE OF DISPOSITION(S): BURIAL	42. SIGNATURE OF EMBALMER: John W. Riley	43. LICENSE NO.: 5641
44. NAME OF FUNERAL DIRECTOR: FOREST LAWN MTY GLENDALE	45. LICENSE NO.: FD 656 / 46. SIGNATURE OF LOCAL REGISTRAR: [signature]	47. DATE MM/DD/CCYY: 07/27/1998

PLACE OF DEATH

101. PLACE OF DEATH: RESIDENCE	102. IF HOSPITAL, SPECIFY ONE: IP / ER/OP / DOA	103. FACILITY OTHER THAN HOSPITAL: CONV. HOSP. / RES. CARE / OTHER
104. COUNTY: LOS ANGELES	105. STREET ADDRESS—(STREET AND NUMBER OR LOCATION): 31589 SADDLETREE DRIVE	106. CITY: WESTLAKE VILLAGE

CAUSE OF DEATH

107. DEATH WAS CAUSED BY: (ENTER ONLY ONE CAUSE PER LINE FOR A, B, C, AND D)

	Cause	Time interval between onset and death
IMMEDIATE CAUSE (A)	RESPIRATORY FAILURE	5 MINS
DUE TO (B)	CORONARY ARTERY DISEASE	10 YRS
DUE TO (C)		
DUE TO (D)		

108. DEATH REPORTED TO CORONER: YES / [X] NO — REFERRAL NUMBER
109. BIOPSY PERFORMED: YES / [X] NO
110. AUTOPSY PERFORMED: YES / [X] NO
111. USED IN DETERMINING CAUSE: YES / [X] NO

112. OTHER SIGNIFICANT CONDITIONS CONTRIBUTING TO DEATH BUT NOT RELATED TO CAUSE GIVEN IN 107: NONE

113. WAS OPERATION PERFORMED FOR ANY CONDITION IN ITEM 107 OR 112? IF YES, LIST TYPE OF OPERATION AND DATE: NO

PHYSICIAN'S CERTIFICATION

114. I CERTIFY THAT TO THE BEST OF MY KNOWLEDGE DEATH OCCURRED AT THE HOUR, DATE AND PLACE STATED FROM THE CAUSES STATED.
DECEDENT ATTENDED SINCE MM/DD/CCYY: 11/15/1995 — DECEDENT LAST SEEN ALIVE MM/DD/CCYY: 07/21/1998
115. SIGNATURE AND TITLE OF CERTIFIER: [signature] MD
116. LICENSE NO.: G21176
117. DATE MM/DD/CCYY: 07/23/1998
118. TYPE ATTENDING PHYSICIAN'S NAME, MAILING ADDRESS, ZIP: JOHN A. HORTON, MD, 1240 WESTLAKE BL, WESTLAKE VILLAGE, CA91361

CORONER'S USE ONLY

I CERTIFY THAT IN MY OPINION DEATH OCCURRED AT THE HOUR, DATE AND PLACE STATED FROM THE CAUSES STATED.
119. MANNER OF DEATH: NATURAL / SUICIDE / HOMICIDE / ACCIDENT / PENDING INVESTIGATION / COULD NOT BE DETERMINED
120. INJURY AT WORK: YES / NO
121. INJURY DATE MM/DD/CCYY
122. HOUR
123. PLACE OF INJURY
124. DESCRIBE HOW INJURY OCCURRED (EVENTS WHICH RESULTED IN INJURY)
125. LOCATION (STREET AND NUMBER OR LOCATION AND CITY, ZIP)
126. SIGNATURE OF CORONER OR DEPUTY CORONER
127. DATE MM/DD/CCYY
128. TYPED NAME, TITLE OF CORONER OR DEPUTY CORONER

STATE REGISTRAR

A B C D E F G H — FAX AUTH. #: 273/27707 — CENSUS TRACT

050161622

This is a true certified copy of the record filed in the County of Los Angeles Department of Health Services if it bears the Registrar's signature in purple ink.

DATE ISSUED AUG 18 1998

Director of Health Service and Registrar

This copy not valid unless prepared on engraved border displaying seal and signature of Registrar.

DE LA RUE

ANY ALTERATION OR ERASURE VOIDS THIS CERTIFICATE

CERTIFICATION OF VITAL RECORD

COUNTY OF LOS ANGELES • REGISTRAR-RECORDER/COUNTY CLERK

CERTIFICATE OF DEATH
STATE OF CALIFORNIA
USE BLACK INK ONLY

STATE FILE NUMBER

39319051820
LOCAL REGISTRATION DISTRICT AND CERTIFICATE NUMBER

DECEDENT PERSONAL DATA

1A. NAME OF DECEDENT—FIRST (GIVEN): Frank
1B. MIDDLE: Vincent
1C. LAST (FAMILY): Zappa
2A. DATE OF DEATH—MO, DAY, YR: December 4, 1993
2B. HOUR: 19:01
3. SEX: M
4. RACE: Caucasian
5. HISPANIC—SPECIFY: YES ☐ NO ☒
6. DATE OF BIRTH—MO, DAY, YR: December 21, 1940
7. AGE IN YEARS: 52
IF UNDER 1 YEAR: MONTHS, DAYS — IF UNDER 24 HOURS: HOURS, MINUTES
8. STATE OF BIRTH: MD
9. CITIZEN OF WHAT COUNTRY: USA
10A. FULL NAME OF FATHER: Francis Vincent Zappa
10B. STATE OF BIRTH: Italy
11A. FULL MAIDEN NAME OF MOTHER: Rosemarie Collimore
11B. STATE OF BIRTH: Unknown
12. MILITARY SERVICE: 19__ TO 19__ NONE ☒
13. SOCIAL SECURITY NO.: 546-56-0064
14. MARITAL STATUS: Married
15. NAME OF SURVIVING SPOUSE (IF WIFE, ENTER MAIDEN NAME): Adelaide Gail Sloatman
16A. USUAL OCCUPATION: Composer
16B. USUAL KIND OF BUSINESS OR INDUSTRY: Music
16C. USUAL EMPLOYER: Self
16D. YEARS IN OCCUPATION: 52
17. EDUCATION—YEARS COMPLETED: 12

1 OF 2

USUAL RESIDENCE

18A. RESIDENCE—STREET AND NUMBER OR LOCATION: 11917 Vose Street
18B. CITY: No. Hollywood
18C. ZIP CODE: 91605
18D. COUNTY: Los Angeles
18E. NUMBER OF YEARS IN THIS COUNTY: 26
18F. STATE OR FOREIGN COUNTRY: California
20. NAME, RELATIONSHIP, MAILING ADDRESS AND ZIP CODE OF INFORMANT: Gail Zappa- Wife, 11917 Vose Street, No. Hollywood, CA 91605

PLACE OF DEATH

19A. PLACE OF DEATH: Residence
19B. IF HOSPITAL, SPECIFY ONE: IP, ER/OP, DOA
19C. COUNTY: Los Angeles
19D. STREET ADDRESS—STREET AND NUMBER OR LOCATION: 11917 Vose Street
19E. CITY: No. Hollywood

CAUSE OF DEATH

21. DEATH WAS CAUSED BY: (ENTER ONLY ONE CAUSE PER LINE FOR A, B, AND C)
IMMEDIATE CAUSE (A) Renal Failure — TIME INTERVAL BETWEEN ONSET AND DEATH: 3 months
DUE TO (B) Matastic Prostate Cancer — 3 years
DUE TO (C)
22. WAS DEATH REPORTED TO CORONER: YES ☐ NO ☒ REFERRAL NUMBER
23. WAS BIOPSY PERFORMED: YES ☐ NO ☒
24A. WAS AUTOPSY PERFORMED: YES ☐ NO ☒
24B. WAS IT USED IN DETERMINING CAUSE OF DEATH: YES ☐ NO ☒
25. OTHER SIGNIFICANT CONDITIONS CONTRIBUTING TO DEATH BUT NOT RELATED TO CAUSE GIVEN IN 21: None
26. WAS OPERATION PERFORMED FOR ANY CONDITION IN ITEM 21 OR 25. IF YES, LIST TYPE OF OPERATION AND DATE.: No.

PHYSICIAN'S CERTIFICATION

I CERTIFY THAT TO THE BEST OF MY KNOWLEDGE DEATH OCCURRED AT THE HOUR, DATE AND PLACE STATED FROM THE CAUSES STATED.
27A. DECEDENT ATTENDED SINCE MONTH, DAY, YEAR: 02/01/90
DECEDENT LAST SEEN ALIVE MONTH, DAY, YEAR: 12/02/93
27B. SIGNATURE AND DEGREE OR TITLE OF CERTIFIER: Cynthia M. Watson M.D.
27C. CERTIFIER'S LICENSE NUMBER: G52886
27D. DATE SIGNED: 12/04/93
27E. TYPE ATTENDING PHYSICIAN'S NAME AND ADDRESS: Cynthia M. Watson, M.D. 530 Wilshire; Santa Monica, CA 90401

CORONER'S USE ONLY

I CERTIFY THAT IN MY OPINION DEATH OCCURRED AT THE HOUR, DATE AND PLACE STATED FROM THE CAUSES STATED.
28A. SIGNATURE AND TITLE OF CORONER OR DEPUTY CORONER
28B. DATE SIGNED
29. MANNER OF DEATH—specify one: natural, accident, suicide, homicide, pending investigation or could not be determined
30A. PLACE OF INJURY
30B. INJURY AT WORK: YES ☐ NO ☐
30C. DATE OF INJURY MONTH, DAY, YEAR
31. HOUR
32. LOCATION (STREET AND NUMBER OR LOCATION AND CITY)
33. DESCRIBE HOW INJURY OCCURRED (EVENTS WHICH RESULTED IN INJURY)

FUNERAL DIRECTOR AND LOCAL REGISTRAR

34A. DISPOSITION(S): Burial
34B. PLACE OF FINAL DISPOSITION—NAME AND ADDRESS: Pierce Brothers Westwood Mem. Park, 1218 Glendon Ave., Los Angeles 90024
34C. DATE MO, DAY, YR: 12/05/93
35A. SIGNATURE OF EMBALMER: Not Embalmed
35B. LICENSE NO.: ---
36A. NAME OF FUNERAL DIRECTOR (OR PERSON ACTING AS SUCH): Pierce Bros. Westwood Village
36B. LICENSE NO.: F-951
37. SIGNATURE OF LOCAL REGISTRAR: Robert C. Mate H
38. REGISTRATION DATE: DEC - 5 1993

STATE REGISTRAR: A. B. C. D. E. F. CENSUS TRACT

VS-11 (REV. 7-92) 185 — MAKE NO ERASURES, WHITEOUTS, OR OTHER ALTERATIONS — 01-9-1-7005

This is to certify that this document is a true copy of the official record filed with the Registrar-Recorder/County Clerk.

NOV 15 1995
19-055617

This copy not valid unless prepared on engraved border displaying the Seal of the Registrar-Recorder/County Clerk.

THE GREAT SEAL OF THE STATE OF CALIFORNIA — EUREKA

REGISTRAR-RECORDER/COUNTY CLERK — COUNTY OF LOS ANGELES • CALIFORNIA

BANKNOTE CORPORATION OF AMERICA

ANY ALTERATION OR ERASURE VOIDS THIS CERTIFICATE

BIOGRAPHICAL NOTES

Bud Abbott (Professional Name); William Alexander Abbott (Name on Death Certificate); **p. 4**—Abbott's long career included vaudeville, burlesque, motion pictures, radio, television and the stage. The majority of his movies were made with Lou Costello. Their most famous skit "Who's on First?" is considered a classic. *Abbott and Costello Meet Dr. Jekyll and Mr. Hyde* and *Abbott and Costello Meet the Keystone Kops* are some examples of their films.

Nick Adams (Professional Name and Name on Death Certificate); Nicholas Aloysius Adamshock (Birth Name); **p. 5**—Adams' first movie was *Mister Roberts*. He became good friends with James Dean after working with him in *Rebel Without a Cause*. Adams came up with the idea for the TV series *The Rebel*. He starred as the soldier Johnny Yuma, a troubleshooter in the badlands. When Adams was found dead, his friends were not convinced that it was an accidental overdose or suicide. They felt his death was a homicide covered up by Hollywood.

Gracie Allen (Professional Name); Grace Allen Burns (Name on Death Certificate); **p. 6**—Gracie Allen was married to George Burns, who played straight-man for her special brand of humor. They made movies together and costarred in their long-running television series *The Burns and Allen Show*. At the end of each show, George would turn to his wife and say, "Say good night, Gracie." The death certificate lists her name as Grace Allen Burns. Her maiden name was used as if it were her middle name, which is quite common.

Irwin Allen (Professional Name and Name on Death Certificate); **p. 7**—Allen spent 45 years as a producer and director. He was considered the father of the disaster movie genre, which began with the *Poseidon Adventure*. For the small screen, Allen produced *Lost in Space* and *Land of the Giants*.

Dame Judith Anderson (Professional Name); Frances Margaret Anderson (Name on Death Certificate); **p. 8**—Twice married, Anderson carried neither of her husbands' names, though she tried a number of names as her stage career advanced. She finally settled on Judith Anderson in 1923. She was made a dame by Queen Elizabeth II in 1960.

Eve Arden (Professional Name); Eve Arden West (Name on Death Certificate, Including Married Surname); **p. 9**—Arden spent her professional career playing weary, worn women. She received an Academy Award in 1945 for Best Supporting Actress for *Mildred Pierce*. Arden created the title character *Our Miss Brooks*, for radio. She carried this role on to television and the movies. Arden is probably best known to younger audiences as the high school principal in the film *Grease*.

Desi Arnaz (Professional Name); Desiderio Alberto Arnaz III (Birth Name); **p. 10**—Arnaz's movie career was just beginning when Word War II broke out. After the war, he served as the orchestra leader on Bob Hope's radio show in 1946 and 1947. He developed the hit television series *I Love Lucy*, with his wife, Lucille Ball. His signature song was "Babaloo."

Fred Astaire (Professional Name and Name on Death Certificate); Frederick Austerlitz (Birth Name); **p. 11**—Astaire began dancing with his sister Adele. He brought choreography to a cinematic artistry. With Ginger Rogers as his costar, he made a number of romantic comedies. *Swing Time* and *Top Hat* were two of his best known films. In one of his most famous scenes, he danced in a room, then up the wall, over the ceiling and back down again.

Mary Astor (Professional Name and Name on Death Certificate); Lucile Langhanke (Birth Name); **p. 12**—Astor's career began in silent films. She received an Academy Award for her performance in the 1941 movie *The Great Lie*.

Eleanor Audley (Professional Name and Name on Death Certificate); Eleanor Zellman (Birth Name); **p. 13**—Audley had a long career in television and films because of her unusual voice quality. She had recurring roles on *Green Acres*, *My Three Sons*, *The Beverly Hillbillies* and *The Dick Van Dyke Show*. She also appeared in several *I Love Lucy*, *Perry Mason* and *Wagon Train* segments.

Gene Autry (Professional Name); Orvon Gene Autry (Birth Name and Name on the Death Certificate); **p. 14**—Best known as the "Singing Cowboy," Autry made 52 motion pictures. *Rim of the Canyon* and *Back in the Saddle* were two of his earliest films. He made many appearances at rodeos and horse shows across the country. He has five stars on the Hollywood Walk of Fame.

Hermione Baddeley (Birth Name and Name on Death Certificate); **p. 15**—Baddeley was a native of the United Kingdom. She began her acting career at a very young age in the *Ealing Comedies*. She was on the stage in London and finally in New York in 1960 in *The Milk Train Doesn't Stop Here Anymore*. She was not interested in series television until Norman Lear persuaded her to take the role of the housekeeper, Mrs. Naugatuck, on the television series, *Maude*.

Bonny Bakley (Familiar Name); Bonny Lee Bakley (Birth Name and Name on the Death Certificate); **pp. 16–17**—Bakley came to Hollywood to make her fame and fortune. She married Robert Blake. Bakley was shot to death on May 4, 2001. The coroner's office issued a death certificate with deferred causes of death and did not issue a cause of death until January 29, 2002.

Lucille Ball (Professional Name); Lucille Ball Morton (Name on the Death Certificate); **p. 18**—Ball began her career as a blonde chorus girl in 1933. Her movie roles came steady but not spectacularly. She changed her hair color to red and her career skyrocketed with the show *I Love Lucy*, which she co produced with her husband, Desi Arnaz. Her special brand of slapstick comedy and timing is legendary.

Ethel Barrymore (Professional Name); Ethel Blythe (Birth Name); Ethel Barrymore Colt (Name on the Death Certificate); **p. 19**—Ethel Barrymore is best remembered for her stage career and for being Lionel Barrymore's sister. She received the Academy Award for Best Supporting Actress in *None But the Lonely Heart* in 1944.

John Barrymore (Professional Name and Name on the Death Certificate); John Blythe (Birth Name); **p. 20**—While the family surname was actually Blythe, that name does not appear anywhere on John Barrymore's death certificate. He was better known for his stage career than for his motion pictures. *A Bill of Divorcement* and *Twentieth Century* were two of his movies. He is Drew's grand uncle.

Lionel Barrymore (Professional Name and Name on the Death Certificate); Lionel Blythe (Birth Name); **p. 21**—Lionel Barrymore spent a lifetime involved in the creative arts. He was not only an actor, but also a composer, etcher and novelist. He was in motion pictures from 1908 until 1953, frequently making as many as three movies a year. He played the mean Mr. Potter in *It's a Wonderful Life*. In his later years, he was confined to a wheelchair.

John Belushi (Professional Name); John Adam Belushi (Birth Name and Name on the Death Certificate); **pp. 22–23**—Belushi got his professional start in *Second City* productions. He went on to *Saturday Night Live*, where his characters blossomed. His films included *National Lampoon's Animal House*, *Blues Brothers* and *Continental Divide*. Belushi died in a hotel bungalow. The Los Angeles County Coroner's office issued a deferred death certificate, which was later followed by an amendment listing the cause of death as acute cocaine and heroin intoxication.

Jack Benny (Professional Name); Benjamin Kubelsky aka Jack Benny (Birth Name and Name on the Death Certificate); **p. 24**—Benny made a career in motion pictures, radio and television using self-ridicule, terrible violin playing and a penny-pinching persona. *The Meanest Man in the World* and *Without Reservations* were two of his films.

Milton Berle (Professional Name and Name on Death Certificate); Milton Berlinger (Birth Name); **p. 25**—Berle's rich, long and full career began in 1914. He was in the first feature-length comedy film *Tillie's Punctured Romance*. His biggest success came in the early small-screen series *Texaco Star Theater* in 1948. Since that time he was in demand as an emcee, lecturer, author, nightclub comedian and television guest star. His moniker was Mr. Television.

Bill Bixby (Professional Name); Wilfred Bailey Bixby (Birth Name and Name on the Death Certificate); **p. 26**—Bixby made his mark on the small screen with shows like *My Favorite Martian*, *The Courtship of Eddie's Father* and *The Incredible Hulk*. He had a few smaller roles in films and on the stage. At the time of his death, he was the principal director of the television series *Blossom*.

Amanda Blake (Professional Name); Beverly Louise Neill (Name on the Death Certificate); **p. 27**—Blake first worked with James Arness in the movie *Stars in My Crown*. She earned the role of Miss Kitty on *Gunsmoke* in 1959. She stayed with the series for 19 years before entering semi-retirement and doing guest appearances and game shows. (An affidavit, which is not shown, adds the name Amanda Blake Gilbert.)

Joan Blondell (Professional Name and Name on the Death Certificate); Rose Joan Blondell (Birth Name); **p. 28**—Twice married, Blondell carried neither of her husbands' names. Her movie career spanned from 1930 until

1979. She was nominated for an Academy Award in 1951 for Best Supporting Actress in *The Blue Veil*. In the movie *Grease*, she played the world-wise waitress, Vi.

Ray Bolger (Professional Name); Raymond Wallace Bolger (Birth Name and Name on the Death Certificate); **p. 29**—Best remembered as Hunk, the Scarecrow, in *The Wizard of Oz*, Bolger went on to become a popular entertainer. Because of his dancing, musicals were the primary venue for his success during his 65-year career. *Where's Charley* and *Babes in Toyland* were two of his films.

Clara Bow (Professional Name and Birth Name); Clara Bow Beldam (Name on the Death Certificate); **p. 30**—Although her career only lasted 14 years, Bow is still remembered as the "flappers' flapper." She had much more success as a silent screen star than with "talkies." Her voice was reported to be so irritating that she was never successful when she had to be heard. Bow's early movies were *Beyond the Rainbow* and *Enemies of Women*.

Fanny Brice (Stage Name and Name on the Death Certificate); Fanny Borach (Birth Name); **p. 31**—Brice's career experiences included burlesque and vaudeville, the stage, motion pictures and radio. She created the role of Baby Snooks for radio. Her first movie was *My Man* in 1928. She appeared in the *Ziegfeld Follies* in 1946 and was the inspiration for the films *Funny Girl* and *Funny Lady*.

George Burns (Professional Name and Name on the Death Certificate); Nathan Birnbaum (Birth Name); **p. 32**—Burns played straight-man to his wife, Grace Allen's character, on radio and on their television series *The Burns and Allen Show*. He earned an Academy Award for Best Actor for *The Sunshine Boys*. *Oh, God!* was another of his films. With his trademark round glasses and cigar, he lived two months beyond his 100th birthday.

Mae Busch (Professional Name and Birth Name); Mae Busch Tate (Name on the Death Certificate); **p. 33**—Busch's acting career spanned from 1915 until 1947. Two of her films were *Love 'Em and Weep* and *Oliver the Eighth*. She was made more popular and famous by Jackie Gleason's weekly comment "...and the ever popular Mae Busch," on his *Jackie Gleason Show*.

Francis X. Bushman (Professional Name); Francis Xavier Bushman (Birth Name and Name on the Death Certificate); **p. 34**—Bushman's screen career lasted from 1911 until 1966. He made his first movie, *The Lady of Lyons*, at age 9. He made the transition from silent movies to talkies and was well known for his piercing blue eyes.

Spring Byington (Professional Name); Spring Dell Byington (Birth Name and Name on the Death Certificate); **p. 35**—Byington began her career with a stock company when she was 14. While still a young woman, she was cast for middle-aged motherly roles. She received an Academy Award nomination for *You Can't Take It with You*. Her television series, *December Bride*, ran for five years.

Eddie Cantor (Professional Name, Birth Name and Name on the Death Certificate); **p. 36**—Cantor was born at a time that must have been very exciting for an entertainer; the theater was in its heyday. Cantor performed in the *Ziegfeld Follies* in 1917, 1918, 1919 and 1923, then he became a star of radio for the next 20 years. His movie career spanned from 1926 until 1952. He helped start The March of Dimes to find a cure for infantile paralysis.

Truman Capote (Professional Name and Name on Death Certificate); Truman Streckfus Persons (Birth Name); **p. 37**—Capote took his stepfather's surname when his mother remarried Joseph Garcia Capote. He was the author of two novels, *Breakfast at Tiffany's* and *In Cold Blood*, that were made into successful motion pictures. The Los Angeles County Coroner's Office issued a deferred death certificate on August 26, 1984. The causes of death, which are not shown, are fatty metamorphosis of liver and phlebitis. The amended death certificate was signed on September 17, 1984.

Richard Carlson (Professional Name); Richard Dutoit Carlson (Birth Name and Name on the Death Certificate); **p. 38**—Carlson had a rich career as a stage and screen actor and director, stage producer and playwright. Two of his science fiction genre movies were *Creature from the Black Lagoon* and *It Came from Outer Space*.

Leo Carrillo (Professional Name); Leo Antonio Carillo (Birth Name and Name on the Death Certificate); **p. 39**—Carrillo's motion picture career spanned from 1927 until 1950, then he switched to the small screen. He is probably best remembered as Poncho in *The Cisco Kid* television series with Duncan Renaldo as Cisco.

John Cassavetes (Professional Name); John Nicholas Cassavetes (Birth Name and Name on the Death Certificate); **p. 40**—Cassavetes was first a star and then became an independent filmmaker and reputable acting teacher. His starring roles were in such movies as *The Dirty Dozen* and *Rosemary's Baby*. His independent films include *Faces* and *Minnie and Moskowitz*. To meet new language and abbreviations mandated by the state of California, his death certificate was amended (not shown) to clarify the place of burial of his cremains.

Jack Cassidy (Professional Name); John Joseph Edward Cassidy (Birth Name); Jack Edward Cassidy (Name on the Death Certificate); **p. 41**—Cassidy's forte was musical comedy on both the large and small screen. *W. C. Fields and Me* and *Death Among Friends* were two of his films. He was once married to Shirley Jones and his sons were teen idols David and Shaun Cassidy. He died in a housefire at his home in West Hollywood, California.

Jeff Chandler (Professional Name); Ira Grossel aka Jeff Chandler (Birth Name and Name on the Death Certificate); **p. 42**—Chandler was nominated for an Academy Award in 1950 for *Broken Arrow*. Most of his roles were action-oriented. His films included *Johnny O'Clock* and *Sword*. The cause of his death—complications after spinal surgery—had many of his friends and coworkers concerned. Many of them signed a petition to have an investigation opened concerning the circumstances surrounding his death.

Lon Chaney (Professional Name); Leonides F. Chaney (Birth Name); Lon F. Chaney (Name on the Death Certificate); **p. 43**—Chaney's birth name is sometimes listed as Alonzo Chaney. Almost all of his work was in the silent movie days. He learned his nonverbal skills at home since his parents were profoundly deaf. He made his mark in horror films, playing the title roles in both *The Phantom of the Opera* and *Hunchback of Notre Dame*.

William Conrad (Professional Name); John William Conrad (Name on Death Certificate); **p. 44**—With his deep and resonant speaking voice, Conrad was in big demand on the radio. He was Matt Dillon in the radio version of *Gunsmoke* for 11 years. He had hopes of being the television character, but his rotund shape did not fit the producer's idea of what Matt Dillon should look like. He did have two successful television series: *Cannon* and *Jake and the Fatman*. His distinctive voice gave him many roles as narrator on shows such as *The Adventures of Rocky and Bullwinkle*, *The Dudley DoRight Show* and *The Fugitive*.

Gary Cooper (Professional Name and Name on the Death Certificate); Frank James Cooper (Birth Name); **p. 45**—Cooper got his start in motion pictures in 1925. He was devastatingly handsome and shy and was known for his nonchalance, quiet strength, "little-boy" quality and charisma. Cooper was nominated for three Academy Awards in addition to the two he received for Best Actor in *Sergeant York* in 1941 and *High Noon* in 1952. He was awarded a Lifetime Achievement Oscar in 1961, but was too ill to attend. His good friend Jimmy Stewart accepted it for him.

Lou Costello (Professional Name); Louis Francis Cristillo (Birth Name and Name on the Death Certificate); **p. 46**—Costello teamed up with Bud Abbott for a long-running comedic partnership. They made such movies as *Buck Privates* and *The Naughty Nineties*, which included their famous "Who's on First" sketch.

Broderick Crawford (Professional Name); William aka Broderick, Broderick Crawford (Birth Name and Name on the Death Certificate); **p. 47**—Crawford began his film career in *Women Chase Men*. He received an Academy Award for Best Actor for his role in *All the King's Men*. The following year, he played Harry Brock in *Born Yesterday*. He is probably best remembered for his television series *Highway Patrol*.

Dorothy Dandridge (Professional Name); Dorothy Jean Dandridge (Birth Name and Name on the Death Certificate); **pp. 48–49**—Dandridge appeared in such films as *Sun Valley Serenade* and *Tarzan's Peril*. She was nominated for an Academy Award for her performance in *Carmen Jones*. It was at first undetermined whether her death from an overdose of Tofranil was an accident or suicide. On June 9, 1966, the coroner's office amended her death certificate to read probable accident.

Brad Davis (Professional Name); Robert Davis (Birth Name and Name on the Death Certificate); **pp. 50–51**—While only 41 at the time of his death, Davis had already made 22 movies. Two of his best known films are *Midnight Express* and *What Really Happened to the Class of '65*. When his death certificate was filed, the cause of death was listed as one of the opportunistic diseases that are often present as a result of AIDS and the HIV virus. The first amendment to the death certificate was to correct the date of cremation. (This amendment is not shown.) The second amendment was to change the cause of death from natural causes to suicide.

Sammy Davis, Jr. (Professional Name, Birth Name and Name on the Death Certificate); **p. 52**—Davis began performing with his dancing family as a child. He was a member of the Frank Sinatra–led "Rat Pack." He had an artificial eye due to an automobile accident. Davis was considered by some to be a variety artist. His audience sense and pacing were innate in him. In 1972, Davis had the number one record in America, "Candy Man." He always considered Las Vegas to be his spiritual home.

James Dean (Professional Name); James Byron Dean (Birth Name and Name on the Death Certificate); **p. 53**—In his short career of three movies, Dean made a lasting impression. Countless young actors have envisioned being the next James Dean. He received Academy Award nominations for Best Actor in *East of Eden* and *Giant*. He was the first actor to be nominated for an Academy Award posthumously, for *Giant*.

Albert Dekker (Professional Name and Name on the Death Certificate); Albert Ecke (Birth Name); **p. 54**—Named for his father; for his professional career Dekker used his original first name and took his mother's maiden name for his surname. His career spanned from 1937 until 1969. *The Wild Bunch* was released the year following his death. His bizarre death was considered by the coroner's office to be accidental, but many at the time believed that it was an elaborate suicide.

Cecil B. DeMille (Professional Name); Cecil Blount DeMille (Birth Name and Name on the Death Certificate); **p. 55**—Considered by many to be the "Father of Hollywood," DeMille rented an old barn in 1914 and made one of the first feature films, *The Squaw Man*. His film, *The Greatest Show on Earth,* received the Academy Award for Best Picture in 1952. DeMille did a cameo as himself in the film *Sunset Boulevard*, which is where the line, "I'm ready for my closeup, Mr. DeMille," originated. His final film was *The Ten Commandments,* in 1956.

John Denver (Professional Name); Henry John Deutschendorf, Jr. (Birth Name and Name on the Death Certificate); **p. 56**—Denver used his middle name for his first name and chose the name of the capital city of Colorado for his surname. A well-known singer/songwriter, 14 of his records were gold and eight were platinum. Two of his most successful songs were "Rocky Mountain High" and "Thank God I'm a Country Boy." He appeared in the movie *Oh God!* and the made-for-television movie *Foxfire*. Denver died in an airplane that he built himself.

Peter Deuel (Professional Name); Peter Elsrom Deuel (Name on Death Certificate & Birth Name); **pp. 57–58**—Success came early for Deuel. He was selected for a role on the television series *Love on the Rooftop*. He then played in three of the Gidget series of motion pictures with Sally Fields. He was a costar on the television series *Alias Smith and Jones* at the time of his death. The Los Angeles County Coroner signed a deferred death certificate on December 31, 1971. The final certificate listing the cause of death as suicide was signed on January 26, 1972.

Walt Disney (Professional Name); Walter Elias Disney (Birth Name and Name on the Death Certificate); **p. 59**—A man of vision and creativity, Disney created the first full length animated films using such characters as Mickey Mouse, Snow White, Cinderella and Peter Pan. His movies for children are legendary and he also developed Disneyland. The legend continues to this day that Disney was cryogenically frozen.

Dominique Dunne (Professional Name); Dominique Ellen Dunne (Birth Name and Name on the Death Certificate); **p. 60**—Dunne's career was just beginning when she was murdered. She was in *The Haunting of Harrington House*, *Poltergeist* and *The Shadow Riders*. She was murdered by her boyfriend while trying to end the relationship. She is the daughter of crime writer Dominic Dunne. The death certificate was amended to correct the date of birth. (This amendment is not shown.)

Jimmy Durante (Professional Name); James Francis Durante aka Jimmy Durante (Birth Name and Name on the Death Certificate); **p. 61**—Durante began his career in vaudeville. During the 30s and 40s, he appeared in two dozen movies. The 50s saw him as a host of various variety shows on television. His self-deprecating act came at his own expense instead of that of others. His "schnozzola" (nose) helped make him famous. Durante would always end his performances with the line, "Good night, Mrs. Calabash, wherever you are."

Harry Essex (Professional Name); Harry J. Essex (Birth Name and Name on the Death Certificate); **p. 62**—His death certificate says that he was a writer/director for 75 years and Essex did maintain an office and wrote daily until just weeks before his death. He wrote for the screen and stage, and he also wrote novels. *Creature from the Black Lagoon* and *It Came from Outer Space* are two of his best known films.

Douglas Fairbanks (Professional Name); Douglas Elton Fairbanks, Sr. (Birth Name and Name on the Death Certificate); **p. 63**—Although some reference works list his surname as Ullman, Fairbanks' death certificate lists his father's name as John Fairbanks. Fairbanks' first appearance in motion pictures was in *The Lamb,* in 1915. By the end of 1916 he had made two dozen more. His last movie was *The Private Life of Don Juan* in 1934. Many of his films were considered swashbucklers.

W. C. Fields (Professional Name); William Claude Durkenfield (Birth Name); William Claude Fields (Name on the Death Certificate); **p. 64**—Fields preferred to use his initials for his professional name, and he also shortened his surname to Fields. He began his professional career as a juggler in vaudeville and progressed to actor and screenwriter. In 1923, he starred in a stage play called *Poppy*. He seemed to use his character in *Poppy* as his model in his movie career. Fields had great chemistry with his costar, Mae West, in *My Little Chickadee*. He turned down the role of the Wizard in *The Wizard of Oz*.

Henry Fonda (Professional Name, Birth Name and Name on the Death Certificate); **p. 65**—Fonda was an actor with a full, rich career. He played men of substance who were trying to do their best. Many of his characters were either hardworking or heroic. *The Grapes of Wrath* and *On Golden Pond* are two films showing such themes. Fonda was the patriarch of an acting family with daughter Jane, son Peter and granddaughter Bridget.

William Frawley (Professional Name); William Clement Frawley (Birth Name and Name on the Death Certificate); **p. 66**—Frawley had a long career in the movies. He often played a pugnacious Irishman. When the part of Fred Mertz came along on *I Love Lucy*, he took it. He stayed for the run of the series. When it ended, he joined the *My Three Sons* series for a five-year run.

Clark Gable (Professional Name and Name on the Death Certificate); Clark William Gable or William

Clark Gable (Birth Name); **p. 67**—Gable was the recipient of the Academy Award for Best Actor for *It Happened One Night*. He was also nominated for *Mutiny on the Bounty* and *Gone with the Wind*. In 1938, after a Hollywood poll, he was crowned the "King of Hollywood" by Ed Sullivan. During World War II, he was awarded the Air Medal and the Distinguished Flying Cross. Gable's last film was *The Misfits*. It was also the last film for his costar, Marilyn Monroe.

Gretchen Gailing (Professional Name); Gretchen Imogene Gailing (Name on the Death Certificate); Gretchen Imogene Hall (Birth Name); **p. 68**—Gailing had a 15-year career as a bit actress. She was usually cast as the beautiful woman behind the star. Her first movie was *Gone with the Wind*. While her roles were specialized, most of them went uncredited.

Janet Gaynor (Professional Name); Janet Gaynor Gregory (Name on the Death Certificate); Laura Gainor (Birth Name); **p. 69**—Gaynor had several small roles before her big break came in 1926. She was selected for the leading lady in *The Johnstown Flood*. In 1927, she received an Academy Award for Best Actress for *Seventh Heaven* and *Sunrise*. This was the first and only time that an actress received the award for multiple roles. She retired in 1938 but made *Bernadine*, in 1957.

John Gilbert (Professional Name and Name on the Death Certificate); John Pringle (Birth Name); **p. 70**—Gilbert was a silent screen star who did not make it into the talkies. *The Big Parade* and *LaBoheme* were two of the movies that made him a worldwide icon. Men wanted to emulate him and women adored him. The big question: after his failure in talkies, people wondered if it could have been his voice quality or the interference by Louis B. Mayer.

Gale Gordon (Professional Name); Charles J. Aldrich, Jr. (Birth Name and Name on the Death Certificate); **p. 71**—Gordon was born with a cleft palate. He had two operations as a child, which resulted in his richly developed voice. He came to California in 1929 to freelance in radio. Radio series where he excelled were *Fibber McGee and Molly* and *Our Miss Brooks*. When he moved to television, he was featured in *The Brothers*, *Our Miss Brooks*, and several of Lucille Ball's series, particularly *The Lucy Show* where he portrayed Mr. Mooney. He was originally chosen for the role of Fred Mertz, in *I Love Lucy*, but the part went to William Frawley.

Betty Grable (Professional Name); Betty Grable aka Elizabeth Ruth James (Birth Name and Name on the Death Certificate); **p. 72**—Grable used to say, "I'm a song and dance girl. I can act enough to get by, but that's the limit of my talents." That was the formula that worked best for her. Her peaches-and-cream complexion photographed perfectly for the new technicolor. Grable was the number-one pinup girl for several decades. She once had her legs insured for one million dollars. *Down Argentine Way* and *Diamond Horseshoes* were but two of her pictures. (Some reference works list her birth name as Ruth Elizabeth.)

Jean Harlow (Professional Name); Harlean Carpenter aka Jean Harlow (Birth Name and Name on the Death Certificate); **p. 73**—Harlow, also known as the "platinum blonde," made some silent movies for Hal Roach. When many stars of the silent era lost their positions when talkies came into vogue, Harlow came into her own. Howard Hughes remade *Hell's Angeles* with Harlow and her career skyrocketed. While she was called a "screen siren," it was more her comedic and dramatic flair that appealed to her audiences.

George Harrison (Professional Name, Birth Name and Name on the Death Certificate); **pp. 74–75**—Harrison was one of the original Beatles. He was known affectionately as "the quiet Beatle." After Harrison's death, the news media attempted to find the home where he died. The address on the death certificate turned out to be bogus. With the threat of a lawsuit, the family cooperated and filed an affidavit to amend the record. The correction also changed the location of the disposition of his cremated remains. (Note that the affidavit is signed by two consultants, instead of mortuary personnel or family members.)

William S. Hart (Professional Name); William Surrey Hart (Birth Name and Name on the Death Certificate); **p. 76**—Hart began his film career in 1914 at age 44. He preferred westerns and insisted on stark realism. He preferred plot and character over action. According to some reference materials, his career ended when he brought suit over the film *Tumbleweeds* for negligent distribution. Other sources list films after this such as *The Movies March On*, *Billy the Kid* and *Show People*.

Brynn Hartman (Married Name and Name on the Death Certificate); Bryann Omdahl (Birth Name); **p. 77**—Brynn Hartman was married to Phil Hartman for 11 years. It appears that after shooting Mr. Hartman on May 28, 1998, she turned the gun on herself. According to the death certificate, she shot herself at 6:21 A.M. and was pronounced dead at 7:09 A.M.

Phil Hartman (Professional Name); Phillip Edward Hartman (Birth Name and Name on the Death Certificate); **p. 78**—Phil Hartman began his professional career with the comedy troupe called the Groundlings. He progressed to *Saturday Night Live* where he stayed from 1986 to 1994. In 1995, he started on *NewsRadio* where he was working at the time of his death. Hartman was shot to death by his wife, Brynn Hartman, who then turned the gun on herself.

Jon-Erik Hexum (Professional Name, Birth Name and Name on the Death Certificate); **p. 79**—Hexum was a young actor who was making his mark in Hollywood when an accident ended it all. He is best remembered for his two television series, *Voyagers* and *Cover Up*. He died six days after an accidental shooting on the set for *Cover Up*. He was handling a prop gun and put it to his temple and fired. He was unaware that even a prop gun expels a wad of paper. This struck him in the temple and caused a quarter-sized piece of bone to be forced into his brain. He was taken off life support and his organs were donated for transplant.

Alfred Hitchcock (Professional Name); Alfred Joseph Hitchcock (Birth Name and Name on the Death Certificate); **p. 80**—Hitchcock got his start in the British film industry. His first film in Hollywood was the 1940 thriller, *Rebecca*. Some of his other most famous works are: *Rear Window*, *Psycho*, and *The Birds*. His trademarks included a cameo appearance by himself in each movie, his greeting of "good evening," and his stout profile for the introduction to his television series.

William Holden (Professional Name); William Franklin Beedle, Jr. (Birth Name); William Franklin Holden (Name on the Death Certificate); **p. 81**—Director Billy Wilder saw the potential in Holden. Wilder cast Holden in *Sunset Boulevard* where he earned an Academy Award nomination. He received the Academy Award for Best Actor for *Stalag 17*, in 1953. Another nomination came his way for *Network*, in 1976.

Hedda Hopper (Professional Name); Hedda Hopper aka Elda F. Hooper (Name on the Death Certificate); **p. 82**—Hopper had a long career in motion pictures. However, it was her career as a gossip columnist for which she is most remembered. In the "golden years," the studio system controlled Hollywood. Hopper was known to be a sympathetic reporter of the studios' activities and their stars. Her arch rival was Louella Parsons.

William Hopper (Professional Name); William De Wolf Hopper (Birth Name and Name on the Death Certificate); **p. 83**—Hopper began his movie career in 1937. He had small roles in a number of movies in the early 40s. He did not care for the industry but being Hedda Hopper's son, he was pushed into acting. When Perry Mason was being cast, he read for the part of Perry. Instead of that role, he was given the character, Paul Drake. It was a good fit.

Curly Howard (Professional Name); Jerome Lester Horwitz (Birth Name); Jerome Lester Howard (Name on the Death Certificate); **p. 84**—Curly Howard was one of the original Three Stooges of stage and screen. He and his brothers, along with outsider Larry Fine, became the interchangeable Three Stooges who entertained millions for decades. Their slapstick, often brutal, and treatment of each other will always be considered classic. *They Stooge to Conga* and *Phoney Express* were two of his films.

Moe Howard (Professional Name and the Name on the Death Certificate); Moses Horwitz (Birth Name); **p. 85**—Moe Howard's first movie was *Soup to Nuts*, in 1930. He was a member of the Three Stooges' family. He made a number of shorts along with feature films. One of his shorts was *Beer Barrel Polecats*.

Shemp Howard (Professional Name and Name on the Death Certificate); Samuel Horwitz (Birth Name); **p. 86**—The last of the family to join the Three Stooges, Shemp Howard did not become a member of the group until his brother Curly retired in 1947. *Of Cash and Hash* and *Rumpus in the Harem* were two of their shorts.

Rock Hudson (Professional Name and Name on the Death Certificate); Roy Harold Scherer, Jr. (Birth Name); **p. 87**—Although Hudson was a shy man, he was able to become active in the Hollywood social community. His films included *Giant*, *Pillow Talk* and *Send Me No Flowers*. Hudson was the first handsome Hollywood heartthrob to start in a television series, *McMillan and Wife*. His last performance was as a guest star in the prime-time soap opera *Dynasty*. He was the first actor of his stature to admit that he was dying of AIDS.

Roy Huggins (Professional Name); Roy Marshall Huggins (Birth Name and Name on the Death Certificate); **p. 88**—Huggins is best known for his work on the small screen. His credits include: *Alias Smith and Jones*, *The Bold Ones: The Lawyers*, *The Fugitive* and *The Rockford Files*.

Richard Jaeckel (Professional Name); Richard Hanley Jaeckel (Birth Name and Name on Death Certificate); **p. 89**—Jaeckel was working as a delivery boy for 20th Century–Fox Studio when they were in need of a baby-faced actor for *Guadalcanal Diary*. After his tour of service during World War II, he returned to film work. He was nominated for an Academy Award as Best Supporting Actor for his work in *Sometimes a Great Notion*. In the 1991-92 television season, he portrayed Lieutenant Ben Edwards on *Baywatch*.

David Janssen (Professional Name and Name on Death Certificate); David Harold Meyer (Birth Name); **p. 90**—Janssen began his professional film career in 1946 in *Swamp Fire*. His small screen success began in 1957 when Dick Powell selected him to star in *Richard Diamond, Private Detective*. In 1963, he began to star in *The Fugitive*. This series lasted four years. *O'Hara, U.S. Treasury* and *Harry O* were two others series that he starred in following *The Fugitive*. The Los Angeles County

Coroner's Office issued a deferred death certificate on February 14, 1980. The final death certificate, which is not shown, was issued March 19, 1980. The cause of death listed was arteriosclerotic cardiovascular disease (hardening of the arteries).

George Jessel (Professional Name); George Albert Jessel (Birth Name and Name on the Death Certificate); **p. 91**—Jessel's professional career began at the age of 9 but his acting career was sporadic. He worked continuously from 1926 to 1930. In 1945, he started producing musicals for Fox. He spent much of his time doing charity work. His peers recognized his efforts by awarding him the Jean Hersholt Humanitarian Award in 1969. His unofficial title was "Toastmaster General of the United States."

Al Jolson (Professional Name); Asa Yoelson aka Al Jolson (Birth Name and Name on Death Certificate); **p. 92**—Jolson ran away from Washington D.C. to New York. In 1899, he changed his surname to Jolson. He introduced "blackface" and sang a few songs in the Southern style in a small nightclub in San Francisco. In 1927, he was the first star in a talking picture, *The Jazz Singer,* where he uttered the first words ever used in a motion picture, "You ain't heard nothing yet!" The *Jolson Story* was a runaway success. He sang to the acting of Larry Parks. Once again, he showed his power to electrify and enchant an audience.

Ruby Keeler (Professional Name); Ruby Keeler Lowe (Name on the Death Certificate); Ethel Hilde Hector (Birth Name); **p. 93**—Keeler made her movie debut in 1933, opposite Dick Powell, in *42nd Street.* Keeler said, "I couldn't act. I had that terrible singing voice, and now I can see that I wasn't the greatest tap dancer in the world either." There is an amendment to the original death certificate (not shown) to change the place of birth from Nova Scotia to Canada.

Percy Kilbride (Professional Name); Percy William Kilbride (Birth Name and Name on the Death Certificate); **p. 94**—Kilbride made scattered movie appearances between 1930 and 1947. In 1947, he created the role of Pa Kettle in *The Egg and I.* Between 1949 and 1955, he worked exclusively in the Ma and Pa Kettle movies. Kilbride and Ralf Belmont were struck by a car on September 21, 1964 while crossing the street. Belmont was killed immediately and Kilbride died from his injuries on December 11, 1964.

Victor Kilian (Professional Name); Victor Arthur Kilian (Birth Name and Name on the Death Certificate); **p. 95**—Kilian could be called a character actor. His specialty was the "brutish villain." *Reap the Wild Wind* and *Blood and Sand* were two of his films. Kilian was victimized by the blacklist in the 50s. Perhaps best remembered as the Fernwood Flasher on television's *Mary Hartman, Mary Hartman*, he was killed by an intruder in his home. There is an amendment (not shown) that changes a blank on the death certificate to read "not embalmed."

Nancy Kulp (Professional Name); Nancy Jane Kulp (Birth Name and Name on Death Certificate); **p. 96**—Kulp's professional career was more prominent on the small screen than in motion pictures. Two of her film roles were in *Three Faces of Eve* and *Who's Minding The Store.* Her two pivotal television roles were on *Love That Bob* and *The Beverly Hillbillies.* She entered politics in the 1980s, running for office in Pennsylvania only to have her Hillbillies costar, Buddy Ebsen, come out publicly in support of her opponent.

Fernando Lamas (Professional Name); Fernando Alvaro Lamas (Birth Name and the Name on the Death Certificate); **p. 97**—Lamas came to Hollywood in 1950 from his native Buenos Aires, Argentina. He already had his film career firmly established in Buenos Aires. His real success came with television where he directed such series as *Mannix, Alias Smith and Jones*, and finally *Falcon Crest.* Lamas left behind a widow, swimming star Esther Williams, and a legacy. Billy Crystal's famous line, "You look marvelous," was a direct spoof.

Dorothy Lamour (Professional Name); Dorothy Lamour Howard (Name on the Death Certificate); Mary Leta Dorothy Slaton (Birth Name); **p. 98**—Lamour is best known for her string of seven "road show" films with Bing Crosby and Bob Hope. *Road to Singapore* and *Road to Bali* gave her the opportunity to use her signature, sarong-draped, demure girl character. She adopted the name Lamour from her stepfather's surname, Lambour.

Burt Lancaster (Professional Name); Burton Stephen Lancaster (Birth Name and Name on the Death Certificate); **p. 99**—Lancaster was one of the few people who could say that he became a star from his first film. That is what *The Killers* did for Lancaster. While he could play a wide range of characters, he did his best work with the bigger-than-life characters like those in *Birdman of Alcatraz* and *From Here to Eternity.* He was nominated for four Academy Awards and received one for *Elmer Gantry.*

Michael Landon (Professional Name and Name on Death Certificate); Eugene Maurice Orowitz (Birth Name); **p. 100**—Landon's first screen success was the now legendary *I Was a Teenage Werewolf.* After several other screen roles, he was given the character Little Joe on *Bonanza.* He next starred in *Little House on the Prairie* and then finally *Highway to Heaven.*

Peter Lawford (Professional Name); Peter Sydney Lawford (Birth Name and Name on the Death Certificate; **p. 101**—Lawford was considered by some to be a reliably good actor, but not a great one. He was a member of Frank Sinatra's "Rat Pack." He became a Washington society insider with his marriage to Patricia Kennedy, sister of the late President John F. Kennedy. Two of his films are *Exodus* and *The Picture of Dorian Gray*.

Rose Louise Hovick aka Gypsy Rose Lee aka deDiego (Professional Name, Birth Name and Name on the Death Certificate); **p. 102**—Considered by some to be the most publicized woman in the world, Lee was one of the most famous strippers of all time. Two of her films are *Babes in Bagdad* and *The Stripper*. The musical *Gypsy* was based on her life.

Liberace (Professional Name and Name on the Death Certificate); Wladziu Valentino Liberace (Birth Name); **pp. 103–104**—Considered to be the consummate showman; using feathers, furs and diamonds, Liberace brought glamor, glitz and extravagance to his piano playing. The Riverside County Coroner discovered that neither the HIV virus nor AIDS was mentioned on his original death certificate. He called for his remains to be brought from Forest Lawn Hollywood Hills Mortuary back to Riverside County for an autopsy and full determination of the cause of death.

Audra Lindley (Professional Name); Audra Marie Lindley (Name on Death Certificate); **p. 105**—Lindley spent most of her career on the small screen. She appeared in several daytime soap operas including: *The Edge of Night*, *Search for Tomorrow* and *Another World*. Her evening television series included *Bridget Loves Bernie*, *Three's Company* and its spin off *The Ropers*. She married James Whitmore but that marriage ended in divorce.

Bela Lugosi (Professional Name and Name on the Death Certificate); Béla Ference Dezso Blasko (Birth Name); **p. 106**—Lugosi began his professional career in his native Hungary. He emigrated to Germany and then to the United States in 1921. Lugosi turned down the role of the Mummy because there were no speaking lines. Boris Karloff got the role and it catapulted him to fame. For many years, there was a bitter exchange between the two. Lugosi played character roles until his appearance in Bram Stoker's *Dracula*. It skyrocketed him to fame and typecast him for the balance of his career.

Ida Lupino (Professional Name, Birth Name and Name on the Death Certificate); **p. 107**—Lupino was born into a theatrical family in England. When she came to the United States, she had roles opposite such luminaries as Humphrey Bogart, John Garfield, and George Raft. Lupino achieved success in such films as *Anything Goes* and perhaps her best role in the *The Gay Desperado*.

Paul Lynde (Professional Name); Paul Edward Lynde (Birth Name and Name on the Death Certificate); **p. 108**—Lynde was a star on Broadway and in the film *Bye Bye Birdie*, but he is perhaps most fondly remembered as Uncle Arthur on the television series *Bewitched*. He also made his fame and fortune as the center square on the game show *Hollywood Squares*. His acerbic wit was perfect in small amounts.

Fred MacMurray (Professional Name); Frederick M. MacMurray (Birth Name and Name on the Death Certificate); **p. 109**—MacMurray normally played "Mr. Nice Guy" characters. He also did some of his best work in roles that called on him to examine the dark side of humanity. *Double Indemnity* and *The Pushover* were two of these. On the small screen he was the father, Steve Douglas, in *My Three Sons*.

Guy Madison (Professional Name and Name on the Death Certificate); Robert Ozell Moseley (Birth Name); **pp. 110–111**—Madison got his start with a small role in *Since You Went Away*, in 1943. He came into his own in 1951 with the television series *The Adventures of Wild Bill Hickok*. The original death certificate was amended to add his birth name.

Marjorie Main (Professional Name); Mary Tomlinson Krebs aka Marjorie Main (Name on the Death Certificate); Mary Tomlinson (Birth Name); **p. 112**—Main began her career as a character actress with such roles a prison matron, a curious landlady, an aunt and a secretary. Her distinctive voice and delivery were assets for her. She received an Academy Award nomination for Supporting Actress in *The Egg & I*. This movie introduced the Kettle family to the movie audiences. She was Ma Kettle in nine films.

Dean Martin (Professional Name); Dean Paul Martin (Name on the Death Certificate); Dino Paul Crocetti (Birth Name); **p. 113**—Throughout his career in music, film, television and the stage, Martin was the epitome of "cool" and was a member of the "Rat Pack." He earned great success with Jerry Lewis in their comedy duo films. Their first movie was *My Friend Irma*, in 1949. The Billy Wilder film, *Kiss Me, Stupid*, formalized his persona as a lush with redeeming qualities. His song "Everybody Loves Somebody Sometime" is cast on his memorial plaque at the cemetery.

Dean Paul Martin (Birth Name); Dean Paul Martin, Jr. (Birth Name and Name on the Death Certificate); **p. 114**—Martin probably earned more fame from his days in the rock group Dino, Desi and Billy, than from his film career. He was an accomplished tennis athlete and starred in the 70s tennis film *Players* with Ali McGraw. His death occurred when he flew into a mountain in Riverside County, California while on a military maneuver. Note that his father's surname, Crocetti, does not show up on this death certificate.

Walter Matthau (Professional Name and Name on the Death Certificate); Walter Matuschanskavasky (Birth Name); **p. 115**—Matthau received an Academy Award for *The Fortune Cookie* and nominations for *The Sunshine Boys* and *Koch*. The chemistry between him and Jack Lemmon is legendary. They were also great friends in real life. Note that the death certificate lists his father's name as Milton Matthow.

Victor Mature (Professional Name); Victor John Joseph Mature (Birth Name and Name on the Death Certificate); **p. 116**—Mature was better known for his physique than for his acting skills. His acting ability was simply overshadowed by his broad shoulders and tapered waistline. He never took himself too seriously. Two of his best roles were in *My Darling Clementine* and *Kiss of Death*.

Hattie McDaniel (Professional Name, Birth Name and Name on the Death Certificate); **p. 117**—McDaniel spent her professional career playing stereotypical domestics. When she received the Academy Award for Best Supporting Actress for *Gone with the Wind*, she was the first person of color to be recognized by the Academy of Motion Pictures Arts and Sciences. No other person of color would win a major award until Whoopi Goldberg in *Ghost*. McDaniel also appeared in *Since You Went Away* and *Song of the South*.

Audrey Meadows (Professional Name); Audrey Cotter Six (Name on Death Certificate); **p. 118**—Meadows is best remembered for her role as Alice in the television series *The Honeymooners*. The surname Meadows came from her father's middle name according to her death certificate.

Sal Mineo (Professional Name); Salvatore Mineo (Name on Death Certificate); **p. 119**—Mineo was nominated for an Academy Award for *Rebel Without a Cause* when he was 16 and for *Exodus* when he was 20. His life and career were cut short when he was stabbed to death in an alley near his home in what turned out to be robbery.

Robert Mitchum (Professional Name); Robert Charles Mitchum (Named on Death Certificate); **p. 120**—Mitchum had something for everyone in his audience. (His tall, muscular frame, his quality of a common man appealed to men.) His voice appealed to both women and men. His work in *The Story of G. I. Joe* was his only performance that earned an Academy Award. His film *Night of the Hunter* was initially a box office flop , but has become a classic. He appeared in *Cape Fear*—the original and also the remake—but in different roles. His death certificate has an affidavit attached (not shown), which changed one digit of his social security number.

Marilyn Monroe (Professional Name); Norma Jean Mortenson (Birth Name; **p. 121**—Monroe had a film career made up of 30 movies. *Niagara* and *How to Marry a Millionaire* were but two of them. Arguably, her best film, *Some Like It Hot,* is still considered by many to be her funniest film of all time. The cause of her death at age 36 is still in question. It has never been determined whether it was an accidental overdose or a homicide.

Clayton Moore (Professional Name); Jack Carlson Moore (Birth Name and Name on Death Certificate); **p. 122**—Moore made a number of films in the 40s. When he became the title character in *The Lone Ranger*, the balance of his career was set. The series ran from 1949 to 1951 and from 1954 to 1957. He continued to make appearances as the Lone Ranger during his entire life. In 1978, the Wrather Corporation, which owned the Lone Ranger, served Moore with a court order barring him from appearing in public in the mask and costume. Public support eventually forced the Wrather people to change their minds.

Vic Morrow (Professional Name, Birth Name and Name on Death Certificate); **p. 123**—Morrow learned his craft in the theater and in Paul Mann's Actor's Workshop. His first movie was *The Blackboard Jungle*. His fame came from his five years on the television series *Combat!* as Sgt. Chip Saunders. Morrow was killed while filming *Twilight Zone: The Movie* when a helicopter crashed beside him decapitating him along with two child actors he was carrying.

Harriet Nelson (Professional Name); Peggy Lou Snyder (Birth Name); Harriet Hilliard Nelson (Name on Death Certificate); **p. 124**—Nelson was first a vocalist in Ozzie Nelson's orchestra. Her first film was a feature introducing the Nelson Family. Their television series, *The Adventures of Ozzie and Harriet,* quickly followed. This series ran for 14 years and epitomized family life in the 50's.

Ozzie Nelson (Professional Name); Oswald George Nelson aka Ozzie Nelson (Birth Name and Name on Death Certificate); **p. 125**—Nelson was multi-talented. He began as an orchestra leader and songwriter. When the Nelson family starred in *The Adventures of Ozzie and Harriet*, he was the star, the producer and a writer.

Lloyd Nolan (Professional Name); Lloyd Benedict Nolan (Birth Name and Name on Death Certificate); **p. 126**—Nolan's professional career spanned 60 years. For much of that time, he played police detectives or gangsters in "B" movies. He had his most famous role on the small screen in *Julia*, playing Diahann Carroll's physician boss.

Ramon Novarro (Professional Name and Name Used on the Death Certificate); José Romón Samaniegos or Ramon Samaniegos (Birth Name); **p. 127**—Novarro got his big break in 1926 when MGM studio decided that *Ben Hur* needed to be recast. Rudolph Valentino set the stage for the latin lover phase of Hollywood. Novarro had found his niche. He was tortured and murdered on Halloween night in 1968 by two brothers who thought that there was $5,000 hidden in his home.

Pat O'Brien (Professional Name and Name on Death Certificate); William Joseph O'Brien, Jr. (Birth Name); **p. 128**—O'Brien had a long career in films. Like so many of his era, he trained on the stage. His two most famous pictures were made just two years apart. *Angels with Dirty Faces* was made in 1938 and *Knute Rockne, All American* was made in 1940.

Carroll O'Connor (Professional Name); John Carroll O'Connor (Birth Name and Name on Death Certificate); **p. 129**—O'Connor played character roles in a number of motion pictures. He auditioned for the role of the Skipper on the television series *Gilligan's Island.* His real success came in three other television series: *All in the Family, Archie Bunker's Place* and *In the Heat of the Night.*

Heather O'Rourke (Professional Name); Heather Michelle O'Rourke (Birth Name and Name on Death Certificate); **p. 130**—O'Rourke had a career that only spanned seven years. She made *Poltergeist* and the two sequels that followed. "They're here!" was her famous line. She died of septic shock following surgery for an acute bowel obstruction.

Louella Parsons (Professional Name); Louella Rose Oettinger (Birth Name); Louella Parsons Martin (Name on Death Certificate); **p. 131**—Parsons was a columnist for 53 years. Her arch rival was fellow columnist Hedda Hopper. These two women controlled the success or failure of producers, directors and budding stars and starlets. Without one or both of their approvals, there was no career.

George Peppard (Professional Name); George William Peppard (Name on Death Certificate); **p. 132**—Peppard had successes on both the large and small screens. His movie credits include *Home from the Hill, Breakfast at Tiffany's* and *The Carpetbaggers.* His television series were *Banecek, Doctors Hospital,* and *The A-Team.*

River Phoenix (Professional Name); River Jude Phoenix (Name on Death Certificate); River Jude Botton (Birth Name); **pp. 133–134**—Phoenix had movie roles in *Explorers, Stand by Me,* and *Indiana Jones and the Last Crusade.* He collapsed and died on October 31, 1993. The Los Angeles County coroner issued a deferred death certificate on November 1, 1993. The final death certificate was filed November 16, 1993, listing the cause of death as acute multiple drug intoxication.

Mary Pickford (Professional Name); (Mary?) Gladys Smith (Birth Name); Mary Pickford Rogers (Name on Death Certificate); **p. 135**—Pickford was affectionately known as "America's Sweetheart." She made her last film, *Secrets: Hollywood on Parade,* in 1933. The death certificate has several pieces of information that are different from what biographers list. Her birth year is 1894 on the death certificate, while others sources list it as 1893. Her occupation is listed on the death certificate as producer for 50 years. The biographers list the years of ownership of United Artists from 1919 until it was sold in 1953, which adds up to only 34 years.

Freddie Prinze (Professional Name and Name on the Death Certificate); **p. 136**—Prinze was just starting what promised to be a successful and interesting career. His first television series was *Chico and the Man.* He was married with a 10-month-old son, Freddie Prinze, Jr., who is one of the hottest rising stars of today. On January 29, 1977, he took his life at his apartment. Notice that on the death certificate his last address is different than the one listed for his wife.

Gilda Radner (Professional Name); Gilda Susan Radner-Wilder (Name on Death Certificate); **pp. 137–138**—Wilder got her professional start with the Toronto Second City improvisational troupe. She progressed on to Not Ready for Prime Time Players on *Saturday Night Live.* She is known for such characters as: Lisa Lupner, Roseanne Roseanna-Dana, Baba WaWa and Emily Litella. Her long battle with ovarian cancer is documented in her autobiography *It's Always Something.* There is an amendment to her death certificate that changes her residence from Connecticut to California.

Dack Rambo (Professional Name); Norman Jay Rambo (Birth Name and Name on Death Certificate); **p. 139**—Rambo was a twin to Orman "Dirk" Rambo. They were discovered by Loretta Young. *The New Loretta Young Show* was their first professional series. Dack Rambo went on to do several more series: *The Guns of Will Sonnett, Dirty Sally, Swords of Justice,* and finally, *Dallas.*

Dirk Rambo (Professional Name); Orman Ray Rambo (Birth Name and Name on Death Certificate); **p. 140**—Rambo was a twin to Norman "Dack" Rambo. According to biographers, they were discovered by Loretta Young in church. She cast them in her series *The New Loretta Young Show.* Dirk Rambo went on to appear in *Dragnet* and *The Virginian.* He was killed in a traffic accident when the car he was driving was hit by another car and caught fire.

Martha Raye (Professional Name and Name on the Death Certificate); Margie (Margy?) Yvonne Reed (Birth Name); **p. 141**—Married six times, Raye carried none of her husbands' names. She was married to Mark Harris at the time of her death. She is remembered as much for her patriotism as for her film work. Many admired her work in *The Bugaloos.* Her television supporting roles were on *McMillan and Wife* and *Alice.*

George Reeves (Professional Name); George Leecher Bessolo (Name on Death Certificate); George Brewer (later changed to Bessolo) (Birth Name); **p. 142**—Reeves learned his craft at the Pasadena Playhouse. He had roles in various movies including *Gone with the Wind* until he entered military service in World War II. Upon his return from the service, he made "B" movies and the serial *The Adventures of Sir Galahad.* Reeves starred in the movie *Superman vs the Mole Men.* His success in the movie led to the *Superman* television series. On June 6, 1959, he was found shot to death in his bedroom. The coroner determined his death to be a suicide, but his friends speculated about whether or not it was a homicide.

Lee Remick (Professional Name); Lee Ann Remick (Birth Name); Lee Remick Gowans (Name on Death Certificate); **p. 143**—Remick's professional career had several phases. Early on, she played saucy flirts. As she matured, she was known for the subtle depth that she gave to her characters. She received an Academy Award nomination for *Days of Wine and Roses. Anatomy of a Murder and The Omen* are two of her best-remembered films.

Edward G. Robinson (Professional Name and Name on Death Certificate); (Emmanuel?) Emanuel Goldenberg (Birth Name); **p. 144**—Robinson was known for playing tough guys and gangsters. He was considered by many to be "The best actor never to win an Oscar." *Little Caesar* and *Soylent Green* were films at opposite ends of his career.

Ginger Rogers (Professional Name and Name on the Death Certificate); Virginia Katherine McMath (Birth Name and Name Added to Death Certificate by Affidavit [not shown]); **pp. 145–146**—Rogers and Fred Astaire were the most legendary dance team in film history. There was a popular bumper sticker that said it all: "Ginger Rogers did everything that Fred Astaire did but backwards and in high heels." While a dramatic actress in her own right, the public preferred her in dance films. Movies like *Swing Time*, *Shall We Dance?* and *The Gay Divorcee* were favorites. The Riverside County coroner gave a deferred death certificate on April 28, 1995. The final death certificate was issued on June 9, 1995.

Roy Rogers (Professional Name and Name on Death Certificate); Leonard Slye (Birth Name); **p. 147**—Rogers was know as the "King of the Cowboys." He succeeded Gene Autry in this title. After a string of cowboy movies, he starred in the television series *The Roy Rogers Show*. His costars were his wife, Dale Evans, and Trigger, "the smartest horse in the movies." Rogers used to be offended when people asked to see his stuffed horse, Trigger. He preferred to call him mounted.

Cesar Romero (Professional Name); Cesar Julio Romero, Jr. (Birth Name and Name on Death Certificate); **p. 148**—Romero was a confirmed bachelor. His first film was *The Thin Man*. Even from this, he was typecast as a callow gigolo. He was the original Cisco in *The Cisco Kid* between 1939 and 1940. His favorite role was in *The Captain from Castile*. On the small screen he is remembered as the Joker on *Batman* and as Peter Stavros on *Falcon Crest*.

Charlie Ruggles (Professional Name); Charles Sherman Ruggles (Name on Death Certificate); **p. 149**—In his professional career, Ruggles played a long line of drunken reporters beginning with his role in *Gentleman of the Press*. He was known for his flexible facial and vocal expressions. On the small screen Ruggles had a recurring role on *The Beverly Hillbillies*. Toward the end of his life, a reporter asked him what his future plans were. With a smile he replied, "Forest Lawn. After you've played everything I have, there ain't no more."

Gail Russell (Professional and Birth Name); Gail Russell Moseley (Name on Death Certificate); **p. 150**—When Russell received her first screen test, she was young, painfully shy and had no acting experience, but she did have extraordinary beauty. *The Angel and the Badman* and *Wake of the Red Witch* were two of the movies that she made with John Wayne. On August 27, 1961, she was found dead in her apartment from acute and chronic alcoholism. This was something that had plagued her from nearly the beginning of her career.

Rosalind Russell (Professional and Birth Name); Rosalind Russell Brisson (Name on Death Certificate); **p. 151**—Russell had a full and varied career. She received four Academy Award nominations for Best Actress for *My Sister Eileen*, *Sister Kenny*, *Mourning Becomes Electra* and for *Auntie Mame*.

Irene Ryan (Professional Name and Name on Death Certificate); Irene Noblitt (Birth Name); **p. 152**—Ryan started her professional career at age 10. During World War II, she toured with Jimmy Durante, Orson Welles and others. Her films were mostly "B" movies. She appeared in a number of television series in minor roles. She was given the role of Granny in *The Beverly Hillbillies*. That series ran from 1962 to 1971.

George C. Scott (State Name, Birth Name and Name listed on Death Certificate); **p. 153**—Scott made his film debut in 1959. The same year he earned his first Academy Award nomination for *Anatomy of a Murder*. He earned three more nominations for *The Hustler*, *The List of Adrian Messenger* and *Patton*. He won the award for *Patton* but refused to accept it.

Dinah Shore (Professional Name and Name on Death Certificate); Frances Rose Shore (Birth Name); **p. 154**—Shore had a varied professional career. She started as a singer in radio and then advanced to making recordings with Xavier Cugat's band. By 1943, she had moved on to motion pictures. When her film career seemed stalled in 1951, she moved to the small screen. She started with a 15-minute show, which aired twice a week. Shore went on to host *The Dinah Shore Chevy Show* and then on to a daily talk show. She was once married to George Montgomery and had a long-term relationship with Burt Reynolds. Her trademark was to blow a kiss at the end of each show.

Jay Silverheels (Professional Name and Name on Death Certificate); Harold J. Smith (Birth Name); **p. 155**—Born in Canada, Silverheels came to Hollywood in 1934 as a stuntman. The majority of his early roles were untitled. From 1949 to 1956, played Tonto on *The Lone Ranger*. He was the first Native American to portray a Native American on television.

Frank Sinatra (Professional Name); Francis Albert Sinatra (Birth Name and Name on the Death Certificate); **p. 156**—Sinatra had several nicknames that showed the admiration and respect that both his friends and fans held for him. He was known affectionately as "The Voice," "Ol' Blue Eyes," and "The Chairman of the Board." Sinatra had a voice that captured the listener whether in song or words. He received the Academy Award for his portrayal of Maggio in *From Here to Eternity*. He continued to have hit recordings into the 90s.

Barbara Stanwyck (Professional Name and Name on Death Certificate); Ruby Stevens (Birth Name); **p. 157**—Between motion pictures and television, Stanwyck's professional career lasted 60 years. She received four Academy Award nominations for *Stella Dallas*, *Ball of Fire*, *Double Indemnity* and *Sorry Wrong Number*. Her two television series were *The Big Valley* and *The Colbys*.

Craig Stevens (Professional Name and Name on Death Certificate); Gail Shikles, Jr. (Birth Name); **p. 158**—(Death Certificate lists his father as Gail Stevens) During Stevens' motion picture career, many considered him adequate at best. The 1958 television series *Peter Gunn* was the first of the suave-but-tough private investigator shows on the small screen. Initially, Stevens imitated Cary Grant, but he soon developed his own hard-edged acting style.

Jimmy Stewart (Professional Name); James Maitland Stewart (Birth Name and Name on Death Certificate); **p. 159**—Stewart was one of the most beloved actors of his time. He played a wide range of characters and was nominated for five Academy Awards for *Mr. Smith Goes to Washington*, *It's a Wonderful Life*, *Harvey*, *Anatomy of a Murder* and *The Philadelphia Story*. He was affectionately known as "Mr. Nice Guy." He dabbled in television in his later years and became a published poet.

Milburn Stone (Professional Name); Hugh Milburn Stone (Birth Name and Name on the Death Certificate); **p. 160**—Stone left home as a teenager to join a traveling theatrical troupe. He moved on to Hollywood in 1935 and played a wide range of characters in a number of "B" movies. Success came in 1955 when he was cast as Doc Adams in *Gunsmoke*, a role he turned into a colorful, endearing character. Some reference material reads that he stayed for the entire 20-year run of the series. Others read that he retired in 1972 due to ill health.

Dorothy Stratten (Professional Name); Dorothy Ruth Hoogstraten aka Dorothy Stratten (Name on Death Certificate and Birth Name); **p. 161**—Stratten was the 1980 Playmate of the Year for Playboy magazine. She had parts in several movies and television programs. She appeared in such films as *Americathon* and *Skatetown U.S.A.* On the small screen, she appeared on *Fantasy Island* and *Buck Rogers in the 25th Century*. She was shot to death by her estranged husband, Paul Snider. He then turned the gun on himself. At the time of her death, she was having a relationship with Peter Bogdonovich, who later dated and married Dorothy's sister.

Sharon Tate (Professional Name); Sharon Tate Polanski (Name on Death Certificate); **pp. 162–163**—Tate was featured in *The Wheeler Dealers*, *The Sandpiper*, *The Fearless Vampire Killers* and *The Valley of the Dolls*. She was married to Roman Polanski and expecting their first child, when she and some house guests were stabbed to death by members of the Manson family. The Los Angeles County coroner's office signed the original death certificate on August 2, 1969. They signed an amendment on December 4, 1969 listing the homicide information.

Robert Taylor (Professional Name and Name on Death Certificate); Arlington Spangler Brugh (or Spangler Arlington Brugh, depending upon the reference material used) (Birth Name); **p. 164**—Taylor was not considered a great actor by some, but he always did a credible job. He was often considered too good looking to be taken seriously. Three of his films include *Magnificent Obsession*, *Johnny Eager*, and *Bataan*. His small screen credits include *Robert Taylor Detectives*. He also succeeded Ronald Reagan as host/narrator of *Death Valley Days* when Reagan began his full-time political career. Taylor was once married to Barbara Stanwyck.

Danny Thomas (Professional Name and Name on the Death Certificate); Amos Jacobs (Birth Name); **p. 165**—The original death certificate uses his professional name, Danny Thomas, but an affidavit to amend a record (not shown) added the name of Amos Jacobs. Some reference material lists his birth name as Muzyad Yokhoob. He had a brief motion picture career, but he is much better known for his television series *Make Room for Daddy*. *The Andy Griffith Show*, *The Dick Van Dyke Show*, *Gomer Pyle* and *The Mod Squad* were four television series that he produced in partnership with Sheldon Leonard and Aaron Spelling. He was the father of Marlo *"That Girl"* Thomas and founded St. Jude Hospital for children in Memphis, Tennessee.

Thelma Todd (Professional Name, Birth Name and Name on the Death Certificate) **p. 166**—Todd, The Ice Cream Blonde, aka Hot Toddy, was a member of the Paramount Pictures' young actors school. The school lasted only a year. She and Buddy Rogers were two of the 15 students. Like most young actresses, she yearned for dramatic roles, but she seemed to be best suited for comedy. *Horse Feathers*, *Duck Soup* and *Speak Easily* were a few of her films. Her death by carbon monoxide poisoning is another of Hollywood's mysteries. Whether it was an accident, suicide, or homicide by gangsters who were trying to take over her nightclub for gambling is the question. The Los Angeles County coroner determined her death to be accidental.

Mel Torme (Professional Name and Name on the Death Certificate); Melvin Howard Torme (Birth Name); **p. 167**—Torme started his professional career at age three. He was a radio personality the next year. By age 15, he was a published composer, and at 18 he was a film actor. *Higher and Higher*, *Good News* and *Girls Town* were a few of his films. On the small screen, he was a frequent guest star on *Night Court*. Music was always more important to him than acting. He could write songs, record albums or author a biography of one of his contemporaries, like Judy Garland or Buddy Rich. The Velvet Frog was a nickname.

Spencer Tracy (Professional Name); Spencer B. Tracy (Birth Name and Name on the Death Certificate); **p. 168**—Tracy has an enviable record. He was nominated for an unprecedented nine Academy Awards. He received the award twice in back-to-back films *Captains Courageous* and *Boys Town* in 1937 and 1938. His last film was *Guess Who's Coming to Dinner*. He did not live to see this movie. He died within a few weeks of the end of production. Tracy will always be linked on screen and off with Katherine Hepburn. While the two were deeply in love, Tracy, being a devout Catholic, could never bring himself to divorce his wife.

Lana Turner (Professional Name and Name on the Death Certificate); Julia Jean Mildred Frances Turner (Birth Name); **p. 169**—Mervyn LeRoy is credited with changing Turner's name from her nickname of Judy. The legend says that in a brainstorming session, he proposed Lenore and she came back with Lana. She was the original "Sweater Girl." She was credited with being discovered in a malt shop in Hollywood. One of her best roles was in *The Postman Always Rings Twice*. She received an Academy Award nomination in 1958 for *Peyton Place*. Her last role was on the small screen in the series *Falcon Crest*.

Robert Urich (Professional Name); Robert Michael Urich (Birth Name and Name on the Death Certificate); **p. 170**—Urich had a special talent for being able to move between drama, comedy, action-thriller or period pieces. If he was typecast, it was that his audience was always happy to have him come into their homes every week. He starred in 15 television series. *Vega$* and *Spencer for Hire* were two of the most popular.

Vivian Vance (Professional Name); Vivian Roberta Dodds (Name on the Death Certificate); Vivian Roberta Jones (Birth Name); **p. 171**—Vance was a stage actress until tapped by Desi Arnaz to join the cast of *I Love Lucy*. That series ran on television from 1951 to 1960. She continued on with Lucille Ball when they moved on to *The Lucy Show*. *The Secret Fury*, *The Blue Veil*, and *The Great Race* were the only three films that she made. She suffered from mental illness for years and eventually became an activist for the cause.

Charles Wagenheim (Professional Name, Birth Name and Name on the Death Certificate); **p. 172**—Wagenheim was a character actor of diminutive size. Frequently cast in unsavory parts, he may be best remembered for his role in *Meet Boston Blackie* and the *Diary of Anne Frank*. He was bludgeoned to death in his apartment just days before veteran actor Victor Kilian was killed in the same manner.

Ethel Waters (Professional Name, Birth Name and Name on the Death Certificate); **p. 173**—Waters launched her professional career at age 17 when she took a dare to enter a local talent contest. She made 10 films and received two Academy Award nominations for *Pinky* and *Member of the Wedding*. She also appeared in the television series *Beulah*.

Marion Robert Morrison aka John Wayne (Professional Name, Birth Name and name on the Death Certificate); **p. 174**—Wayne started his professional career by working on the Fox lot during summer vacations from college. After a string of successful films, he received his Academy Award for Best Actor in *True Grit*. His movies like *The Green Berets* were popular with the public but not the critics.

Clifton Webb (Professional Name and Name on the Death Certificate); Webb Parmelee Hollenbeck (Birth Name); **p. 175**—Webb's career focused on dance work. He became one of New York's leading ballroom dancers. He received an Academy Award nomination for his first film *Laura*. He also received Academy nominations for *The Razor's Edge* and *Sitting Pretty*.

Jack Webb (Professional Name, Name on the Death Certificate and Birth Name); **p. 176**—Webb is an example of someone who found a niche and made a career of it. He started in radio doing detective melodramas. He took his last, *Dragnet*, to the small screen. His production company, Mach VII, gave television such series as *Emergency* and *Adam 12*. On the day of his death, the Los Angeles Police Department lowered their flags to half mast.

Orson Welles (Professional Name); George Orson Welles (Birth Name and Name on the Death Certificate); **p. 177**—Welles is remembered more as a director than as an actor. His film *Citizen Kane* is perhaps the most discussed, if not the finest movie ever made in the United States.He received an Academy Award for Best Original Screenplay for *Citizen Kane*, but his thinly-disguised portrayal of media titan William Randolph Hearst would both make and break his career. Even his radio program

War of the Worlds was so believable that thousands thought this country was really being invaded by martians.

Mae West (Professional Name, Birth Name and Name on the Death Certificate); **p. 178**—West's professional trademark was her seductiveness, which was made up frequently with innuendo and double entendre. *Klondike Annie* and *My Little Chickadee* were two of her movies. She is often credited as discovering Cary Grant, remarking when she saw him for the first time, "If he can talk, I want him."

Mary Wickes (Professional Name); Mary Isabella Wickes (Birth Name and Name on the Death Certificate); **p. 179**—Wickes did not consider herself a comedian, but rather an actress who played comedy. Like so many others, she learned her craft on the New York stage. She went to Hollywood to reprise her role from *The Man Who Came to Dinner*. Wickes played the hook-nosed Sister Mary Lazarus in the *Sister Act* films. Her last television series was the *Father Dowling Mysteries*.

Billy Wilder (Professional Name and Name on the Death Certificate); Samuel Wilder (Birth Name); **p. 180**—Wilder was a consistent and prolific filmmaker. His films *The Lost Weekend*, *Sunset Boulevard* and *The Apartment* earned Academy Awards for Best Film. *Some Like it Hot* was another favorite film.

Walter Winchell (Professional Name, Birth Name and Name on the Death Certificate); **p. 181**—Winchell made a journalistic discovery that "people are interested in people." He created a demand for juicy tidbits about celebrities. He spent the rest of his professional career attempting to satisfy this demand. He had a syndicated daily column and weekly radio program that, between the two, reached millions.

Natalie Wood (Professional Name); Natalie Wood Wagner (Name on the Death Certificate); Natasha Nikolaevna Gurdin (Birth Name); **p. 182**—Wood started her professional career at age four. She received three Academy Award nominations. *Rebel Without a Cause*, *West Side Story* and *Love with the Proper Stranger* were the films where her ability was recognized. Her death by drowning was considered an accident by the Los Angeles County coroner. To others, it is still subject to speculation.

Loretta Young (Professional Name); Loretta V. Louis (Name on the Death Certificate); Gretchen Young (Birth Name); **p. 183**—Young made her first motion picture appearance at age four. She received the Academy Award for Best Actress for *The Farmer's Daughter*. She received another nomination for *Come to the Stables*. When she retired from motion pictures, she hosted *The Loretta Young Show*. She always made her entrance in a beautiful gown. Grace and charm were her hallmarks.

Robert Young (Professional Name); Robert George Young (Name on the Death Certificate); **p. 184**—Young had a strong work ethic. During the 30s, he made as many as nine films per year. *The Enchanted Cottage* and *They Won't Believe Me* were two of his best films. His small screen successes were *Father Knows Best* and *Marcus Welby*.

Frank Zappa (Professional Name); Frank Vincent Zappa (Birth Name and Name on the Death Certificate); **p. 185**—Zappa was first and foremost a musician. He was considered tireless, intimidating, and well-organized. His movie credits include *Head*, *200 Motels* and *Baby Snakes*. An amendment to his death certificate changed the time of death and the name and address of his physician. (This amendment is not shown.)